D1567093

Naval Science 2

Naval Science 2

Maritime History, Leadership,
and Nautical Sciences for
the NJROTC Student

3rd Edition

CDR Richard R. Hobbs, USNR (Ret.)

NAVAL INSTITUTE PRESS
ANNAPOLIS, MARYLAND

Naval Institute Press
291 Wood Road
Annapolis, MD 21402

ISBN: 978-1-61251-393-5 (hardcover)
According to the Library of Congress, this textbook and its companion instructor's answer guide are ineligible for cataloging-in-publication data.

♾ Print editions meet the requirements of ANSI/NISO z39.48-1992 (Permanence of Paper).
Printed in the United States of America.

22 21 20 19 18 17 16 15 14   9 8 7 6 5 4 3 2 1
First printing

Contents

Acknowledgments

One of the most satisfying aspects of my professional career throughout the past thirty years has been my association with the NJROTC program. I am convinced that this program represents one of the finest and most worthwhile endeavors in existence to serve American youth. Given my admiration for the program and the people who are involved in it as administrators and instructors, preparing this textbook was certainly a very gratifying experience for me.

Special thanks for their assistance with reviewing and critiquing the technical portions of this edition go to two of my former Advanced Placement Physics students Jeff Finn and Scottie Luddy, now practicing electrical engineers. The NJROTC unit at Annapolis Senior High School in Annapolis, Maryland, graciously supplied several of the NJROTC cadet photos that appear in the leadership section. Many of the photographs of vintage naval artwork, vessels, and historical figures came from the website of the Naval History and Heritage Command, and those of more recent naval ships, aircraft, equipment and people came from the website of the Chief of Naval Information, as did much information on current naval activities and operations. The pictures of spacecraft and their stunning photography of the Sun, Moon, planets, and other bodies in our solar system and beyond appearing in the nautical sciences section were mostly obtained from the National Air and Space Administration photo archives website.

Finally, a special tip of the hat goes to Chris Robinson, the freelance commercial artist who created all of the maps for this edition, and to freelance editor Pelham Boyer, whose excellent editing contributed much to it. As always, my thanks and appreciation goes to the people of the Naval Institute Press, and especially production editor Marlena Montagna, without whom this textbook would not have been possible.

Maritime History

Influence of Sea Power on Western Civilization

Sea power is the ability to use the sea to meet a nation's needs. It means being able to defend a nation's own sea-lanes and being able to deny an enemy the use of the sea in time of war.

Sea power played a major role in the development of early Western civilization. In many wars throughout history, a single major victory at sea made winning possible. Defeat of the enemy's fleet kept it from supplying its land forces. The victor was then able to attack the enemy's homeland, thus winning the war on land.

Early Seafarers

Early people feared the seas. They saw them as barriers. Gradually, however, they learned to use the water, both as a way to get food by fishing and as an easier way to travel and conduct trade. Travel by water was faster, cheaper, and safer than travel over land. Before long the countries bordering the Mediterranean Sea that carried on the most trade became the richest and most powerful in that region. Ports and cities on navigable rivers became centers of culture and commerce.

The first European people to use sea power were the sailors and traders of ancient Crete, a large rocky island south of Greece. Some four thousand years ago (2500–1200 BC) the Cretans dominated their neighbors on the shores of the Aegean Sea, countries now known as Greece and Turkey. This was inevitable because of Crete's geography. The island was too rugged for farming, and it sits right on the major sea routes of the eastern Mediterranean.

The **Phoenicians** were the next to master the sea in this region. Centered in modern-day Lebanon, their ships roamed the coastlines of North Africa and the Mediterranean Sea from about 2000 to 300 BC. Their ships carried tin from Britain, amber from the Baltic Sea, and slaves and ivory from western Africa. The Phoenicians established great ports at the city-states of Tyre and Sidon in what is now Lebanon.

These port cities were at the end of the Asian caravan routes, which brought in the trade goods and wealth of Asia. Phoenician ships carried these goods to the coastal trading cities around the Mediterranean and to northern Europe. The Phoenicians also started colonies and trading stations, which grew into new centers of civilization. The Phoenician alphabet became the written language of traders, and the Phoenicians were the first to use money as a means to facilitate trade. Later, the Phoenician alphabet became the basis for our own alphabet. The greatest of the Phoenician colonies grew to be the empire of Carthage in North Africa, later the main opponent of Rome.

Next came the Greeks. Famous Greek authors—Herodotus, Thucydides, and Homer—wrote detailed, semifictional accounts of early sea power. One of the better known of these tales is about the Trojan War. It is based on an actual series of conflicts fought between 1200 and 1190 BC to control the Hellespont, now called the Dardanelles (Turkish Straits), in order to take control of the Aegean–Black Sea trade. By 500 BC the Greek city-states had achieved a high level of civilization, and their trading ships and naval vessels sailed the entire Mediterranean. Many prosperous Greek colonies developed in Asia Minor (Turkey), Sicily, Italy, France, and Spain. They took over sea control from the Phoenicians.

Early trading vessels were clumsy craft, easy prey for armed robbers in smaller, swifter craft. So merchants began to crew vessels with hired seagoing soldiers to protect their ships and to patrol the seaways. Navies thus came into being, using special ships called **galleys** (which had oars and sometimes sails) crewed by trained fighting men.

Greece vs. Persia

By 492 BC Greek expansion had run into the mighty forces of Persia (modern-day Iran) moving westward into the eastern Mediterranean. The Greeks were able to hold off two Persian invasions in the next twelve years but then were forced to withdraw from their northern lands in Thrace and Macedonia. In 480 BC Xerxes, the Persian king, undertook a huge invasion to try to conquer the Greeks once and for all. Knowing that sea power would be necessary for a victory, Xerxes built a navy of 1,300 galleys. This fleet followed his 180,000-man army westward

A galley of the type used in the Mediterranean circa 500 BC. Galley tactics were simple: overtake, ram or grapple, board, and capture in hand-to-hand fighting. At other times galleys patrolled the sea routes over which most ships traveled. *U.S. Naval Institute Photo Archive*

around the coast of the Aegean Sea, guarding his flank and carrying his supplies.

Themistocles, the Greek commander, realized that the only way the Persians could be stopped was to break this Persian **sea line of communication** supporting Xerxes' army from Asia Minor. He convinced the Greeks to build a naval force of 380 **triremes,** a type of multidecked war galley. Greek strategy was to hold the Persian army at bay at the narrow pass of Thermopylae, while the Greek fleet struck the Persian fleet in a series of hit-and-run attacks in the waters among the Greek islands. But a traitor showed the Persian army a secret mountain pass, enabling the Persians to surround and destroy the Greek defenders at Thermopylae.

Xerxes' army now continued south to plunder the abandoned city of Athens. The Greeks took up new positions at the Isthmus of Corinth. Meanwhile their fleet moved south to the waters around the island of Salamis, near Athens, to protect their eastern flank.

Bad weather and the Greek hit-and-run attacks had by this time reduced the Persian fleet to eight hundred vessels. There were only three hundred Greek triremes left to oppose them. Splitting his force, Xerxes sent two hundred galleys to block the retreat of the Greek fleet around Salamis. The remaining six hundred galleys moved directly against the Greek fleet in the narrow strait between Salamis and the shore. But in the narrow strait the Persians lost the advantage of numbers, since only the lead ships had contact with the Greek fleet, which was better armed. So the Greeks were able to prevail. About half the Persian fleet was sunk, with great loss of life, compared to a Greek loss of only forty ships. Xerxes watched the unfolding disaster from a throne set up on a hill overlooking the battle. Upon realizing his fleet was wiped out, he ordered his army to begin a long retreat.

Following this battle, there was a short period of peace and prosperity in Greece, thereafter known as the **Golden Age of Athens.** Theater, sculpture, writing, and philosophy flourished.

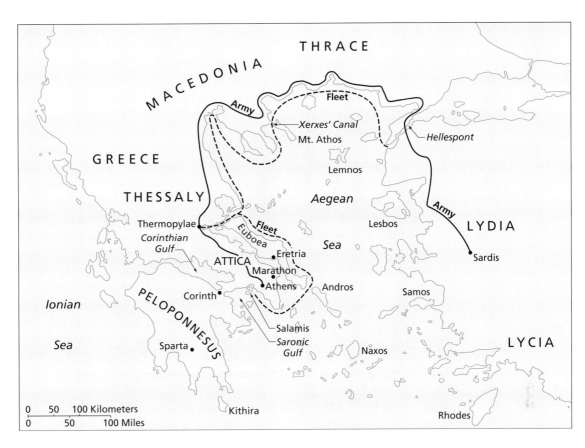

Route of the Persian fleet and army against the Greeks in 480 BC.

An ancient Greek trireme of the type that defeated the Persians at Salamis. There were three decks of oars and rowers, one above the other on each side of the ship. Often the rowers were slaves. *U.S. Naval Institute Photo Archive*

The concept of democracy in government was born. Thus the foundations of Western civilization were laid, and the key event that made this possible was the sea battle of Salamis in 480 BC.

During the next 150 years Greek civilization moved steadily eastward, conquering most of what was the Persian Empire. Under Alexander the Great of Macedonia, Greek culture spread throughout the entire eastern Mediterranean. The great port of Alexandria in Egypt was established. Persia was driven from the seas, and the reign of the Phoenicians was ended. Macedonia became the world's greatest sea power, conquering most of the civilized Western and Middle Eastern world.

Rome vs. Carthage

The Greeks controlled the eastern Mediterranean for the next two centuries. In the western Mediterranean, however, Greek expansion was checked by the rising sea power of **Carthage,** a city-state in North Africa founded in the late eighth century BC by the Phoenicians. But on the Italian peninsula, a new power was emerging—Rome. In 275 BC the Romans conquered Italy, including the Greek colonies in the south. In the process they absorbed the Greek culture, helping to continue the advance of Western civilization. In their way, however, was a strong rival—

Carthage. In 265 BC, the first of several bitter conflicts between the two powers began, in Sicily. Together these conflicts were known as the **Punic Wars** (*Punic* is a Latin variation of the word "Phoenician," or *Punicus*).

At the beginning of the Punic Wars, Rome saw what sea power and a strong navy could do. The Carthaginian navy protected Carthage from attack by the Romans, harassed Roman sea commerce, and plundered the Roman coast.

The Romans studied Greek sea tactics and eventually improved on them. As the Punic Wars progressed, Roman seamanship and tactics overcame the Carthaginians, driving them from the sea. The first Punic War gave Rome the island of Sicily as a province, and the second Punic War gave Spain to Rome. The third Punic War began with an amphibious invasion of North Africa. By the time it was over, Carthage had been burned and Carthaginian power had been destroyed forever.

The *Mare Nostrum*

The Roman Empire was now free to spread throughout the Mediterranean. The Roman navy cleared the Mediterranean of pirates, moved and supported Rome's armies, and defeated any hostile fleets.

In the first century BC, rebellious Romans and their Egyptian allies under the command of Mark Antony and Queen Cleopatra tried to overthrow the Roman Empire during the confusion following the assassination of Julius Caesar. The rebellion was crushed, however, in 31 BC at a great sea battle near Actium (Greece). The Roman admiral Agrippa destroyed the Egyptian fleet with blazing arrows and pots of flaming charcoal. In an earlier battle at Naulochus, Agrippa had defeated Pompey, Caesar's other rival to power, and secured the western Mediterranean. The Battle of Actium put the whole eastern Mediterranean in the Roman Empire.

For more than five centuries after Actium, trade vessels could move freely from the Black Sea to Gibraltar with little fear. The Mediterranean had become the Roman *Mare Nostrum* (Our Sea); all coasts, ports, and naval bases were controlled by Rome. On land and sea the *Pax Romana* (Roman Peace) was established, the longest period of peace in world history. Roman law, government, art, language, and religion were firmly established in western Europe, the Middle East, and North Africa. Western civilization today can be traced to Rome and to the earlier Greek contributions.

The Middle Ages

Eventually, Rome's greatness began to decline, a result of social, political, and economic breakdowns too extensive to discuss here. As Rome declined, the empire broke up into two parts. The Eastern, or Byzantine, Empire had its capital at Constanti-

nople (after 1930 called Istanbul), and the Western Empire kept its capital at Rome. Barbarian invaders from northern and central Europe conquered Rome and deposed the last emperor in AD 476.

For the next thousand years, Europe was in turmoil, and there was a constant threat of Muslim/Arab expansion into the Mediterranean from northern Africa. The period of western European history from the fall of Rome until about the eleventh century has been called the **Dark Ages,** because of numerous invasions of barbaric tribes, incursions of North African Moors, religious bigotry, and a general lack of education among the masses of people. Only in the region around Constantinople, where much of the Roman tradition was preserved, was there a general advance of culture during this period.

Meanwhile, in northern Europe the **Vikings** from Scandinavia explored, raided, conducted trade, and settled in wide areas of Europe, the eastern Mediterranean area, and the North Atlantic region from the late eighth to the eleventh centuries. They used wooden sailing vessels called **longships,** with shallow-draft hulls and oars that facilitated travel through the open ocean as well as shallow coastal areas and rivers. At first the Vikings mainly sailed across the Baltic Sea to raid in the Baltic States, but by the late eighth century they had ventured across the North Sea to Northumbria, in northern England, where their exploits here and elsewhere gave rise to a perception of them as brutal raiders seeking only to plunder and take slaves. Many of them, however, went on to settle permanently in northern England, Scotland, and France.

In the 800s they reached Iceland, which they settled over the next several centuries, and by the twelfth century they had sailed as far west as Greenland and modern-day Newfoundland and Labrador, in Canada. There is even some evidence that they may have ventured as far south as present-day New England in America. The Viking age ended with the establishment of Christianity as the dominant religion in Scandinavia and the formation of the Nordic kingdoms of Norway, Denmark, and Sweden in the eleventh and twelfth centuries.

In the eastern Mediterranean, the Byzantine Empire, centered in what is now Turkey, defeated the advancing Muslims at

A replica of a Viking longship, built for the television History Channel dramatic series *Vikings*. When not under sail the vessel could be propelled by oars.
www.history.com

Constantinople in AD 717. The Byzantines thereafter prospered and blocked additional westward Muslim overland expansion. The Muslims became largely content with piracy on the Mediterranean and with strengthening their control over their huge North African and Middle Eastern territories. Muslim fleets dominated the Mediterranean at this time. By the eleventh century, though, Christendom was ready to contest Muslim control. The Muslims were expelled from Sardinia and Sicily and pushed into southern Spain. The **First Crusade**, initiated by Pope Urban II in 1095, recaptured Jerusalem and nearly swept the Arabs from the Mediterranean. Unfortunately the excessive violence often inflicted on the Muslim population by the Crusaders during this and subsequent crusades in the Middle East fostered a resentment within the Muslim culture toward northern and western Europeans that would endure for the next ten centuries.

Over the next three hundred years, the religious fervor that had brought on the Crusades turned more to commercial expansion by the Italian states. Their merchant fleets took advantage of the Muslim retreat. Venice profited most from the increased trade and became the biggest center of commerce between Asia and Europe. It hired out ships to Crusaders and gave the Arabs commercial favors, thus profiting from both sides. Venice acquired Crete and Cyprus in the course of these events. By 1400 Venice was at the height of its power, with a fleet of three thousand ships. In the late eleventh century, the Crusades began gradually to hasten a reawakening of culture and education in western Europe. This movement flourished in the thirteenth through sixteenth centuries. This time is referred to as the **Renaissance** (the Rebirth) in western European history.

By the fourteenth century the north German port cities were on the opposite end of much of the Venetian trade. In 1356 they formed the Hanseatic League, or the Hanse, which grew to dominate the northern and western European economy. The Baltic and North Seas became to some degree in the north what the Mediterranean had been for centuries in the south.

But by now the Muslim cause had been taken over by the aggressive Ottoman Turks. They swept across the Dardanelles into southeastern Europe and captured Constantinople in 1453. The fall of the Byzantine Empire removed the barriers to Muslim advances into Europe. The Turks swept to the very gates of Vienna, Austria. Muslim fleets sought domination of the Mediterranean and control of the profitable east–west trade.

The Battle of Lepanto

For some time the divided Christian states could not get organized to oppose the Turks, but after the Turkish conquest of Cyprus in 1570, fear of the Turks finally drew the states together. Spain and the Italian states agreed to combine their fleets for a conclusive battle with the Ottoman Turks. The winner would have a significant effect on the course of Western civilization.

The Christian fleet, commanded by Don John of Austria, was composed of some two hundred galleys, mostly Venetian and Spanish. The Ottoman fleet, commanded by Ali Pasha, numbered about 250 galleys. Though most of the galleys on both sides had one or two guns at their bows, for their main offensive weapon the Turks still relied on the bow and arrow. Many soldiers in the Christian galleys, however, were armed with the **arquebus,** an early type of musket. The opposing fleets came together in the Gulf of Lepanto near Patras, Greece, in 1571. This was just a few miles south of where Agrippa had defeated Antony in the Battle of Actium sixteen centuries earlier. In the terrible battle that took place, the Christian navies crushed their Turkish opponents. Some 30,000 Turks died. All but sixty of their ships were captured or destroyed. Some 15,000 Christians captured earlier by the Turks and used as slaves to row the galleys were freed by the victory.

As a result of the Battle of Lepanto, the Ottoman Turks were prevented from expanding any further along the European side of the Mediterranean. They never again seriously challenged control of the Mediterranean, although Muslim pirates continued to harass merchantmen in these waters for the next 250 years.

Lepanto was the end of the **age of the galley.** By the time of Lepanto, the Mediterranean had begun to decline as the center of world maritime activity. It had served for two thousand years as the cradle of western European civilization and commerce. Its period of greatest influence was the age of the galley. But the Turkish hold on the Middle East had caused seafaring nations to seek new routes to Asia. The **Age of Discovery** had dawned, and with it came new types of ships better designed for sailing in the open ocean. They had deeper drafts, and high towers called "castles" fore and aft from which to attack any enemies who might come aboard amidships. The ships' increased size and weight required multiple masts to carry sufficient sail to propel them, as opposed to the old single-masted, shallow-draft Mediterranean galleys and Viking longships. Advances in met-

The Battle of Lepanto in 1571. The battle ended Muslim attempts to move further into Europe and control the Mediterranean Sea. *British National Maritime Museum*

allurgy and gunpowder led to their being armed primarily with guns vice spears, arrows, and stones. Crude magnetic compasses allowed mariners to better find their way when out of sight of land in midocean.

The Age of Discovery

The Age of Discovery was a new age of sea power. Brave explorers in wooden ships sailed the world's oceans and founded colonies while seeking religious freedom and fortunes for king and country. The hardships were great, but the lure of freedom, gold, and adventure was greater. As before, the nations with sea power became rich and powerful. Inevitably, rivalries arose, and wars were fought between opposing great powers.

The Portuguese were the first to seek a new sea route to the East Indies and the rest of Asia. Prince Henry the Navigator hired explorers to try to find a route to the East by sailing around Africa. Bartholomeu Dias rounded the Cape of Good Hope at the southern tip of Africa in 1488. This proved that a sea route to Asia existed, although it was long and difficult. Vasco da Gama sailed from Portugal to India in 1498, opening a Portuguese trade route to the Indies and China and establishing colonial trading sites. Portugal's leadership was brief, though, for it was soon overwhelmed by neighboring Spain.

Contributing about five thousand dollars in royal jewels, Queen Isabella financed Christopher Columbus on his first voyage of discovery in 1492. It was certainly the most profitable investment in history. Searching for a new and better all-water route to the Far East, instead he discovered the New World, thus helping put Spain into a position of European leadership. Soon Spanish—along with Portuguese, English, Italian, French, Dutch, and Swedish—seafarers were sailing across the Atlantic to new markets, new wealth, and new conflicts.

Through sea power, Spain established a huge empire. Millions in gold, silver, and jewels poured into the royal treasury. Treasure-laden ships sailed in groups escorted by warships to protect them against pirates and warships of rival nations. This was an early example of a **convoy,** a method used for centuries afterward to protect merchant shipping.

At the time, national wealth was thought to be measured by the amount of treasure in the royal vaults. The total wealth of the world was considered to be a fixed quantity. Thus, to become richer and more powerful, a nation had to make some other nation poorer through capture of its trade and colonies. This **mercantile theory** kept the world in almost continuous conflict well into the 1800s.

England Challenges Spain

In 1570 Pope Pius V called upon King Philip II of Spain to drive the Muslims from Europe and the Mediterranean. At the same time, the pope asked Philip to crusade against the "heretic and usurper" Queen Elizabeth I in Protestant England. Having proved himself and his great fleet at Lepanto, Philip accepted this task.

Elizabeth, on the other hand, wanted to protect her throne against the Catholic Mary Queen of Scots. She began to strengthen England's defenses against the attack she knew would soon come from Spain. After securing England's flank by an alliance with the king of France, she secretly released her fortune-seeking seamen to raid Philip's treasure ships from the New World, a practice called **privateering.** And she began rebuilding her navy.

The privateering of the English "seadogs"—Sir Francis Drake, Martin Frobisher, and Sir John Hawkins—was extremely successful and pleased the queen. In 1578 Sir Francis Drake, the most famous of the English raiders, sailed his *Golden Hind* into the Pacific through the Strait of Magellan and raided Spanish cities and shipping along the west coast of South America. He returned to England in 1581 via the Cape of Good Hope, laden with gold, silver, and jewels worth half a million pounds sterling (equal to many millions in today's dollars). Queen Elizabeth accepted the treasure and knighted Drake on the quarterdeck of his ship.

Elizabeth had a significant advantage in her superb seamen. The widespread privateering had created a group of men who had great knowledge of ships and the sea. With these seadogs in command of the world's best sailors, England prepared to meet Spain in a great contest for supremacy on the seas.

Defeat of the Spanish Armada

In the early summer of 1588 Philip sent forth what he believed to be an unbeatable naval **armada** (large fleet of warships). Its purpose was to stop the English raids on his ships and ports and to bring England back into the Catholic Church. The **Spanish Armada** consisted of a fleet of 124 galleons with 1,100 guns. It was crewed by eight thousand sailors and carried 19,000 soldiers, all under the command of the Duke of Medina-Sidonia.

To oppose it the English had reinforced the queen's thirty-four men-of-war with 163 armed merchantmen, 16,000 men, and two thousand guns. The English fleet was under the overall command of Charles Howard, lord admiral of England.

So the scene was set. The Armada had fewer guns but had superior total firepower. The English had smaller ships and long-range **culverins** (a type of cannon). The English had an advantage in maneuverability, clear decks, and range. King Philip's orders were to "grapple and board and engage hand to hand." (A **grapple** is a group of large metal hooks with a central shaft, attached to a heaving line and used for latching onto an object such as a ship.) But the English intended to fight with guns

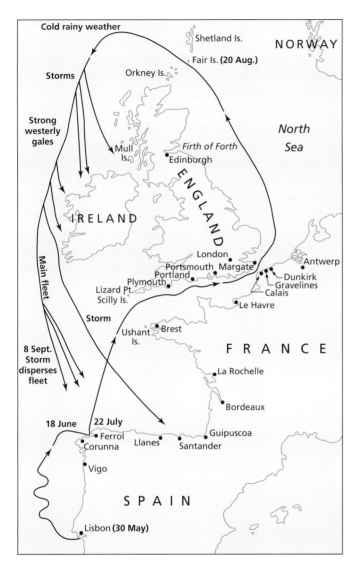

The route of the Spanish Armada, 1588. The British defeated the Armada in the English Channel near Calais, France, after which the Spanish fleet fled northward around Britain and Ireland to try to return home. Bad weather and storms caused many of the Spanish ships to founder along the Irish coast.

alone, for they carried fewer soldiers. The sailors and marines doubled as antiboarding defenders and cannoneers.

During their first encounters in the English Channel, each side used more than 100,000 rounds of shot. Spanish fire had little effect, because of the distance kept by the English ships. The English pounded the Spanish ships, causing many casualties on the packed decks but little damage to the hulls.

Ignoring a chance to attack the English off Plymouth, the Spaniards sailed on up the channel. The English picked away at them with little effect. But by the time Medina-Sidonia sought rest and resupply in the neutral French port of Calais, he found that he had fired all of his heavy shot. During the night, Howard

sent eight **fireships** (ships loaded with combustibles that were set afire and sent drifting among enemy ships, meant to burn any they might hit) into the Spanish ships anchored at Calais, forcing the Spaniards out in confusion during darkness. The next day the English and their Dutch allies attacked without fear of the now-silent Spanish guns, facing only small boarder-repelling pistols and muskets.

However, the English supply system also proved to be inadequate. After Howard had sunk two Spanish ships, driven three onto the rocks, and littered the enemy decks with casualties, he too ran out of ammunition. But the Spanish were already on the run. With the wind against them and the English behind them, the Spaniards fled northward into the North Sea, intending to round Britain and Ireland to get home.

If the English ammunition had held out, they probably would have crushed the Spanish Armada then and there. As it was, hunger and thirst, storms, and poor navigation finished the task for the English. About forty of the Spanish ships sank at sea, and at least twenty were wrecked on the rocky shores of Scotland and Ireland. In October, only about half of the great naval force that Philip had confidently sent to conquer England returned to Spain.

The failure of the Armada marked the beginning of Spain's decline. The defeat of the Armada was a signal to other seafaring nations, especially England, France, and the Netherlands, to strike out for colonies and commerce around the world. The fact that these efforts often involved taking over territories and trade routes claimed by the king of Spain made little difference to the mariners. They did not attempt to conquer Spanish colonies in Central and South America. But pirates and privateers often plundered the **Spanish Main,** stretching from Colombia and Panama to the islands in the Caribbean. Asia, Africa, and North America east of the Mississippi River were considered wide open for colonization and trade.

England Builds Its Empire

England's efforts at colonization in the seventeenth century were paid for by private groups who received **charters** (licenses) for that purpose from the Crown. The first successful colony in North America was founded in 1607 at Jamestown, Virginia. Later colonies in Massachusetts, Pennsylvania, and Maryland were begun by groups seeking religious freedom. The last colony on the East Coast was Georgia (1732), the settlers of which had volunteered as a way to get out of debtor's prisons.

With the English, French, and Dutch all eagerly seeking colonies, conflict was inevitable. Between 1665 and 1674 the English and Dutch fought three fierce naval wars. The English were the winners, and one of their gains was the Dutch colony of New Amsterdam, which the English soon renamed New York. Between 1689 and 1763, the English fought a series of wars with the French, now their only serious rival at sea. During the **Seven Years' War** (1756–63), known in America as the **French and Indian War,** the two powers fought what amounted to a world war, with land and sea battles occurring in almost every part of the globe. England's ultimate victory gained it many new possessions, the main one in North America being Canada.

Whatever may have been happening among the "superpowers" of the time, throughout this period of nearly two centuries the colonies on a thin strip of cultivated land on the East Coast of North America managed to survive only because of the sea. It was across the Atlantic Ocean that all of the settlers had come, bringing with them only the bare necessities of life and their Old World traditions. And it was across this same ocean that additional colonists, livestock, and hardware came, to sustain and expand what the hardy first folk had begun. The sea provided them with an industry, particularly in New England, where they soon discovered some of the richest fishing grounds in the world. Virginians used the sea to send large quantities of tobacco to the Old World, which had taken an almost instant liking to it. Within and among the colonies, the inland rivers and coastal waters became waterborne highways. On these highways the products of inland regions were traded for imported goods and sent on their way to the larger coastal communities and then overseas, primarily to England.

Born of the sea, maintained by the sea, and enriched by the sea, England's American colonies had by 1760 grown in population to more than 1.5 million people. By 1775 they had grown to 2.5 million. American seamen and American-built ships made up about one-third of the entire English merchant marine. With the **Treaty of Paris** in 1763, the war in North America between France and England ended. England was supreme, and its navy and merchant fleets controlled the world's seas.

Critical Thinking

1. Describe the main factors that influenced whether a country developed into a sea power in the ancient Mediterranean until the demise of the Roman Empire in AD 476.

2. Research and describe the mercantile theory and its proponents during the Age of Discovery in Europe.

Chronology

2500–1200 BC	Crete dominates Mediterranean
1200 BC	Trojan War
480 BC	Battle of Salamis
275 BC	Rome conquers Italy
31 BC	Battle of Actium
476	Last Roman emperor deposed
793–1066	Age of the Vikings
1095	First Crusade
1492	Columbus discovers America
1571	Battle of Lepanto
1588	Spanish Armada defeated
1607	Jamestown colony established
1756–63	Seven Years' War (French and Indian War)

Study Guide Questions

1. What is meant by a nation's sea power?

2. A. How did navies start?
   B. What was their purpose?

3. What was the major type of warship used in ancient times?

4. Why did ancient Crete develop into the first sea power in the Mediterranean?

5. How did the Phoenicians contribute to Western culture?

6. Which great Middle Eastern empire was the main enemy of ancient Greece?

7. What was King Xerxes' invasion plan against Greece?

8. What was the Greek plan of battle at the Battle of Salamis?

9. A. Who followed the Greeks as the leader in Western culture?
   B. Which country was their principal enemy during their rise to power?
   C. What were the wars between these countries called?

10. What two sea battles won the Mediterranean for Rome after Caesar's death?

11. What is the period of western European history from the fall of Rome until about the eleventh century often called?

12. Who were the Vikings, and where did they explore and settle?

13. A. Which of the Italian states became a great commercial and naval power during the Crusades?
    B. How did it do this?

14. What was the result of the Battle of Lepanto?

15. Which country led the way to the Age of Discovery with early explorations around Africa?

16. What changes occurred in Spain as a result of the discovery of the Americas?

17. Which country rose to challenge Spain as the leading sea power in the sixteenth century?

18. For what purpose did the Spanish Armada sail in 1588?

19. Which country challenged English colonialism in North America first?

20. What was the main result of the French and Indian War in America?

New Vocabulary

triremes	piracy
culverin	convoy
fire ship	mercantile theory
galley	privateering
invasion	armada
flank	maneuverability
sea line of communication	grapple
plunder	ammunition
rebellion	charters

2

The American Revolution, 1775–1783

While England and France were busy fighting each other in the Seven Years' War from 1756 to 1763, the American colonies grew and prospered. When the war was over, British officials looked to the colonies as a way to raise money to help pay off the debts built up during the long conflict. They felt the colonies had benefited unfairly. They believed that, unlike Englishmen at home, the colonists had not borne their fair share of the taxes and restrictions. England thus passed the Revenue Act and began enforcing taxes on sugar imports to the colonies in 1763. Then, by the Stamp Act of 1765 and other similar acts, it tried to reassert Parliament's power in the colonies. The colonists thought all this was unfair and soon became upset over the way Britain was treating them.

In 1767 Parliament passed the Townshend Act, which taxed paper, lead, and tea. All over the colonies people protested. Anti-British feelings were especially strong in Boston. There on the evening of 5 March 1770 an angry crowd of protesters including an African American named Crispus Attucks gathered and began to taunt British soldiers. One thing quickly escalated to another, and in a scuffle that followed the soldiers shot and killed Attucks and several other people—considered the first casualties of the American Revolution. The incident was played up in the press and soon became known as the **"Boston Massacre."** It made many colonists want to seek revenge.

Three years later, irate Bostonians disguised as warlike Indians boarded a merchant ship and dumped some British tea into the harbor rather than pay taxes due on it. Parliament soon responded to this **"Boston Tea Party"** with the Coercive Acts, which closed the port of Boston, abolished the right of the people of Massachusetts to select their own council, and restricted other civil liberties.

These were the events that led to the American Revolution, which began at Lexington and Concord in April 1775. "The die is cast," wrote King George III. "The colonies must either triumph or submit." There was no longer the possibility of a peaceful settlement.

The first American campaign of the Revolution was the siege of Boston that began following the battles at Lexington and Concord. British army forces were occupying the city, and a number of militias from the New England colonies surrounded them. The main action during the siege was the Battle of Bunker Hill in June 1775, one of the bloodiest encounters of the war. In July George Washington took command of the assembled militias and transformed them into the Continental Army. Later that month the Continental Congress petitioned King George III to restore liberty to the colonies in a final attempt to avoid war with England, but the king refused to accept the petition, and the colonists knew that they must prepare for war. It would be another year, however, before the colonies declared their independence from Britain.

Problems for British Sea Power

The Royal Navy, though in 1775 the mightiest in the world, soon found out that it would not be easy to fight the Americans. For one thing, the British had been getting much of their shipbuilding materials, such as tar, pitch, turpentine, and timber for masts and hulls, from the colonies. Now, of course, the colonies would not supply these materials to England. In addition, following the Seven Years' War, inadequate funding for upkeep and repairs had left many British warships rotting at their docks. It would be several years after the conflict began before there were enough ships to meet wartime needs. What ships were available at the outset would be used mostly for transporting troops and attempting to protect commercial shipping. In addition, the British also soon found that many officers in the Royal Navy believed the Americans were English citizens and refused to fight against them.

Another force that had earlier been on England's side was now turned against it—the privateers, armed American merchant ships that had helped the British win the French and Indian War. Now these privateers, with the blessing of the Continental Congress, set out to capture British ships and goods. During the course of the war, some 55,000 American sailors would serve on almost 1,700 privateers and would capture almost 2,300 British merchant ships.

The 1,800-mile-long American coast presented a big problem for the British. How could they defend their merchant ships from privateers in English waters, patrol the American coastline to keep ships from supplying the colonies with arms and other goods, and at the same time supply British land troops with the weapons and other things they needed?

The Birth of the American Navy

The month before Washington had taken command of the Continental Army, a group of Maine backwoodsmen under Jeremiah O'Brien won the first sea fight of the Revolution. The Patriots captured a small British merchant sloop and used her to capture the British armed cutter *Margaretta* and all of the supplies she was taking to British troops in New England.

This action was similar to most of the naval warfare waged by the colonies throughout the war. Every colony except New Hampshire commissioned ships, and Virginia and South Carolina had fairly large squadrons. Nearly all of these ships were small. They operated all along the Atlantic seaboard, in river mouths, bays, and coves. They carried on coastal commerce and attacked British supply boats and parties whenever the opportunities and odds were favorable. But most importantly, they kept open the coastal lines of communication on which so much of the life in the colonies depended.

Partly because of this "coastal cavalry" force, the Continental Congress was reluctant to establish a navy. Many representatives thought that no warships built and manned by colonists would be able to stand up to the powerful ships of the Royal Navy. Others thought that the break with England would only be temporary and that establishing a navy would bring retribution against the colonies when "normal" relations were resumed. Still, the colonies needed supplies to wage war, and capturing them from British ships was a good way to get them. When Congress learned that two unescorted transport ships loaded with supplies for the British army in Quebec had sailed from England, it decided that the time had come to launch the Continental Navy.

On 13 October 1775 the Continental Congress took the step that the U.S. Navy regards as its official birth. It approved a plan for buying, fitting out, and arming two vessels, the *Andrew Doria* and the *Cabot*, to intercept the British supply ships. As the war progressed, more ships were built. By war's end the Continental Congress would commission more than fifty armed warships of various types. The ships seized war supplies and munitions bound for the colonies, conveyed diplomats to Europe and back, and would take some two hundred British merchantmen as prizes, forcing the Royal Navy to divert ships to patrol sea-lanes and protect merchant shipping throughout the war.

Soon after taking command of the army, George Washington on his own initiative commissioned seven ships to capture some of the supplies that were streaming in by sea to the British troops in Boston. They made up what came to be called **"Washington's Navy."** In November 1775 his "navy" took muskets, shot, and a huge mortar, which Washington's poorly armed forces needed desperately, from British ships. In the short time that it was in existence, its ships took some thirty-eight of these prizes.

On 10 November 1775 the Continental Congress established a Marine Corps of two battalions. The Marine Corps still celebrates this date as its birthday.

In the early days of the Revolution, men were eager to serve in the Continental Navy. As the war continued, however, recruiting them became more difficult, due to a combination of strict discipline, low pay, and the rewards that could be obtained from privateering.

It took a lot of seamen to man an eighteenth-century warship. A typical three-masted frigate might have eighteen to twenty sails or more—most with separate rigging that had to be tended by one or more sailors—with more needed to set or furl them. A dozen men were required to man each long carriage gun in the main battery, and additional men were needed for the secondary guns and other shipboard duties. Typically only the guns on an engaged broadside were manned, but that still required a total gun crew of over 250 men on a typical 44-gun frigate. The 42-gun *Bonhomme Richard,* for example, captained by John Paul Jones in 1779, had a total crew of over 350 officers and men.

Sometimes the Continental authorities were forced to resort to the practice of **impressment** to crew the ships, wherein men were forced to serve by taking them on board against their will. Finding men to serve in the Continental Navy would be a problem throughout the war, and ships were sometimes unable to go to sea because they lacked sufficient crews.

First Naval Operations

The first Continental naval squadron was composed of six small schooners, brigs, and sloops donated by several states and assembled at Philadelphia. They were placed under the command of Esek Hopkins, a Rhode Islander. On 22 December 1775 the first American naval flag was raised on one of them, the *Alfred,* by the senior lieutenant in the Continental Navy, John Paul Jones. More would be heard of him later.

On his squadron's first cruise, in February 1776, Hopkins took it to New Providence (later Nassau) in the Bahamas, where he was able to overcome two British forts and take more than eighty artillery pieces, powder, and naval stores. On its way home the squadron captured several British ships loaded with more British arms, which it took as well.

A few weeks later, when Hopkins took the squadron south to Providence, Rhode Island, troubles began to multiply. Several of the ships began to break down, an epidemic of smallpox

Sketch of a U.S. frigate of the late eighteenth and early nineteenth centuries. *U.S. Naval Institute Photo Archive*

Action on the gun deck of an American frigate during the Revolutionary War. *U.S. Naval Institute Photo Archive*

sent a hundred men ashore, and General Washington wanted another hundred men he had loaned to the squadron returned. There was no money to pay those who were left. It was nearly impossible to recruit men for such duty when the crews of the coastal privateers got better shares of the prizes they captured, plus quick payoffs for their efforts.

Thus the Nassau expedition turned out to be the last time American ships would put to sea as a squadron during the war. Later, various officers who had been in the squadron set out by themselves in their ships and took on many British ships in hard-fought individual actions.

One such officer was LT John Paul Jones. With his sloop the *Providence,* in a single month, August 1776, he captured sixteen enemy vessels and destroyed many others. Later, as captain of the makeshift frigate *Alfred,* Jones cruised off the New England coast and raided enemy shipping and fishing in that area. One of the ships he captured carried British winter uniforms, and soon ten thousand American soldiers were wearing them. John Paul Jones would become legendary among early American naval leaders.

The Battle of Lake Champlain

Less than a month after the opening battles of the Revolution in Massachusetts, Ethan Allen captured Fort Ticonderoga on the southern end of Lake Champlain. Then, in the fall of 1775, American colonial forces invaded Canada, hoping that such action might persuade the Canadians to join them against the British. BGEN Richard Montgomery took Montreal in November. Then, joined by Patriot soldiers under GEN Benedict Arnold, he attacked Quebec on 31 December but could not capture the city. Montgomery was killed, and Arnold was wounded. The Americans stayed and bombarded the city through the winter. In May, after the ice had melted on the St. Lawrence River, British reinforcements arrived by ship, forcing Arnold and his Patriot troops to retreat toward the colonies. When it became apparent to the American garrison at Montreal that they could not hold out against the British reinforcements, the garrison joined with Arnold in his retreat south, abandoning the city on 17 June. The British, under MGEN Sir Guy Carleton, governor general of British North America, pursued them.

When Arnold and his men reached Crown Point near the southern end of Lake Champlain in June 1776, he assembled a ragtag flotilla of sixteen craft to oppose the British. In response the British constructed their own larger naval force at the northern end of the lake, and by October they were ready to proceed against the Americans.

Strength was not on Arnold's side, but he outfoxed the British. On 11 October he hid his flotilla at Valcour Island, about halfway down the western side of the lake near Plattsburgh, until the enemy fleet sailed past on its way south before a strong north wind. Then the American force attacked from upwind, forcing the British to turn and attack against the wind. Over the next two days the Americans inflicted much damage on the superior British fleet, though they lost most of their own ships in the process. Afterward the Americans ran their few surviving craft ashore, burned them, and escaped into the woods. Carleton and his forces resumed their southerly advance, eventually stopping at Crown Point. By this time winter was approaching, and Carleton returned to winter quarters in Canada, forsaking any further advances into the colonies.

This action came to be called the **First Battle of Lake Champlain,** to differentiate it from a second battle that would be fought near there during the War of 1812. The battle could not be considered a "victory" in the usual sense, because Arnold lost all his ships. However, the Patriots were able to stop the southerly British advance and thus gain time to regroup and train their forces until the following spring. (Unfortunately for the Patriots, the hero of this battle, General Benedict Arnold, would later be called a traitor when he changed sides in 1780 over disputes with the Continental Congress and was appointed a general in the British Army, in which he served until war's end.)

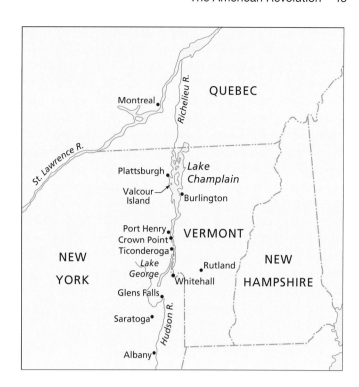

Map of Lake Champlain and surrounding region.

Washington Saves Philadelphia

While these events were taking place in upstate New York, farther to the east and south things were not going well. After the Battle of Bunker Hill in June 1775, the siege of Boston had stalemated, and the British general Sir William Howe still held the city. However, when the Americans placed cannon from the captured Fort Ticonderoga on Dorchester Heights overlooking the city in March 1776, the situation became untenable for the British, and Howe decided to evacuate the city. The Continental naval forces there were not large enough to stop the British from evacuating by sea, so Howe's troops and a thousand **Loyalists** (colonial troops loyal to the British) escaped in ships to Halifax, Nova Scotia, to await reinforcements. Washington took his Continental Army south to New York City to fortify it and prepare for campaigns in New York State and New Jersey.

After the reinforcements arrived, General Howe sailed south from Nova Scotia with the main British army to join British generals Sir Henry Clinton and Charles Cornwallis for an assault on New York City (then a community of less than 50,000 people on lower Manhattan Island), arriving on 5 July 1776, the day after the **Declaration of Independence** was signed. Five hundred British ships anchored off Staten Island. The Americans did not have a single warship, and the few small craft they had could not keep the enemy out of New York. Altogether, the British landed more than 30,000 well-equipped and well-trained troops. Washington's opposing troops numbered only about 20,000, and many of them were untrained militiamen.

By late fall, General Howe's superior forces had driven the Patriots from Long Island and Manhattan, and then from White Plains, New York. General Washington's army fled again and again before the advancing British. By December 1776 the American forces had been reduced to only a few thousand men by casualties and desertion, and also because most of those whose enlistments had run out by then had gone home to take care of their families for the winter. The British would occupy New York City for the rest of the war.

During the fighting in Manhattan, Washington authorized the use of the first **submersible** in warfare, a large one-man wooden capsule designed and built by David Bushnell, fitted with two hand-cranked screws, one on top and the other in front. Called the *Turtle*, on the night of 6 September 1776 it made its way out into the harbor and attempted to sink General Howe's flagship with an explosive charge. The attempt failed, and the *Turtle* was sunk later that fall by the British, along with its transport ship. Bushnell claimed to have later salvaged it, but its final fate is unknown.

After consolidating their victory at New York, the British sent a contingent of troops to capture Newport, Rhode Island, which they did without opposition in December. Meanwhile, Washington and his remaining troops crossed the Hudson River into New Jersey to escape the pursuing British. In early December Washington and his men crossed the Delaware River into Pennsylvania to escape the enemy yet again, thus avoiding a major confrontation that could have ended the war then and there. Things looked bleak for the Patriots. The Continental Congress abandoned Philadelphia, fearing a British attack there as their next move. As Thomas Paine, the famous Patriot pamphleteer, wrote during this time, "These are the times that try men's souls . . . but he that stands by [his country] now, deserves the love and thanks of man and woman."

Then in late December, Washington launched a bold counterattack. On Christmas night 1776, in a raging sleet storm, the nearly frozen American soldiers quietly rowed through the ice floes on the Delaware River back to the New Jersey shore. Their surprise attack on the enemy troops (Hessian soldiers, mercenaries from Hesse, in what is now Germany) at Trenton was a huge success. One week later, Washington surprised the British again, this time at Princeton, and his men won another complete victory, thus regaining initiative along with control of most of New Jersey.

The British then returned to New York City for the winter, while Washington and his troops wintered in Morristown, New Jersey. They had saved the colonial capital at Philadelphia from the enemy, and more importantly, the tide was turning. The Patriots would be ready to fight again with the coming of spring.

The Crucial Year: 1777

British forces poured across the Atlantic into America during the spring and early summer of 1777. The British prepared to use the same three-pronged plan of attack that had failed the year before because of the delays caused by the naval operations on Lake Champlain. LTGEN John Burgoyne, who had succeeded General Carleton in command of the British army in Canada, would move south from Montreal with eight thousand men down the western shore of Lake Champlain to the Hudson Valley. An army of pro-British **Tories** (called Loyalists by the English) and Indians would advance eastward from Lake Ontario. The main army, commanded by Howe, would march north from New York City. The three forces would meet in Albany, New York, after destroying all Patriot forces in their paths, thus splitting the colonies in half.

A drawing of the submersible *Turtle*, designed and built by David Bushnell during the Revolutionary War. *The Naval History and Heritage Command*

Burgoyne's troops, who had retained control of Lake Champlain after defeating the American flotilla there the previous fall, moved south from Canada as planned and recaptured Fort Ticonderoga in early July. In late August, however, Patriot militia beat a force of Tories and Indians near Fort Stanwix in the Mohawk River valley in central New York and forced it to return to Canada. The plan probably still would have worked if Howe had proceeded northward from New York City as originally intended. But he decided to first go by ship south into the Chesapeake Bay to take Philadelphia, in the process reengaging and defeating Washington's army, before proceeding to meet Burgoyne at Albany.

On 25 August 1777 Howe landed 15,000 men on the shores of the Chesapeake Bay about fifty miles south of Philadelphia. Howe's use of water transport had kept Washington guessing about his intentions for two months. When he finally received word that Howe's armada of 260 ships had entered the Chesapeake, Washington quickly marched most of his army south of Philadelphia to Brandywine Creek to block the British advance. But the Patriots were no match for the superior British force, and after a two-day battle on 10 and 11 September the British marched in triumph into Philadelphia as the Continental Congress fled once again. Howe then quartered his army comfortably in Philadelphia for the winter, while Washington's remaining troops faced terrible cold and hunger at Valley Forge, northwest of the city. However, as events were to turn out, though Howe had taken Philadelphia, by not following the British master plan he contributed to the eventual defeat of the British in the colonies.

The Turning Point: The Battle of Saratoga

Meanwhile in New York Burgoyne had continued to advance southward after recapturing Fort Ticonderoga, and by late July 1777 he had reached the upper Hudson River just north of Albany. However, he was now by himself with his force in upstate New York, and he was in trouble. His supply line was stretched through the wilderness, and his men were running short of food. Through the summer of 1777, militiamen from New York and New England constantly harassed his troops.

Almost in desperation, Burgoyne on 19 September marched his men European-style through an open field to try to break through the American lines near Saratoga, New York. They made easy targets for colonial sharpshooters, who were firing from behind trees. When the British retreated, the Americans followed, only to be driven back by British bayonets. The two forces took turns advancing and retreating. On 7 October Burgoyne led his trapped Redcoats in a final attempt to break through American lines. Once more, Daniel Morgan's riflemen mowed them down. The British retreated when GEN Benedict Arnold led a wild counterattack. Burgoyne had lost 1,200 men

and was surrounded by a total of 15,000 American militiamen and regulars under MGEN Horatio Gates. Burgoyne finally surrendered on 17 October 1777.

Saratoga marked the turning point of the war in two ways. First, after Burgoyne's defeat, the British government was less willing to carry on the war. Lord North, England's prime minister, offered to repeal the British tax laws that had caused the war if the Patriots would stop fighting and remain under British rule. But by now the leaders of the Revolution were dedicated to winning freedom for a new nation.

Even more important, the American victory at Saratoga now brought the French into the war on the American side. A few months after declaring independence, the Continental Congress had sent Benjamin Franklin to France. He tried to convince the French that joining the American cause was the best way for them to take world leadership away from England. After Saratoga the French finally decided that the Americans had a chance of winning the war, and they signed a treaty of friendship with the former colonies on 6 February 1778. In June, France declared war on England and began actively helping the Patriots win their freedom. A year later Spain joined the war as France's ally, followed by the Netherlands in 1780.

The naval battle on Lake Champlain the year before had set the stage for Saratoga. Saratoga helped bring France and, later, Spain and the Netherlands into the war on the American side. These allies made American victory and independence possible.

The War at Sea

American naval efforts in American waters during the war were mostly just a nuisance to Britain. By 1780 only a few of the forty converted merchantmen and thirteen frigates built for the Continental Navy remained in American hands. Though these vessels captured many British ships, they did not affect the outcome of the war. The small naval forces of the coastal states were also largely ineffective, as British ships were able to sail freely up and down the coast throughout most of the war.

American privateers were the biggest problem for the British in the offshore waters of the Atlantic. They hurt British trade in the West Indies, delayed troop transports bringing reinforcements, and captured arms and supplies that the colonial forces badly needed. The British were never able to put enough ships on station to contain them. However, privateering also took away men, ships, and weapons that the Continental Navy could have used. Despite the problems they caused, the privateers did not greatly harm the British war effort. Washington had been right when he said that naval power would decide the outcome of the war, but in the end it was French, not American, naval power that made the difference.

American exploits in more distant waters, however, were impressive. The tiny Continental Navy and several American

John Paul Jones was one of the first naval heroes of the new American republic. As the inscription on his tomb under the Naval Academy chapel reads, "He gave to our Navy its earliest traditions of heroism and bravery." *The Naval History and Heritage Command*

naval heroes won glory overseas during the war. The most famous of them was **John Paul Jones,** who took the war to European waters with inspiring results.

Jones received command of the new 18-gun *Ranger* in June 1777 and sailed to France. In the spring of 1778 Jones took the *Ranger* around Britain and Ireland, where he captured the HMS *Drake* and several merchant ships.

One year later, Jones was given command of an old 42-gun converted French merchantman, which he renamed the *Bon-*

homme Richard in honor of Benjamin Franklin, who had written *Poor Richard's Almanac.* In August 1779 Jones sailed in command of a small squadron that included the American frigate *Alliance,* with thirty-six guns, and three smaller French vessels. The captain of the *Alliance* was an unpredictable Frenchman named Pierre Landais.

At dusk on 23 September 1779 Jones's squadron was trailing a large English convoy off the northeast coast of England when its two escorts approached. The British warships were the 50-gun HMS *Serapis,* under CAPT Richard Pearson, and the 20-gun *Countess of Scarborough.* Jones immediately ordered an attack, but the small French ships turned away. Later, though, the French frigate *Pallas* took the *Countess* after a sharp fight.

The *Richard* and the *Serapis* both began to fire broadsides at each other as soon as they came into range. Early in the exchange, however, two of Jones's 18-pounder cannons exploded on the lower gun deck, killing all the crewmen there and blowing a huge hole in the deck above. Jones saw that his only hope was to try to lay the *Richard* alongside and take the *Serapis* by boarding. He ordered grapples heaved, and then he seized one of the **forestays** (forward rigging lines that help support the masts) from the British vessel and tied it to the *Richard*'s **mizzenmast** (the mast farthest aft) himself. For the rest of

The *Bonhomme Richard*, commanded by CAPT John Paul Jones, engages HMS *Serapis* on 23 September 1779. The *Alliance* is in the background to the right. *The Naval History and Heritage Command*

the battle, the two ships swung together stern to bow and bow to stern, their guns firing directly into each other.

After two hours of fighting, the crew of the *Richard* had cleared the topside weather decks of the *Serapis,* but the *Richard* was full of holes. At this point the *Alliance* reappeared. A glad shout went up from the Americans, but it was quickly drowned out when the *Alliance* fired a broadside that ripped into the *Richard* instead of the *Serapis*. The *Alliance* fired two more broadsides into the *Richard* and then withdrew. Landais later told a friend that he had hoped to become the victor by sinking the *Richard* and capturing the *Serapis* himself. Jones would later bring charges against Landais, who would be dismissed from the French Navy.

The *Richard* slowly began to sink. At this point Captain Pearson of the British ship asked if Jones was ready to strike. Jones replied with the immortal words, "I have not yet begun to fight!" At about 2130 hours an American seaman dropped a grenade through an open hatch on the *Serapis*. The grenade hit powder cartridges in the British vessel, and the explosions killed many of her gunners.

Jones's crew now came topside to fight hand to hand. The fighting continued for an hour, until at 2230 Captain Pearson tore down his flag with his own hands. He had been shaken by the explosions and the ferocity of the hand-to-hand fighting and was afraid his tottering mainmast would collapse.

The battered *Richard* went down two days later, and Jones raised the American flag on board the *Serapis*. Then, avoiding the British ships that were trying to find him, he sailed his squadron and prizes to Holland.

The Closing Campaigns

With France now its enemy, Britain could no longer concentrate all its efforts in the colonies. The British were now determined to stand on the defensive in the north, mount an offensive in the south, and take the war to the West Indies.

In April, soon after the French alliance with the American colonies, a dozen French warships under the command of VADM the comte d'Estaing sailed for America. Sir Henry Clinton, who had succeeded Howe in command of the British forces in the colonies after the failed 1777 campaigns, feared a possible French attack on New York, so in June 1778 he abandoned Philadelphia and marched his army through New Jersey to reinforce New York City. D'Estaing took eighty-five days to cross the Atlantic, an extraordinarily long time even by the standards of that era. Had he arrived sooner, he might have caught General Howe's fleet in the Delaware, where it was transporting Clinton's artillery and supplies by water to New York. But d'Estaing arrived too late, and Howe delivered Clinton's supplies on 29 June. Clinton then stationed frigates in New York Harbor to warn of the approach of the French naval forces.

When d'Estaing arrived off New York on 11 July, General Washington proposed to launch a land attack while d'Estaing attacked by sea. But the French ships could not get into the shallow harbor, so d'Estaing headed for Newport to assist American forces there in an attack against that seaport the following month. After a strong storm and attacks by British warships damaged his ships, the attack was aborted, and he made for Boston. In November, after a short stay there, d'Estaing sailed away to the Caribbean to engage British forces in the islands over the winter of 1778–79. Meanwhile, Washington and his troops spent the winter months consolidating their positions in New York and New Jersey, where they would remain for most of the following year. The British, wanting to concentrate their forces in New York, abandoned Newport in October 1779, after which it would become a French naval base for the duration of the war.

The Southern Campaigns

After the departure of the French, the English decided to take advantage of their absence and take the war into the southern colonies. Accordingly, in December 1778 a British force of 3,500 troops sailed from New York to invade Savannah, Georgia. It captured the city after a brief fight, and proceeded to take control of most of the rest of Georgia by mid-January 1779. The British then attempted to capture Charleston, South Carolina, but they were not successful and spent the summer consolidating their positions in Georgia.

In the Caribbean, d'Estaing heard from General Washington of the British invasion in the south and determined to help the small American force there recapture Savannah. Accordingly he sailed with his fleet for Savannah, arriving there on 1 September 1779. Following a three-week siege of the port, in October the combined French and American forces assaulted the city. But the attack failed, and a dejected d'Estaing, who had been wounded during the assault, sailed for France.

In Morristown, Washington's troops began suffering through another difficult winter, in many ways worse than the one at Valley Forge. Confident that these troops were not a threat to New York City, Clinton mounted a major offensive in the south in February 1780. His large fleet, with eight thousand troops under Lord Cornwallis embarked, set sail for Charleston and surrounded the American forces there. The city had held off the British for three years, but Clinton's new force was overwhelming, and the city fell on 12 May. Soon the British had control of all of South Carolina, and in the fall they began invading North Carolina. Washington, with most of his troops tied down in New York and New Jersey, was powerless to stop the British. The last Continental naval squadron had been captured in Charleston Harbor, so the Continental Navy was never again an effective fighting force.

In August 1780 Clinton received word that a French fleet bringing 5,500 soldiers under the comte de Rochambeau had arrived in Newport, Rhode Island, to reinforce General Washington. Fearing a prospective attack on New York, Clinton left Cornwallis in command in the south and hurried back with six warships to New York.

In October GEN Nathaniel Greene's troops defeated a Tory force at King's Mountain, South Carolina, and in January 1781 General Morgan destroyed a British force under LCOL Banastre Tarleton at Cowpens. Cornwallis followed Morgan and Greene through North Carolina. He won a battle at Guilford Courthouse, but he lost so many men that he had to retreat to Wilmington, North Carolina, and asked the Royal Navy to send help to him there. Help did not arrive, and in May 1781 he led his remaining 1,500 troops into Virginia, convinced that he could not campaign further in the Carolinas. After his departure, local southern forces under General Greene soon regained control of North Carolina, and by three months later they had recaptured all of South Carolina except for Charleston.

The Battle of Yorktown

Cornwallis marched first to Petersburg, where there was another contingent of British troops, and with the combined force of about 7,200 troops he successfully conducted military operations throughout central Virginia. The marquis de Lafayette, an influential young Frenchman who had been appointed a general in the Continental Army in 1777, and GEN "Mad Anthony" Wayne commanded about five thousand ragged militia in the area, and these troops kept Cornwallis under observation. Then in August, under orders from Clinton, Cornwallis entrenched his army at Yorktown on the lower Chesapeake Bay, where he could expect to receive British naval support. Lafayette immediately sent word of Cornwallis' move to General Washington.

In the meantime, French general Rochambeau, who had brought 5,500 troops to Newport the previous August to aid Washington, learned in May 1781 that contrary to earlier arrangements, no additional French troops would be coming. In spite of this, he and Washington agreed to attack Clinton's superior force in New York City. Washington wrote to the French minister at Philadelphia to ask him to urge RADM the comte de Grasse, then in command of French naval forces fighting the British in the West Indies, to come to New York from the Caribbean to assist. Rochambeau, however, was convinced that the British threat in the south was greater. He wrote letters of his own to de Grasse urging him to bring not only his fleet but also French troops to the Chesapeake Bay. De Grasse received the letters in July at Haiti.

On 14 August 1781 the reply on which everything hinged arrived at Washington's headquarters. De Grasse reported that he would be coming to the Chesapeake Bay with more than twenty-five warships and three thousand troops in September. Realizing that without de Grasse's support he could not successfully attack New York City, Washington ordered 2,500 Americans and four thousand of General Rochambeau's troops to march from New York to Yorktown. He left the remaining troops behind to protect West Point and to distract Clinton in New York. A French squadron also sailed south from Newport carrying siege artillery and munitions. Washington hoped to bring all these land and sea forces together to battle the British at Yorktown.

On 5 September the American and French troops passed through Philadelphia, and General Washington learned that de Grasse had arrived in the Chesapeake Bay. On the evening of 14 September Washington and Rochambeau greeted Lafayette and Wayne at Williamsburg, Virginia, and then set up siege lines around Yorktown. The next morning Washington learned that on 5 September off the Virginia Capes de Grasse had battled to a standoff a British fleet that had come down from New York and that the French fleet from Newport had safely arrived on 10 September. On the 13th, after spotting the combined French fleet at anchor off Yorktown, the commander of the remaining British ships decided to return to New York in order to bring back Clinton with a large relief force of troops to aid Cornwallis. The stage was set for the attack against Cornwallis, now isolated at Yorktown without any hope of assistance from the British fleet.

Twenty thousand French and American troops attacked Yorktown on 9 October. For eight days the combined land forces fired artillery at the British while the French fleet bombarded them from the bay. American and French forces also stormed two key defensive positions and kept the British from fleeing across the York River to Gloucester. The British fleet that had retreated to New York returned to the Chesapeake with Clinton and six thousand British troops, but it was one week too late to help Cornwallis. He had surrendered his entire army of some seven thousand troops and eight hundred sailors from British ships in the York River to General Washington on 19 October 1781.

Aftermath

The British loss at Yorktown marked the end of the fighting in the colonies. The conflict then shifted to the West Indies, the Mediterranean, and India. England, tired of war, now faced the powerful combined forces of France, Spain, and the Netherlands in Europe. King George III gave up all hope of defeating the colonists, though he would keep the 30,000 troops still in Canada, the American colonies, and Florida in place, while other British forces attacked the French and Spanish in the Caribbean. He hoped by disrupting American coastal trade and encouraging Indian attacks on western settlements he could demoralize the colonials and bring them back under British rule once the French, Spanish, and Dutch were defeated.

In February 1782 Lord North resigned, and the new pacifist cabinet in Parliament decided not to launch any more offensive attacks in North America. England sent a representative to Paris to discuss peace with the Americans. The American delegation, headed by Benjamin Franklin, John Jay, and John Adams, insisted on American independence. England still held New York, Charleston, and Savannah in the colonies, but the pressure in Europe was working to the Americans' advantage.

The treaty that the Americans and the British drew up gave the colonies their full independence. They would not be under British rule or protection in any way. The colonies received a territory that extended west to the Mississippi, north to the Great Lakes, and south to Florida. The U.S. Congress declared the war over on 11 April 1783, but it was not until 3 September that the American and British representatives signed the *Treaty of Paris (1783)*, the American part of the overall accord called the *Peace of Paris* that formally ended the war for all participants.

Critical Thinking

1. Describe the major advantages and disadvantages of each of the two combatants of the American Revolutionary War, 1775–83.

2. Elaborate on the statement that sea power played a major role in America gaining its independence during the American Revolutionary War.

Chronology

1775	American Revolution begins; Congress establishes Navy; British evacuate Boston
1776	Battle of Lake Champlain; British invade New York; Washington crosses Delaware
1777	British capture Philadelphia; Burgoyne surrenders at Saratoga
1778	France allies with America; British capture Savannah
1778–81	British southern campaigns
1779	Jones defeats *Serapis*
1780	Charleston surrenders
1781	Battle of Yorktown; Cornwallis surrenders
1783	Congress declares war over; Peace of Paris signed

Study Guide Questions

1. As a result of the Seven Years' War, whose worldwide colonial possessions did Britain obtain?

2. A. Why did the British Parliament begin to lay burdensome taxes on the American colonies?
   B. What happened in 1773 as a result of the Townshend Act?

3. What did the British response to the Boston Tea Party lead to in April 1775?

4. What naval materials did the colonies supply to the Royal Navy?

5. When was the Marine Corps established?

6. What were the problems of recruiting a crew in the early Continental Navy?

7. How did the American invasion of Canada in 1775 turn out?

8. A. Who was the American commander at the first Battle of Lake Champlain in 1776?
   B. What was the important outcome of the battle?

9. A. What was the overall British plan to defeat the Americans in 1777?
   B. What happened?
   C. Why was the Battle of Saratoga vital to the American cause?
   D. What were the names of the opposing generals in this battle?

10. Who was the great American diplomat who brought about the French alliance early in 1778?

11. Who is considered the greatest American naval hero of the Revolutionary War?

12. A. Where did John Paul Jones have his famous battle with HMS *Serapis*?
    B. What was the name of the ship commanded by Jones?
    C. What was Jones's strategy in the fight?

13. What was Jones's famous reply when the British captain asked if he was ready to strike his colors?

14. What major ports and colonies were captured during the British southern campaign?

15. A. What crucial naval confrontation made victory at the Battle of Yorktown possible?
    B. Who were the American and French commanders at Yorktown?

16. A. After Yorktown, where did the British concentrate their war effort?
    B. When did the war officially end?

New Vocabulary

militia	reinforcements
broadside	forestay
impressment	mizzenmast
artillery	topside
garrison	weather decks
desertion	grenade
submersible	power cartridge
counterattack	mainmast
sharpshooters	entrench

The Growth of American Sea Power

When the Treaty of Paris ended the Revolutionary War in 1783, the new nation was badly in debt. The government did not have authority to raise money through taxation, so there were no funds for maintaining ships or building new ones. The Continental Marines, established in 1775, were disbanded, and the Continental Navy went out of existence when its sole remaining warship, the frigate *Alliance,* was sold. The officers and men who had served in the Continental Navy returned to their peacetime jobs of merchant shipping and shipbuilding.

American merchant mariners and shipbuilders soon found, however, that the British were not going to make life easy for them. The British government issued a series of *Orders in Council* (royal decrees) that sought to keep Americans out of the West Indies trade, limited exports to English colonies, and made it illegal for British subjects to buy ships built in America. Later, as the war with Napoleon intensified, they also forbade trade with France or any of its colonies.

Thus, American merchants had to find new overseas markets for their trade. Some looked to China, but it was far away, and getting there took a lot of time and money. Now that the protection of the British flag had been removed, American ships trading in the Mediterranean and eastern Atlantic region became subject to harassment by pirates from the Barbary states of Morocco, Algiers (now Algeria), Tunis (modern-day Tunisia), and Tripoli (modern-day Libya). They had been capturing ships and holding crews for ransom in these waters for hundreds of years. European nations such as Britain, France, and the Netherlands had long paid these countries tribute money so they could sail these waters in safety, but the United States had no such arrangements. In 1784 and 1785 three American ships were seized by the Barbary pirates. Faced with the threat of continued seizures of its shipping and having no navy to prevent it, the United States concluded treaties with Morocco in 1786, and with the other three Barbary states ten years later, under which the United States would pay tribute in return for freedom from harassment by the pirates.

A New American Government

In 1789 the Articles of Confederation were replaced by the U.S. Constitution. The Constitution authorized Congress "to provide and maintain a navy," but other needs in the new nation were more pressing. Besides, a war had started between Portugal and Algiers, and this made it possible for American merchantmen in the Mediterranean to join with Portuguese and Spanish convoys for protection. The need for a navy did not seem urgent.

One of the first acts of the new U.S. government helped American merchants. The government decided to impose tariffs (taxes) on incoming foreign trade goods, giving an immediate advantage to U.S. shipping. Additionally, British West Indian planters needed and began welcoming U.S. ships and the goods they carried, despite the Orders in Council that prohibited such trade.

With these incentives, U.S. shipping and shipbuilding grew rapidly until 1793. In that year Portugal and Algiers declared a truce, and soon thereafter a pirate fleet captured eleven U.S. ships in the Atlantic. In addition, in 1790 the Napoleonic Wars had broken out in Europe, and France had declared war on Britain. British warships had then begun to seize neutral vessels trading with France, and French privateers had begun capturing neutral vessels trading with British possessions, such as the West Indies. The time had come for the United States to give serious consideration to building a navy.

The Navy Act of 1794

Not all Americans were in favor of building a navy. Those who lived inland did not want to be taxed for something they felt would benefit mainly those who lived along the coast. So the Navy Act that Congress eventually passed in 1794 provided for only six frigates; also, to appease opponents, their construction would stop if the United States made peace with Algiers. In 1796 this happened, but President Washington convinced Congress to allow work on three of the frigates to be completed. Washington's secretary of war, GEN Henry Knox, who administered naval affairs in the new government, knew they might one day be used against the frigates of the Royal Navy or France. So he directed that they be built larger than the standard 38-gun Royal Navy frigates of that time, in order that they would be faster and could carry more guns. The *United States, Constitution,* and *Constellation,* all rated at forty-four guns, were launched in 1797. (Warships of the sailing era were rated according to the number of long-barreled carriage-mounted guns they carried. For example, ships of the line, corresponding to the battleships of a later day, carried from fifty to a hundred or more, often on multiple gun decks; larger frigates, twenty-eight to forty-four; and smaller frigates, twenty to twenty-four guns. Any additional guns they might carry, such as short-barreled *carronades,* were not counted in these totals, so ships of the same ratings might have differing numbers of total guns.)

The British realized early in their war with Napoleon's France that they would need trade goods carried in U.S. ships, and so they stopped seizing them. The British and the Americans worked out these and other maritime differences in Jay's Treaty, which the two countries signed in 1797.

The French were outraged by this agreement, and they increased their raids on U.S. ships. In one year French privateers

The HMS *Victory*, commissioned in 1764, a three-decked ship of the line with 104 guns. Now a museum ship at Portsmouth, England, she was Admiral Horatio Nelson's flagship at the Battle of Trafalgar and is the only surviving such ship of that era. *HMS Victory National Museum of the Royal Navy*

The 44-gun frigate USS *Constitution*, launched in 1797. The ship has survived for over two centuries and is kept in sailing trim in Boston Harbor. She is the oldest U.S. ship still in commission. *The Naval History and Heritage Command*

in the West Indies and along the U.S. Atlantic coast seized over three hundred U.S. merchant ships. In the fall of 1797 President John Adams sent three representatives to Paris to try to work out a settlement. The French wanted these men to pay a huge bribe to begin the talks, but the envoys refused. Americans everywhere responded to the French demand with the slogan "Millions for defense, but not one cent for tribute!" Ironically, this occurred at the same time that the United States had been paying tribute for some time to the Barbary states for safe passage of its shipping through the Mediterranean.

In any event, the **French XYZ Affair,** as this came to be called, put Congress in the mood to finish building the six frigates authorized in 1794. The *Congress* and the *Chesapeake,* thirty-eight and thirty-six guns, respectively, would be launched in 1799, and the *President,* forty-four guns, in 1800. In addition, several New England states built and donated frigates to the Navy. On 30 April 1898 Congress created the Navy Department, and President Adams appointed Benjamin Stoddert to be the first Secretary of the Navy. In May, Congress authorized U.S. vessels to seize armed French ships that were found cruising in American coastal waters. The United States had started an undeclared naval war, the **Quasi-War with France.**

Quasi-War with France, 1798–1800

In July 1798, Congress extended its earlier authorization and allowed U.S. ships to capture armed French ships anywhere they met them on the high seas. Stoddert was then able to send a series of Navy expeditions to the West Indies, where most of the French privateers were based. After two small expeditions were unsuccessful, Stoddert sent a more powerful force of twenty-one ships in four squadrons to the West Indies. There, U.S. vessels were allowed to use British bases and had the support of the Royal Navy. U.S. officers and seamen learned much as they served together with what was then the finest navy in the world.

Commodore Thomas Truxtun was one of the Americans who worked hard to profit from the lessons he learned from the Royal Navy. In his ship the *Constellation,* Truxtun fought the two most famous battles of the Quasi-War. The first took place in February 1799, when the *Constellation,* on patrol in the Caribbean, encountered the French frigate *Insurgente.* After a brief fight the *Constellation* holed *Insurgente*'s hull so many times that her captain had to surrender. In the second battle a year later, the *Constellation* fought the French frigate *Vengeance* to a draw after a five-hour battle off Guadeloupe.

Finally, in October 1800, after more than two years of undeclared war, a peace treaty was signed between France and the United States. One of the provisions in the treaty was a very unpopular clause canceling U.S. claims against the French attacks on U.S. merchant ships. Partly because of all the uproar the treaty caused, Thomas Jefferson was able to defeat John Adams in the presidential election of 1800.

During the war the U.S. fleet had grown rapidly. Several more warships, including the sloop (then a small three-masted, square-rigged ship) *George Washington* and frigate *Philadelphia,* were built and commissioned. By war's end there were fifty vessels, six thousand seamen, and over five hundred commissioned officers and midshipmen serving in the U.S. Navy, as well as 1,100 Marines in the U.S. Marine Corps.

War with Tripoli and the Barbary Pirates, 1801–1805

As part of his campaign for the presidential election of 1800, Jefferson had promised to reduce government spending. The Navy cost the country over two million dollars every year, so making the Navy smaller was one way for Jefferson to keep his promise after he was elected. He sold off almost all the American warships that Stoddert had acquired during the quasi-war with France except the sloop *Enterprise* and thirteen frigates, and he laid up seven of those in reserve. He authorized only small gunboats to be built during his administration. In the event of any future hostilities, these would be stationed along the Atlantic coast, together with land fortifications and shore batteries, to repel any invasion.

Meanwhile, the Barbary pirates began to cause more trouble. When the *George Washington* arrived in Algiers with a tribute payment in September 1800, the **dey of Algiers** (the Algerian leader) ordered her captain, William Bainbridge, to take passengers and the tribute payment to the sultan in Constantinople. When Bainbridge refused, the dey aimed the guns of the fortress at the ship and forced Bainbridge to carry out his orders. After this incident, other Barbary states increased their tribute demands. Jefferson refused to pay them. In May 1801, when the United States did not meet the tribute demands of the **pasha** (ruler) **of Tripoli,** the pasha declared war on the United States. In response, Jefferson sent a squadron consisting of the frigates *President, Philadelphia,* and *Essex* and the 12-gun sloop *Enterprise* to the Mediterranean to protect American shipping.

That summer, the *Enterprise* blockaded the port of Tripoli for eighteen days and then left for Malta. On the way she met and defeated a Tripolitan cruiser, the *Tripoli.* The other U.S. warships convoyed American merchantmen through the Mediterranean. But by the end of summer, most of the crews' enlistments were running out, so the squadron had to return home.

A more powerful squadron was prepared for the next year. It arrived in the spring of 1802, under the command of CAPT Richard Morris. He attempted another blockade of Tripoli, but the blockade was ineffective because of a lack of shallow-draft vessels that could attack Tripolitan small craft. The Americans were able only to capture one Tripolitan cruiser and destroy another, and the pasha refused to lower his price for peace. Morris retired to Gibraltar for most of the rest of the year. Embarrassed by these failures, President Jefferson ordered Morris to return with his squadron to the United States, where Morris was subsequently replaced by Commodore Edward Preble.

The officers serving under Preble at first did not like their commander, because he was very strict. After seeing their leader in action, however, the officers were proud to be called **"Preble's Boys."** Preble had been worried at first because his officers were all younger than thirty, saying at one point, "They have given me nothing but a pack of boys!" But the young officers' aggressive spirit and quick minds soon won Preble's respect.

Preble was sent back to the Mediterranean in mid-August 1803 with the frigates *Constitution* and *Philadelphia.* When Preble arrived in Gibraltar in September 1803, he found that Morocco had broken its 1786 treaty with the United States by capturing a U.S. vessel. He quickly sent the *Philadelphia,* under Captain Bainbridge, and a schooner to blockade Tripoli. Then Preble assembled a powerful force in the Moroccan port of Tangier. The emperor of Morocco was impressed by Preble's display of strength, so much so that thereafter he kept his treaty with the United States without demanding any further payments.

The *Philadelphia Incident*

On 31 October, while she was blockading Tripoli, the frigate *Philadelphia* had run aground and been captured. Her crew of more than three hundred was then held for ransom. Unfortunately, the Tripolitans were able to free the U.S. warship from the reef she was on and anchored her near the guns of the pasha's castle, within easy range of shore batteries and armed Tripolitan vessels.

Commodore Preble learned of *Philadelphia*'s capture in late November while cruising off Italy. In December he sailed with the *Constitution* and the *Enterprise* to Tripoli to take stock of the situation. On his arrival Preble saw that the *Philadelphia* was too well defended to be recaptured. He decided to destroy her so that Tripoli could not use her.

LT Stephen Decatur Jr. volunteered to lead a raiding party to burn the *Philadelphia.* On 16 February 1804 Decatur and his men slipped into the harbor in a captured Tripolitan ketch renamed the *Intrepid.* Decatur disguised himself in Maltese

The burning of the captured frigate *Philadelphia* on 16 February 1804. *The Naval History and Heritage Command*

Stephen Decatur, promoted to captain at age twenty-five by President Jefferson as a result of his heroism during the war with Tripoli in 1804, was the youngest to achieve this rank in U.S. naval history. *The Naval History and Heritage Command*

dress and stood next to his vessel's Sicilian pilot. Some of his seventy volunteers, also in disguise, stayed on deck, but most stayed hidden out of sight below.

As the *Intrepid* came near her target, a Tripolitan guard warned the vessel to stay away. The pilot told the guard that the *Intrepid* had lost her anchors in a storm and asked to be allowed to tie up. The guard agreed, but then, just as the *Intrepid* was passing her lines, the guard became suspicious and shouted an alarm.

Decatur immediately ordered "Board!" and led his men over the side. The few Tripolitan guards on duty in the *Philadelphia* put up little fight. Several were killed, and the rest jumped overboard. Decatur's men set fire to the ship, and the *Philadelphia* was soon engulfed in flames. The Americans then reboarded the *Intrepid* and escaped safely to the squadron, despite being fired upon by the Tripolitan fort and several warships.

When news of that exploit reached the United States, Decatur was hailed as a hero and given a captain's commission. At twenty-five he was the youngest man to reach that rank in the short history of the U.S. Navy.

Attack on Tripoli

During the summer of 1804, Preble tried to convince the pasha of Tripoli to release the crewmen of the *Philadelphia* but was refused. Preble decided he would have to use force. He obtained half a dozen gunboats, plus some other craft, from the king of Naples and attacked Tripoli on 3 August. Nine Tripolitan gunboats came out to challenge them. The Tripolitans were ready to board and fight hand to hand, but the Americans surprised them by leaping into the lead enemy gunboat while the squadron kept the others away. During the ensuing fighting, the blade of Decatur's cutlass broke off, and he would have been killed if a seaman named Reuben James had not thrust his own head under a sword meant for Decatur.

As Decatur was towing his prize out of the harbor, he learned that his younger brother James had been shot as he stepped on board to take control of another enemy gunboat that had surrendered. That gunboat was trying to escape when Stephen Decatur overtook her, boarded her, and killed her captain in a hand-to-hand fight.

By the time Preble called an end to the battle, the Americans had captured three enemy gunboats. Following this attack, the pasha of Tripoli offered to return the U.S. crewmen for $150,000 in ransom money and to demand no more tribute. Preble rejected the offer and ordered his forces to bombard Tripoli. The Americans continued the bombardment during the next few weeks, but no more enemy gunboats came out to fight the U.S. vessels.

President Jefferson and the U.S. public were spurred to action by Preble's feats. They hoped that a final victory would end the war with Tripoli and make all of the Barbary states stop demanding tribute. Jefferson sent a powerful U.S. naval force to the Mediterranean, and he ordered CAPT Samuel Barron to replace Preble. The United States gave Preble a hero's welcome when he returned to Washington.

The American naval force kept Tripoli blockaded through the early part of 1805, and plans were made for a better blockade and more attacks on the city in the summer, when more gunboats were to arrive from America.

In the meantime, however, William Eaton, a bold U.S. naval agent to the Barbary states, devised a scheme to topple the pasha from his throne. He convinced the pasha's dethroned older brother, Hamet, then in exile with the Mamelukes (a centuries-old military class) in Egypt, to join a ragtag army of about four hundred Muslim and European mercenaries he had put together to attack Tripoli and restore the throne to Hamet.

Eaton's army, which included a small contingent of U.S. Marines led by LT Presley O'Bannon, marched some six hundred miles westward from Egypt through the North African desert in March and April 1805. On 27 April this force attacked and captured the port city of Derna, across the Gulf of Sidra from Tripoli, with the help of two brigs (a two-masted square-rigged ship) and a schooner from the naval squadron. After the capture O'Bannon raised the Stars and Stripes over the city's harbor fortress, marking the first time the American flag was raised over captured foreign soil. Later, tradition has it that Hamet presented his Mameluke sword to O'Bannon in recognition of his bravery in capturing the city and defending against counterattacks over the next several weeks. This action was later memorialized by the phrase "to the shores of Tripoli" in the "Marine Corps Hymn," and a commemorative Mameluke sword is still presented today to each new U.S. Marine officer upon commissioning.

Unfortunately, Eaton's triumph was short-lived. In June came word that the United States had signed a treaty with the pasha at Tripoli ending the war. In return for $60,000 in ransom and a promise that the United States would no longer support his brother, the pasha agreed to release the captive *Philadelphia* crew members and end all further demands for tribute payments. Eaton was ordered to take Hamet and evacuate Derna, which he reluctantly did, abandoning most of his army. The vengeful pasha later executed most of those left behind.

America Moves toward War with England

As mentioned previously, throughout the 1790s Napoleon Bonaparte's France had been at war with most of Europe. In 1797 he attempted to conquer Egypt but was defeated by Britain's ADM Lord Nelson at the Battle of Abu Qir Bay in August 1798. Still, he was able to seize control of the French government in 1799, and the following year he forced Spain to cede to France the Louisiana Territory in America. In 1802 the British and French agreed to peace in the Treaty of Amiens, but Napoleon knew that further conflict with the British was inevitable. Besides, the Louisiana Territory was far away and difficult to administer. So in 1803, as a way to finance his anticipated war against England,

Napoleon sold the Louisiana Territory to the United States for $15 million. Napoleon also hoped that this would cause the United States to look with favor toward France in its coming struggle with Britain, which began again later in 1803.

For two years following the resumption of war between France and Britain, the U.S. merchant marine made great profits as the leading remaining neutral carrier of ocean commerce. But in 1805 that changed. At the Battle of Trafalgar that year, the British fleet under Admiral Nelson smashed the combined fleets of France and Spain, France's ally, making Britain ruler of the seas. At the Battle of Austerlitz in December 1805 in Austria, however, Napoleon crushed the combined Austrian and Russian armies, which made France master of the European continent. England and France then struck against each other's sea lines of communication, an action that inevitably would involve the United States.

Again, as had happened in the mid-1790s, U.S. merchant ships were subjected to harassment and capture as prizes on the high seas. British Orders in Council once again closed French ports to foreign shipping, and French decrees ordered French privateers to seize any ships trading with England or carrying British goods to continental European ports. Nevertheless, U.S. merchants continued to make great profits by trading in desperately needed supplies with both sides.

Gradually, however, American sentiment turned against the British. According to British naval custom, British warship captains could, if short of crew members, stop any British merchantmen and take the men needed to fill their own crews, a procedure called "impressment." But problems arose when the British began seizing seamen off U.S. ships, claiming they were deserters from the Royal Navy. This may have had some basis in fact, for conditions in the Royal Navy were often bad and U.S. merchant seamen made good wages. It was not uncommon for British warships to lose significant parts of their crews to desertion whenever they visited an American port during these years. Nevertheless, many Americans were upset by these British abuses of power at sea.

In addition to the bad feelings created by the trade restrictions and impressments of Americans, there was also lingering resentment against Britain and the Royal Navy; the American Revolution had ended just twenty years before. Moreover, although Britain had ceded the **Old Northwest Territory** (comprising the modern-day states of Ohio, Indiana, Illinois, Michigan, and part of Wisconsin) to the United States after the Revolution, the British still maintained a large presence there, and they and their countrymen in Canada had often incited the Indians in the region to violence against American settlers.

The Chesapeake Affair

Bad as the growing number of impressments on U.S. merchant ships was, feelings against the British became even more inflamed when an American warship was boarded at sea and some of her crew were forcibly removed. In 1807 the U.S. frigate *Chesapeake,* with thirty-six guns, was set upon by the HMS *Leopard,* fifty guns, off Cape Henry, Virginia. The *Chesapeake* was fired upon and forced to surrender, after which the British took four of her seamen. One was soon hanged as a British deserter.

The nation was outraged, and there were many demands for a declaration of war against England. President Jefferson, however, was greatly opposed to any American involvement in European wars. So he tried to stop the movement toward war by having Congress pass an embargo (suspension of trade) of exports of needed raw materials and food to Europe. He hoped that this would force the European powers to respect U.S. rights.

All that the embargo did, however, was cause severe economic strain for U.S. shipping companies in New England and for farmers in the south and west. Soon smuggling became rampant, further draining revenue from the government. And neither Britain nor France stopped impressing American seamen or seizing U.S. merchant ships. In 1809 Congress yielded to popular demand and repealed the embargo, replacing it with an act that permitted trade with all ports except those under British or French control. Impressments and ship seizures by both England and France continued unabated. By 1810 the English had taken over a thousand American ships and had impressed more than six thousand U.S. citizens into duty with the Royal Navy. France had seized over eight hundred American merchant ships.

Final Moves toward War

James Madison became president in 1809. The next year congressional elections brought into office young "War Hawks" from the south and west. These men called for an end to pacifism and urged an invasion of Canada as punishment for the outrages at sea. Madison did not want war, so he urged Congress to make one last try to halt the harassment at sea by reimposing the embargo of imported goods of any nation that would not do away with restrictions on U.S. trade.

In response, Napoleon quickly repealed all French decrees against U.S. shipping, hoping this would bring the United States into the war against Britain if the British did not follow suit. Britain did not repeal their Orders in Council, so Madison continued to enforce the embargo of British goods. This angered the British and made them think that the United States was teaming up with France against them. Britain kept up the impressment of sailors on the high seas and harassment of American merchant ships; "Freedom of the seas!" became the War Hawks' slogan. Britain and the United States were moving toward war.

Matters reached the boiling point when in April 1811 the British frigate *Guerrière* stopped a U.S. merchantman off New York and impressed one of the ship's seamen, a native of Maine.

Commodore John Rodgers was sent to sea in the 44-gun *President* to protect U.S. shipping. On the evening of 16 May off the Virginia Capes, the *President* came upon a ship that refused to identify herself. It is unclear who fired first, but the *President* soon silenced the stranger by pouring broadsides into her. The ship turned out to be the British sloop of war HMS *Little Belt.* She managed to limp into Halifax, Nova Scotia, with thirty-two dead and wounded crewmen. Rodgers was hailed as a hero for avenging the *Chesapeake* affair of 1807.

Also in 1811, the British in the Northwest Territories incited Tecumseh, a Shawnee Indian chief, to unite the tribes there against American settlers. The usual horrors of Indian warfare followed. In November, GEN William Henry Harrison led a well-trained U.S. frontier army against the Indians at Tippecanoe Creek in Indiana Territory. He won an important victory, and Tecumseh fled to Canada to join British forces.

New England senators and congressmen did not want to go to war, for in spite of the harassment at sea their voters back home were getting rich if only one ship in three made it to port. But the War Hawks, under the strong leadership of Henry Clay, Speaker of the House, and Senator John C. Calhoun, finally persuaded Madison to ask Congress to declare war. On 18 June 1812 the United States declared war on Britain, for impressment, interference with neutral trade, and plots with the Indians in the Northwest. Even after the declaration of war, however, many merchants in New England continued illegally trading with Canada, a practice that would go on for most of the war.

The War of 1812

The U.S. Navy in 1812 had only eighteen warships, seven of them frigates. Many were in need of repairs, and all were short of crew. Supplies of wood that had been selected and set aside for shipbuilding, as well as naval stores, had been used up. Several hundred useless little gunboats built by Jefferson lay rotting in rivers and harbors along the East Coast. The same congressmen who voted the nation into war had, only seven months before, voted down a plan to build a dozen large ships of the line and twenty frigates.

Britain, on the other hand, had more than six hundred men-of-war, including some 250 ships of the line and frigates. Fortunately for the United States, most of this fleet was in Europe blockading the ports of Napoleon's France. Faced with these odds, the U.S. naval strategy was clear—try to protect the nation's shores and coastal trade routes with squadrons of the small gunboats, while harassing British sea commerce with privateers and the British Navy with opportunistic attacks by the few larger U.S. warships that were still in service.

In the early days of the war, U.S. land forces launched an invasion into Canada, but because this operation was poorly planned and met stiff British and Canadian opposition, it was unsuccessful. The Canadians captured a U.S. fort at Mackinac Island in Lake Huron, giving the British control of the upper Great Lakes region. Then the British chased the Americans out of Detroit, built a fleet on Lake Erie, and helped Tecumseh and his Indian allies continue fighting in the Northwest Territory.

The War at Sea

Things at sea went considerably better for the United States at first. Several significant victories were won by American warships in one-on-one encounters with British men-of-war. The first of these occurred on 19 August 1812, when the USS *Constitution,* commanded by CAPT Isaac Hull, one of Preble's Boys, encountered HMS *Guerrière* off the coast of Nova Scotia. Of all British ships, Americans hated *Guerrière* most, because of her role in impressing American seamen a year earlier.

British CAPT James Richard Dacres of the *Guerrière* opened fire first, but Hull calmly told his gunnery officers to wait. By six o'clock that evening Hull had brought the *Constitution* to within a hundred yards of his opponent. With both ships running before the wind, he ordered his first broadside fired. Exchanges of broadsides followed. Dacres saw his shot rip through the rigging or bounce harmlessly off the heavy oaken hull of the American ship, earning for her the nickname "Old Ironsides." The U.S. captain first aimed his fire at the enemy ship's waterline, making gaping holes through which water poured in. Next he aimed at the masts. Within twenty minutes the *Guerrière*'s mizzenmast had been knocked off. It was soon followed by the foremast and mainmast. The battle was over, and Dacres surrendered. The *Guerrière* sank the next day.

Other High Seas Battles

In October 1812 another famous battle took place far across the Atlantic, when the 44-gun frigate *United States,* under the command of Stephen Decatur, met the British 38-gun frigate *Macedonian.* In two hours Decatur wore the enemy down and captured the ship, a valuable prize. Several other one-on-one engagements were fought over the next several months, with the U.S. warships victorious in most.

The opening months of the war at sea had given the Americans much success. Not only had three British frigates and several smaller men-of-war been beaten, but Lloyd's of London, the major insurer of British merchant ships of the time, reported that nearly five hundred merchant ships had been captured by Yankee privateers and commerce raiders.

Despite these victories, the U.S. Navy also suffered some significant losses. The most important of these happened on

The USS *Constitution* defeats the British frigate HMS *Guerrière* on 19 August 1812. During the battle a number of British cannonballs bounced off her hull, giving her the nickname "Old Ironsides." *The Naval History and Heritage Command*

CAPT James Lawrence in the USS *Chesapeake* uttered some of the most famous words in U.S. naval history when, fatally wounded during the battle with HMS *Shannon* in 1813, he told his crew, "Don't give up the ship!" *The Naval History and Heritage Command*

1 June 1813, when the HMS *Shannon,* under command of CAPT Philip Broke, defeated the U.S. frigate *Chesapeake,* now commanded by CAPT James Lawrence, off Boston Harbor. During the conclusion of the fierce fifteen-minute battle Lawrence was mortally wounded, and while being carried below he cried out the immortal words "Don't give up the ship!" More than two hundred men were killed or wounded on both sides. The *Chesapeake* was sailed into Halifax, Nova Scotia, by a prize crew, followed by the *Shannon,* which had pumps going to keep her afloat. Captain Lawrence died on the way.

British Sea Power Prevails

The early victories at sea had given the United States new pride and respect. By 1813, however, the British had driven the French from the sea and were therefore able to increase the number of ships patrolling the U.S. coast and blockading American ports. Once they returned from their victories, hardly any of the American warships could get to sea again for the duration of the war. Thus, after 1813 most of the burden of fighting the British at sea fell to privateers. More than five hundred of them were commissioned during the remainder of the war, most from Massachusetts, New York, and Maryland. Though they carried the war to the British and captured over 1,300 vessels by war's end, they could not take the place of a powerful navy. They could do nothing to stop the British blockade of East Coast ports. Consequently, by 1814 U.S. exports had fallen in value to only about one-tenth of what they had been in 1811. A Boston newspaper gave a gloomy picture of conditions at the time: "Our harbors blockaded; our shipping destroyed or rotting at the docks; silence and stillness in our cities; the grass growing upon the public wharves."

The Jeffersonians had claimed that no enemy could gather enough ships to blockade the entire U.S. coast, so it was not necessary to have a seagoing navy to protect seagoing commerce. The United States and its merchant marine paid a high price for that mistake.

The Great Lakes Campaigns

After war had broken out in June 1812, a shipbuilding race had begun on Lake Ontario between the British naval commander, Sir James Yeo, and his American counterpart, Commodore Isaac Chauncey. Both men had talent for building and organizing, but neither was willing to fight without overwhelming superiority. The result was a series of naval skirmishes throughout the war on the lake, which decided nothing, and blockade efforts, which lasted only until the other side built a new and bigger ship. This went on until war's end, when both sides had two-decked 58-gun men-of-war and were building 110-gun dreadnoughts, larger than any in service on the ocean at the time. None of these, however, saw significant action during the war.

Because control of Lake Erie was key to control of the remaining Northwest Territory (Ohio had been granted statehood in 1803), both sides saw it as an important objective in the early days of the war. Detroit had been surrendered to the British at the outbreak of war, and the British controlled the entire Northwest Territory down to Ohio, where American GEN William Harrison was sustaining a difficult defense against the British and their Indian allies. The British had a small squadron of armed vessels on the lake, but the Americans had no warships there at all. To remedy this situation President Madison sent a contingent of shipwrights to Presque Isle (now Erie, Pennsylvania) to begin building a small U.S. fleet. Later, twenty-

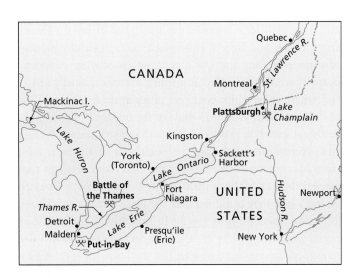

The theater of operations in the eastern Great Lakes in the War of 1812.

seven-year-old Master Commandant Oliver Hazard Perry was sent there to take operational command.

When Perry arrived in the spring of 1813, he found things in a bad state. Work had begun on two 20-gun brigs that would be better than anything the British had on the lake, but winter had delayed their completion and outfitting until July. Perry named one brig the *Niagara;* he named the other the *Lawrence,* for his good friend the late captain of the *Chesapeake,* and chose it for his flagship. Meanwhile, Commodore Yeo sent CDR Robert Barclay, a distinguished Trafalgar veteran, to command the British Lake Erie squadron.

After overcoming one obstacle after another, Perry finally went on patrol in August with his two brigs and seven other vessels. When Barclay sighted Perry's squadron, he beat a hasty retreat to his base at Malden, on the northwest corner of Lake Erie, to await completion of a new flagship, the 20-gun brig *Detroit.* Perry moved west and consolidated his forces at Put-in-Bay, in a group of islands opposite Malden.

By September things at Malden were getting desperate, as some 14,000 Indian allies of the British there were running out of food. It was imperative that Barclay move promptly to regain control of the sea lines of communication through Lake Erie to Malden. So, early on 10 September, despite knowing he was going against a superior force, Barclay sailed forth to meet Perry in a battle that would ultimately decide the fate of the entire Northwest Territory. Besides the *Detroit* he had the 17-gun ship *Queen Charlotte* and four smaller vessels.

Sighting the British, the American squadron came before the wind (turned to sail in the direction it was blowing) and approached the enemy. Flying from the masthead of the *Lawrence* was Perry's blue battle flag, inscribed with Captain Lawrence's dying command, "Don't Give Up the Ship." Perry took some punishment from the *Detroit's* long guns. Then at close range he opened up with his carronades, as well as rifle fire from a contingent of Kentucky marksmen manning the tops (platforms high up the masts) in his rigging. Soon nearly every man topside on the British ship, including most of her officers, was dead. If Master Commandant Jesse Elliot, in command of the *Niagara,* had done the same to the *Queen Charlotte,* the battle would have quickly been over. But Elliot harbored a grudge that he, not Perry, should have been placed in command of the squadron and chose to remain out of the *Charlotte's* range. So for the next two hours Perry and the *Lawrence* battled four British vessels, which gradually shot her to pieces and killed or wounded half her crew. At that point Perry had himself rowed through a hail of fire to the *Niagara* and took command from Elliot.

With his fresh new flagship, Perry steered across the British line, firing double-shotted broadsides, for which the British had no real defense. One by one the British ships struck their colors, and at 1500 Barclay surrendered the remainder of his squadron. After returning to the *Lawrence,* Perry wrote the now-famous

Scene on a U.S. postal stamp commemorating Oliver Hazard Perry being rowed from his damaged flagship USS *Lawrence* to take command of the *Niagara* during the Battle of Lake Erie during the War of 1812.

The Naval History and Heritage Command

dispatch about the victory to General Harrison: "We have met the enemy and they are ours." Lake Erie was now firmly under American control. The Kentuckians pursued the retreating British and Indians ashore, defeating them in the Battle of the Thames. Tecumseh was killed in this battle, ending support for the British cause. Detroit was thus recaptured, and the Northwest Territory was secured.

The Final Year of the War

As war was breaking out between the United States and Britain in 1812, the British and their allies were beginning to achieve success against Napoleon's forces in Europe. In December 1812 Napoleon's armies in Russia were virtually annihilated.

His defeat at Leipzig in October 1813 and his abdication of the French throne in April 1814 freed more and more British assets for deployment in the war against America. Soon the British had blockaded much of the southern coast. A large expedition against Louisiana was prepared. In July 1814 a British force based at Halifax, Nova Scotia, invaded and captured parts of eastern Maine, which they would hold until war's end. Another force was assembled to proceed to the Chesapeake Bay and attack Washington, D.C., and Baltimore.

In the summer of 1814 ships of the Royal Navy entered the Chesapeake Bay, swept aside a little flotilla of barges and Jeffersonian gunboats and landed four thousand troops without opposition on the west bank of the Patuxent River. From there they marched on Washington, overwhelming the militiamen trying to defend the city on 24 and 25 August. Government officials, including President Madison, fled in panic, and British officers ate the dinner that had been prepared for him at the White House. The British then set fire to the White House, the Capitol, and other public buildings. They did this partly in retaliation for Americans' having burned several towns in Canada earlier in the war, as well as for the effect they thought such action would have on American morale. The Americans themselves burned two warships at the Washington Navy Yard to keep them from falling into enemy hands.

The British next turned their attention to Baltimore. They regarded this city as a "nest of pirates," because it was the home port of a great many privateers that had been raiding British merchantmen at sea. A British army of nearly five thousand men stopped before the city's defenses to wait for a fleet of frigates and bomb (mortar) vessels to subdue Fort McHenry, located at the entrance to the inner part of the harbor.

The night-long bombardment that began the evening of 13 September failed to bring down the large U.S. flag waving defiantly over the fort. Francis Scott Key, a U.S. civilian being held aboard one of the British vessels, witnessed the stirring

Fort McHenry then and now. The enhanced old engraving (left) depicts the attack on the fort the evening of 13 September 1814. The photo (right) shows the fort as it is today. Note how the grounds of the fort jut out into the inner harbor, protecting it and the old port of Baltimore from seaborne attack.

The Naval History and Heritage Command

http://baltimore.org

sight and wrote the words of "The Star-Spangled Banner," which later became our national anthem. Unable to get past the fort, a few days later the British reembarked their troops on their ships and sailed away.

Meanwhile, while these events were unfolding in Washington and Baltimore, in Canada a force of Canadian and British troops fresh from the campaign against Napoleon was preparing, under the command of Sir George Prevost, governor general of Canada, to advance down into the United States along the old Lake Champlain route used by Burgoyne during the Revolution. To oppose them the United States had only a small contingent of troops at Plattsburgh, on the western shore of the lake, and a small naval squadron under the command of Master Commandant Thomas Macdonough, another of Preble's Boys.

Prevost began his march down the western side of the lake in late August 1814. In a week he reached Plattsburgh and began to engage the American garrison. To prevent the Americans from attacking Prevost's force from the lake as it advanced,

Thomas Macdonough's victory at the Battle of Lake Champlain, September 1814. The U.S. victory caused the British to retreat into Canada and sign the Treaty of Ghent, ending the War of 1812.

The Naval History and Heritage Command

the British had built a small flotilla of ships consisting of a 37-gun frigate, two schooners, a brig, and a dozen armed, oar-powered galleys. To oppose them Macdonough had built a roughly comparable force of a 27-gun corvette, a 20-gun brig, a schooner, brig, and ten galleys, all in little more than a month, and had anchored them in Plattsburgh Bay to await the arrival of the British flotilla coming down to support Prevost. On 11 September the two opposing naval forces met in what later would be called the Battle of Plattsburgh, or **Second Battle of Lake Champlain.** After a furious two-hour battle, with hundreds of casualties on both sides, the Americans emerged victorious, and the British squadron surrendered. For the second time in the war, and only the second time in history, an entire British fleet had been defeated. Prevost's land force beat a hasty retreat back to Canada the next morning.

Macdonough's victory had a profound effect on peace negotiations, which had been taking place in Ghent, in Belgium, for some time. The Duke of Wellington, who had defeated Napoleon at Waterloo, offered his opinion that the cost of any new offensive would vastly outweigh any probable gains and that peace should be made at once, without demands for territory. The British government dropped their demand for territorial concessions and so notified the delegates at Ghent, thereby paving the way for conclusion of a peace treaty by year's end. On Christmas Eve 1814, the **Treaty of Ghent** was signed. It returned the two countries to the *status quo ante bellum* (the status before the war) with regard to territory, with the British reaffirming the American ownership of the Northwest Territory and agreeing to leave Maine, and the Americans agreeing to return land they had captured in Canada. It made no mention of impressments or of neutral shipping rights at sea, since the British had repealed the Orders in Council and stopped impressments of American sailors when the war against Napoleon ended earlier that year.

Battle of New Orleans

News traveled slowly in the early nineteenth century. Thus, even though the peace treaty ending the war had been signed in Europe, fighting continued in America. The British expedition to Louisiana had finally arrived off the mouth of the Mississippi River on 8 December 1814, after having been delayed several weeks by privateer actions in the Azores. Soon the British had swept through a flotilla of gunboats arrayed against them, and on 23 December they landed eight miles below New Orleans

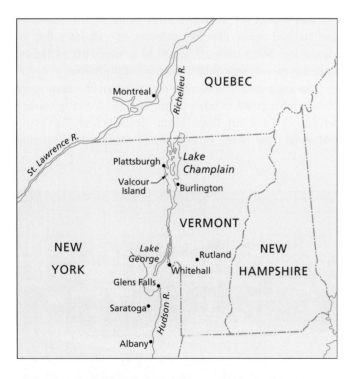

Map of the Lake Champlain region where the famous battle of September 1814 was fought.

and began skirmishing with U.S. general Andrew Jackson and his defenders. By the end of the first week in January, more than eight thousand British veterans under MGEN Sir Edward Pakenham were ashore and ready to attack. Upstream, Jackson's force had grown to four thousand men, including a contingent of ex-pirate Jean Lafitte's men and a naval battery manned by gunners from the disabled schooner *Louisiana*.

On 8 January 1815 Pakenham foolishly marched his men in a frontal assault against Jackson's strong position between the Mississippi and a swamp, where the Americans had dug in to prevent encirclement. Jackson's riflemen, firing from behind cotton bales and earthworks, mowed the British down. When the smoke cleared, Pakenham and over two thousand of his troops were dead or wounded, and the rest were in flight.

The peace treaty finally arrived in the United States on 11 February, and Congress ratified it six days later. By and large, the treaty was welcome in both countries, since they had much more to gain from trade with each other than from war. The U.S. Navy had won new respect, and American diplomats were treated with honor worldwide. The victories of the navy both at sea and on the Great Lakes had united the nation and started a great naval tradition. The United States had become a world power, respected as never before.

The United States Advances as Sea Power Prospers, 1815–1860

The nation and the Navy emerged from the War of 1812 stronger and more confident than ever. Within a few months of the Battle of New Orleans, hundreds of U.S. merchantmen were plying the world's trade routes. The chief task of the U.S. Navy between 1815 and 1860 was promoting and protecting this trade everywhere on the globe. The Navy now enjoyed prestige and popularity because of its successes in the war. For the first time, the Navy was able to build up after the end of a war, with public support. Whaling became a major industry in New England ports. And some of the most "romantic" days in the history of sailing were about to unfold. American clipper ships would soon become the queens of the sea.

The advances of the ongoing industrial revolution began to have an effect on life at sea. The science of oceanography came into being. Better instruments, nautical charts, and clocks improved navigation and helped American firms compete for world trade. Steam propulsion came into the world of sea power, at first in the form of paddle-wheeled merchant steamers and warships, then later with screw-propeller-driven vessels. With it came the iron hull, armor, and heavier ordnance firing *shells* (thin-walled projectiles filled with explosives) instead of solid shot. No major wars, and consequently no major sea battles, were fought between 1815 and 1860. For the first time, wars in Europe did not directly affect American progress. Americans went their way, across the seas and across the continent.

In the 1850s the man largely responsible for the improvement of naval ordnance was CDR John Dahlgren. He developed large bottle-shaped guns, thick in the breech and tapered toward the muzzle, which could fire heavy spherical shells filled with explosive charges. They were much more effective and longer in range than the contemporary smaller-caliber cannon with cylindrical barrels, little changed in nearly two centuries. Smaller guns with rifled barrels and elongated projectiles were also developed about this time, but they were not as reliable as the smooth-bore Dahlgren guns, which became the weapons of choice for the main batteries of naval warships for the next thirty years.

Administrative practices in the major navies of the world also saw much change in response to the new naval technological advances. In the United States, in 1842 the Navy replaced a three-member Board of Navy Commissioners that had been in place since 1815 with a departmental system more closely adapted to the new era of steam propulsion. There were five bureaus, each headed by a senior officer: Navy Yards and Docks; Construction, Equipment, and Repairs; Provisions and Clothing; Ordnance and Hydrography; and Medicine and Surgery. The bureau chiefs all reported to the Secretary of the Navy.

Until that time officer training in the worlds' navies had consisted primarily of young boys signing on to ships as midshipmen and then being taught how to be officers by their seniors and by civilian "professors of mathematics" who were attached to ships. Training quality varied from ship to ship and was very inconsistent. For several years there had been a movement to bring the education of midshipmen ashore and consolidate the training at one location to provide consistency and improve the quality of instruction. Finally, in response to the demands of the growing steam Navy for more capable officers and enlisted men to man it, and a mutinous incident involving a midshipman on the USS *Somers* in1842 that created popular support for better training, the Secretary of the Navy ordered the establishment of the **U.S. Naval Academy** at Annapolis, Maryland, in 1845, and school ships and other training facilities for enlisted personnel. In 1850 Congress abolished flogging of sailors, and in 1862 it ended the traditional daily ration of grog (mixture of rum and water) to shipboard personnel.

Piracy and Protection

Often American traders sailed into areas of rebellion and turmoil—the type of situation in which piracy flourishes. The war with Tripoli had ended that country's acts of piracy against U.S. shipping, but when the United States fell behind in tribute payments to Algiers in 1807, the dey of Algiers ordered his corsairs (pirates) to resume capturing U.S. merchantmen. This situation persisted throughout the conflict with Britain. After the war, Congress declared war on Algiers, and naval operations conducted during 1815 and 1816 finally ended this threat; treaties were subsequently signed with Algiers and the other Barbary states that stopped the need to pay tribute. To make sure that the deys and pashas did not revert to their old ways, American naval squadrons continued their presence in the Mediterranean from then until the Civil War, operating from a base at Port Mahon, Minorca.

When revolts against Spain began in Latin America in the early nineteenth century, Spain and some of the new South American countries issued **letters of marque** (official documents commissioning vessels as privateers) to various ships sailing under their flags, authorizing them to stop and board enemy merchant vessels in the Caribbean and Gulf of Mexico. However, many of these ships, as well as rogue pirates, began harassing all shipping in the region. Jean Lafitte was the most notorious American pirate; he and his men had been given pardons because of their assistance to General Jackson at New Orleans in 1815 but had returned to piracy after the war. He established his base on an island at the mouth of the Mississippi River.

Between 1815 and 1822 nearly three thousand merchant ships were attacked by pirates in the West Indies. By 1822 the damage to American trade had become so great that the United States decided to put an end to the pirates there once and for all. A West Indies Naval Squadron, under the command of Commodore James Biddle, was sent to the area. Biddle captured or destroyed thirty pirate vessels in less than a year, but his large ships could not pursue the smaller pirate vessels into the coves where many lurked. Spanish officials in Cuba and Puerto Rico refused Biddle permission to pursue pirates who beached their vessels and escaped ashore. Yellow fever and malaria caused many deaths in the American crews.

In February 1823 Commodore David Porter was given command of the West Indies Squadron. Porter learned from Biddle's operations. He gathered a squadron of smaller vessels, gunboats, and the first steam-powered paddle wheeler to be used in naval operations. Over the next two years he followed the pirates into the coves and inlets. His larger ships escorted merchantmen at sea. By mid-1826 a new commodore, Lewis Warrington, had succeeded in driving Lafitte and other pirates out of the Caribbean. For the first time in three centuries, the ships of all nations could sail those waters without fear of being plundered. After the pirate threat was eliminated, the West Indian Squadron became known as the Home Squadron, and its ships routinely conducted patrols in the region over the next twenty years.

Whaling

Colonial Americans had begun whaling in the early 1700s. Sailing out of New Bedford, Nantucket, and other New England seaports, whalers flourished until the Civil War. After the War of 1812, the whaling industry grew rapidly. Between 1830 and

A whaleboat with a harpooner in the bow about to harpoon a whale; the whale ship is in the background processing an earlier catch. The whaling industry was profitable, but whaling was a dangerous job with severe living conditions. *The Naval History and Heritage Command*

1860, many fortunes were made by the owners of whaling vessels. In the mid-1840s the Americans had over seven hundred whaling ships, about three-quarters of the world's total, and they sailed the world over in search of their prey.

Life aboard the whaling ships was primitive and dirty. Many crewmen died from disease and injuries, but the lure of shares of the profits of successful voyages pushed men on. Many sea stories of the era have been passed down from writers of the day and have become a part of American history and adventure. Probably the most famous of these is *Moby Dick*, by Herman Melville.

In the 1860s, however, the era of American whaling rapidly declined. In 1859 oil was discovered in Pennsylvania, and it began to replace whale oil for lighting and heating. Later, natural gas was also used for these purposes. The flexible whalebone used for hoopskirts, corset stays, buggy whips, and umbrella ribs was replaced by other materials as dress styles and needs changed. During the Civil War, Confederate raiders attacked and destroyed many Northern whaling fleets, and the trade never revived. Weather and the Arctic ice claimed most of the surviving American whaling fleet in the 1870s.

The Slave Trade

Unfortunately, in the 1700s an infamous **"triangular trade"** had developed in the Atlantic, subsequently persisting well into the nineteenth century—the major part of which was the slave trade. Much of the wealth and prosperity of New England in the eighteenth and early nineteenth centuries was founded on this slave trade. The rich businessmen and shipowners and their families never saw the loads of human misery for which they were responsible.

In North America this triangular slave trade most often originated in the New England colonies, from which the slave ships sailed, loaded with rum made in New England's distilleries from West Indies molasses. The ships sailed to West Africa, where the rum was exchanged for slaves; from there, the slaves were taken to be sold in the West Indies, from whence they were taken to the Americas. Then another cargo of sugar and molasses would be carried back to New England. The equatorial route across the Atlantic Ocean from Africa was called the "Middle Passage." Many slaves died during this voyage due to the terrible conditions on board the slave ships. Over 15 million black Africans were transported to slavery in the Americas over this route.

Although in the early nineteenth century laws in Britain, France, and the United States were put into effect prohibiting the slave trade, and intermittent antislavery patrols from all three navies put to sea to enforce them, these measures failed to do much to stop the illegal human trafficking. The high demand for slaves to harvest sugar cane in the Caribbean islands, as well as cotton and other commodities in the American south, would keep the slave trade going until the start of the Civil War in 1861.

The Mexican War, 1846–1848

Americans began moving into Texas in the 1820s, when that territory was still a part of Mexico. By 1835 nearly 30,000 Americans had settled in the area, and many problems had started with the Mexican government. On 2 March 1836, after a year of skirmishing, Texans declared their independence and organized the Republic of Texas, with its "Lone Star" flag. Meanwhile Mexican army forces under General Santa Anna entered Texas and on 6 March overran a small Texan garrison at the Alamo, a fortified mission near San Antonio. They killed all the defenders, including its commander, Jim Bowie, and the frontiersman folk hero Davy Crockett. About six weeks later, rallying under the cry "Remember the Alamo!," Sam Houston and eight hundred Texans routed the Mexican army and captured Santa Anna at the Battle of San Jacinto. Santa Anna signed a treaty ending hostilities and recognizing Texan independence, though this treaty was never ratified by the Mexican government.

For the next ten years Texas enjoyed a de facto (actual) independence from Mexico. The Mexican army did not make any further serious attempts to subjugate it. More American settlers poured

The landing of 12,000 American troops under GEN Winfield Scott at Veracruz during the Mexican War in 1847. The landing was made without casualties while U.S. ships fired on shore batteries in the fort and city. *The Naval History and Heritage Command*

into Texas, and the new government claimed the Rio Grande as its southern border. But Mexico, as mentioned, had never recognized the independence of Texas or the Rio Grande border and repeatedly warned that any attempt by the United States to annex Texas would bring war.

Similarly, in California armed revolts had driven out the Mexican government's representatives, resulting in its being almost as free of Mexican control as was Texas during these same years. In March 1845 Texas was annexed by the United States and admitted to the Union as a state. In anticipation of resulting hostilities with Mexico, U.S. troops under GEN Zachary Taylor moved to garrison the disputed Rio Grande boundary. Secretary of the Navy George Bancroft ordered the Navy Home Squadron to support him and informally arranged for a small group of frontiersmen and scouts under Army captain John Frémont to enter and "explore" California.

In April 1846 elements of Taylor's command were killed in skirmishes with Mexican troops, whereupon Congress declared war on Mexico, on 13 May 1846.

When war was declared, a four-ship Pacific Squadron, under command of Commodore John Sloat, was operating from a base in Mexico. He sailed to California and in July occupied Monterey, the capital of Mexican California, and Yerba Buena (later San Francisco) without a fight. He then fell ill and was relieved by Commodore Robert Stockton. Stockton combined his naval personnel with Frémont's group and other Army troops that had fought their way across the New Mexico–Arizona Territories and formed a small army. It proceeded to capture Los Angeles, San Diego, Santa Barbara, and other California settlements. Soon thereafter the Mexican defense force signed the Treaty of Cahuenga in January 1847, ceding California to the United States and ending the war on the West Coast.

The United States had now brought the entire Southwest under the American flag and for all practical purposes had won the war. The Mexican government, however, did not recognize the treaties with Texas and California, so President James K. Polk planned to carry the war into the heart of Mexico. Zachary Taylor's army, though greatly outnumbered, spent the next few months defeating Mexican forces in a number of battles in northeastern Mexico. This was not enough to conclude the war, so Polk ordered GEN Winfield Scott to assemble an army of 14,000 men to take the capital, Mexico City.

Since Mexico had no navy, there were no sea battles. Nevertheless, sea forces carried out operations that led to a successful end to the war. Scott's army was loaded in Army transports and sailed to join with the Navy's Home Squadron, which was blockading Mexico's east coast. The transports and the Home Squadron met at Veracruz in March.

In the largest U.S. amphibious operation carried out before World War II, over a hundred ships landed the American force on 9 March 1847 without losing a man. As the ground forces surrounded Veracruz, the Navy took up bombardment positions off the major Mexican fort there. A naval battery was sent ashore to aid the Army in its bombardment of the city. The fort and the city were pounded into submission in less than two weeks.

With the port in American hands and supply lines clear, Scott and his army swept into Mexico. A series of tough engagements were fought before the Army and Marines captured Mexico City on 14 September 1847. When the city fell, General Scott decided to impress the populace by posting a guard of brightly uniformed Marines at an old castle then known as the Halls of Montezuma, in deference to an old Aztec ruler. This action was later immortalized in the first line of the "Marine Corps Hymn."

The Treaty of Guadalupe-Hidalgo ended the Mexican War in February 1848. By its terms, Mexico recognized the U.S. annexation of the New Mexico–Arizona Territory and California and set the Rio Grande as the U.S.–Mexican border, thus indirectly recognizing U.S. sovereignty in Texas. The United States had now reached its second seacoast. This fulfilled the growing American ideal of **Manifest Destiny,** the dream of a country stretching from coast to coast, and was the most important result of the Mexican War. As always, such a great victory meant both immense benefits and increased responsibilities for the American people. A navy would now have to be maintained in the Pacific to defend the nation's new shores and protect the many merchant ships that were soon to ply the trade routes to Asia.

The Clipper Ships

Just as the Mexican War was about to start in 1845, the most colorful and dramatic era of commercial sailing ships began. The square-rigged clipper ship *Rainbow* slid down the ways in New York that year. The era of the **clipper ships** was beginning.

American ships had begun trading with China in the 1780s. By 1825 American trade with that country was second only to that of England, and the U.S. Navy established the East India Squadron to protect American ships and interests in the western Pacific. In 1840 this rich commerce stopped, during the Opium War between China and Britain. Trade was reopened in 1842, when Commodore Lawrence Kearny sailed into Canton, China, with the USS *Constellation* and *Boston* of the East India Squadron. Kearny used a combination of courtesy, firmness, fairness, and show of force to lay the foundation for a trading treaty signed by China and the United States a year later.

The British clipper ship *Cutty Sark* on display near London prior to a fire that burned most of the original ship during renovations in 2007. She was one of the better known of these graceful sailing vessels plying the world's oceans. Built in 1869, she was one of the last of the "tea clippers" in the China trade. *Volkmar Rudolf*

The trade with China always involved a race against time. In the early days it took as much as a year and a half for a round trip between New England and China. The Chinese trade offered tea, silk, porcelain, ivory, and other luxuries. Profit was so great that one successful trip would pay for a ship. But time was important, especially for tea, which could spoil on a long voyage. Therefore, Yankee shipbuilders sought to build a ship that would cut the sailing time to and from China, and later the island of Java. The clipper ship was their answer, so called because their sleek hulls seemed to "clip" the waves rather than plow through them. The clippers were the most beautiful sailing ships ever to ply the seven seas; in their time, they were also the fastest. In 1845, the *Rainbow,* mentioned earlier, set a new standard for a voyage from Canton, China, to New York City, making the trip in a record time of eighty-eight days. By the 1850s, American "China clippers" were routinely sailing between New York and Hong Kong in about ninety days.

The end of the Mexican War in 1848 opened up the Pacific coast to American shipping. Later that year, gold was discovered in California. Now the clipper ships had another very profitable route, hauling thousands of gold seekers between East Coast ports around the Cape of Good Hope to California.

The clippers had their greatest year in 1853, when 145 of them sailed from East Coast ports for San Francisco. In all, 161 clippers were built between 1850 and 1855. But then the ship-building boom collapsed. The completion of a railroad across the Isthmus of Panama in 1855 made the long, dangerous trip around South America unnecessary. Over the much shorter distance, larger and slower ships could haul bulk cargoes and more passengers much more cheaply. Moreover, clipper ships were expensive to build and operate. With profits down, the fast American clippers could not carry enough passengers or cargo to make further construction of them worthwhile. For a time the tea trade with China and Java and transport of passengers and wool between England and Australia kept them going, but competition from British clippers and the opening in 1869 of the Suez Canal, which steamships could use but not sailing ships, led to their demise by the 1880s.

Opening the Door to Japan

After trade with China had been reestablished in 1842, the next objective of American foreign trade was Japan. After a brief relationship with Portuguese traders and missionaries in the late sixteenth and early seventeenth centuries, in 1637 Japan had expelled all foreigners from the country. No foreigners had been allowed to enter the country during the 215 years since. Moreover, a Japanese law in 1825 had decreed that any foreign ship that attempted to anchor in a Japanese harbor was to be destroyed. Any seamen coming ashore were to be arrested or killed, and any Japanese who left to visit foreign countries were to be killed upon their return. Such isolation, of course, kept Japan in a feudal state, with few technological, scientific, or social advances.

Cultural misunderstandings impeded U.S.-Japanese relations as well. When the U.S. East India Squadron tried to open the door to trade in 1846, Commodore James Biddle was treated in an insulting manner. In an incident when he was pushed by a Japanese guard, he chose not to make an issue of the matter. He was not aware that this caused him to "lose face," a major failure in Asian culture. Afterward the Japanese would not even consider talking with such a "weak" individual; they rejected Biddle's trade proposals and towed his ships out to sea.

But the lure of the Japanese market, the need for a coaling station for ships crossing the Pacific to China, and demands for protection of shipwrecked sailors caused Americans to want to open the door to Japan. President Millard Fillmore chose Commodore Matthew Calbraith Perry to head a naval expedition to Japan. Perry, the younger brother of Oliver Hazard Perry, the hero of Lake Erie, was the perfect man for the job. He had more diplomatic experience than any other naval officer. He had forty-four years of naval service and had taken part in most important naval actions since 1808. Perry's mission was to carry a letter from the president to the emperor of Japan and to conclude a treaty that would satisfy all three main American objectives.

Perry's seven ships sailed in November 1852 from the United States and arrived in Hong Kong the following spring. Leaving three ships at Okinawa, he entered Japanese waters with two steam frigates and two sailing sloops of war and anchored in Tokyo Bay off Nagasaki on 8 July 1853. The Japanese had never seen steamships, and they could not fail to be impressed with the fact that Perry had all guns loaded and ready for action.

Perry put into practice all the things he had learned from previous attempts to trade and negotiate with the Japanese. He ordered away the Japanese guard boats and refused to deal with anyone whose rank was lower than his own. For a week the commodore refused to allow himself to be seen, while the Japanese fretted and debated about what was to be done.

Finally, on 14 July, a thirteen-gun salute echoed over the anchorage as Perry stepped into his barge. One hundred Marines

The second landing of Commodore Perry and his officers to meet the imperial commissioners at Yokohama, Japan, in February 1854. The resulting Treaty of Kanagawa was signed in March, opening several Japanese ports to American shipping. Other parts of the treaty led to an agreement opening Japan to trade with the United States and other nations.
The Naval History and Heritage Command

in well-starched dress uniforms, a company of seamen, and two Navy bands preceded the barge in fifteen gunboats as a guard of honor. Perry was flanked by two huge African American seamen who served as bodyguards, the first blacks the Japanese had ever seen. In front of them marched two young midshipmen carrying the president's letter in a beautiful rosewood box. After the letter was delivered to representatives of the Japanese shogun, the ruler of Japan, Perry announced that the squadron would depart for China in a few days but would return in the spring with more ships for a reply to the president's letter.

He returned in February with a much larger squadron. The Japanese had been convinced by his first visit that America was a nation worthy of trading with. When the Americans returned, more ceremonies took place, and there were exchanges of gifts. The Americans were given silks and carvings and other handicrafts. The Japanese received firearms, tools, clocks, stoves, a telegraph, and even a one-quarter-size locomotive, complete with tender, coaches, and circular track. The track was quickly laid, and the Japanese envoys were treated to rides on the little cars, their robes flying in the breeze as the train went around at twenty miles per hour.

After more than a month of detailed talks, the Japanese and Americans signed in March 1854 the Treaty of Kanagawa, which complied with nearly everything in President Fillmore's letter. It provided for the opening of the ports of Shimoda and Hakodate to American shipping, the protection of shipwrecked American seamen, and start-up of an American consulate at Shimoda. Four years later a follow-on treaty opened Japan fully to trade with the United States. Other similar treaties were soon signed with other European nations, establishing trade with them as well.

The Perry mission was regarded as the most important "peacetime battle" of the nineteenth century for the U.S. Navy. Perry was showered with honors upon his return to America. The great American author Washington Irving wrote of his exploit, "You have gained yourself a lasting name, and have won it without shedding a drop of blood or inflicting misery on a human being." Truly a new era was about to dawn for America as a trading nation in the Pacific, and the U.S. Navy had helped make it possible.

Critical Thinking

1. Many of the most famous of early American heroes of the sea lived and became famous during the era of the growth of American sea power from 1783–1860. Pick several of these and describe the characteristics that they had in common that led to their achieving heroic status.

2. Research the roles that Marines played in the ship's company aboard warships during the period from 1783–1860 and what they do as members of a ship's company today.

3. Relate the various phrases in the "National Anthem" with the events that occurred during the British attack on Fort McHenry in Baltimore during the War of 1812.

Chronology

1783	Treaty of Paris
1789	U.S. Constitution adopted
1794	Navy Act passed
1798–1800	Quasi-War with France
1801–1805	War with Tripoli
1807	*Chesapeake* affair
1812	War of 1812 begins; *Constitution* vs. *Guerrière*;
1813	Battle of Lake Erie
1814	Washington burned; Battle of Lake Champlain; Baltimore attacked; Treaty of Ghent
1815	Battle of New Orleans
1830–60	American whaling flourishes
1846–48	War with Mexico
1845–75	Era of the clipper ships
1854, 1858	Treaties of Kanagawa with Japan

Study Guide Questions

1. What occurred in the United States in 1789 that enabled Congress to authorize construction of a navy?

2. What were the names of the first three U.S. frigates?

3. How were warships rated in the days of sail?

4. Who was the U.S. naval officer who fought the two most famous battles of the Quasi-War with France?

5. A. What was the outcome of the Quasi-War?
   B. Why was John Adams defeated in the next election?

6. How did the term "Preble's Boys" come into being?

7. A. What was the *Philadelphia* incident?
   B. Who was the hero of the exploit?

8. A. How did William Eaton finally get the war against Tripoli to end in 1805?
   B. What phrase in the "Marine Corps Hymn" refers to this operation?

9. What caused American sentiment to turn against the British in the years leading up to the War of 1812?

10. What was the *Chesapeake* affair?

11. What was the U.S. naval strategy for the War of 1812?

12. A. What naval battle fought in August 1812 helped sagging U.S. spirits?
    B. Who was the U.S. naval officer involved?
    C. What famous nickname was the USS *Constitution* given because of this battle?

13. What famous battle cry was uttered by CAPT James Lawrence in the battle between the USS *Chesapeake* and HMS *Shannon*?

14. What was the result of the British blockade of U.S. ports during the War of 1812?

15. What was the result of the Battle of Lake Erie?

16. A. What famous anthem was written during the British attack on Baltimore in 1814?
    B. Who wrote it?

17. What was the significance of the battle at Plattsburgh on Lake Champlain in 1814?

18. When and where was the peace treaty ending the War of 1812 signed?

19. A. Why was the Battle of New Orleans fought after the peace treaty ending the War of 1812 was signed?
    B. Who was the U.S. general who won the battle?

20. What benefit did the U.S. gain from the War of 1812 around the world?

21. What was the chief task of the U.S. Navy following the War of 1812?

22. Who was the most notorious of the American pirates in the 1820s?

23. What caused the U.S. whaling industry to decline in the 1860s?

24. A. What was the infamous triangular trade carried on in the Atlantic from precolonial times to the start of the Civil War?
    B. Describe the route the trade used and the cargoes carried.

25. What was the outcome of the war with Mexico in 1846–48?

26. A. What were the clipper ships?
    B. What were their main routes?

27. What was the "Manifest Destiny" in the United States in the mid-1800s?

28. What was the outcome of Perry's mission to Japan in 1853–54?

New Vocabulary

ransom	waterline
tribute money	skirmish
tariff	letter(s) of marque
expedition	triangular trade
impressment	clipper ship
embargo	lose face

4

The Civil War, 1861–1865

By the late 1840s the United States had crossed the North American continent, a result of both the Mexican War and the lure of gold and fertile farmlands in the western territories. The Canadian boundaries had been established in Oregon Territory. The U.S. Navy had beaten the Barbary States in the Mediterranean and the pirates in the West Indies. The threat of a foreign attack on U.S. territory had been eliminated, so American maritime interests concerned themselves with overseas trade. Clippers, whalers, and **packets** (ships sailing on a schedule) loaded with immigrants caught the imagination of Americans. But one other thing haunted American life during the first half of the nineteenth century—slavery.

The issue of slavery was not of prime importance to the average American of the early 1800s. The majority of Southerners were small farmers who could not afford slaves, and most Northerners were small farmers or tradesmen who had never come into contact with any. Many influential plantation owners and politicians in the South had vested interests in the issue, however, because the cultivation and harvesting of tobacco, rice, indigo, and, above all, cotton, on which most of the Southern economy depended, would not be profitable without slavery. By contrast, the Northern economy was based on commerce and industry far more than on agriculture. Although the triangular slave trade profited northern merchant ship owners, many influential politicians and abolitionists in the North regarded slavery as a moral evil. As time progressed, these regional views spread throughout the respective populations of the North and South.

In 1800 the population of the country was about evenly split between North and South, but over the next fifty years immigrants from Europe steadily added to the population of the North, while Southern population growth stagnated. By 1850 only about a third of the national population lived in the South. Southern politicians became alarmed at the loss of political power in the House of Representatives that this trend caused, especially in light of the prospective addition of new states formed from the territories of the Louisiana Purchase of 1803. They were concerned that if parity in the Senate were not maintained, they would become a perpetual minority in Con-

gress, unable to block any measures that would threaten their whole way of life in the South. Thus they pressed for admission of the new states as slave states, so that their political power base in the Senate would remain strong.

Conversely, Northern politicians wanted to limit the spread of slavery into new territories and states, both to restrain Southern political power and to address the moral issue. This led to the passage of the Missouri Compromise of 1820, which stipulated that a balance between slave and free states had to be maintained as new states entered the Union. This balance lasted until the passage of the Kansas-Nebraska Act of 1854, which eliminated the Missouri Compromise and made it possible for slavery to be introduced into any new territory based on the decision of the residents there.

The Kansas-Nebraska Act was of great concern in the North, because of the danger of the potential spread of slavery it represented. Moderate politicians such as Abraham Lincoln and abolitionists throughout the North began actively working to oppose the act and any further spread of slavery. In the South, politicians convinced their constituents that the North was threatening their culture and way of life. This perceived threat was greatly intensified in 1859 when the militant Northern abolitionist John Brown raided the federal arsenal at Harper's Ferry, Virginia (now West Virginia), and called for a general insurrection of Southern slaves.

Extremists on both sides became willing to go to war to ensure that their views prevailed. This situation was exacerbated by a nationalist premise on the part of many in the South, reinforced by ongoing nationalist movements throughout Europe, that if the federal government failed to protect their interests, Southern states had the right to secede from (leave) the Union. The Unionist response was that because the Preamble to the Constitution stated that the Union derived its power from the people as a whole, no state could elect to secede without due process of Congress.

Against this backdrop of tension the presidential election of 1860 took place. The newly formed Republican Party had nominated Abraham Lincoln. Lincoln was convinced that the Constitution prohibited the federal government from taking any action to abolish slavery where it already existed, but he objected on moral grounds to any further spread of slavery to any new states. To Southerners this meant that if Lincoln were elected president, they would soon become a permanent minority not only in Congress but also in the Electoral College. In response to Lincoln's nomination, South Carolina immediately announced that it would secede from the Union if he were elected.

The Democrats had two candidates in the election—one from the North, the other from the South—and the remnants of the Whig party nominated a third. As a result, Lincoln won the election with just 40 percent of the popular vote, even though he got only a smattering of votes from the South and no Southern electoral votes. On 20 December South Carolina carried out its threat to secede from the Union, declaring that the election results did not represent the will of the Southern people. Six other Southern states soon followed South Carolina's lead. In February the Confederate States of America was formed, with Jefferson Davis as its first president. The Confederacy at this point consisted of South Carolina, Mississippi, Florida, Alabama, Georgia, Louisiana, and Texas.

A great shuffling of personal loyalties now began within the officer corps of the U.S. Army and Navy. These men had to choose between the flag they were sworn to protect and, for some, their home ties to the Southern states. For many, the home ties proved stronger. They resigned their commissions and headed south to serve the Confederacy. Among the many such officers were Robert E. Lee, who had been recognized as the Army's most promising officer, and Matthew Fontaine Maury, the Navy's first oceanographer. Union feeling was much stronger in the Navy enlisted rates, however. Most of the experienced career petty officers, boatswain's mates, gunners, quartermasters, and leading seamen stayed with the Union.

Southern militias quickly took over many federal coastal forts and bases throughout the South, leaving only four remaining in Union hands: Fort Pickens at Pensacola (Florida), Fort Taylor at Key West (Florida), Fort Jefferson on the Tortugas, and Fort Sumter in Charleston Harbor. Due to their remote positions and strength, the first three were beyond immediate danger. The Civil War was to start, however, at Fort Sumter, in Charleston.

The South Carolinians set up batteries facing the fort and on 1 April notified Confederate president Davis that all was in readiness. On the 11th, the Confederate general, Pierre Beauregard, demanded that Fort Sumter surrender. MAJ Robert Anderson, the Union garrison commander, refused. At dawn on 12 April, Beauregard fired the shot that officially began the American Civil War. Fort Sumter returned the fire. The next

A contemporary engraving showing the bombardment of Fort Sumter in Charleston Harbor in April 1861. *The Naval History and Heritage Command*

day its administration buildings were set on fire by hot shot, threatening its magazines, so most of the powder had to be wet down or thrown into the harbor. On the 14th, Anderson hauled down the flag. The fort was evacuated and the troops carried away by a small Union naval force that had been standing by off the harbor entrance.

On 15 April President Lincoln called for 75,000 volunteers for three months to suppress the rebellion. News of this, plus the fall of Fort Sumter, brought Arkansas, Tennessee, North Carolina, and Virginia into the Confederacy, but the western counties of Virginia left that state and came back into the Union as West Virginia.

Resources and Preparations

The U.S. Army had only about 16,000 regulars in uniform when the Civil War began. It was composed mostly of volunteer state militiamen. Of the 31 million Americans, however, 22 million lived in the North, while only nine million, including 3.5 million slaves, lived in the South. The North's greater population would prove decisive. Before the war ended, the North would have over 2.5 million men in uniform, including some 200,000 African Americans. The Confederates would put about one million men in uniform.

In heavy industry, the North was overwhelmingly superior to the South. The South had little industry, except some textile manufacturing. The South had no foundries or metal works to make heavy guns or iron plating and few skilled workers. Its transportation system was inadequate, especially the railroads, which were barely able to handle peacetime needs. The North had an efficient rail system that was in full operation.

Even though the Union navy was not prepared for the war, it was able to build and grow. The South, on the other hand, had hardly any shipyards, few merchant seamen, and no navy at all when the war began. It tried to commission privateers and commerce raiders and build blockade runners for commerce and gunboats and armored warships, called **ironclads,** for harbor defense and riverine warfare, but it could never challenge Northern sea power.

Despite its agricultural economy, the South was not self-sufficient in food. Much of the plantation land was used to grow cotton and tobacco, of value only if it could reach a market. Large areas of the South were dependent on the importation of foodstuffs from its western states, especially Texas and Arkansas. When the Mississippi River fell under Union navy control in 1863, food from the West was cut off. This, along with the Union naval blockade of Southern ports, would have the Confederacy on the verge of starvation by the time the war ended.

The Southern leadership had no idea of the economic demands of modern war, so it was not able to foresee its battlefield needs. One very important belief in the South was that the Northern blockade, by cutting off "King Cotton" from British and French markets, would force those countries to help the Southern cause for economic reasons. This proved to be a vain hope, though there was much sympathy for the South in Europe. When exports of cotton from the South dwindled, Europeans turned to alternative sources of supply in Egypt and India.

In spite of these handicaps, however, the South had some undeniable strengths. Key among these was the high quality of its officer corps, most of the finest members of which had recently worn the blue uniform. Also, the South was a vast territory, not easily invaded or held by anything other than a large and expensive army. Finally, the majority of Southerners were very loyal to the Confederate cause, a fact that gave the Southern leaders much comfort and enabled them to fight on against great odds. For a comparison of the assets of the North and South and the advantage the North had over the South at the start of the Civil War, see the table below.

COMPARISON OF NORTH AND SOUTH IN 1860		
	NORTH (%)	SOUTH (%)
Population	71	29
Wealth produced	75	25
Farm acreage	65	35
Value of crops	70	30
Railroad mileage	72	28
Factories	85	15
Iron production	96	4
Bank deposits	81	19
Naval ships	100	0

Union Navy Role: Blockade

When the war started, Jefferson Davis knew that the South must get help abroad. In order to force the economic issues, he authorized privateering on 17 April, granting letters of marque to ships of any nation that would prey on Northern shipping. He also declared an embargo on cotton, in the hope that keeping it in the South would cause prices to rise and entice blockade runners to carry it to foreign markets, as well pressure England and France to enter the war on the side of the South.

Lincoln's immediate response was to begin a naval blockade of all Southern ports from the Virginia Capes to Texas. Davis thought that Lincoln's action would so anger the British and French merchants and textile businesses that foreign privateers would be attracted to the Southern cause, tempted by the great profits that could be made. Second, he believed that this Northern action would eventually force the British and French to at least recognize and assist the South, if not openly join it as allies.

Davis was wrong on both scores. Both British and French shipyards built fast schooners and cruisers for the South to use as blockade runners, but they observed the Union blockade themselves. Trade with the North was far more important to them than was trade with the South. Furthermore, in addition to new sources of cotton in Egypt and India, the Europeans already had huge inventories of raw cotton from the 1860 crop. Davis undoubtedly would have helped the Confederate cause much more if he had tried to ship out all the cotton he could before the Union blockade could become effective. This might have built up some cash reserves for purchasing war materials that could have been smuggled in by blockade runners.

Proclaiming a blockade and making one effective are two different things, however. When Lincoln gave his Navy the task, there were only forty-two ships in commission, with only three of them in home waters, to blockade and patrol 3,550 miles of Confederate coast, with 189 harbors and navigable river mouths. Gideon Welles, Lincoln's Secretary of the Navy, was a man who understood naval administration and the role of the Navy. He began a shipbuilding program and bought and adapted many vessels of the American merchant marine. By December 1861, Welles had 264 vessels in commission and had established an adequate blockade off all the major cotton ports: Wilmington, North Carolina; Charleston, South Carolina; Savannah, Georgia; Pensacola, Florida; Mobile, Alabama; Galveston, Texas; and the entrances to the Mississippi River.

Every kind of ship, tugboat, and even paddle-wheel ferry-boat was commissioned, equipped with one or two guns, and staked out along the Southern coast. They quickly stopped Confederate coastal shipping and made privateering and blockade running a hazardous business. Crews were recruited from every walk of life and often sent to sea without any training. However, in most ships, career men or merchant mariners served as a

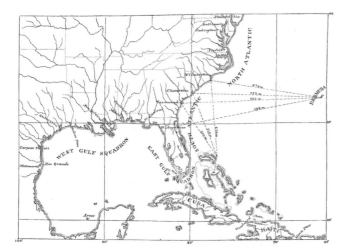

Contemporary map showing the various Union blockading squadrons and bases. *The Naval History and Heritage Command*

nucleus of trained men, and they quickly whipped the new men into shape. Men learned fast when they were under shore-battery fire, and they were kept busy trying to stop enemy blockade runners throughout most of the war.

The expansion of the blockade, however, presented one problem. The farther from Union territory the ships were, the more dependent on coal and other supplies they became. Consequently, a plan was developed to establish a series of bases at strong points along the Confederate coast. These sites would be captured mainly by amphibious assault, garrisoned strongly, and then used to support the blockade. By the end of 1862, the Union had secured Port Royal, South Carolina; Hatteras Inlet, North Carolina; and Jacksonville, St. Augustine, and Pensacola, Florida. Once these bases were established and the blockade was tightened around Florida that state was practically put out of the war, because its inland transportation was so poor. The loss of Florida deprived the South of its salt mills, which were essential for the preservation of ham and bacon for Southern troops. The Confederates were never able to get rid of these naval bases deep in their territory. These coastal actions, though not as well known as several of the major land battles, were ultimately significant factors in the Union victory.

Defeats and Diplomacy

The first major land battle of the war was the First Battle of Bull Run in July 1861. It had ended in a Northern defeat just a few miles from Washington, D.C. The battle put an end to any ideas of a quick victory over the Confederacy. Lincoln extended enlistments from the original three months to three years. The North's battered Army of the Potomac dug in around the capital, expecting a Confederate attack that never came.

By October the South was anxiously hoping that British and French ships would run the blockade in order to pick up the cotton crop that had just been harvested. In order for this to happen, the South needed the Confederacy to be recognized as an independent nation. To try to accomplish this, Davis sent two ambassadors to Europe on a British steamship, the *Trent,* sailing from the West Indies. James Mason was en route to England, John Slidell to France. They were, however, intercepted on 8 November by CAPT Charles Wilkes and his Union sloop *San Jacinto.* Wilkes overhauled the British ship, stopped her on the high seas, and removed Mason and Slidell by force, an action in direct violation of international law.

As a result of this **Trent Affair** there were immediate cries for war in England, and the English fleet was mobilized. However, the matter was settled diplomatically, by releasing the prisoners to British custody. France, which was planning to take advantage of the Civil War by sending an expeditionary force to Mexico, also came near to recognizing the Confederacy. Naval events, however, caused both nations to hold off.

River Campaigns

Bull Run had temporarily stopped military activity in the East, but not in the upper Tennessee and Mississippi River valley regions. Events were about to take place that would foreshadow the defeat of the Confederacy.

In February 1862 a joint force of Navy gunboats and Union army volunteers under the command of a little-known brigadier general, Ulysses S. Grant, captured Fort Henry in north-central Tennessee. The river Navy was a development of the times, adjusting to the circumstances of the war. The Union river gunboats became the first ironclads in the United States. Grant conceived of them as mobile artillery. Under Flag Officer Andrew Foote, the Navy's river squadron demolished Fort Henry and had already accepted its surrender when Grant's army arrived.

Grant then marched overland for an attack on Fort Donelson some twelve miles away on the Cumberland River, while four ironclads and two wooden gunboats moved against the river face of the fort. Here the Navy was thwarted, because the

Theater of operations in the Gulf of Mexico and the Mississippi and Tennessee River valleys.

twelve large guns constituting the fort's battery were on high bluffs overlooking the river. The Confederate shot fell on the unarmored upper decks of the ships, putting them out of action. Grant took the fort from the land side after attacking its fortifications for several days, accepting the unconditional surrender of ten thousand Confederate troops on 16 February. In recognition of his victory, he was henceforth dubbed "Unconditional Surrender" (aka U.S.) Grant by the Northern press.

Grant next moved up the Tennessee River to Pittsburg Landing at Shiloh, Tennessee, where he fought one of the bloodiest battles of the war with the Confederates on 6–7 April. But for the covering gunfire from two Union gunboats, Grant's left flank would have been destroyed and the battle lost. The gunboats fired into the Confederate positions all night, one shell per minute. The next morning, when Grant attacked, it was this section of the Confederate line that broke, giving Grant his costly victory.

Following the losses of forts Henry and Donelson, the Confederates had to abandon their big fortress at Columbus, Kentucky, since all river transport to the place had been stopped. While Grant was engaged at Shiloh, the Union general John Pope moved on down the Mississippi River to Island No. 10, where the river swings in an S curve at the Kentucky–Tennessee line. A major Confederate fortress there guarded the route southward on the river.

On 4 April the Union gunboat *Carondelet* succeeded in running the Confederate batteries, placing her in position to destroy the enemy guns on the Tennessee side. Pope's men could now cross behind her, and Island No. 10 surrendered on 7 April; Pope took seven thousand prisoners. All of western Kentucky and much of western Tennessee were now under federal control. The Union forces consolidated and made preparations to move on Memphis.

The Battle for New Orleans

New Orleans was the South's largest and most important port city. While Grant was making a military name for himself by winning the strategically important central Mississippi Valley, another of the great Union heroes of the war began his move on this key city. Captain David Glasgow Farragut assembled an assault fleet at Ship Island off the nearby Mississippi Gulf coast in March: four sloops, a paddle-wheeler, twelve gunboats, and twenty-one converted mortar-boat schooners under the command of CDR David Dixon Porter, son of the War of 1812 hero of the same name. Farragut, an adopted older brother of Porter, had been in the Navy for fifty years, having served continuously since the War of 1812. This was to be his biggest battle yet.

In mid-March Farragut's force began navigating through the delta toward a Confederate log barrier several miles upriver. Unexpected silting and sand bars in the channel resulted in very

ADM David Farragut would emerge from the Civil War at age sixty as the Union's most famous naval hero. *The Naval History and Heritage Command*

slow going, and it took a month to get all his ships upriver to the barrier. By this time Farragut had lost the advantage of surprise, and virtually the whole Confederacy knew of his approach. At the barrier there were two forts, Fort Jackson on the left bank and Fort St. Philip on the right. On 18 April Porter's gunboats began a steady 5-day-long fire on the forts. On the 20th sailors from two of the gunboats succeeded in creating a narrow breach in the barrier that would allow Farragut's ships to pass through in single file. On the 24th, just after midnight, the fleet started the dangerous trip.

Farragut organized the assault force in three divisions, plus one division of mortar boats, which was to remain at the barrier and protect the rear. At 0315 the assaulting ships arrived at the barrier and started to take heavy fire from the forts. The Union warships received numerous hits, but plowed through the hail of shot past the barrier and proceeded upriver into the midst of a small defensive Confederate fleet consisting of the ironclad CSS *Manassas* and a dozen gunboats. The superior Union fleet soon blasted the defenders out of the water, sinking the gunboats and forcing the *Manassas* to be run aground. Farragut proceeded up the river to New Orleans, and on the 25th anchored his fleet off the quays of the port. The next day, on 26 April, the city surrendered; the two bypassed forts gave up two days later. An occupying force of Union army troops under MGEN Benjamin Butler arrived on 1 May.

The South's leading port was now in the hands of the Union. It was a disaster for the Confederacy. The British and French, who had been thinking about recognizing the South, now thought differently. After all, if a major port could not be held, there did not seem to be much chance that the Confederacy could survive. Thereafter, they no longer seriously considered recognizing the South, though shipyards in both nations continued to build blockade runners and cruisers for the Confederacy.

The *Monitor* and the *Merrimack*

In the mid-1800s European navies had started to develop ironclad warships as a countermeasure to red-hot cannon shot, which could easily penetrate and set fire to wooden warships. At first iron plating was applied to the sides of wooden sailing ships and also to the decks of steamships, but by 1860 the Royal Navy was building steam-driven warships made entirely of iron. By the start of the Civil War most European navies either had in commission or were building some of these ships.

The conservative senior leadership in the U.S. Navy was slow to accept the idea of ironclad warships. At the start of the war the Union navy's most powerful ships were six steam-powered but unarmored frigates. Soon after the beginning of hostilities, however, the Union commissioned half a dozen ironclad gunships for service on the Mississippi River. The Confederates, realizing the potential value of ironclads in defending against the overwhelming numbers of mostly wooden sailing vessels of the Union fleet, at first tried to purchase some from France and England. These efforts were unsuccessful. In the summer of 1861 they began to convert several wooden ships into ironclads just as the Europeans had initially done, by adding iron armor plating to the sides and to the main deck over vital areas.

The most ambitious of these conversions was made to the USS *Merrimack,* a new steam frigate partially burned and then scuttled by Union forces when they withdrew from the Norfolk Navy Yard early in the war. The Confederates raised the vessel, placed her in dry-dock, and set about converting her into the first Confederate ironclad. Stephen Mallory, the Confederate navy secretary, directed the plan. Mallory believed the vessel to be the best means of driving the Union blockaders from the mouth of the Chesapeake and reopening Norfolk as a cotton port.

The ship could make only four knots and drew too much water for safe navigation in the rivers, but she was something entirely new and a real danger to any wooden vessel. She was 275 feet long, with a beam of fifty-one feet and draft of twenty-one feet. Her main deck supported a **casemate** (armored superstructure) framed with twenty-inch pine beams, overlaid with four-inch oak planks and two layers of iron plates. The sloping sides of the casemate would cause solid shot to bounce off harmlessly. The casemate had fourteen gun ports, four on each broadside and three each fore and aft. Renamed as the CSS *Virginia,* she mounted twelve guns, including six 9-inch Dahlgren guns and two 6-inch and two 7-inch rifled guns. When her builders later heard about Union plans to build an ironclad too, they fitted a heavy iron ram on the *Virginia*'s bow.

When the work was nearly completed, CDR Franklin Buchanan, a former U.S. naval officer who had been the first superintendent of the U.S. Naval Academy, was named commanding officer of the *Virginia.* He mustered a crew of about 350 men. If the ship could get under way in time, it could smash to matchwood the five wooden Union navy ships blockading Norfolk and the lower Chesapeake Bay, and the Union troops in Newport News and Fortress Monroe in Hampton Roads would have to evacuate.

Work continued through the summer to the end of February 1862, the project slowed by the lack of iron plate and other metal parts. In early March, the *Virginia* was finally ready to fight.

In August 1861 spies had brought word to Lincoln that the Confederates had salvaged the *Merrimack* and were working to convert it to an ironclad. Secretary of the Navy Welles appointed an Ironclad Board, and Congress was persuaded to appropriate $1.5 million for construction of ironclad steamships. The board reviewed dozens of proposals and selected three for contracts. By far the most radically different and innovative of these three successful proposals was submitted by John Ericsson, a Swedish-born shipbuilder in Brooklyn, New York.

Even before receiving his contract Ericsson began to work feverishly on the ship, incorporating as he went along over forty patentable innovations. The ship went from the drawing board to completion in only a hundred days, an astonishing achievement. Described by some critics as a "cheese box on a raft," the craft was 172 feet long, with a beam of 41 feet and a draft of eleven feet. Her hull had only a foot or so of freeboard, so as to present a very small target. Her battery was two 11-inch Dahlgren guns in a heavily armored turret, placed amidships on the main deck, which was otherwise mostly bare and flat, save for a small pilothouse forward. The deck was armor plated also, and an overhang protected the screw and rudder. Through steam power, the fourteen-ton turret could be rotated 360 degrees. The ship, named the *Monitor,* was commissioned on 25 February 1862, with LT John L. Worden, USN, as commanding officer.

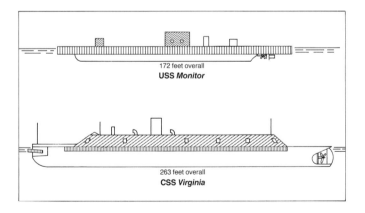

This comparison chart shows the difference in size between the USS *Monitor* and the CSS *Virginia.* The *Monitor* was smaller and more maneuverable, but the *Virginia* had more guns. *The Naval History and Heritage Command*

Watercolor of the USS *Monitor* by Oscar Parkes.
The Naval History and Heritage Command

After a brief testing period, the ship was ordered to proceed to Hampton Roads, at the entrance to Norfolk harbor.

The Battle of Hampton Roads

In early March, the North and South appeared to be in an unstable balance in the East, though things had begun to go badly for the Confederacy in the West. President Lincoln finally persuaded GEN George McClellan to plan a move on Richmond from the south, landing his forces at Fortress Monroe at Hampton Roads and moving up the peninsula to the Confederate capital. Only the threat of the CSS *Virginia* hung over the optimistic expectations of the Union commander. If the *Virginia* got loose in Hampton Roads, it would not only doom the wooden blockade vessels but also destroy his whole plan to move on Richmond.

On 8 March the *Virginia* steamed out from the Norfolk Navy Yard and headed down the Elizabeth River toward the anchored Union blockade ships, the USS *Cumberland* and the USS *Congress.* As the *Virginia* moved toward the two ships, the *Cumberland* began firing, but the shots merely bounced off the sloping iron sides. Buchanan fired a few shots, but his intent was to ram. The *Virginia* plowed into the side of the *Cumberland,* and then backed off. The Union sloop sank quickly, taking with her more than a third of the crew. The *Virginia* suffered only two casualties but lost her ram when backing off from the sinking ship.

Buchanan then turned on the *Congress,* which had run aground while trying to escape to the protection of Union shore batteries. The ironclad slowly and carefully placed herself in position to rake the Union ship. Finally, at a range of only 150 yards, she fired one shell after another into the trapped ship. The *Congress* became a flaming wreck, many of her crew killed and wounded. Her commanding officer was killed, and his successor ordered the colors struck to end the slaughter. Buchanan ordered Confederate boats sent to accept the surrender and take off the crew as prisoners. During this operation, however, some

Confederate sailors were killed by Union troops on shore. In retaliation Buchanan ordered the *Congress* bombarded with red-hot shot. While topside to observe this, Buchanan was hit in the leg by a Union minié ball and had to be relieved in command by LT Catesby Jones.

Jones now turned his attention to the USS *Minnesota,* another blockader run aground. But this ship was too far into the shoal waters to be accurately fired on. The *Minnesota* was hit several times by the *Virginia* and some small Confederate ships from the James River squadron that had joined the fight, since they were no longer blockaded. After three hours of trying to get closer, the *Virginia* broke off and retired to an anchorage under Sewell's Point in Norfolk. She had suffered only minor damage, and she was ready for action again the next day.

The *Monitor,* meanwhile, had been laboring in heavy seas in the Atlantic toward Hampton Roads. She arrived the night of 8 March, her entrance to the area lit by the burning *Congress.* Worden was directed to anchor near the *Minnesota* to protect her from further damage.

Early in the morning of 9 March, Union sailors saw the smoke of the *Virginia* as she came out of her anchorage. The Confederate ship took a different channel so she could get much closer to the *Minnesota.* Worden weighed anchor and placed

the *Monitor* between the *Virginia* and the helpless wooden vessel. Then began a ferocious four-hour gunnery duel at close range between the two ironclads. The *Monitor* kept so close that the *Virginia* had trouble bringing her guns to bear. The Union ship, much smaller and with half the draft of her opponent, was much more maneuverable, but even with her larger guns she could not penetrate the Confederate's armor. Finally Jones broke off with the *Monitor* and concentrated on the *Minnesota,* quickly setting the ship on fire.

Now, however, the *Virginia* went aground. The *Monitor* closed in, believing she could finish off the Confederate. Jones, however, shifted his fire from the *Monitor*'s turret to the small pilothouse forward. A lucky shot exploded ahead of the viewing slits, temporarily blinding Worden and seriously wounding him in the face. LT Samuel Greene, the executive officer, was in the turret. It took him twenty minutes to get the word and proceed to where he could conn the ship. In the meantime, the helmsman kept steering according to Worden's last order, which was to "sheer off." As a result, the *Monitor* withdrew toward Fortress Monroe, during which time the *Virginia* freed herself from the bottom. The *Virginia* had been damaged and was leaking badly at the bow. Even though the *Monitor*'s shot had not penetrated the iron plates, many were cracked, as was much of the wooden

Painting by contemporary artist J. O. Davidson depicting the action between the USS *Monitor* and CSS *Virginia* during the Battle of Hampton Roads in March 1862. *The Naval History and Heritage Command*

An old photograph showing the damage done to the *Monitor's* turret, taken shortly after the battle.

The Naval History and Heritage Command

superstructure. Jones decided to retire to the shelter of the Norfolk Navy Yard for repairs.

The battle thus came to an indecisive end. But clearly the age of ironclad vessels had arrived. With it a whole new set of naval tactics had to be developed by the world's navies. The timely arrival of the *Monitor* and numerous other Union vessels enabled General McClellan to launch his peninsular campaign against Richmond. Norfolk was captured, and the *Virginia* was blown up by her own crew to prevent capture. The *Monitor* sank a year later in a gale off the Carolina Capes, taking down part of her crew. She would be an important influence in naval ship design, however, for more than forty years. (The wreck of the *Monitor* was located in 1973, and many artifacts and parts, including her anchor, propeller, engine, turret, and the two Dahlgren guns, have been recovered and are on display at the Mariners Museum, Newport News, Virginia.)

The Union continued to build additional ironclads similar to the *Monitor*—known, in fact, as "monitors"—for coastal warfare and by war's end had about fifty of them, some of them double-turreted. They also built a number of **casemate ironclads,** similar to the CSS *Virginia* but with masts, as well as armored steamships, for ocean duty. Unlike the Union, the Confederacy lacked the resources to build many more ironclad warships, though by war's end it had built several additional *Virginia*-type casemate ironclads and a number of armored steamships. Many of these used cotton bales as backing for a thin layer of iron plating, which was by then in very short supply in the Confederacy.

Lee Gains Time

McClellan launched his attack on the Virginia Peninsula on 17 March 1862, only a week after the famous Battle of Hampton Roads. Lincoln realized that the war would not end unless Lee and his Army of Northern Virginia were crushed, despite the Union victories in the West. By 5 April McClellan had landed some 121,500 soldiers of his Army of the Potomac on the peninsula and had begun his advance from Fortress Monroe, after taking Yorktown. A month later Norfolk was taken. But the slow Union advance enabled Lee to gather his forces and prepare the defenses before Richmond.

In a series of sharp engagements called the Seven Days' Battles, Lee pushed McClellan back from Richmond. By August McClellan had to evacuate the peninsula and reorganize the defenses of Washington. In September Lee crossed the Potomac into Maryland in the first invasion of the North. He hoped to detach Maryland from the Union and move into Pennsylvania. He wanted to impress the North with the horrors of war and perhaps gain diplomatic recognition and military aid from the European powers by this grand undertaking.

On 17 September, on Antietam Creek near Sharpsburg, Maryland, however, Lee met McClellan's reorganized and reequipped army in the bloodiest one-day action of the entire war. Over 12,000 thousand Union and 13,000 Confederates fell in battle that day. Lee was forced to withdraw to Virginia. The immediate threat to Maryland, Washington, and the North was stopped, but Lee had gained some time and prolonged the life of the Confederacy.

The Emancipation Proclamation

Antietam was an expensive victory for the North, but it served to hearten the Union. Lincoln took the opportunity to announce his preliminary Emancipation Proclamation on 22 September 1862. In it he promised freedom to all slaves within areas of the ten Confederate states still in rebellion as of 1 January 1863. He was in no position to enforce such an edict, but it was a great psychological move. Although it did not free slaves in the border states or in certain Confederate areas already controlled by the Union, the proclamation rallied many Northerners who were only lukewarm about continuing the war. It also made a significant difference in European attitudes. The war now became a cause for the liberation of the slaves, which Europe favored, not just a war to save the Union, about which most Europeans were indifferent. It thus ended any chance that France or Britain would intervene in favor of the South in the war.

Also, many liberated slaves joined the Union forces. Lincoln's proclamation could not enforce immediate freedom for slaves in the Confederacy, of course. But the Emancipation Proclamation encouraged the passage by Congress of the Thirteenth Amendment to the Constitution in 1865, which finally ended all slavery in the United States. (The 2012 movie *Lincoln* is an excellent portrayal of the events surrounding the passage of the Thirteenth Amendment.)

Vicksburg

After capturing New Orleans in April 1862, Farragut was convinced that his next most logical move would be to take the port of Mobile, thereby eliminating the last major Gulf cotton exporting port of the Confederacy. But the top priority of President Lincoln and his advisers was to secure the Mississippi River for the Union. Accordingly, by direction of Lincoln, Farragut was ordered to fight his way up the Mississippi until his ships met a small force of Union gunboats coming down from the upper part of the river. Each would capture any Confederate towns and settlements they passed along the way. They would meet at Vicksburg, Mississippi, where the Confederates were building heavy fortifications, and attempt to neutralize or capture it, thus placing the entire Mississippi River under Union control.

In late May Farragut arrived first, just south of Vicksburg, because the gunboats had encountered some unexpectedly heavy Confederate resistance on their way down the river. While waiting for the gunboats to arrive, he decided to run up past the Confederate shore batteries with eight of his larger ships and bombard them as a prelude to capturing the city. He soon found that his fire was not effective against the well-emplaced Confederate batteries high on the bluffs overlooking the river. Meanwhile the gunboats had finally arrived, and he joined up with them just north of the city.

Reasoning that his naval forces alone would not be able to take this "Gibraltar of the Mississippi," as it came to be called, Farragut called for Army troops to storm it from the landward side before the Confederates could finish preparations to repel such an assault. The requested Army forces never came, however, and the Confederate buildup continued as the Union force sat at anchor and waited.

In mid-July the Confederate ironclad CSS *Arkansas,* just completed at Yazoo City, Mississippi, suddenly appeared on the scene and promptly attacked Farragut's anchored ships, inflicting a number of casualties. Faced with this new threat and with the river level falling as summer progressed, Farragut felt obliged to return to New Orleans. Upon his arrival there he received the welcome news that he had been promoted to the rank of rear admiral, the first to achieve that rank in the U.S. Navy.

A few days after Farragut's departure the *Arkansas* followed downriver to help Southern forces fighting at Baton Rouge. There she became disabled and had to be burned by her crew to avoid capture, thus ending her short twenty-three-day career. Meanwhile, the Union gunboats retreated three hundred miles upriver to a base at Helena, Arkansas. Thus by default a five-hundred-mile stretch of the lower Mississippi was reopened to the Confederacy, at least for the next several months.

In October the flotilla of Union gunboats and transports, now called the Mississippi River Squadron and numbering some sixty craft, was placed under the command of David Dixon Porter, now made an acting rear admiral. Soon thereafter the squadron was given the task of carrying supplies and providing support for some 32,000 Union troops under General William Tecumseh Sherman marching downriver to take part in another attempt to capture Vicksburg, while General Grant approached by rail down through Mississippi with another force of 40,000. However the Confederates cut Grant's supply lines, causing him to retreat. Meanwhile Porter and Sherman reached the Yazoo River just north of Vicksburg in December, but without assistance from Grant, Sherman's force was repulsed.

With the coming of spring in 1863 and a fall in the river level, Grant was able to march his troops down the western side of the river to a point about ten miles south of Vicksburg. They were ferried across the river in late April by a number of Porter's gunboats and transports, which had made a daring run down past the Confederate batteries on the cliffs at Vicksburg. The crossing was the largest amphibious operation undertaken in the war to that time. Grant then proceeded to attack the city's southern defenses, while Sherman moved in from the north. However, both assaults on the now impregnable fortifications failed, and Grant settled in for a siege of the city.

For forty days and nights, Porter's gunboats rained destruction on Vicksburg, while the Army tightened its noose. Vicksburg's defenders took shelter in caves and lived on horse meat and rats. Finally, on 4 July 1863, weakened by starvation, the 30,000 Confederate defenders surrendered. Grant paroled the Vicksburg prisoners and sent them home under a pledge to take no further part in the war. Four days later, when they heard of the fall of Vicksburg, the last Confederate fort at Port Hudson in Louisiana surrendered, and the Mississippi River was clear of all Confederate forces from Illinois to the Gulf of Mexico. The Confederacy was split, cut off from any further support from its western states or Mexico.

Turning Point

Despite the Union victories in the Mississippi Valley, General Lee and his Army of Northern Virginia were still very much in

A contemporary lithograph showing Admiral Porter and his force of gunboats and transports making a hazardous run down the Mississippi past the elevated Confederate batteries at Vicksburg on the night of 16 April 1863. A Confederate scouting party set fires on the west side of the river so that the advancing vessels would be illuminated for their gunners. *Currier & Ives*

the war. In May 1863 Lee took on the Army of the Potomac at Chancellorsville, Virginia, and won a resounding victory over Northern general Joseph Hooker. Lee lost his most talented general officer at Chancellorsville, however, when Thomas J. "Stonewall" Jackson was accidentally killed by his own men in the darkness as he returned from a reconnaissance mission.

The victory spurred Lee to plan another invasion of the North. It was a desperate gamble to crush the Union's will to carry on the war. With an army of 75,000 men, he marched up Virginia's Shenandoah Valley and emerged near the town of Gettysburg, Pennsylvania, on 1 July. At Gettysburg he ran into a Union army of 90,000 men under the command of GEN George Meade. There followed one of the bloodiest and most decisive battles of the war.

After some initial Confederate successes on 1 July, the Confederates were thrown back several times in attacks against the Union flanks the following day. On 3 July, Lee ordered an all-out frontal assault against Cemetery Ridge, after an intensive two-hour artillery barrage. At about 1400, a force of 15,000 men in gray, most under the command of MGEN George Pickett, moved in front of the ridge and began an ill-advised charge across an open field into the very teeth of the Union lines. Artillery and small-arms fire cut down thousands. Some Confederate troops managed to reach the Union lines but were killed or thrown back. Pickett's failed charge decided the battle. Lee was forced to begin a retreat back to Virginia that night, leaving behind 20,000 casualties from the three-day battle.

The North had now achieved two great victories on successive days—Gettysburg and Vicksburg. The tide of the war had changed; there was no longer any hope of the South's winning. Lee's task now was to try to keep his army intact by avoiding major battles, so as to make possible a settlement that would keep the Confederacy alive.

Charleston

From the beginning of the war, Secretary Welles and the North had looked upon Charleston as the hotbed of secession and a nest for blockade runners. Especially galling was Fort Sumter, where Union forces had been humbled in the first battle of the war. Charleston was not as important as New Orleans, Wilmington, or Mobile, but it was of high symbolic value to both sides. The Union navy had blockaded it since the start of the war and had sunk stone-laden ships in the secondary channels to block them.

Charleston Harbor was heavily defended by well-placed fortifications. Besides Fort Sumter there were five smaller forts guarding the approaches to the harbor. It was impossible to approach the harbor entrance without coming under fire from these forts. Further, the main ship channel went directly past Fort Sumter. The Confederate generals in charge of the

Charleston defenses, P. G. T. Beauregard and Roswell Ripley, were engineers, and they had laid out an extensive earthen and sandbagged defensive system that was far more efficient than masonry forts. They emplaced many heavy guns of the latest design with rifled barrels that fired shot of great penetrating power. Underwater, they had placed obstacles such as heavy piles, a log-and-chain boom, rope barriers to foul propellers, and a field of torpedoes (mines). In addition to these defenses, inside the harbor the Confederates had built two ironclad gunboats, which periodically made destructive forays out into the Union's wooden blockade fleet.

The North believed that its new monitors could force their way into the harbor at Charleston. In April 1863 Union admiral Samuel DuPont, the commander of the blockading fleet, was ordered to launch an attack against Charleston with his ironclads. He personally believed that Charleston could not be taken without support from Army troops on land; nevertheless, on 7 April he launched an attack with seven new monitors, the casemate-type ironclad *New Ironsides,* and the armored gunboat *Keokuk.* The ships were slow in getting started, and the lead monitor became fouled in her own minesweeping apparatus. The column plodded up the channel, anchoring periodically to avoid running aground.

The head of the Union column finally arrived at the outer barrier at Fort Sumter in midafternoon. Soon the entire column became a target for the most accurate and concentrated fire yet seen in the war. The Confederates had zeroed in their heavy guns and could hardly miss. Hundreds of Southern shells hit the Union ironclads. The *Keokuk* was heavily damaged after being struck more than ninety times, and sank the next day. The other ironclads made it out, jarred, damaged, and turrets jammed, but with only one death.

Though the ironclads had withstood the punishment, their own fire on the Confederate works had been ineffective. Fort Sumter had been hit more than fifty times, but its fighting efficiency remained unaffected. The earthworks were undamaged. DuPont had served well on the blockade station for over two years, but he had attempted the impossible. The admiral reported to Lincoln that Charleston was impregnable to naval attack alone and that a major amphibious assault involving a large Army force was necessary. Both the president and the Navy Department reluctantly agreed, but the political pressures were such that DuPont was relieved shortly thereafter.

In July 1863 ADM John Dahlgren arrived on the scene as DuPont's relief. The Army sent down General Gillmore of the Corps of Engineers. Together, the two hoped to place Charleston under siege and force its surrender. Thereafter, a series of land and sea assaults took place. Several of the outer islands were taken by amphibious landings, but only after weeks of terrible casualties were the secondary forts secured. The guns were then turned on Fort Sumter, which was reduced to rubble by

September. Nevertheless the Confederates refused to surrender it or Charleston, and both would hold out for another year and a half, despite additional naval and amphibious assaults.

The Davids and the *Hunley*

During the siege of Charleston, the Confederates introduced two new kinds of warships there: a semisubmersible boat called a "David" and a submarine. Davids were semisubmersible fifty-foot, cigar-shaped, steam-powered torpedo boats fitted with a sixty-kilogram (about 130 pounds) spar torpedo on the bow. Named for the prototype, the CSS *David,* the boats carried a crew of four and were designed to operate low in the water, with ballast tanks that could be filled for an attack so that only a raised conning tower and the stack for the steam engines were visible above water. The boats were supposed to ram a Union ship hard enough to make their spar stick in the hull like a spear, then back off while the explosive was detonated by yanking a long cord. A number of blockading Union vessels were attacked outside Charleston Harbor by the *David* and her sisters. In October 1863 the powerful casemated Union ironclad *New Ironsides,* one of the other two ironclads that had been approved along with the *Monitor* two years before by Navy secretary Welles' Ironclad Board, was badly damaged by the *David.* A dozen of these Davids would eventually be built for the Confederate navy by war's end.

After the success of the *David,* the Confederates in Mobile, Alabama, began working on a more sinister vessel. This was the *Hunley,* the world's first true submarine warship. It was originally designed to pull a torpedo fastened at the end of a line into the side of an enemy ship after submerging and going underneath it, though later it was fitted with a spar torpedo instead.

The *Hunley* was built of a section of iron boiler about forty feet long, four feet wide, and four feet high. The bow and stern each contained a ballast tank that could be flooded to make the vessel submerge and pumped out to make her rise. A set of leather bellows provided for air circulation. A small conning tower on top had four tiny glass observation ports through which the captain could see where he was going. The vessel was powered by eight or nine men turning a crankshaft attached to a propeller at the stern. During the first sea trials in Mobile, the

An archeologist works inside a salvaged section of the *Hunley* on display at the Lasch Conservation Center in Charleston, South Carolina. *Courtesy of Friends of the Hunley*

Hunley's crew had drowned. The vessel was shipped by rail to Charleston, where three more crews drowned in trials. General Beauregard prohibited her from being submerged again, and tactics were changed to make the *Hunley* operate more like a *David,* attacking with a spar torpedo.

On the night of 17 February 1864, the *Hunley* crept out of the harbor and headed toward the Union blockade line. Approaching the Union sloop *Housatonic,* the *Hunley*'s commanding officer, LT George Dixon, rested the men and then had them flood the ballast tanks until the deck was awash. Then they cranked hard to plunge the spar torpedo into the ship's side. But something went wrong after the spar was set, and the charge exploded before the *Hunley* could get away. The *Housatonic* sank in less than five minutes, followed shortly thereafter by the *Hunley* and her fifth brave crew. This was the first undersea boat to sink an enemy ship in battle. Insofar as is known, no other attempts were made to build a submarine during the Civil War. (The *Hunley* was raised in August 2000 from about thirty feet of water off Charleston and transported to that city. Remains of her crew were found still aboard and were interred in Charleston's Magnolia Cemetery in 2004. The salvaged *Hunley* was placed on display at the Warren Lasch Conservation Center in Charleston.)

An old photograph of a Confederate David submersible taken shortly after the Civil War (left) and a contemporary drawing of the submarine CSS *Hunley* (right). *The Naval History and Heritage Command*

Confederate Privateers, Cruisers, and Blockade Runners

Although the Confederates commissioned many privateers during the early days of the war, by mid-1862 most had been sunk or captured by Union naval forces. Their efforts were hampered somewhat by the Declaration of Paris of 1856. The declaration, signed by all major European countries except Spain, declared privateering illegal. Early on, however, the Southern privateers forced many Union merchant ships to transfer to foreign registry in order to avoid them.

The most effective Confederate navy effort against Union merchant shipping, however, was commerce raiding by about a dozen commissioned naval cruisers. These cruisers were mostly foreign-built with Confederate financing, with foreign crews and Southern officers. They ranged far and wide over the world's oceans, capturing U.S.–flagged vessels wherever they encountered them. After capturing their prizes and making prisoners of their crews and any passengers, the cruisers simply burned them. They continued the decline of the Northern merchant marine begun by the privateers. Some shipping companies went out of business.

Ultimately, over 1,600 American merchant ships transferred to foreign registry during the war, many of these in 1863, when the Confederate cruiser CSS *Alabama* ran amok on the high seas. Altogether, the raiders burned and sank some two hundred ships, about 5 percent of all Union merchant ships that sailed during the war. Costly as this was, these losses did not have much effect on the outcome of the war, mainly because more and more cargo was carried by the reflagged neutral ships, safe from Confederate attack. However, American merchant shipping was dealt a blow from which it never recovered, even up to the present day.

Besides wreaking havoc on Northern merchant shipping, another effect the cruisers had was weakening the Union blockade. In the last years of the war over a hundred Union warships were kept busy tracking down a dozen Confederate raiders.

Another more profitable Confederate maritime enterprise that arose during the war was **blockade running.** By some estimates as many as 1,500 blockade runners saw service during the Civil War. The more successful ones were specially designed fast, side-wheeler steamships with low silhouettes, collapsing funnels, and shallow drafts. They operated out of ports such as Wilmington, North Carolina, and many other shallow harbors along the Confederate coastline. Because the Union did not have sufficient ships to effectively blockade the entire 3,500-mile Southern coast until near the end of the war, blockade running was a very profitable business, worth the risks involved. Salt that usually sold for $6.50 a ton would bring $1,700 a ton in Richmond, and coffee jumped from $249 a ton to $5,500. Even in 1863, however, when the Union blockade was beginning to make its presence felt, the odds of capture were only one in four. In 1864 blockade runners brought in from foreign markets, among other commodities, eight million pounds of meat, 1.5 million pounds of lead, half a million pairs of shoes, and 69,000 rifles and forty-three cannon. All this was paid for by five million dollars' worth of exported cotton the blockade runners carried to foreign markets that year.

Captain Semmes and the *Alabama*

The most famous and successful of the Confederate cruiser skippers was CAPT Raphael Semmes. His first ship, the CSS *Sumter,* captured seventeen Union ships before being cornered by the Union navy in Gibraltar. Semmes sold her and made his way to England. There he learned a new cruiser was being built in a British shipyard for a Confederate agent, without British government approval.

On her trial run, the ship was sailed to the Portuguese Azores, where officials looked the other way when a chartered British ship transferred a battery of six 32-pounders and other armament to the ship. Semmes then took the ship outside territorial waters to perform a commissioning ceremony. He read his Confederate navy orders, mustered his crew of volunteers and English and Irish adventurers, and raised the Confederate ensign. Now the CSS *Alabama* was a ship of war.

Semmes took twenty ships in the North Atlantic over the next two months, then sailed to the Caribbean. He captured a number of ships there and then moved into the Gulf of Mexico. Off Galveston he tricked a Union gunboat away from other Union navy support and quickly sank her. For eighteen months Semmes cruised the world's oceans—the Caribbean, South Atlantic, Indian Ocean, Bay of Bengal, and South China Sea. On 11 June 1864, his crew exhausted and his ship badly in need of repairs, he brought the *Alabama* into the French port of Cherbourg and requested docking.

Confederate admiral Raphael Semmes. During the Civil War he commanded the Confederate commerce raider CSS *Alabama,* which drove most Union commercial shipping from the North Atlantic during much of the conflict.
The Naval History and Heritage Command

In the harbor the *Alabama* was spotted by the American consul. He telegraphed CAPT John Winslow of the U.S. seven-gun sloop *Kearsarge,* then off Holland. Three days later the Union ship arrived off Cherbourg. French authorities now refused Semmes docking rights, so he refueled and challenged Winslow to a single-ship duel outside French territorial waters.

On 19 June the *Alabama* steamed out of port, following the *Kearsarge* into international waters. A French ironclad followed and anchored at the three-mile limit, and an English yacht, the *Deerhound,* stood by to observe the action. Thousands of spectators lined the shore to watch the battle. The ships fired a number of broadsides without much effect, because of the long range. Then the *Kearsarge* came about, and the two ships steamed in broad circles half a mile apart seeking to rake each other. Soon the *Kearsarge* took control of the situation. The *Alabama* did not have the speed to outmaneuver her opponent, and much of her ammunition was defective. After an hour of battle, the *Alabama* was sinking, while the *Kearsarge* was only slightly damaged.

Semmes tried to beach his ship, but Winslow cut in front and raked the *Alabama* again. Water rushing into the Confederate ship extinguished her boilers, and Semmes struck his colors. As the *Alabama* began to sink, the *Deerhound* came in to pick up survivors. Semmes and forty of his crew were taken to England, escaping capture.

The *Alabama* had captured more than sixty Union ships during her commerce raiding, destroying most at sea. The Northern steamship lines had suffered huge losses. Because the raider had been built in Britain, the British government later had to pay $15.5 million in claims as the result of an international court ruling in Geneva, Switzerland.

The Confederate raider CSS *Alabama* was finally sunk in June 1864 in a fierce engagement with the U.S. Navy sloop *Kearsarge* off Cherbourg, France. Here, sailors in the *Kearsarge* cheer as Semmes strikes his colors. Note the 11-inch Dahlgren gun in the center. *The Naval History and Heritage Command*

Other Confederate raiders also enjoyed much success against Northern shipping. One, the CSS *Shenandoah,* commanded by CAPT James Waddell, wreaked such havoc among Union whaling ships in the Aleutian Islands near Alaska that the American whaling industry was all but destroyed.

The Battle of Mobile Bay

Following their victories at Vicksburg and Gettysburg, the Union armies shifted their attention to central Tennessee. In several fierce battles around Chattanooga, Grant opened the northwestern door to Georgia. Promoted by Lincoln in March 1864 to become supreme commander of all Union armies, Grant now went to Virginia to consult with Lincoln and devise a strategy to bring a successful end to the war, as well as to closely supervise the final push against Lee's remaining forces in central Virginia. He left General Sherman in command of the western army, with orders to march on Atlanta, Georgia.

The impending Atlanta campaign facilitated now-Admiral Farragut's long-cherished plans to close off the last of the Confederacy's Gulf ports, Mobile, Alabama. Sherman figured that a naval assault on Mobile would cause the Confederates to move units defending Atlanta to the Gulf. In July 1864, therefore, Farragut was given four monitors to shield his fourteen wooden ships and an amphibious troop contingent to besiege and capture the forts guarding the entrance to Mobile Bay.

Mobile was a strategic port for the South. It had been the leading cotton-shipping port of the United States before the war. Accordingly, the Confederates had prepared defenses for the harbor stronger than those of any other on the Gulf coast. Three formidable forts guarded the outer entrance to the bay. Fort Gaines on Dauphine Island and Fort Morgan protected the main entrance channel, with Fort Powell to the northwest guarding a shallower channel not usable by deeper draft ships. Ships had to pass directly under the guns of Fort Morgan to enter Mobile Bay. Pilings formed a submerged obstruction two miles long from Fort Gaines toward the main channel. A triple line of two hundred moored torpedoes (mines) extended that barrier to within a quarter of a mile of Fort Morgan. A buoy marked the eastern end of the minefield, which left only a 150-yard-wide channel for blockade runners.

Key to the Mobile defenses was a brand-new Confederate ironclad, the CSS *Tennessee,* an improved version of the CSS *Virginia,* from which Admiral Buchanan flew his flag. The ship, though better built than the *Virginia,* still had design flaws. It had a speed of only six knots, its steering chains from the wheel to the rudder were exposed topside, and its gun-port shutters easily jammed. Three other small gunboats completed the little Confederate fleet with a total of sixteen guns, compared to Farragut's battle force of eighteen ships and 159 guns. The Union monitors were no faster than the *Tennessee,* but they had heavier armor and 15-inch and 11-inch Dahlgren smoothbore guns, compared to the Confederate's 7-inch and 6.4-inch rifles.

In the morning of 4 August 1864 Farragut landed the Army troops on Dauphin Island to lay siege to Fort Gaines, which was largely undefended on the landward side. The next day his fleet started up the channel, with the four monitors in line ahead on the eastern side of the channel closest to Fort Morgan and the other fourteen ships on a parallel course slightly behind, in a second line on the western side. The latter ships were lashed together in pairs, each Union frigate having a gunboat secured alongside to port, with the frigate *Brooklyn* and gunboat *Octorara* the first pair. As the two lines of ships neared the fort, they began to exchange fire with it. At this point the commanding officer of the leading Union monitor *Tecumseh* sighted the *Tennessee* approaching from within the bay, followed by three gunboats. He turned toward the minefield to attack her, neglecting his navigation. Suddenly, when only a hundred yards from the Confederate ironclad, the *Tecumseh* struck a mine that exploded and ripped out her bottom. The ship sank almost instantly, taking most of her crew of a hundred down with her.

The other monitors kept going, however, in order to avoid disaster. Meanwhile, the *Brooklyn,* with the *Octorara* alongside, heard confused reports about objects in the water ahead and stopped dead in the middle of the channel. All the ships of the

Battle of Mobile Bay—the crucial moment. In this painting by contemporary artist Louis Preng, Admiral Farragut orders his force to bypass the sinking monitor *Tecumseh* and pass the Confederate minefield into Mobile Bay, beyond Fort Morgan. *The Naval History and Heritage Command*

Union frigate line following behind were now in danger of colliding with one another.

Farragut was faced with the most important decision of his career. He climbed into the rigging of his flagship, the USS *Hartford,* second in line, and surveyed the scene. He saw that he must go ahead into the danger of the minefield or turn back with a major naval defeat on his hands. He took a calculated risk, figuring that most of the mines had been in the water so long that they were probably ineffective because of leakage. He shouted out the famous words "Damn the torpedoes!" Then he ordered Captains James Jouett of the gunboat *Metacomet,* which was alongside, and Percival Drayton of the *Hartford:* "Four bells! Captain Drayton, go ahead! Jouett, full speed!"

The ships moved through the minefield, often bumping and scraping the easily seen black mines. Not a single one detonated. The entire Union battle line swept into the bay and into the charging Confederate force.

Admiral Buchanan on the *Tennessee* tried desperately to ram the *Hartford,* but the frigate skipped out of his way. As the rest of the Union frigates cleared the fort, one by one they were engaged by the *Tennessee,* but no serious damage was done to either side. By this time, all of the ships had moved several miles north of Fort Morgan, so the fort's guns could not help the Confederate ships. Now the Union ships started closing in on the Confederate gunboats. One Confederate gunboat was forced to surrender, another was beached, and the third escaped to the city. The *Tennessee* retired under the guns of Fort Morgan.

Farragut anchored the Union fleet four miles north of Fort Morgan and ordered the crews to breakfast. They had barely finished when Buchanan charged forth again in the *Tennessee.* He wanted to sink the *Hartford.*

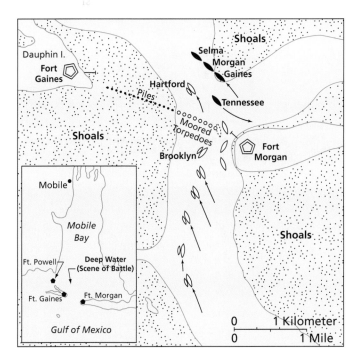

Map of the opening action of the Battle of Mobile Bay, showing Farragut's ships lashed side by side attempting to pass Fort Morgan, with the Union monitors acting as cover between. The Union monitor *Tecumseh* has just been sunk by a mine abreast Fort Morgan, and the Confederate ironclad *Tennessee* is approaching from the north.

The Union ships weighed anchor, surrounded the Confederate, and began to fire point-blank. Buchanan could do little but maneuver slowly. Two of the Union monitors rammed the *Tennessee,* damaging themselves more than their enemy. Then the *Hartford* bore down and, after smashing into the Confederate, fired a broadside into her from ten feet away. The shots bounced harmlessly off her casemate. The *Tennessee,* plagued by faulty ammunition throughout the battle, was able to get off only a single last shot at her opponent.

Then the Union monitors joined the fight. Before long the *Tennessee*'s gun ports were jammed and her steering chains cut. The stack was shot away, so her gun deck was filled with suffocating heat and smoke. Admiral Buchanan was wounded. As the entire Union fleet closed in for the kill, Buchanan authorized the *Tennessee*'s captain to raise the white flag. It was the end not only of the battle, but also of the Confederate navy. The forts quickly surrendered. No serious attempt to capture the city itself would be made until the spring of 1865, but the war had now passed the city by, and Mobile was lost to the Confederacy.

Sherman, who had been moving slowly toward Atlanta, now broke loose and defeated the Confederates in three sharp battles. The city fell on 2 September 1864. He then set out with 60,000 shock troops with light rations, living off the countryside, and in what became known as **Sherman's March to the Sea** cut a devastating path sixty miles wide to the coast, wiping out the Confederacy's last agricultural area and isolating it from its southernmost states. Savannah fell to his forces in December, and he then surged northward into the Carolinas toward Charleston. With his forces closing in on the city, Sherman finally accomplished what the Navy could not—Charleston surrendered on 18 February 1865. Grant's master plan had now confined Lee to the Petersburg–Richmond area. Wilmington, North Carolina, connected to Richmond by rail and defended by Fort Fisher, was now the only port still open to Confederate blockade runners.

Fort Fisher

Fort Fisher was the key to Confederate defenses at the mouth of the Cape Fear River in North Carolina. Wilmington is located up the river. The port continued to receive a trickle of foreign war supplies through the winter of 1864–65 despite the Union blockade. An attempt to capture Fort Fisher was made in late December 1864, but this was unsuccessful because the Army supplied a force that was less than half the number requested by the Navy for an amphibious assault. General Grant was so dissatisfied with Army general Benjamin Butler's performance that he sent him home.

Both sides prepared for the next assault. The Confederates heavily reinforced Fort Fisher and repaired and extended the fortifications. Meanwhile, Grant sent GEN Alfred Terry to head an Army landing force of eight thousand men, the number the Navy had requested in the first place. With Admiral Porter's fleet bombarding in direct support, Terry's force landed on 13 January 1865 and dug in north of the fort, cutting off any hope of help from Wilmington. Terry had his men dig trenches and works to within five hundred yards of the fort, while Porter's fleet rained shells on the besieged defenders.

On 15 January the Navy renewed its firing. A Navy landing force of 1,600 sailors and four hundred Marines then landed on the seaward face of the fort, in coordination with an attack by Terry's army from the north. The Navy–Marine Corps effort was repulsed with over three hundred casualties, and the survivors regrouped on the landing beach. The Army succeeded in breaching the northern parapets just as the defenders were recovering

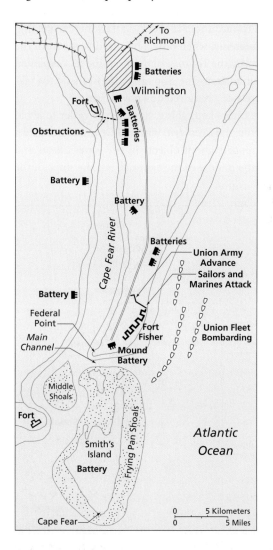

The naval amphibious assault on Fort Fisher, near Wilmington, North Carolina. This was the only successful large-scale joint amphibious assault against a strongly fortified position during the Civil War. It showed that well-planned Army-Navy assaults could succeed against the best defenses.

from the naval assault. Calling for fleet support, Terry's forces moved forward, with the shells of the naval bombardment falling just ahead. Caught between Terry's forces and the naval landing force, the 1,800 Confederate survivors surrendered.

When Navy secretary Welles informed Lincoln of the victory at Fort Fisher, the president exclaimed, "Why, there is nothing left for your ships to do!" And that was true.

The Fort Fisher expedition was of special interest to contemporary military strategists because it was the only successful large-scale joint amphibious attack against a strongly fortified position during the war. It showed the value of heavy supporting fire from ships. It also showed that well-planned Army-Navy assaults could be successful against even the best defenses.

Strategically, the capture of Fort Fisher blocked Wilmington, thus ending, as Lincoln saw, the Navy's primary role in the war. Despite occasional setbacks, the Navy had accomplished every job it had been assigned on the rivers in the West and on the Gulf and Atlantic coasts, and it had driven the Confederates from the seas. The final act of the war was about to take place between Lee and Grant near Richmond.

Lee Surrenders

Grant was now in a position to outflank the Confederate defenses of the Richmond–Petersburg area. He kept up relentless attacks through the winter, suffering heavy casualties. Grant's losses, however, were quickly replaced. Though Lee suffered smaller losses, he had no reserves upon which to call. In desperation, Lee launched a final attack on Grant's lines on 25 March 1865. He was repulsed with heavy losses and forced to abandon Petersburg. On 9 April, at the village of Appomattox Court House, Virginia, Lee surrendered his command to General Grant in the parlor of Wilmer McLean's home.

Like Lincoln, Grant sought only to conclude the war and return the nation to peace. He gave Lee's men food and allowed them to keep their horses for the spring plowing. He paroled the Confederate officers and men on the strength of their word and sent them home. But for a few skirmishes, the war was over. On 14 April 1865 the now-retired major general Robert Anderson raised the same flag over Fort Sumter that he had lowered as a major exactly four years earlier. On 10 May Jefferson Davis was captured near Irwinville, Georgia, by a detachment of the 4th Michigan Cavalry. The Confederate government ceased to exist. The Union was preserved.

Aftermath of the Civil War

Nearly 540,000 servicemen from both sides died during the Civil War, the nation's most costly wartime toll. About five billion dollars were spent by both sides. Destruction in the South was devastating, and the region was stricken with poverty and famine for many years. The spirit of defeat oppressed its people even longer.

Many changes occurred during the war. Because of the scarcity of whale oil, for example, petroleum, which had been discovered at Titusville, Pennsylvania, in 1859, was used to make kerosene for lamps throughout the nation by war's end. Food canning was developed by Gilbert Van Camp in Indianapolis; the Union army soon was living on canned meats and vegetables. Mines came into being as an effective weapon of war; some thirty-five Union ships were sunk by Confederate mines, more than from any other cause. Torpedoes on the ends of spars were tried. Ironclad ships were proven effective. The idea of a submarine, though not entirely successful, was resurrected. Balloons were used as observation platforms; they did not achieve much success, but the idea of aerial reconnaissance began.

Medical care of wounded men received great attention, and the U.S. Navy fitted out its first hospital ship, the *Red Rover,* a side-wheeler put into service in 1862 at St. Louis, on the Mississippi River. The ship was staffed by female nurses and had operating rooms, elevators, bathtubs, and ice vaults. Dorothea Dix and Clara Barton, who later founded the American Red Cross, recruited both men and women to perform nursing duties at the battlefronts and in Army hospitals.

Cameras were used to record the sights and scenes of war for the first time. Railroads and the telegraph, though existing before the war, became indispensable communication links.

The Navy itself had grown to more than seven hundred ships. Nearly 60,000 officers and men were serving in a Navy that had numbered only about nine thousand at the start of the war. That the Navy played a vital role in the victory of the Union is unquestionable.

Confederate general Robert E. Lee proved to be the superior tactician in the field, but the overall grand strategy of the Union under Lincoln and Grant gradually forced him into submission because of lack of men, food, and military supplies. Despite the final defeat of Lee in Virginia, the battles around the edges of the Confederacy were really the decisive ones. The Navy played a relatively small role in the holding and maneuvering actions in the eastern theater, except for the final battle for Fort Fisher, which sealed Lee's fate at Petersburg and Appomattox.

The Confederacy's attempts to sustain itself by *interior lines of communications* (roads and railroads), as the continental school strategists would later call them, failed in the face of the superior naval power around it. Movement by sea forces over water proved to be faster and much more effective than movement by land forces over the poor roads and railroads of the South. These geopolitical and strategic lessons on maritime sea power versus continental land power would be studied by generations of military strategists in the years following the Civil War.

Critical Thinking

1. Was the American Civil War inevitable? Elaborate on your reasons why or why not.

2. Research the life of LT George Dixon, the captain of the Confederate submarine *Hunley*. What legendary artifact was discovered near his body when the submarine was raised from Charleston Harbor in 2000?

3. The USS *Monitor* was the first of a new design for warships, but she was not the last of her class. Research how many more *Monitor*-class warships were built, the operations in which they participated, and when the last one was decommissioned.

Chronology

1861	Civil War begins; Trent Affair
1862	*Monitor* vs. *Virginia;* New Orleans surrenders; Battle of Antietam
1863	Battle of Gettysburg; Vicksburg surrenders
1864	*Hunley* sinks *Housatonic;* CSS *Alabama* sunk; Battle of Mobile Bay
1865	Fort Fisher surrenders; Lee surrenders

Study Guide Questions

1. What were the two different economies that had developed in the North and South?

2. What political development caused the Southern states to secede from the Union?

3. What was the significance of the Fort Sumter surrender?

4. In spite of the odds, why were many in the South persuaded that they would be able to establish the Confederacy as an independent nation?

5. What maritime miscalculations did Jefferson Davis make in the early days of the Civil War?

6. How did the U.S. Navy set about accomplishing its blockade?

7. What was the Navy's amphibious strategy to support the Union blockade?

8. A. What was the Trent Affair?
   B. How was it settled?

9. What were the military and diplomatic gains achieved by the Union victory at New Orleans?

10. What was the significance of the battle between the USS *Monitor* and CSS *Virginia?*

11. What was the significance of the Union victory at Vicksburg?

12. What great battle was the turning point of the war in the East?

13. Why was the Confederate effort with privateers unsuccessful?

14. A. What was the principal effect of the Confederate commerce raiders?
    B. Which cruiser was the most successful?

15. What was the result of commerce raiding by the cruiser CSS *Shenandoah?*

16. A. What command decision did Admiral Farragut have to make at Mobile after the Union ironclad *Tecumseh* was sunk?
    B. What was Farragut's famous order?

17. What did General Sherman finally accomplish in 1865 that the Navy could not, following his famous march to the sea?

18. What was the importance of Fort Fisher at Wilmington, North Carolina?

19. What were some of the major developments and inventions that came about during the Civil War?

20. What were the geopolitical and strategic lessons of the Civil War in regard to sea power versus land power?

New Vocabulary

secede	turret
ironclad	monitor
blockade	diplomatic recognition
blockade runner	artillery barrage
casemate	detonate
broadside	parapet

5

America's Rise to World-Power Status

The usual postwar demand to save money quickly reduced the U.S. Navy in size after the Civil War. Ships were expensive. So they were tied up at piers, and their crews went back to farms and factories or headed west to seek adventure and fortune. Within five years the fleet had dwindled from nearly seven hundred ships to fewer than two hundred. Only fifty of these were in commission, and most were already obsolete.

The decline persisted, despite calls for a stronger navy and merchant marine by concerned naval officers and other far-sighted people. There was a great increase in overseas trade, but the new steamships were not flying the U.S. flag.

In addition to decreasing the Navy's size, Congress and some older officers also wanted the fleet to go back to sail, because of the cost of coal. Existing boilers and engines were replaced with smaller ones or removed. Captains were warned that if they used too much coal, they might have to pay for it themselves.

For European navies this was a time of technological progress, much of it stimulated by studies of naval actions during the Civil War: the development of self-propelled torpedoes, improved armor plate, large rifled guns, and powerful engines. In 1873 the British launched the prototype (first model) of the modern battleship; it could steam to America and back without refueling. But a series of American secretaries of the Navy did nothing to stop the decline of U.S. sea power.

By 1878 fewer than six thousand men remained in the U.S. Navy, most of them foreigners. There were too many officers in the upper ranks and few ships to assign them to, resulting in slow promotions and little incentive for younger officers. By 1881 the U.S. Navy ranked twelfth in the world, and over 80 percent of its men were not U.S. citizens. Naval officers often had to learn four or five languages to communicate with their crews.

Educational Renaissance

Following the Civil War there were, however, some important advances made in the professional training and education of U.S. naval personnel, both officer and enlisted. These were accomplished through the dedication, professionalism, and loyalty of a handful of superb officers.

The U.S. Naval Academy, which had been moved to Newport, Rhode Island, during the war, was returned to Annapolis, Maryland, in 1865. Under new superintendent ADM David Porter and commandant LCDR Stephen B. Luce, the academy acquired a brilliant staff of young administrators and instructors, veterans of the war. They raised academic standards, expelling midshipmen who did not measure up. They instituted an honor system, set up a program of athletics, and encouraged creative expression and healthy social activities. By 1869 the academy's engineering curriculum and physics department had achieved a high academic reputation that continues to this day. In the early 1870s the department attracted a brilliant young immigrant from Germany named Albert Michelson, who, after graduating and serving as an instructor at the academy, went on to head the department of physics at the University of Chicago. He became the first American recipient of the Nobel Prize for Physics in 1907, for measuring the speed of light.

In 1873 the **U.S. Naval Institute** was established on the grounds of the Naval Academy. Composed of officers and civilian instructors at the academy interested in reform, the institute had as its purpose the advancement of professional and scientific knowledge about the U.S. Navy, other world navies, and the maritime industry. It soon became a major forum for ideas to improve the fleet. In 1875 it began publishing a journal called the U.S. Naval Institute *Proceedings.* The *Proceedings* was a leader in criticizing the condition of the fleet, pointing out both the commercial benefits and naval requirements of a strong American maritime force. This professional journal is still the foremost naval and maritime publication of its type in the world. Eventually the Naval Institute also became an important publisher of books on naval matters.

Also in 1875, Luce, now a commodore, was instrumental in starting a system of training naval enlisted men on station ships before they were transferred to training vessels to be taught gunnery and seamanship. This was the forerunner of the Navy's modern training system for enlisted men.

In 1884, after a brilliant career in sea billets (job assignments on board ships), including the Naval Academy training squadron, Luce convinced the Secretary of the Navy to establish the **Naval War College** in Newport, Rhode Island. Luce had argued that naval warfare of the future would require senior officers well schooled in the broad principles of grand strategy, modern fleet tactics, naval history and policy, and international law. The college was the first institution of its kind in the world. Among the excellent officers selected by Luce for the first Naval War College staff was CAPT Alfred Thayer Mahan, professor of naval history, who would soon make history himself.

Today's naval training programs for both officers and enlisted personnel stem directly from Commodore Luce's efforts. He also started fleet exercises as a means of battle practice, and until his death in 1917 at the age of ninety, he fought tirelessly for improvements in ships and gun design. His work contributed immensely to improving the morale of the service following its post–Civil War decline.

Mahan and Sea Power

In 1886 Commodore Luce was ordered to sea duty again, and Captain Mahan was appointed to relieve him as president of the Naval War College. As Mahan studied naval history in preparation for assuming his duties, he became convinced that the importance of sea control in human history had never been fully appreciated or properly communicated. He soon became one of the foremost proponents of sea power as a means to achieve world-power status. In 1890 he published his findings in *The Influence of Sea Power upon History, 1660–1783,* which became world famous as the foremost text on sea power and naval strategy. He published two more such studies, in 1892 and 1897.

Mahan argued that it was command of the sea that had enabled Britain to create its empire, reap the profits of maritime commerce, and defeat the land powers that tried to challenge it on the trade routes of the world. He believed that a seafaring nation could, if led by an enlightened and dynamic government, use the sea to become a world power. For the United States, or any other nation desiring to become a world power, the lesson was clear—national survival depended on control of the sea. The country needed to build a fleet of ships that could defeat any enemy fleet at sea and break up any blockade that might be deployed against it. To support this fleet, overseas bases were needed as coaling stations anywhere sea communications might be threatened. And, for security purposes, such bases would best be located in overseas colonies under the control of the aspiring maritime power.

Mahan's work was a brilliant study of maritime history and naval strategy. It immediately received acclaim worldwide, especially in Europe and the Far East, where it was used to help justify the large naval construction programs in which the major nations in these regions were then engaged. It also seemed to justify the new imperialism that had become rampant among these nations in the last part of the nineteenth century. Mahan was honored by the queen of England and given honorary degrees. Kaiser Wilhelm II of Germany ordered that copies of Mahan's work be placed on all ships of the German navy. The Japanese government provided copies to all its army and naval officers, political leaders, and schools. At home, Mahan's ideas were welcomed by advocates of a strong navy—in particular, by a rising young politician named Theodore Roosevelt—and by proponents of American expansion across the Pacific, the annexation of Hawaii, and the building of a canal across either Nicaragua or Panama.

RADM Alfred Thayer Mahan. He had a profound influence on naval strategy and tactics worldwide after publication of his book *The Influence of Sea Power upon History, 1660–1783* in 1890. *The Naval History and Heritage Command*

Postwar Foreign Naval Developments

During the years following the American Civil War, the British began using iron for all new warship construction. In 1872 the French introduced the use of steel, and soon the British followed suit. Other improvements in armor, propulsion, and armament followed. As a result of their naval building programs, the British had become the preeminent naval power in Europe by the 1890s. Meanwhile, the Germans, in order to be able to challenge the British for control of the North Sea region and not wanting to fall behind them, embarked on a strong naval building program of their own. At the same time they began imperialistic moves into the western Pacific, taking control of several of the islands there in order to establish colonies and bases.

In the Pacific, the island nation of Japan had been made aware of the advances in Western naval and other military technology by the contacts with American commodore Matthew Perry in the 1850s, whose visits had opened the door to trade with the West. Soon thereafter, in addition to trade, the Japanese sought an infusion of military technology from the West.

The strategic problem facing Japan in the last half of the nineteenth century was in many ways similar to that facing Britain in Europe. Both were island nations located off continents that were dominated by aggressive land powers. What Japan feared most during these years was the emergence of China as a naval power and the march of Russia toward ice-free ports in the region.

The Japanese had realized that neither of these potential adversaries could bring full strength to bear against them as long as they themselves remained in control of the seas in the western Pacific. Thus, Japan too had begun a vigorous naval shipbuilding effort in the latter part of the nineteenth century. Officers and officer candidates were sent abroad to attend naval schools in Britain and the United States. By the 1890s, they were building warships as good as any built in the United States and Europe.

Thanks to its naval superiority, Japan defeated China in the Sino-Japanese War of 1894–95, forcing the Chinese to withdraw from Korea, surrender to Japan the islands of Formosa and the Pescadores, and relinquish control of Port Arthur in Manchuria. After the Chinese withdrawal, Korea became an independent state but soon came under the control of Russia. Later, Japan would gain worldwide acknowledgment as the major power in the region when it defeated the Russian Far Eastern fleets during the Russo-Japanese War of 1904–1905, gaining control of southern Sakhalin Island and Korea as a result. It is worth noting that in both these conflicts the Japanese launched major preemptive naval attacks on enemy forces prior to formal declarations of war.

The United States Rebuilds Its Navy

Partly in response to the naval building programs overseas and partly because of a need for foreign markets for growing volumes of U.S. manufactured goods, in the early 1880s pressure began to mount in the United States to rebuild its Navy and merchant marine. Both had suffered neglect since the end of the Civil War. Congress established the Naval Advisory Board in 1881, and in 1883 it authorized the building of three new protected cruisers of the latest European design. These were followed in 1886 with authorizations for America's first battleships, the *Texas* and the *Maine*. Though these proved suitable only for coastal defense, they provided opportunities for American shipyards to learn how to build modern warships. They also helped establish the American steel industry, along with the coal and rail industries, because of the steel armor plating used in these ships. By the end of the 1880s, American shipyards were producing fine cruisers, such as the *New York* and *Olympia*, that compared favorably with any in the foreign navies.

The building program continued into the 1890s, spurred on by Mahan's publications on sea power. The Naval Act of 1890 called for the construction of three new first-class battleships—the *Indiana, Massachusetts,* and *Oregon*—plus additional cruisers, torpedo boats, and gunboats. In 1892 Congress authorized the battleship *Iowa,* which was somewhat heavier and faster than the *Indiana* class. In 1897, one of the greatest American proponents of Mahan's views on sea power, Theodore Roosevelt, became Assistant Secretary of the Navy in the McKinley administration. Roosevelt firmly believed that war with Spain over Cuba was inevitable, and he insisted that the U.S. fleet continue to be built up to maximum readiness. Thus, at the eve of the Spanish-American War in 1898 the United States had a fleet that was respectable by any measure: four first-class battleships, two second-class battleships, two armored cruisers, ten protected cruisers, and a number of gunboats, old monitors that could be used for coastal defense, and torpedo boats.

The Spanish-American War of 1898

For years Americans had resented Spain's harsh rule over Cuba, the most important Spanish colony in the New World. Cuban revolutionaries had been inciting insurrections against this rule for more than twenty years, producing by 1895 a state of near anarchy and open rebellion. Spanish authorities had been ruthless in their attempts to suppress the rebellion and retain control of the island, killing thousands of civilians. Partly in response to this human suffering, and certainly because of economic concern over some $50 million worth of American investment in sugar cane plantations and over $100 million in annual sugar trade, support grew in the United States for intervention in Cuba. Some even advocated annexing it from Spain by force if necessary. **Yellow journalism** (stories written to incite an emotional response) in U.S. newspapers, including publication of a letter stolen from the Spanish ambassador describing President William McKinley as "weak," further whipped up American sentiment in support of war with Spain.

In February 1898 McKinley sent the battleship USS *Maine* to Havana to protect American lives and property. On the evening of 15 February a huge explosion ripped the ship apart, sinking her in minutes, and killing 266 of her 354 officers and crew. Most Americans at the time immediately blamed the Spanish for the explosion, even though the Spanish government expressed sympathy and denied any part in the incident. (Several studies in recent years have indicated that the probable cause was a coal-dust explosion in a forward coal bunker, which set off ammunition in a nearby magazine.) In any event, the loss of the *Maine* brought the nation to the brink of war with Spain.

Both nations tried to head off war by negotiation during the next couple of months, but war was inevitable. Under the leadership of Assistant Secretary Theodore Roosevelt, the Navy prepared for war. Recognizing that the Spanish-owned Philippine Islands in the Pacific region could be made a key U.S. base to protect its Asian trade, in late February Roosevelt cabled

Remember the *Maine!* The loss of the *Maine,* sunk in the harbor of Havana, Cuba, on 15 February 1898 by an explosion of unknown origin, set off the war of 1898 with Spain. Above, the *Maine* rests on the bottom the day after she blew up. *The Naval History and Heritage Command*

Commodore George Dewey in his flagship *Olympia* at Hong Kong to make ready the U.S. Asiatic Fleet to attack the Spanish fleet at Manila. He dispatched the cruiser *Baltimore* across the Pacific to deliver a load of shells to Dewey.

Because Cuba would be a primary objective of the war and Puerto Rico a close second, the bulk of the U.S. fleet was concentrated in the Atlantic. In mid-March the new battleship *Oregon,* completed in San Francisco two years before, was ordered to leave immediately and begin an amazing 15,000-mile, sixty-six-day trip to join the U.S. Atlantic Fleet by way of Cape Horn.

The Spanish government alerted Admiral Cervera, commander of the home fleet at Cadiz, to prepare to sail to the Caribbean to defend the colonies, destroy the American fleet and naval base at Key West, and blockade the American coast. Though Cervera pointed out that his fleet was not ready to take on the superior U.S. Atlantic Fleet, he reluctantly steamed from Spain to the Cape Verde Islands on 9 April with four cruisers and two destroyers.

News of his sailing immediately caused a war scare all along the U.S. East Coast. To calm the frightened populace, the Navy hauled out some of its obsolete Civil War monitors and stationed them in various port cities for harbor defense, and the Army placed several old Civil War cannons along the coast. Also, a so-called Flying Squadron, with a battleship and three

cruisers, under Commodore Winfield Schley, was detached from the Atlantic Fleet and based at Norfolk for protection of the Atlantic seaboard should Admiral Pascual Cervera's ships proceed there. The main part of the fleet, consisting of three battleships and three cruisers under RADM William T. Sampson, was ordered to Key West, ready for offensive operations against Cuba and Puerto Rico.

On 22 April the Navy Department directed Admiral Sampson to set up a blockade of Cuba. On 25 April Congress declared that a state of war had existed with Spain as of 21 April. On the 29th, Admiral Cervera's Spanish fleet left the Cape Verdes and steamed to the defense of Puerto Rico. Cervera knew the poor state of his ships and the lack of training of his crews; he firmly believed he was sailing into destruction. Other European countries, however, believed that Spain would defeat the United States in a long war. Mahan, however, predicted that America would win in "about three months."

Operations in the Pacific

News of the formal declaration of war reached Commodore Dewey by cable in Hong Kong the day after the cruiser *Baltimore* arrived with her load of ammunition. He was given twenty-four hours to get under way for the Philippine Islands and commence operations against the Spanish fleet at Manila.

Besides his flagship *Olympia* Dewey had three other cruisers, including the *Baltimore,* two gunboats, and a cutter. The Spanish squadron, under the command of ADM Patricio Montojo, consisted of his flagship, the cruiser *Reina Christina,* and six other light cruisers and three gunboats, all of them in poor condition. Montojo realized he would have no chance at sea, so he planned to fight at anchor under the shore batteries at Cavite, a naval station south of Manila.

Dewey left Hong Kong on the 27th and arrived at Manila Bay shortly after midnight on 1 May. He made for Manila, twenty-two miles across the bay. As dawn broke, the enemy squadron was sighted off Cavite. Dewey in *Olympia* at the head of his column of ships immediately turned south and proceeded to within five thousand yards of the enemy, at which point he gave the famous command to his flagship's commanding officer, "You may fire when you are ready, Gridley."

With that the American ships began a series of oval-shaped firing runs past the Spanish ships, each ship firing both at the enemy ships and the shore batteries behind them. After two

ADM George Dewey engaged and destroyed the entire Spanish fleet at Manila Bay during the war with Spain in 1898, without a single American casualty and only seven wounded in action. *The Naval History and Heritage Command*

hours, Dewey retired for a time to rest the crew and allow them to have breakfast. When the smoke cleared, Dewey saw that the Spanish fleet was in shambles. All major vessels had been sunk or abandoned, and only a few gunboats remained. At 1100 Dewey resumed battle, and in another hour he had wiped out the remainder of Montojo's squadron. He then anchored off Manila to hold the Philippines against any outside interference and to await the arrival from the United States of a force of Army troops that would secure the city.

While waiting for the troops to arrive, Dewey was confronted by five German warships that entered the harbor hoping to acquire some of the Philippine islands for their nation's empire. Dewey stood his ground and threatened to fire on any ships that tried to interfere with him. The Germans sailed away. A year later, however, Germany bought the Caroline, Marshall, Mariana, and Palau Islands, and many others, from Spain. They would become fiercely important factors in later naval history.

En route to the Philippines, the USS *Charleston,* one of the escorts of the American troop convoy en route to Manila, stopped off at the Spanish island of Guam. Her commander took command of the colony in the name of the United States without firing a shot.

On 13 August the force of 11,000 troops arrived in Manila Bay. The Spanish colonial government surrendered after putting up only token resistance. Thereafter began a three-year insurrection by the Filipinos, who wanted immediate independence. Finally, a workable American commonwealth administration was established that was supported by both Americans and Filipinos. The turning over of the Philippines to the United States under the eventual peace treaty would permanently involve the United States in the affairs of the Far East. The Republic of the Philippines would receive full independence after World War II.

Though not directly involved in the war, the Hawaiian Islands had become very important to the United States as a

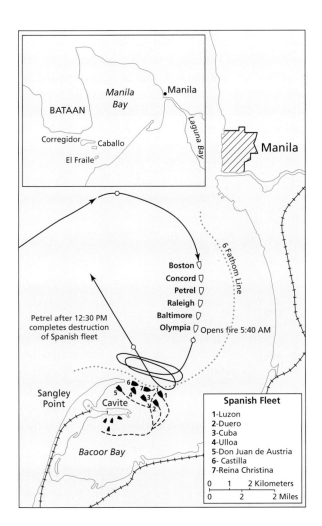

Maneuvers of opposing forces in the battle at Manila Bay on 1 May 1898.

base for operations in the Philippines and for growing American business interests in the Pacific. Some years earlier, in 1894, the Americans in Hawaii had formed a provisional government and asked for immediate annexation by the United States. The request had been denied by President Grover Cleveland, who considered the Hawaiian queen the legitimate government. After Dewey's overwhelming victory in Manila Bay, however, the expansionists in Congress were so strengthened that by mid-1898 they were able to pass a joint congressional resolution for the annexation of Hawaii. In 1900 it became a U.S. territory, and in 1959 it would become our fiftieth state.

Operations in the Caribbean

As these events were unfolding in the Pacific, in the Atlantic region Admiral Sampson assumed that Admiral Cervera would head directly for the Spanish port of San Juan, Puerto Rico, after leaving the Cape Verde Islands. Thus Sampson lifted the blockade of the Cuban coast opposite Key West and headed toward San Juan. When he arrived off San Juan, there was no sign of Cervera. Sampson spent time in a useless bombardment of San Juan's defenses, suffering eight casualties and some damage from the shore batteries.

While Sampson was using up his coal and ammunition off San Juan, the wily Cervera brought his fleet near the French island of Martinique for refueling. Refused entrance by the French, he proceeded to the Dutch island of Curaçao. After refueling there, he sailed northwest toward Cuba.

The American consul in Martinique had cabled Washington as Cervera passed that island. The Navy Department then ordered Schley's Flying Squadron to sail from Norfolk to Key West. Cervera had in effect outmaneuvered the Americans, by guessing that Sampson and Schley would do what they did. With the Atlantic Squadron split, the Spaniards eluded both its parts and headed toward the back door of Cuba, at Santiago. Meanwhile, the *Oregon,* just entering the Caribbean after its circumnavigation of South America, stood a chance of steaming alone into the midst of the Spanish fleet.

Word of Cervera's stop at Curaçao, however, indicated that the *Oregon* was safe and that Cervera was probably headed toward Cuba. There were three ports in Cuba large enough to handle Cervera's fleet: Havana, Cienfuegos, and Santiago. The Navy Department concluded that Cervera probably would try to reach Havana, possibly stopping at Cienfuegos for coal. Accordingly, Sampson ordered the Flying Squadron to go around the western end of Cuba to blockade Cienfuegos, while he guarded the approaches to Havana. Both the department and Sampson were incorrect again. Cervera had steamed directly to the isolated southeastern port of Santiago de Cuba, arriving on 19 May.

Meanwhile, Commodore Schley headed toward Santiago, after determining that the enemy was not at Cienfuegos. His squadron arrived off Santiago de Cuba on the morning of the 29th. There he saw the *Cristóbal Colon,* Cervera's best cruiser, at the harbor entrance. He laid off the harbor for two days, then bombarded it for a few minutes at extreme range with little

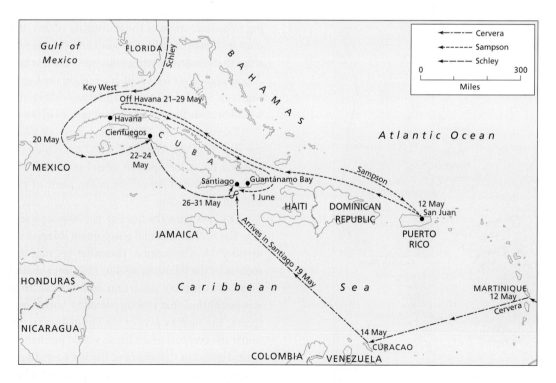

Maneuvers of the opposing U.S. and Spanish fleets in the Caribbean campaign of the Spanish-American War.

effect. On 1 June Admiral Sampson arrived with his squadron, plus the *Oregon*. As senior officer present, Sampson took command of all U.S. naval forces and established a close blockade of the port.

Battle of Santiago de Cuba

On 10 June a force of U.S. Marines from the *Oregon* went ashore at Guantánamo Bay and, after a week of fighting, drove away the Spanish garrison. This gave the fleet a secure anchorage only forty miles from Santiago, one that could be used as a coaling and maintenance base for Sampson's blockading force at Santiago. Guantánamo would be an important American naval base ever after, under a subsequent treaty with Cuba.

Sampson now called on Washington to have Army troops land and take the Spanish batteries at Santiago, so he could go in with small boats and sweep the Spanish minefield before forcing an entrance to the harbor. The Army was eager to oblige, in order to take part in the war. On 20 June MGEN William Shafter arrived with an Army expeditionary force of 16,000 men. He had orders to cooperate with the Navy and land near Santiago to capture the batteries. With naval assistance, Shafter landed without opposition at Daiquiri, sixteen miles east of Santiago, on 22 June.

But Shafter had other ideas about how to conduct the operation. Instead of making his objective the Spanish batteries, he went charging into the jungle, with the intent of capturing the city. He thought this would either force Cervera out into the waiting blockaders or cause him to surrender or be destroyed in the harbor.

Shafter's army found the going very rough and slow. His men were hampered by barbed-wire entanglements, poor trails, heatstroke, and typhoid fever. On 1 July the Spaniards made a strong stand at El Caney and San Juan Hill, inflicting nearly

1,500 casualties before retreating to the city's main defense lines. During this battle, LTCOL Theodore Roosevelt's Rough Riders and a regiment of African American cavalrymen swarmed up nearby Kettle Hill on foot and threw the Spaniards off. (Roosevelt had resigned his post as Assistant Secretary of the Navy in order to get into battlefield action.)

Shafter, shocked by his losses and ill with fever, considered retreating to escape from the Spanish forces, which were now much larger than his own. As a last resort, however, he called on the Navy to try to force the entrance of the harbor to relieve the pressure on his men. Sampson was very upset by this request, as it was asking him to risk the fleet in a narrow, twisting, mined channel to save the Army, when the Army had not carried out its mission of silencing the shore batteries. On Sunday morning 3 July, the exasperated Sampson turned over command of the blockading force to Commodore Schley and sailed eastward along the Cuban coast in his flagship, the cruiser USS *New York*, to meet personally with Shafter. The blockade had been further weakened that morning with the departure of the USS *Massachusetts* for Guantánamo to refuel.

Though the situation looked bad to the Americans, it looked worse to the Spanish. The Spanish authorities in Havana, feeling that Santiago would probably soon fall, had directed Cervera to escape at his first chance. Seeing the blockade weakened, the Spanish admiral chose this opportunity to attempt it. The *Infanta Maria Teresa*, Cervera's flagship, headed directly for the harbor mouth at 0935 on 3 July. She was followed at ten-minute intervals by three armored cruisers and two destroyers.

The American fleet, somewhat relaxed in Sunday blockade routine, was caught by surprise but quickly recovered. The Americans, under way toward the harbor entrance as the Spaniards exited, turned west to run along the coast. By now both sides were firing at each other, the American battleships

The Battle of Santiago de Cuba. Cervera came out of the harbor from anchorages behind Morrow Castle and ran into Schley's blockading force. All the Spanish ships were sunk or beached, with only one American killed and one wounded. *The Naval History and Heritage Command*

concentrating on the *Teresa.* The enemy shells were missing the American ships, but soon the *Teresa* was in bad shape. Hit repeatedly by 8-inch and 12-inch shells, her wooden decks ablaze, she nevertheless led her battle line out of the harbor and tried to ram the cruiser *Brooklyn,* Schley's flagship, before turning west. The *Brooklyn,* on Schley's orders, turned sharply away to the east, crossing the bow of the *Texas* and almost causing a collision. The *Brooklyn* was then temporarily out of the fighting as she circled to recover her position.

The confusion enabled the Spanish to clear the harbor, but soon the faster speed and superior firepower of the American warships made the Spanish ships blazing torches. They turned into the beach, one at a time, to run aground and surrender rather than to sink and lose all hands. As the *Brooklyn* and battleships *Texas* and *Oregon* cut down the Spanish cruiser *Vizcaya,* Captain Philip of the *Texas* called to his jubilant crew, "Don't cheer, boys, the poor devils are dying." The *Oregon* overtook the last and fastest Spanish cruiser, *Cristóbal Colon,* about seventy miles west of Santiago. With 13-inch shells slamming all around, the *Colon* ran onto the beach and surrendered. The two Spanish destroyers were cut to pieces by the battleship *Indiana* shortly after they cleared the harbor mouth and before they could fire a single torpedo.

Sampson, on the *New York,* steamed valiantly westward to try to get into the battle but never made it. A bitter dispute later arose between him and Schley over who deserved credit for the victory. Schley was also later roundly criticized for his tardiness in blockading Santiago and his wrong-way turn when Cervera emerged.

The entire action took a little more than three hours. One American was killed and another wounded. Spanish losses were heavy, over three hundred killed and 150 wounded, with 1,800 captured, including Admiral Cervera. The Spanish fleet had been annihilated by a superior fleet, despite the latter's tactical errors and surprisingly poor marksmanship.

End of the War

The Battle of Santiago de Cuba had given the American people another Fourth of July victory. In only two months the U.S. Navy had destroyed the Spanish fleets in both the Pacific and Caribbean. Santiago surrendered its 22,000 troops on 14 July to General Shafter, after a brief siege assisted by long-range naval bombardment. An expeditionary force was sent to Puerto Rico; it quickly overcame all resistance after capturing San Juan, the capital. American arms were victorious everywhere by the end of July, and the U.S. Navy made plans to cruise against the Spanish mainland. Before that happened, the Spaniards sued for peace. The two countries signed a peace treaty in Paris on 10 December 1898. Spain recognized the independence of Cuba and turned over Puerto Rico, the Philippines, and Guam to the United States.

Probably the most important long-term consequence of the war was America's new overseas possessions. The United States now had distant territories and bases that made a seagoing navy a necessity. It had become a formidable naval power. But the new possessions in the Pacific posed many problems.

Attempts to find solutions to these problems would dominate much of the U.S. Navy's thinking for the next forty years. Most perplexing was the issue of how to defend the Philippines against a militaristic, expansionist Japan. The Philippine Islands were some eight thousand miles from the U.S. West Coast and only a few hundred miles from Japan; their defense would require naval superiority in Far Eastern waters. This, in turn, would require base facilities in the Pacific far beyond anything the United States had in 1898. Thus, in addition to annexing Hawaii, early in 1899 the United States laid claim to Wake Island, and later the same year it annexed part of the Samoa Islands, including a fine harbor at Pago Pago. In the face of growing anti-imperialist sentiment at home, however, that was as far as Congress could go.

Spain, having lost all its principal colonies, decided to divest itself of all of its remaining empire and concentrate on domestic development. In 1899 it put up for sale all its remaining Pacific possessions—nearly a thousand islands. The United States was not interested, so Germany acquired many of them, including several located between the United States and the Philippines.

The Rise to World-Power Status

The first decade of the twentieth century saw major changes in the world balance of naval power. In the United States, the recent victories over Spain had kindled a national pride in the Navy and helped convince Congress to accept as a national goal the building of a navy that would be second only to that of Great Britain. The chief rivals of Britain and the United States soon became Germany and Japan.

While Mahan had provided the basic philosophy for the American rise to major power status in the years following the turn of the century, the forceful young leader who made it all happen was Theodore Roosevelt. Following the war with Spain, he had returned as a national hero and won the governorship of New York in 1898. Two years later he was selected as President McKinley's vice-presidential running mate. When McKinley was assassinated in 1901, Roosevelt assumed the presidency.

Beginning in 1903, the Navy began building two capital ships (large warships) a year, a trend that would continue for about the next fifteen years, throughout the Roosevelt administration and that of William Howard Taft, who succeeded him from 1909 to 1913. The size of these ships continually increased, both in displacement and armament. In 1905 Congress authorized the battleships *Michigan* and *South Carolina,* both of which would have eight 12-inch guns arranged in two pairs of turrets fore and aft.

Then in 1907 came a warship that would set the standard for all capital ships thereafter—the British battleship *Dreadnought.* Her main battery (primary armament) consisted of ten 12-inch guns mounted in five turrets. Because the U.S. ships authorized in 1905 were still on the building ways, this gave her two and a half times the firepower of any other battleship then afloat. She was also the first large ship to be powered by turbine engines, which gave her a maximum speed of twen-

A contemporary photograph of the British battleship HMS *Dreadnought.* She set the standard for all subsequent capital ships. At the time of her launching she had two and a half times the firepower of any other battleship then in existence. *The Naval History and Heritage Command*

The U.S. Navy's first practical submarine, the USS *Holland,* under way during sea trials in Long Island Sound in 1899. *The Naval History and Heritage Command*

ty-one knots, faster than any other battleship. The *Dreadnought* became the type name for all such big-gun battleships launched after her, and all the battleships that preceded her came to be called **predreadnoughts.** In 1912 the British pioneered the use of oil instead of coal as fuel for large battleships, with the launching of the first battleships of the 27,500-ton *Queen Elizabeth* class. These developments were soon reflected in subsequent warships built by other world-class navies, including that of the United States.

Advances also were being made in other fields of naval technology. In 1900 Roosevelt urged the Navy to buy its first submarine, the *Holland,* named after her inventor. Submarines developed rapidly after this in all of the world's major navies. Roosevelt was also a prime supporter of experiments with manned aircraft, which had begun in 1898 and culminated with the Wright brothers' first successful heavier-than-air flight at Kitty Hawk, North Carolina, in 1903. In 1910 Eugene Ely flew an airplane off a platform built on the bow of the cruiser USS *Birmingham.* A few months later, he made the world's first arrested shipboard landing. His aircraft was brought to a stop by lines strung across the deck of the cruiser *Pennsylvania,* thus setting the stage for the development of the aircraft carrier.

But hardware was not the only area in which the U.S. Navy improved in the years following the turn of the century. The technology being incorporated into the newer ships demanded highly specialized and trained crews to operate them. Because of their relatively high standards of living and education, young Americans who enlisted in the Navy soon became very good sailors proficient in the new technology. And since the Navy was doing so many interesting things during these years, enlistment and reenlistment rates were high. By the time World War I broke out in 1914, U.S. naval personnel were among the world's best.

Though the American merchant marine could not compete very well in world markets, owing to wage competition

A replica of the Curtis-Ely Pusher biplane that launched naval aviation by making the first flight off the deck of a warship, the cruiser USS *Birmingham,* on 14 November 1910, with Eugene Ely at the controls. *CHINFO, Tony Curtiss*

and corporate taxes, the lack of commercial business in the United States had the advantage of keeping American shipyards interested in building quality warships. This produced a whole generation of shipyard workers who became warship-building specialists. They were backed by a now-thriving steel industry that had grown mightily since the days, just twenty years earlier, when nobody had known how to roll steel plate. These capabilities would stand the nation in good stead through two world wars in the twentieth century.

International Relations

Toward the end of the nineteenth century, Great Britain, traditional enemy of the United States since revolutionary times, had begun to display a new friendship toward this nation. Britain alone of the major European powers supported American objectives during the Spanish war of 1898. In 1903 the British agreed to a settlement of the Alaskan-Canadian boundary favorable to America. They also conceded exclusive control of the proposed canal across Panama to the United States.

The same could not be said of Germany, however. There had been confrontations in Samoa since 1889. The Germans had challenged Commodore Dewey in Manila Bay in 1898 for control of the Philippines and had bombarded the Venezuelan coast to force settlement of international debts in 1902. Then in 1904 Germany threatened to collect debts in the Dominican Republic by force. In response to this latter action, Roosevelt proclaimed what came to be called the **Roosevelt Corollary** (extension of a previous doctrine) to the long-standing **Monroe Doctrine** of 1823, which prohibited foreign interference in the Americas. Roosevelt stated that henceforth the United States had the right to use military force in lieu of foreign intervention in any situation involving wrongdoing by or collapse of government in any Latin American nation. There followed many such actions by the United States in various revolution-torn countries in Latin America and the Caribbean throughout the remainder of the twentieth century.

Thus, in a background of some international tension between the U.S. and various foreign countries in general, and Germany in particular, Congress set out on a building program to surpass that of Germany, so that the United States and not Germany would be the nation that had a navy second only to that of Great Britain.

Germany continued to arouse American anger by the arrogant utterances of its kaiser, by the brutal way in which it developed its new colonies, and by its purchase from Spain, as mentioned before, of the Carolines, the Marshalls, and the Marianas in the Pacific, all islands located between the U.S. mainland and the Philippines. The leadership within the Navy prepared plans for possible war with Germany. In the process it assumed incorrectly that such a war would be solely a naval conflict, fought between capital ships of the two fleets. This misconception heavily influenced the U.S. warship-building program in the early years of the twentieth century in favor of the construction of large battleships rather than cruisers and small destroyers. As a consequence, the latter would be in short supply for escort duties and antisubmarine warfare during World War I.

In the Pacific region, when the Sino-Japanese War of 1894–95 showed the weakness of the Chinese government, several of the European powers began to move into the region, seeking to establish "spheres of influence" in China, backed up by naval squadrons. This caused American merchants to fear that they would lose access to Chinese markets if the United States did not establish a sphere of influence of its own there. The U.S. government, however, was opposed to such a course of imperialist action. A solution was found by Secretary of State John Hay, who in 1899 drafted a paper calling for assurances from each power that China would be open to the trade of all friendly nations, a policy that came to be known as the **Open Door Policy.**

Hay's policy did not prove to be a final solution, however. To protect their interests, the major powers kept warships in the area, which caused the Chinese to become resentful. In 1900 this led a group of Chinese who called themselves the Society of Righteous and Harmonious Fists, or "Boxers United in Righteousness"—referred to as simply the "Boxers" by many in the West—to begin a campaign to rid their nation of foreigners by force. This campaign came to be called the **Boxer Rebellion.** Russia seized upon the opportunity presented by the Boxers to tighten its grip on Port Arthur, occupy Manchuria, and dominate Korea. This in turn led to conflict with the Japanese, who also had designs on these places, and ultimately it led to the Russo-Japanese War of 1904–1905. After the conclusive Battle of Tsushima in May 1905, in which the Japanese soundly defeated the Russian fleet, the Japanese government requested that President Roosevelt end the war. Though the resulting Treaty of Portsmouth did so in 1905, it made no provision for territorial gains or payment of war reparations to Japan, which angered the Japanese and soured relations between Japan and the United States. Having eliminated its Russian competition, in 1905 Japan established a **protectorate** (a relationship of protection and partial control) over Korea, annexing it as a permanent part of its territory in 1910.

In 1906 the Japanese were further agitated by a new San Francisco School Board policy of segregating the school children of Japanese immigrant laborers who had come into the area following the war with Russia. The situation was soon blown up into a full-scale international incident, and some in Japan threatened to go to war with the United States. The situation was resolved in 1907 only when Roosevelt persuaded the board to rescind its policy.

Later in 1907 Roosevelt wanted to impress the Japanese and the other major nations of the world with a demonstration of the sea power behind American diplomacy. Roosevelt had some years earlier expressed his concept of effective diplomacy by quoting an old African proverb: "Speak softly and carry a big stick." American sea power was Roosevelt's "big stick." In December Roosevelt sent sixteen of the most powerful U.S. battleships on a fourteen-month voyage around the world. It was a triumphant cruise of 46,000 miles, with stops in twenty foreign ports, including Japan. Its ships painted white, the fleet was supposed to symbolize peace as well as strength.

The **Great White Fleet,** as it came to be called, was a great success. The ships performed well, and their crews were excellent ambassadors of goodwill. The cruise provided good training for the fleet and showed that there was great need for bases and coaling stations in the Pacific. Though the voyage was overshadowed somewhat by the launching of the British battleship *Dreadnought,* it proudly demonstrated the might of America to the world.

The Japanese victory over Russia in 1905, plus the war scare in 1906–1907, caused leaders in the Navy to begin to consider

A contemporary cartoon lampooning Roosevelt's "Big Stick Diplomacy."
Louis Dalrymple

The Great White Fleet arriving at San Francisco, 6 May 1908, during its voyage around the world. *The Naval History and Heritage Command*

Japan a threat against American interests in the western Pacific, especially the Philippines. Accordingly, beginning in 1911, a series of color-coded war plans was developed by Navy and Army planners that would specify American strategy in the event of any future conflict with Japan. Collectively called **War Plan Orange,** these plans would form the basis of U.S. strategy in the Pacific theater in World War II.

The Panama Canal

For over three centuries, Europeans and Americans had talked of a canal across the narrow Isthmus of Panama between the Atlantic and the Pacific. A dangerous journey of thousands of miles around South America would be replaced by a fifty-mile trip across the isthmus if a canal could be built. The California Gold Rush, which began in the 1840s, revived ideas of a canal. Many gold seekers sailed to Colon, hiked across the isthmus to Panama City, and picked up ships for San Francisco. In 1855 an American company completed a railroad across the isthmus for travel of people and shipment of freight between the oceans.

In 1881 a French company headed by Ferdinand de Lesseps, the engineer who had successfully built the Suez Canal, bought the railroad and began a Panama canal project. It was a disaster, owing to financial mismanagement and disease. By 1889 yellow fever and malaria had killed over 22,000 workers, and the project was largely abandoned, though some nominal work on it continued.

Mahan reinforced the idea of the canal in his writings on sea power. He foresaw the need to connect the Atlantic and Pacific by a canal so American naval and merchant ships could move quickly between the nation's coasts. The sixty-six-day trip of the battleship *Oregon* around South America during the Spanish-American War illustrated Mahan's point. It was clear that with new territories in the Pacific, the United States must have either a canal or two separate navies.

In 1901 a treaty was concluded with Great Britain in which the two nations agreed to total American control of such a canal (if built), including fortification and defense; it replaced an earlier treaty negotiated in 1850 that had prohibited such a canal under the exclusive control of either nation. At first the United States favored a canal across Nicaragua, but in 1903 it was able to purchase the construction rights and abandoned equipment from the French company for the site in Panama. Now the United States had to secure treaty rights from Colombia, which at that time controlled Panama. A preliminary treaty was worked out with a Colombian diplomat in Washington. However, the Colombian senate refused to approve the treaty, hoping to hold out for more money.

Colombia had made a mistake. The people of Panama wanted a canal for the jobs it promised. They had repeatedly revolted against Colombia to gain independence over the years, so now they were easily convinced by Canal Company agents to revolt again. They were encouraged also by President Roosevelt, who was eager to build the canal. He sent the gunboat USS *Nashville* to the Panamanian city of Colon, supposedly to maintain "perfect neutrality and free transit" of the isthmus, according to the terms of an 1846 treaty with Colombia.

The *Nashville* arrived on 2 November 1903, and the next day the Panamanian revolutionary government raised its flag and declared itself the head of the independent Republic of Panama. When Colombian troops arrived by ship to put down the revolt, the commanding officer of the *Nashville* made ready his guns and politely told them they could not land, because the presence of troops ashore would violate American treaty obligations to maintain "perfect neutrality." Within hours, the USS *Dixie* arrived with a force of U.S. Marines to act as a police force ashore to assist the new government. On 6 November the United States formally recognized the Republic of Panama as a sovereign nation.

Building the Panama Canal. The work was hard and had to be done under the most challenging conditions. For the cuts through the interior highlands, rock had to be blasted away with dynamite, then hauled off a load at a time by rail cars over temporary tracks laid for the purpose. Many hundreds of workers died during the project. *Detroit Publishing Co. Photograph Collection/Library of Congress*

The battleships USS *Arkansas* (left) and USS *Texas* go through the Gatun Locks in the Panama Canal in 1919, heading back to the Pacific Fleet after duty in the North Atlantic during World War I. The canal was opened in August 1914, just as the war began in Europe. *The Naval History and Heritage Command*

Fifteen days after the revolution, a treaty was concluded with Panama, which gave the United States a Canal Zone ten miles wide "in perpetuity" for ten million dollars and a $250,000 annual payment. The treaty was ratified by the U.S. Senate on 23 November. (The canal would be returned by the United States to Panamanian control on 31 December 1999.)

Construction of the canal began again in 1904. The U.S. Army Corps of Engineers used all its technical skill and organizational ability and built the canal in ten years. An average of 39,000 men worked daily. Building dams, they created Gatun Lake in the interior of the isthmus, eighty-five feet above sea level. By means of three sets of locks, each a thousand feet long and 110 feet wide, ships were raised to the lake to transit the isthmus and then lowered again to sea level on the other side. The canal was opened on August 1914, just as the First World War began in Europe. The Navy now had its priceless canal. All of Mahan's criteria for America to become a major world power through sea power had been met.

Critical Thinking

1. Research the British battleship HMS *Dreadnought* and the many innovations it incorporated that caused it to become the standard for the modern battleship.

2. Research the role the Panama Canal plays today in enabling ships of all nations to pass back and forth between the Atlantic and Pacific oceans without going around the Cape of Good Hope in South America, considering the question of whether or not it is still of vital importance to the U.S. Navy.

3. The U.S. relationship with Britain changed a great deal over the nineteenth century, from one of sworn enemies at the beginning of the century to cooperation and friendship by the end of it. Research how this change evolved over the century and what the major milestones in the evolution were.

Chronology

1865	Civil War ends
1873	Naval Institute established
1884	Naval War College established
1890	Mahan publishes sea power study
1898	Spanish-American War
1907	HMS *Dreadnought* launched; voyage of Great White Fleet
1914	Panama Canal opens

Study Guide Questions

1. What happened to the U.S. Navy after the Civil War?

2. What developments were taking place in foreign navies in the post–Civil War years?

3. A. When and where was the U.S. Naval Institute started?
   B. What is its purpose?
   C. What journal does it publish?

4. What were Alfred Thayer Mahan's principal arguments for sea power in 1890?

5. Why did pressure begin building for the United States to rebuild its Navy and merchant marine in the 1880s?

6. What ships comprised the U.S. fleet at the start of the Spanish-American War in 1898?

7. What happened in Havana Harbor that finally set off the war between the United States and Spain?

8. How was the U.S. Atlantic Fleet divided in response to Spanish admiral Cervera's sailing toward the Caribbean?

9. What was Commodore Dewey ordered to do with the Asiatic Fleet at Hong Kong at the start of hostilities?

10. A. Where did Commodore Dewey meet the Spanish fleet in battle?
    B. What was Dewey's famous order to start the battle?

11. A. Where was the major battle fought in the Caribbean Sea area?
    B. Who were the opposing commanders?
    C. What was the outcome of the battle?

12. What territories did the United States acquire from Spain as a result of the war?

13. Who was primarily responsible for the rise of the United States to world-power status in the early years of the twentieth century?

14. What naval development occurred in England in 1907 that would revolutionize warship design?

15. What events caused friction between the United States and Japan in the first decade of the twentieth century?

16. What was the name of the set of war plans drawn up beginning in 1911 to prepare for possible Japanese threats against the Philippines?

17. A. What was the "Great White Fleet"?
    B. What was its purpose?

18. A. What was the Roosevelt Corollary announced in 1904?
    B. Toward which nation was it initially directed?

19. What heavily influenced Congress to authorize building mainly battleships for the U.S. fleet during the pre–World War I years?

20. How did American interest in a Panama Canal develop?

New Vocabulary

prototype	predreadnought
imperialism	corollary
coal bunker	sphere of influence
circumnavigation	isthmus
dreadnought	protectorate

6

World War I, 1914–1918

The late 1800s and early 1900s were characterized by increasingly aggressive competition among the world's major powers for control of world resources and for economic, military, and political power. The naval building races that had begun between the European powers in the West and between Russia, China, and Japan in the East were one aspect of this competition. The United States came late to this naval building program, and it took part primarily because it was required as a condition of its rise to world-power status.

In the Taft administration from 1909 to 1913, and even more in the early years of the Wilson administration that followed, the main focus of the United States was turned inward, toward domestic reforms. The era was marked by a movement called **progressivism,** which focused on individual rights, anti-trust legislation against big business, banking reform, conservation of natural resources, and nonintervention in the affairs of Europe unless U.S. interests were directly threatened.

Meanwhile, the European powers were engaged in a series of actions that would inevitably lead to war in 1914. Since the late 1800s imperialism had been rampant in both Europe and the Far East. The European powers competed with one another for colonies in Africa and the Pacific region, while Japan acquired Korea, Taiwan, and territory on the Chinese mainland as a result of its victories over China in 1895 and Russia in 1905. Diplomacy in Europe had been overtaken by **militarism.** This meant that the primary political preoccupation in the major nations was not domestic programs but the buildup of armies. In countries with diverse populations, a series of nationalistic movements began to take place among ethnic minorities longing for independence. Finally, a series of entangling alliances arose. These alliances were designed to enhance the security of the participating nations, but they actually made war more likely, because they made it mandatory for the major powers to defend one another in the event of attack.

Europe went to war on 28 July 1914, when Austria-Hungary declared war on Serbia. Within a week all the great powers of Europe had been drawn into the war by the various interlocking defense treaties. On one side was the **Triple Entente,** consisting of France, Britain, Russia, and Serbia (referred to as the Allies); on the other side were the **Central Powers,** Germany and Austria-Hungary. At the end of 1914 the Ottoman Empire (modern-day Turkey) entered the war on the side of the Central Powers. In 1915 Italy joined the Allies, as did most of the North African nations by war's end. President Woodrow Wilson wanted to keep the United States neutral in the conflict, though most Americans supported the British and French.

Opening Strategies

At sea the two main enemies were the British home fleets and the German High Seas Fleet. The British had two home fleets: the Grand Fleet, based at Scapa Flow in the Orkney Islands of Scotland, and the Channel Fleet. The mission of the twenty-four frontline battleships and battle cruisers of the Grand Fleet was to prevent the escape of German ships into the Atlantic, to guard the North Sea, and to engage and destroy the German High Seas Fleet in battle. The main task of the Channel Fleet, with seventeen second-line battleships, was to keep the English Channel safe for passage of British troops and supplies to France.

The German fleet was based in the estuaries of the Weser and Elbe Rivers. It was supposed to guard the German coast from British attack and defeat units of the British fleet whenever possible.

The Central Powers occupied an interior land position. They had an excellent railroad system to shift forces quickly to either the western front in France or the eastern front in Russia. They controlled the central agricultural areas of Europe. By contrast the Allies were geographically separated and lacked adequate communications. Thus Germany had a geographical advantage in the land struggle but was at a disadvantage at sea. Its ships would have to go through the North Sea to get into the Atlantic, and this would be difficult in the face of the British fleet at Scapa Flow.

Britain, on the other hand, was dependent on imported foodstuffs for survival. She could, however, call on nearly half the world's merchant shipping and economic resources in every

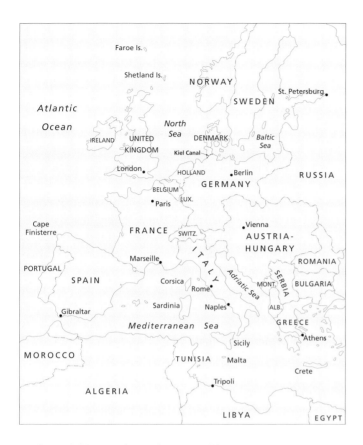

The European theater of operations, World War I.

corner of the globe—as long as it controlled the oceans. At the outbreak of war the Germans intended to quickly defeat France on land, hold Russia at bay, and keep their High Seas Fleet intact as a bargaining chip at a peace conference. In the meantime, they also planned to hurt the British merchant and naval fleets with far-ranging cruisers and raiders and to whittle down the strength of the home fleets in small actions.

In Britain there were two conflicting ideas on how to fight the war. One group wanted a peripheral strategy, depending mainly on the navy to blockade Germany and gradually weaken the German ability to fight by a series of amphibious operations. The continental Allied powers would carry the war to Germany on land. The other group wanted to place the main British army on the continent to assist France and drive toward the heart of Germany. The latter group won out. During the first months of the war, Britain was able to transport a quarter of a million troops across into France because of its control of the English Channel. These troops represented a key factor in helping to stop the first German offensive across Belgium toward Paris in September 1914. Thereafter both sides consolidated their positions and constructed miles of soggy, rat-infested trenches, from which their troops faced each other across an empty no-man's-land stretching 350 miles across Europe. Periodically each side tested the other's lines by charging against them, only

to be cut down by rapid-fire tripod-mounted machine guns, a relatively new infantry weapon developed in the late 1890s. This condition of stalemate lasted for months, with terrible loss of life on both sides.

In the North Sea, meanwhile, the British and German navies fought several times, with the British victorious every time. After January 1915 the German surface forces mostly retired to port behind protective minefields, where they stayed for most of the rest of the war.

The Pacific Theater

In 1898 Germany had acquired a naval base at Tsingtao, China, and had purchased many Pacific islands from Spain in the years following. Subsequently, many of these new acquisitions were developed into coaling stations and colonies. Thus, when war broke out in 1914, half a dozen German cruisers were operating in the Pacific, under VADM Graf von Spee. Japan had been resentful of the German presence in the region ever since Germany had been instrumental in forcing Japan out of Port Arthur at the end of the Sino-Japanese War. Japan had signed an alliance with Britain in 1902. Hence, when war was declared in 1914, Japan cited the alliance and demanded the withdrawal of German warships from China and Japan and the surrender of Tsingtao.

When war broke out, von Spee was at Ponape, in the Caroline Islands, with four of his cruisers. Von Spee reasoned that

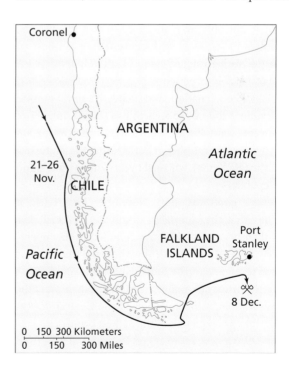

German admiral von Spee's route of attack on the Falkland Islands, December 1914.

if he lingered in the western Pacific he would eventually be hunted down, so he decided to proceed to the west coast of South America, where he could get support from friendly Chile. On the way he picked up two more cruisers at Easter Island. He arrived off Chile in October 1914.

The British had a force of cruisers operating off the coast of Brazil, homeported at the British colony of Port Stanley in the Falkland Islands. Several of these sailed around Cape Horn and engaged the Germans off Coronel, Chile, in November but were driven off with two cruisers sunk. Von Spee then decided to proceed around the cape to Port Stanley in December, hoping to capture the base and its coal supplies. The British, however, had sent two additional cruisers to the Falklands to join six others already there, so when von Spee arrived on 8 December he found himself outnumbered. He tried to flee back west, but he was overtaken and his ships were cut to pieces by the superior British force. This battle eliminated the last major German surface force outside the North Sea.

Gallipoli and Jutland

In late 1914 the British war command concluded that if it could force the straits of the Dardanelles and capture Constantinople (modern-day Istanbul), the Allies could supply men and war materials through Russia to the eastern front, thereby ending the war in a matter of months. The key to this plan was to capture the Turkish peninsula of Gallipoli, which commanded the approaches to the Dardanelles and the Sea of Marmara.

Accordingly, but only after much delay that allowed the Turkish defenders to reinforce and secure their positions, an amphibious assault was launched against Gallipoli in late April 1915. Because of a lack of experience, poor reconnaissance, bad planning, a lack of coordination, and ineffective naval gunfire support, the landings did not go well. Still, a sizable number of Allied troops were eventually landed. However, they were soon pinned down by an equal number of Turks under the aggressive command of Mustafa Kemal, who eight years later would found the Turkish Republic.

The stalemate continued until November 1915, when it became obvious that the campaign would not succeed. The Allied forces then began to withdraw, completing this operation by January 1916. (The successful withdrawal under fire is still considered to be one of the most remarkable amphibious evacuations in the history of modern warfare.) As a result of the failed Gallipoli campaign, Bulgaria joined the Central Powers and helped Germany conquer all of the Balkan countries.

In January 1916 a new, more aggressive admiral was given command of the German High Seas Fleet—VADM Reinhard Scheer. He was determined to find favorable opportunities to do battle with the British fleet in order to reduce its numbers and perhaps win control of the North Sea. Accordingly, in May the fleet sortied from its base at Jade Bay and proceeded toward the coast of southern Norway, opposite Denmark's Jutland Peninsula, to raid Allied shipping there. Altogether, there were some one hundred German ships, including sixteen dreadnought and six predreadnought battleships and a number of cruisers and destroyers in scouting positions.

Unknown to the German commander, however, the British Grand Fleet had sailed for the same area the day before from its bases at Scapa Flow and the Scottish firths (openings of rivers into the sea). The Royal Navy had earlier broken the German naval code and now had gathered radio intelligence that tipped them off about the German plans. Under the command of British admiral Sir John Jellicoe were about 150 ships, including twenty-eight dreadnoughts and several squadrons of cruisers and destroyers.

First contact was made at about 1530 the afternoon of 31 May between opposing cruiser forces. Within minutes, two British cruisers had been sunk by German cruisers, which were superior in armor and armament. But the main action was yet to come. At about 1650, a division of four British dreadnoughts came into range of the German main body and began a running battle to the north, with Jellicoe's main body of twenty-four battleships proceeding to join the action from the northwest. About 1800 a long column of Jellicoe's battleships succeeded in **capping the T** on Scheer's force. (*Capping* or *crossing the T* is a classic naval tactic. A commander attempts to maneuver

The North Sea–Skagerrak area, site of the Battle of Jutland.

his column of warships into position ahead of an enemy column at right angles to it, thus forming the shape of the letter *T*, with the enemy ships moving up the stem. This gives his ships full broadside capability against the enemy ships, while they can bring only their forward guns to bear.) Before they could do much damage, Scheer turned away to disengage. Jellicoe refused to follow, fearing that his force might be led into minefields or waiting submarines.

Several times later that night and into the early morning hours the next day the two opposing fleets maneuvered close to each other. Several short but hard-fought encounters took place. Finally, Scheer decided to preserve his remaining ships and retreat in a southeasterly direction back to base, despite any British forces he might encounter along the way. At about 0230 Scheer succeeded in breaking through the British rear, with the loss of only an old predreadnought and two light cruisers. Jellicoe, again not wanting to risk German minefields, decided not to pursue. The Battle of Jutland, as this action came to be called, was over. Scheer made it back to Jade Bay later that afternoon with most of his force intact. The British had lost six cruisers and eight destroyers, while the Germans had lost one old predreadnought, five cruisers, and five destroyers.

The Germans were pleased by their good showing against the world's most powerful navy. After Jutland, however, they did not want to risk their High Seas Fleet again, so it mostly stayed in port for the rest of the war. Gradually many of the fleet's personnel were transferred to the submarine force, a decision that caused a severe loss of morale within the German navy. This in turn would ultimately spread and contribute to the collapse of all of the German military forces two years later. The Battle of Jutland is considered to be the most important action fought between surface forces in the Age of Steam.

In America, the Battle of Jutland shocked the Wilson administration. It demonstrated that the British fleet was not supreme, and that the United States might yet find itself facing Germany on the high seas without British protection. In response to the battle, plus a new threat of German U-boat warfare, in August 1916 a large new naval shipbuilding program was rushed through Congress. Ten battleships, six battle cruisers, ten scout cruisers, fifty destroyers, and sixty-seven submarines were to be built within the next three years.

Undersea Warfare

When war broke out in August 1914, Britain imposed a blockade against Germany, hoping that this would deny the Germans vital foodstuffs and raw materials. But the blockade did not seriously hurt Germany at first, because of previously stockpiled materials, development of substitutes, and imports from neutrals by way of the Baltic Sea. As a response to the blockade, in February 1915 Germany declared the waters around Britain

A British sailor on the stern of a torpedo-boat destroyer prepares to drop depth charges on German U-boats in the North Atlantic. *U.S. Naval Institute Photo Archive*

and Ireland a war zone, and warned that any British or Allied ships operating in these waters would be subject to attack by submarines and surface ships. The declaration also warned that neutral ships might be attacked as well, since they could easily be mistaken for enemy ships.

The German surface raiders were kept at bay by the British home fleets, but not so the German submarines, or **U-boats**, as they were called. Beginning in February the U-boats sank an average of almost two merchant ships per day. Then in May the *U-20* sank the British passenger liner *Lusitania* off the south coast of Ireland. Among the dead were 128 U.S. citizens. Americans at home were outraged to the point of demanding war over this blatant violation of international law, which prohibits such attacks on unarmed merchant and passenger ships without prior warning. But as Germany had calculated, the United States government was not ready to go to war. (Besides passengers, the ship was later determined to have been carrying small-arms ammunition and possibly war munitions to England, though the latter has never been proven.) President Wilson urged patience, and he demanded that Germany stop all attacks on passenger vessels, and end its unrestricted submarine warfare. In response to this, in June the kaiser proclaimed that henceforth no large passenger liners would be attacked.

In August a British passenger steamer the *Arabic* was sunk with the loss of three American lives. This brought U.S. protests to the point of threatening war. The kaiser then proclaimed that no passenger liners of any size would be attacked until their crews and passengers had been given the chance to escape. Shortly afterward the German naval chief of staff further ordered that thenceforth all U-boat attacks would be conducted from the surface. The German navy responded by ending all U-boat activity around the British Isles, thus ending the first phase of U-boat warfare in the North Sea. For the rest of the year the Germans shifted the focus of U-boat warfare to the Mediterranean, where more than a hundred Allied ships were sunk by year's end.

Early in 1916 the German general staff thought that the United States had become more understanding about German submarine warfare, so the surface attack measure was rescinded, and unrestricted submarine attacks on armed merchant shipping in the British Isles area were resumed. Outside the war zone, the old order still applied. Then in March the unarmed French steamer *Sussex* was torpedoed in the English Channel by a U-boat that mistook her for a warship. Casualties included three injured Americans. This led President Wilson to threaten to break diplomatic relations with Germany. The German government replied with the **Sussex Pledge,** promising that henceforth passenger ships would not be targeted and that merchant ships would not be sunk until the presence of weapons had been established, and then only after provisions were made for the safety of passengers and crew, in accordance with international law.

Admiral Scheer decided that U-boat warfare against merchant shipping could not possibly succeed under these restrictions, so he recalled most of his U-boats and directed that those left attack only warships. He decided to try to use cruisers to lure British forces to locations where waiting U-boats could torpedo them. Thus it was that about a dozen German U-boats were deployed when the Grand Fleet sortied for the cruise that would lead to the Battle of Jutland.

By late 1916 the German general staff had begun to realize that Germany was losing the war—simply because it had not yet won it. Time was on the side of the Allies. Germany could not continue this stalemate, because the British blockade was beginning to hurt. The U-boat offered the only hope of victory. A study by the chief of the German naval staff concluded that if major unrestricted submarine warfare were started by February 1917, Britain would be starved into submission by June, before the summer harvest.

The Germans calculated that even if American aid were started, it would be too late to do any good. They believed the Allies would not start convoys, and they figured that Allied antisubmarine tactics would not be successful in combating the large number of improved German U-boats. They were to be proven wrong on each of these assumptions.

On 1 February 1917 the kaiser ordered his U-boat fleet to begin unrestricted submarine warfare in designated "blockade zones" in the eastern Mediterranean and around Britain, France, and Italy. Any Allied or neutral ships found in these areas were liable to be sunk without warning. By the end of April, the Germans had sunk over two million tons of shipping, exceeding even their own estimates. Britain's economy and war industry were severely damaged. It quickly became clear that if the sinkings continued at this rate, Britain would soon have to surrender.

America Declares War

American public opinion had swung strongly to the side of the Allies by the end of 1916, mainly because of German U-boat warfare and American civilian casualties. When Germany proclaimed its policy of unrestricted submarine warfare in February 1917, President Wilson severed diplomatic relations and ordered American merchantmen bound for the war zone to be armed. He hoped that these actions would force Germany to go back on its decision.

In early March, British intelligence intercepted a secret German note to Mexico. In it, Germany's foreign secretary, Arthur Zimmermann, tried to convince Mexico to join Germany in the event of war with the United States. In return, Germany would help Mexico recover land it had relinquished to the United States after the Mexican War, comprising the states of Texas, Arizona, and New Mexico. When the British revealed the contents of this note to the U.S. government, there was an uproar. All remaining support for the German cause in Washington evaporated, even among those who had strongly supported neutrality. By late March, seven American merchant ships had been sunk by U-boats without warning off the British Isles. Wilson hesitated no longer. On 2 April he sent his war message to Congress, stating, "The world must be made safe for democracy. . . . The right is more precious than peace." On 6 April Congress declared war on Germany.

The Convoy System

Shortly before war was declared, President Wilson had sent RADM William Sims to London to confer with the British. The ship on which he was traveling struck a German mine near Liverpool, and he came ashore among the survivors. He proceeded to London, arriving a few days after the American declaration of war. He immediately went into consultation with ADM Sir John Jellicoe, now the First Sea Lord. Sims learned that Britain was losing the war and would have to surrender by October if the U-boat sinkings could not be stopped.

Sims was very surprised that the British had not started a **convoy system** to protect merchant shipping. This tactic of grouping merchantmen under destroyer escort had proven successful in the English Channel. But British admirals believed it unwise to bunch merchant ships at sea, fearing collisions and claiming that destroyers should not be used for such a "defensive" role. A group of younger British naval officers, however, had wanted to try the convoy approach. Sims conferred with them and was convinced that the concept would work. He went directly to the British prime minister, David Lloyd George, and strongly recommended that the convoy be tried. The prime minister agreed and directed the admiralty to do so.

In the meantime, Sims cabled President Wilson to send every destroyer possible to Britain to help in antisubmarine warfare. The first destroyers arrived in May. By July, thirty-seven American destroyers were in Britain and assigned to antisubmarine work, mostly escorting convoys under British command.

Sims was appointed Commander, United States Naval Forces Operating in European Waters. He concentrated on all aspects of antisubmarine warfare. He had to convince the top officers in the U.S. Navy, and Secretary of the Navy Josephus Daniels as well, about the value of the convoy. While the British started convoys on 30 April at Sims' urging, it took the U.S. Navy until July to accept the idea. By that time, the success of the convoy system had been proven in actual operations. Escorts of convoys sank more U-boats than ever before, convoys sailed without collisions, and port schedules were greatly improved. Convoys could sail on direct routes, not having to zigzag to avoid U-boats. This saved both time and fuel. From May onward, losses dropped steadily. Adoption of the convoy system was a key factor in saving Britain from defeat in World War I.

Antisubmarine Operations

No one single method of warfare, however, could defeat the U-boats. In addition to the convoy, the following methods were used to finally bring the menace under control.

Surface Warfare

The destroyer came to be the main surface vessel designed for combating the submarine. Along with its guns and torpedoes, the destroyers also carried a new weapon called the **depth charge.** Designed by the British early in the war, depth charges were canisters of TNT fitted with devices that would detonate at preset depths. Depth charges could be rolled off the stern from racks or fired from simple launchers called "Y guns," so named because of their shape. By 1918 destroyers carried from thirty to forty depth charges, each containing three hundred pounds of TNT. The United States built 273 destroyers during and immediately after the war.

Another ship designed by the U.S. Navy especially for antisubmarine warfare was the **submarine chaser.** This was a wooden patrol vessel 110 feet long, with a 3-inch gun forward and depth charge rack aft, and a top speed of about fourteen knots. Subchaser patrols were established in the North Sea and across the southern end of the Adriatic Sea in the Mediterranean, to bottle up Austrian submarines. Over four hundred of these little ships were built in various U.S. boatbuilding yards, and they were very helpful in convoying and other antisubmarine functions.

It was not enough just to escort and patrol against lurking submarines, however. Locating the submarine under the water was the key to destroying it. In 1915 the **hydrophone** was invented. This device could pick up underwater noises and indicate their bearing, though not the range. If two or three ships, each with a hydrophone, found a submarine, however, they could determine by cross bearings almost exactly where the submarine was located, drop depth charges there, and destroy their prey. When three ships worked together in this manner, the system was called **triangulation.** The subchasers were fitted with hydrophones in 1917 and proved to be even better equipped than the destroyers to hunt the U-boats. This was the beginning of what is now called sonar, underwater sound detection and ranging equipment.

Mines

The blockade of German submarine bases with surface ships did not prove to be very effective. So, the Allies laid gigantic minefields to prevent U-boats from getting into the Atlantic. One of these minefields was laid across the Dover Strait, from England to Belgium. Because this field could be patrolled against German minesweepers, it proved to be the most effective. The Dover Strait Barrage destroyed at least twelve U-boats and completely closed the strait to German submarine traffic.

The largest minefield, however, was the North Sea Mine Barrage, which ran from Scotland almost to the Norwegian coast. This field consisted of over 70,000 mines, most of them laid by the U.S. Navy. There is no positive information available

A squadron of subchasers getting under way to head for home at the end of World War I. The small ships were designed by the U.S. Navy especially for antisubmarine patrols in the North Sea and the Mediterranean. They were built by several small boat-building companies in New England and the Midwestern United States.
U.S. Naval Institute Photo Archive

on how effective the field was. It is believed that at least one submarine was sunk and a number of others damaged.

A minefield, however, is often far more dangerous in the minds of those who must try to cross it than it may actually be. How many U-boats declined to try to make the trip through the minefield is unknown. It is documented that morale among the submariners was falling fast at this time, partly because of the minefields. And it was the German submarine force that led mutinies that undermined the whole German fleet as the war neared its end.

Air Warfare

Air operations had been carried out by the British against submarines since early in the war, without much success. With the advent of the convoy, however, careful coordination of air patrols with convoy schedules began to pay off. The early airplanes flying these missions had no effective weapons with which to sink submarines, but they did attack and damage a number of them, and this served to discourage the U-boats. Improved weapons and detection methods would make the airplane an important antisubmarine weapon during World War II.

America's Role

The U.S. Navy did not take part in the dramatic surface warfare actions that occurred in the early years of the war. Our Navy's role was mainly to patrol and convoy the huge numbers of troops and enormous amounts of supplies needed by the ground forces on the western front after the American entrance into the war. By midsummer 1917, just a few months after the United States entered the war, 50,000 troops a month were crossing to France. A year later, 200,000 were crossing each month. All told, over two million Americans crossed the Atlantic to the war zone, and not a single troopship or soldier was lost to U-boats.

On land, these American forces were vital in stopping major German land offensives against the Allies in early 1918 and again in July 1918, during the Second Battle of the Marne. American forces, including over 25,000 Marines, bore some of the heaviest fighting at Château-Thierry, Belleau Wood, and the Meuse-Argonne fronts and succeeded in throwing the Germans back. Large-caliber naval guns mounted on railway flatcars helped destroy German railroads, bridges, and ammunition dumps during the first Allied offensive in late summer 1918.

The American shipbuilding industry built several thousand merchant ships to carry supplies and war material to England and France. These supplies, along with the manpower and the highly successful convoy system of the U.S. Navy, were essential in helping the Allies to victory.

Allied Victory

Fortunately for the Allies, the Americans had entered the war at the decisive time. Russia had surrendered to the Germans in late 1917 after the communist-inspired Russian Revolution and terrible defeats on the eastern front. (**Communism** is an economic and social system wherein all property is owned by a classless society rather than by individual citizens of a state. The Bolshevik Revolution in Russia in 1917 marked the first time a communist political party had ever gained control of an entire nation.) This released large numbers of German troops to the western front, where they outnumbered the Allies for the first time since 1914. New tactics and equipment—aircraft, tanks, and mobile artillery—had been adopted by the Germans. They mounted fierce drives, and the Americans arrived just in time to help stop them.

But Germany could not keep up its last offensives. It had temporarily avoided starvation with the capture of Romania and the Russian Ukraine in early 1916, but the British blockade gradually caused widespread famine and shortages of war material. By October 1918 its submarines were defeated, and the Allies were advancing rapidly toward Germany. Its High Seas Fleet began to mutiny, because ships could not sortie without heading into certain death. The convoy system had not only destroyed the U-boats but had also made the Allies overwhelmingly powerful on the sea and in the field. The German people were starving and near revolution. On 9 November 1918 Kaiser Wilhelm II abdicated and fled to exile in Holland. Two days later, on the eleventh hour of the eleventh day of the eleventh month, Germany surrendered to the Allies in a railway car near Paris.

Critical Thinking

1. What were the lessons learned by America and its allies as a result of the unrestricted submarine warfare carried out by Germany during World War I?

Chronology

1914   World War I begins; von Spee beaten at Falklands
1915   Gallipoli assault; *Lusitania* sunk by U-boat
1916   Battle of Jutland
1917   Germany begins unrestricted submarine warfare; America declares war on Germany; convoying begins to Europe; American troops arrive
1918   Russia signs nonaggression treaty with Germany; Germany surrenders

Study Guide Questions

1. What was the main focus of the United States during the Taft administration from 1908 to 1913?

2. A. Which nations formed the Triple Entente in World War I?
   B. Which nations formed the Central Powers?

3. A. Which two navies were the principal enemies in World War I?
   B. What sea became the major area for hostilities in the Atlantic region?

4. A. What geographic advantage did the Central Powers have?
   B. What major geographical disadvantage did Germany's navy have?
   C. What great disadvantage did Britain have?

5. What strategies did the enemy navies set out to follow to win the war?

6. What major amphibious operation was carried out by the Allies in 1915–16?

7. A. Who was the commander of German surface forces in the Pacific when war broke out?
   B. When and where did the German threat in the Pacific region end?

8. What major battle took place in the North Sea in 1916? What were the results?

9. What did Germany do in 1917 to try to bring the war to a favorable conclusion?

10. What two events nearly caused the United States to go to war with Germany in 1915 and 1916?

11. What event in early 1917 caused all remaining congressional support for Germany to cease?

12. What tactic caused Allied shipping losses from U-boat attacks to decline after May 1917?

13. What new weapons began to be used by destroyers against submarines in World War I?

14. What weapon was used in large numbers to prevent egress of German U-boats into the North Atlantic?

15. What was the U.S. Navy's principal role in World War I?

16. What turned the tide of the war on land for the Allies in 1918?

17. When and where did Germany surrender to the Allies?

New Vocabulary

progressivism
militarism
stalemate
sortie
stockpile
unrestricted submarine warfare
convoy system
depth charge
subchaser
hydrophone
triangulation
sonar
mine barrage

7

The Interwar Years

When World War I ended, the victorious Allies conferred at Versailles, France. They imposed their demands on a defeated Germany the following June. The resulting Treaty of Versailles included a requirement that Germany pay the Allies **reparations** (payments for economic injury), eventually set at $33 billion, an amount far beyond Germany's ability to pay. This provision served to foster much resentment on the part of many Germans toward the Allies for years to come.

As part of the treaty inserted at President Wilson's insistence, the Allies agreed to form the **League of Nations,** an organization in which the nations of the world would join together to ensure peace and security for all. But because the league included a mutual-defense provision, which stated that an attack on one would be defended by all, the U.S. Congress refused to accept the treaty, despite many attempts by Wilson to gain support for it. Finally, in July 1921, after Wilson had been replaced as president by Warren Harding, Congress passed a resolution to end the war and ratified separate peace treaties with the Axis powers that October.

Another treaty provision that was a severe blow to German morale was that most of the newer German warships had to be turned over to the Allies. Germany was allowed to retain only half a dozen predreadnought battleships and cruisers and twelve destroyers, but no submarines. However, before the Allies could take ownership of the forfeited vessels, the German navy succeeded in scuttling them all at Scapa Flow, where they had been ordered to proceed at the end of hostilities. The furious Allies then decreed that almost all of the remaining German navy's ships had to be turned over to the Allies.

Naval Disarmament Treaties

Soon after World War I a headlong rush back to "normalcy" had quickly made itself felt across the United States. Isolationism gained in favor. Naval building projects were vetoed; the country listened to the demands of pacifists to cut military spending. In 1921 there was a business recession, felt not only in the United States but also in other major industrial nations.

It seemed to President Harding that it was time for the Allies to come to an agreement on arms limitations.

In November 1921 Britain, France, Italy, and Japan were invited to send representatives to a conference in Washington on naval disarmament. At the opening of the conference the United States stunned the conferees with sweeping proposals to drastically reduce the standing navies of each of the major naval powers. Among other things, the United States, Britain, and Japan would agree to a 5:5:3 ratio in battleship tonnage. After several weeks of negotiations, the **Washington Naval Disarmament Treaty** was signed. This limited the total tonnage of capital ships and placed limitations on the tonnage and armament of these ships and cruisers. The treaty limited battleships to nine 16-inch guns and cruisers to 8-inch guns. No limitations on total tonnage of cruisers were included.

As a concession to the Japanese, who felt that the treaty forced on them third-rate naval status, a so-called nonfortification clause was inserted. This specified that no further fortifications in the Pacific area would be carried out by Japan, by the United States in any of its possessions west of Hawaii, or by the British anywhere east of Singapore or north of Australia. Another treaty simultaneously "guaranteed" the territorial integrity of China.

There were, of course, some Americans who voiced opposition to the treaty provisions. The United States would not remain one of the strongest naval powers in the world if it followed the agreements. But most Americans, concerned with the weak economy and wanting to stay isolated from events in Europe, could not be persuaded to spend money on warships. As might have been expected, soon after the treaty was signed all the world powers except the United States began major heavy-cruiser building programs. In the **London Conference of 1930,** the United States, Britain, and Japan agreed to a 10:10:7 ratio in tonnage of cruisers and parity in tonnage of destroyers and submarines. The agreement also defined a heavy cruiser as having 8-inch guns and a light cruiser as having 6-inch or lower-caliber guns.

Additional naval disarmament conferences were held on several occasions in succeeding years, but none really accomplished anything of significance. For all practical purposes, there were no further treaty limitations on navies after 1936, when the ban on capital-ship construction expired.

In 1928 American isolationism led to another unusual attempt to avoid international conflict, in the form of the **Kellogg-Briand Pact.** This was a treaty worked out between Frank Kellogg, President Calvin Coolidge's secretary of state, and French foreign minister Aristide Briand. Under its terms fifteen nations tried to outlaw war by agreeing thenceforth not to use the threat of war in their dealings with each other. Eventually more than sixty nations signed the treaty.

Unfortunately, even though it still remains in effect today, this idealistic treaty never achieved its purpose, because it had no provisions for enforcement. To get around the treaty, many signatory nations have simply continued to wage war without formal declarations. Nevertheless, it is still considered to be an important *multilateral treaty* (a treaty to which three or more sovereign states are parties), because it has served as one of the bases of international law prohibiting the unlawful threat or use of force by one nation against another either to coerce it or to acquire territory.

In the late 1920s and early 1930s Presidents Coolidge and Herbert Hoover, faced by the aggressive building programs of the Europeans and Japan, reluctantly put construction bills before Congress, but pacifists, isolationists, and others who naively wanted the United States to adhere to the ideals of the Kellogg-Briand Pact forced Congress to reduce the programs to virtually nothing. It was not until President Franklin Roosevelt was inaugurated for his first term in 1933 that any substantial American naval warship building resumed.

Rise of the Dictatorships

After a short period of prosperity immediately following World War I, the economies of much of the world, including the United States, began to waver in the 1920s. Periods of recession and labor unrest alternated with almost dizzying heights of prosperity. Europe's faltering economy collapsed because of widespread inflation, first in Germany, driven by reparations, and then in other major nations. Revolution swept across Russia, and riots and strikes erupted throughout Europe. Finally, in 1929, the U.S. stock market collapsed. The great World Depression was on.

In this climate of worldwide despair, anyone with a radical plan to end the depression—and a voice loud enough to be heard—could move crowds of disillusioned people to follow them. Benito Mussolini had come into power in Italy in 1922, reawakening a vision of the grandeur of ancient Rome in the eyes of his followers. He inspired Italian workers to build up the country's military might so that he could reestablish Rome as the center of Mediterranean power. At the same time, Adolf

Hitler, playing on the theme of German superiority, founded the Nazi Party in Germany. By 1932 the party dominated the German government. When unrest swept Berlin in 1933, Hitler was named chancellor. Nazi Germany under his rule came to be called the **Third Reich** (third empire), a term used to distinguish it from the First Reich (German Holy Roman Empire, 862–1806) and the Second Reich (German pre–World War I Empire, 1871–1918).

In Japan, during the early 1920s moderates were fairly successful in keeping the militarists out of political control. However, in 1924 the U.S. Congress passed an immigration bill classifying the Japanese as "undesirable Orientals." The act prohibited them from entering the United States under any circumstances. The militarists were now able to arouse national resentment against the United States and political support for themselves. Once in control, the militarists selectively assassinated their political foes and began to build up the imperial armed forces.

By the early 1930s, the military dictatorships in Italy, Germany, and Japan were seeking to regain prosperity for their peoples by conquering their neighbors. The democracies—Britain, France, and the United States—refused to take effective countermeasures against these aggressive acts. This lack of military response helped bring on World War II.

In 1931 the Japanese leaders felt themselves sufficiently strong to invade China from their bases in Korea, which they had annexed in 1910. The United States and Britain protested the move as a violation of the Washington Treaty but did nothing more. A protest by the League of Nations did nothing to stop Japan's three-month conquest of Manchuria. Japan simply

Adolph Hitler rose to power in Germany by becoming chancellor of the Third Reich in 1933. He had risen to prominence in Germany on themes of national economic self-sufficiency and *lebensraum* (living space) for the German people. *United States Holocaust Memorial Museum*

withdrew from the league. The militarists recognized that they had achieved the naval superiority to do whatever they wished in the western Pacific, and they had—the disarmament treaties had ensured that they would.

In 1935 Hitler withdrew Germany from the league and refused to continue abiding by all treaty limitations imposed on German armaments and military service. The Germans began to rebuild their armed forces, including capital ships and submarines for a new German navy. In response, the British got Germany to agree to naval building quotas limiting its surface warships to 35 percent of British tonnage and submarines to 45 percent. Also in 1935 the Italians invaded Ethiopia, annexing that country in 1936 and renaming it Italian East Africa. When the League of Nations denounced that act as "bald aggression" and imposed economic sanctions, Italy purchased war supplies from Germany, withdrew from the league, and with Germany formed the Rome–Berlin Axis.

In early 1939 Hitler abolished the Anglo-German naval limitation agreement, freeing Germany to build as many warships as it wanted, of whatever kind and tonnage. By the time war broke out in September 1939, when Hitler invaded Poland, the German navy consisted of two 31,000-ton battleships, two 42,000-ton battleships nearing completion (the *Tirpitz* and *Bismarck*), three 20,000-ton "pocket battleships" (smaller than usual to comply with treaty limitations in force when they were designed), nine cruisers, a number of destroyers, and fifty-six submarines. Germany would continue to build U-boats throughout the war at a furious rate. Before it was finally defeated in May 1945, Germany would send nearly 1,200 submarines into action against Allied shipping.

U.S. Navy in the Prewar Years

After the naval disarmament treaties, U.S. Navy strategists changed their planning, as reflected in War Plan Orange, the contingency war plan that had been developed some years earlier for a possible Pacific war. The strategists' new plans envisioned the probability of having to make a comeback from an initial loss of bases in the Philippines and Guam. They foresaw that the Navy would probably have to fight its way back across the Pacific, operating for long periods far from its bases while seizing enemy bases and converting them for U.S. use. The Navy faced three problems: (1) how to free the fleet from dependence on established bases; (2) how to isolate and attack enemy bases

A biplane takes off from the USS *Langley,* the U.S. Navy's first aircraft carrier. *The Naval History and Heritage Command*

protected by land-based air units; and (3) how to invade and hold heavily defended enemy bases.

The U.S. Marine Corps took on the task of working out the third problem. From this effort came the **amphibious doctrine** that was to be put into effect in World War II. This doctrine emphasized the concepts of command and control, close air support, naval gunfire support, patrol tactics, and the development of new amphibian vehicles and landing craft. This amphibious capability, when expanded to meet the needs of the war, would produce an unstoppable assault force. Many historians regard the amphibious doctrine as the most far-reaching tactical innovation of the war.

During the same time, sophisticated naval aircraft and aircraft carriers came into use. Naval aviation had originally been looked upon as merely a reconnaissance arm of the fleet. But all this changed in 1921, when GEN Billy Mitchell proved in a test that an airplane could sink a battleship with bombs. Mitchell's feat convinced Navy leaders to convert a collier into the Navy's first aircraft carrier, the *Langley,* and to get the treaty powers to consent to the U.S. construction of the carriers *Lexington* and *Saratoga.*

Finally, with carriers, their aircraft, and amphibious forces working far from established home bases, a **logistic support** (resupply) **system** had to be devised that would keep these forces in operation. First, there was the problem of mobile fuel and supply support. This problem was solved by the development of highly versatile at-sea replenishment capabilities—support ships that moved with the fleet and resupplied it while under way. This innovation is sometimes regarded as "the secret weapon" that strategists believed would win the Pacific war.

When a Marine amphibious force captured a new area, new bases on that captured territory would have to be built rapidly. For this task the Naval Construction Battalions (NCBs, or **Seabees**) were formed. The Seabees could create operating bases in any environment, from jungle to rocky atoll. The bases, with facilities tailored to the needs of the area commander, could be rapidly built as soon as the land was cleared. Shortly thereafter the base would be in full operation.

Final Steps toward War

By 1936 the League of Nations was little more than a squabbling group, neither able nor willing to halt the drift toward world war. The aggressive dictatorships had withdrawn their memberships. In 1936 Germany remilitarized the Rhineland, in defiance of the Treaty of Versailles. In 1937 Japan began a war with China with a full-scale invasion, quickly conquering most of the eastern half of the country. During these Chinese operations Japan repeatedly bombed U.S. missions, schools, churches, and hospitals, even sinking the U.S. Navy gunboat *Panay*. The United States limited its response to verbal and written protests. In 1938 Hitler invaded Austria. Betrayed by traitors from within, that nation became a province of Germany.

British prime minister Neville Chamberlain now decided that the only way to avert war was to come to some agreement with Italy and Germany. He undertook what has become known as a policy of **appeasement.** Under this policy, Britain and France made a series of concessions to Hitler and Mussolini in return for "promises of peace." In one of these deals Britain persuaded the league to recognize the Italian conquest of Ethiopia, an act that effectively destroyed the league. Next, Britain and France agreed to the takeover of Czechoslovakia by Germany.

But Hitler next demanded the free city of Danzig and a large segment of western Poland. Britain and France finally drew the line, abandoned the policy of appeasement, and aligned themselves with Poland. The Soviet Union, which had been angered by the British-French sellout on Czechoslovakia, in August 1939 signed a nonaggression pact with Germany. In effect this meant that if Germany went to war with the West over Poland, the Soviets would not enter the conflict. The pact also had a secret provision, never divulged by the Soviets until 1989: in exchange for their agreeing not to enter the war, Germany agreed to let the Soviets have the Baltic States of Estonia, Latvia, and Lithuania. In addition, Poland was divided up along the Narew, Vistula, and San Rivers, with the eastern part reserved to the Soviets, the western part to the Germans.

Hitler was thus freed of any Soviet threat from the east. On 1 September 1939 his armies invaded Poland in a massive offensive, starting World War II. Britain and France, henceforth referred to as the **Allies,** declared war on Germany two days later. On the 17th the Soviets invaded the eastern part of Poland. Later they would also subjugate Estonia, Latvia, and Lithuania, and would try, but fail, to invade Finland.

American Drift toward War

Between 1935 and 1939, as the Washington disarmament treaties collapsed, the United States retreated into a policy of isolationism and neutrality. When the Europeans declared war on each other, President Franklin Roosevelt established the **Neutrality Patrol,** which had as its task the reporting and tracking of **belligerent** (engaged in war fighting) ships and aircraft approaching the United States or the West Indies. Actually, President Roosevelt regarded the Neutrality Patrol as a means of preparing for the war he saw coming. The patrol enabled him to refit some ships and recall reserves to active duty for training and assignment at sea.

The American people were certainly opposed to the totalitarian governments and aggression of the Axis powers and Japan, but they wanted to stay out of the war. As the Nazi blitzkrieg rolled over Poland and conquered Belgium, Holland, Luxembourg, Norway, Denmark, and France—all by June 1940—President Roosevelt began to see the defeat of Britain as a possibility. He asked for assurances that the British fleet would not be turned over to Hitler in that event. Prime Minister Winston Churchill replied that he could not guarantee this, since he probably would not be prime minister following a British defeat.

Faced with the potential loss of the Royal Navy, which in effect served as the first line of U.S. defense, Congress finally recognized the necessity of expanding the U.S. Navy as Roosevelt had requested. Congress passed the Two-Ocean Navy Act, authorizing the president to build for each ocean a fleet sufficient to meet American defense needs.

Events started to move faster for the United States. In September 1940 Roosevelt concluded with Churchill a deal in which the United States gave Britain fifty of its oldest destroyers and ten Coast Guard cutters in return for ninety-nine-year leases on sites for bases in the West Indies, Newfoundland, and Bermuda. In March of the following year, the famous **Lend-Lease Act** was passed, allowing the United States to "loan" war materials to Britain. This put U.S. industry on a wartime production level, because, as Roosevelt declared, America had become the "arsenal of democracy." The United States later seized Axis ships in American ports, froze German and Italian assets in the United States, occupied Greenland, and took over the defense of Iceland from Britain.

A lend-lease destroyer protects a convoy beneath a watchful American torpedo-bomber. *The Naval History and Heritage Command*

In early 1941 high-ranking U.S. and British officers met secretly in Washington and drew up what was called the **ABC-1 Staff Agreement.** This agreement put the U.S. Navy in the war on the side of the Allies, since by its terms the Navy would be sharing escort duties for transatlantic convoys to Britain. The agreement also called for secret meetings between American and British chiefs of staff to make strategic plans. A key decision to come out of the meetings was that in the now-likely event that the United States was drawn into the European conflict and also a war with Japan, the defeat of Germany and liberation of

Europe would be the first priority. Operations against Japan in the Pacific theater would be mainly defensive in nature until the Axis powers in Europe could be defeated; resources thus freed would then be brought to bear against the Japanese.

While the foregoing events were taking place in Europe and America, the situation in the Pacific had deteriorated. The Japanese war with China had stalemated, and an attempted invasion of the Soviet Union had failed. The Japanese then turned their attention toward U.S. and European possessions in the western Pacific. When France fell to Germany in 1940, the Japanese quickly declared a protectorate over Indochina, taking control of the valuable rice crop and occupying the air and naval bases there. They also informed the Dutch authorities in the East Indies that the oil resources on those islands would now be "developed jointly" with them. It was clear that the Japanese were out to dominate the East Indies and its mineral resources. In reaction to this aggressive behavior, President Roosevelt immediately placed an embargo on the sale of aviation gasoline and scrap iron to Japan. Steel was added to the embargo two months later.

An embargo on oil was sure to be the next U.S. move. It came in July 1941, along with a freeze on all Japanese assets in the United States. Thus the Japanese could no longer pay in cash for Dutch East Indies oil. In November the United States proposed that if Japan would evacuate China and sign a non-aggression pact in regard to Southeast Asia and Indochina, their access to oil would resume. Japanese militarists would accept nothing less than full cooperation in their effort to conquer China, however, so they planned to seize the oil resources they needed in the Dutch East Indies by force. They would then move against remaining European holdings throughout the region, while keeping the United States at bay by strikes against the Philippines and the U.S. Pacific fleet at Pearl Harbor. War was now inevitable.

Meanwhile, in the Atlantic region, although some earlier encounters had taken place between German submarines and U.S. naval escorts, it was not until 16 October 1941 that the first casualties were sustained by the two undeclared enemies. On that date, a U.S. destroyer was damaged by a torpedo, with the loss of eleven men. In early November a naval tanker and the destroyer USS *Reuben James* were sunk with heavy losses. That caused Congress to remove the last feature of the U.S. neutrality policy—U.S. merchant ships were now armed and authorized to carry lend-lease goods directly to Britain.

However, it remained for the Japanese to bring the United States totally into the war. On 7 December 1941, the Japanese launched a surprise carrier attack on Pearl Harbor, Hawaii. The following day, Congress declared war on Japan. On 11 December, Germany and Italy declared war on the United States. The United States declared war on those countries that same day.

Critical Thinking

1. Why were the efforts to establish treaties limiting the size and armament of warships during the interwar years from 1918–41 doomed to failure? Is there any relevance of this to modern nuclear nonproliferation treaty efforts?

Chronology

1918	Treaty of Versailles
1921	Washington Naval Disarmament Treaty
1929	U.S. stock market collapses
1933	Hitler becomes German chancellor
1937	Japan invades China
1938	Germany invades Austria
1939	World War II begins in Europe
1940	France falls to Germany
1940–41	United States enacts Japanese embargoes; U.S. declares war on Axis powers

Study Guide Questions

1. What provision of the Treaty of Versailles ending World War I caused much resentment by the German people toward the Allies for years to come?

2. A. What was the League of Nations?
   B. What defense provision did it have?

3. What provision of the Treaty of Versailles dealt with the German navy?

4. A. What were the five major naval powers invited to the naval disarmament talks in Washington in 1921?
   B. What did the 5:5:3 ratio in the proposed disarmament treaty refer to?

5. Why did the United States not embark on any large warship building programs in the 1920s?

6. How did the worldwide economic problems of the 1920s allow the dictatorships to arise in Europe?

7. What did Hitler do regarding the German military forces after assuming power in 1933?

8. In the Pacific, what three problems did the Navy and Marine Corps have to solve?

9. What effect did Billy Mitchell's test sinking of a battleship by aerial bombing have on Navy leaders?

10. A. Who are the Seabees?
    B. What is their mission?

11. What was the British policy of "appeasement" toward Germany and Italy?

12. What action by Hitler's Germany in 1939 began World War II in Europe?

13. What was the decision reached at the ABC-1 Staff meeting in 1941 about the priority of fighting the war in the Atlantic versus the Pacific theaters?

14. What were the final U.S. economic acts that made war with Japan inevitable?

New Vocabulary

reparations	dictatorship
isolationism	appeasement
disarmament	belligerent
militarist	blitzkrieg

8

World War II ~ THE ATLANTIC WAR, 1939–1945

When Germany invaded Poland in September 1939, the German army used a revolutionary new tactic called *blitzkrieg* (lightning war). Rather than move overland on foot, German troops used motor vehicles and tanks supported by dive-bombers to advance deep into enemy territory before the defenses could react. Germany overran western Poland by the end of the month. In mid-September, under th secret terms of the nonaggression pact negotiated with Hitler, the Soviet leader Joseph Stalin invaded and captured eastern Poland.

For the next six months the war entered a quiet phase, during which Germany massed troops and equipment along the **Maginot Line,** a massive system of fortifications built by the French in the late 1930s along their border with Germany. In April 1940 Hitler invaded Denmark and Norway. In May German troops maneuvered around the Maginot Line and rapidly advanced across Belgium, the Netherlands, and France. All three of these countries were soon overcome.

British troops that had been sent into France to counter the initial German buildup now hastily retreated to the city of Dunkirk on the English Channel. There, in an amazing operation over a nine-day period from late May to early June, nearly 340,000 English soldiers were successfully evacuated across the channel to England by a nine-hundred-vessel fleet of mainly. civilian tugboats, yachts, and other small craft—all this in spite of continual air attacks by the German air force, the **Luftwaffe.**

In June 1940 German troops entered Paris, and France surrendered. An armistice between the two was concluded a week later. A new French government, called **Vichy France,** was set up by Marshal Philippe Pétain. By terms of the armistice agreement, it was given nominal sovereignty over the southeastern two-fifths of France not yet occupied by German military forces, and it controlled most of the surviving French military forces. Never recognized by the Allies, the Vichy government was in fact under German control throughout its existence until the defeat of Germany in 1945. Meanwhile, in London, French general Charles de Gaulle organized a resistance movement called the **Free French.** It rejected the Vichy government and did what it could to support the Allies throughout the war.

It would eventually form the nucleus of the Fourth Republic, whose government was headed by de Gaulle after the war.

In September 1940 Hitler sponsored the **Tripartite Pact,** wherein Germany, Italy, and Japan formed an alliance as the **Axis powers.** They were subsequently joined by Hungary, Romania, Slovakia, Bulgaria, Yugoslavia, and Croatia. The following April the Soviet Union signed a nonaggression pact with Japan. Spain, though declaring itself a nonbelligerent, nonetheless was sympathetic toward the Axis powers and often offered them material support throughout the war.

The Battle of Britain

In just three months Hitler had conquered most of western Europe, leaving only the United Kingdom to oppose him, and German troops were massing along the French coast opposite Britain, just twenty miles away across the English Channel. The threat of invasion was imminent. But Hitler first wanted to destroy the Royal Air Force (RAF) and the British will to resist. To accomplish this, over the next year he used the Luftwaffe to launch against Britain the greatest air assault the world had ever known.

In what become known as the **Battle of Britain,** as many as a thousand sorties a day were carried out by Luftwaffe bombers against targets throughout all of England at first, then later concentrated against London. To counter them Royal Air Force pilots flying the famous Spitfire fighters often flew six and seven missions a day, inflicting heavy losses on the attackers. Inspired by Prime Minister Winston Churchill, the British people never lost their will to resist, despite massive losses. In September of 1940 it became clear to Hitler that the German attacks were not going to decimate the RAF, and he abandoned his plans for a cross-channel invasion. By June 1941, the Luftwaffe had suffered significant losses of both aircrews and planes, while the RAF was still as strong as ever; Hitler was forced to finally end the bombing campaign. Over 150,000 Londoners had been killed or injured. "Never in the field of human conflict was so much owed by so many to so few," said Churchill in praise of the courageous performance of the RAF.

The European theater, World War II.

was a back-and-forth affair that depended on which side was being better resupplied at the moment.

In early 1941 both British and American intelligence began picking up information that Hitler was about to invade the Soviet Union, in spite of the nonaggression pact the Soviets and Germans had signed. Both governments informed the Soviets, but the Soviet premier, Joseph Stalin, chose to disregard the warnings. Then in June Hitler launched a major invasion of the Soviet Union, forcing it to join forces with the Allies. Over the next four years fighting along the eastern front in the Soviet Union would be some of the bloodiest the world had ever known. Altogether there would be over 25 million Soviet and five million German casualties in that theater.

Despite these events taking place in Europe, the majority of Americans wanted no part in the European conflict. President Franklin Roosevelt, however, reelected for a third term in 1940, felt differently. As mentioned in the last chapter, he took many measures to prepare America for war and to gear up American military industrial production to wartime levels. Roosevelt felt that the United States had a moral obligation to assist Britain and its allies, and he did all that he could to support them in their war effort against Germany and the other Axis powers.

The Japanese surprise attack on Pearl Harbor on 7 December 1941 stunned the American people and galvanized them into action. America was now ready to go to war. Three days after the Japanese attack, Germany and Italy joined Japan in declaring war on the United States. The second of two world wars had come to America.

A reorganization of Navy commands followed the Pearl Harbor attack and the declarations of war. ADM Ernest J. King became commander in chief of the U.S. fleet. He would also become the Chief of Naval Operations in March 1942. It was under his guidance that the U.S. Navy would contribute to the defeat of Germany in the Atlantic and achieve victory over Japan in the Pacific.

America Joins the Allies

In late 1940 Hitler sent GEN Erwin Rommel and his **Afrika Korps** (motorized German infantry and armored divisions in North Africa) into North Africa, where it had much early success, driving back the British and advancing into Egypt. For a year and a half after that, the North African campaign

A restored British World War II–era Spitfire fighter of the type that defended against German air attacks during the Battle of Britain 1940–41. *Arpingstone*

ADM Ernest King, Chief of Naval Operations during much of World War II. King played a major part in formulating the strategy that led to victory in the Atlantic and the Pacific wars. His leadership philosophy was summarized in his statement, "I can forgive anything except for three things which I will not tolerate—stupidity, laziness, and carelessness." *The Naval History and Heritage Command*

The Battle of the Atlantic

When World War II broke out in September 1939, the German admiral in charge of U-boat operations, ADM Karl Dönitz, tried to send as many submarines to sea as possible to disrupt the flow of food and war materials to Britain. At first he was hampered in his efforts by the small number of German U-boats (only fifty-six when war started) and by the distances they had to proceed in order to get to the western Atlantic sea-lanes from their bases in Germany. Once Norway and France had been conquered, however, the situation changed. While secondary bases of operation were being established in Norway, Dönitz personally supervised the construction of fortified submarine bases along the French Atlantic coast at Brest, Lorient, St. Nazaire, La Pallice, and Bordeaux. Submarines operating out of these bases could cut in half their transit times to the hunting grounds in the western Atlantic. Moreover, German submarine production was continually increasing. By July 1940 there were many more U-boats on station in the Atlantic at any given time than there had been in the opening months of the war.

Because of a limited number of available escorts and the lack of any effective convoy organization, Allied losses to the U-boats began to mount rapidly. Admiral Dönitz often used wolf-pack tactics, with as many as twenty or thirty U-boats coordinating their attacks. Often the targeted merchantmen near the U.S. East Coast were silhouetted by bright lights ashore. By fall of 1940, German U-boats were sinking about 300,000 tons of Allied shipping per month. German successes were making such an impact on oil supplies that fuel rationing had to be imposed in the northeastern United States.

A particularly difficult phase of the North Atlantic sea war involved the Allied convoys to the Russian port of Murmansk, on the Barents Sea. During the German offensives into the Soviet Union in 1942 and 1943, Allied assistance to Soviet forces was slowed to a trickle. Sometimes less than 40 percent of a given convoy made it to Murmansk, but the perseverance of the Allied merchantmen and Allied escort ships finally broke Germany's efforts to destroy the convoys. Some historians believe that the supplies received through Murmansk were a decisive factor in preventing Russian surrender to the Germans during the war.

President Roosevelt and Prime Minister Churchill realized that little could be done against the Germans in Europe until the submarine menace had been brought under control in the Atlantic. Every effort was made to defeat the U-boats. By early 1941 enough escort vessels had been built so that most merchant vessels could be convoyed at least part of the way on each side of the Atlantic. In addition, improved radar was developed that allowed convoy escort ships to detect and track surfaced U-boats. By May 1941 the code of the German Kriegsmarine (navy) had been broken by British code breakers, allowing the British to decipher Dönitz's instructions to his wolf packs at sea and steer convoys away from them.

Increasingly effective coastal air patrols inhibited U-boat operations off the U.S. Atlantic seaboard by late 1941 and in the Gulf of Mexico and off South America by 1942. British patrols flying out of Iceland did the same for the western approaches to Britain. Eventually all these efforts began to pay dividends. In 1940 twenty-six Allied vessels were sunk for every U-boat lost. By 1942 that ratio had been cut to thirteen to one. This was still serious, because by then the Germans were producing about twenty new U-boats per month, but the tide was turning. By 1943, with the addition of escort carrier and hunter-killer

A depth-charge attack on a German submarine in the North Atlantic.
The Naval History and Heritage Command

groups and sufficient numbers of escorts to accompany convoys all the way across the Atlantic, the rate of exchange had fallen to just two vessels lost for every U-boat sunk.

Thereafter, continued improvements in radio-direction-finding techniques and hunter-killer operations kept the U-boats pretty much under control and out of the Atlantic sea-lanes until the war's end in 1945. After the liberation of France in 1944, most U-boats operated from bases in Norway. Toward the end of the war, U-boats fitted with breathing tubes called **snorkels** (which permitted them to operate diesel engines while submerged instead of running on short-lived batteries) attempted a last blitz against Allied shipping in British waters. Some even patrolled once again in U.S. waters, but these efforts came too late to affect the outcome of the war.

Notable among U.S. antisubmarine group exploits was an incident involving the submarine *U-505* in June 1944. She had been tracked from the time she left her base in Brest until she headed home northward from a cruise in the south Atlantic. With this information CAPT Dan Gallery and his group, led by the escort carrier *Guadalcanal,* intercepted *U-505* and blasted her to the surface with depth charges and *hedgehogs* (small depth charges fired in salvos). The defeated crew set demolition charges, opened sea valves, and abandoned ship, but before the U-boat could sink a specially trained American salvage party boarded it. They disconnected the demolition charges, closed the sea valves, and captured the U-boat and her entire crew. They then pumped out the waterlogged boat and towed her to Bermuda. After the war the *U-505* was restored, and she has since been on display at the Museum of Science and Industry in Chicago, Illinois.

In all, the Allies lost 2,775 merchant ships, amounting to 23 million tons during the Battle of the Atlantic. Of this, 14.5 million tons were sunk by German U-boats. The Germans entered 1,175 U-boats into the war, of which they lost 781. They used the capital ships they had at the beginning of the war and those completed during the conflict as independent surface raiders. Though these ships scored some notable successes, most of them were eventually hunted down by the Allies and either sunk or blockaded in port.

The War in Europe and Africa

In the spring of 1942 the German armies were consolidating their positions in France and North Africa. Nowhere were things going well for the Allies. American military leaders and

A boarding party from the USS *Guadalcanal,* under the command of CAPT Dan Gallery, captures the German submarine *U-505* on 4 June 1944. This was the first boarding and capture by U.S. naval forces since 1815. *The Naval History and Heritage Command*

Stalin in the Soviet Union wanted to bring the war directly to Hitler with an invasion in Europe. But cooler British heads prevailed, convincing President Roosevelt that the Allies were not ready for such a major undertaking in the face of Hitler's superior forces.

Still, the Allies had to do something in order to recover the initiative. Winston Churchill proposed an invasion of French North Africa in order to take the pressure off British forces in Egypt. Field Marshal Erwin Rommel, the "Desert Fox," commanding the elite German Afrika Korps, was heading toward Suez, the loss of which would be extremely serious for the Allies. Churchill believed an Allied invasion would also have the secondary benefit of drawing German forces away from the beaches of Europe to Africa. Once there, they could not be easily returned to the continent, because of increasing Allied control of the Mediterranean Sea area.

Operation Torch was the code name given to the Allied invasion of North Africa. It was planned for 8 November 1942. This became the first Allied offensive operation against the Axis in the European–North African theater. American amphibious forces making up the Western Naval Task Force were to come from East Coast ports and converge on French Morocco. They were to land on three beaches near the primary objective, the port of Casablanca.

Area of operations for Operation Torch, the invasion of North Africa by the Allies. Arrows show the landing sites. American forces landed at the three beachheads in Morocco while combined British and U.S. forces landed at the two Algerian cities.

The big question mark of Operation Torch concerned the Vichy French forces in the area, since at that time Morocco had been a French protectorate for many years. Would they resist the landings? The invasion thus became a political problem as well as a military one. If the French decided to offer serious resistance, they might well be able to hold off the Allies until German reinforcements arrived. This could doom the invasion and set up a major disaster for the Allies in North Africa.

As it turned out, the Vichy French navy and some shore batteries put up a spirited defense at Casablanca, but this was quickly eliminated by U.S. Navy gunfire. The French then quickly surrendered and joined forces with de Gaulle's Free French (in accordance with secret orders from Marshal Pétain, the French leader in Vichy). In response, Hitler's armies immediately occupied the previously unoccupied parts of France.

Operation Torch, though anything but smooth, met all of its objectives. It showed, however, that the Allies were by no means ready to invade Hitler's Europe. Much more training, larger forces, and better equipment would be necessary.

The North African operations set up one of the first major defeats for the Axis. Shortly before the Allied landings in Morocco and Algeria, British field marshal Bernard Montgomery's Eighth Army routed the Afrika Korps at El Alamein, thus removing the threat to Suez. The Allies then squeezed the Germans and Italians between them into Tunisia. In May the fighting in North Africa ended with the defeat and capture of the entire Afrika Korps, about 275,000 troops, and all of its remaining equipment. Rommel escaped to Germany in the closing days of the campaign. As an indirect result of the Allied victory in Africa, most of the main units of the Vichy French naval fleet were subsequently scuttled at Toulon.

On the Eastern Front

In the winter of 1942–43 the Soviets had surrounded and defeated an entire German army at Stalingrad, an industrial city on the Volga River. By the end of the five-month battle in February 1943, they had taken 330,000 prisoners in one of history's most savage confrontations. The Battle of Stalingrad turned the tide on the eastern front. The Soviet advance thereafter would not stop until the Soviet army, known as the Red Army, entered the German capital of Berlin two years later.

The Casablanca Conference

In January 1943 President Roosevelt and Prime Minister Churchill met in the famous **Casablanca Conference** in Morocco. General de Gaulle was also there, representing the Free French forces. Soviet Premier Stalin was also invited to attend but declined because of the critical battle for Stalingrad taking place at that time. The leaders' military chiefs and aides, including Admiral King for the United States, were also in attendance. Churchill and Roosevelt decided that before any major offensives could succeed elsewhere in Europe, antisubmarine warfare in the Atlantic had to be given top priority. Second, the Allied leaders agreed that the next offensive operation against the Axis would be an invasion of Sicily in July. At King's insistence, Churchill agreed to send more military resources to the Pacific to take advantage of the reconquest of Guadalcanal. Finally, in what was considered at the time a very bellicose statement, the leaders announced that the Allies would demand nothing short of the unconditional surrender of Germany, Italy, and Japan.

Operation Husky: Invasion of Sicily

With the success of North Africa still fresh in the minds of all, Allied forces under the overall command of GEN Dwight Eisenhower prepared for the massive invasion of Sicily, code named **Operation Husky**. This was to be the first major attempt to take the home territory of an Axis nation. On 9 July 1943 the invasion took place on beaches on the southern and southeastern sides of the island. LTGEN George Patton commanded the U.S. Seventh Army, while Field Marshal Montgomery commanded the British Eighth Army. Over 580 ships landed and supported some 470,000 Allied troops on the island. They were opposed by some 270,000 Italian and German infantry and air force support troops.

Soon the Axis forces were in full retreat, chased by General Patton's tanks and Montgomery's infantry forces. Patton proved to be a masterful field commander, rapidly moving his armor to best advantage and chasing the retreating Axis forces toward Messina and an evacuation of the island. Only about one-third of the Axis troops escaped to Italy with their equipment.

By 17 August Sicily was under Allied control. The Sicilian campaign was a major triumph for the Allies, for it largely eliminated Italy from the war. In late July a coup deposed Benito Mussolini as head of the Italian government and put him into "protective custody." His successor, Marshal Pietro Badoglio, said publicly that he would continue the war against the Allies, but in private he began negotiations that would lead to surren-

The Casablanca Conference, January 1943. President Roosevelt is seated in the foreground (left), next to British prime minister Winston Churchill. Their military chiefs of staff are standing behind, including Admiral King to Roosevelt's right.
The Naval History and Heritage Command

der. In the meantime, Eisenhower's staff began immediate planning for the invasion of Italy itself.

The Italian Campaigns

Initially the Allies had planned, once Sicily was secured, to simply cross the Strait of Messina between Sicily and the toe of Italy and fight their way northward against both Italian and German troops stationed there. However, the coup against Mussolini convinced the Allies that a more aggressive plan could be adopted—an attempt to quickly capture all of Italy and isolate the remaining German forces there. They decided that in addition to the crossing at Messina they would launch an invasion at Salerno, in order to capture the seaport at Naples, then surge north from there to secure Rome and invade northern Italy.

The landings at Salerno were dubbed **Operation Avalanche** and were scheduled for 9 September. Meanwhile, the new Italian government negotiated an armistice with the Allies; it was signed on 3 September and announced the day before the scheduled landings at Salerno. Thus, when Montgomery's Eighth Army crossed into Italy from Sicily on the 3rd it met little resistance and proceeded rapidly northward toward Salerno to link up with the invading Allied force when it landed there.

Much to the consternation of the Germans, when the armistice was announced on 8 September, most of the Italian naval fleet of over two hundred vessels steamed out of Italian ports and surrendered to the Allies at Malta and North Africa, thus avoiding their falling into German hands.

The Allies still had to contend with the German occupation forces, however. When the amphibious landings at Salerno occurred on 9 September, the Allied landing forces, primarily the U.S. Fifth Army, under LTGEN Mark Clark, met fierce resistance. German forces had the beaches zeroed in, and they had prepositioned motorized vehicles and tanks on heights overlooking them. The Luftwaffe was standing by to turn the landing zone into an inferno. In spite of these defenses, a precarious beachhead was secured, but with heavy losses. The beachhead was repeatedly saved by naval gunfire support. Noting the reliance of Allied forces on the supporting warships, the Nazis hurled the bulk of their airpower at these ships. Three destroyers were sunk, and many ships were damaged.

But the beachhead held. German tactical errors in the field halted their counterattacks in mid-September. A strategic error by Field Marshal Rommel withheld German reinforcements from the north—when they could probably have made the difference. On 16 September Montgomery's Eighth Army joined forces with Clark's Fifth Army, and the Germans withdrew to defensive positions north of Naples. That great port city was occupied by the Fifth Army on 1 October. The port was a shambles, and the harbor was cluttered with sunken, booby-trapped ships scuttled by the Germans. Clearance of the harbor was assigned to the Seabees, who managed to do it, despite incredi-

ble obstacles, within four months. Meanwhile, the Allies began their buildup for further movement northward. The Germans had consolidated their forces at the **Gustav Line,** the strongest of a series of fortified defensive lines between Naples and Rome. To bypass these defenses, the Allies planned an "end run"—an amphibious assault on Anzio Beach, some thirty-seven miles south of Rome. The planning was complicated by the fact that many of the Allied forces in the Mediterranean theater were being transferred to England in preparation for the great invasion of France across the English Channel.

Nevertheless, the landing was made on 22 January 1944 with only two reinforced divisions. The initial landing met with little resistance, but the Germans quickly moved in to stop any forward movement by the relatively small Allied invasion force. Allied reinforcements poured into the small area, but the Germans kept reinforcing their surrounding forces at a similar rate, building up powerful artillery defenses that continuously pounded the enclosed Allies. A major Allied seaborne supply route was established between Anzio and Naples over the next several months. It wasn't until the seasonal rains ceased in May that the Allies finally broke the German hold on Monte Cassino, the key fortress on the Gustav Line, and surged northward. The Germans broke off all contact at Anzio when this happened, and the victorious Allies swept unopposed into Rome on 4 June.

Two days later the focus of attention in Europe became coastal France, where the great cross-channel operation against Hitler's **Festung Europa** (Fortress Europe) began. The rest of the Italian campaign received little public attention. Nevertheless, the fighting went on there, as the Germans slowly but steadily retreated northward. It would take another year of

Troops of the U.S. Fifth Army disembark from landing craft at the Anzio beachhead January 1944. *The Naval History and Heritage Command*

fighting before the remaining German forces in northern Italy surrendered, on 2 May 1945.

The successful Italian campaigns involved some of the heaviest fighting in the war and resulted in over 100,000 American casualties, but they prevented German forces in Italy from reinforcing northern France after the invasion at Normandy, and they secured the Mediterranean Sea for the Allies.

Operation Overlord: Invasion of Normandy

Hitler had calculated that the Allies would be invading his Festung Europa no later than the spring of 1944. He ordered the commander on the western front, Field Marshal Karl von Rundstedt, and his deputy, Field Marshal Rommel, to build a great "Atlantic Wall" of concrete fortifications to keep the Allies out. Von Rundstedt felt that static defenses were useless against naval gunfire, so he organized highly mobile inland divisions, centered around Calais, which could rush to any spot where an invasion occurred.

Rommel, on the other hand, felt that Allied airpower would prevent the mobile divisions from getting to the seacoast. So he concentrated his efforts on beach defenses, counting heavily on mines. He also had concluded that the Allies probably would invade at the Normandy beaches, rather than at Calais, the English Channel's narrowest point. He was right. The Allies had begun to prepare for a major amphibious invasion of the Normandy coast, about 170 miles southwest of Calais, under the code name Operation Overlord.

In the early spring Eisenhower began a strategic air attack against Germany designed to eliminate aircraft factories and ruin the Luftwaffe. By April the raids had decimated the German air force to the point where the Allies could count on a thirty-to-one superiority over the Normandy beaches. Next, the Allied air forces struck at the railroad marshaling yards, bridges, and the trains and tracks themselves, wreaking such havoc that it was almost impossible for any military traffic to move by rail anywhere in France. These air attacks made the subsequent landings possible, because Overlord would not have been successful without Allied air superiority over the beaches.

D-day at Normandy

The invasion at Normandy was originally set for 1 May 1944, but Eisenhower postponed the date to 1 June in order to get an additional month's production of landing craft.

The physical conditions of tide, visibility, and weather all were of utmost importance to the planners. The tide was especially crucial. It had to be rising at the time of the initial landings, so the landing craft could unload and retract without becoming stranded. At the same time, the tide had to be low enough to expose sunken obstacles so underwater demolition teams could destroy them.

The Allies finally selected one hour after low tide for the first landings. This meant that each succeeding wave of boats would come in on higher tides, with less beach to cross. Only three successive days each month would provide the desired tidal heights. The closest dates to 1 June were 5, 6, and 7 June. Eisenhower selected 5 June as his first choice for **D-day** (debarkation

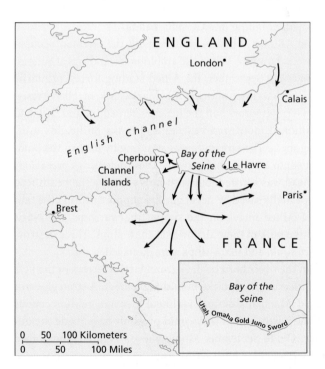

GEN Dwight Eisenhower briefing troops before the Normandy invasion.
National Archives

The Allied landing areas on D-day in Normandy, 6 June 1944. U.S. forces landed on Utah and Omaha Beaches; British and Canadians landed on Gold, Juno, and Sword. Breakout occurred in mid-August, and Paris was liberated on 24 August.

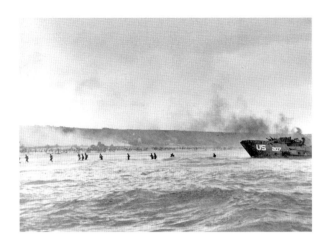

D-day at Normandy. Troops wade ashore from their landing craft at Omaha Beach. Note the extensive fortifications along the beach in the background and the steep embankment beyond. Once ashore, troops faced withering German machine-gun fire as they crawled through the obstacles and up the slope. *The Naval History and Heritage Command*

The principal objective of the landings, beyond establishing the beachhead itself, was to capture the port city of Cherbourg so the enormous flow of logistical supplies required to support the invasion could be handled quickly.

The landings took place on 6 June 1944—a day later than planned because of bad weather, which would have limited air support. In commemoration of the event, this date has been memorialized as "D-day" ever since. Minor opposition was encountered on four of the five beaches, but at Omaha Beach crack German troops were well dug in and opposed the landing fiercely, causing heavy casualties. Many of the Germans assigned to the other beaches had been lured inland to counter Allied paratroops—dropped there for just that reason.

The Allied troops consolidated their beachhead while expanding south and west to cut off Cherbourg, on the Cotentin Peninsula. By the 24th the 40,000 Germans in Cherbourg were surrounded. A U.S. naval force of battleships, cruisers, and destroyers was called in to pound the heavily fortified Cherbourg into submission. The Germans put up a determined counterbattery (return) fire. The battleships prevailed, but not before three destroyers and the battleship USS *Texas* were hit. On 25 June the Germans surrendered Cherbourg, and the Allies began the salvage of the wrecked harbor. It was back in commission and receiving cargo within two weeks.

Despite the German resistance ashore, the Allies advanced. Taking advantage of a weak spot in the German lines found by GEN Omar Bradley's First Army, General Patton drove through

day), and then chose H-hours (times for operations to begin) from 0630 to 0755 for the best tidal conditions for each beach.

The Allies planned to land on five beaches located in the French province of Normandy between the Cotentin Peninsula and the Orne River mouth, near the city of Caen. The Americans were to land at Omaha and Utah Beaches on the right flank, and the British were to hit Gold, Juno, and Sword on the left flank.

Navy LSTs off-load cargo at one of the American invasion beaches at Normandy. Note the large number of Allied ships participating in the landing in the background and the barrage balloons tethered above the beach to deter air attacks. *The Naval History and Heritage Command*

The U.S. cemetery at Colleville-sur-Mer near Normandy, France. The remains of some 9,400 U.S. service members who were casualties on D-day are buried here. *American Battle Monuments Commission*

with the U.S. Third Army, creating a major breakout and trapping 50,000 German troops. On 24 August Paris fell, and General Eisenhower assumed command of the Allied ground forces on the continent. The Germans were in full retreat. A new Free French government under Charles de Gaulle replaced what was left of the Vichy regime.

In retaliation for the Allied landing at Normandy, a week after the first waves went ashore Hitler began a bombardment of London using the **V-1 flying bomb.** This was a primitive type of unmanned, pulse-jet powered cruise missile developed by the Luftwaffe at Peenemunde after the losses suffered during the Battle of Britain. Because they flew at altitudes of between two and three thousand feet and their pulse-jet engines made a distinctive loud buzzing sound, they soon came to be called "buzz bombs." They flew at speeds of more than 350 miles per hour until a predetermined time, when their engines cut off and they dove on their targets. At the peak of these attacks over a hundred of them a day were launched toward London and southeast England, until October 1944 when the last launch sites in France within range of Britain were overrun by Allied forces. Sporadic attacks with air-launched versions continued until March 1945.

A German V-1 flying "buzz bomb." They were the first and most numerous of several "Vengeance" weapons developed to attack Britain following the Allied invasion of Normandy.

Altogether over eight thousand of these "Vengeance" series of weapons were launched against Britain.

Operation Anvil: Invasion of Southern France

Only one more invasion remained to be staged in the European theater. **Operation Anvil** (later renamed Operation Dragoon at the behest of Churchill) was to take place on the French Riviera on the shores of the Mediterranean Sea near Marseilles. The operation, originally planned to complement the landing at Normandy, had two objectives: to gain another port for supplies flowing into France and to draw German forces away from the primary beaches in Normandy. The landing had to be delayed until 15 August, however, because of a shortage of landing craft. By then the area around Normandy was secure, but a port on the Riviera was still highly desirable, as was the liberation of southern France that such a landing would facilitate.

ADM Henry K. Hewitt was given the assignment to conduct this first daylight landing in the Mediterranean. The assault was preceded by 1,300 bombers, which pounded the German defenses for nearly an hour and a half, and by over half an hour of heavy naval shore bombardment. The landing craft moved in under a canopy of rockets fired by amphibious ships. The rockets, naval gunfire, and bombing eliminated German resistance, and Free French and American forces quickly took the offensive. Within two weeks they had captured the port of Marseilles, the naval base at Toulon, and the Riviera cities of Nice and Cannes. The Allies then surged northward through the Rhône Valley, joining with Patton's forces near Dijon on 12 September. Most of France, Belgium, and Luxembourg had been liberated by that time, and the Germans were settling in behind their west wall, the **Siegfried Line** (a prepared defensive line that ran along the western border of the old German empire).

Germany Is Defeated

The rapid movement of Allied forces through France was made possible mainly because of their complete control of the air. When winter weather arrived, however, air cover was reduced because of poor flying conditions. On 16 December von Rundstedt launched a major counteroffensive, called the **Battle of the Bulge,** in the Ardennes area of Belgium. The Nazis made quick advances through a break in the U.S. lines before being stopped by massive attacks on their flanks by Allied armies. The Germans had surrounded elements of the U.S. 101st Airborne Division at the Belgian town of Bastogne. After several days of fierce fighting, the German commander demanded that the cut-off Americans surrender. The American commander, BGEN Anthony C. McAuliffe, gained instant and lasting fame for himself and his troops when he sent back one of the most eloquent replies in the annals of military history: "Nuts!" The terrible siege was broken on 27 December, when the U.S. Third Army, led by General Patton, broke through the German lines. The Battle of the Bulge was Germany's last offensive.

In early 1945 the Allies resumed their attacks on the German Reich—Americans, British, French, and Canadians on the western and Italian fronts, and the Soviets on the eastern front. In March the Allied forces reached the Rhine River, and the U.S. Navy was called on to make its last direct contribution in the fight against Germany. Navy landing craft, which had been carried across Belgium by trucks and trains, helped ferry elements of Bradley's armies over the river in most of their initial crossings.

Then, on 7 March, the First Army captured the Ludendorff Bridge at Remagen, establishing a major bridgehead across the Rhine. The bridge held up for ten days under heavy German artillery fire. This was sufficient time for major forces to cross the river. The final push from the west was now on, while the Russians surged toward Berlin from the east. On 25 April U.S. and Soviet forces met at the Elbe River. They had cut Germany in half from west to east.

On 28 April Mussolini was captured and killed by Italian antifascist guerrillas while trying to escape to Switzerland. Two days later, Hitler, besieged in his bunker in Berlin by Soviet forces, committed suicide after naming Admiral Dönitz as his successor. On 7 May 1945 hostilities ceased in Europe. The representatives of the German army, navy, and government signed the unconditional surrender document at Eisenhower's headquarters in a little red schoolhouse in Reims, France. World War II was over in Europe after five years, eight months, and six days of death and destruction.

Critical Thinking

1. The Allied effort to hunt down and eventually sink the German battleship *Bismarck* was one of the most storied events of World War II in the Atlantic. Research the exploits of the *Bismarck* and how she came to her end off the coast of France in May 1941.

2. Convoy tactics were one of the most significant factors that led to the defeat of the German U-boat offensive in the Atlantic in both world wars. Research how convoys were formed and how they defended against the U-boat threat.

Chronology

1939   World War II begins
1940   France falls to Germany
1941   Japan bombs Pearl Harbor; Germany, Italy and Japan declare war on the United States
1942   Allies invade North Africa
1943   Sicily attacked; Italy invaded
1944   Anzio landing; *U-505* captured; D-day at Normandy; Allies liberate Paris; Battle of the Bulge
1945   World War II ends in Europe

Study Guide Questions

1. What was the Maginot Line in Europe?
2. What French city was the site of an amazing evacuation of trapped English troops in May 1940?
3. What actions took place during the Battle of Britain in 1940–41?
4. Who was the senior U.S. naval leader who took over the leadership of the U.S. Navy following Pearl Harbor?
5. What was the Battle of the Atlantic?
6. What was the German U-boat wolf-pack tactic?
7. Why was the German conquest of Norway and France important to U-boat warfare?
8. What famous antisubmarine group exploit was carried out under the leadership of CAPT Dan Gallery in June 1944?
9. What factors finally led to the defeat of U-boat warfare in the Battle of the Atlantic?
10. What was Operation Torch?
11. What battle turned the tide for the Allies on the eastern front in 1942–43?
12. What was the most significant result of the Sicilian campaign of 1943 for the Allies?
13. Where did the Allies stage an invasion in January 1944 to try to accomplish an "end run" around the Gustav Line in Italy?
14. A. Where did the massive Allied invasion of northern France take place in June 1944?
    B. By what name has 6 June 1944 been called ever since?
15. A. What were the German "buzz bombs"?
    B. When and where were they used?
16. What was the last major German offensive against the Allies?
17. When and where did Germany surrender to Allied forces?

New Vocabulary

wolf-pack tactics
snorkel
demolition charge
unconditional surrender
beachhead
counterbattery fire
buzz bombs

World War II ~ THE PACIFIC WAR, 1941–1945

9

When the United States restricted the sale of oil to Japan in July 1941 in response to Japanese expansion into Indochina, the Japanese had to find an alternative source of oil. The Dutch East Indies were the only possible source of supply in the western Pacific region. Thus, American strategists reasoned, a military move into the Indies would be the next logical step for the Japanese. To deter such a move, President Roosevelt had directed that the battleships and aircraft carriers of the U.S. Pacific Fleet be moved from the West Coast to Pearl Harbor, Hawaii. In October the civilian government of Japan fell and was replaced by a military government headed by General Hideki Tojo. In November a special Japanese envoy arrived in the United States to assist the Japanese ambassador in negotiations to resume the flow of western oil.

Unknown to the Japanese, the United States had an advantage in the negotiations, in that American code breakers had some months earlier succeeded in breaking the Japanese diplomatic code. Thus, Washington knew that a deadline for the negotiations had been set for late November, after which something bad would happen. The Japanese proposed that if the United States and its allies would recognize its territorial gains in China and grant it access to oil, Japan would not attack Southeast Asia or Indochina. The United States countered with a proposal that if the Japanese would agree to evacuate China and sign a nonaggression pact guaranteeing that they would not invade any European or American holdings in the region, their access to oil would resume.

No reply was forthcoming from the Japanese. In late November there came an ominous development—a Japanese naval expeditionary force was sighted heading toward the Malay Peninsula, where it would presumably launch an invasion as a response to the final U.S. proposal. But unknown and undetected was another Japanese force at sea. This one, which included all six of Japan's large carriers and numerous escort ships, under the operational command of ADM Chuichi Nagumo, was headed east across the Pacific toward Pearl Harbor, Hawaii.

In Washington on 6 December American cryptologists intercepted a last fourteen-part diplomatic message to the Japanese delegation, directing it to destroy all codes and break off diplomatic relations with the United States. The last paragraph directed that this be done at 1300 Sunday 7 December, Washington time—0730 at Pearl Harbor.

The Attack on Pearl Harbor

Masked by stormy seas and heavy rain, the Japanese strike force had approached to within two hundred miles north of Oahu, Hawaii, by the early morning of Sunday, 7 December.

Because of a threat of subversive activity, most American aircraft at the air base at Pearl Harbor on Oahu had been lined up in neat rows, to guard them against sabotage. The eight battleships of the Pacific Fleet were all anchored at Battleship Row in the harbor to permit weekend liberty. There were also some ninety other ships either anchored or moored alongside piers in the harbor. Fortunately, the two carriers *Lexington* and *Enterprise* then stationed at Pearl Harbor were at sea, delivering planes to Midway and Wake Islands.

At 0600 the six carriers of the Japanese strike force turned into the wind and launched over 180 planes to attack the battleships and also destroy the parked aircraft, so that there could be no counterattack.

At 0800 the first of the attacking Japanese planes reached the harbor and radioed back the signal "Tora . . . Tora. . . . Tora," a code word meaning complete surprise had been achieved. At this time most American sailors and airmen were finishing breakfast or just relaxing. Suddenly death and destruction began raining from the skies. The attack struck all parts of the harbor at once, because all the Japanese pilots had predesignated targets. Within moments the battleship *Arizona* exploded and sank after a bomb set off her ammunition magazines. Soon all remaining battleships and ten other ships were sunk or badly damaged. By 0945 the attack was over. Altogether, some 2,400 American servicemen had been killed and another 1,280 had been wounded. Nineteen ships had been sunk or severely damaged,

Pearl Harbor, Hawaii, just before the Japanese attack on 7 December 1944, looking southward. Ford Island is in the center of the harbor. Hickham Field is toward the upper left on the main shore, and the tank farm is midway between. "Battleship Row" is to the left of Ford Island, with the *Nevada* and *Arizona* anchored adjacent to the lower-left point. *The Naval History and Heritage Command*

A closer shot of Battleship Row, taken from an attacking Japanese aircraft. The battleship *Nevada* is to the lower left, followed by the *Arizona* with repair ship *Vestal* outboard, then the *Tennessee* with *West Virginia* outboard of her, and the *Maryland* with *Oklahoma* outboard. The *West Virginia* and *Oklahoma* have just been torpedoed; the white smoke in the background is from Hickham Field. *The Naval History and Heritage Command*

The USS *Arizona* burning and sinking after being hit by bombs of Japanese carrier planes. Over 1,100 crewmen were killed in the attack. *The Naval History and Heritage Command*

The USS *West Virginia* damaged and sinking after being hit by several bombs and seven aerial torpedoes. Saved from capsizing by her brave crew, she was salvaged and extensively repaired and modernized in time to rejoin the Pacific Fleet and take part in the invasion of the Philippines in October 1944. She would play a major role in the subsequent battles in Leyte Gulf and in the invasions of Iwo Jima and Okinawa. *The Naval History and Heritage Command*

including all eight of the battleships. Over 350 planes had been destroyed or heavily damaged on the ground.

Fortunately for the United States, a large tank farm near the harbor containing some 4.5 million barrels of oil had been spared. Loss of this oil would have hindered later American naval operations even more than the damage done to the ships. Also, important repair yards and machine shops, which would make possible the eventual salvage and return to duty of fourteen of the nineteen ships disabled by the attack, were practically untouched.

The Japanese had also predeployed some twenty submarines into the area, but because of the shallow depths of the harbor, these could not participate in the attack. They did, however, launch five **midget submarines** that attempted to penetrate the harbor defenses. Insofar as is known, none of them reached their targets (though recent analysis of an old Japanese photo taken during the attack seems to show one near the surface in the middle of the harbor; it may have fired its two torpedoes into the capsizing battleship USS *Oklahoma*). They were all either beached or sunk during the attack, and several were recovered intact years later. In general, the Japanese submarines would not play a major role in the Pacific War.

The next day, calling 7 December 1941 "a date which will live in infamy!" President Roosevelt asked Congress to declare war on Japan. Three days later Germany and Italy joined Japan in declaring war on the United States.

Despite the attack's apparent success at the time, there were several things that would come back to haunt the Japanese. Their leaders never thought they could conquer America. But they hoped by inflicting major damage at Hawaii, they would so demoralize the American people that they would press for a quick peace that would ensure Japanese dominance in the western Pacific. However, rather than demoralize their American enemy, as had the sneak attacks on their Chinese foes in 1894 and the Russians in 1904, the attack on Pearl Harbor roused and infuriated the American public in general, and the U.S. Navy in particular, as nothing else could have. Americans would be willing to endure any hardship and make any necessary sacrifice to achieve ultimate victory.

Until then, the prevailing view among the senior leadership of most of the world's navies had been that the battleship was the dominant ship in naval warfare. After Pearl Harbor, the United States and its allies had no choice but to build their offense in the Pacific around the aircraft carrier. The Japanese would hold to a belief in the superiority of a battleship-centered strategy until the end. History would show that the carrier, not the battleship, would be the dominant naval weapon in the Pacific in World War II, as it has been in all the major navies of the world since.

Early Japanese Successes

With the American fleet crippled in Pearl Harbor, the other parts of the Japanese master plan swung into action. Japanese forces landed on the Malay Peninsula to begin their successful push toward the great British base at Singapore. They took Thailand without resistance. Within days they made landings in the Philippines to guard their sea lines of communication to their main objective, the oil of the Dutch East Indies. By mid-December they had made their first landings near the oil fields on the island of Borneo, followed by an advance southward toward Java, the main island of the archipelago. Java was especially rich

The USS *Arizona* Memorial at Pearl Harbor, Hawaii. Note the remnants of the sunken battleship visible beneath the memorial. Over 1,100 of her deceased crew are interred in it, and oil from ruptured fuel tanks still occasionally bubbles to the surface. *CHINFO*

in the natural resources that Japan needed. Japanese troops landed on the U.S. territories of Wake Island and Guam and at British Hong Kong. All these would fall to the Japanese by year's end.

In January 1942 the ABDA (American, British, Dutch, and Australian) defense command was formed. Its headquarters was on Java. It was never very effective, because of the small forces at its disposal and disagreements over what it should do. The Dutch considered defense of Java the principal goal. The British and Americans believed that a successful defense of Java was impossible and that the best ABDA could do was delay the Japanese so they could not move their forces farther into the Southwest Pacific and isolate Australia. Meanwhile, the Japanese methodically moved through the Indies, raiding Darwin, Australia's northernmost port, and invading Portuguese Timor, thus effectively isolating Java from any major reinforcement.

ABDA naval forces made several unsuccessful attempts to stop the Japanese advance. Finally, on 29 February, the Japanese defeated the ABDA forces in the Battle of the Java Sea. The majority of ABDA ships, including the American cruiser USS *Houston,* were sunk by aircraft and destroyer-fired torpedoes. The Japanese were then free to invade and capture Java; by 9 March the island was forced into unconditional surrender. Before the end of March all of the Dutch East Indies were in Japanese hands, and the rich oil wells of Java, Borneo, and Sumatra were providing an inexhaustible supply of fuel and other resources.

The Japanese had attained all of their objectives in the south, and at the same time they had conquered Burma and the Andaman Islands in the Indian Ocean. They had driven the battered British Indian Ocean Fleet into East African ports. Moreover, they had accomplished all of this in less than half the time they had planned and with no significant losses. Flushed with their success, they even considered invading Australia, to extend their southern defensive perimeter even further. However, they soon realized they did not have sufficient resources to attempt to do that. Instead they planned to bypass and isolate Australia by advancing via New Guinea and the Solomon Islands to New Caledonia, Fiji, and Samoa.

On 11 March, two days after the fall of Java, GEN Douglas MacArthur was ordered out of the Philippines by President Roosevelt. He slipped away from his command post on Corregidor in Manila Bay on a PT boat and made his way to the southern Philippines. From there he flew to Australia to take command of the defense of that nation. As he left the Philippines, he promised the Filipinos, in his now-famous words, "I shall return." In April and May the last Filipino and American defenders of the Philippines were overrun on Bataan Peninsula and Corregidor. The survivors suffered every form of human brutality as they were forced on an eighty-mile "Death March" up the Bataan Peninsula to their prison camps.

The Japanese Defense Perimeter

The Japanese had now established their defense perimeter. Anchored by Rangoon in the Indian Ocean area, it included all of the Dutch East Indies and northern New Guinea on the south, extending to include Rabaul on New Britain and Kavieng on nearby New Ireland in the southwest. It then crossed the Pacific northward to newly captured Wake, Guam, and the British Gilbert Islands. On the northern flank Japan was protected by bases in the Kurile Islands. Japan had also improved its many bases in the islands acquired from Germany during World War I—the Carolines, Marshalls, and Marianas. Japan

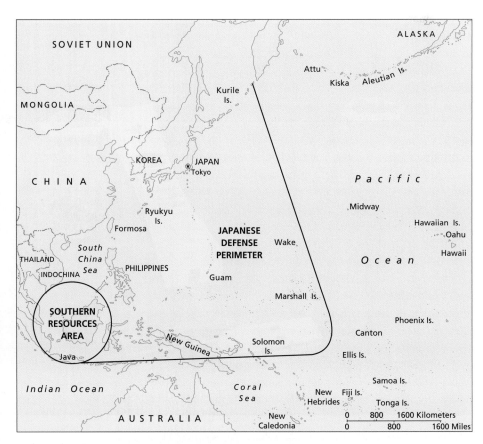

The Pacific theater, World War II, showing the Japanese defense perimeter.

made Truk in the Carolines into its "Pearl Harbor" of the central Pacific and developed Rabaul into a major forward base for further expansion southwestward.

Only on the central perimeter, near Midway Island, did a gap exist. The commander in chief of the Japanese navy, ADM Isoroku Yamamoto, who had planned the attack on Pearl Harbor, wanted to seal this gap with an assault on Midway, but the Japanese General Staff felt it was too risky. It was too far from the home islands and well within range of American bombers from Hawaii; if it were seized, it would be difficult and dangerous to maintain a garrison there and keep it resupplied.

U.S. Pacific War Plans

Because the primary focus of Britain at the time of the attack on Pearl Harbor was on resisting invasion while contesting the Axis powers for control of Europe and North Africa, and the Soviets had signed a nonaggression neutrality pact with Japan, it was soon acknowledged that the main burden of fighting the Japanese in the Pacific would fall to the United States. Into the confusion of successive defeats in the Pacific came the new commander in chief of the Pacific Fleet, ADM Chester W. Nimitz. He arrived at Pearl Harbor on Christmas Day and assumed command in a brief ceremony aboard a submarine on 31 December. It was up to him to win the biggest naval war the United States had ever faced. Nimitz was quiet and unruffled, inspiring confidence. There was no question who was running the show. Nimitz was to prove equal to the monumental task he had been assigned.

Admiral King's first instructions to Nimitz were clear: (1) cover and hold the Hawaii-Midway line and thereby maintain communications with the U.S. West Coast; and (2) maintain communications between the West Coast and Australia by holding a line drawn north to south from Dutch Harbor in the Aleutian Islands of Alaska, through Midway to Samoa, then southwest to New Caledonia and Port Moresby, New Guinea. Forces were to be sacrificed if necessary to delay any Japanese advances in the Dutch East Indies in order to hold that line of defense. Reinforcements would be sent to the Pacific if and when they became available. In the meantime, the United States was going to have to make a major effort in the Atlantic in order to keep the sea-lanes open to Britain and thwart the massive German threat facing the British and Soviets.

The fires had hardly been extinguished at Pearl Harbor in December 1941 before the U.S. Navy began to finalize both short- and long-term plans for the conduct of the war against the Japanese. The war in the Pacific was going to be primarily a naval war, and planning had already been done for the conduct of such a war. A contingency plan for an island-hopping campaign across the Pacific, called War Plan Orange, had been drawn up thirty years earlier by naval planners at the Naval War

ADM Chester Nimitz, with Admiral King, devised much of the Pacific war strategy. He personified the true meaning of the phrase "an officer and a gentleman." *The Naval History and Heritage Command*

College in Newport, Rhode Island. It had been much refined in the years since.

Given the orders to hold the line of defense across the mid-Pacific and to protect the sea-lanes to Australia, Admiral Nimitz knew his task would be a grim one for the first months while the small ABDA naval forces fought a delaying action in the Dutch East Indies. But after that, there was no question in his mind that the U.S. Navy would have to take the offensive.

Limited Offense Becomes the Best Defense

Admiral Nimitz knew that the Japanese were planning additional moves to the southwest. Unknown to the Japanese, not only their diplomatic but also their naval code had been broken by U.S. naval intelligence. Thus, on many crucial occasions throughout the war Japanese plans were known ahead of time. This allowed successful countermeasures to be planned and executed. Nimitz felt that he could best defend the sea-lanes to Australia by attacking Japanese bases in the central Pacific with carrier task forces, in a series of hit-and-run raids. This would cause much concern in the Japanese high command. Yamamoto himself was afraid that the Americans might even attempt a raid on Tokyo and endanger the emperor's life.

VADM William "Bull" Halsey was selected as the man to strike the Japanese bases. He was to conduct raids at widely separated locations so as to cause the Japanese the most anxiety. In the process Halsey hoped to make them believe that there were more U.S. naval forces in the region than they had thought existed. Back home, the press exaggerated the effects of the raids and greatly boosted American public morale, and so the raids achieved part of their purpose.

Then came an electrifying surprise U.S. attack on the Japanese home islands. In April 1942, Halsey's carrier striking force boldly sailed deep into Japanese waters with sixteen long-range Army B-25s lashed to the flight deck of the aircraft carrier

The Doolittle raid on Tokyo on 18 April 1942. B-25s are spotted on the deck of the USS *Hornet*. After the successful attack, when asked where the planes had come from, President Roosevelt said, "From Shangri-La," a mythical land of eternal youth in Tibet. Later in the war, a newly built U.S. carrier was given the name *Shangri-La* in memory of the attack.
The Naval History and Heritage Command

USS *Hornet*. The plan was to launch the bombers on a one-way mission to the Japanese home islands as soon as the force approached within maximum range. They would then continue on to land in China, since they would not have sufficient fuel to return to the carrier. On 18 April the planes, led by Army lieutenant colonel James Doolittle, each with a five-man volunteer crew, successfully took off when the *Hornet* had come within 660 miles of Japan. They made air raids on Tokyo, Nagoya, and Kobe. None of the B-25s were lost over Japan. Then, as planned, they flew on into China. There most of the crews crash-landed the planes or parachuted safely to ground in friendly territory, though some were captured in Japanese-controlled areas and executed. One plane made it to Vladivostok in the Soviet Union, where its crew was kept for a year before returning home.

The Japanese armed forces were stunned. Their boast that the sacred territory of the Land of the Rising Sun would never be attacked had been proved wrong. Yamamoto's previously disapproved plan to capture Midway in order to close the gap in the Japanese defense perimeter was now revived, and the attack was scheduled for June. Another Japanese move into the Coral Sea to cut the sea-lanes to Australia was put into action for early May. A third Japanese offensive, a two-pronged thrust into the Solomon Islands and toward Port Moresby in New Guinea, also was started. Nimitz, aware of these intentions through decoding of Japanese messages, planned his own actions carefully.

Battle of the Coral Sea

To stop the Japanese moves toward the Solomons, Nimitz directed his carrier task groups to converge on the Coral Sea. In mid-April he sent the carrier *Lexington* and her group to join RADM Frank Jack Fletcher's *Yorktown* carrier group already operating in the Coral Sea. At month's end he ordered Admiral Halsey, who had just returned to Pearl Harbor with the *Enterprise* and *Hornet* after the Doolittle raid, to make best speed to the area with those two carriers. Halsey, however, would not complete the 3,500-mile transit in time to participate in the inevitable battle.

During the first week in May the *Yorktown*, now joined by the *Lexington*, had several uneventful skirmishes with Japanese forces in the Coral Sea area, following which Fletcher assumed tactical command of both carriers. On 7 May planes from Fletcher's carriers found the Japanese carrier *Shoho* en route to cover an invasion force at Port Moresby and sank her with thirteen bomb and seven torpedo hits.

A restored B-25 like those flown in the Doolittle raid of 1942 takes off from the deck of the USS *Ranger* (CV 61) in 1992. *CHINFO, Terry Mitchell*

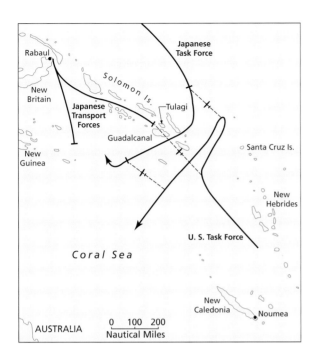

The carrier *Lexington* was struck by two torpedoes launched by attacking Japanese planes during the Battle of the Coral Sea and had to be abandoned and later sunk. *The Naval History and Heritage Command*

The Battle of the Coral Sea. This was the world's first all-carrier air and sea battle. It turned back the Japanese advance into the South Pacific for the first time in the Pacific War, and kept open the supply route to Australia.

On 8 May the climactic action in the Battle of the Coral Sea was fought when the Japanese carriers *Zuikaku* and *Shokaku* and the two American carriers found each other and launched air strikes nearly simultaneously. It would be the first great combat between carrier forces, with neither fleet ever coming in sight of the other.

The waves of attacking American aircraft and their Japanese counterparts hit the two opposing task groups at almost the same time. The Japanese carrier *Shokaku* was severely damaged, and both American carriers were hit. The *Lexington* was struck by two torpedoes, which ruptured her fuel lines and caused major explosions; the carrier had to be abandoned and was later sunk by one of her own escorting destroyers. The *Yorktown,* hit by one bomb and several near misses, limped away and started back to Pearl Harbor for repairs. Halsey, arriving too late for the battle, followed back a few days later with the *Enterprise* and *Hornet.*

The Battle of the Coral Sea turned back the Japanese advance for the first time in the Pacific War. Even though the American losses were somewhat greater, the strategic victory was clearly on the side of the United States. While only one Japanese carrier had been sunk, another had been damaged, and the third had lost so many aviators it was kept out of the subsequent Midway operation. Nagumo's Midway strike force would be short three carriers for the major action of Yamamoto's grand plan.

Battle of Midway

As mentioned earlier, in the early days of the Pacific War following the attack on Pearl Harbor the Japanese General Staff would not approve ADM Yamamoto's desired attack on Midway Island. But the successful and shocking Doolittle raid on the home islands in April changed that. Yamamoto soon convinced them that an attack at Midway was necessary, both to prevent another such raid and also to draw out the remaining American carriers so he could engage and hopefully sink them. This would force the Allies to stop fighting and negotiate a peace treaty favorable to Japan.

On 27 May 1942 the Japanese Combined Fleet set out from the Inland Sea toward Midway with the mission of destroying the remaining U.S. carrier fleet, in order to complete the unfinished business left over from the attack on Pearl Harbor six months before. Yamamoto's Combined Fleet had immense numerical superiority over the American forces in the Pacific. The Combined Fleet was a huge armada of eleven battleships, eight carriers, twenty-three cruisers, and sixty-five destroyers. It was pitted against Nimitz's small Pacific defensive force of three carriers, eight cruisers, and fourteen destroyers. But Yamamoto devised a curious battle plan that split his forces into four separate groups, spread all the way from the Aleutian Islands off Alaska to Midway, in an attempt to trap the unsuspecting U.S. fleet and replicate the World War I Battle of Jutland. The key to the impending action, however, was U.S. intelligence. Nimitz had deduced all the major movements in the Japanese plan through radio intercepts and code breaking. The Americans were not going to be surprised—much to the astonishment of the Japanese.

Yamamoto deployed his forces into three groups that would strike against Midway, and a fourth group, called the Japanese Northern Area Fleet, that would conduct simultaneous attacks against Dutch Harbor, Adak, Kiska, and Attu in the Aleutian Islands chain off Alaska. Most historians consider the Aleutian Islands actions to have been a diversion intended to draw defending forces away from Midway, but others point out that the Japanese also reasoned that conquest of the Aleutian Island chain would block any Allied advance on Japan across the northern Pacific.

The three groups proceeding against Midway consisted of a four-carrier strike force under Admiral Nagumo; an occupation force consisting of a light carrier, several battleships, troopships, cruisers and destroyers; and several hundred miles to the rear, a so-called main body, a powerful battleship force including the 64,000-ton superbattleship *Yamato,* on board which Yamamoto was embarked for the battle. By late May Nimitz had deduced from intelligence the timing of Yamamoto's planned attack. He ordered Admiral Fletcher with the *Yorktown* and ADM Raymond Spruance, who had relieved Halsey upon his return from the Coral Sea area, to proceed with the *Enterprise* and *Hornet* from Pearl Harbor to Midway to engage the Japanese invasion force. They arrived on 2 June, whereupon Admiral Fletcher took tactical command of all three carriers.

The first action took place the next day in the Aleutians, with several mostly ineffective bombing raids on Dutch Harbor by planes from the Japanese Northern Fleet carriers. The rest

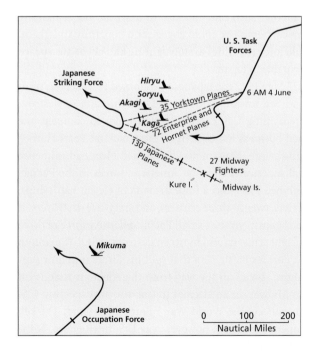

The Battle of Midway. This battle was the turning point of the Pacific War. The Japanese lost four carriers, plus the best of their carrier pilots.

of the northern Japanese force proceeded to attack unoccupied Adak Island, followed by amphibious assaults on undefended Kiska and Attu on 6 and 7 June. The Japanese would occupy both for a year, until they were eventually recaptured by American and Canadian forces.

At about the same time as the Japanese raid on Dutch Harbor, a scout plane ranging some seven hundred miles to sea from Midway alerted the defenders there to the approach of Yamamoto's occupation force. Midway planes attacked that force later that day and night but caused little damage. Fletcher drew his carriers in to within two hundred miles of Midway to await Nagumo's carrier force.

At dawn on 4 June Nagumo launched his first attack of 108 bombers and Zero fighters against Midway, with an equal number held in reserve. Catalina patrol planes reported the approaching Japanese aircraft and the location of the carrier force that had launched them. Fletcher ordered Spruance to advance toward the enemy carriers and attack them with planes from the *Enterprise* and *Hornet,* while the *Yorktown* recovered some search planes launched earlier.

Meanwhile, all available aircraft on Midway took off to engage the approaching enemy. Bombers and torpedo planes headed for the carriers, while fighters intercepted the approaching Japanese air strike. The American fighters proved to be no match for the agile Zeros and were quickly shot down. The Japanese bombers proceeded to Midway and set fire to hangars and blew up buildings but did not damage the runways there.

Nagumo now was faced with several hours of fast action and difficult decisions. His carriers were successively attacked by five waves of torpedo planes and bombers from Midway, none of which scored a hit and almost all of which were shot down. Then an American submarine penetrated his formation and fired torpedoes, all of which missed. Finally, the Japanese aircraft flying back from the Midway strike radioed that another attack was needed to destroy the runways.

At this point Nagumo received word of the American carrier task force from a scout plane. He changed course to approach it and directed that the contact-detonating bombs that were being loaded on his reserve aircraft for the second Midway strike be replaced with armor-piercing bombs and torpedoes for an attack on the U.S. carrier force. The off-loaded bombs were left lying on deck until they could be returned to their magazines. At the same time, the Japanese planes returning from Midway appeared overhead, and Nagumo ordered that they be recovered before launching his attack on the American carriers. He reported his intentions to Admiral Yamamoto, in his battleship group 450 miles to the rear.

Nagumo's force was now attacked by three low and slow waves of torpedo planes from the American carriers, all of which were shot down in flames before they could score a hit by Japanese Zeros flying cover. Their sacrifice would not be in

A Navy TBD Devastator torpedo bomber launches a torpedo against a Japanese carrier during the Battle of Midway. *The Naval History and Heritage Command*

vain, however. Nagumo had now turned back eight attacks in three hours without a scratch. But his luck had run out. About to launch their counterattack, the four Japanese carriers turned into the wind. Suddenly, a wave of dive-bombers from the *Enterprise* and *Yorktown* that by great good fortune had just found Nagumo's carriers came screaming down from 15,000 feet on a dive-bombing attack. They met almost no resistance from the Japanese Zeros, which had been pulled down to meet the low-level torpedo attacks.

The Americans caught the Japanese carriers with planes on their flight decks about to take off, other planes refueling, and the off-loaded bombs lying around. American bombs hit the carriers *Soryu, Kaga,* and *Akagi* and turned them into flaming torches in minutes. All three would sink during the night. Only the carrier *Hiryu,* farther north, escaped this attack. Her dive-bombers and torpedo planes followed the *Yorktown*'s planes back and crippled the U.S. carrier with three bomb hits. Additional hits by torpedo planes caused Fletcher to abandon his flagship and turn tactical command over to Admiral Spruance.

About the time the *Yorktown* was being abandoned, her search planes discovered the *Hiryu* and reported her location and course. A short time later another wave of dive-bombers from the *Enterprise* set the *Hiryu* on fire with four direct bomb hits. She would sink the next morning.

Yamamoto was now without aircraft carriers to protect his main body of heavy warships. A few hours after midnight on 5 June Yamamoto canceled the Midway operation rather than

The sinking carrier *Yorktown* lists heavily to port after being struck by torpedoes fired by a Japanese submarine during the final action of the Battle of Midway. *The Naval History and Heritage Command*

expose his unprotected surface forces to daylight dive-bombing attacks in the morning. He ordered his entire invasion force to retire to the west. Spruance spent most of the day trying to catch and attack them, but he was unsuccessful.

Meanwhile the four retiring occupation force cruisers came under attack by a U.S. submarine. In the process of dodging torpedoes, two of them, the *Mogami* and *Mikuma,* collided. On 6 June Spruance located the damaged ships and sank the *Mikuma.* The final action came later that day when the *Yorktown,* under tow after being abandoned, was torpedoed by a Japanese submarine. She sank the next day, along with an escorting destroyer that had been alongside.

The Battle of Midway was the turning point in the Pacific War. The Japanese loss of four carriers and a cruiser was compounded by the loss of their best carrier pilots. This loss of pilots would be one of the chief causes of Japan's ultimate defeat at sea. The Japanese would never be able to launch another major offensive. From that point on, the best they could hope for was a military stalemate that would allow them to hold on to their remaining conquests in the western Pacific.

The Battles for Guadalcanal

After the defeat of the Japanese at Midway, both Admiral Nimitz and General MacArthur believed that the time was ripe to start an Allied counteroffensive while the enemy was still off balance. For the Japanese, this meant building an airfield on the island of Guadalcanal so its aircraft could be used to cover their flank while they completed the conquest of New Guinea. For the Allies (primarily Americans), it meant launching an operation to lessen the Japanese threat to the Australian sea-lanes, protecting Port Moresby on New Guinea, and establishing an advanced base from which to strike Rabaul. All the earlier planning incorporated in War Plan Orange had been focused upon recapturing the Philippines, if lost, by a drive across the central Pacific. However, the Japanese threat to the sea lines of communication with Australia diverted much of the Allied effort to the south.

When in July 1942 cryptologists provided intelligence that the Japanese were about to construct an airfield on Guadalcanal, that island became the focal point of a series of naval actions and battles and a prolonged struggle between U.S. Marines and Japanese ground forces. Japanese long-range bombers operating from such an airfield would be a serious threat to the sea lines of communication between the U.S. West Coast and Australia, whereas under Allied control it could be used to support subsequent operations against Japanese island bases throughout the region.

On 7 August a large force of Marines landed at Guadalcanal and on nearby Tulagi Island, covered by three carriers and a surface force of cruisers and destroyers. Opposition on the ground at Guadalcanal was light, because most of the Japanese on the island at the time were construction workers. By the next day the Marines captured the unfinished airstrip and set up a defensive perimeter around it. During the day Japanese aircraft from Rabaul began attacking the unloading amphibious ships in the sound north of Guadalcanal but were driven off by planes from the American carriers.

That night the Japanese attacked the landing force with a strong force of cruisers that came down the passage, called "the Slot," between the major Solomon Islands and extending from Rabaul to Savo Island, north of Guadalcanal. In the resulting **Battle of Savo Island** between the Japanese cruisers and Allied warships covering the amphibious ships, the Allies lost four heavy cruisers. This was to be the first of many such attacks and Japanese attempts to ferry troops to counterattack the Marines on the island. The sound north of Guadalcanal used by the Allied amphibious force staging the landings would become known as "Ironbottom Sound," because of the many ships that would be sunk there during the campaign.

By 20 August the Marines and Seabees had the airstrip, which they called Henderson Field, completed and in operation, and the first planes were flying sorties and bringing in supplies.

When the Japanese learned that the Americans were making the airfield on Guadalcanal operational, they realized that they had to try to recapture it. They began pouring troops onto the island at night, bringing them down the Slot by fast transports and destroyers with such regularity that the Marines called the reinforcing enemy ships the "Tokyo Express." In response more Marines were sent to the island, so that by

The mud and heat of the jungles of Guadalcanal made fighting there a terrible ordeal. U.S. forces had to fight not only the enemy but also the disease and discomfort of the jungle. *The Naval History and Heritage Command*

mid-October there were about 23,000 Marines facing a total of about 22,000 Japanese troops. Meanwhile, a large Japanese fleet of carriers, battleships, and cruisers was hovering to the north, preparing to launch planes to the airfield as soon as their troops captured it.

Night naval battles and bombardments by the Japanese fleet and aircraft wreaked havoc on American forces. But the Marines on the island held, and they inflicted ten casualties for each of their own men lost. In August and September, Fletcher lost two of his carriers when they were torpedoed by Japanese submarines; the *Wasp* was sunk, and the *Saratoga* was badly damaged. Afterward Admiral Nimitz replaced Fletcher as commander of the remaining carriers with Admiral Halsey, who was soon thereafter promoted to commander of the entire South Pacific area of operations. Then, in the nearby Battle of the Santa Cruz Islands on 24 October, Admiral Halsey gambled his last two carriers against the Japanese fleet and lost. The *Hornet* was sunk and the *Enterprise* heavily damaged, leaving no operational U.S. carriers in the Pacific.

Additional Marines continued to arrive on the island; they numbered some 50,000 by February 1943. They continued their hard-fought advance, pushing the Japanese into the jungle interior. Finally, the Japanese concluded that Guadalcanal would have to be abandoned. On 9 February 12,000 half-starved Japanese survivors slipped out of the jungle and made an escape on fast destroyers. Guadalcanal was secured. Whereas after the Battle of Midway it became clear that the Japanese could not win the war, after the successful battles for Guadalcanal it became increasingly apparent that the United States and its allies would.

Strategy of 1943–44: Continuous Pressure

A consolidation and planning period took place following the success on Guadalcanal and other successes on New Guinea. Events in Europe dictated that it would be mainly up to U.S. forces, assisted when possible by some from Australian and New Zealand, to prosecute the rest of the war in the Pacific. At the Casablanca Conference in January 1943, it was decided to proceed through the remaining Solomon Islands toward the giant Japanese base at Rabaul. The program put into effect for the rest of 1943 and early 1944 called for the elimination of the Japanese outposts in the Aleutians; intensified submarine attacks on the Japanese lines of communication from the Dutch East Indies; and the isolation of Rabaul, by MacArthur's forces assisted by South Pacific naval forces. A two-pronged advance across the Pacific would follow, with the objective of reaching the **Luzon** (northern Philippines)–**Formosa**–**China coast geographic triangle** by late 1944. From there, attacks against the Japanese home islands could be launched.

One line of advance would proceed across the central Pacific by way of the Gilberts, Marshalls, Marianas, Carolines,

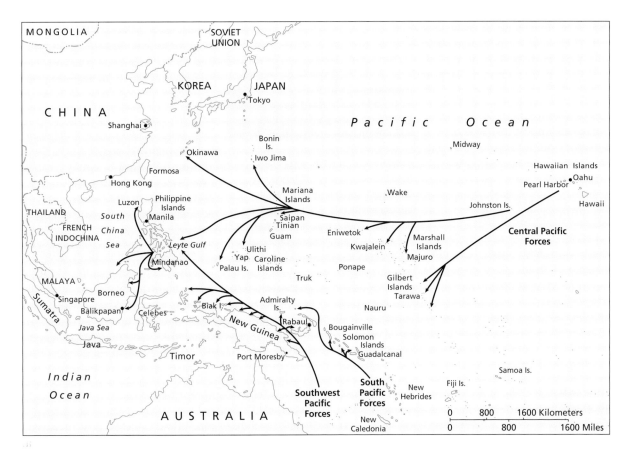

The planned lines of advance across the Pacific in 1943–44.

and Palaus toward the northern Philippines or Formosa, using naval forces commanded by Nimitz. The other line of advance would be across the Southwest Pacific via the north coast of New Guinea to the southern Philippines, using combined U.S. and Allied forces under the overall command of MacArthur.

The reconquest of Attu and Kiska in the Aleutian Islands took place over the summer months of 1943. By August the Aleutians had been fully returned to American control, and they were never again threatened by the Japanese. Though some thought was given to establishing a third line of advance across the North Pacific via these islands, the Joint Chiefs finally decided that the foggy, cold North Pacific, with its rocky islands, was not suitable for such a major offensive.

In an effort to boost Japanese morale, on 18 April 1943 Admiral Yamamoto and his staff had set out on an inspection trip to Japanese bases in the Solomons. Because coded messages that outlined his itinerary had been broken by U.S. naval intelligence, American long-range fighters from Henderson Field were able to intercept his plane over Ballale Island, near Bougainville, and shoot it down, killing Yamamoto. This was a major blow for the Japanese, for they had lost their most able commander. For the next twelve months, until March 1944, the campaign against Rabaul progressed on two fronts—through

the Solomons and on New Guinea. During this time the U.S. fleet fought some forty-five major naval battles and conducted seventeen invasions in the Solomons and the southwest Pacific. Successful campaigns by MacArthur on eastern New Guinea were made possible by the Solomons operations, and by March 1944 Rabaul had been encircled and bypassed, isolating 90,000

A Hellcat fighter after a bad landing aboard a U.S. carrier during the Pacific War. *The Naval History and Heritage Command*

Japanese troops without hope of resupply or escape. It became a backwater as the war progressed westward along the northern New Guinea coast and northward toward the Philippines. MacArthur made rapid progress leapfrogging along the northern New Guinea coast, and by the end of July he had secured most of the island.

By early 1944 several new carriers had joined the Pacific fleet; these became known as the **Fast Carrier Task Force,** under the command of ADM Mark Mitscher. Designated Task Force 58 when a part of ADM Raymond Spruance's Fifth Fleet, it would be redesignated Task Force 38 whenever it operated as part of ADM William "Bull" Halsey's Third Fleet. It would be the main striking force in the central and western Pacific until the war's end in 1945.

The Submarine War in the Pacific

The submarine war in the Pacific was in many ways a mirror image of the Battle of the Atlantic. In the Atlantic it was the goal of German U-boats to interdict Allied shipping in order to strangle Britain, but in the Pacific the roles were reversed; it was the American submarines that attempted to gain a stranglehold against Japanese shipping. In this endeavor they were aided somewhat by the Pacific geography—shipping lanes to Japan from their sources of supply in Malaya, Borneo, Sumatra, and Java often passed through narrow straits between islands. This made interdiction easier for American submarines than for their German counterparts in the Atlantic. To build up their numbers, submarines were mass-produced during the war by American shipyards, just as escort destroyers and Liberty and Victory merchant ships were. For the Pacific, specially designed big submarines, nearly twice the size of German U-boats, were developed to carry greater fuel and torpedo loads for extended long-distance patrols against the Japanese.

The Japanese, on the other hand, never placed much emphasis on their submarine fleet. Their subs mainly targeted warships rather than auxiliary and merchant shipping. They generally underestimated the potential of the submarine throughout the war. This philosophy had been reinforced by the poor showing of their submarines at Pearl Harbor and during the following early months of the war. Though they had some successes, including about ten merchant ships sunk off the U.S. West Coast, they were insignificant compared to those of the U.S. submarines in the Pacific War.

Interestingly, however, the only direct Japanese military attacks on the U.S. mainland during World War II were made by Japanese submarines. In February 1942 the Japanese sub-

A Japanese float plane is catapulted from the deck of the submarine *I-25* off Oregon to launch one of the three attacks on the U.S. mainland made by Japanese naval forces in World War II. *The Naval History and Heritage Command*

marine *I-17* surfaced near Santa Barbara, California, and shelled an oil refinery with its 5.5-inch deck gun. The only damage was to a pump house and oil well. In June the submarine *I-25* surfaced in the mouth of the Columbia River in Oregon near midnight one evening and fired seventeen shells from its deck gun at an old Civil War–era fort, hitting only a nearby empty baseball field. In September of that year the same submarine surfaced off the Oregon coast and launched a small floatplane that managed to release two incendiary bombs into the forest near Brookings, Oregon, in an attempt to start a forest fire. The attempt was unsuccessful because of recent rains. Following the attack, the plane returned to the submarine, which submerged and sailed away. (Fifty years later its Japanese pilot, who survived the war, returned to Brookings and presented his sword to the townspeople.)

From late 1944 until early 1945 the Japanese also attempted to attack the U.S. and Canadian mainland by launching some nine thousand **"wind ship weapons,"** consisting of hydrogen-filled rubberized-silk and later paper balloons that carried small incendiary and antipersonnel bombs. They were released from the Japanese home island of Honshu into the jet stream, which carried them across the Pacific. Around nine hundred of these made it to the United States, and some reached as far east as Michigan. The only known casualties resulting from these balloon bombs were six civilians (five children and a pregnant woman) on a picnic in Oregon.

Making the situation worse for the Japanese was the fact that their antisubmarine operations were never very successful either. Because of a general lack of escort ships, the Japanese

A Japanese merchant ship heads for the bottom after being torpedoed by a U.S. submarine during the Pacific War. This photo was taken through the periscope of the successful attacker. *The Naval History and Heritage Command*

were never able to adopt the convoy techniques that were so successful in the Atlantic against the German U-boats, and they never developed radar. Consequently, by mid-1943 Japanese merchant shipping losses to submarine attacks were very heavy. Essential raw materials could no longer be delivered from the southern resources areas to support the Japanese war industry or military forces.

Altogether in the Pacific War, U.S. submarines sank over 1,100 merchant vessels, totaling over five million tons. In addition, American submarines sank some two hundred naval warships and auxiliary ships. The submarine was in many ways the naval weapon that won the war for the United States and its allies in the Pacific.

Saipan

June 1944 found U.S. forces engaged in arguably the greatest military effort in history. At the very time the Normandy landings were taking place in Europe, the United States was about to send a huge amphibious force against Saipan in the central Pacific. The mammoth task of projecting 127,000 troops on 535 ships some three thousand miles from Pearl Harbor and providing them with fast carrier task force support against the entire Japanese Fleet was just as complex as the D-day invasion in Europe.

Following air strikes by U.S. Army planes from newly won bases in the Marshalls and Navy carrier planes, as well as bombardment by Fifth Fleet battleships, the landings began on 15 June. Heavy casualties were sustained, but by the end of the day 20,000 Marines were ashore. By 17 June the American offensive had captured the main airfield and had begun to push the Japanese back.

Battle of the Philippine Sea

After the devastating losses at Midway and in the Solomons Islands campaign that followed, a new Japanese Mobile Fleet had been formed from the decimated Combined Fleet, under the operational command of ADM Jisaburo Ozawa. In mid-June 1944 Ozawa with his fleet was approaching Saipan from the west in the Philippine Sea, with orders both to attack the American invasion force at Saipan and to engage in a climactic battle with Task Force 58 and other units of the U.S. fleet covering the invasion there. The Japanese thought victory in such a battle might return to Japan the initiative in the western Pacific, which had been lost at Midway two years before and give them a good chance to win the war.

Even though Ozawa correctly estimated that task Force 58, with its fifteen carriers, seven battleships, and numerous escort ships, was twice as strong as his own force of nine carriers and five battleships, he thought he would have several advantages in the forthcoming action. The easterly trade winds would enable him to conduct flight operations while advancing, while the American carriers would have to reverse course to the east each time; his planes were unarmored and lighter, giving them a striking radius of three hundred miles, as opposed to two hundred for the American carrier aircraft; and he expected Japanese aircraft based on the nearby islands of Rota and Guam to attack the Americans first, greatly reducing Task Force 58's superiority in numbers before the Mobile Fleet went into action. He intended to stand off beyond the range of the American planes and shuttle-bomb the American carriers to destruction with multiple attacks by crisscrossing planes from his carriers and the island bases. However, unbeknownst to Ozawa his force had been detected and was being shadowed by American submarines, who were keeping Admiral Spruance, the Fifth Fleet commander, appraised of Ozawa's movements. On 18 June, Spruance ordered Admiral Mitscher and his Task Force 58 to steam out between the approaching enemy and the landing forces on the island. But Mitscher's search planes found nothing, and Spruance, always mindful of his primary orders—"Capture, occupy, and defend Saipan, Tinian, and Guam"—ordered Mitscher to return to shield the beachhead.

Ozawa's main body had three large carriers and three smaller ones surrounded by cruisers and destroyers in two circular formations. One hundred miles ahead of the main body was VADM Takeo Kurita, with a force of battleships, cruisers, and three light carriers to act as bait to draw out the American forces and to provide antiaircraft protection for the main body. From Japan, Admiral Soemu Toyoda, commander in chief of the Japanese navy, radioed Ozawa that "the fate of the Empire depends on the issue of this battle; let every man do his utmost!"

As previously mentioned, Ozawa had counted heavily on getting air support from nearby Japanese air bases in the Marianas. But unfortunately for Ozawa, he did not know that only thirty operational planes remained on damaged airfields after devastating Allied raids on these bases on 11 and 12 June, or that many of his pilots had returned from recent operations against MacArthur from the island of Biak sick with malaria. Not aware that the odds were heavily against him because of these factors, he moved to close with Task Force 58.

Early on the morning of 19 June a Zero from Guam detected Task Force 58, and soon a number of planes from Japanese bases on Guam and other nearby islands were on their way to attack it. They were spotted on radar, however, and intercepted by F6F Hellcats launched from Mitscher's carriers while still some distance away, near Guam. A fierce air battle ensued, during which thirty-five Japanese planes were shot down. At 1000 American radar detected another large swarm of enemy planes approaching, this time from the enemy carriers, and soon all available TF 58 carrier aircraft were launched to meet the new threat. Several additional raids were intercepted as the day progressed. Nearly all the attacking planes were shot down before they could get close enough to TF 58 to do harm, and the remainder either failed to inflict significant damage or retired to the Japanese carriers.

In eight hours of furious air warfare that day, a total of 350 Japanese planes were shot down in what came to be called the "Marianas Turkey Shoot." At the same time, two American submarines slipped through the screening ships of Ozawa's main body and fired torpedoes at two carriers. The *Albacore* torpedoed Ozawa's new carrier flagship *Taiho,* and the *Cavalla* put three torpedoes into the carrier *Shokaku*. Both carriers exploded a few hours later, with great loss of life. But Ozawa and his staff survived and transferred to the carrier *Zuikaku*.

Ozawa ordered a general retirement to refuel, intending to resume battle the next day—even though he had only a hundred carrier planes left. He believed erroneous reports from his surviving pilots that TF 58 had been crippled. Mitscher's scout planes searched for Ozawa's ships the next morning but found nothing. Then late in the afternoon a scout plane found the Japanese and reported their position. Mitscher immediately changed course toward them and launched his planes for an attack when he thought they were just within maximum operating range. Unfortunately, they turned out to be sixty miles farther away than reported.

Just before sunset the Americans found the Japanese force and attacked it, sinking two oilers and a carrier and damaging two other carriers, a battleship, and a cruiser. Ozawa managed to get seventy-five of his fighters into the air. Only ten survived, and the crippled Mobile Fleet sailed away with only thirty-five planes and three undamaged carriers left. Japanese naval air capability had been destroyed, and the Marianas invasion was able to continue, opposed only by the Japanese garrisons on the islands.

As evening fell after the final engagement of the battle, Admiral Mitscher daringly ordered all the landing lights on his carriers and searchlights on the escort ships turned on to assist the returning pilots. Still, many planes were lost. They had to ditch in the sea, out of fuel. But of 209 aviators who had engaged the enemy that day, all but forty-nine were recovered, either on the flight decks or from the water by destroyers and floatplanes. Fortunately, none of the lit-up carriers fell prey to Japanese submarines known to be lurking in the area.

With the Mobile Force defeated and out of the area, TF 58 was able to concentrate on providing full assistance to the

The Battle of the Philippine Sea, sometimes called the "Marianas Turkey Shoot." A Japanese bomber plunges toward the sea after being hit by antiaircraft fire during the battle. *The Naval History and Heritage Command*

invading forces on Saipan and subsequent invasions of Tinian and Guam. Now sustained shore bombardment could be brought to bear before the troops landed, greatly reducing American casualties. Both Saipan and Tinian were secured by the end of July, and organized resistance had ceased on Guam by 10 August.

Japan had lost its direct air route into the Carolines. The United States had acquired logistic bases for additional steps toward the Philippines, advance submarine bases for attacks on Japanese communications and sea-lanes to the Indies, and air bases from which new long-range B-29s would soon be bombing the industrial cities of Japan.

Return to the Philippines

The next series of invasion plans had yet to be decided when Spruance and other senior naval commanders returned to Pearl Harbor to rest and plan their future operations. The Fifth Fleet was redesignated the U.S. Third Fleet, under the command of Admiral Halsey, with Vice Admiral Mitscher remaining in command of the Fast Carrier Task Force, now redesignated Task Force 38.

In its two drives across the Pacific, in seven months MacArthur's forces had moved nearly 1,500 miles from the Admiralties to the island of Morotai. In ten months Nimitz's forces had advanced over 4,500 miles from Hawaii to the Palaus. The time had now arrived to make a final choice of the next objective.

Convinced that the central Philippines were weakly defended, Halsey sent Nimitz an urgent message recommending that the Palaus and Yap be bypassed and that ground forces intended for these operations instead be turned over to MacArthur for an invasion of Leyte Island in the central Philippines. The Joint Chiefs concurred and directed Nimitz and MacArthur to combine forces for the invasion of Leyte on 20 October and then Luzon in December, after securing Morotai and Peleliu in the Palau Islands. Nimitz would then invade Iwo Jima and Okinawa early in 1945.

Morotai was captured in one of the easiest conquests of the war, but in overcoming Peleliu's defenses the Marines incurred the highest combat casualty rate (40 percent) of any amphibious assault in American history. The Japanese had put a new strategy into effect, one of **defense in depth**. Rather than expend most of their efforts trying to repel the invaders at the beaches, the defenders had prepared defensive positions well behind the beaches, taking full advantage of the natural terrain. Hardened fortifications were constructed, and there were no more useless banzai bayonet charges. The Marines landed on 17 September and quickly captured the airfield, but after that progress was costly and slow. It was not until February 1945 that the island was cleared of Japanese defenders. By that time the Marines had suffered ten thousand casualties, including nearly two thousand dead.

Long before February, however, the other airfields and anchorages in the Palaus had been brought under American control. Had they remained in Japanese hands, they would have been a threat to the Leyte invasion and later operations in Luzon.

The Invasions of Leyte and Luzon

The stage was now set for the invasion of Leyte. More than 60,000 assault troops landed on Leyte by sunset on D-day, 20 October. From then on it was a tough fight in the interior of the island. General MacArthur waded ashore a few hours after the first landing, accompanied by President Sergio Osmena of the Philippines, thus fulfilling his promise made two years before that he would return.

By late December MacArthur's Sixth Army had secured the most important sections of the island, but Japanese troops in the mountains would continue organized resistance well into the summer of 1945. While the fighting for Leyte continued, MacArthur's forces moved on to Luzon only slightly behind schedule. In mid-December two Army regiments captured an air base in southwestern Mindoro, 150 miles south of Manila. The invasion of Luzon itself started on 9 January 1945, when four Army divisions landed along the shores of Lingayen Gulf. By then the Japanese navy was incapable of any serious opposition, because most of its remaining naval forces in the area had been wiped

out in the Leyte Gulf by Allied forces supporting the Leyte landings in October. Their most significant reaction was the first use of kamikaze suicide plane attacks against Admiral Thomas Kinkaid's supporting naval forces and Mitscher's Fast Carrier Force, once again redesignated Task Force 58. (The word kamikaze means "divine wind." This referred to a typhoon that reputedly saved Japan in 1281 by destroying a Mongol fleet that was sailing to invade the home islands.) Army units reached Manila on 3 February, and after six weeks of bitter building-to-building fighting, by mid-March Manila Bay was open for Allied shipping. Organized Japanese resistance ended by late June 1945.

Iwo Jima

The conquest of the Marianas had provided bases from which the large Army B-29 bombers could make devastating air raids on the Japanese industrial cities. But between the Marianas and Japan was the volcanic island of Iwo Jima. As long as the Japanese held the island, the Japanese home island defenses would be alerted when bombers were en route, and fighters would be scrambled to intercept them.

The three-thousand-mile round trip was much too long for Allied fighters to accompany and defend the bombers. Damaged bombers were often lost in the sea on the return trip because they consumed too much fuel to fly that distance. The Americans determined to put an end to this dangerous situation. In U.S. hands the island's airfields could be improved to handle emergency landings for the big bombers and to provide a base for fighter planes to escort them over Japan.

D-day at Iwo Jima was set for 19 February 1945. Despite the three-day naval bombardment and covering fire during the

GEN Douglas MacArthur, fulfilling his promise to return to the Philippines, wades ashore at Leyte on 20 October, accompanied by Philippine president Sergio Osmena. *The Naval History and Heritage Command*

Some of the more than five hundred amphibious craft en route to the assault beaches at Iwo Jima. Mount Suribachi looms in the background. *The Naval History and Heritage Command*

Marines coming ashore during the landings at Iwo Jima. Note the battleships in the background providing fire support. *The Naval History and Heritage Command*

The famous photograph of U.S. troops raising the flag atop Mount Suribachi taken by Joe Rosenthal in the midst of the successful assault on Iwo Jima. The moment was later memorialized by a lifelike statue based on the photo, the Iwo Jima Monument near Arlington National Cemetery in Washington, D.C. *The Naval History and Heritage Command*

War correspondent/photographer Joe Rosenthal (left) during a moment of relaxation following the assault on Iwo Jima. *The Naval History and Heritage Command*

movement to the beachhead, the assault waves quickly piled up on the beach, because the amphibian tractors were unable to climb the crumbling volcanic ash. Many landing craft broached (turned sideways in the surf) or ran into earlier boat waves. The Marines, stranded on the steep beach, soon were hit by withering machine-gun, mortar, and heavy gunfire from weapons that had withheld their fire earlier so as not to reveal their positions. Through this holocaust the Marines inched forward, isolating Mount Suribachi and reaching the edge of the nearest airfield. Of 30,000 Marines who hit the beach that first day, 2,400 became casualties.

The fighting continued through the night, and the next day the airfield was captured. The assault on Mount Suribachi then began. After three days of blasting and burning out pillboxes and sealing up caves with grenades, flamethrowers, rockets, and demolition charges, the Marines surrounded the mountain, and a patrol reached the summit and raised the American flag. By good fortune, the flag-raising was photographed by a war correspondent. A sculpture later made from the iconic photo and placed near Arlington National Cemetery in Washington, D.C., immortalizes the moment and has provided inspiration ever since to the American people.

While the vicious fighting was in progress on Iwo Jima, the supporting naval forces of TF 58 and the amphibious support force were hit by numerous kamikaze attacks. The carrier *Saratoga* was badly damaged, and the escort carrier *Bismarck Sea* sank after a huge explosion blew off her stern.

Instead of taking five days as originally planned, the conquest of Iwo Jima took over a month. It was not until 25 March that the last Japanese troops made their final attack. When the fighting ended, only two hundred Japanese had been captured; all the rest were killed. For the first time casualties among the assault forces, however, exceeded those of the Japanese defenders. Over 19,000 Marines and sailors were wounded, and nearly seven thousand were killed. Admiral Nimitz said the Marines on Iwo Jima made "uncommon valor a common virtue."

Battle of Okinawa

The war was now closing in on the home islands of Japan. From the middle of February 1945, carrier aircraft began striking Japanese cities with high explosives and incendiaries. On 25 February, even before Iwo Jima was secured, fighters from TF 58 supported two hundred B-29s in a massive raid on Tokyo, burning out two square miles of the enemy capital and destroying 150 Japanese aircraft. Afterward, TF 58 steamed past Okinawa, bombing the island's airfields and taking intelligence photographs. The final gigantic amphibious assault and battle of the Pacific War was about to begin.

Weeks of heavy raids and softening-up attacks on Japanese bases on Kyushu and Okinawa preceded the assault on

An invasion beach at Okinawa. In the background, part of the huge invasion force is busy off-loading supplies to support the forces ashore. *The Naval History and Heritage Command*

A Japanese kamikaze suicide plane attacks the USS *Missouri* during the Okinawa landings. The plane caused only minor damage. Its dead pilot was buried at sea by the crew the next day. *The Naval History and Heritage Command*

the island. On 1 April a force of 1,300 ships carrying 182,000 assault troops arrived off the island, having come from bases all over the Pacific. Over 100,000 Japanese defenders awaited their attack from well-prepared positions, as on Iwo Jima and Peleliu. The Japanese troops on Okinawa knew that they were the last obstacle to an Allied invasion of their home islands. Many had pledged to fight to the death to prevent the island from falling.

Almost from the beginning, ships of the invasion fleet were subjected to fierce kamikaze attacks. On the morning of 6 April, the Japanese began their last major counterattack of the war. Over 350 Japanese kamikazes flew out of Kyushu to strike the fleet. Meanwhile, the last surviving Japanese surface force, made up of the superbattleship *Yamato,* the light cruiser *Yahagi,* and eight destroyers, sailed south from the Inland Sea, propelled by the last 2,500 tons of fuel oil in Japan. It was to be a one-way trip for both aircraft and ships. Since the ships did not have enough fuel to return, their mission was to drive through the invasion fleet, inflicting as much damage as possible, and then beach themselves at the invasion site, firing until all their ammunition was expended and they were destroyed.

En route to Okinawa the kamikazes sank several U.S. picket destroyers, but not before warnings had been radioed by the sinking ships. Met by combat air patrol fighters from TF 58, 150 of the planes were shot down. The remaining two hundred made it to the Okinawa area. There they were mostly destroyed by fighter planes and intense antiaircraft fire. Meanwhile, the *Yamato* force was allowed to proceed far enough southward so it would not be able to retreat to safety. Then Admiral Mitscher struck with the full force of his carrier aircraft. Only two destroyers survived the attack and made it back to base.

For the next three months the carrier task forces and other ships of the U.S. Third and Fifth Fleets suffered hundreds of kamikaze attacks as they supported the Okinawa invasion and thrust their power into the Japanese home islands. On 21 June 1945 Okinawa was declared secure after the defending Japanese general and his chief of staff acknowledged defeat by committing suicide. During the battle for the island the U.S. Navy had suffered the loss of sixty-eight ships and over four thousand sailors—more than either the Marines or the Army incurred in the hard going on the island.

But the U.S. Navy stayed, and Okinawa was secured. The battle had cost the Japanese 100,000 men and seven thousand airplanes. Okinawa was the end of the fighting for the Japanese. Emperor Hirohito told his Supreme War Council on 22 June that they must find a way to end the war. Fire-bombing raids were turning Japanese cities into ashes, and their navy and air force were gone. In April the Soviet Union had informed the Japanese that it would not renew the nonaggression pact. With Germany having surrendered in May, entrance of the Soviets into the Pacific War was imminent. Since the war in Europe was over, British armed forces were now able to play a much larger role in the final months of the Pacific campaign.

The Final Days

Bringing an end to the war was not easy, however. There were still powerful factions in the Japanese military forces that favored a fight to the bitter end. The Japanese people would never accept a surrender that did not preserve the emperor and imperial system. The Japanese made peace gestures to the Soviets during negotiations for extension of their nonaggression pact. But the Soviets remained silent—so silent that Stalin did not even tell the United States or Britain about the peace initiatives during their final wartime meeting in Potsdam, Germany, in late July.

However, the United States knew about the peace initiatives, because U.S. intelligence was reading the messages between the Foreign Ministry in Tokyo and the Japanese ambassador in Moscow. On 26 July the **Potsdam Declaration** spelled out the terms of surrender for Japan, specifying that unconditional

An Army B-29 Superfortress prepares to take off from the air base on Tinian Island for a raid against the Japanese home islands. Tinian, about four miles south of Saipan, was captured in late July 1944 after the invasion of Saipan. Soon the Seabees had built six 2,400-meter runways there for use by Army planes flying bombing missions against the remaining Japanese strongholds in the western Pacific. Similar planes from Tinian would later drop the atomic bombs on Hiroshima and Nagasaki. *The Naval History and Heritage Command*

The "Little Boy" atomic bomb dropped on Hiroshima on 6 August 1945. *The Naval History and Heritage Command*

surrender would pertain only to the military forces and that all possessions except the four home islands—Hokkaido, Honshu, Shikoku, and Kyushu—would have to be given up. No provisions concerning the emperor were made, since the Allies had not yet decided on that question. This omission caused much concern in Japan.

As the Soviets stalled and the Japanese procrastinated, the combined U.S. and British fleets, the most powerful ever assembled in history, ranged freely up and down the Japanese coast, shelling and fire-bombing the cities virtually at will. Meanwhile the Americans and British were in the later stages of planning for a massive invasion of the Japanese home islands, code-named **Operation Downfall**. Events were moving faster than these plans, however. On 16 July the United States successfully exploded the world's first atomic device at Alamogordo, New Mexico. Within hours several **atomic bombs** were en route to the Army B-29 bomber base at Tinian in the Marianas.

After a thorough assessment of the probable consequences of the planned invasion of Japan, with estimates of up to a million or more casualties on both sides, versus those anticipated from dropping an atomic bomb, President Harry Truman decided to use the A-bomb to try to end the war without the necessity of an invasion.

In the early morning of 6 August 1945 a B-29 Superfortress bomber, named the *Enola Gay* after the pilot's mother, took off from Tinian with an atomic bomb aboard and headed for Hiroshima, an industrial city on the Inland Sea. Six hours later, at

0815 Hiroshima time, the bomb was released over the target. Exploding with a blast equivalent to sixteen kilotons of TNT, it utterly destroyed the city. Despite the destruction at Hiroshima and the dropping of leaflets warning of the consequences of further delay, the Japanese military elements in the government refused to consider unconditional surrender. So on 9 August another U.S. aircraft dropped a second atomic bomb, on the industrial port of Nagasaki.

Meanwhile, the Soviets realized that the end was very near and that they had to get into the Pacific War immediately if they were to get in on the victory. Despite the fact that their non-aggression pact with Japan was still in effect, on 8 August the Soviet Union declared war on Japan and moved its forces into Manchuria and Korea, sweeping the Japanese occupation forces before them.

Faced with the ultimate destruction of Japan, Emperor Hirohito told his Supreme Council to accept the Potsdam Declaration. They agreed, but only on the condition that the imperial system remain. The U.S. Secretary of State, James Byrnes, speaking on behalf of the Allied governments, accepted the condition subject to stipulations that the emperor submit to the authority of the supreme allied commander during the occupation of Japan and that the Japanese people decide on the emperor's final status in free elections at a later date. The council, with the

Hiroshima, Japan, after the atomic bomb explosion. Only a few steel and concrete buildings remain standing. *The Naval History and Heritage Command*

The Japanese surrender delegation aboard the USS *Missouri* for the final ceremony that formally ended World War II. This was the first time the Japanese had surrendered to a foe in more than two thousand years. *The Naval History and Heritage Command*

concurrence of the emperor, agreed to these stipulations on 14 August. The next day, with another carrier raid already airborne over Tokyo, the Third Fleet received the order to "cease fire."

In the next two weeks the Allies converged on Tokyo Bay. On Sunday morning, 2 September 1945, the Japanese foreign minister and representatives of the Imperial General Staff boarded the battleship USS *Missouri* at anchor in Tokyo Bay and signed the surrender document on behalf of the emperor, the government, and the Imperial General Headquarters. GEN Douglas MacArthur signed the acceptance as supreme allied commander for the Allied powers. FADM Chester Nimitz signed as representative for the United States. Following him were representatives of the United Kingdom, China, the Soviet Union, Australia, Canada, France, the Netherlands, and New Zealand. Shortly thereafter, General MacArthur moved into his Tokyo headquarters to direct the occupation of Japan. World War II was over.

Critical Thinking

1. Research the main provisions of the contingency plan War Plan Orange first drawn up by naval planners in 1911. How were its provisions carried out during the war in the Pacific during World War II?

2. The admiral in charge of Pearl Harbor, ADM Husband Kimmel, was relieved of command and forced to retire after the sneak attack by the Japanese in December 1941. His descendants have tried to reverse this action ever since. Research the attack and form an opinion on whether the admiral should have been found culpable with regard to the attack. Justify your position.

3. Much intrigue surrounds the role that the Japanese minisubmarines played during the sneak attack on Pearl Harbor in December 1941. Research this issue and state the probable role of the midget submarines during this action.

4. Historians have often criticized Japanese admiral Yamamoto's deployment of his ships before the Battle of Midway. Discuss how he might have better deployed them and what the results of the battle might have been had he done so.

5. President Truman's decision to end World War II by the use of atomic weapons has been a contentious issue ever since. State the pros and cons of this decision and the consequences that resulted from it.

Chronology

1941	U.S. halts oil sales to Japan; Japan bombs Pearl Harbor
1942	MacArthur leaves Philippines; Doolittle raid on Japan; Battle of Coral Sea; Battle of Midway; Marines land on Guadalcanal
1943	Guadalcanal secured; Aleutians recaptured
1944	Rabaul bypassed; Battle of Philippine Sea; assault on Saipan; New Guinea secured; MacArthur invades Philippines; Battle for Leyte Gulf
1945	Iwo Jima landing; Battle of Okinawa; atomic bomb dropped on Hiroshima; Soviets declare war on Japan; Japan surrenders

Study Guide Questions

1. After the United States restricted the sale of oil to Japan in 1941, where was their only remaining possible source of supply?

2. What did the Japanese do to cause the United States to declare war on Japan?

3. A. What targets were successfully attacked by the Japanese at Pearl Harbor?
   B. What key land assets were missed?

4. What major miscalculations did the Japanese make about Pearl Harbor?

5. What were Nimitz's orders at the start of the Pacific War?

6. What was the name of the war plan for the Pacific War that had been developed and refined at the Naval War College?

7. What was the ABDA defense alliance?

8. What American general was ordered to leave the Philippines in March 1942?

9. Where was there a gap in the Japanese defense perimeter?

10. What were the Japanese hopes for the conduct of the war in 1942?

11. A. What was the Doolittle raid on Japan in April 1942?
    B. What change in Japanese war strategy did it cause?

12. A. What battle was the first great combat of the Pacific War between carrier forces?
    B. What was the result of the battle?

13. How did Nimitz know about Japanese intentions at the Battle of Midway?

14. Why is the Battle of Midway regarded as the turning point of the Pacific War?

15. On what island in the Solomons did the Japanese and Allied forces converge to determine the outcome in the southwestern Pacific?

16. Where were "Ironbottom Sound" and "the Slot" located?

17. What name was given by American personnel to the Japanese operations that attempted to reinforce Guadalcanal?

18. What was the fundamental difference between the submarine wars in the Atlantic and the Pacific?

19. What happened to the Japanese commander Admiral Yamamoto in April 1943?

20. What central Pacific island was the target of one of the greatest military efforts in history in June 1944?

21. What was the principal effect of the Japanese defeat in the Battle of the Philippine Sea?

22. What was the new Japanese defense strategy put into effect on Peleliu in late 1944?

23. When and where did General MacArthur make good on his promise to return to the Philippines?

24. A. What were the kamikazes?
    B. Where did they first appear?

25. Why was it necessary for Allied forces to secure Iwo Jima?

26. Why did the Japanese mount a fanatical defense of the island of Okinawa?

27. What three events in early August 1945 made it imperative for the Japanese to accept the Potsdam Declaration for their surrender?

28. When and where did the Japanese sign the surrender document?

New Vocabulary

cryptologist	defense in depth
defense perimeter	kamikaze
scout plane	pillboxes

10

The Cold War Era, 1945–1991

Even before the surrender of Japan, the American public had begun to bring pressure on Congress to dismantle the greatest military force ever assembled in human history and "bring the boys home." Knowledgeable Americans knew that the United States had acquired worldwide responsibilities by becoming a superpower. The country could not retreat into isolationism as it had done after World War I. Nevertheless, the rush to demobilize was so swift that the American armed forces were soon rendered almost impotent.

Of a wartime Navy of nearly 3.5 million, within a year barely 500,000 remained. Of an Army strength of over eight million, only one million remained a year after the war ended, and that deterioration continued to a low of only 600,000 by 1950. This drastic reduction in strength made it difficult at times to man even the smaller number of ships left in commission. Nearly all naval construction was halted, and two thousand vessels were decommissioned. Many of these were laid up in "mothballs" for future use in an emergency, with their engines, hulls, and guns covered with protective coatings. Of those ships that did remain in commission, many sat alongside their piers with half crews, unable to get under way.

The American public had become complacent. There appeared to be no remaining enemies in the world, and besides, the United States had a monopoly on the atomic bomb. It was assumed by many that the newly created United Nations (UN) could solve in a peaceful manner any disputes that might arise.

In the face of this attitude, the Soviet Union quickly resumed the offensive in its war against capitalism. It soon demonstrated that its strategic long-term goal of a communist-dominated world remained unchanged. The wartime alliance with the West had been only a temporary tactical maneuver.

While Americans pinned their hopes on the United Nations, sped their demobilization, and slashed their defense budget, the Soviets made only a token demobilization. At the war's end they had formally annexed the Eastern European nations that had been ceded to Stalin in the beginning of the war by Nazi Germany. In addition, over the next several years they converted the remaining Eastern European states, most of which they had liberated from the Nazis and subsequently occupied, into satellite states, which collectively became known as the "Eastern Bloc." They installed in the bloc states Soviet-style communist regimes, which employed Stalin-like measures to suppress the population. In Asia they retained control of Manchuria and northern Korea, which they had overrun during the closing days of the Pacific War and installed communist regimes in them as well. The United States was unable to effectively contest any of these actions. The U.S. Army and Navy were both too weakened by postwar demobilization, and American public opinion was solidly against starting another war. America had only two options: make a diplomatic protest or use the atomic bomb. The former could accomplish nothing without any power to back it up, and there was no stomach for the latter, even in the face of blatant Soviet aggression.

The United States did, however, continue to develop its atomic weapons technology, testing new and improved weapons at test ranges at Bikini Atoll and other unoccupied Pacific islands during the ensuing years. For a while the United States had a monopoly on this technology, but soon the Soviet Union developed nuclear capabilities as well, detonating its first test weapon in 1949. Thereafter both governments spent massive

The demobilization of the fleet progressed rapidly in the years following World War II, as indicated by this aerial view of some of the mothballed ships at San Diego, California, in 1950. *The Naval History and Heritage Command*

A U.S. atomic bomb test on Bikini Atoll in 1946. The ships around the blast were mostly ex–Japanese navy ships placed there to measure the effects of the blast on surface ships. *The Naval History and Heritage Command*

amounts upgrading both the quality and quantity of their nuclear arsenals, in what become known as the **nuclear arms race**. It would continue more or less unabated throughout the next forty years. Eventually other nations also developed nuclear capabilities, with the United Kingdom detonating its first bomb in 1952, and France and the People's Republic of China doing so in the 1960s.

To arouse Americans who were again seeking a "return to normalcy," in March 1946 President Truman invited Winston Churchill to make a speech at Westminster College in Fulton, Missouri, in which he would issue a strong warning concerning the USSR. In this speech Churchill stated, "From Stettin in the Baltic to Trieste in the Adriatic an iron curtain has descended across the continent. . . . From what I have seen of our Russian friends and allies during the war, I am convinced that there is nothing they admire so much as strength, and there is nothing for which they have less respect than for weakness, especially military weakness." Thus was born the term given to the barrier between the West and communism—the **iron curtain.**

Unification of the Services

Along with demobilization came a reappraisal of the entire U.S. defense structure. Under the slogan of **"unification,"** many in government and in the Army and Army Air Forces component

proposed a centralized military establishment that would, they hoped, make the shrinking peacetime defense budgets stretch farther. The Navy came under special criticism. Several loud voices stated that the Navy had become an unnecessary extravagance, because there was no naval power anywhere in the world to oppose it.

The Army Air Forces sought independent status as the U.S. Air Force. They pointed to its strategic bombing role in Europe and Japan and to the fact that only it had the ability to deliver the atomic bomb, since Navy planes were not large enough. Some Army Air Forces generals questioned the need for a navy at all, arguing that any future wars, unlikely as they were, could be won cheaply and quickly by bombing. They saw the proposed Air Force as the nation's new first line of defense.

Fleet Admiral Nimitz, by now the Chief of Naval Operations, took a more realistic view. He felt that no one weapons system would be adequate to provide for all aspects of national defense or to protect the nation's growing world interests, most of which were dependent upon free use of the seas. After long debate, Congress finally passed the **National Security Act (NSA)** of July 1947. The new law created the **Department of Defense,** headed by a secretary of defense, with subordinate Departments of the Army, Navy (including the Marine Corps), and Air Force, and the Joint Chiefs of Staff. Under the terms of the NSA, the secretary of defense became a member of the president's cabinet, while the secretaries of the services did not have cabinet rank. The act established the Air Force as a separate service and gave it responsibility for strategic bombing and for combat operations in support of land armies. The Navy retained its carrier aviation and its land-based reconnaissance wing. The Army kept its traditional roles. Secretary James Forrestal became the nation's first secretary of defense.

Under the same act, the **National Security Council,** with permanent members including the president, vice president, secretary of state, and secretary of defense, became the nation's top national-security policy body. The National Security Act also provided for the creation of the **Central Intelligence Agency (CIA).**

The Truman Doctrine, the Marshall Plan, and the Cold War

Several events that occurred during the months before approval of the National Security Act made a significant impact on the congressional decision to maintain a strong Navy–Marine Corps team, with all of its component forces. The post–World War II Soviet moves into the Eastern European, Balkan, and Baltic nations had gone unopposed, but when the Soviets tried to expand into Iran and the countries bordering the eastern Mediterranean, President Truman, as commander in chief, took steps that caused Congress to become more aware of the danger. Strong pressure in the United Nations by the United States caused the Soviets to back down and get out of northern Iran.

In 1946–47 George Kennan, a prominent American diplomat stationed in Moscow, published his view that "the main element of any United States policy toward the Soviet Union must be that of a long-term, patient but firm and vigilant containment of Russian expansionist tendencies." This policy of **containment** became the cornerstone of U.S. foreign policy for the next four decades.

In the spring of 1947 President Truman applied this containment policy to counter Soviet moves toward Greece and Turkey. In Greece, there had been civil war since the closing days of World War II, with communists supported by the Soviets seeking to overthrow the legitimate government, which had returned to power there after the war. The Soviets had been threatening Turkey since the war as well, because Stalin wanted access to the Dardanelles, through which Soviet ships from Black Sea ports had to transit to reach the Mediterranean.

In March 1947 in a speech before Congress, President Truman enunciated the **Truman Doctrine,** thus formalizing the containment policy. Truman stated, "It must be the policy of the United States to support free peoples who are resisting attempted subjugation by armed minorities or by outside pressures. . . . We must assist free peoples to work out their own destinies in their own way." In support of the doctrine, Congress

voted substantial economic aid to both Greece and Turkey. U.S. military bases were established in both countries, bases that are still there today. U.S. Navy units were sent to the Mediterranean as a diplomatic show of force. Soviet expansion toward the Mediterranean was thus checked.

This was the beginning of the permanent deployment of the U.S. Sixth Fleet in the Mediterranean Sea. Truman said that U.S. policy was "to support the cause of freedom wherever it was threatened." Thus the Navy found itself projecting American foreign policy at the same time as it was struggling in the halls of Congress for its very existence.

In June 1947 Secretary of State George Marshall announced Truman's plan to provide economic aid for reconstruction of European countries. This plan, formally named the European Recovery Program, became known as the **Marshall Plan.** Its purpose was to restore the economies of the war-ravaged countries in Europe and, in the process, make it more difficult for the Soviets to make more inroads there. Although the Soviet Union was invited to participate, it refused to do so, and it prohibited any of its new satellites from accepting the American assistance, since Stalin believed that this might lead to their defection to the West. The Soviet leaders denounced the plan as American economic aggression.

Thus began an era of political, military, and later economic contention between the Western democracies, headed by the United States, on one side, and the communist bloc, dominated by the USSR, on the other, that would extend over much of the next forty-five years. The **Cold War** had begun.

The North Atlantic Treaty Organization (NATO) and Warsaw Pact

As American political and economic policy began to assert itself, several Soviet actions solidified Western determination. In 1948 the Communist Party executed a sudden **coup d'état** (change of government by force) in Czechoslovakia, seizing complete control of the country and causing the death of the Czech president. Many Americans and Europeans now began to see how aggressive the forces of Soviet-backed communism really were.

The next incident was the **Berlin Blockade,** in June 1948. The Soviets clamped a blockade on all materials entering or leaving the western section (the British, French, and U.S. zones) of the occupied city of Berlin by road, rail, or canal. This action was an attempt to cut off the army garrisons of the Western Allies in the city and starve West Berlin into capitulation to the Soviets and their East German satellite. The allies responded with a massive airborne supply operation called the **Berlin Airlift,** which lasted eleven months. During this time over two million tons of supplies were flown into the city, one-fourth of it carried by Navy planes.

In response to the growing Soviet menace, the United States, Canada, and their Western European allies agreed in 1949 to create the **North Atlantic Treaty Organization (NATO)**. In this treaty, all the participants agreed that "an armed attack against one or more . . . shall be considered an attack against them all." The nations that initially signed this military alliance were Belgium, Britain, Canada, Denmark, France, Iceland, Italy, Luxembourg, the Netherlands, Norway, Portugal, and the United States. Others would join later, including West Germany in 1955 and many of the former Eastern Bloc countries after the end of the Cold War.

On the communist side, in 1949 the Soviets established the Council for Mutual Economic Assistance (COMECON) as the economic organization of the Eastern Bloc communist countries. Later in the 1950s, most of the other major socialist and communist countries of the world joined as "observers" as well. In 1955, following the acceptance of West Germany into NATO, the Eastern European Mutual Assistance Treaty, more commonly referred to as the **Warsaw Pact,** created the military counterpart to NATO among the Eastern Bloc nations. This organization would contend with the NATO countries from then until the demise of the Soviet Union and the end of the Cold War in 1991.

Throughout the balance of the Cold War from the early 1950s on, Soviet turboprop Bear and supersonic Badger reconnaissance aircraft continually monitored U.S. and NATO maritime exercises throughout the Mediterranean Sea and Atlantic Ocean areas. In the 1980s some of these aircraft were based in Cuba. From there, they flew surveillance missions all along the Atlantic seaboard of the United States. Often they were intercepted and escorted by U.S. and NATO fighters, a situation that kept tension high throughout these years.

The Far East

In the Far East, the end of World War II and the defeat of Japan fanned the flames of smoldering nationalism (desire for national independence) and **anticolonialism** (opposition to foreign control) into major insurgencies trying to take control of weak governments. Communist backing was often a major factor in these revolutions.

The government of Nationalist China, headed by Chiang Kai-shek, was driven from the mainland to Taiwan by Mao Zedong's communists in December 1949 after five years of civil war. The vacuum left by British and French withdrawals from Southeast Asia in the early 1950s stimulated insurgencies in

In 1949 the United States, Canada, and their Western European allies created the North Atlantic Treaty Organization (NATO), a military alliance designed to enhance the security of the Western democracies. Here, NATO defense ministers including then U.S. Secretary of Defense Robert Gates, meet at NATO headquarters in Brussels, Belgium, in October 2010. *Department of Defense, Jerry Morrison*

Burma, Thailand, Malaya, and Indochina. Indochina erupted into open warfare. The Dutch were forced to leave the East Indies after a revolution by the Indonesian people. The British granted independence to India, Pakistan, and Ceylon.

The Potsdam Conference in 1945 had decreed that Korea, a former Japanese possession, would be temporarily divided, with the Soviets occupying the part north of the thirty-eighth parallel and the United States occupying the southern part of the country. The Soviets quickly established a puppet communist regime in the north and trained a large army. In May 1948 they established the People's Democratic Republic of Korea (DPRK), usually called North Korea, with its capital in Pyongyang.

In the south, the United States and the United Nations helped establish the Republic of Korea (ROK), usually called South Korea. In free elections, the South Koreans elected Syngman Rhee as the first president and set up their capital at Seoul in July 1948. Not until U.S. forces began their evacuation did an American advisory group start to train an ROK army. This was still ill-equipped and poorly organized when the last of the American garrison forces departed in June 1949. American lack of resolution had set the stage for another war involving the United States. A year later, on 25 June 1950, the North Korean army crossed the thirty-eighth parallel in a full-scale invasion of South Korea.

The Korean War

The North Korean invasion of South Korea, backed by the Soviet Union and the Chinese, had two main purposes. The first was to unify Korea into a communist state. The second purpose was to establish a geographic dagger pointed at the center of Japan, where General MacArthur's occupation rule prevented communist subversion from gaining a foothold.

As soon as President Truman learned of the invasion, he directed the U.S. delegate to the United Nations Security Council to call an emergency meeting. The USSR was boycotting the council, and with no Soviet veto to block action, the Security Council condemned the North Korean act as a breach of world peace and ordered military sanctions. The United States undertook the direction of military operations. President Truman ordered the Joint Chiefs of Staff to take any action necessary to aid South Korea and repel the invasion. The Joint Chiefs named GEN Douglas MacArthur commander in chief, Far East. He was later named supreme commander of United Nations forces.

The UN Security Council called on other member nations to come to the aid of South Korea and to assist the United States with military forces. Eventually fourteen other countries sent military and naval contingents, and many others sent medical and material aid.

The South Koreans were soon overrun by fifteen well-equipped North Korean divisions. Seoul fell only three days

The Korean theater of operations, 1950. The arrows show the major lines of advance of the North Koreans in June 1950.

after the invasion, and the "Reds," as the North Korean communists were called, proceeded southward with little opposition. General MacArthur tried to stem the tide with three U.S. Army divisions from Japan, but by late July only an area about twenty-five miles west by eighty miles north of Pusan remained in allied hands. This zone was called the "Pusan Perimeter."

Fortunately, at this point American reinforcements and equipment began pouring into the Pusan Perimeter. Aided by naval bombardment, air strikes, and U.S. Marines, the defenders began to inflict severe casualties on the attacking North Koreans. By the third week of August, after being stalled for three weeks on the Pusan Perimeter, the North Korean drive had lost steam, and General MacArthur began plans for possibly the most daring amphibious assault ever conceived.

Operation Chromite: Inchon

By September 1950 a stalemate had been reached along the Pusan Perimeter. The UN forces were growing ever stronger and could undoubtedly have broken through the weakening

North Korean lines, but at great cost. General MacArthur did not want to incur those losses, so he proposed an exceptionally complex amphibious assault on Inchon, the port of Seoul, capital of South Korea. The objective was to capture Inchon and Seoul, thus cutting the supply line to the North Korean armies on the Pusan Perimeter. This would isolate over 90 percent of the North Korean army and, for all practical purposes, destroy North Korea's capability for making war.

The proposed landing at Inchon, however, presented extreme difficulties. The only approach to the port was through the Flying Fish Channel, a tortuous, thirty-mile run through mudflats that became visible each day at low tide. The range of tide at Inchon is one of the greatest in the world—twenty-nine feet on the average, sometimes as much as thirty-six feet. If the landing were unsuccessful, the tank landing ships (LSTs) of the landing force would later be trapped, sitting high and dry on the tidal mudflats.

D-day for the Inchon landing was set for 15 September, because it was only on the three days beginning on that date that the tides would meet amphibious requirements. The Marine brigade, a key force in the defense of the Pusan Perimeter, was withdrawn to form the nucleus of the 1st Marine Division, which would spearhead the landing. Carrier air support would be provided from three U.S. carriers offshore in Task Force 77.

A cruiser-destroyer force threaded its way up the Flying Fish Channel on 13 September to bombard the North Korean fortifications on the islands of Wolmi-do and Sowolmi-do, which protected the harbor and city. There was a spirited exchange of fire; three destroyers were hit, but the shore and air bombardment on 13–14 September was sufficient to enable the landing to proceed on schedule the following morning.

At 0630 on the 15th, the first waves stormed ashore at Green Beach on Wolmi-do. The island was secured in thirty-one minutes. Sowolmi-do followed quickly, thanks to 40 mm fire from one of the support ships. The main landing followed in the late afternoon. Red Beach was in downtown Inchon, the only place heavy equipment such as tanks, bulldozers, and trucks could be landed. Blue Beach was on the southern outskirts of the city on a muddy, narrow beach too soft to take heavy equipment.

At 1730 the first wave hit Red Beach. Not until the fourth wave landed did the defenders begin any serious opposition, but by that time the troops ashore were securing enemy strongpoints and advancing toward their first objective line, a thousand yards inland. The landings went on throughout the night and the next day, as bulldozers tore down the seawall to facilitate landing heavy equipment. Twenty-four hours after the first landings at Inchon, the Marines shifted their command post ashore and declared the landing phase of the operation concluded. Before the enemy could regroup, Kimpo Airfield outside Seoul was captured, on 18 September, and the Marines closed in on the capital. The Inchon operation proved to be one

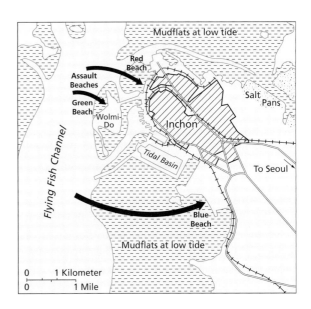

A diagram of the Inchon landing, showing Green Beach on Wolmi-Do, Red Beach on the seawall of the city, and Blue Beach to the south. Blue Beach became the main logistics beach after the initial landings.

Marines climbing the seawall at Red Beach during the Inchon landings.
The Naval History and Heritage Command

of the most successful amphibious assaults in military history. "The Navy and Marines have never shone more brightly," General MacArthur remarked.

Breakout at Pusan

On the day after the Inchon landing, the U.S. Eighth Army, under the command of GEN Walton Walker, began a major offensive to break out of the Pusan Perimeter. The North Koreans were now in an untenable military situation. With their main supply route through Seoul severed and their only other supply route, along the east-coast road, under steady naval bombardment, the North Koreans had no means of logistic support. When the Inchon invasion force turned southward and met the Eighth Army coming north from Pusan on 26 September, for all practical purposes the war in South Korea was over. On the 28th, Seoul fell. Not all fighting had ceased, but the North Koreans had no hope of victory. All that remained was "mopping up." In that process, over 125,000 North Korean soldiers were taken prisoner.

After much debate in the United Nations, that body authorized General MacArthur to proceed north of the thirty-eighth parallel to destroy the remnants of the North Korean forces. While the Eighth Army advanced against heavy opposition toward the North Korean capital of Pyongyang, the ROK army, now reorganized, reequipped, and trained in the hardships of war, roared a hundred miles northward in ten days along the east coast against little opposition. On 19 October, the Eighth Army captured Pyongyang.

Chinese Intervention

Despite warnings that his invasion of communist North Korea might bring communist Chinese intervention, MacArthur's forces continued to drive northward toward the Yalu River boundary with Chinese Manchuria. MacArthur's intelligence officers did not believe the Chinese would enter the war in force. They believed that if the Chinese were going to do it at all, they would have done it when the allies had their backs to the sea at Pusan. Thus MacArthur sent the Eighth Army north from Pyongyang and the X Corps north from Hamhung. On 26 October elements of the ROK army arrived at the Yalu.

There was an eighty-mile gap between the two northward-moving UN forces, because there were no east-west communications or roads. Chinese forces began to advance southward into this gap. Elements of the ROK army met the Chinese in several heavy encounters in late October and early November. On 2 November, Chinese forces attacked units of the Eighth Army near Unsan.

MacArthur warned the Joint Chiefs on 6 November that if the movement of Chinese forces across the Yalu continued, his army faced destruction. Nevertheless, on 24 November MacArthur gave the order for his forces to begin a drive to the Yalu. That same day, the first U.S. elements reached the Yalu, at Hyesanjin. Then on 25 November 1950, 200,000 Chinese troops, called Volunteers of the People's Liberation Army, or sometimes simply the Red Chinese, launched a major offensive, sweeping the allies before them and cutting off a large group of Marines at the Chosin Reservoir, north of Hungnam.

The next two weeks saw the United Nations forces fight their way back southward in full retreat, even as the cold and snow of the Korean winter closed in. In temperatures as low as twenty-five degrees below zero, Marines and other allied forces were often forced to fight their way out of surrounded positions. Navy and Marine planes pounded the Chinese forces in the hills. Under this umbrella, the Marines finally reached the coastal city of Hungnam on 9 December. During the next two weeks, 105,000 troops, 90,000 Korean refugees, thousands of vehicles, and tons of bulk cargo were loaded onto waiting amphibious vessels in the greatest "amphibious operation in reverse" ever conducted. On Christmas Eve 1950, the last troops departed, and Navy underwater demolition teams blew up all port facilities before leaving.

The forces evacuated from Hungnam were sped southward and reintroduced into the fighting below the thirty-eighth parallel, where the bulk of United Nations forces had retreated by 15 December.

GEN Matthew Ridgway took command of the Eighth Army on 26 December, following the death of General Walker in a jeep accident. The Eighth Army slowed its retreat but could not stop the Chinese advance before losing Seoul again on 4 January 1951. In late January Ridgway began a slow advance toward the Han River south of Seoul, a methodical drive that culminated in the recapture of the South Korean capital on 15 March. UN forces made more advances in the succeeding months, particularly along the east coast, where they reached a point about fifty miles north of the thirty-eighth parallel. But there the war bogged down for both sides.

Dismissal of MacArthur

General MacArthur had hated the limitations placed upon him after the Chinese intervened. He particularly wanted to be allowed to follow Chinese aircraft in "hot pursuit" over the Yalu River into Manchuria and to bomb Chinese staging bases on the north bank of the river. The Western European allies put great pressure on the United States to forbid such action. They feared that the war would escalate and eventually involve the Soviets, because the USSR had signed a mutual defense treaty with China. This opinion was shared by the U.S. State Department, and its view prevailed with the president.

When he was unable to persuade President Truman to accept his recommendations, in March 1951 General MacArthur sent Joseph Martin, the minority leader of the House of Representatives, a letter attacking the president's policies. When Martin made the letter public, President Truman relieved MacArthur for insubordination, replacing him with General Ridgway.

In his letter, MacArthur pointed out that "here we fight Europe's war with arms, while the diplomats there still fight it with words. . . . [If] we lose the war to Communism in Asia the fall of Europe is inevitable, win it and Europe most probably would avoid war and yet preserve freedom. . . . We must win. There is no substitute for victory."

GEN Douglas MacArthur was commander in chief of U.S. forces during the first nine months of the Korean War. He was relieved by President Truman in April 1951 after public disagreements over war strategy. Lieutenant General Walker, commander of ground forces in Korea during the first part of the war, is seated in the rear. *The Naval History and Heritage Command*

Truce Talks

By June 1951 the severe casualties inflicted on the Red Chinese had begun to make an impression. The USSR's ambassador to the United Nations suggested that armistice talks might be held, and the United Nations leaders agreed. Thereafter began over two years of almost fruitless negotiations at Panmunjom, a small village along the thirty-eighth parallel. Meanwhile, fierce fighting continued, although neither side attempted a major offensive to capture territory.

Dwight Eisenhower was elected president in November 1952. A major promise of his campaign had been to bring an end to the Korean War. This stimulated new efforts in the truce talks, and finally, after more than two years of negotiations, an armistice was signed on 27 July 1953. The agreement divided the two Koreas along a boundary near the thirty-eighth parallel but based on the existing cease-fire line. It established a **demilitarized buffer zone (DMZ)** two and a half miles wide, centered on the border between the two countries, into which neither side could send military forces. The agreement also put a cease-fire into effect and dealt with the **repatriation** (return) of prisoners of war. South Korea had kept its freedom, gaining in the process about 1,500 square miles of territory, at a cost of 70,000 South Korean, 34,000 American, and five thousand other UN casualties on the battlefields. In addition, several million Korean civilians are believed to have died during the course of the war.

A major issue in the truce talks concerned prisoners of war (POWs). Many North Koreans and Chinese taken prisoner in the south refused to go back to their countries. Furthermore, after American POWs were returned, they brought with them many tales of inhumane treatment in North Korean prison camps and failure to comply with international conventions concerning treatment of POWs. The issue of North Korean treatment of American POWs would continue to be a topic of discussion between U.S. and North Korean representatives at Panmunjom for years to come. Eventually all remaining POWs on both sides were repatriated, but for the next sixty years Panmunjom would continue to be the site of talks between the two Koreas and the United States whenever contentious issues arose.

Korean War Aftermath

Encouraged by the outcome in Korea, communist guerrillas led by Ho Chi Minh intensified their war against the French in Indochina, which had been a French protectorate since the 1800s. In 1954 the French were defeated in battle at Dien Bien Phu. This event resulted in the partition of Indochina into North and South Vietnam, Laos, and Cambodia. As we will see below, this set the stage for even more trouble in the region a few years later.

Unfortunately, provocative behavior on the part of the North Koreans did not end with the Korean War armistice. In the following years many incidents occurred that showed their continued willingness to test the resolve of South Korea and the United States. One of the worst of these took place in January 1968, when a U.S. intelligence-gathering ship, the USS *Pueblo* (AGER 2), was attacked and captured by the North Koreans fifteen miles off Wonsan Harbor. The ship was forced into Wonsan Harbor, where the crew was removed to a detention site; there they would remain for the next eleven months. Only after agreeing to a false confession (which was later repudiated) was the U.S. negotiating team at Panmunjom finally able to obtain the crew's release. The ship was put on display as a tourist attraction at Wonsan. This incident marked the first time in over 150 years that a U.S. warship had been captured on the high seas by a foreign power.

Photo of the captured Navy intelligence-gathering ship USS *Pueblo* on display as a tourist attraction at Pongyang, North Korea, in September 2011. *Michael Day*

Thereafter the bellicose behavior of North Korea was toned down for most of the rest of the century. But soon in the new millennium, provocative behavior toward South Korea and the United States would resume.

New Naval Capabilities

Although the Korean War did not bring peace to a troubled world, it had some positive consequences for the U.S. Navy. The prewar contention by some that naval warfare was obsolete was largely discredited. The Korean War had shown that naval shore bombardment, carrier air strikes, close air support, amphibious assault, and logistic support from the sea were all necessary parts of any military operation. Congress thereafter authorized the building of six large *Forrestal*-class aircraft carriers, and plans for new classes of amphibious and mobile logistics ships were drawn up.

On 1 November 1952 a new threshold in nuclear warfare was crossed with the test explosion by U.S. scientists of the first **hydrogen bomb,** on Eniwetok Atoll in the Pacific. Whereas the explosive power of atomic bombs is rated in terms of how many thousands of tons (i.e., **kilotons**) of TNT they are equivalent to, hydrogen bombs are rated in terms of millions of tons of TNT (i.e., **megatons**). In August 1953 the Soviet Union detonated its version of the super-explosive bomb. As President Eisenhower expanded U.S. military power to cope with the growing Soviet Cold War threat, there was a greater spirit of cooperation among the Joint Chiefs of Staff. They now realized that all components of the U.S. armed forces had definite roles in limited war, as well as in deterring possible nuclear war with the Soviet Union. This new cooperative spirit would show itself many times in various crises throughout the remainder of the Cold War and thereafter, when joint forces from all services would often be called upon to protect U.S. interests around the globe.

Approval of the new carrier construction program won for the Navy its battle to be a part of the nation's **strategic nuclear striking force.** The *Forrestal* class was designed to launch planes capable of carrying nuclear bombs. The difficulty of locating and neutralizing mobile nuclear-equipped carrier forces was certainly a deterrent that any aggressor would have to consider seriously.

While the new carriers were being built, an even farther-reaching naval technical development occurred. Under the direction of the Navy's hard-driving CAPT (later ADM) Hyman G. Rickover, the world's first nuclear-powered submarine, the USS *Nautilus,* put to sea in January 1955. It was soon followed by a fast-growing fleet of **nuclear attack submarines.** During the remainder of the twentieth century, the use of nuclear power for submarines, and later some surface ships, would be as significant for the U.S. Navy as the shift from sail to steam had been during the Civil War era.

Underwater hydrogen bomb test "Baker" in the Pacific Test Range at Bikini Island in 1956. This huge ball of radioactive water soon rose to form the mushroom-shaped cloud characteristic of nuclear detonations, then fell back to envelope the test ships shown in the photo in the radioactive base surge. *The Naval History and Heritage Command*

The next significant development was an intermediate-range, nuclear-tipped ballistic missile named the Polaris, which could be launched from a submerged submarine. Simultaneously, a new class of submarines that could launch it was built. The USS *George Washington* went into commission in 1959 as the first of the new fleet of **ballistic missile submarines.** These new submarines, and the succession of improved missiles they would carry, would join the Army's land-based **ICBMs** (intercontinental ballistic missiles) and the Air Force's manned bombers to become a significant leg of the nation's **triad** (three pronged capability) of strategic deterrence, for the balance of the century and beyond. Several classes of nuclear-powered aircraft carriers and other surface warships followed.

During the 1960s, a whole new generation of mobile logistic ships designed for underway replenishment (**UNREP**—alongside replenishment while under way) joined the fleet. These had the capability of servicing whole task groups at sea at speeds up to twenty knots. Improvement in large helicopters added the new dimension of vertical replenishment (**VERTREP**—replenishment via helicopter) to mobile logistics. Today, all U.S. Navy surface ships at sea receive the bulk of their resupply of "beans, bullets, and black oil" (food, munitions, and fuel) in UNREP and VERTREP operations.

Similarly, in the 1960s and 1970s new ships transformed the amphibious squadrons of the Atlantic and Pacific Fleets into twenty-knot operational groups capable of landing fully equipped Marine battalions on enemy beaches. The advent of nuclear weapons required the modification of amphibious doc-

VADM Hyman G. Rickover. Always controversial and often irascible, he earned by his dedication and perseverance the title "Father of the Nuclear Navy." For forty years he almost singlehandedly led the Navy's postwar development of probably the most sophisticated weapon system the world has ever known—the nuclear submarine. *The Naval History and Heritage Command*

In response to Soviet construction of missile sites in Cuba, President John F. Kennedy ordered a quarantine against all Soviet shipments of military weapons and equipment to Cuba in October 1962. *National Archives*

trine, emphasizing mobility and dispersal. The helicopter also made a major impact on amphibious warfare, resulting in the tactic of **vertical envelopment,** which is the airlift of troops and equipment to landing areas behind the selected assault beach. There they can prevent enemy reinforcements from opposing the landing and impede delivery of logistic support to enemy defenders in the amphibious objective area.

The Cuban Missile Crisis

As potentially explosive as most of the serious incidents between the United States and communism in the late 1940s and 1950s were, in 1962 an event that came to be called the Cuban missile crisis was the most dangerous of all Cold War crises to that date. It was a direct confrontation between the United States and the Soviet Union.

In October 1962, high-flying Air Force U-2 reconnaissance aircraft photographed Soviet medium-range (MRBM) and intermediate-range (IRBM) nuclear ballistic missile launching pads under construction in Fidel Castro's Cuba. Photographs from earlier missions had also shown surface-to-air missile batteries being erected, and electronic gear, construction equipment, and even suspected crated missiles being unloaded from Soviet-flag freighters in Cuban ports. The ballistic missile sites made it obvious that the Soviets were trying to overcome the superiority of America's nuclear-armed strategic military forces by placing many large American cities well within the 700-mile range of the Soviet IRBMs.

Many years later it was learned that, unbeknownst to the United States, Soviet forces in Cuba had also received some one hundred tactical nuclear warheads for their long-range artillery rockets and IL-28 bombers stationed in Cuba.

Faced with this Soviet threat, President Kennedy had only two choices: do nothing, which would make the United States

vulnerable to Soviet nuclear blackmail, or force the Soviets to remove the missiles, even at the threat of nuclear war. After an agonizing appraisal of the alternatives, the president called upon the U.S. Navy to establish a **quarantine** (a selective blockade) of Cuba. Having made the decision, the president told ADM George Anderson, then CNO, "Well, it looks as if everything is in the hands of the Navy."

Admiral Anderson replied, "Mr. President, the Navy will not let you down."

On the evening of 22 October, the president went on national television and told the American people and the world that the Soviet Union had placed nuclear missiles in Cuba. He stated that "any nuclear missile launched from Cuba by the USSR against any nation in the Western Hemisphere would be regarded as an attack by the Soviet Union on the United States, requiring a full retaliatory response." He announced that "a strict quarantine of all offensive military equipment under shipment to Cuba is being initiated," and that any ship bound for Cuba carrying such cargo would be turned back. Soviet premier Nikita Khrushchev branded the U.S. charges lies and warned that the quarantine was an act of "piracy" that would lead to war. Work on the missile sites continued unabated.

Over the next three days 180 Navy ships became involved in the operation, establishing a quarantine line on an arc five hundred miles to the east of Cuba. Naval vessels and aircraft continuously conducted reconnaissance missions over and around the island. Intelligence reported that a number of Soviet ships were on their way to Cuba and nearing the quarantine line. The whole world waited with bated breath. Would they turn back? Would they have to be boarded and captured? Would they have to be sunk?

On 24 October, for the first and only time in U.S. history, American military forces were placed on Defense Condition (DEFCON) 2, the highest readiness condition short of war. Strategic nuclear-armed Air Force bombers, many of them airborne and flying holding patterns worldwide, were placed on fifteen-minute standby to go into attack mode. Thirty thousand U.S. Marines embarked in amphibious ships near Cuba made preparations to invade the island. Tension rose. Nuclear war seemed only hours away. Later that day, however, the Soviets responded to the quarantine by turning back fourteen of the ships bound for Cuba, which were presumably carrying offensive weapons. Others slowed down or turned away. Secretary of State Dean Rusk is reported to have remarked, "We're eyeball to eyeball, and I think the other fellow just blinked."

On 26 October a Soviet charter ship approaching the quarantine line was stopped, boarded and searched, and allowed to proceed when found not to be carrying any contraband. This established the right to stop and search suspected quarantine violators.

That day and the next, President Kennedy offered to end the quarantine and promised not to invade Cuba, if the Soviets would remove their missiles. He also made a secret deal with Khrushchev to remove certain U.S. nuclear MRBMs deployed with NATO forces in Turkey and Italy that were of particular concern to the Soviets, in order to provide an additional incentive.

Some forty years after the crisis, in a history conference held in Cuba in 2002, it was learned that on the 27th a U.S. destroyer participating in the quarantine, the USS *Beale,* had dropped a small grenade, used for underwater signaling, on a suspected Soviet Foxtrot-class submarine during a "holddown" operation. This procedure, consisting of maintaining sonar contact until an unidentified submarine was forced to surface, was routine in those days in the Cold War whenever such an unidentified submerged submarine was discovered by U.S. Navy warships. The submarine was armed with a fifteen-kiloton nuclear torpedo, which it was authorized to fire if its hull was penetrated. Because of the circumstances at the time, her captain was infuriated by the grenade attack and wanted to arm and launch the torpedo, but fortunately he was dissuaded by one of the other two officers aboard whose concurrence was required to do so. Instead the submarine surfaced

The destroyer *Joseph P. Kennedy* about to stop and inspect a Soviet-chartered Lebanese freighter bound for Cuba during the Cuban missile quarantine in October 1962. The ship was allowed to proceed when the search found no contraband. *The Naval History and Heritage Command*

for air in the midst of the blockading ships, and a devastating nuclear exchange was narrowly avoided.

On 28 October, Khrushchev formally capitulated and agreed, much to the chagrin of Cuba's dictator Fidel Castro, to remove all Soviet missiles from Cuba. Nuclear holocaust was averted, and the world breathed more easily. Khrushchev's attempt to overcome American nuclear superiority had failed in the face of American sea power, but as a result a buildup of the Soviet navy that had begun in the late 1950s was intensified, under the leadership of Admiral of the Fleet of the Soviet Union Sergei G. Gorshkov. By the 1970s that momentum would give the Soviets a navy second only to that of the United States. Later President Kennedy was criticized by some for not taking advantage of the opportunity to demand the removal of Castro's communist regime as well as of the Soviet missiles, but this dissipated as time passed and the true magnitude of the crisis was more fully revealed.

After Kennedy called off the quarantine in November, the Soviets removed all of their other tactical nuclear weapons from Cuba, thus ending Castro's grandiose vision of Cuba's becoming a miniature nuclear superpower in the region. The missiles that were subject to the secret accord between the president and Khrushchev were quietly removed from Italy and Turkey the following spring.

In 1963, as an aftermath of the crisis, the United States and the Soviet Union agreed to establish a direct communications link—the famous teletype "hotline"—between the two governments for use in the event of any future serious confrontations. A limited nuclear test ban treaty was also negotiated between the two countries in July of that year.

The Vietnam War

Vietnam had been a part of French Indochina since the mid-1800s, when France had acquired control of the area now comprising Vietnam, Laos, and Cambodia as a result of imperialist expansion into the region. During World War II Vietnam had been occupied by the Japanese. It declared its independence following the Japanese defeat in 1945. The French, however, tried to reassert their control, in a war that lasted from 1946 to 1954. In that year, as mentioned above, the French suffered a major defeat by communist forces led by Ho Chi Minh at Dien Bien Phu, leading to complete French withdrawal two years later.

After the French defeat a Geneva accord established along the seventeenth parallel of latitude a partition between North and South Vietnam, similar to what was done in Korea following World War II. The communists under Ho Chi Minh were given control of North Vietnam, called the Democratic Republic of Vietnam. South Vietnam, called the State of Vietnam, was placed under the control of anticommunist nationalists led by Bao Dai. The latter state later became the Republic of Vietnam.

The partition was supposed to be temporary, lasting until free elections would unify the country two years later, and it incorporated a five-mile demilitarized zone on each side.

In 1955 a new leader, Ngo Dinh Diem, was chosen by Bao Dai. Diem organized the government into the Republic of Vietnam and declared himself president. He was backed by President Eisenhower and the Southeast Asia Treaty Organization.

Communist China and the Soviet Union poured assistance into North Vietnam. Fearing that this would soon lead to expansion southward by North Vietnam, President Eisenhower offered South Vietnam military aid, including seven hundred advisers, and economic assistance in the amount of $200 million a year. Initially this American aid brought great prosperity to South Vietnam. However, Diem ran a corrupt and dictatorial government, composed largely of politicians and military officers who had earlier sided with the French. They carried with them a legacy of defeat and were never fully supported by the population. Ho Chi Minh, on the other hand, was regarded as a hero by most Vietnamese, both in the North and the South, because of his role in the defeat of the French. These facts would bear heavily on the eventual outcome in the embattled country.

When it came time for the 1956 elections to settle issues of national unification and type of government, Diem, fearful of defeat at the polls, refused to allow them. Civil war flared immediately. Communist rebels in the south, called the National Liberation Front (NLF), or Vietcong, received the support of communist North Vietnam. They resorted to massacre and terrorization of the peasantry to force it to support the NLF. When he took office in 1962, President John Kennedy, following the advice of the Joint Chiefs and Secretary of State Dean Rusk, decided to increase the number of American military advisers in South Vietnam to 23,000 by the middle of 1963. They soon were piloting helicopters and returning Vietcong fire. The NLF, now reinforced by thousands of troops from North Vietnam, was spreading its control over the countryside, murdering five hundred village leaders, teachers, and businessmen each month. In response to this deteriorating situation, in November 1963 South Vietnamese military leaders staged a coup. They assassinated Diem and seized control of the government.

The Tonkin Gulf Incident

Open involvement of the United States in the war began in August 1964, during the presidency of Lyndon Johnson. The destroyer USS *Maddox* was patrolling in the Gulf of Tonkin, off the North Vietnamese coast, on an intelligence mission. The ship was outside the three-mile limit then recognized by the United States but within the twelve-mile limit claimed by North Vietnam. On 2 August the *Maddox* was attacked by three North Vietnamese patrol boats, which fired torpedoes and machine guns at her. In the ensuing battle, one of the patrol boats was left dead in the water.

President Johnson ordered the destroyer to resume its patrol in the gulf as an expression of American rights to freedom of the seas. The following night, during stormy weather, another North Vietnamese torpedo attack was reported by the *Maddox* and the nearby destroyer *C. Turner Joy,* though in later years evidence seemed to indicate the alleged attack may never have occurred. In any event, the president ordered aircraft from the carriers *Constellation* and *Ticonderoga* to bomb North Vietnamese patrol boat bases and an oil storage depot in retaliation. Two days later, Congress passed the **Tonkin Gulf Resolution,** which gave the president a free hand to employ necessary measures to "repel any armed attack" or "prevent further aggression." This resolution, along with subsequent congressional financial appropriations, formed the legal basis for America's escalating involvement in the Vietnam War.

In February 1965, after heavy American casualties were sustained in a Vietcong mortar attack on the Pleiku Air Base, President Johnson retaliated with carrier air attacks on barracks and port facilities in North Vietnam. A terrorist attack three days later killed twenty-three Americans in an enlisted

North and South Vietnam as they were until 1972, showing the DMZ at 17 degrees north latitude and the location of Yankee Station in the Gulf of Tonkin, where many ships of the U.S. Navy were deployed during the war.

men's hotel. The president now ordered the U.S. Marines to land at Da Nang to protect a major air base located there and to develop and defend additional bases in the northern part of South Vietnam to prevent North Vietnamese incursions across the DMZ. The Marines landed on 8 March and shortly thereafter joined South Vietnamese forces in "search and destroy" missions against the Vietcong.

With the commitment of the Marines, the general U.S. buildup began. Amphibious assaults and combat air support from the Seventh Fleet steadily grew in size and strength. Army combat troops arrived and took over the Chu Lai base in April 1967, while Marines, now numbering more than 70,000, operated from a series of bases from Da Nang north to the DMZ. The Marines were supported by 26,000 U.S. Navy Seabees in the northern area. They fought regularly against regiment-sized North Vietnamese units and thousands of Vietcong. An example of this fighting was a siege at Khe Sanh in early 1968, in which surrounded Marines inflicted heavy casualties on the enemy for over six months.

The U.S. Navy involvement was massive. The Seventh Fleet had as many as five carriers operating in and around "Yankee Station" in the Tonkin Gulf continuously for the next five years. Their movements were often monitored by one or more Soviet intelligence-gathering trawlers (AGIs) operating in the gulf. Over sixty amphibious assaults were made on South Vietnamese beaches, in missions designed to eliminate pockets of Vietcong and North Vietnamese forces that had been located by intelligence. By 1968 President Johnson had committed more than half a million American servicemen to South Vietnam. Air Force B-52 bombers from bases in Guam and Thailand flew hundreds of massive Rolling Thunder bombing raids against enemy targets.

In addition to seaborne activities, the Navy also conducted numerous inshore commando, river, and coastal patrol operations. A whole new "brown-water Navy," named the Mobile Riverine Force, was created. It consisted of armored monitors, armored troop carriers, **swift boats** (heavily armed, shallow-draft fast patrol boats), and a wide variety of other patrol and minesweeping craft. Riverine patrols roamed through the numerous canals and rivers of the Mekong Delta south and west of Saigon. Air-cushion vehicles patrolled the coastal sounds, the Plain of Reeds, and many rivers. Thousands of armed helicopters and helicopter gunships zipped through the air to strike known and suspected enemy concentrations. Offshore, Navy swift boats and U.S. Coast Guard cutters, in Operation Market Time, interdicted attempts by the North Vietnamese to infiltrate troops and supplies by sea. Special Forces, SEAL (Sea, Air, Land) teams, UDTs (underwater demolition teams), and Vietnamese sea commandos (highly trained Vietnamese with Navy SEAL and U.S. Marine advisers) conducted hundreds of raids and ambushes against the elusive enemy.

A Navy swift boat speeds down a river to attack the Vietcong during the Vietnam War. *The Naval History and Heritage Command*

A temporary American helicopter base built during the Vietnam War. *Wally Beddoe/USMC Combat Helicopter Ass'n (www.popasmoke.com)*

Restrictions Hinder Victory

In spite of the increased American involvement, however, the war dragged on for several years. There was no declaration of war by Congress, and political indecision in Washington made effective military prosecution of the war difficult if not impossible. Many bombing restrictions in North Vietnam and prohibitions against mining North Vietnamese waters were imposed, mainly out of concern over provoking a reaction from the Soviet Union or China.

Continuous attacks by carrier- and land-based aircraft along the famous **Ho Chi Minh Trail,** the overland communist supply route through the Laotian and Cambodian jungles, could not stop a steady flow of combatants and material from North Vietnam. There rarely was anything resembling a battlefront. Instead, guerrillas popped up from jungles, villages, and rice paddies where only moments before peaceful-looking farmers had tended their crops.

The Chinese, Soviets, and other communist-bloc nations kept their North Vietnamese allies amply supplied with weapons, ammunition, and equipment, mainly through the port of Haiphong. U.S. ships and aircraft were under strict orders not to fire on any "third country" (foreign-flag) shipping, even when it was observed off-loading cargo to the enemy, again out of concern over provoking the Soviets or the Chinese.

For a time in late 1967, it began to look as though the communists were being beaten in the field. Then, on 30 January 1968, during Tet (the Buddhist New Year), they struck at major cities all across South Vietnam. They created havoc in Saigon and held the provincial capital of Hue for twenty-five days.

This "Tet Offensive" was eventually beaten back. The North Vietnamese and Vietcong suffered many casualties and gained no battlefield objectives. But the offensive stimulated a growing peace movement in the United States, supported by many college students, leftists, liberals, and others. The president found his administration under increasing pressure to get out of the Vietnam War due to the rising toll of casualties and material costs, as well as the growing protests at home. Finally, President Johnson announced a unilateral bombing halt of North Vietnam and invited Hanoi to peace talks in Paris. He announced at the same time that he would not seek reelection.

Vietnamization

As the peace talks dragged on through 1969, newly elected President Richard Nixon began withdrawing Americans from Vietnam. He insisted that America still sought the original objective, to ensure that the South Vietnamese had the right to choose and maintain their own form of government. He believed the way to attain that was to help the Vietnamese take over all aspects of their government and military operations.

Accordingly, a massive training program called **Vietnamization** was undertaken to prepare the South Vietnamese to administer their affairs and operate in an effective manner. In the civilian area, training was given to local government offi-

Upon taking office in 1969, President Richard Nixon, shown here with Secretary of State Henry Kissinger, Vice President Gerald Ford, and Chief of Staff Alexander Haig, introduced a new strategy called "Vietnamization," aimed at ending American involvement in the Vietnam War by transferring all military responsibilities to South Vietnam. *National Archives*

cials, civil servants, teachers, dock managers, builders, farmers, industrialists, medical personnel, and police forces. An effort called Civic Action helped in nearly every conceivable way to make the South Vietnamese self-supporting. Good roads, bridges, airports, and harbor facilities were built by the Seabees and U.S. Army and civilian engineers and financed by American tax dollars. One of the best internal transportation systems in Asia was created for the struggling nation.

By the end of 1970 some 93 percent of South Vietnam's population had been brought under government control, from a low of only 42 percent three years before. A succession of weak governments after Diem's assassination had been replaced by a stable and freely elected government, which, headed by President Nguyen Van Thieu, appeared to be in control of the nation's destiny.

While Vietnamization appeared to be going well, fighting flared up again in early 1972, despite the Paris peace talks, which had been going on fruitlessly for nearly three years. In response to the North Vietnamese attacks, President Nixon authorized renewed bombing of North Vietnam, including Hanoi. The communists were thrown back with heavy losses, but the fighting continued. Finally, the president authorized the mining of Haiphong Harbor. Within a week the enemy was desperate for supplies, because communist-bloc ships were unable to proceed into the harbor from the Gulf of Tonkin for off-loading. Two dozen ships were trapped in the harbor, unable to depart. The communists stopped all significant military action and came back to the peace table. On 27 January 1973 all parties to the war signed an accord ending the fighting and providing for the peaceful withdrawal of the remaining American advisers by March 1973.

The Fall of South Vietnam

The United States made promises to support the South Vietnamese government and military forces. However, many of these promises were dependent largely on President Nixon himself. But the president, though notably successful in foreign affairs, had become embroiled in the Watergate scandal. As the Washington political scene became more and more confused, congressional interest in virtually everything other than the domestic political situation waned. Any connection with Vietnam had come to be regarded as a political liability by congressmen after the revelations of the My Lai Massacre in 1969 and the Pentagon Papers controversy in 1971. This feeling, plus the terrible cost of American involvement in the war—some 150 billion dollars and over 56,000 deaths, as well as the widespread internal political turmoil—left little support in Congress for South Vietnam.

President Nixon finally chose to resign in August 1974, rather than face the possibility of an impeachment trial over the Watergate affair, with the further disruption of governmental functions that would cause. The vice president, Gerald Ford, took over the reins of government, hoping to heal the wounds of the controversy. In this atmosphere, any proposal to maintain the necessary level of financial and military aid to South Vietnam met with very limited response from Congress and the American people.

America's preoccupation with domestic political affairs encouraged the Vietcong and North Vietnamese to violate all provisions of the cease-fire agreement. They began bringing in massive reinforcements through the northern provinces of South Vietnam. In March 1975, two years after American withdrawal, South Vietnam's ability to withstand communist pressure collapsed. By the end of April, the whole country had capitulated to North Vietnam and the NLF. Two weeks earlier, the American-supported Cambodian government had fallen to the Khmer Rouge, a fanatical communist insurgent group in that country. Laos was taken over by the communist Pathet Lao in early December. Communism had triumphed in Indochina, after nearly thirty years of constant warfare.

Vietnam War Aftermath

After the Vietnam War, massive cutbacks took place in the numbers of Navy ships and personnel. The number of active-fleet ships dropped from about 650 in 1972 to about 450 by 1978. During these same years, the number of Navy personnel dropped from about 600,000 to some 525,000, and Marine Corps personnel, from around 200,000 to 190,000. These downward trends continued until the early 1980s, when worldwide events such as the Falklands War, the Iran-Iraq conflict, and the rise of international terrorism caused the trend to be reversed at least for a while.

Even before the U.S. withdrawal from Vietnam, sweeping changes were being planned in personnel policy, administration, technology, and weapons in the Navy. The old Navy bureau organization was changed to five **material systems commands,** in the interest of improving efficiency and of keeping up with the rapid pace of technological advances. These commands— Air Systems, Sea Systems, Electronics Systems, Supply Systems, and Facilities Engineering—were placed under the Chief of Naval Material. That chief, along with the Chief of Naval Personnel and the Chief of the Bureau of Medicine and Surgery, reported directly to the Chief of Naval Operations.

In the early 1970s a program to update many personnel administrative practices was initiated by ADM Elmo Zumwalt, who was, at the age of forty-nine, the youngest CNO in the history of the Navy. He made many changes, promulgated by means of a series of directives called "Z-Grams." Reforms such as beards, more liberal hairstyles, and civilian clothes on liberty, motorcycles on bases, and other departures from tradition excited many of the younger people and worried older hands. Efforts were instituted to make the Navy more attrac-

ADM Elmo Zumwalt, Chief of Naval Operations from July 1970 to July 1974. Perhaps more than any other post–World War II CNO, he modernized the Navy and brought it in line with modern organizational theory. *The Naval History and Heritage Command*

tive to women and minorities, and these met with much success after some initial setbacks.

In 1972, following passage of the Equal Rights Amendment by Congress, all military services began to change policies that had heretofore restricted women to service only in administrative and support roles. For the first time women were admitted to the service academies, all officer training corps programs, and flight schools. In the Navy the first women were assigned to shipboard and air squadron billets formerly reserved to men. Then in 1978 Congress approved a change to federal law to permit the assignment of women to sea-duty billets in all tenders, oilers, and other types of auxiliary ships and noncombatant aircraft.

Disarmament Treaties

In 1972 President Nixon and Soviet premier Brezhnev signed the Strategic Arms Limitation Treaty (SALT I), the first of several such treaties. One provision contained an **antiballistic missile** (small guided missiles able to intercept and destroy incoming ballistic missiles) defense-system agreement, henceforth called the **ABM Treaty.** Under this treaty, no further antiballistic-missile systems capable of intercepting either strategic land-launched or submarine-launched ballistic missiles (**ICBMs** or **SLBMs**) could be developed by either country. Another provision froze the numbers of ICBMs and SLBMs at then-existing levels.

These treaties had the effect of ensuring that the existing balance of power in strategic weaponry between the two countries would remain stable at then-current levels, thus reaffirming the doctrine of **mutual assured destruction** (MAD), which would serve as a deterrent to nuclear war throughout the remainder of the Cold War. This doctrine held that if both sides in a prospective nuclear war had an overwhelming number of nuclear-armed ballistic missiles, the destruction of each side by the other should war erupt would be assured, thus deterring either side from starting such a war.

The Falklands War

In early 1982 a major maritime event took place in the South Atlantic off the coast of Argentina. The Falkland Islands, long the subject of an ownership dispute between the United Kingdom and Argentina, were taken over by an Argentine occupation force on 2 April. In response, the British, whose colonists had occupied the islands since 1833, gathered a UK invasion force consisting of two ski-jump carriers, several amphibious ships, five submarines, and about thirty escort, auxiliary, and support ships. The ships sailed in groups from England to the South Atlantic, arriving off the Falklands in late April. For the next two months the battle for control of the Falklands raged, involving nearly all elements of modern naval warfare. The Argentines finally capitulated on 4 June, but not before the British had lost several ships, including two frigates and a transport ship, to air-launched Exocet missiles fired from Argentine attack planes. Several others were damaged. One of the Argentines' few capital ships, the cruiser *General Belgrano*, was torpedoed and sunk by a British nuclear attack submarine.

Though not directly involved, the U.S. Navy benefited greatly from the lessons learned by the British during the war, many of which caused dramatic changes. The conflict effectively quieted many skeptics in Congress who had begun to question the need for maintaining fifteen carriers and their associated support ships. It contributed to this force level being kept unchanged throughout the 1980s. Also, the 1950s and 1960s had seen a trend toward the use of aluminum vice steel plate in the construction of most U.S. and British warships, as a

Many valuable lessons were learned about the survivability of modern warships during the Falklands War. Here, HMS *Avenger* aids HMS *Plymouth* after the latter was hit by Argentine bombs. *The Naval History and Heritage Command*

means of compensating for the increased weight of habitability features and new electronic gear. One of the major problems on many of the British warships hit during the Falklands campaign, however, was uncontrollable burning of their aluminum structures. Most U.S. warships built since have incorporated steel plate wherever possible, and fire-retardant, shrapnel-resistant insulation is applied to any aluminum plating used.

Grenada and Panama

In late October 1983, in response to a takeover of the Caribbean island nation of Grenada by Cuban-backed communist forces, a joint U.S. task force with elements of all services conducted a major amphibious operation and took control of the island in three days. Forces from several nearby Caribbean island governments also took part in the operation. In the process, about six hundred American citizens, mostly students attending medical school there, and eighty foreign nationals were evacuated to safety. Later, U.S. forces helped the Grenadians reestablish their representative government and rebuild damaged buildings and other facilities.

Relations between the United States and Panama had steadily deteriorated throughout the 1980s. By 1988 the country had become a major staging area for drug smuggling to the United States, and its dictator, GEN Manuel Noriega, was indicted on drug-trafficking charges by a U.S. federal grand jury. In response, the Noriega government became increasingly belligerent toward U.S. interests in Panama, causing the United States to impose economic sanctions in retaliation. In May 1989 a national election voted Noriega out of power, but he refused to accept the result and had the vote annulled.

In December 1989, following a series of incidents that culminated in the killing of a U.S. Marine lieutenant by Pan-

Area of operations during the Falklands War of 1982.

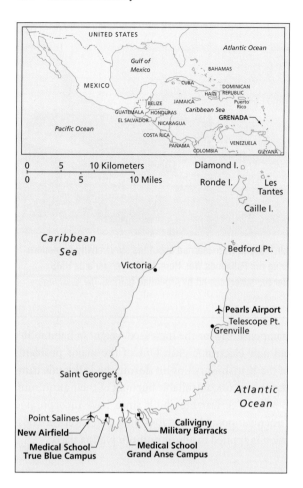

The invasion of the island of Grenada by a joint U.S. task force in October 1983 underscored American resolve to resist communist takeovers of democratic governments in the Western Hemisphere during the 1980s. *The Naval History and Heritage Command*

Part of the huge cache of Soviet-made arms and ammunition recovered during the Grenada operation in October 1983. Note the Cuban Economic Office label on this crate of 7.62 mm ammunition. *The Naval History and Heritage Command*

Marines patrolling a street in Panama during Operation Just Cause in 1989. *The Naval History and Heritage Command*

amanian Defense Force (PDF) troops, the Noriega government declared that a state of war existed between the United States and Panama. Early in the morning hours of 20 December 1989, President George H. W. Bush sent a combined invasion force of 12,000 U.S. Army, Navy, Air Force, and Marine Corps troops to remove Noriega and return the country to the control of the officials who had been lawfully elected in May. These forces joined another 12,000 U.S. military personnel, mostly Army, already stationed in the Panama Canal Zone.

The intervention, called **Operation Just Cause,** was the largest U.S. military operation in the 1980s. Some fierce fighting occurred, but rapid envelopment by coordinated airborne and armored U.S. forces quickly overcame most PDF strongholds. By the end of the day most military objectives had been achieved, and only scattered pockets of resistance remained. Democracy was restored to Panama. Noriega eluded capture for some months, eventually surrendering to U.S. authorities in January 1990. He was later transported to the United States,

where he served a lengthy prison sentence after being convicted on drug-trafficking charges.

In 2010 he was extradited to France, where he served a year in prison after being convicted of money laundering, and in 2011 he was extradited back to Panama. He is currently serving a twenty-year prison sentence there for human rights violations that occurred during his rule.

Rise of Terrorism

One of the more unfortunate trends that marked the 1980s was the rise of terrorism worldwide, especially in connection with events in the Middle East. Principal among these events was the

Iran-Iraq War, which lasted most of the decade. Of only slightly less importance was the issue of a homeland for the Palestinian Arabs, a question that has caused almost continuous strife between Israel and neighboring Arab states for decades. Many of the more extreme Arab groups involved in both struggles, unable to challenge Israel and the Western nations militarily, turned to international terrorism to advance their causes. Since many of the terrorist acts involved U.S. allies or U.S. citizens or both, our armed services, especially the Navy and Marine Corps, were asked to respond to several of the crises—but not always with beneficial results.

Following a takeover of the U.S. embassy in Tehran, Iran, by a group of radical students, fifty-two American diplomats and citizens were held hostage there for 444 days between November 1979 and January 1981. After a failed rescue attempt at one point by helicopters from the carrier USS *Nimitz*, extensive negotiations by the Carter administration, along with help from the Algerian government, resulted in the release of the hostages on the day of President Reagan's inauguration on 20 January.

One of the most tragic events occurred after a Marine force was asked to join a UN peacekeeping effort in Lebanon in 1983. On 23 October a suicide bomber driving a truck full of explosives attacked the headquarters building at Beirut Airport that housed some of the peacekeeping force. The explosion resulted in the deaths of 241 Marines and naval personnel in the building at the time.

Other terrorist actions during the 1980s included additional instances of the taking of civilian and military hostages of U.S. and several other Western nationalities worldwide, car bombings, assaults against civil facilities, such as airports and train stations, and airliner bombings and hijackings. In the early part of the decade, a number of these actions were shown to have been directly sponsored by the erratic Libyan leader COL Muammar Qaddafi, who had established several terrorist

Libya, under its ruler Colonel Muammar Qaddafi, sponsored terrorist attacks in Europe in the mid-1980s and provoked incidents with the U.S. Sixth Fleet in the Gulf of Sidra, ultimately resulting in a retaliatory attack on Libyan terrorist bases in April 1986.

training bases within Libya. In the mid-1980s Qaddafi began to make threats to limit freedom of navigation in the Gulf of Sidra, in the Mediterranean off Libya's northern shore. In March 1986 there were several incidents involving U.S. naval air and surface forces, during which surface-to-air missiles were fired at Navy aircraft and Libyan patrol boats were sunk.

Finally, on 15 April 1986, in retaliation for the continuing threats and several Libyan-sponsored terrorist acts against U.S. citizens in Europe, and with the agreement of most of our European allies, a combined attack was carried out against Libyan terrorist support bases. Air Force F-111s based in England struck army barracks, an airport near Tripoli, and the port of Sidi Bilal. Carrier-based A-7s and F/A-6s attacked other barracks at Benghazi and an airfield at Benina. Qaddafi himself

There was not much left of the U.S. Marine headquarters in Beirut following the terrorist bombing in 1983. *The Naval History and Heritage Command*

A Soviet-built Libyan guided-missile corvette burns in the Gulf of Sidra after a clash with U.S. naval aircraft in March 1986. *The Naval History and Heritage Command*

narrowly missed being killed during the course of these raids, in which only two U.S. Air Force F-111 crewmen were lost.

Following the 1986 attacks, most of Qaddafi's attentions were turned inward toward maintaining and strengthening his autocratic rule of the country, often through oppressive human-rights violations against his real or imagined opponents. Although the 1986 attack had a dramatic effect on reducing Libyan-sponsored terrorism, it did not completely eliminate it. In December 1998 terrorists from Libya bombed a Pan American Airways jet in flight over Lockerbie, Scotland, killing all 259 people aboard, including 179 Americans. Qaddafi's repressive policies would eventually lead to his death at the hands of revolutionaries during the Arab Spring uprisings in 2011.

The Persian Gulf

In September 1980 a war began between Iran and Iraq that would progress through several phases until August 1988, when a truce was negotiated that would end most of the open warfare. Though the proximate cause of the war was a long-standing border dispute, there had also been many years of political and ethnic tension between the two countries. The first years of the conflict turned into a war of attrition, during which neither country was able to achieve significant inroads into the territory of the other, despite many casualties on both sides. During much of the conflict from the mid-1980s onward, the war erupted into the Persian Gulf, with each side trying to disrupt the oil-tanker trade of the other and thereby gain economic advantage. Soon tankers of all nations transiting the gulf, especially the Strait of Hormuz, were subject to air and mine attacks by both nations. Because of the American political posture in the area—the United States had generally assumed the role of peacemaker—and perhaps also because the U.S. has always been less dependent on Middle Eastern oil than most other Western nations and therefore less vulnerable, the United States played a major role in keeping the Persian Gulf open for transit by oil tankers of all nations during the latter stages of the Iran-Iraq War. Throughout 1987 and 1988 U.S. frigates and cruisers served as escorts, accompanying and protecting tankers transiting the gulf.

These operations were not conducted without cost. In May 1987 the frigate USS *Stark* (FFG 31) was attacked and hit by two Exocet missiles launched from an Iraqi aircraft while the ship was on radar picket duty in the gulf. In April 1988 the USS *Samuel B. Roberts* (FFG 58) was almost cut in two by a mine but was saved by the damage-control efforts of her crew. Then, in July 1988, an unfortunate incident demonstrated the limitations of even the most modern equipment in this type of situation. The Aegis cruiser USS *Vincennes* (CG 49), in the middle of a battle against Iranian gunboats in the Strait of Hormuz, mistakenly shot down a civilian Iranian airliner that approached the ship in a seemingly threatening manner over the strait. All 290 people aboard the plane died.

Many mine-warfare ships, mainly in the Naval Reserve fleet, engaged in mine-clearing operations following the end of hostilities in the gulf. These operations continued until early 1990, at which time all the mines released by both sides during the war were considered to have been neutralized.

The Demise of the Soviet Union

The Soviet economy, never very strong since World War II, suffered throughout the early 1980s from both low productivity and lack of modern technology. To a great extent this state of affairs resulted from restrictive communistic policies concerning private property and the accumulation of personal wealth, as well as an emphasis on military spending. These, in conjunction with years of Cold War military posturing and a provocative foreign policy, had severely limited any infusion of money and technology from the West.

Against this background Mikhail Gorbachev came to power as premier of the Soviet Union in 1985. Both as a means of internal economic reform and an attempt to win favor with Western nations, Gorbachev initiated a series of liberal reforms

The USS *Fox* provides escort to the tanker *Gas Prince* during the Iran-Iraq War in the Persian Gulf, July 1987. *CHINFO*

The last of the Soviet premiers Mikhail Gorbachev (left) signs the INF treaty with President Ronald Reagan (right) in December 1987. *National Archives*

reduced many tensions. It eliminated **intermediate-range nuclear missiles** (those with ranges between three hundred and 3,400 miles) in Europe. Relations with Western nations were also improved by many state visits, summit meetings, and further arms-control negotiations conducted throughout the late 1980s, as well as by a loosening of controls over the satellite states of Eastern Europe that had been dominated by the Soviet Union since World War II.

All of Gorbachev's domestic efforts, however, proved to be insufficient to hold back a rising tide of democracy that, once set in motion, rapidly engulfed the Soviet Union. The populations of the satellite states took advantage of the erosion of Soviet control to generate successful self-determination movements. These eventually resulted in complete independence of all the former satellite states by 1990. Perhaps the most important, and surely the most emotional, symbol of the new European order occurred in November 1989 with the demolition of the **Berlin Wall**. It had divided East and West Berlin in Germany for thirty years and symbolized the repression of the satellite nations behind the so-called iron curtain. Germany itself was formally

and policies collectively called *glasnost* (a new openness in foreign relations) and *perestroika* (internal political and economic reforms). In 1987 an important bilateral arms-reduction agreement called the INF (Intermediate-range Nuclear Forces) Treaty was negotiated between the United States and USSR that

One of the most emotional symbols of the Cold War era was the Berlin Wall that had been constructed by the East Germans in 1961, pictured here in 1975. Note the wide no man's land "death strip" behind it, built to provide a clear line of fire at any fleeing refugees attempting to escape across it. Later much of the surface on the West Berlin side was whitewashed and covered with colorful graffiti. The wall was demolished in 1989. *Edward Valachovic*

reunited a year later. The Warsaw Pact alliance between the USSR and the former satellite nations was disbanded in February 1991.

But most amazing to most Western analysts was the rapid rise of the democratic movement within the Soviet Union itself. Simultaneously with the loss of the satellite states, people in most of the republics making up the Soviet Union staged their own demonstrations for self-rule. Quickly rising to the foremost position was the Russian republic, led by Boris Yeltsin, who only a few years earlier (1988) had been thrown out of the Soviet Politburo (governing leadership group) for urging Gorbachev to proceed more quickly with the liberalization program.

Things came to a head in August 1991, when the remaining old-line communists in the Politburo attempted to stage a coup. They arrested Gorbachev and detained him and his family for three days at his vacation home on the Crimean Peninsula, on the Black Sea. The Soviet army, however, declined to support the coup and refused to attack the Russian parliament building in Moscow, from which Yeltsin was leading the opposition to the coup. The overwhelming support for both Yeltsin and Gorbachev from the people of Moscow, and indeed the whole Soviet Union, proved decisive. Within days the situation was fully resolved. Gorbachev was returned to Moscow, and the coup leaders were themselves arrested.

Yeltsin had now become the most powerful leader in the disintegrating Soviet Union. In early December he made the dissolution official by proclaiming the existence of a new Commonwealth of Independent States, made up of the former Soviet republics. On Christmas Day 1991, Gorbachev resigned, and the Soviet Union was formally dissolved. The red, white, and blue prerevolutionary Russian flag was raised over the Kremlin.

The Cold War was over. The Western democracies, led by the United States, had successfully prevailed against almost fifty years of challenge from Soviet communism.

Critical Thinking

1. The United Nations was established following World War II to try to prevent a third world war from ever occurring. Research the United Nations and the role that it has played in the major military conflicts over the last twenty years. State whether you think it should continue to be supported by the United States. Justify your conclusion.

2. Research the probable consequences that might have occurred if GEN Douglas MacArthur's request to carry the Korean War into China in 1951 had been granted by President Truman.

3. There were many similarities between the way the Vietnam War was conducted throughout the late 1960s and the Korean War a decade earlier. Research the reasons for the prohibition against direct attacks against North Vietnam by U.S. forces throughout most of that war.

Chronology

1946	Churchill "iron curtain" speech
1947	Truman Doctrine and Marshall Plan; unification of U.S. armed forces; Cold War begins
1949	NATO created
1950–53	Korean War
1955	Warsaw Pact created; *Nautilus* launched
1962	Cuban missile quarantine
1964–73	Vietnam War
1968	*Pueblo* incident
1980–88	Iran-Iraq War
1982	Falklands War
1983	Grenada invasion
1986	Attack on Libyan terrorists
1989	Panama invasion
1991	Cold War ends; USSR dissolved

Study Guide Questions

1. What happened to the U.S. armed forces after World War II ended?

2. What were the only two possible American response options to Soviet takeovers of Eastern European nations following World War II?

3. What term was originated in 1946 by Winston Churchill to describe the conflict of interests between the West and the Soviet Union?

4. What was the objective of postwar "unification" of the U.S. armed services?

5. What was the final result of congressional deliberations on armed-forces unification?

6. What events caused the beginning of the U.S. Sixth Fleet deployments to the Mediterranean?

7. What was President Truman's plan for reconstruction of war-torn Europe?

8. A. What two Soviet actions in the late 1940s caused the Western democracies to create a formal alliance to counter the spread of Soviet communism?
   B. What was this alliance called?
   C. What Soviet-sponsored military alliance was formed in response?

9. A. Where did the Potsdam Conference draw the boundary line between North and South Korea?
   B. Which major nations aligned themselves with North and South Korea?

10. What were the objectives of the North Korean invasion of South Korea?

11. Who was the supreme commander of UN forces in Korea?

12. What made the landing at Inchon so risky?

13. What happened on 25 November 1950 that changed the whole complexion of the Korean War?

14. Why was General MacArthur relieved by President Truman?

15. Where were the Korean truce talks held?

16. What was the historical significance of the *Pueblo* crisis in 1968?

17. What new kinds of submarines became part of the U.S. fleet in the 1950s?

18. A. What was the American response to the discovery of Soviet intermediate-range missiles in Cuba in 1962?
    B. What was the result?

19. What did the USSR do as a result of the Cuban confrontation?

20. Where was the dividing line between North and South Vietnam after 1954?

21. What triggered civil war in South Vietnam in 1956?

22. What controversial event brought the United States into the war on a major scale?

23. What official and common names were given to the communist South Vietnamese insurgents?

24. A. What was the "brown-water Navy"?
    B. Where did it operate?

25. What restrictions were placed on the conduct of the war by U.S. civilian leadership?

26. What effect did the Tet Offensive of 1968 have in the United States?

27. What was the final outcome of the Vietnam War?

28. What effects did the Falklands War of 1982 have on the U.S. Navy?

29. What happened on the island of Grenada in 1983?

30. Why did the United States take military action in Panama in 1989?

31. Why did the United States conduct an attack against Colonel Qaddafi's Libya in April 1986?

32. What was the role of the U.S. Navy during the Persian Gulf warfare in the 1980s?

33. What profound change took place in the early 1990s that brought an end to the Cold War?

New Vocabulary

superpower	range of tide
demobilization	demilitarized zone (DMZ)
communism	armistice
arms race	kiloton
iron curtain	megaton
containment	quarantine (blockade)
communist bloc	helicopter gunship
coup d'état	"third country" shipping
geographic dagger	ski-jump carrier

11

The 1990s

The end of the Cold War in 1991 brought with it a greatly diminished threat of nuclear warfare between the superpowers. Still, there were many serious issues that would concern the U.S. Navy and the other U.S. armed services for the remainder of the decade and into the new millennium. On the international scene, these issues included the problem of the nuclear stockpile of the former USSR; continuing conflict in the Middle East, southern Europe, and elsewhere; proliferation of nuclear weapons among third-world nations; the international illegal drug trade; and global terrorism, much of it directed against the United States and other Western nations. On the domestic scene there was concern over internal strife caused by the post–Cold War downsizing of the services and the increasing role of women in the military, drug trafficking within the United States, and domestic terrorism.

Russia and the Former Soviet Union

Immediately upon taking over the leadership of the former Soviet states that constituted the new commonwealth, President Boris Yeltsin found himself faced with several very serious problems. Most important were the issues of how to revitalize the economies of Russia and the other former Soviet states, what to do with the armed forces, and how to control the formidable former Soviet nuclear arsenal.

In pursuit of economic support for his new commonwealth, Yeltsin immediately established friendly working relations with Western heads of state. After receiving assurances that Yeltsin now controlled the Soviet nuclear-weapons stockpile, the United States and other Western nations started sending much aid in various forms.

In 1991 the first of several important strategic-arms-reduction agreements between the United States and the Russians was signed. Called the Treaty on the Reduction and Limitation of Strategic Offensive Arms, or the START I Treaty, it cut total numbers of strategic nuclear warheads in both countries by 25 to 35 percent. Later that year President Bush announced a unilateral withdrawal of all U.S. land-based tactical nuclear

President George H. W. Bush and Russian President Boris Yeltsin sign the START II treaty at the Kremlin in Moscow in January 1993. *National Archives*

weapons from overseas bases and all sea-based tactical nuclear weapons from U.S. ships, submarines, and aircraft.

In January 1993 Bush and Yeltsin signed the second Strategic Offensive Arms Reduction and Limitation Treaty (START II), considered the broadest disarmament pact in history. Its terms called for both sides to reduce long-range nuclear arsenals to between three thousand to 3,500 warheads within a decade and to eliminate completely their land-based multiple-warhead missiles. Many nuclear missiles on both sides were dismantled and destroyed. In late 1996 Yeltsin announced that from that time on, no Russian-controlled nuclear missiles would remain aimed toward any of the Western states. In early 1997 President Bill Clinton announced that several of the former Soviet satellite states would be permitted to join the North Atlantic Treaty Organization (NATO). The Czech Republic, Hungary, and Poland did so in 1999, and several others have joined since. Only a few years earlier such an idea would have seemed incredible to most in the West.

The Middle East

The peace in the Persian Gulf area following the end of the Iran-Iraq War in 1988 unfortunately proved to be short-lived. With his forces no longer engaged in the war with Iran, Iraq's leader Saddam Hussein was free to attempt other more aggressive military adventures to the south.

Operations Desert Shield and Desert Storm

In August 1990, suddenly and without warning, Iraqi forces under Hussein staged a brutal invasion of neighboring Kuwait. That country was captured quickly, along with thousands of Western civilian oil-field workers and their families, who were then detained and used as hostages against Western reprisal. Saudi Arabia, fearful of becoming the next victim of Hussein's aggression, quickly appealed to the United Nations and especially to its own ally, the United States, for help. In an unprecedented show of unanimity against such aggression, the UN passed a trade embargo against Iraq, restricting movement and sale of all goods, including oil and food products, into and out of Iraq. Simultaneously, the United States embarked upon **Operation Desert Shield,** deploying the largest U.S. military and naval force assembled since the Vietnam War to Saudi Arabia.

By the end of 1990, some 450,000 U.S. military personnel and 100 U.S. Navy ships were engaged in operations in support

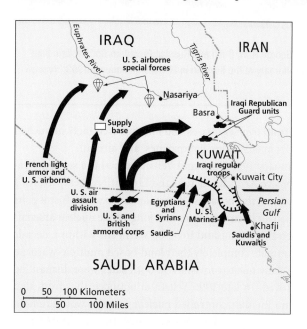

Theater of operations in Operation Desert Storm, 1991. GEN Norman Schwarzkopf's strategists deceived the Iraqis into believing the main thrusts into Kuwait would come north from Saudi Arabia and from an amphibious assault near Kuwait City. However, most of the coalition forces engaged in a swift flanking movement to the west into southern Iraq, cutting off the Iraqi forces in Kuwait from any hope of escape or resupply.

Iraqi dictator Saddam Hussein kept the Middle East in turmoil throughout the 1980s and 1990s by his aggressive behavior toward neighboring nations and oppressive treatment of minority populations within his own country. *Iraqi state television*

of Desert Shield. Forces from many other nations also joined U.S. forces there to form the so-called UN coalition. U.S. and allied ships patrolled in the Persian Gulf, Arabian Sea, and Red Sea, enforcing the UN trade embargo against Iraq. Among the forces deployed in the Saudi desert were thousands of U.S. Marines. Navy hospital ships, largely staffed with Naval Reserve medical personnel, deployed off the Saudi coasts ready to handle any casualties. And maritime sealift transported the bulk of the heavy equipment and supplies needed to sustain the operation.

The UN Security Council imposed a deadline of 15 January 1991 by which time Hussein had to have all of his forces out of Kuwait or face military action. Hussein did not leave Kuwait. On 16 January a massive air assault on every target of military significance in Iraq and Kuwait turned Operation Desert Shield into *Desert Storm*. Tens of thousands of air sorties (attack missions) were launched by U.S. Navy, Army, and Air Force planes and helicopters and those of other coalition forces. The coalition soon achieved air superiority and quickly shot down any offensive-minded Iraqi aircraft that managed to get airborne.

On 23 February an allied ground offensive into Kuwait and southern Iraq began, under the overall command of GEN H. "Stormin' Norman" Schwarzkopf, U.S. Army. The U.S. and coalition forces made short work of the now demoralized Iraqi troops, most of whom had been heavily bombed and cut off from all resupply of food and munitions by the air campaign. By 26 February Kuwait City had been secured, and on the evening of 27 February President Bush announced a cease-fire, which became permanent on 8 April. Victory for the coalition forces was complete, thus ending the largest air and ground offensive fought since World War II.

Aftermath of Desert Storm

Following the end of hostilities in Operation Desert Storm, Hussein devoted much effort to reestablishing control over his country. Part of this effort involved the suppression of ethnic Kurds in northern Iraq and Shiite Muslims in southern Iraq, both of whom had tried to initiate revolts against him after Desert Storm.

In late 1991 and 1992, U.S., British, and French warplanes began enforcing UN-imposed **no-fly zones** (areas over which

Two no-fly zones shown on this map were imposed on Hussein's Iraq by the UN and enforced by U.S., British, and French warplanes between 1991–92 and the beginning of Operation Iraqi Freedom in 2003.

hostile aircraft are prohibited from flying) over the northern and southern part of Iraq, designed to protect the Kurds in northern Iraq and Shiites in the south from further oppression by Hussein. The no-fly zones would continue to be enforced up to the start of *Operation Iraqi Freedom* in 2003.

In August 1996 Hussein staged a threatening movement of some 45,000 troops and three hundred tanks toward UN-protected Kurdish territory in northern Iraq. In response, in September President Clinton ordered a joint U.S. Navy–Air Force strike against Iraqi air-defense systems and bases in the southern part of the country. Some sixty cruise missiles were launched from four surface ships and an SSN in the Persian Gulf and two B-52 bombers from Guam. All Iraqi air defense targets were hit, but no target was completely destroyed. Never-

A Tomahawk missile is launched against Iraqi air-defense installations by the cruiser USS *Shiloh* (CG 67) in the Persian Gulf in September 1996. *CHINFO*

theless, Hussein appeared to have "gotten the message," and the troops and tanks were withdrawn shortly thereafter.

In addition to threats against the Kurds and Shiites, there was also growing concern especially in the late 1990s over Hussein's efforts to enlarge Iraq's stocks of weapons of mass destruction (WMD). In defiance of UN mandates and sanctions, UN weapons inspectors were often denied access to alleged weapons production sites. Finally in the fall of 1998 the alarm over this issue had grown to the point that in September the U.S. Congress at President Clinton's urging passed an act supporting Iraqi opposition group efforts to remove Hussein from power. Then in December a 4-day bombing campaign was conducted by the United States and Britain against Hussein's WMD research and development installations. Code-named *Operation Desert Fox,* the attacks also included strikes against the barracks and command headquarters of Hussein's elite Republican Guard army forces. Over 600 air-launched cruise missiles and bombs were launched from U.S. Air Force and British aircraft, and some 325 Tomahawk cruise missiles were fired from U.S. Navy ships in the Persian Gulf.

Despite these measures, Hussein's efforts to thwart UN weapons inspections and continue his alleged WMD development program continued, ultimately resulting in Operation Iraqi Freedom in 2003.

Conflict in the Balkans

Unfortunately, after the demise of the Soviet Union conflict broke out in several of the countries formerly under its control. In 1991 a civil war began in the Balkan country of Yugoslavia, which had been a client state of the Soviet Union. Yugoslavia's six republics—Slovenia, Croatia, Bosnia-Herzegovina, Serbia, Montenegro, and Macedonia—began to break apart for two reasons: economic difficulties caused by the end of Soviet aid and long-standing friction between ethnic groups in its population. In June 1991, after Croatia and Slovenia both declared their independence from the former Yugoslavia, fighting broke out between ethnic Serbs in Croatia, who claimed part of that republic for Serbia, and the Croat police force. Soon the conflict broadened into Bosnia-Herzegovina, between Serbs, who claimed part of that republic as well, and Muslims and Croats, who claimed the rest. The fighting in the region would continue for five years, and included several prolonged instances of attempted ethnic cleansing and other crimes against humanity.

After months of bloody fighting that included atrocities on both sides, in late 1991 the UN imposed an oil, trade, and weapons embargo against the remnant government of Yugoslavia (which was supplying troops and arms to the Serbs) and Serbia in an attempt to end the fighting. The embargo had little effect, however, and the fighting and atrocities continued. Economic sanctions against Serbia and Montenegro were imposed the

Yugoslavia and its six republics as of 1991.

following May, also with little effect. By the end of 1992 the situation had deteriorated to the point that Yugoslavia ceased to exist for a time as a separate nation. It was briefly reconstituted as the Federal Republic of Yugoslavia by Serbia and Montenegro from 1992–2006, but was never recognized as an independent sovereign state by the international community.

In October 1992 the UN established a no-fly zone prohibiting flights of military aircraft over Bosnian air space; the prohibition was extended to cover all types of aircraft in early 1993. The UN also proclaimed so-called safe areas around several cities, including the nearly leveled city of Sarajevo in southeastern Bosnia, control of which had been a strategic objective of both sides in the conflict. At least one Navy carrier battle group and a Marine amphibious ready group were continually stationed in the Adriatic Sea, both to support Navy operations and to serve as a show of force.

Fighting continued for two more years until late 1995, when the United States joined other NATO forces under the auspices of the United Nations to try to bring a halt to the conflict by a heavier application of force. In August and September 1995, in **Operation Deliberate Force,** Navy and Marine Corps planes from the carrier *Theodore Roosevelt* joined with NATO aircraft from an airbase at Aviano, Italy, to conduct air strikes against Serb military positions south and east of Sarajevo. Altogether 3,500 sorties were flown against 350 separate targets.

Finally, in December 1995 the presidents of Bosnia and Herzegovina, Serbia, and Croatia signed a treaty to end the war. It was negotiated in Dayton, Ohio, with much involvement by the U.S. State Department. The pact called for Bosnia and Herzegovina, Croatia, and what was then still the Federal Republic of Yugoslavia to agree to fully respect the sovereign equality of one another and to settle disputes by peaceful means. For several years thereafter NATO and then the European Union (EU)

deployed troops there, including at one point some 20,000 U.S. Army troops, to keep order following the accords.

The present-day states that succeeded Yugoslavia, with their dates of independence, are as follows: Slovenia, Croatia, and Macedonia (1991); Bosnia and Herzegovina (1992); Montenegro, and Serbia (2006); and Kosovo (2008). Kosovo is not as yet fully recognized as a sovereign state by the entire international community.

Other Problem Areas

Problems broke out in other areas of the world as well. In January 1991 a long civil war erupted in the formerly Soviet-aligned African state of Somalia after the cessation of aid from the Soviet Union, when several clan-led rebel armies forced longtime president Mohammed Siad Barre to flee the country. In his absence several of these groups began battling among themselves for territory, soon producing widespread anarchy and famine. The situation was particularly acute because nearly every adult male in the country possessed at least one firearm, owing to the supply of weapons remaining there from the old Soviet Union.

In December 1992, 28,000 U.S. troops, including 1,800 Marines, took part in the UN-sponsored **Operation Restore Hope,** which was intended to bring in food supplies and restore some order to the country.

Although clan warlords signed a peace accord in March 1993, much sporadic violence continued. Finally in October, following an incident at Mogadishu in which an Army Black Hawk helicopter was shot down and an ensuing gun battle between U.S. soldiers and clan members resulted in eighteen dead and eighty wounded Americans, President Clinton set March 1994 as the date by which all U.S. forces would leave the country. About two thousand Marines were kept offshore for several months thereafter as potential cover for the remaining UN troops.

In mid-1996 Navy–Marine Corps amphibious ready groups were called upon on two occasions to assist in evacuation of U.S. nationals and other noncombatants from the African nations of Liberia and the Central African Republic of Bangui, both of which were experiencing outbreaks of ethnic violence, famine, and disease. The Marines also reinforced the U.S. embassy in Monrovia, Liberia, during that crisis.

In the spring of 1998 much apprehension arose over the issue of nuclear-weapons proliferation when India and Pakistan each exploded nuclear test devices in response to the other's doing so. Escalating conflict between the two nations that might have led to a regional nuclear war was halted by the diplomatic efforts of the Clinton administration, acting in conjunction with the United Nations. Fortunately, both nations were deterred from continuing on a course that could have led to nuclear destruction of both sides. The issue of nuclear non-

An improvised submarine built by drug smugglers in Equador.

Osama bin Laden, head of the al-Qaeda terrorist organization until his death in 2011. He masterminded the 9/11 attacks on the United States in 2001, then managed to elude capture for the next ten years.

proliferation in the region continues to be a major international concern.

Drug Trafficking

Throughout the 1990s and beyond, the Navy and all the other U.S. armed services have been called upon to support both international and domestic efforts to suppress the illegal drug trade. In the 1990s, illicit drug producers in South America increasingly began transporting their drugs to the United States by way of Central America, using boats, improvised submarines, low-flying aircraft, and tractor-trailers hauling smuggled drugs along with legitimate cargo. In response, all services have lent support with their various intelligence agencies worldwide. They also have conducted joint drug-interdiction training exercises with host-nation (partner) forces, particularly in Central and South America. Ground radar and airborne surveillance assets of the Navy and other services have also been used to track and intercept boats and aircraft suspected of drug smuggling. On the domestic scene, all services conduct extensive drug-awareness and testing programs designed to discourage the use of all illegal drugs and other banned substances by service personnel.

International Terrorism

In early August 1998 U.S. embassies in Kenya and Tanzania were virtually destroyed by terrorist car bombs. These attacks were determined by U.S. intelligence services to have been masterminded by a wealthy exiled Saudi Arabian terrorist named Osama bin Laden, who had proclaimed a *holy war* (war motivated by religious extremism) against the United States for its part in the action against Iraq in the early 1990s.

In retaliation for these bombings, on 20 August 1998 President Clinton ordered cruise-missile attacks to be carried out against two targets: terrorist training camps run by bin Laden in Afghanistan and a factory in Sudan believed to be involved in manufacturing chemical weapons for him. Over seventy Tomahawk missiles were fired during the attacks on the two facilities by U.S. Navy ships in the Persian Gulf and in the Red Sea. Though he was thought to have been present at the Afghanistan site at the time of the attack, bin Laden escaped injury and would go on to become the most infamous terrorist of modern times after the 9/11 attacks on the United States in 2001.

Domestic Events

The 1990s proved to be somewhat turbulent times at home as well, both for the Navy and the other armed services. In response to the end of the Cold War threat, a downsizing and consolidation of forces among all U.S. armed services began that would progress well into the new millennium. Added to the natural tensions caused by this throughout the decade were several widely publicized, unfortunate incidents of fraternization and sexual misconduct in the Navy and the other services.

In 1993 Congress repealed the Combat Exclusion Law, thus allowing women to serve on combatant ships and aircraft. However, they were still restricted from serving in assignments in which they might be exposed to frontline combat, or from serving aboard submarines.

In April 1995 the threat of domestic terrorism was again highlighted when a powerful bomb exploded in front of the Federal Building at Oklahoma City, Oklahoma, killing or maiming scores of innocent people. In July a year later, a bomb detonated at the 1996 Olympic Games in Atlanta, Georgia, killing one person and injuring several others. In the same month came an explosion and crash of TWA Flight 800 into the sea off the coast of Long Island, New York, killing all 230 passengers and crew; Navy divers participated in a salvage operation that lasted until late fall 1996 and eventually resulted in the recovery of most of the bodies of those killed and most of the wreckage of the plane. At first it was thought that terrorism may have played some part in the incident, but it was later determined that the most likely cause of the explosion had been an electrical discharge into a vapor-filled fuel tank.

Critical Thinking

1. Following the liberation of Kuwait with Operation Desert Storm in 1991, should coalition forces have continued to advance into Iraq to remove Saddam Hussein from power at that time? Justify your answer.

Chronology

1990	Iraq invades Kuwait
1991	Operation Desert Storm; war in Bosnia begins; no-fly zones in Iraq established
1992	Operation Restore Hope
1995	Oklahoma federal building bombed
1996	TWA Flight 800 salvage; missile attack on Iraq
1998	Attack on bin Laden terrorist base

Study Guide Questions

1. What were the main provisions of the START II disarmament treaty signed by the United States and the Russian Commonwealth in 1993?

2. A. What action caused the United States to engage in massive military operations in the Persian Gulf area in 1990–91?

   B. What were these operations called?

   C. What was the outcome?

3. What was the purpose of the no-fly zones imposed by the UN in Iraq in 1991–92?

4. What provocative actions did Hussein carry out in Iraq throughout much of the 1990s?

5. A. What major terrorist actions against the United States occurred in Africa in 1998?

   B. Who masterminded these?

   C. What was the U.S. response?

6. Where in Europe did fighting break out in 1991?

7. What other trouble spots in Africa involved the U.S. Navy and Marines in the 1990s?

8. What event in 1998 caused much concern over nuclear nonproliferation issues?

9. What incident of domestic terrorism took place in Oklahoma in 1995?

New Vocabulary

new millennium	mastermind
no-fly zone	holy war
economic sanctions	

12

The New Millennium

The advent of the new millennium would mark the beginning of an era of new and often nontraditional missions for the U.S. Navy and Marine Corps. One main issue that had become increasingly alarming during the latter 1990s would dominate—**global terrorism.** To this would be added another major problem that had last been confronted around the turn of the 19th century—**piracy.** Worldwide, **humanitarian missions** (for relief of human suffering) would be another important priority. Against this backdrop, several innovative changes would be made to the ways in which carrier strike groups and Marine expeditionary forces were made up and deployed, in order to better support and carry out Navy missions. Later in the decade the U.S. Navy would be given a new, additional mission of sea-based **ballistic-missile defense (BMD)** of our homeland as well as those of our allies in Europe and the Far East.

Unfortunately, funding for adequate numbers of trained personnel, ships, and aircraft to support the pace of operations in support of these worldwide missions in the years since the beginning of the new millennium has been a persistent problem, especially since the 2007 recession. By 2005 the total number of Navy ships had decreased from some 589 during the latter part of the Cold War in 1985 to 283, a number that has not changed much since. At the same time the demands of the wars in Iraq and Afghanistan created shortages in numbers of qualified personnel to man these ships. It became necessary to adopt such measures as rotating crews to deployed ships from those undergoing maintenance and overhauls, a practice unheard of in times past. This state of affairs has not been made any easier by the mandated federal funding cuts of the recent past, and it will undoubtedly present many challenges in the foreseeable future.

Early Events

In August 2000 the guided-missile destroyer USS *Cole* (DDG 67), in port in Aden, Yemen, for a routine fuel stop, suffered a large hole blown in her port side by a bomb-laden boat crewed by two suicide bombers. Seventeen U.S. sailors were killed, and thirty-nine others were injured. The terrorists conducting the attack were subsequently linked to the terrorist Osama bin Laden. The damaged ship was carried back to the Ingalls Shipyard in Pascagoula, Mississippi, on board a civilian transport ship. There the ship was repaired and would be relaunched in September 2001, ironically in the same week as the terrorist attacks on the World Trade Center and the Pentagon.

In April 2001 the often contentious U.S. relationship with China experienced another low when a Navy P-3 reconnaissance aircraft flying a mission over international waters in the South China Sea suffered a midair collision with a Chinese fighter jet that came too close. Following the collision the Chinese plane crashed into the sea, killing its pilot. The American plane made an emergency landing on China's Hainan Island, south of the mainland. The twenty-four men and women of its crew were held for the next eleven days until they were released into U.S. custody. They received a hero's welcome when they returned to the United States a few days later. The plane was later dismantled by the Chinese, who returned it in pieces to the United States in early July.

In June 2002 the United States formally withdrew from the 1972 antiballistic-missile (ABM) defense treaty that had been

A hole was blown in the side of the guided-missile destroyer USS *Cole* by terrorists during a fuel stop in Aden, Yemen, in August 2000. Seventeen crew members were killed. The ship was repaired and returned to duty a year later. *CHINFO*

Navy lieutenant Osborn, pilot of the Navy P-3 involved in the midair collision with a Chinese fighter jet in April 2001. *CHINFO*

The south tower of the World Trade Center in New York City moments after it was hit by an airliner commandeered by al-Qaeda terrorists on the morning of 11 September 2001. Smoke is billowing from the damaged north tower alongside. *www.TheMachineStops.com*

negotiated with the old Soviet Union, thus freeing the Navy to pursue the development and deployment of an ABM version of its Standard shipboard air defense missile, the SM-3. This would pave the way for the ballistic-missile defense mission in the later years of the decade. Such a missile and its supporting radar systems would have been prohibited under the 1972 treaty.

Terrorist Attacks of 11 September 2001

As the nation entered the new millennium, ominous signs began to appear that the threat posed by global terrorism would continue to assert itself, as evidenced by the bombing of the USS *Cole* in August 2000. Then, on the morning of 11 September 2001 (henceforth referred to as **9/11**), the unthinkable happened. Both of the World Trade Center towers in New York City were hit and set afire by hijacked airliners. A short time later a third hijacked plane hit the Pentagon in Washington, D.C. A fourth plane, presumably headed toward targets in Washington, D.C., crashed into the countryside in western Pennsylvania, most likely as the result of a scuffle between its hijackers and the passengers and crew.

Both Trade Center towers collapsed later that morning, causing nearly three thousand people to lose their lives. As a result of the attack on the Pentagon, 189 people were killed. President George W. Bush immediately called the terrorist attacks an act of war. He vowed to retaliate against the terrorist organizations responsible for them (later determined to be bin Laden and his al-Qaeda terrorist organization, then understood to be based primarily in Afghanistan). The Navy immediately deployed ships of the Atlantic and Pacific Fleets off the East and West Coasts to help guard against further terrorist attacks. Air National Guard planes flew combat air patrols over New York City, Washington, D.C., and other large cities throughout the country. Within a few weeks, some 50,000 reservists of all ser-

vices were given mobilization orders to augment Air National Guard units, help guard U.S. airports, and provide other support. This homeland defense effort was designated **Operation Noble Eagle.**

Operation Enduring Freedom

In the days following the 11 September attack, plans were made to retaliate against bin Laden and al-Qaeda, and any countries that supported them, beginning with the Taliban government in Afghanistan. When the Taliban would not give up bin Laden, the United States at the direction of President George W. Bush deployed military assets to the region in preparation for a large military confrontation. These deployments included the aircraft carriers USS *Theodore Roosevelt* (CVN 71) and *Carl Vinson* (CVN 70), plus other carriers and support ships in the Arabian Sea; over a hundred Air Force fighter-bombers; and a large contingent of U.S. special operations forces. Many other nations pledged to support the American effort.

On 8 October 2001, **Operation Enduring Freedom** began with air strikes by Navy and Air Force planes on strategic targets throughout Afghanistan. These were accompanied by humanitarian airdrops of food to relieve the suffering of the Afghan population. Much of the ground fighting was left to the Northern Alliance, a loose coalition of rebel Afghan tribes in northeastern provinces that had long been fighting the Taliban.

By late November the Northern Alliance, supported by relentless air attacks by U.S. Navy and Air Force planes, and by

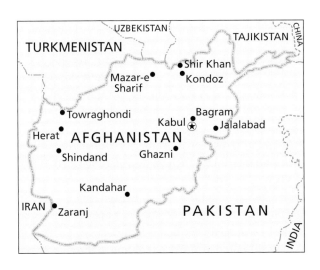

Map of Afghanistan, showing major cities and surrounding countries.

An Osprey vertical-lift aircraft discharges a squad of Marines supporting Operation Enduring Freedom in a desolate desert in Afghanistan. *CHINFO*

American Special Forces personnel on the ground, had seized control of most of the country from the Taliban. Several key al-Qaeda officials had been captured or killed, but bin Laden himself escaped. Most of the remaining Taliban and al-Qaeda sought safe haven either in Pakistan or in the remote mountains in Afghanistan. An international conference in Bonn, Germany, laid the framework for political reconstruction of the country. Though the conference also stipulated that all remaining Afghan militia forces were to be placed under control of the new government, in reality most of the militias continued to affiliate with regional and tribal leaders, a situation that would be a source of continuing problems for the new regime. In October 2004 Hamid Karzai became the first democratically elected president of Afghanistan, an office he would continue to hold until mid-2014.

In late 2001 and early 2002, peacekeeping forces from NATO countries and many other nations arrived in Afghanistan and joined American forces to keep peace and provide training for Afghan military forces and civilian police. Although for a time things were relatively quiet, eventually Taliban insurgent activity began to increase, and as in Iraq in later years, **improvised explosive devices (IEDs)** and suicide bombers began to take an increasing toll. Thousands of regular and reserve Navy personnel served in nontraditional roles in Afghanistan during these years. Surface line officers served as artillery battery commanders; Navy divers assisted with explosive ordinance disposal; and Seabees and other sailors engaged in all manner of support activities throughout the country. A large number of civilian security contractors were also employed to assist in the peacekeeping and training roles.

In spite of the best efforts of the U.S. and allied peacekeeping force, insurgent activity continued to rise. In 2010 President Barack Obama ordered a surge in the number of American troops deployed to Afghanistan, with a new emphasis on shift-

ing most combat and security patrol responsibilities to the Afghan National Army. At the same time a campaign against al-Qaeda leaders in refuge in Pakistan, and later in other countries, began, often using **unmanned aerial vehicles** (drones) armed with air-to-ground missiles to attack and kill them. In 2011 and 2012 the United States and its allies began to draw down the number of troops serving in Afghanistan. Most if not all remaining NATO and American military personnel are presently scheduled to be withdrawn by late 2014.

Operation Iraqi Freedom

By 2002 continuing defiance by Iraq's Saddam Hussein of the terms of the 1991 cease-fire agreement ending Operation Desert Storm had become a major issue for the United States. Hussein had prevented UN weapons inspection teams from inspecting key sites on several occasions, and there were alarming intelligence estimates (later disproved) that Iraq was accumulating a growing stockpile of **weapons of mass destruction**—chemical, biological, and, of special concern, nuclear weapons. There were also claims by some that Hussein was harboring al-Qaeda terrorists, though these were never substantiated. In late 2002 President Bush declared that if the UN did not take more effective action to force Hussein to disarm, the United States might have to take unilateral military action against Iraq.

When the UN Security Council and several other countries pressed for more time to seek a diplomatic solution, the United States decided to move toward war if Hussein and his sons did not agree to leave Iraq. On 17 March 2003 President Bush gave him forty-eight hours to leave the country. He did not do so, and on 19 March the United States, along with coalition partners Britain and several other nations, began **Operation Iraqi Freedom** with extensive air and missile attacks against the capital, Baghdad, and other key military targets. The initial attacks, using what were dubbed "shock and awe" tactics at the time by Defense Secretary Donald Rumsfeld, were intended

A Predator drone. These drones have daylight and infrared cameras and can be equipped with a variety of laser-guided munitions, such as the missile shown here. *CHINFO*

to take out most of Iraq's command and control organization while killing many of Iraq's key leaders, including, ideally, Hussein himself. In the days that followed, a large number of American-led coalition troops invaded Iraq from the south in a blitzkrieg-like advance toward Baghdad, while other airborne forces parachuted into northern Iraq, where they teamed up with Iraqi Kurds fighting there. By 9 April these forces had succeeded in capturing Baghdad, and on 1 May, on board the carrier USS *Abraham Lincoln* (CVN 72), President Bush declared that major combat had ended.

Hussein and his sons managed to elude capture for a time, but in July both sons were killed by coalition forces, and Hussein himself was captured near Tikrit, north of Baghdad, in December. He would eventually be convicted of crimes against humanity by an Iraqi court and executed in December 2006. Massive efforts were begun to rebuild Iraq's infrastructure

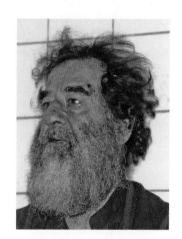

Iraqi leader Saddam Hussein as he appeared when captured by U.S. forces in December 2003. He was eventually executed in 2006 for multiple crimes against humanity, including the murder of hundreds of thousands of Iraqi citizens during his ruthless twenty-four-year rule of Iraq. *U.S. government photo*

(basic communications, transportation, and other vital facilities and services), and to train Iraqi military and civilian police forces to eventually take over responsibility for keeping order in the country. As in Afghanistan, many of these efforts were assisted by Navy personnel serving in nontraditional roles. These efforts would go on for the remainder of the U.S. presence in Iraq.

The Coalition Provisional Authority transferred sovereignty to the Iraq Interim Government in June 2004, and its first president, Ghazi al-Ujayl al-Yawr, was elected in January 2005.

Unfortunately, the capture of Baghdad and Hussein did not end all hostilities in Iraq. Roadside IEDs and suicide bombs and other attacks by insurgent forces and terrorists sympathetic to Hussein's old regime and to al-Qaeda continued throughout the decade and into the next, until and beyond the U.S. withdrawal, eventually resulting in the deaths of thousands of American military personnel and other coalition troops, as well as Iraqi civilians.

As the war progressed from the early days of Operation Iraqi Freedom to what would become an eight-year-long U.S. presence, American public opinion increasingly grew in favor of withdrawal. This trend was exacerbated by an increasing body of evidence that indicated that in fact there had been no weapons of mass destruction in Iraq at the time of the invasion in 2003, despite many intelligence estimates to the contrary at the time. By 2009 the country had stabilized to the point that troop reductions could begin, and on 1 September 2010 President Obama officially proclaimed the end of U.S. combat operations in Iraq, thus ending Operation Iraqi Freedom. On 15 December 2011, Defense Secretary Leon Panetta, at a flag-lowering ceremony in Baghdad, officially declared the war in Iraq over. The last U.S. troops left Iraqi territory on 18 December 2011.

Operation Unified Assistance

In late December 2004, in the midst of the wars in Iraq and Afghanistan, a huge tsunami generated by a strong undersea earthquake in the Indian Ocean basin devastated much of the seacoasts of Indonesia, Sri Lanka, Thailand, southern India, and several other countries in South and Southeast Asia. By some estimates as many as 370,000 people were either killed by the tsunami itself or by its effects shortly thereafter. In response, the United States initiated Operation Unified Assistance, deploying eight U.S. Navy ships, including the carrier USS *Abraham Lincoln* and the amphibious assault ship USS *Bonhomme Richard* (LHD 6), along with P-3 aircraft from Kadena, Japan, and heavy-lift cargo aircraft from the U.S. Air Force, to assist in the recovery effort. By the time the operation ended in February 2005, helicopters from the amphibious ships USS *Fort McHenry* (LSD 43) and *Essex* (LHD 2) had logged over two thousand missions in support of the relief efforts, and some 12 million tons

Damage resulting from the 2004 Indian Ocean tsunami at a coastal town in Sumatra. *CHINFO, Philip McDaniel*

of supplies had been flown to the region by Navy and Air Force planes. Several thousand casualties had been treated by U.S. medical personnel, mainly on board the hospital ship USNS *Mercy* (T-AH 10), sent to the region as part of the humanitarian response.

Piracy

Although sporadic outbreaks of piracy have occurred for many centuries around the globe, not since the war with Tripoli in 1803 did these represent a significant threat to freedom of navigation on the high seas until the late 1990s. At that time, there began to be increasing international concern over fishing vessels, other ships, and seamen being captured and held for ransom by pirates in the waters of the Gulf of Aden off Somalia. At first these attacks had been in retaliation for international fishing violations in Somali territorial waters following the start of the civil war there in 1991, but by the mid-1990s they had become a source of income for destitute Somali fishermen. By

the start of the new millennium these attacks had escalated to merchant vessels and yachts of all sizes and descriptions. They were taking place from mother ships well beyond Somali territorial waters, from the Gulf of Aden to the north of Somalia around the Horn, and well into the Arabian Sea and Indian Ocean to the east. They represented a significant threat to ships of all maritime nations.

In response to this threat, the U.S. Central Command ordered Task Force 150, consisting of several destroyers that had been assigned to the area as part of Operation Enduring Freedom, to conduct antipiracy patrols. In 2002 TF 150 became a combined task force, including ships from four other nations. By the middle of the decade this force had grown to a multinational force of some fifteen ships on rotational assignments from as many as twenty-five nations, with the command of the force rotating among the participating nations. However, restrictions regarding the use of force and the disposition of any pirates captured rendered the task force incapable of preventing a steady increase in the number of hijackings. By 2008, at the height of Somali piracy, the pirates held more than thirty ships and over six hundred hostages, and more than $100 million in ransoms had been paid. Thereafter both the number of attacks and successful hijackings began to decline, both because of more aggressive UN mandates governing the antipiracy force and also better countermeasures, including armed security guards on the merchant ships themselves.

Today, in addition to the multinational task force, NATO, the European Union (EU), and individual ships from various countries operating independently all conduct antipiracy operations off the Horn of Africa. International antipiracy forces routinely conduct raids ashore in Somalia to confiscate pirate weapons, equipment, and fuel. Patrol aircraft fly over the shoreline to relay pirate activity to nearby warships. As of the end of 2012, the pirates held only seven ships and 177 crew members. No further ships were captured in 2013, and only a single freighter has been captured as of this writing thus far in 2014.

One of the more storied incidents of this piracy occurred in April 2009, when four heavily armed Somali pirates boarded the American containership *Maersk Alabama* 240 miles off the Somali east coast, in the Indian Ocean. It marked the first time a U.S.-flagged ship had been seized by pirates since the early

1800s. The ship, with a crew of twenty, counting her master, Richard Phillips, was bound for the port of Mombasa, Kenya, with some 17,000 tons of cargo, including relief supplies for Somalia, Uganda, and Kenya.

When the pirates boarded, most of the crew barricaded themselves in the engine room, where they could maintain control of the ship, while Captain Phillips and two other crewmen remained on the bridge. When the pirates could not gain control, they grew frustrated and decided to leave the ship in one of its covered orange motorized lifeboats, taking Captain Phillips with them as a hostage.

The next day the U.S. destroyer *Bainbridge* (DDG 96) arrived on the scene, having been dispatched from the combined piracy task force upon receipt of word of the hostage situation. The frigate *Halyburton* (FFG 40) and the amphibious assault ship *Boxer* (LHD 4) arrived on scene the following day. The *Maersk Alabama*, under the command of her chief engineer, resumed course toward Mombasa; meanwhile a standoff situation developed with the pirates on the lifeboat, which had begun to slowly proceed toward Somalia.

Another two days went by, during which Captain Phillips made an unsuccessful escape attempt and the pirates at one point opened fire on a small boat from the *Halyburton*. By now the lifeboat was nearly out of fuel, and the *Bainbridge*'s captain convinced the pirates to let the ship take it in tow toward Somalia. One of them came on board the *Bainbridge* to negotiate and receive treatment for a wound received while on board the *Maersk Alabama*. Unbeknownst to the pirates, however, a contingent of Navy SEALs had boarded the *Bainbridge* during the night and taken concealed firing positions on the fantail. When the remaining pirates came out into the open to escape the heat in the enclosed lifeboat, the SEALs opened fire, killing all

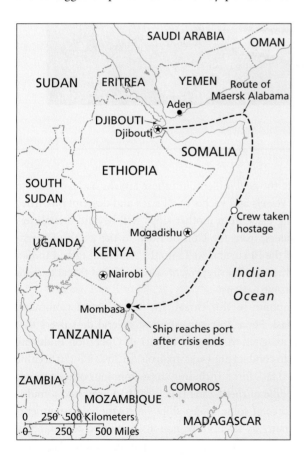

Map showing the area of pirate attacks off Somalia in the mid-2000s and the route of the *Maersk Alabama* during the confrontation in 2009.

The lifeboat from the containership *Maersk Alabama* in tow behind the guided-missile destroyer USS *Bainbridge* following the successful rescue of Captain Phillips. The amphibious assault ship USS *Boxer* is standing by in the background. *CHINFO*

CAPT Richard Phillips (right) with CDR Frank Castellano, the commanding officer of the *Bainbridge,* after his successful rescue by Navy SEALs. *CHINFO*

The hospital ship USNS *Comfort* anchored off Colombia in 2011 following her assistance at Haiti the year before. *CHINFO, Jonathen Davis*

three of them and saving Captain Phillips. He was subsequently taken on board the *Bainbridge,* and after recovering from his ordeal, he was flown home and reunited with his family, which had been keeping vigil in Vermont. The bullet-pocked lifeboat is on display at the UDT-SEAL museum in Fort Pierce, Florida.

Interestingly, this incident would not be the last encounter of the *Maersk Alabama* with Somali pirates. They attempted to board her four more times over the next two years during subsequent transits through the area, each time being repulsed by security teams by then embarked. The incident was made into a 2013 movie, *Captain Phillips,* released by Columbia Pictures.

Relief Efforts in Haiti

The value of the Navy's humanitarian mission was exemplified by the Navy's response to a major earthquake in Haiti that occurred on 12 January 2010, killing an estimated 220,000 people in and around the capital city of Port-au-Prince and injuring or rendering homeless a million more. Much of the infrastructure, such as electrical power and water and sewerage, was either destroyed or rendered unusable, and local morgues and medical facilities were overwhelmed with tens of thousands of bodies and injured people. Within a week the carrier *Carl Vinson* had arrived on scene with an enhanced air wing of nineteen helicopters; soon the carrier had distributed over 600,000 emergency rations and 100,000 bottles of drinking water. The carrier was the first of an eventual seventeen Navy ships that came to render assistance in the first days of the recovery efforts, including the hospital ship USNS *Comfort* (T-AH 28). Altogether over

ten thousand Marines and sailors helped to clear the harbor and make it functional once more, as well as assisting in many other ways.

Tsunami in Japan

On 11 March 2011 there occurred a magnitude-9 earthquake off the coast of Japan, the largest ever to have hit Japan and the fifth largest in recorded history. The earthquake triggered a powerful tsunami that impacted the western coastline of Japan's northern islands with forty-foot waves, killing thousands of people and wiping out entire coastal towns and villages. But perhaps the worst effect was severe damage to four nuclear reactors at a coastal nuclear power plant at Fukushima, on the northeastern coast of the large island of Honshu. Primary and backup power for cooling water was lost, and three of the reactors melted down, with accompanying major release of radiation. Soon this

A tsunami resulting from an offshore earthquake comes ashore in Japan in March 2011. *Reuters/Kyodo*

contamination found its way into ground and sea water, forcing evacuations for miles around.

Within hours the U.S. Seventh Fleet was deploying ships to the area in a massive **humanitarian assistance and disaster relief (HA/DR)** operation. More than 3,600 sailors and Marines served in the lead elements of the relief forces, delivering tons of food and water and helping with the evacuation of some eight thousand American citizens there. Ultimately some twenty-four ships and 15,000 sailors and Marines took part, doing everything from harbor clearance to providing technical support and barges of cooling water for the stricken nuclear power plant at Fukushima.

The Death of bin Laden

The capture or killing of Osama bin Laden, the terrorist who had masterminded the 9/11 al-Qaeda terrorist attacks on New York and the Pentagon in 2001, had been a high priority for the United States ever since the attacks took place. Bin Laden had successfully eluded capture for almost a decade; numerous leads had led to nothing. For some time it was known that he had avoided the use of cell phones ever since the United States had launched missile strikes against his bases in Afghanistan and Sudan in 1998. Thus a key tactic in the intelligence community after 2002 was to track the movements of his couriers, who personally conveyed directions to his subordinates in the al-Qaeda organization. Finally, in late 2010, leads were developed that led to a walled compound in Abbottabad, Pakistan, which the U.S. intelligence community placed under intensive surveillance. Eventually officials concluded that bin Laden was in fact living there, with his youngest wife and family. Soon thereafter options were developed by the CIA and the Joint Special Operations Command (JSOC) to attack the compound and kill or capture bin Laden.

President Obama met with his National Security Council (NSC) on 14 March 2011 to review the options. These consisted of either an attack by Air Force stealth B-2 bombers with precision-guided bombs or a ground assault by commandos. Should the latter course of action be decided upon, the commandos would be a Navy SEAL team. Since there was some concern about collateral damage if the former option were adopted, at the next NSC meeting a week later, the raid by a SEAL team was decided upon. It was given the secret operational code name **Neptune Spear.** For the next month intensive rehearsals were conducted with great secrecy in the United States and

Map of Pakistan showing Abbottabad where Osama bin Laden was in hiding.

at Bagram Air Base in Afghanistan, where a full-scale replica of bin Laden's compound was built in an isolated part of the base.

By the end of April all was in readiness, and the director of the CIA, Leon Panetta, under orders from the president, directed VADM William McRaven, director of JSOC, to proceed with the raid on 1 May. At 1500 that day the president joined selected officials in the White House Situation Room to monitor the operation.

Shortly after 2300 on the dark, moonless night of 1 May 2011, two Army stealth helicopters took off from the Jalalabad air base in eastern Afghanistan with twenty SEALs from SEAL Team 6 and one military working dog. The dog was included to give warning of approaching Pakistanis or escapees from the compound. The aircraft entered Pakistani airspace undetected and proceeded to the target in Abbottabad. About ninety minutes later they were hovering over the compound. The original plan was to have one group of SEALs in one of the helicopters fast-rope onto the compound's roof, while the other, including the dog, landed inside the walls to secure the perimeter. This plan had to be abandoned, however, when one of the helicopters hit a wall in a downdraft and crash-landed into the compound. Fortunately none of the SEALs were injured, and they proceeded to attack the compound's guest house. Meanwhile the other SEALs landed in their helicopter outside the walls and quickly scaled them to join their fellows.

After neutralizing the residents of the guest house, the SEALs gained

The bin Laden compound at Abbottabad, Pakistan, a few days after he was killed by members of Navy SEAL Team 6 on 1 May 2011. It was later destroyed by the Pakistani government. *www.wikimedia.com, Sajjad Ali Qureshi*

entrance to the three-story main house with explosives and crept up the stairs toward the bedroom on the third floor, where it was presumed that bin Laden was. The house was pitch dark, because CIA operatives had cut the power to the compound. On the way up the SEALs encountered one of bin Laden's sons, whom they shot and killed when he tried to rush them. Bin Laden suddenly peered at them from the third floor and then retreated into his bedroom; one of the SEALs shot him, hitting him in the head. The SEALs quickly followed and discovered him lying on the floor. When he reached for two nearby weapons, he was shot again and killed. The SEAL team leader radioed, "Geronimo Echo KIA," a previously arranged code indicating that bin Laden was dead. When this news reached the Situation Room, President Obama proclaimed, "We got him!"

All this action took place in the first fifteen minutes of the raid. After shooting bin Laden the SEALs photographed his body and took DNA samples. They then searched the house and moved survivors into the courtyard, where they were later taken into custody by Pakistanis. They removed computer hard drives, DVDs, and other electronic equipment for later analysis and bagged and carried bin Laden's body to another reserve Army helicopter that had landed outside. Finally, before leaving they blew up their damaged helicopter with demolition charges. (Unfortunately, the rotor assembly was later recovered intact by the Pakistanis, a loss that compromised the stealth technology built into it.) The raid had taken thirty-eight minutes from start to finish.

The SEALs returned in the helicopters to Bagram, where bin Laden's body was transferred to a Marine Osprey aircraft for transport to the *Carl Vinson* in the North Arabian Sea. He was buried at sea within twenty-four hours, as required by Muslim custom. The Chairman of the Joint Chiefs of Staff, ADM Michael Mullin, called Pakistan's army chief at about 0300 local time to inform him and the Pakistani government of the completed raid. They had not been informed previously because of security concerns. The Pakistani government later destroyed the compound, fearing that it would otherwise be turned into a shrine and serve as a lingering reminder of a massive Pakistani intelligence failure.

The Arab Spring Revolts

Throughout the first decade of the new millennium there was a rising tide of dissatisfaction among the populations in all of the Arabian countries in North Africa and the Middle East. There had long been substandard living conditions in these countries, high unemployment in some, and in most repression of women, lack of personal liberty, and autocratic rule. As the Internet became more widely accessible, especially among the younger generations in these countries, the wide gulf between their standards of living and societal norms, versus those of the United States and many other countries worldwide, had become increasingly apparent, adding to their malaise. This unrest finally culminated in open protests that began in Tunisia

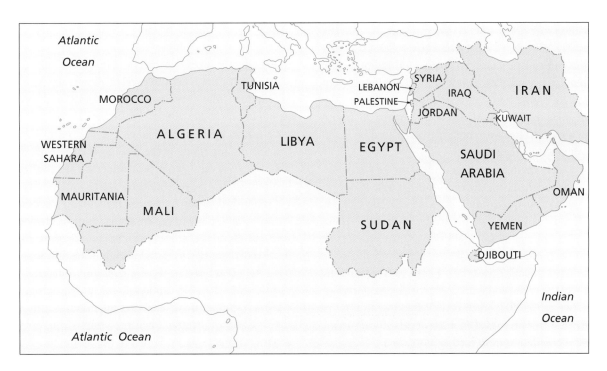

Map showing the principal nations of North Africa and the Middle East affected by the Arab Spring movement 2010–12.

Libyan dictator Muammar Qaddafi shortly before his death at the hands of Libyan rebel fighters.

Jesse Await

in December 2010 after the public self-immolation of a protester upset over corruption in the government and numerous human-rights violations. The protests quickly spread to neighboring Egypt and eventually to most of the other Arab nations throughout the North African and Middle Eastern regions. They were collectively dubbed the **Arab Spring** movement by an American journalist, because they were reminiscent of similar "Spring of Nations" protests staged across Europe in 1848 and those of the "Prague Spring" of 1968 in Prague, Czechoslovakia.

In many of these countries there were attempts to mollify protestors with promises of increased revenue sharing from the sale of oil exports, with some of these overtures at least partially successful, but in countries such as Tunisia and Egypt, where there is not much oil production, this was not an option. Violent protest ultimately erupted into open rebellion, resulting in the overthrow of the government of Tunisia in January 2011, and that of Egypt a month later, with both being replaced by much more liberal democratic regimes.

Both of these changes in government occurred without significant bloodshed, but such was not the case in Libya, ruled by the always outspoken and oftentimes erratic dictator Muammar Qaddafi. Violent demonstrations erupted there in February 2011, and soon the opposition controlled most of Benghazi, the second-largest city. Before long they also took control of the outskirts of Tripoli, the capital. However government forces were able to retake much of the coastal territory between the two cities after much bloody fighting and many civilian casualties. This prompted an international effort to protect the civilian population from further bloodshed.

On 17 March 2011 the United Nations Security Council adopted a resolution imposing a no-fly zone over Libya and authorizing "all necessary measures" to protect civilians. Two

days later, France, the United States, and the United Kingdom intervened with a bombing campaign against pro-Qaddafi forces. They were soon joined by a coalition of some twenty-seven other nations from Europe and the Middle East. U.S. naval forces played a major role in this effort, called **Operation Odyssey Dawn.** Participating Navy ships included two attack submarines and one of four recently converted guided-missile/special-operations submarines, the USS *Florida* (SSGN 728), as well as several Aegis destroyers, the USS *Kearsarge* (LHD 3) amphibious ready group, and the amphibious command ship USS *Mount Whitney* (LCC 20). Altogether the Aegis ships and submarines launched more than 220 Tomahawk cruise missiles at Libyan targets, while Harrier "jump jets" (capable of vertical takeoff and landing) from the *Kearsarge,* along with Royal Navy and French aircraft, decimated Libya's air-defense system and destroyed Libyan armor.

By late August, with the help of the coalition air and material support, the anti-Qaddafi fighters had captured Tripoli, ending Qaddafi's forty-two years of autocratic rule. Qaddafi reconstituted his government for a short time at Sirte, declaring that city to be Libya's new capital, but in October rebel fighters captured Sirte and killed Qaddafi in the street. The liberation of Libya was complete. In August 2012 the transitional rebel government turned over power to a newly elected General National Congress, which was tasked with forming an interim government and drafting a new constitution.

Concurrently with the fall of the Qaddafi government in Libya, the Arab Spring movement resulted in either new democratic governments or significant liberalizing reforms in the existing governments of most of the other Arab countries in the region. A bloody insurrection against the oppressive regime of President Bashar al-Assad in Syria is still ongoing as of this writing, with the rebel Free Syrian Army requesting arms and air support from the United States, Israel, and western European nations to counter assistance being supplied to the Assad government by Russia and Iran.

In Iran the effects of the Arab Spring were not as dramatic. There were several large prodemocracy demonstrations held beginning in early 2011, but these were soon brutally suppressed by the hard-line Islamist government. Of greater concern to the United States, Israel, and Western European democracies was the issue of Iran's uranium-enrichment program. This program had been ongoing since the 1950s, but steadily accelerated into the new millennium, causing increasing concern that it would ultimately lead to the production of nuclear weapons. Despite steadfast Iranian denials of this intention, beginning in 2006 the UN Security Council began to impose increasingly severe economic sanctions on Iran for not stopping its enrichment program.

Iran's response was to threaten to restrict or close the adjacent Strait of Hormuz to oil tanker traffic. This would be

Syrian president
Bashar al-Assad.
*Fabio Rodrigues
Pozzeborn/ABr*

Ballistic Missile Defense

As mentioned at the start of this chapter, the 2002 U.S. withdrawal from the Soviet-era Antiballistic Missile Defense Treaty cleared the way for the development of the antiballistic missile (ABM) version of the ship-launched Standard missile, the SM-3, capable of intercepting and destroying incoming ballistic missiles. In the years since, steady improvements have continued to be made both to the missile and its supporting Aegis ballistic missile defense (BMD) radar systems. The capabilities of the system were dramatically demonstrated in 2008, when a SM-3 missile fired from an Aegis cruiser brought down an errant U.S. satellite 130 miles above the North Pacific. Currently there are some thirty Aegis BMD-capable cruisers and destroyers in service, roughly split between the Atlantic and Pacific fleets. More retrofits of older Aegis ships and acquisitions of additional new Aegis BMD ships are planned for the future as quickly as funding allows.

especially troublesome for European Union (EU) nations who import much of their oil through the strait. Both the United States and the EU threatened appropriate military action to keep the strait open if Iran should attempt to close it. Although more recently some progress has been made with diplomatic efforts to get Iran to curtail its enriched uranium production, both the United States and Israel have threatened to take unilateral military action against Iran if it continues to enrich uranium to the degree necessary to build nuclear weapons.

It remains to be seen what the long-term outcomes in the Syrian and Iranian situations will be, and how the liberal reforms spawned by the Arab Spring movement in other Arab nations in the region will fare in the future.

An Iranian patrol boat fires a missile during exercises in 2012 in the Strait of Hormuz as a show of force in reprisal for U.S. and EU sanctions against Iran's nuclear development program. *Iranian Press TV*

Trouble with North Korea

In the years since the Korean War the North Korean dictator Kim Jung-il had steadily built up North Korea's armed forces. At the start of the new millennium they were the fourth largest in the world, behind those of China, the United States, and India. Throughout these same years he had paid little attention to the welfare or human rights of his citizenry, prompting President Bush in 2002 to refer to North Korea as an "outpost of tyranny."

Thereafter, the uneasy truce that had existed between North Korea, on one side, and South Korea and the United States, on the other, began to deteriorate. In the mid part of the decade North Korea announced that it would begin aggressive uranium-enrichment and underground nuclear bomb test programs that might lead to the development of nuclear weapons, in violation of the international nuclear nonproliferation treaty. They conducted two such underground tests, in 2006 and 2009. In March 2010 North Korea torpedoed and sank a South Korean patrol boat. For months it steadfastly denied all allegations that it had done so, and responded to them by severing most accords between the two countries. In November it shelled a nearby South Korean island.

In 2011 Kim Jung-il died from a heart attack and was succeeded by his youngest son, Kim Jong-un, who would soon prove to be an even more unpredictable, irascible, and brutal leader than his father. North Korea continued to develop its uranium-enrichment program and conduct provocative missile tests, culminating in the launch of a space satellite in December 2012.

Things went from bad to worse in 2013. In February it conducted a third underground nuclear test. Then in March the North Korean government announced intentions to launch **preemptive** (surprise) nuclear strikes against South Korea and the United States, followed a few days later by announcements that it was withdrawing from all nonaggression pacts with South Korea, and that it had abrogated the long-standing 1953 Korean War Armistice agreement. On 30 March it declared that it was in a "state of war" with South Korea. In response to these actions, two U.S. Air Force nuclear-capable B-2 stealth bombers were flown, with wide publicity, across the Korean Peninsula to demonstrate American resolve to maintain its nuclear shield over South Korea. Also, several BMD-capable Aegis destroyers and a cruiser were stationed in the Sea of Japan to detect, track, and intercept any threatening missiles that might be launched by North Korea.

North Korea subsequently toned down its provocative behavior toward South Korea and the United States, most likely in response to urgings from its ally China after diplomatic pressure from the Obama administration. However, it has continued its vigorous uranium enrichment, underground nuclear testing, and missile-test programs, despite numerous international sanctions and diplomatic protests from the United States, South Korea, Japan, the United Nations, and even China. Many international organizations, including the UN, accuse Kim Jong-un and North Korea of having one of the worst human rights records of any nation on Earth, including murder, enslavement, torture, and prolonged starvation of its citizenry.

Future military plans in response to the provocative behavior of North Korea call for the United States to assist South Korea to build six more Aegis destroyers to add to the three it already has, and for Japan to upgrade several of its destroyers with the Aegis BMD system. Additional land-based ABMs will also be added to those already in place on the U.S. West Coast, in California and Alaska, by 2017. Most military intelligence analysts have asserted that North Korea does not as yet have the capability to deliver a nuclear warhead on any of its current missiles, nor does it have the wherewithal to launch an invasion into South Korea on its own initiative without assistance from China, which it is very doubtful it would receive. It remains to be seen what the eventual outcome of this latest round of volatile behavior by North Korea will be.

Terrorism and Violent Extremism

Unfortunately, the threat of worldwide terrorism and violent extremism continued unabated into the new millennium. During the years since 9/11 there have been several significant instances of both, at home and abroad.

The highest incidence of terrorist attacks in the world over the last decade outside war zones is said to have taken place in India, most of them in Mumbai (formerly Bombay), the most populous city in that country. After a series of bombings over several years involving public transportation facilities, in November 2008 the worst of these attacks occurred when a rad-

ical group staged a three-day bombing campaign in the center of the city, killing 166 people and injuring more than three hundred. All the terrorists were eventually hunted down and killed or captured by local authorities. Similar attacks on a smaller scale have resulted in hundreds of casualties in dozens of countries across the globe.

In the United States there were two particularly violent incidents of such attacks. On 5 November 2009, at Fort Hood, Texas, an Army base engaged in readying Army troops for deployment in Iraq and Afghanistan, an Army psychiatrist, MAJ Nidal Hasan, opened fire on enlisted personnel, killing thirteen and injuring thirty. Although officially classified as an act of workplace violence, many, including the surviving victims and their families, have called it a terrorist attack, since the perpetrator had been in contact with an al-Qaeda cleric for some months before.

On 15 April 2013 a particularly horrifying incident took place at the end of that year's Boston Marathon in Massachusetts—two bombs exploded near the finish line, killing three spectators and injuring hundreds. The perpetrators were soon identified as two immigrant brothers with ties to Muslim extremists. After a four-day manhunt by federal, state, and local agencies, one was killed and the other was tracked down and captured. The surviving brother, Dzhokhar Tsarnaev, later stated that their attack had been in retaliation for the wars in Iraq and Afghanistan.

In addition to these incidents of violent extremism and terrorism, there were also a number of other cases involving lone gunmen opening fire in such public places as schools, universities, shopping malls, a theater, and at a gathering of constituents of a U.S. congresswoman. Though not classified as terrorist acts per se (in itself), they nevertheless had similar impacts on all those affected by them.

Unfortunately, such acts as those described above will continue to be a concern in the foreseeable future. Although a great deal of time and energy is continually expended by the military services and by other agencies of the federal, state, and local government to try to prevent them, it behooves all Americans to maintain personal vigilance and awareness of their surroundings and to report potentially dangerous situations to proper authorities.

Cyber Warfare

The new millennium saw the introduction of a new form of information warfare, called **cyber warfare.** This refers to the intentional intrusion, called "hacking," into computers or computer networks by agencies of foreign governments for the purpose of sabotage or espionage. In the years since 2000 this type of Internet-based attack on all kinds of U.S. computer networks has steadily increased, to the point that nowadays hardly a day goes by without some kind of attempt to infiltrate some network in the United States, be it government, military, industrial, or commercial. The term **cyber terrorism** refers to attempts by extremists or terrorists to damage or destroy vital computer networks by such means as the use of powerful computer viruses, or to use the Internet to further their agenda. As with other physical forms of terrorism, it is often difficult to identify and track down the perpetrators of such attacks and to take effective countermeasures against them.

It has been estimated that billions of dollars in losses have occurred due to computer-based industrial espionage in the United States. Also, a significant amount of classified material and information on technological developments within all the military services has been lost due to cyber attacks on Department of Defense (DOD) information networks.

In response to the possible threat to national security represented by these kinds of attacks, in May 2010 the **U.S. Cyber Command** was formed, headquartered at Fort George G. Meade, Maryland. It has component commands in all three of the military services. Its mission is to defend all Department of Defense computer networks against cyber attacks and to ensure the freedom of action of the United States and its allies in **cyberspace** (the online realm of the Internet and other computer networks), as well as their ability to deny this freedom to potential adversaries when required. The Department of Homeland Security has a similar mission in respect to other government and private and commercial users of the Internet.

Equipment Issues

The strain on the ships, aircraft, and personnel carrying out the many missions of the U.S. Navy in the new millennium has been unprecedented, particularly in the face of the increasing fiscal constraints of the last few years. Extended deployments, coupled with insufficient funding for periodic maintenance and overhaul, have taken a continuing toll on both hardware and people.

As regards ships and aircraft, notable problems that have arisen include degraded readiness of Aegis cruisers and destroyers due to deferral of costly maintenance for their radar and weapons systems; reduction in the expected length of refueling cycles (time intervals between refuelings) of the nuclear-powered aircraft carriers now in service, because of extended deployments; and the ending of the service lives (length of time they can be safely flown) of carrier aircraft, such as the F/A-18, years earlier than anticipated because of the strain from unexpectedly high numbers of catapult launchings and arrested landings. At the beginning of the millennium it was thought that the U.S. fleet would have some 315 ships in service by 2012–13, as a result of new construction and major rehabilitation of older ships. But every year since the mid-2000s the Navy has

An FA-18 Super Hornet readying for launch. Much concern has arisen over a probable decrease in the service lives of these aircraft because of the unanticipated increased demands of naval operations in recent years. *CHINFO*

had to make do with less than 285 ships, because of drawdowns in the shipbuilding and maintenance budgets.

Personnel Issues

The new millennium has been a challenging time as well for personnel in all of the U.S. military services, especially the Navy. The demands of the two simultaneous wars in Iraq and Afghanistan resulted in many men and women serving multiple tours of duty in the war zones, in some cases five or six or even more. As has been previously mentioned, large numbers of sailors found themselves serving in nontraditional roles in the conflicts, especially in Afghanistan. Many Navy Reservists were recalled with little advance notice from civilian life to active duty for year-long individual assignments, as were many Marine reserve units. Because of increasing use of all manner of improvised explosive devices (IEDs) by insurgents in both wars, there was a steady increase in the number of war veterans returning home with debilitating head injuries or amputations. Severe posttraumatic stress disorder (PTSD) is another common problem faced by many veterans of both wars.

On a more positive note, much progress continued to be made in the new millennium toward more fully integrating women into all aspects of military service, including roles formerly restricted only to men. Women had begun serving on board surface warships and piloting combat aircraft during the 1990s, and they flew many combat support missions in both Iraq and Afghanistan. Nearly 250,000 women have served in all services in combat support roles in both wars. In 2010 the Department of the Navy announced a change in policy that would allow qualified junior women officers to serve on fleet ballistic-missile submarines, a reversal of a long-standing ban on women serving in submarines. In November 2012 the first twenty-five of these graduated from submarine school and reported for duty. In January 2013 the Defense Department lifted a statutory ban that prohibited women from serving in frontline combat assignments, thus opening the way for them to volunteer to serve in these roles whenever qualified to do so.

In December 2011 Congress formally ended the previous prohibition of openly gay (homosexual) personnel of both sexes from serving in the U.S. armed forces.

A Look Back—and Ahead

The last few decades were very challenging ones for our Navy. In the Vietnam years of the sixties and seventies, the Navy had nearly a thousand ships and 600,000 people in uniform. By 2005 these numbers had declined to under 285 ships and 370,000 people, and this despite the demands of fighting two simultaneous wars. Joint operations with the other services and combined

Women have made significant gains in equality of military service in recent years, as evidenced by this female Marine in full combat gear serving alongside her male counterparts in Afghanistan. *CHINFO*

operations with multinational forces are now the rule rather than the exception. Technology continues to drive toward new concepts in weapons and equipment at an ever-accelerating pace.

Steadily increasing budgetary constraints since the demise of the Soviet Union and the end of the Cold War have forced us to realize that we cannot always acquire every new weapon or program we may want or all the new ships we may need. The international drug trade and violent extremism and terrorism at home and abroad have shown that our modern enemies are not always easily identifiable and often cannot be directly attacked, at least not by traditional means.

In spite of all this, our Navy continues to perform its mission with distinction, meeting every challenge both at home and abroad. Many trying times surely lie ahead as we continue to try to deal with the tragic events that have afflicted our country in recent years, but there is no doubt that each generation of Navy men and women will do its best to continue to protect America and our way of life from all enemies, both foreign and domestic.

Critical Thinking

1. In the years following the terrorist attack on the World Trade Center buildings on 11 September 2001, many increased security measures were implemented in the United States to try to lessen the threat of future attacks. Research the security measures that have been taken and state which of these appear to have been most effective and which have been least so. What additional measures would you recommend be taken in the future?

2. In recent years much controversy arose concerning President George W. Bush's decision to invade Iraq in 2003 and remove Saddam Hussein from power. State the major pros and cons that have been advanced concerning this issue and suggest alternative courses of action that might have been taken.

3. There was much criticism in some quarters within the United States about the extent of American aid rendered to antigovernment forces in the countries involved in the Arab Spring uprisings of 2010–11. Identify the pros and cons of such interventions, and make the case either for or against future interventions in countries such as Iran and Syria.

4. Research the current state of U.S. ballistic-missile defense and the directions it might take in the next decade.

Chronology

2000	Attack on USS *Cole*
2001	Terrorist attack on World Trade Center and Pentagon; Operation Enduring Freedom begins in Afghanistan
2003	Operation Iraqi Freedom begins in Iraq
2004	Operation Unified Assistance in Indonesia
2009	*Maersk Alabama* piracy incident
2010	Relief mission in Haiti; Arab Spring revolts begin; Operation Iraqi Freedom ends
2011	Relief mission in Japan; Operation Odyssey Dawn in Libya; death of Osama bin Laden; Congress repeals ban on gays in military
2012	First women report for duty on board submarines
2013	Pentagon lifts ban on women in combat roles; North Korea abrogates 1953 armistice

Study Guide Questions

1. What happened to the total number of ships in the U.S. Navy fleet in the twenty years between 1985 and 2005?

2. What happened to the guided-missile destroyer USS *Cole* in August 2000?

3. What was the significance of the June 2002 U.S. withdrawal from the 1972 ABM Treaty?

4. A. What terrorist attack against America took place in September 2001?
   B. What military action took place as a direct result of the attack?

5. A. What were the major concerns that led the United States to undertake Operation Iraqi Freedom in 2003?
   B. When did it end?

6. What was Operation Unified Assistance in 2004?

7. What happened to the containership *Maersk Alabama* in April 2009 off the coast of Somalia?

8. What happened in Haiti in January 2010?

9. What were the worst effects of the earthquake and tsunami in Japan in March 2011?

10. A. Why did it take almost ten years to track down Osama bin Laden after the 9/11 attacks on the Pentagon and New York City?
    B. Who conducted the raid on bin Laden's compound in Pakistan in May 2011?
    C. What was the outcome?

11. What was the Arab Spring uprising that began in March 2011?

12. A. What contentious announcements were made by the North Korean government in March 2013?
    B. What did the United States do in response?

13. What significant issues have arisen since the year 2000 that affect the ability of the U.S. fleet to carry out its missions?

14. What were some of the factors that had a negative impact on armed service personnel during the wars in Iraq and Afghanistan?

New Vocabulary

millennium	containership
piracy	humanitarian assistance
improvised explosive device (IED)	stealth technology
ballistic missile	self-immolation
antiballistic missile (ABM)	jump jet
special forces	uranium enrichment
nontraditional roles	preemptive strike
weapons of mass destruction	refueling cycle
coalition	service life
infrastructure	cyber warfare
tsunami	cyber terrorism
	cyberspace

Leadership

NJROTC Leadership

You have now had at least a year of NJROTC. You may have been advanced to petty officer third class or petty officer second class, with leadership duties in a squad or platoon. You may be a member of the color guard, drill team, or rifle team.

If you have advanced to a higher level, that is great. If not, keep trying. You too will advance when you are qualified and there are openings. In the meantime, you are an experienced cadet who can, and should, help the new young men and women who are coming into the unit as cadets in Naval Science 1. Everyone must help so the unit will be a good team.

As a squad leader, assistant squad leader, platoon guide, or other leader within your unit, you will have special responsibilities during your unit's marching practices, parades, inspections, and other functions. Know your responsibilities. As a leader, you will have others to look after, guide, and train.

Your first rule must be to **set the best example possible.** Your own uniform should be neat, pressed, and shipshape, with a clean cap, shirt, skivvy shirt, and shined shoes. Awards and insignia must be neat and without dangling threads. When questioned, it is better to be able to answer by showing as well as telling. For example, "The NJROTC patch is sewn on the left sleeve of the shirt, like this"; or, "Shoes should be polished to a bright shine, like this." Your *NJROTC Field Manual* is a good reference on how to wear the uniform correctly.

You will find that your own correct wearing of the uniform, taking directions, snappy saluting, and sharp marching will be a better guide than many things you say. Your subordinates will learn by watching and following your example. If you tell them how to do something and then do not do it that way yourself, you have wasted your time. In fact, you will have done both yourself and the unit damage. Subordinates will do as you do before they will do as you say. Leadership and responsibility begin with setting the example yourself.

The Leader

Leadership depends upon three things: the leader, the followers, and the job to be done. Each leader will have his or her own way of guiding, directing, and inspiring followers. Although the approach of each leader may be different, each may be equally successful in getting good results.

After learning to be good followers the first year, NJROTC cadets have many leadership opportunities at all levels. The NJROTC needs effective leaders in squad, platoon, company, and staff positions. Leaders are also needed for various teams, the color guard, and committees. The effectiveness of the leaders at the top levels depends on the effectiveness of the leaders at the lower levels. Cadet officers rise to top positions by working their way up. As they mature in experience, age, and rank, they gradually become better leaders.

There are few "born leaders." Even "natural leaders" have to develop through experience. They must learn to handle increasingly complex situations, as well as learn from their successes and failures. Some people do have a flair for leadership, quickly developing confidence and poise in a leadership role. Perhaps

The first role of a good leader is to set a good example. The sharp-looking members of this color guard at a drill competition at RTC Great Lakes Illinois are certainly doing that. *CHINFO, Mike Miller*

they have the looks, stature, command voice, or other physical qualities that set them apart. Maybe they are outstanding students, good athletes, or inspiring speakers. Any of these things might give them a bit of a head start, but these individuals must also have the initiative, desire, and willingness to become leaders. Sometimes people who were early leaders fade away as new leaders arise in the group. Some people make excellent leaders after a slow start. Leadership is not easily taught or easily learned, but leaders can be made.

A leader must be able to use his or her experience in each new situation, as well as learn something new. To improve, successful leaders must analyze themselves and their leadership style. In this way, they can learn which methods do not work and thus gradually develop skills that will help them do the job successfully. The NJROTC program seeks to help each cadet gain leadership experience that will be useful in almost any situation.

Follow the Leader

Having spent a year as a first-year cadet, you have experience as a **follower**. If you received a promotion, you must have done well. You are now in a position to guide and help new cadets in the unit this year.

You already have learned that you must first be a good follower before you can become a good leader. Also, you know that even high-ranking cadet officers in your unit must take orders from the cadet commander, and he or she in turn from the naval science instructors. They, in turn, must follow school and program policies and directives, and so on.

To be a leader, you must first try to do the job you are given. You must be dedicated to this job and be willing to do the required work with your teammates. Resist the temptation to pass off an unpopular order or job assignment as imposed on you by a senior. Rather, take responsibility for the order or task yourself, as in, "We need to do this," as opposed to "(he or she) wants us to do this."

As a leader you must be more disciplined than your followers, because you will influence them. You must always set a good example, because your subordinates will imitate your bad actions as well as your good. You must be careful that your appearance, dress, and conduct set high standards at all times.

As a cadet officer, you will not make decisions upon which the lives of others or the success of a critical mission depend. Nevertheless, your decisions will still be important to your unit. But your experience at this level is a good beginning. You are

One of the more interesting aspects of participation in the NJROTC is the opportunity to take field trips and partake in fun activities, as these cadets are doing at the Naval Station Great Lakes marina. *CHINFO, Andre McIntyre*

the one who must study the pros and cons of an issue, collect input from your group, and then make the decision on how the group can best get the job done. You will have a responsibility toward your seniors, your subordinates, your job, and your unit. You will have to develop the habit of working effectively with others. There are three basic things to remember as you develop your leadership abilities: **know your business; know yourself; know your personnel.**

The NJROTC has several optional programs and other activities in which you can take part that will help you learn to be a good cadet officer and leader. Units can send interested cadets to basic leadership training and leadership academies, summer programs of one or two weeks' duration at one of several military bases around the country. In addition, weekend field trips to various Navy bases, ships, and air stations are a good way to learn more about the Navy and its people. These programs and activities will greatly build your knowledge of the Navy and the military and the skills required to lead people effectively.

Personal Relationships

To do his or her job, a leader must associate with seniors, peers, juniors, and the general public. These associations are called **personal relations.** Just as in the regular Navy, a cadet's relationships with all these groups will greatly influence how effective a leader he or she is.

Few truly great leaders of the world have reached their positions without having outstanding personal and social traits. These traits make up the leader's personality. **Personality** is having the ability to talk to large groups and still make each person feel that he or she is being talked to alone. It is a "magnetic" personal quality that allows the leader to satisfy every person's desire for recognition. This is a basic requirement for anyone who wants to lead others.

Many great leaders of the past, such as President Abraham Lincoln, President Andrew Jackson, and Admiral Chester Nimitz, achieved much because they got along so well with people. People felt comfortable and welcome in their presence.

This special quality of leadership is really just an unselfish, friendly interest in people. It may be just a cordial "good morning" when starting the day or a question about how work is going. Such interest from the senior makes the junior feel important. It shows a subordinate that he or she is valued as an individual.

A leader must have the cooperation of those with whom he or she is working. A leader with a warm, friendly personality makes people feel that he or she is glad to be a member of their organization. This feeling, this being proud of the other people in the same group, is called **esprit de corps,** pride in the organization.

Respect of subordinates is not something that can be commanded; it must be earned. Subordinates expect their leaders to have an interest in and concern for their affairs. However, a leader should not be their "buddy" but rather their counselor and guide. A leader must be friendly and interested in his or her followers. Such friendly concern does not destroy discipline or break down the chain of command. If juniors feel that their leader knows their needs and will do everything he or she can for them, they will trust that leader.

If there is one key to successful leadership, it is probably **fairness.** This is the one thing that every effective leader must practice. Subordinates should receive all to which they are fairly entitled. Fairness in an NJROTC unit means things like an equal opportunity to serve as leaders, an equal chance to work on projects and committees or to be on the color guard or drill teams, and recognition for jobs well done.

Essential Qualities of Leadership

A person must have certain traits or characteristics in order to be an effective leader. Some of these are outlined here.

Loyalty. Loyalty to country is a must for anyone in the military service. There is also loyalty to seniors, which means a willingness to serve them reliably and well. Similarly, there is loyalty to juniors, which means consideration for their welfare and interests. Remember the **golden rule of loyalty:** to build loyal and committed juniors it is important first to be loyal and committed to them.

There are other forms of loyalty: loyalty to relatives, to friends, to beliefs, and finally, to oneself. As the well-known adage goes, "To thine own self be true, and it must follow as the night the day, thou canst not then be false to any man."

Courage, Physical and Moral. The most traditional trait of a leader is courage. At one time this meant physical courage only, deeds of daring that involved the danger of death. Today it implies a willingness to attempt a mission in spite of its danger. Training, education, drill, and professional preparation are the best ways to lay a foundation for physical courage.

Moral courage means being able to stand up for one's beliefs, to call things as one honestly sees them, to admit a mistake. Most people know the difference between right and wrong. Most try to remain true to their principles in spite of fears and pressures by others. It takes moral courage to do right in the face of these things. Most young leaders will make

There are many forms of physical courage, as this cadet is learning while patching a pipe in a damage-control trainer at Great Lakes, Illinois. *CHINFO, Dwayne Rider*

occasional honest mistakes. No one, however, should attempt to lie or "cover up" or intentionally break the law.

In civilian life as in the military, courageous leaders stand up for their people, always show a belief if their unit's ability to get the job done, and make tough decisions without passing the buck.

Honor, Honesty, and Truthfulness. *Honor* means a proper sense of right and wrong. An NJROTC cadet is expected to be a person of honor, one whose integrity is above reproach. Honor is an important characteristic for any person. *Honesty* means refusing to lie, cheat, or steal. Honesty is so important to leadership that it is written into the honor codes at all the service academies. There are no degrees of honesty. Either individuals are honest, or they are not. *Truthfulness* means telling things the way they truly are, without deception. Navy people must be able to put the greatest confidence and trust in their shipmates. This is possible only if they are men and women of honor, honesty, and truthfulness. A leader must have these qualities if he or she is to command respect, confidence, and obedience.

Truthfulness is the heart of personal integrity, and nothing damages one's integrity more thoroughly and instantaneously than telling an untruth. Sometimes subordinates are tempted to avoid telling a superior things they know he or she does not want to hear, but all effective leaders need to be able to count upon their subordinates to give them the bad news as well as the good, so they can make the best decisions possible.

Faith is another word for confidence. There are several kinds of faith: faith in oneself, faith in one's leaders, faith in subordinates, and faith in the cause for which one is working. Faith in oneself is self-confidence, and that increases the respect one receives from others. If one loses faith in one's leaders and subordinates, he or she trusts no one and is loyal to none. Such a person loses the trust and loyalty of seniors and juniors alike.

Faith in a cause is essential to victory. A weakening of faith is almost always followed by a lowering or complete loss of morale, disintegration, and defeat. A naval leader who believes with all his or her heart in the service, the fleet, his or her ship, captain, division, and himself or herself will see this attitude reflected in everyone around him or her.

Sense of Humor. The ability to see humor in a situation is a valuable asset. One should not play the clown, however. Often a humorous remark at the right time and place can ease tension and restore morale. Laughter can be like a curing medicine. A leader who can see humor in a difficult situation, when such exists, does much to relax his or her subordinates, restore their confidence, and cause them to think positively.

Modesty. A truly great person can afford to be modest; lesser individuals cannot afford to be otherwise. A truly great person can be modest because his or her accomplishments speak louder than any words. While a person should be proud of strengths and abilities, one must not develop too high an opinion of oneself. Modesty, quiet dignity, even humility indicate great character and experience. Self-magnification is improper, often unpleasant, and normally unsuccessful. Excessive concern with one's own importance is likely to cause a leader to consider mainly his or her own welfare, instead of the welfare of subordinates and the command.

Self-Confidence. Self-confidence develops with increased experience, skills, professional knowledge, and positive attitude. Self-confidence helps eliminate the fear of failure. To develop self-confidence, a leader must be willing to accept responsibility and tackle jobs that he or she may at first feel inadequate for or uncomfortable doing. If an occasional failure does occur, remember that it has happened to everyone at one time or another. The ability to bounce back, to learn by experience, and to do a better job next time marks a leader.

Common Sense, Good Judgment, and Tact. Common sense and good judgment enable a person to make good decisions. Common sense means being able to see and react to things as they really are. Good judgment comes with training and discipline and means the ability to analyze facts and draw correct conclusions. The more knowledge a person has, the better qualified he or she is to make good judgments. Tact is the ability to use good judgment to speak and act in a diplomatic way, so as not to offend either one's seniors, peers, or juniors.

Good leaders use common sense and good judgment in solving problems. They take into account similar experiences of

The sport of orienteering makes use of many of the traits needed to be successful as a leader. This group of NJROTC cadets is planning the route it will take on an orienteering exercise in a forest in southern Maryland. *NJROTC unit, Annapolis High School*

others. They recognize and appreciate the needs and personalities of their subordinates.

Health, Energy, and Optimism. These attributes cannot exist apart from one another. Good health is a priceless asset that few appreciate until it is lost. A good leader will learn when to delegate some jobs in order to avoid harming his or her health through overwork. A planned program of daily exercise and periodic breaks from the job will keep the mind, body, and spirit sharp. Without health and personal energy, there is little stamina to withstand the demands of leadership.

Without health and energy, it is difficult to be optimistic. The optimistic person is a winner who looks at the bright side of the problem, expresses the "can do" attitude, and inspires both juniors and seniors with his or her enthusiasm to do the job. The opposite of an optimist is a pessimist, who always looks for reasons why a job can't be done. An effective leader is usually an optimistic winner.

Sense of Responsibility. This is the ability to see and do what must be done. It enables leaders to think independently and to use initiative in their jobs. A responsible leader will accept any assignment, whether pleasant or unpleasant, and stay with that task until it is properly completed.

Concern for People. NJROTC leaders must get to know their subordinates. They should know all cadets in their classes and most of the cadets in their unit. Field trips, unit drills, parades and formations, and social events, such as military balls, are good times to get to know other members of a unit. Nothing inspires confidence and morale in a subordinate like their superior's knowing their name and expressing genuine interest in them, their welfare, and the jobs that they do.

Seniors must know their juniors in order to evaluate them. One of the most important jobs of a leader is choosing subordinates for promotion and advancement. A leader is known by the people he or she develops into new leaders.

All hands must be kept informed. They should know what is going on, when things are going to happen, what is expected of them, and why. People are far more likely to cooperate if they know the reason they must do something.

Finally, the virtue of caring and commitment shines brightest whenever a senior follows through with promises made to subordinates. In the military and in civilian life as well, a guiding principle is *never promise what you can't deliver.* Although followers always appreciate that there are times when unexpected changes affect promises made, they will quickly lose respect for the leader who neglects commitments for reasons of expedience, laziness, or personal gain.

In Summary

We have discussed some of the more important qualities of leadership, although there are many others. We have arrived at three conclusions:

- **Leaders must know the capabilities of each member of their group** and how to coordinate them to do their assigned jobs well.
- **Leaders must be self-confident.** They must have an optimistic winning attitude, be able to keep on track to accomplish the goal, and know when it is better to stress the job or the individual.
- **Leaders must be willing to take increased responsibility.** People who can carry out orders cheerfully, complete their work step by step, use their imagination to improve it, and then, when the job is done, look forward to their next job, should be able to lead successfully.

Critical Thinking

1. Which leadership qualities do you think are most important for a cadet leader in the NJROTC to master? Why?

2. Compare and contrast the leadership qualities required for a cadet leader in the NJROTC with those needed by a petty officer or commissioned officer in the Navy or one of the other armed services.

Study Guide Questions

1. How can you help incoming Naval Science 1 cadets?

2. What are the three things upon which leadership depends?

3. What are the three basic things to remember as you develop your leadership abilities?

4. Explain the statement, "Respect of subordinates is not something that can be commanded; it must be earned."

5. What is the difference between physical and moral courage?

6. Why is humor (at the right time and place) an asset to a leader?

7. Explain the statement, "A truly great person can afford to be modest; lesser individuals cannot afford to be otherwise."

8. Why are common sense and good judgment essential qualities of a leader?

9. Why is maintaining good appearance, dress, and conduct important?

10. Summarize some of the most important things a leader must be and do.

New Vocabulary

subordinate	loyalty
pros and cons	honor
trait	modesty
personal relations	judgment
personality	tact
esprit de corps	optimist, pessimist

Approaches to Leadership

Having discussed traits of leadership, let's talk about how to apply one's abilities in the leadership role. This is a question all leaders must answer for themselves. Different leaders approach problems in different ways; all may get good results. In this chapter we will talk about some of the ways to achieve the best results.

Webster's *New World Dictionary* defines **authority** as "the power or right to give commands, enforce obedience, take action or make final decisions." The person in authority is the person in charge. This is the best definition for authority in the Navy. To be in charge is exciting. As with everything else in this world, however, there is another side to the coin. In fact, in the Navy, there are two special burdens on the leader. With authority goes **responsibility**, and with them both goes **accountability.**

The commanding officer has total responsibility for all things within his or her command. He or she is totally responsible for the performance of the ship and crew. There is no way to avoid or delegate this responsibility. Whoever has authority is also held accountable for all that occurs in that command. A leader who is unsuccessful in a mission or brings disaster to the ship or crew must answer for what happened. A naval leader is accountable for deeds and results—not good intentions. It must be this way. Without this accountability, there would be no confidence or trust in those who are in authority. Men and women will not trust leaders who are not accountable for what they do.

Authority in Civilian Life

Authority is a little different in civilian life. It does not carry the same amount of accountability. But it does mean a responsibility to influence and guide the things others do. Civilian leaders may be held accountable in many cases only if they break the law, cause financial harm, or in the case of sports, fail to perform or to have a winning record.

In spite of this, they should still be willing to accept the responsibility of carrying out their acts in a highly professional manner. Your parents have authority over you because they are responsible for your actions—and legally, they are responsible for what you do until you are an adult.

Your teachers have the responsibility for teaching you, and are held accountable by the principal and superintendent. Local police, civil, and school authorities have a responsibility to keep law and order. They get their authority from the people, through laws.

Your naval science instructors have authority over you and your fellow cadets. This authority arises from the agreement each cadet makes when he or she becomes a member of the cadet corps. The authority also comes from the school district and the Navy. These authorities require your instructors to present the NJROTC course in the best way possible.

Discipline and Self-Discipline

Discipline is an orderly way of doing things. In both military and civilian life, discipline is a way of guiding people toward the right actions. Discipline, properly handled, is not harsh or unfair. Therefore, it is not something to fear.

Self-discipline is control of yourself. It is an inner quality that comes from the experiences and training you have had. There are certain jobs you have to do yourself—like keeping your room clean, being home on time, attending classes, doing your homework, and wearing your uniform when required. Self-discipline is what makes you do those things, even when there are other things you'd rather do.

The NJROTC program is designed to teach self-discipline. It helps cadets learn how to manage their time well. Cadets learn to follow directions and make decisions. These are the traits needed by leaders in both military and civilian life. Without orderly conduct, it would be impossible for a military organization to function.

Self-disciplined people make the military, and all society, work. Self-disciplined people are dependable. They will take care of their responsibilities on their own. Self-discipline begins with self-control. This must be practiced. Self-control will help build better habits. The person who has self-control can stand up to hardship and danger. Self-disciplined people follow regulations well. They have high morale.

Drill and Discipline

One way of learning self-discipline is to take part in **unit drill** and **ceremonies.** In order for drills to be good, the unit must practice regularly until every routine is perfect. Drill teaches self-discipline, because it requires the unit to act as one person. Every cadet must know what to do, because everyone must act together. When the order "By the right flank, march!" is given, everyone must carry out the order at the same time. Anyone not doing so will not only stick out like a sore thumb but may get run over!

Drill in uniform can give each cadet a sense of belonging. It is a matter of "All for one, one for all!" When cadets wear the uniform correctly, they will look good. By "looking good" as a unit, each cadet has a sense of belonging to a super group. Drilling is not a punishment or an endless routine. It is a good way to build pride in each member of a unit and in the whole unit. Practice, preparation, and more practice are the hallmarks of well-prepared and well-led organizations.

Likewise, unit ceremonies require each participant to have the self-discipline to practice and learn the part he or she is assigned to carry out or do. A well-conducted and sharp performance on the part of all who take part immediately gains the respect and admiration of all honored guests and spectators. On the other hand, a sloppy or poorly conducted ceremony has the opposite effect on all who observe it.

Military drill is a good way to learn self-discipline for the good of the unit. This squad is looking sharp at a drill competition at RTC Great Lakes Illinois. *CHINFO, Mike Miller*

Leadership Styles

There are several styles of leadership. Each is very different from the others. They range from **autocratic** to **democratic styles.** Most leaders' styles fall somewhere in between the two extremes.

The autocratic type of leadership is direct and impersonal, and it gets a fast response. The autocratic leader (left) doesn't consult with his group. This style is needed sometimes, but the democratic leader (right), who takes into account the needs and feelings of his or her people, will find that this style usually works better.

Autocratic Style. The autocratic, or authoritarian, style of leadership is centered on the leader. It is direct and often impersonal. It demands a fast response, as in a drill or an emergency situation. The autocratic leader has the responsibility to direct a group effort. Subordinates don't openly question this leader's commands. They are seldom free to use their own initiative. The emphasis is on carrying out orders.

The autocratic leader uses position as the basis for leadership. He or she isn't much concerned about relationships with subordinates. This approach won't build a closely knit group. It doesn't encourage a free exchange of ideas between the leader and the group.

Autocratic leadership will get the job done quickly. Groups working under this type of leader produce well for short periods of time, when the leader is present. But production usually goes down over longer periods and when the leader isn't around. Followers depend so much on the leader that they can't act independently when the leader is not there.

The purely autocratic approach has its place for all leaders in certain situations. But in most day-to-day conditions, the leader should be more sensitive to the needs of subordinates. Then he or she will get a better response when direct orders are really required.

Democratic Style. The democratic style means participation of followers, as well as the leader, in the leadership process. It is more time consuming. It requires skills in dealing with people. It is good for long-term situations.

The democratic leader encourages the group's members to help set up procedures, make decisions, and discuss problems. To make the democratic style work, a leader needs cooperation from his or her people. The democratic leader can encourage his or her subordinates to do their part. They will accept his or her leadership. Then everyone will be more willing to work to get the job done. The democratic leader allows people some leeway or freedom in carrying out their tasks, as long as they get the job done. The people doing the job can then have some of the authority for getting it done. They develop pride in their work, and teamwork grows.

Democratic groups produce better over longer periods of time than autocratic groups do. They can also keep producing when the leader is not present.

Range of Leadership Styles

How should the leader try to get people to do the job? **Effective leadership is based on results.** Use of authority alone may not always produce the best results. Conversely, a completely democratic style in which the leader avoids taking responsibility and simply goes along with the group is seldom appropriate either. Within the range of leadership styles from autocratic to democratic, there are five different approaches to leadership.

Telling. In the telling style, the leader keeps all authority and gives the group little freedom. The leader decides and the group follows. The group does not take part in the decision making.

Selling. In the selling style, the leader "sells" and the group accepts. The leader makes the decision, then persuades the group that this decision is the "best" for the group. The leader shows how the group will benefit from carrying out the decision.

Testing. In the testing style, the leader tests, the group reacts, and then the leader decides what to do. The leader states the problem and picks a possible solution. He or she lets the group

react to this solution and may accept suggestions. He or she then makes the final decision and informs the group.

Consulting. In the consulting style, the leader presents the problem and asks for ideas from the group members. The group makes recommendations. The leader then selects a solution and informs the group of his or her decision.

Joining. In the joining style, the group decides and the leader follows. Here the leader is just another member of the group. He or she agrees to carry out whatever decision the group makes.

No matter what leadership style they use, leaders cannot be everywhere all the time, nor can they—or should they—try to do everything themselves. Therefore, regardless of their style, it is frequently necessary for leaders to **delegate** (give) authority to individuals and groups in order to get the job done. For example, the commanding officer (CO) of a ship might delegate to the officer of the deck (OOD) authority to conduct a routine maneuver in a safe manner at a time when the CO is not on the bridge.

When delegating authority, it is important to set clear and concise limits for the individual or group to operate within, as well as to specify the goal and any time constraints that apply. As long as the individual or group can stay within the given limits, decisions as to how to proceed can be made by the individual or group without any further presence of or direction by the leader. Should it become necessary to exceed the limits, the leader must be so advised, in all except emergency conditions, before proceeding. Depending on the situation, alternatives may be presented for consideration and approval by the leader, or further directions may be requested from him or her.

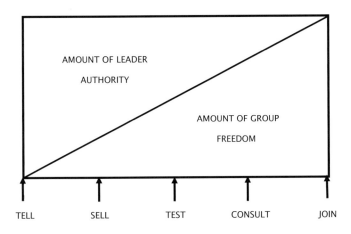

The styles of leadership, on a scale from most autocratic to most democratic.

Each of the five approaches to leadership shown here has a place in different situations. The skillful leader knows when and how to use the best approach to get the desired results.

Good communication requires effort on the part of both the sender and the receiver. These cadets at an NJROTC field-day competition are practicing these skills during a relay race. *NJROTC unit, Annapolis High School*

Leadership and Communication

To become a good leader one has to be able to **communicate**. The four skills necessary for communication are reading, writing, listening, and speaking. Let's discuss each of these briefly.

Reading. The ability to be an effective reader is essential to any leader. He or she must be able to read directives and understand them so he or she can have the group carry them out. On longer articles, instructions, or books, it is a good idea to scan the material first, to pick out the main ideas. Next, the material should be read for details.

Writing. The second skill is to write in a way that others understand. The leader must often give written orders and instructions, so this is a very important skill. There are four important steps to be followed for effective writing. These are:

Step 1: *Clarify your purpose for writing.* Be able to say why you are writing, who will read it, and what you expect the reader to do after reading it.

Step 2: *Limit the subject* to material that suits your purpose as stated in Step 1. Do not waste readers' time with extra material.

Step 3: *List ideas* that you want to get across to your reader. As you read and research your material, write down ideas. You can add to or change these ideas later.

Step 4: *Organize ideas* into groups. This really amounts to an outline. Main ideas are followed by important subheadings and, in turn, by supporting information. In an essay or research paper, the main ideas can be listed under two or three main topics. An outline will help keep you on course and save you time when you actually start writing.

Listening. The art of **listening effectively** is picked up through practice and hard work. Poor listeners often try to place the entire burden on the speaker. There also are persons who want only to hear themselves speak. This is no way to build respect or to manage people effectively. By practicing the following rules, anyone can become a better listener. A good listener will be a better leader.

- *Get ready to listen.* Do not place all the responsibility on the speaker. You must be alert!
- *Take the responsibility for understanding.* Do some thinking as you listen. If you just listen to words, you will miss the purpose of the speech. In your mind, put the speaker's ideas into your own words. Repeat what you thought you heard to be sure. Don't go away in doubt.
- *Listen to understand,* rather than to disagree. Listen and wait; try to understand first and evaluate second. Emotions should not cloud the matter. Question only after a speech or lesson is finished.
- *Listen for the main ideas.* If you are listening to a teacher or other speaker, take notes. Come to classes and lectures prepared to do so. Taking notes will make you more alert for the main ideas.

Alert listening requires effort. Still, it is the best way to get knowledge and understanding.

Speaking. The fourth skill is speaking. Everyone speaks, but not everyone effectively communicates! A speaker must make listeners understand what he or she is trying to say. You probably have listened to someone attempt to give directions and have been more confused than instructed by what he or she said. Obviously, that person did not communicate effectively.

A speaker should use words that the listeners will understand. You will "turn off" your listeners if you use words they don't understand.

Since leadership means getting things done through other people, you must be able to speak well. Of course, giving orders or instructions is not the same as giving a speech. But the same rules hold true in either case. These rules can be used for any speaking you may have to do as a student, cadet leader, or public speaker.

To speak well, you must organize your materials. There are five basic steps for preparing an effective speech. Some steps are like those for writing a paper.

Step 1: *Determine the purpose* for the speech. Having "zeroed in" on your purpose, stick to it. Don't wander in your research or your writing.

Step 2: *Narrow the scope of your topic.* Do not try to cover too much in one speech. You will bore your listeners if you do. Most really good speeches can be given in fifteen minutes or less. The longer the speech becomes, the sleepier the audience becomes. They tune you out!

Step 3: *Choose a subject of interest to you and your audience.* Keep in mind the maturity of your listeners. Do not rely just on what you know about the subject. Do some research. Use examples such as stories, events, and people. And be sure your information is correct!

Step 4: *Make an outline* to organize your speech. Note facts and figures, so you don't make mistakes.

Step 5: *Practice your speech.* Say it in front of a mirror or use a tape recorder. Time it. Listen to yourself. Plan to use gestures. "Running through" your speech a few times out loud will give you confidence.

There will be more on communicating effectively and instructing in *Naval Science 3.*

Critical Thinking

1. Which of the leadership styles described in this chapter would work best in your NJROTC unit? Why?

2. What are some of the most important skills necessary for effective communication by cadet leaders in your NJROTC unit? Why do you think these are important?

Study Guide Questions

1. What does authority mean in the Navy?

2. What is the commanding officer of a naval vessel responsible for?

3. What is the difference between civilian authority and naval authority?

4. Why do parents have authority over their children?

5. Who gives authority to law enforcement and school officials to carry out their responsibilities?

6. Where do naval science instructors get authority to teach and manage the NJROTC unit?

7. What is the first step toward developing self-discipline?

8. Why does military drill help in learning self-discipline?

9. What are the two extreme styles of leadership, and what are the features of each?

10. Upon what is effective leadership based?

11. What are the five styles of leadership in the range from autocratic toward democratic?

12. What are the four skills necessary for effective communication?

13. What are the four important steps for effective writing?

14. What are the four rules for being a good listener?

15. What are the five basic steps to follow in preparing a speech?

New Vocabulary

authority	autocratic
responsibility	democratic
accountability	persuade
self-discipline	delegate
morale	

Leadership Skills

People behave in ways that will best satisfy their needs. Survival—the need for food, air, and water—is the most basic human need. Higher needs, such as those for friends, job, and respect, are felt only after the most basic physical and safety needs are satisfied.

Food and safety, however, seldom bring happiness and a sense of accomplishment. The satisfaction of higher needs brings a sense of well-being and pride. These are necessary for an intelligent, mature human being. While survival needs are similar for all people, higher needs vary greatly among individuals, mainly because of the environment in which the individual has grown up.

This chapter will talk about things that influence the behavior of people. Some knowledge of human nature and what makes people behave as they do is important for a leader.

Satisfying Needs

It is not necessary to talk about the basic needs for food, water, and shelter. Everyone understands these things. A hungry person will seldom work well, for his or her mind is on an empty stomach and visions of a good meal. Once that need is satisfied, however, the person's job and desires for approval, recognition, and achievement will take over quickly. These higher needs may never be completely satisfied. But that is probably a good thing, for that might stop new ideas and limit initiative.

One of the foremost writers on the topic of people's needs as motivators was Abraham Maslow. According to Maslow, needs are arranged from the lowest, such as food and shelter (the physiological), to the highest (self-fulfillment), in an order called the **hierarchy of needs.** In this theory, individuals will try to satisfy all or nearly all of the needs at lower levels before they are ready or motivated to go after those at higher levels. For example, if someone suffers from hunger, most of his or her energy will be spent in finding food, not in seeking a sense of belonging or knowledge, until the need for food is satisfied, and so on.

A leader, therefore, must be sure that the basic needs of subordinates are satisfied. He or she must then try to satisfy their

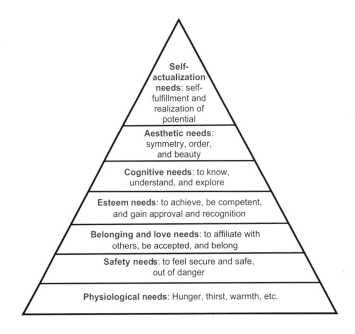

Maslow's Hierarchy of Needs. Maslow believed that needs that are lower in the hierarchy must be at least partly satisfied before those that are higher can become important sources of motivation. *Based on* A Theory of Human Motivation, *by Abraham Maslow*

higher needs. A leader can do this by ensuring that their work gives them the rewards of belonging, status, and getting ahead. The leader must assign jobs in such a way that each person does his or her part well and all work toward the goal. In this way, not only will individual needs be satisfied, but the group will develop teamwork.

Most people seek growth in their work. People desire to learn new skills and move on to more challenging work. They want job responsibilities that use their technical knowledge and ability. They want to become skilled in their trade, because mastery of the job adds to their sense of achievement. Doing a good job, first of all, must be personally rewarding.

But people also desire proper recognition for doing a job well. This increases the drive to succeed. While it is necessary to

177

call attention to mistakes (which everyone makes), recognition of mistakes alone will decrease a person's desire to achieve. It is well to give the deserved compliments first after inspecting a job. Then follow this with constructive criticism, if needed.

Most people want to contribute to the success of their unit and organization, but they generally need a boost or reward (however slight) for doing a good job. This is not selfish; it is human nature and a factor that a leader must consider.

Increasing Motivation

Punishment by the leader is sometimes necessary. This may include putting a subordinate on report, reprimanding him or her, or advising the individual that he or she will not be recommended for advancement unless he or she shows an improvement in attitude and results.

While punishment may make people do what they should, it alone cannot motivate, because motivation is an inner force. The motivated person is **self-starting** and **self-controlled**; he or she does what is necessary to get the job done by himself or herself. What are the things that make people want to do a better job? Many surveys have been done over the years to try to determine these things. In the civilian business world, such matters directly affect production, relationships with unions, public goodwill, and profits. In the Navy, these things directly affect morale, readiness, and reenlistments.

Such surveys have found that there are nine main motivating factors. In order of importance, these are:

1. Feeling that one's work is important
2. Opportunity to do interesting work
3. Opportunity for self-development and improvement
4. Good pay
5. Chance for advancement
6. Respect as an individual
7. Chance to produce work of high quality
8. Knowing what is going on in the organization
9. High degree of freedom on the job.

Items most often put at the bottom of any such listing are the threat of disciplinary action, not having to work too hard, and working under close supervision. Note that each of these is negative, whereas the nine above are all positive.

To help motivate workers, therefore, a leader must give each one the chance to develop his or her abilities and talents. He or she must allow them to use their initiative and judgment within the constraints the leader sets up.

Morale

Morale is the state of mind of an individual. Living conditions, food, quarters, discipline, pay, and duties all affect morale. How

Feelings that what one is doing is important contribute greatly to the morale of an organization. This group of NJROTC cadets being addressed by a Navy admiral obviously reflects this by their obvious interest and drop-attentive attitude. *CHINFO*

important a person feels in a group plays a big part in how good or how bad his or her morale is. Everything that makes a person feel well and satisfied builds up morale, and everything that bothers him or her lowers morale.

High morale is the result of effective leadership. No direction of human activity is possible without it, and no failure is final until morale is destroyed. Morale is based on the belief of the leader in the follower, of the follower in the leader, of each in themselves, and of both in the cause.

To have high morale, an individual must first have standards and goals that make daily life meaningful. Second, he or she must know what must be completed or solved in order to reach those goals; there must be satisfying rewards. Third, a person's basic goals must be in line with other members of the group, so that his or her morale can be kept high during periods of stress.

The leader must realize that high morale is present only in groups that are disciplined and efficient. Morale can be measured by inspections of personnel and their equipment. Interviews can help determine if morale is high or low. A key fact to remember about morale is that nothing will destroy it so surely as inactivity and boredom. At the same time, relaxation and freedom are essential. The leader must plan a schedule with a proper mix of work and play to keep up morale.

Building Morale

The following are some general rules for building high morale in a unit. A leader should:

- Make people confident in his or her ability.
- Stay in touch with individuals' problems and wishes.

- Be consistent and fair in assigning duties and in giving rewards and punishments.
- Show people that he or she respects them and is proud to be with them.
- Keep well informed of attitudes.
- Be accessible.
- Participate in planning and carrying out unit activities.
- Actively supervise lower-ranking leaders to be sure that they do their jobs with the unit's welfare in mind.
- See that people have plenty of opportunity for further education.
- Always be friendly, courteous, and tactful.
- Know each individual by name.

Conversation and Leadership

It is "good business" for a leader to stay in touch with each of his or her subordinates. Personal contact with his or her people is one of a leader's most effective ways of letting them know they are important. This will result in higher morale and will greatly contribute to the efficiency of the command. A leader must believe that each person has something of value to say, that the person may know something the leader doesn't know. Both will benefit from the friendly exchange.

Starting a Conversation. A leader should begin a conversation with a subject of interest to the subordinate. Unit activities, school athletics, clubs, or other programs can be good subjects for "breaking the ice." One does not walk up to subordinates or casual acquaintances and suddenly ask about their health, financial status, details about the family, or hobbies.

A leader should remember three things when starting a conversation. First, no one wants their private affairs pried into. Second, many people like to talk about themselves to someone they can trust, who will listen and understand. And third, the key to getting acquainted is a sincere and unselfish interest in the people being approached. Probably the best opening subject is their work. This is not only of interest to the person but also of genuine interest to the leader.

The following are some conversation starters that may be helpful.

- A question about what they are doing or planning to do
- A comment on their skill or speed in doing the work
- A suggestion for improvement, if this seems needed
- An explanation of the importance of the work
- A question about how the activity can be improved
- A remark regarding similar activities
- A question about their earlier experience with similar work.

Any of these starting points can lead into other topics, if the leader is sincerely interested in getting acquainted and will listen well.

Listening. Listening is a skill the effective leader must have. Few things make a person feel so important or so good about themselves as really being listened to by someone they admire or respect. It takes willpower and practice to forget about personal problems or other concerns when trying to listen to someone. It simply is not possible to listen to a person while thinking about something else. Thinking about other things is bound to show through even if you indicate with smiles, frowns, and other signs that you are trying to follow the person's story.

Everyone can become a good listener. These are some hints that should help.

- Stop working when someone is talking to you; not to do so can be considered insulting and is a sure way of ruining a conversation.
- Accept the speaker as a fellow human being with an interesting personality. While the courtesies of rank should be observed, the speaker must be respected as an individual who has something to contribute.
- Do not interrupt continually with insignificant corrections or arguments.
- Do not belittle the speaker's experiences, plans, accomplishments, or possessions with greater ones of your own.
- Probably one of the worst things a listener can do is to tell other people what they mean or to anticipate the point of their story when they have scarcely begun. This is not only discourteous but can keep one from getting the vital facts. Give the speaker a chance, even if you think you know what he or she is driving at.

These NJROTC cadets are demonstrating good listening skills as they pause from their work to talk with a senior naval officer during a visit to a naval training center. *CHINFO, Scott Thornbloum*

One of the keys to meaningful conversation is to show interest and attention by a pleasant demeanor and by looking into the eyes of the person to whom one is speaking. Here a young NJROTC cadet is having a good exchange with a senior Navy officer during a leadership academy at a Navy training facility. *CHINFO, Scott Thornbloom*

Ending a Conversation. Ending a conversation is almost as important as starting or keeping one going. The leader should not abruptly end a conversation that he or she has started. Ending a conversation without damaging the pride or feelings of the other fellow is an art every leader should develop. Consideration and good listening are the keys to this art.

Once a leader becomes known for being willing to listen, having an open mind, a good memory, and the ability to grasp the point and settle problems, the person who may be inclined to talk too much will shorten his or her chatter. Others, grateful for the attention they know they will get, will respect the leader's time, make their "pitch," and depart.

Attentive, patient, open-minded listening is one of the biggest skills in leadership.

Conclusions about Leadership

To be a leader, then, one must do many things. Among these, the leader must

- Understand, guide, and teach.
- Manage, administer, and supervise.
- Have a dedication and sense of responsibility that inspire others.
- Set a good example at all times.
- Know people's needs and understand how these needs affect human behavior.
- Know how to deal with people and how best to use resources.
- Listen effectively and give counsel wisely.
- Plan ahead.

This sounds like a monumental task for anyone. But leadership, like any other skill, is learned with patient study and practice. The NJROTC cadet leader must keep in mind that promotion depends a lot upon the effort and preparation he or she puts into each task assigned.

Critical Thinking

1. Which of the leadership styles described in this chapter would work best in your NJROTC unit? Why?

2. What are some of the most important skills necessary for effective communication by cadet leaders in your NJROTC unit? Why do you think these are important?

3. High morale and good motivation often go hand-in-hand for good students. What are some things that could be done in your high school to increase student morale and improve student performance?

Study Guide Questions

1. After the basic human needs are satisfied, what higher needs will influence human behavior?

2. What should the leader try to give subordinates?

3. What is a good "rule of thumb" when making an inspection of a job?

4. What must the leader do to motivate followers?

5. A. What is morale?
   B. What three things are essential to high morale in an individual?

6. What things are sure to destroy good morale?

7. Why are frequent contacts with personnel important to building morale?

8. What are three helpful rules to consider when starting a conversation?

9. Why is listening an essential skill for an effective leader?

New Vocabulary

hierarchy of needs	self-starting
motivation	self-controlled
constructive criticism	reprimand

Nautical Sciences

Maritime Geography

Geography is the study of where things are on the Earth. It is also more than that. It is about the relationship of things in a given area—natural resources, land, climate, economics, people, and governments. For naval science students, an important part of geography has to do with the location of key places of maritime significance, the waters around them, and the transportation routes between them, by both land and sea. Also of particular interest are the relationship of geography and politics, called **geopolitics,** and a related field of study called military geography.

In this unit, we will talk about many of these aspects of geography. You will learn where important maritime countries and places are located, and many things about the oceans and seas around them. We will call our approach to this subject "maritime geography."

Understanding geography requires the use of maps. In geography, a map is the most basic tool. Although there are some maps included in this unit that depict the various regions discussed, it would be very helpful if you refer to a large globe or world map as well, to find the places we talk about. To assist in the correct pronunciation of place names and some other terms, the more difficult ones in the following chapters are followed by syllabic pronunciation guides.

Why Study Geography?

Geography has been considered an important subject for study since ancient times. Knowledge of geography is needed if you want to be a good citizen of your country and the world. Only by knowing your own country will you be aware of its strengths and needs. Geography helps supply such knowledge.

But citizens today need to know about more than just their own country. All of us are also citizens of the world. An intelligent citizen must be concerned about problems in other lands, as well as in their own. Only by understanding other people and their needs can we hope to create a peaceful world. Not all nations are blessed with great resources, and few if any have all the resources they need. We need the resources other countries can provide to maintain our standard of living.

We also must be aware of the dangers posed by possible enemies. Our nation wishes to maintain its independence and security and to support the ideals of peace, freedom, and democracy everywhere in the world. But it is clear that some other nations do not have such good intentions. They seek to change governments and bring nations under their control. And their objectives are not just political and social. They want to control the world from geographic strongpoints so they can spread their economic, political, and military control across the globe. All U.S. citizens should understand these geopolitical goals.

The World Ocean

When we speak of the world ocean, we mean the 71 percent of Earth's surface covered with saltwater. If you were to add freshwater surfaces to those of saltwater, you would find that barely one-fourth of Earth's surface is land. Since nearly three-fourths of our world is water, it is clear that the seas are of great importance to life on Earth. The science of oceanography deals with this vital aspect of all life.

The world ocean is the political, economic, and military lifeblood of much of the world. It carries raw materials, food, and manufactured products throughout the world. It provides the people of the world protein-rich seafoods. It is also an important source of minerals.

The continents are large islands in this vast ocean. They divide the world ocean into five major **ocean basins.** The five ocean basins, in order of size, are the Pacific, Atlantic, Indian, Southern, and Arctic. The Southern Ocean basin was identified as such by the International Hydrographic Organization in the year 2000 and comprises parts that used to be traditionally considered within the South Atlantic, South Pacific, and Indian Ocean basins.

Smaller, partially enclosed subdivisions of the oceans are called **seas.** There are many "seas" that are really only part of the oceans listed above. Some of the more important from the standpoint of location and natural resources are the Mediterranean Sea, Caribbean Sea, North Sea, Baltic Sea, Black Sea, Red Sea, Arabian Sea, South China Sea, Sea of Japan, Barents Sea, and Bering Sea. There are a number of important gulfs, or pockets of the seas that reach into the continents. Most notable of these are the Gulf of Mexico, the Persian Gulf, and the Gulf of Aden. You should be able to locate all of these on a world map or a globe.

A body of water similar to a gulf but usually, though not always, smaller is a **bay,** defined as a large body of water opening into a sea. Examples are the Chesapeake Bay on the U.S. East Coast and San Francisco Bay on the West Coast. A **sound** is similar to a bay, except that it connects between two or more inlets or parts of a sea, like Long Island Sound off New York.

Only in the last hundred years or so have the scientific instruments been available for making accurate charts and maps of the ocean floor. These show that the ocean floor is just as varied as the land surfaces. Submarine (underwater) geography includes deep-sea ridges like mountain ranges, seamounts like mountain peaks on land, basins and plains like valleys and surface plains on land, and great trenches even deeper than the Grand Canyon. These features fall within the study of **ocean-ography,** which is covered in unit 2.

On the edges of the oceans are the world's seaports and naval bases from which ships sail forth. **Seaports** are harbors, towns, or cities having access to the sea and containing facilities for cargo handling and ship maintenance of all kinds. A naval base may or may not be located at a seaport. It has facilities for sustaining naval warships and auxiliary vessels. The routes all these ships travel are the strategic waterways of the world.

Military Geography

From ancient days until World War II, military geography was largely a matter of opposing armies finding suitable places to fortify and defend. It might have also involved finding terrain that would be helpful in fighting a battle—hills, rivers, forests, and so on. At sea, the ancients looked for sheltered coves along coastlines, or the **leeward side** (side away from the wind) of islands, where seas were calm. Here their oarsmen might be more effective in ramming enemy vessels. Narrow channels with shoals made defense easier for those familiar with the area.

In World War I, military geography began to be considered. By World War II, every aspect of geography had become important in military planning. Global warfare had begun. Planners had to think about fighting and supporting armies in deserts, jungles, polar regions, mountains, and islands around the world. Supply lines, routes of communications, and transport became crucial. Man-made features such as cities, roads, railroads, bridges, airfields, and harbors often decided success or failure. In the Korean and Vietnam Wars the geopolitical effects were worldwide. The same has been true of the turmoil in the less-developed nations of Africa, Asia, and Central America since then.

Natural resources of all kinds have become necessary for military victory. Vital materials must be shipped over long sea-lanes (routes across the sea) from distant places. Soils have to grow enough food to support millions of personnel overseas as well as home populations. Increasing amounts of water, coal, and petroleum are needed to support industry and fuel military vehicles. Raw materials, transportation, and distance have become crucial to victory in war and to national survival.

Today, as in World War II, every aspect of world geography is taken into account by military planners. Because we depend on foreign sources for many natural resources, as well as on overseas bases and alliances, the maritime aspects of military geography are very important. Sea communications routes, through geographic choke points such as straits, island groups, and canals, are more important than ever before.

1

Maritime Geography of the Western Seas

The sea-lanes of the Atlantic are among the most heavily traveled in the world ocean. The main shipping lanes go between the East Coast of the United States and Western Europe, the two most industrialized regions of the world. The heaviest bulk cargo traffic is carried in huge tankers between the Persian Gulf–area oil fields and Western Europe, traveling the long route around the Cape of Good Hope in South Africa. (The jumbo tankers are too large to go through the Suez Canal, the route taken by smaller tankers and general-cargo ships on their way to both U.S. and European ports from Asia.) The United States imports a large percentage of its total oil needs, and much of that comes across Atlantic sea-lanes from the Persian Gulf, Venezuela, and Nigeria. The Atlantic also provides the water routes between Europe and South America and the Caribbean, and between Gulf of Mexico and East Coast ports and Latin America.

The most important military sea-lanes are those between the United States and its Western European NATO (North Atlantic Treaty Organization) allies and those to the oil-rich countries of the Middle East. In time of war, almost all aid sent from North America to Western Europe would be transported via the North Atlantic sea-lanes. The United States itself, however, is greatly dependent on oil from the Middle East and strategic minerals from Africa and South America. We also need European, South American, and African markets for U.S.-manufactured products and agricultural produce.

Atlantic Ocean

The Atlantic Ocean consists of two sub-basins roughly separated by an enormous underwater mountain range called the **Mid-Atlantic Ridge.** The western sub-basin lies between North and South America, and the eastern sub-basin is between Europe and Africa. The portion of the Atlantic Ocean north of the equator is called the North Atlantic, and the portion to the south is the South Atlantic. The total ocean has an area of about 29 million square miles, extending over about 20 percent of the Earth's surface. Its average depth is about 12,800 feet. The deepest spot in the North Atlantic is in the Puerto Rico Trench,

28,231 feet deep. In the South Atlantic it is the South Sandwich Trench, 27,113 feet deep, about four hundred miles east of South Georgia Island, off Argentina.

The Mid-Atlantic Ridge dominates the midocean floor. Only a few islands emerge above sea level along the ridge; most of the peaks crest one to two miles beneath the surface. These islands are Iceland and the Azores in the North Atlantic and Ascension Island and Tristan da Cunha in the South Atlantic.

Minerals. Few mineral deposits in the Atlantic Ocean's floor can be worked profitably. Those that are mined are located in the shallow waters of the continental shelves (the gradually sloping extensions of the continents out to water depths of between a hundred to two hundred meters [about three hundred to six hundred feet]). The largest mining operations in the Atlantic are for sands and gravels along the Atlantic seaboard of the United States.

The largest single offshore mining operation in the world is based on Ocean Cay in the Bahamas. Aragonite sands, composed mostly of calcium carbonate, are dredged up. They are used in the manufacture of cement, glass, and animal feed supplements. A cement industry also is operated in Iceland, based on shell sands. Phosphates for fertilizers are mined in a number of spots along the shores of all continents facing the Atlantic.

The most important mining operations in the Atlantic are the oil wells in the Gulf of Mexico off the coasts of Texas, Louisiana, and Mexico. Also, there is much oil production in the North Sea between Great Britain and Norway.

Fishing. The North Atlantic has been the scene of major commercial fishing for more than a thousand years. On both sides of the ocean there are major fisheries. Cod, haddock, flounder, and ocean perch are found in the Grand Banks off the Canadian province of Newfoundland and the northeast coast of the United States. Tasty blue crabs are caught all along the eastern seaboard of the United States, in especially large quantities in the Chesapeake Bay and off the Carolina and Florida coasts. Lobsters are a high-value harvest from the New England coast, the Caribbean, Brazil, and South Africa. Herring, sardines, and anchovies are caught in the North Sea's Dogger Bank and in the Norwegian Sea in the far north. Tuna are caught all along the U.S. East Coast, the west African coast, and in the Caribbean.

The Atlantic has some of the most heavily fished areas in the world, providing a total catch of some 24 million tons annually, about 20 percent of the world total.

Ports and Naval Bases. The major U.S. Atlantic ports are Boston, New York, Baltimore, Norfolk, and Charleston. There are many other ports of lesser importance from the standpoint of annual volume. These ports, however, are also very important to coastal shipping and the general prosperity of the nation.

The major naval bases on the East Coast of the United States are at Newport, Rhode Island; New London, Connecticut; Norfolk, Virginia, home port of the Second Fleet; King's Bay, Georgia; and Mayport (near Jacksonville), Florida, home port of the Fourth Fleet. A major naval shipyard is located at Portsmouth, Virginia. Large commercial shipyards that handle major naval shipbuilding programs are located at Bath, Maine; Quincy, Massachusetts; and Newport News, Virginia.

On the eastern side of the Atlantic, the U.S. Navy maintains an important naval air station at Keflavik, Iceland, and a much-used naval base at Rota, Spain. The major ports of Britain are Liverpool, London, and Southampton. The largest and busiest Atlantic port of Western Europe is Antwerp, Belgium. Other important Western European ports are Rotterdam, Netherlands (Holland); Bremerhaven and Hamburg, Germany; Le Havre, France; Copenhagen, Denmark; Oslo, Norway; and Lisbon, Portugal. Almost all direct support for U.S. forces in Germany goes through Antwerp or Bremerhaven. You should know the location of these ports. They all figure prominently in U.S. trade, and all are vital to the defense and economies of Western Europe.

On the western side of the South Atlantic are some important South American ports. A large amount of bauxite ore for making aluminum is exported from Georgetown, Guyana. Tropical woods, quinine, and natural rubber are exported from Belém, near the mouth of the Amazon River in Brazil. The great Brazilian cities of Rio de Janeiro and São Paulo–Santos export iron ore and import U.S.- and European-manufactured products used in that huge country. Buenos Aires, Argentina, and Montevideo, Uruguay, export beef to the United States, and beef and wheat to Europe. They import manufactured products from the United States and Europe.

West African ports of special trading interest to the United States include Casablanca, Morocco, for lead and cobalt; Monrovia, Liberia, for iron ore; Lagos, Nigeria, for oil; Accra, Ghana, for cocoa and gold; and Cape Town, South Africa, for gold, diamonds, platinum, and chromium, among other strategic minerals.

Strategic Geography. When we use the word "strategic" with "geography," we are referring to areas on Earth's surface that are important from a military standpoint. The Atlantic side of the European coast has a number of strategic waterways. The two most important of these are the Strait of Gibraltar and the Danish straits of the Skagerrak (Skăg′-e-răk) and Kattegat (Kăt′-e-găt).

The Strait of Gibraltar is the western entrance to the Mediterranean Sea. It also is the door to the Atlantic Ocean for Russian Black Sea Fleet and Mediterranean Squadron naval vessels. Under the control of Britain, Gibraltar is also vital to allied interests in southern Europe and North Africa.

Russian naval vessels from the Baltic Sea Fleet must go through the Danish straits to get into the North Sea and North Atlantic. The main Russian naval bases and shipbuilding cities on the Baltic

The Strait of Gibraltar.

Baltic Sea ports and bases. The strategic straits of the Skagerrak and Kattegat are the only access in and out.

Sea are St. Petersburg and the Russian enclave of Kaliningrad in Lithuania. Other important Eastern European ports are Riga in Latvia and Gdynia (Ga-din′-ē-a) and Gdansk (Ga-dänsk′) in Poland.

Another area that is strategic from the standpoint of defending allied shipping in the North Atlantic is known as the Greenland–Iceland–United Kingdom (G-I-UK) gap. This is a wide expanse of water between Greenland, Iceland, the Faeroe Islands, and northern Scotland. It is through this seaway that Russian naval warships and submarines from the Northern Fleet, based at Murmansk on the Barents Sea, have to proceed to gain access to the Atlantic Ocean. During the Cold War, a major objective of the United States and its NATO allies was to monitor passage of Eastern Bloc submarines through the Strait of Gibraltar and the G-I-UK gap, since they might have posed a threat to the North Atlantic shipping lanes in the event of the breakout of actual war.

Caribbean Sea and Gulf of Mexico

The Caribbean Sea has an area of roughly one million square miles, with two deep basins separated by the underwater Nicaragua Rise. The rise runs from the hump of Honduras and Nicaragua in Central America northeastward past Jamaica to Haiti. This shallow rise, only two hundred to a thousand feet deep, takes up almost one-fourth of the Caribbean Sea area. To the north is the Yucatán basin with the Cayman Trench, the deepest part of the sea at 25,216 feet. The southern and western half of the sea, extending from Costa Rica to Haiti, and then eastward to the islands of the Lesser Antilles, is as deep as 16,400 feet.

The Lesser Antilles, small islands bordering the eastern limits of the Caribbean, are on a ridge of very active volcanoes. Mount Pelée, on the island of Martinique, killed 30,000 people during a violent volcanic eruption in 1902. More recent but less damaging volcanic action has occurred on several of these islands since then. In January 2010 a major earthquake in Haiti, on the island of Hispaniola, killed some 220,000 people.

Currents from the equatorial Atlantic flow into the Caribbean from the southeast along the coast of northern South America. Part of this current, called the Gulf Stream, continues north into the Gulf of Mexico before moving eastward again between Cuba and Florida, and then up the East Coast of the United States. The prevailing winds, which to a large extent follow the currents, bring strong hurricanes into the area and up the East Coast in the late summer and fall of the year. Almost every year these huge storms cause great property damage and loss of life somewhere in the Caribbean islands, on the Gulf Coast, or along the eastern seaboard of the United States.

The Gulf of Mexico has an area of 598,000 square miles and an average depth of 4,960 feet. From the Yucatán Peninsula of Mexico in the south around the gulf clockwise to the southern tip of Florida, the continental shelf extends far to sea. In the north it has been broadened even farther by silt carried out to sea by the Mississippi River.

Minerals. The Caribbean in general has fewer mineral resources than do other ocean basins. The exception to this is the cluster of Venezuelan oil fields around Lake Maracaibo (Mär-ä-ki′-bō), actually a brackish bay connected to the Caribbean by a narrow inlet. Oil drilling operations there make that country the world's fifth-largest producer of petroleum. Venezuela is one of the top exporters of oil to the United States.

The Gulf Coast of Louisiana and Texas is also rich in oil produced from offshore rigs. Oil and natural-gas fields are also being developed along the Mexican coast near Tampico. The worst oil-pollution catastrophe in history occurred in the Gulf in the spring and summer of 2010. Called the **Deepwater Horizon oil spill,** it occurred when some 4.9 million barrels of oil escaped into the gulf following the explosion of the Deepwater Horizon well, spreading an oil slick that extended all across the southern Gulf of Mexico and onto adjacent beaches. Oil gushed from the broken drilling head some five thousand feet beneath the surface for eighty-seven days until the well was finally capped on 15 July 2010.

Fishing. A great deal of fishing is done by the people of the many Caribbean islands. Most of this is small scale—that is, catches are brought ashore and consumed fresh. The most important commercial fishing operations are for shrimp and menhaden in the Gulf of Mexico. There is a large shrimp catch along the U.S. and Mexican Gulf Coasts. This is where almost all of the shrimp consumed in the United States is caught. There was a lengthy interruption of this fishing in the gulf in 2010 because of the pollution associated with the Deepwater Horizon oil spill.

Menhaden fishing is the most mechanized. Small boats pump their catch into larger carrier vessels. The fish are then brought ashore and processed into fish meal and fish oil for export, mostly to less-developed countries. Fish meal is a high-protein product used for fish cakes, sauces, animal feed, and fertilizer, and the like.

There also are large numbers of delicious Caribbean lobsters, called langusta, caught around all the islands. Some are frozen into packages of expensive lobster tails. Langusta differ from Maine lobsters only in that they do not have large claws. Blue crabs are also caught along the U.S. Gulf Coast, some for canning but most for the fresh market.

Ports and Naval Bases. Houston, Texas, and New Orleans, Louisiana, are the major U.S. ports on the Gulf Coast. Other important ports are Galveston and Port Arthur, Texas; Mobile, Alabama; and Tampa, Florida. Veracruz is the most important Mexican port. Barranquilla (Bär-räng-ke′-yä), Colombia, and Maracaibo and La Guaira (La Gwī′-ra) (port of Caracas), Venezuela, are important in those nations. The capital cities in the Greater and Lesser Antilles are the major ports of each of those islands. The largest and most important of these cities is Havana, Cuba. The island of Aruba, in the Netherlands Antilles, not far from Lake Maracaibo, is a major oil-refining site. Port of Spain, Trinidad, is one of the busiest shipping hubs in the Caribbean, exporting both agricultural products and manufactured goods produced in the region.

The Antilles are a favorite area for luxury passenger cruise ships. To escape the winter, Americans cruise out of Port Everglades (Miami), Florida, and San Juan, Puerto Rico, on pleasure voyages to exotic Caribbean ports such as St. Thomas, Jamaica, and Barbados.

The United States has no major naval bases on the Gulf Coast. There are large commercial shipyards that host naval shipbuilding programs at Mobile, Alabama, and Gulfport and Pascagoula, Mississippi, and a major naval support activity at Panama City, Florida. There is a major naval air training complex at Pensacola, Florida, and small naval air bases at Key West, Florida, and Corpus Christi, Texas. There is an important U.S. naval base in the Caribbean at Guantánamo (Gwän-tä′-na-mo) Bay, Cuba, described in more detail below.

Strategic Geography. Certainly the most important strategic spot in the Caribbean is the **Panama Canal**. Splitting the Central American peninsula within the Republic of Panama, the canal is the main route for most ocean traffic between the Atlantic and Pacific. The Canal Zone was run by the United States for most of the last century, but it was turned over by treaty to Panama in 1999.

The Panama Canal has always been vital to U.S. interests. From the naval standpoint, it has been the best way to transfer all but the largest ships of the Atlantic and Pacific fleets rapidly back and forth in the event of tension or war. There is no question of its importance as a choke point of international trade. While the canal is probably not as important to U.S. defense as it once was, its loss to an enemy power would severely harm U.S. and Western Hemisphere security and economic interests.

There are two more sets of larger locks under construction, planned for completion in 2015, when the current original locks will be a hundred years old. A competing railway across Columbia is also under discussion, as is a revival of an old plan to build a rival canal across Nicaragua. Both would be built and operated by China.

Cuba is the largest island in the Caribbean, and with a population of over 11 million it is also the most populous. Only ninety miles from Florida, Cuba has been a major problem for the United States ever since communist dictator Fidel Castro took power in the early 1960s and made it an ally of the former Soviet Union. There is a base to support submarines at Cienfuegos in southern Cuba. A large number of gunboats are based

The Gatun Locks on the Atlantic side of the Panama Canal. Two more sets of larger locks are under construction, scheduled for completion in 2015.
Sara Morrison

in various small ports around the island. Several interior airfields base fighter squadrons that fly modern fighter and attack aircraft.

For three decades prior to the demise of the Soviet Union, a constant stream of Soviet ships and aircraft supplied Soviet goods to Cuba. With the cargo came military equipment and advisers, which together made the Cuban armed forces one of the largest and best-equipped military forces in the Western Hemisphere. It nearly became a nuclear power around the time of the Cuban Missile Crisis in 1962, until all nuclear arms were removed by the Soviet Union shortly thereafter. Cuba has served as a base of operations for revolutionaries throughout the Caribbean and Latin America, and its forces supported communist insurgencies in Africa and Central American throughout the 1970s and 1980s. It was then and remains the only developing country to have projected power on the world stage in a manner similar to a major global power. The United States broke diplomatic ties with Cuba in 1961, when Castro openly embraced communism and announced his alliance with the Soviet Union. A low-key relationship was resumed in 1977, but there have been no serious moves to reopen embassies or exchange ambassadors since. Following the demise of the Soviet Union in the early 1990s, all Russian aid to Cuba stopped, throwing it into a state of severe economic depression that has persisted to the present day. In 2009, following the retirement of Fidel Castro as Cuban president and the assumption of that office by his brother Raúl, President Obama reversed a long-standing policy that had prohibited travel and financial dealings by U.S. citizens with Cuba.

When relations were broken, the United States made sure that the treaty granting the United States a naval base at **Guantánamo Bay,** in far southeastern Cuba, stayed in effect. "Gitmo," as naval personnel call it, is the Navy's main training base for the U.S. Atlantic Fleet. It has a fine harbor and good facilities. Except for an occasional hurricane in the fall, the weather is excellent most of the year for all types of fleet training, including aircraft operations and missile firing. The U.S. Marines maintain a force at Gitmo for defense of the base and its facilities.

U.S. naval base at Guantánamo Bay, Cuba. *CHINFO*

The main gate of Camp Delta, the detention camp at Guantánamo Bay where detainees from the wars against terrorism are kept. *CHINFO, Michael Holzworth*

There is also a large **detention facility** (prison camp), called Camp Delta, staffed by Army guards and Navy medical personnel that serves as a holding and interrogation facility for al-Qaeda, Taliban, and other detainees who have come under U.S. control during the war on terrorism. There has been a great deal of political discussion in the United States about how to deal with the remaining prisoners there and whether or not to close the facility.

The Arctic Ocean

The Arctic is the smallest of the major oceans and ocean basins. It has an area of about 4.7 million square miles and an average depth of 3,400 feet. Almost all of the water area and much of the contiguous northern land mass is covered over by ice in the winter months, and some two million square miles of it is ice covered year round. The deepest part of the ocean is the Abyssal Plain, running across the North Pole at a depth of 15,091 feet. The Arctic basin is divided by three major submarine ridges, which separate four large undersea plains and a number of smaller ones. The continental shelf north of Alaska, Canada, and Greenland extends about fifty to 125 miles from shore. However, the continental shelf north of Asia extends from three hundred to more than six hundred miles toward the pole. The portion of the Asiatic continental shelf under the Barents Sea north of Russia and Scandinavia extends more than a thousand miles to sea, past Spitsbergen (Spĭts′-bûr-gan) and Franz Josef Land.

Until the nineteenth century, with the exception of a few attempts at exploration, there was not much interest in the region, because of its inhospitable cold climate and the thick ice covering most of the surface that made travel and habitation difficult or impossible. There were some attempts to navigate the so-called **Northwest Passage** across the top of North America between the Atlantic and Pacific Oceans through the Arctic

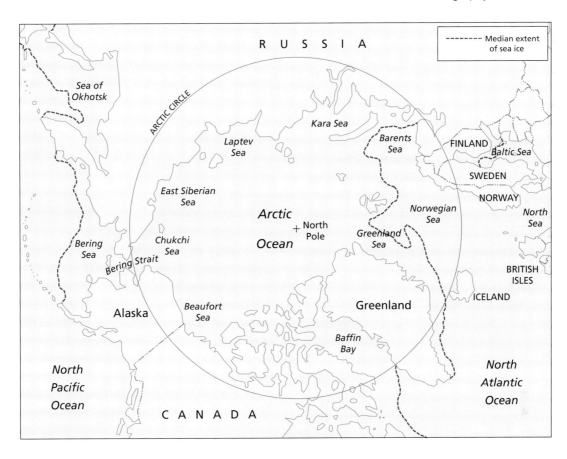

Arctic Ocean, showing the Arctic seas. The dashed red lines show the mean (average) extent of sea ice covering the region in a typical recent year. *NOAA*

Ocean, and the **Northeast Passage,** later called the **Northern Sea Route,** along the Russian northern coast, but these were largely abandoned because they were not navigable most of the year. However, the global-warming trend in evidence in recent years has begun to change all that and spark a sharp increase in interest in the region on the part of many countries, including the United States. Seasonal sea ice is now retreating at a rate unexpected even a few years ago. In 2012 the extent of sea ice reached the lowest level in recorded history, opening up more of the Arctic to navigation, fishing, and commercial exploitation than at any time in perhaps the past several thousand years. Even so, the depth of water in both potential sea routes through the Arctic greatly limits the size of containerships and bulk carriers that can transit them, and the passages are only open three or four months of the year, making commercial traffic through them not economically feasible.

Minerals. At one time not much was known about the extent of oil and gas reserves in the Arctic, but as the climate has continued to warm, much more exploration has been done. At present, current U.S. Geological Survey data suggest that the region may hold as many as 66 billion barrels of oil reserves and more than 200,000 billion cubic feet of natural gas. Along the

Asian side of the Arctic Ocean are five seas: Chukchi (Chŏŏk´-chē), East Siberian, Laptev, Kara, and Barents. Much geologic exploration for minerals has been done there in the last few years. Large oil and natural-gas deposits probably exist in the Laptev Sea north of Siberia.

The continental shelf off Alaska has been the scene of much oil drilling ever since major oil discoveries were made there in the late 1960s and early 1970s in Prudhoe Bay on the North Slope region of northern Alaska. An eight-hundred-mile trans-Alaska pipeline was completed in 1977 at a cost of eight billion dollars. More than 600,000 barrels of oil flow south though it daily from Prudhoe Bay to Valdez (Val-dëz´), Alaska, where tankers take the oil on board for delivery to West Coast refineries.

In March 1989 the largest oil tanker spill in U.S. history occurred when one of these tankers, the 987-foot *Exxon Valdez,* carrying 1,260,000 barrels of crude oil taken on at Valdez, ran aground on a reef in the Gulf of Alaska some twenty-five miles south of that port. The resulting oil slick from 260,000 barrels lost in the mishap spread some 470 miles into the gulf. Many formerly clean Alaskan beaches and tidal basins were covered with inches of black sludge. Although some two billion dollars was ultimately spent by the Exxon Corporation to try to clean

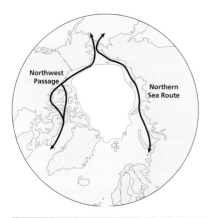

Illustration of the Northwest Passage and the Northern Sea Route.

up the mess, some remnants still remain, and some wildlife habitats are still not back to normal.

As a result of the *Exxon Valdez* disaster, nowadays North Slope oil must be transported in double-hull tankers, and these must be escorted by at least two tugboats. Land-based radar continuously monitors the positions of the ships throughout their transits. Nearly 400 local fishing boat owners are trained to deploy floating oil boom containment barriers in the event of any future spill in the region.

Large oil deposits have been found in the continental shelf off the Beaufort (Bō'-furt) Sea coast of Canada, some four hundred miles east of Prudhoe Bay. Large natural-gas deposits are now being tapped in the area of Melville Island, in the Queen Elizabeth Islands. More recently, huge oil and gas deposits were discovered on the shelf of the Barents Sea off Norway and northwestern Russia, but the challenges posed by setting up drilling facilities in these waters are daunting. Some progress has been made in accessing the Norwegian fields, but thus far the potential expense of developing the Russian fields has been prohibitive.

Getting oil and natural gas out of the Arctic is not easy. The frigid cold, prolonged gale-force winds, and icing and freezing

The oil tanker *Exxon Valdez* aground in the Gulf of Alaska south of Valdez in 1989. There ensued one of the largest oil spills in American history. The cause of the grounding was later determined to be incompetent navigation by the tanker's captain and crew.

of lubricants and equipment make drilling extremely expensive and hazardous. The Arctic Ocean itself is almost always covered with constantly moving ice floes. Engineers have created artificial islands built from sand and gravel dredged up during the summer melt, sometimes poured through holes cut in the seven-foot-thick ice. It has even been proposed to build drilling facilities in the Arctic entirely under water, reminiscent of the rigs in the 1989 science fiction movie *The Abyss* (20th Century Fox). Much of the year the crude oil must be heated in order to flow satisfactorily through the pipelines and drilling rigs, because of the extreme cold. But the demand for fossil fuel products in the world is so great that no effort is being spared to solve the problems.

Fishing. Only in the Barents and Norwegian Seas can commercial fishing take place. There, catches of cod, haddock, redfish, and halibut are taken annually for the fresh-fish markets in Europe and the Russian states. The global-warming trends of recent years have resulted in an apparent northerly migration of all these species, with resulting greatly increased catches in the region. Some whaling is still done there by a small Icelandic whaling fleet.

Ports and Naval Bases. As previously mentioned, Prudhoe Bay is a major oil terminal on the North Slope of Alaska. Murmansk, Russia, a port on the Kola Peninsula adjacent to the Barents Sea, is ice-free much of the year, and is an important port for the Russian navy's Northern Fleet and for fishing fleets based there. The Northern Fleet has its administrative headquarters at Severomorsk, a coastal town about twenty-five kilometers (km) north of Murmansk. Narvik, Norway, is a significant fishing port and a loading place for high-grade iron ore from Swedish mines at Kiruna (Kir'-u-nä), about 125 miles inland.

Strategic Geography. As mentioned above, there are no viable commercial sea lanes across the Arctic Ocean at the present time. However, if recent climate change trends continue into the coming years, further reduction of ice in both the Northwest Passage and the Northern Sea Route during summer months may make these routes more lucrative in the future. In 1958 the American nuclear submarine USS *Nautilus* became the first vessel ever to reach the North Pole under the ice. Since then, U.S., Soviet, and, more recently, Russian nuclear submarines have made many patrols under the ice, and Russian surface warships and patrol aircraft have dramatically increased their activity in the region. Engineers occasionally propose having submarine tankers cross the Arctic Ocean under the ice, cutting thousands of miles off the surface routes between U.S. and Canadian Beaufort Sea oil fields and northern Europe. Since the great-circle routes across the Arctic offers the shortest distance between Asia and the United States and Northern Europe for both submarines and aircraft, the region would almost certainly be a major operational area in the event of any future war between littoral countries in the region.

The moderating trend of climate change in recent years has led to much-increased interest in the region by all five nations with shores bordering the Arctic: the United States, Canada, Russia, Denmark, and Norway. The potential hydrocarbon resources cited above are the main focal point of this interest, but also issues concerning mineral rights, increased fishing, trade, tourism, and military presence in the region are becoming increasingly contentious. The five nations listed above, plus Finland, Iceland, and Sweden in 1996, formed an organization called the Arctic Council, which meets twice a year to discuss issues of concern in the region. Many other nations participate in observer status, including China, India, Japan, and South Korea.

Mediterranean Sea and Black Sea

The Mediterranean Sea is a shallow, long, landlocked sea about 1.1 million square miles in area. Its average depth is 4,921 feet, but there are some deep basins west and south of Italy. The Hellenic Trough, south of Greece, is the deepest area, more than 16,700 feet deep. The Mediterranean lies in a broad trench between the European and African continents. It stretches about 2,500 miles from the Strait of Gibraltar on the west to Israel on the east. The word "Mediterranean" comes from the Latin words *medius,* meaning "middle," and *terra,* meaning "land"; together they mean the sea "in the middle" of the lands (of Europe, Asia, and Africa).

The Mediterranean is divided into two basins, east and west of the Strait of Sicily. The continental shelves are very narrow around the Mediterranean, though most of the Adriatic Sea and Gulf of Gabes (Gä′-bes), off Tunisia, have sea floors that are actually continental shelves. Great sediment beds extend far to sea from the mouths of the Nile River in Egypt, the Rhone (Rōn) River in France, and the Ebro (Ē′-bro) River in Spain.

The Mediterranean basin is one of the most active volcanic areas in the world. There are at least eleven active volcanoes in the Aegean (I-jē′-an) Sea, in a belt from Athens to Rhodes. Four of these are islands, and the others are submerged. Many more underwater volcanoes are in the western Mediterranean, to the north and west of Sicily, and around the Balearic (Bal-ē-ar′-ik) Islands and Corsica. The whole Mediterranean area, especially Greece, Turkey, and Yugoslavia, often has severe earthquakes. The Eurasian and African geological plates push in on the sea from both sides. Volcanic lava from the interior of the Earth wells up at huge pressure, causing volcanoes and earthquakes at the fault line where these plates meet.

The Black Sea is located above Turkey on the eastern end of the Mediterranean, between Europe and Asia. It has an area of about 180,000 square miles, with maximum depths of slightly over seven thousand feet. It connects with the Mediterranean through the Turkish straits and the Sea of Marmara. In many respects it is a landlocked saltwater lake; its mineral content has become so high that the sea supports little life except in the surface layers. Some scientists have speculated that it was formed by overflow from the Mediterranean when the ice melted after the last ice age some ten thousand years ago. Its formation may have given rise to the story of the great flood in the Bible, and perhaps to the legend of the sinking of Atlantis. Photography of the bottom by remote-controlled submersibles has found evidence of ancient land-based habitation.

The Mediterranean was the cradle of Western civilization. For nearly seven thousand years there has been recorded history in the eastern Mediterranean. Egypt, Crete, Phoenicia (Fi-nish′-e-a), Greece, and finally Rome led the parade of culture and trade across the sea in ancient times. The Romans called the Mediterranean *Mare Nostrum,* which means "our sea."

During the Middle Ages, Christian and Muslim cultures clashed in the Crusades. The clash ended in what can be thought of as a geographic compromise: Christians settled to the north and west in Europe, and Muslims settled to the south and east in Africa and Asia.

Minerals. No readily accessible mineral deposits have been located in the Mediterranean. Far below the sediments on the sea floor, however, drillers have found large beds of rock salt, sulfur, potash, and gypsum. All would be valuable for the chemical and fertilizer industries. At the present time these minerals can be mined only from deposits on Sicily and other islands.

Oil wells are being drilled offshore along the Adriatic coast of Italy, in the Gulf of Gabes off Tunisia, and off the Nile Delta in Egypt. Although geologic studies seem to indicate that there is oil and natural gas along much of the Mediterranean coastline, there is no equipment at present that can reach the depths necessary to get it.

The Black Sea. The region has gained notoriety in recent times because of the 2014 Olympic Winter Games held in Sochi, Russia, and the subsequent annexation of Crimea and incursions into eastern Ukraine by Russia.

Fishing. The Mediterranean basin supports a fishing industry twice as valuable as that of any ocean. Catches bring high prices, because most Mediterranean peoples consider fish a luxury food, like steak. Thousands of small fishing boats bring in small catches. Hake, sole, red mullet, and many other species of fish have recorded catches in excess of a million tons each year. The actual total is probably much larger, since many local fishermen do not report accurate numbers.

There is danger of large-scale pollution in the Mediterranean. This pollution threatens to destroy the balance of life in the sea. Overfishing is likewise making some kinds of fish scarce in some areas. The man-made pollution is worsened by the fact that this sea is almost totally landlocked. It loses by evaporation almost three times as much water as it gets from rainfall and runoff from land. Only the flow of water from the Atlantic keeps the sea at the same level over time. There is also a small flow from the Black Sea through the Turkish straits.

A dramatic example of the effect of humans on the ecology of the eastern Mediterranean can be seen by looking at the changes that have taken place there since 1970. In that year a high dam was completed across the Nile at Aswan (A-swan′), Egypt. This stopped the seasonal flood of fresh water and plant food into the sea by way of the Nile. Because of this, a fishing industry that had existed since the dawn of Western civilization has now almost ceased to exist near the mouth of the Nile.

Ports and Naval Bases. The Mediterranean Sea has always been very important to the countries around it. It is still so today. Great port cities are located in all of the countries bounding the Mediterranean coast: Barcelona and Valencia in Spain;

The Turkish straits consist of the Bosporus and the Dardanelles, the only linkage between the Mediterranean and the Black Sea.

Marseilles (Mar-say′) in France; Genoa, Naples, and Venice in Italy; Piraeus (Pi-rē′-as), the port of Athens, Greece; Istanbul (Is-tan-bōō-l′), Turkey; Beirut (Bay-rōō-t′), Lebanon; Haifa (Hi′-fa) and Tel Aviv (Tel′ a-vēv′), Israel; Alexandria, Egypt; Algiers (Al-jirz′), Algeria; Odessa (O-děs′-a) on the Black Sea arm in Ukraine; and a host of others.

The Southern Command of NATO has its headquarters near Naples, with another important base at Izmir (Iz-mir′), Turkey. There is a large U.S. Navy support activity at Naples, and the home port of the flagship of the U.S. Sixth Fleet is at Gaeta (Gä-â′-tä), Italy, about halfway between Rome and Naples. There is a Navy air station at Sigonella, Sicily. The main Spanish naval base is at Barcelona, a favorite port of call for U.S. naval ships. The principal French base is at Toulon (Tōō-lon′), near the beautiful Riviera cities of Nice (Nës) and Cannes (Kăn), also favorite places for U.S. Sixth Fleet sailors. The Italian navy's headquarters is at La Spezia (La Spā′-tsyä), and its fleet's biggest southern base is in Taranto (Tä′-rän-tō).

The Russian Black Sea fleet headquarters is located at Sevastopol on the Crimean Peninsula, which Russia annexed by treaty with the Ukrainian government in March 2014. The Ukraine had maintained a small naval fleet at Sevastopol as well, consisting mainly of aging Soviet-era ships. Major shipyards for merchant and naval surface ships are located at Nikolayev (Nik-a-lä′-yaf), near Odessa. It remains to be seen what future developments will take place in the region as a result of ongoing tension between the governments of Russia and the Ukraine.

Strategic Geography. We have talked about the Strait of Gibraltar as the doorway to the Atlantic Ocean from the Mediterranean Sea. There are two other key **choke points of navigation** associated with the Mediterranean area: the Turkish straits—the Bosporus (Bos′-per-as) and the Dardanelles (Därd-n-elz′)—and the Suez Canal.

In peacetime the Turkish straits are open to all ships by international agreement. In wartime, however, the straits may be closed to any nation at war with Turkey. Turkey is a member of NATO. Russian and Ukrainian naval vessels from Black Sea ports freely use the straits to support and relieve the ships of their navies in the Mediterranean.

The Suez Canal is a vital waterway for the ships of all nations. Over this narrow path through the Egyptian desert passes most surface cargo between Europe and Asia. As was proved in the Arab-Israeli wars in 1967 and 1973, the canal can be blocked quickly with mines or a few sunken ships.

The Arab Spring movement that began in 2010 fomented major unrest, political turmoil, and in some cases open revolt amongst almost all the countries of the eastern Mediterranean region. It resulted in major changes in government in many of them, a process that is still ongoing today.

Critical Thinking

1. Many of the strategically important choke points identified in this chapter would probably be of prime importance in a worldwide conflict such as World War II. What do you think are the most important of the Western choke points today, and why?

2. Do you think the Panama Canal still has strategic importance today? Should the United States have relinquished control of it to Panama in 1999? Justify your response.

3. Research the main sea transportation routes for oil through the Mediterranean Sea region and where they would be most vulnerable to possible interference or closure by belligerent countries nearby.

Study Guide Questions

1. What are the most important military sea-lanes in the Atlantic for the United States? Why?

2. A   What are the two Atlantic sub-basins?
   B. Where is the deepest spot in the North Atlantic? The South Atlantic?

3. What are the principal mineral and mining industries of the Atlantic and its gulfs and seas?

4. Where are the major fishing areas of the Atlantic?

5. What are the major naval bases on the U.S. Atlantic coast?

6. Which two European ports handle most of the support traffic for U.S. land forces in Germany?

7. What are some important trade goods the United States imports from Africa?

8. A. What does strategic geography mean?
   B. What are the choke points of navigation leading to and from the Atlantic basins?

9. Why is the Greenland–Iceland–United Kingdom gap important to the allies?

10. What severe storms occur each fall season in the Gulf of Mexico and Caribbean Sea?

11. A. Which two minerals are the chief resources of the Gulf of Mexico and Caribbean areas?
    B. Where are these minerals being mined?

12. Where are the major naval air and surface bases in the Caribbean and Gulf of Mexico?

13. A. What is the vital navigational choke point of the Caribbean area?
    B. What is the principal importance of this waterway to the United States?

14. Which Caribbean nation and government is a great worry to the United States? Why?

15. Why is the naval base at Guantánamo Bay important?

16. Where is the deepest part of the Arctic Ocean?

17. What valuable resource is being obtained from the continental shelf off Alaska and Canada in the Arctic Ocean?

18. Why would the Arctic probably become a major operational area in event of a war between the United States and any Asiatic country?

19. How has the high dam on the Nile River at Aswan, Egypt, affected the ecology of the eastern Mediterranean?

20. A. What are some famous and important ports of the Mediterranean?
    B. Where are some of the important naval bases in the Mediterranean?
    C. Where is the home port for the U.S. Sixth Fleet flagship?

21. A. What are the names of the important Turkish straits?
    B. Why are these straits important to the NATO allies—and to the Russians and Ukrainians?

New Vocabulary

lobster	sound (water body)
langusta	seaport
ocean basins	strategic geography
bay (water body)	choke point

2

Maritime Geography of the Eastern Seas

Oil—its source and the sea routes over which it travels—dominates most trade in the seas south of Asia. From the Persian Gulf and Arabian Sea, the routes go westward to the Red Sea and Suez, and eastward through the Strait of Malacca and the seas around China to Japan. Trade moves from eastern Africa, India, Indonesia, and western Australia to Suez. It moves from China, Japan, Indonesia, and the islands of the Pacific to the West Coast of the United States and South America. Suez to Singapore, the most important British lifeline of past years, is still a major route of trade and travel between Asia and the West.

Because of the strategic importance of the Middle East—its warm-water ports; its oil; and its hundreds of millions of peo-

ple, many trying to survive under weak governments and in poor environments—U.S. naval forces operate routinely in the Indian Ocean. The U.S. Fifth Fleet flagship has its home port in Manama, Bahrain. The United States tries to maintain friendships in the region despite political and economic unrest. Third-world nations are trying to improve the lives of their people and must look to the seas to do so.

In recognition of the growing importance of Africa to world trade and international security, in 2008 the United States formed the U.S. Africa Command. Headquartered in Stuttgart, Germany, it is one of nine unified combatant commands of the U.S. armed forces. It is responsible for all U.S. military operations in Africa, with the exception of Egypt, which is within

The USS *America* (CVA 66) transits the Suez Canal with her escort ships in the 1980s. *CHINFO, W. M. Welch*

the area of responsibility of the U.S. Central Command, which in turn is responsible for operations in the Middle East, Central Asia, and North Africa. The main naval force of the Africa Command is a combined joint task force headquartered at Djibouti on the Gulf of Aden.

The Suez Canal, Red Sea, and Gulf of Aden

The Suez Canal is a vital waterway for Western Europe as well as the Middle Eastern nations. On this narrow water path through the Egyptian desert, linking the eastern Mediterranean Sea with the Red Sea, most surface cargo between Europe and Asia passes. As was proved in the Arab-Israeli wars in 1967 and 1973, the canal can be blocked quickly with mines or a few sunken ships.

The Red Sea is a warm, very salty sea stretching some 1,300 miles southeast from the Egyptian port of Suez to the Strait of Bab el Mandeb. It is only ninety to two hundred miles wide, with an area of 169,000 square miles. The Axial Trough, in the very middle of the narrow sea, is the deepest, at 9,580 feet near the Saudi Arabian port of Jidda (Jid′-a).

Minerals. The Red Sea has no known oil deposits. It is a possible future source of valuable metals, however. Pools of boiling hot brine are found in the Axial Trough. These waters are rich in dissolved metals, including zinc and copper, in the seabed muds. Someday it may be possible to mine these minerals.

Fishing. There is not much fishing in the Red Sea. Many kinds of fish are caught, but except for sardines near the Gulf of Suez, there is no major fishery. Lights are used to attract fish to the nets, since coral reefs make bottom trawling risky and expensive.

Ports and Naval Bases. The port of Suez on the southern end of the canal is important because it is the southern anchorage for ships waiting to go through the canal northward to the Mediterranean Sea. Port Said (Sä-ēd′) on the northern end of the canal is important for the same reason. Massawa (Me-sä′-wa) is a port and naval base in Eritrea, which gained independence from Ethiopia in 1991. Further south is the major port city of Assab. Jidda, a seaport in Saudi Arabia, serves as a port of entry for the Moslem holy city of Mecca, about forty miles inland.

Djibouti (Jŏ-boō′-tē), the capital city and port in the nation of the same name, is the major African port on the Horn of Africa, on the Gulf of Aden. It not only serves its own country but also is the main port for shipment of Ethiopian imports and exports. It is also the site of a Navy antipiracy base, called Camp Lemonnier, the home of the **Combined Joint Task Force for the Horn of Africa** (a multinational multipurpose naval force) within the U.S. Africa Command. The major port of the area is Aden, capital of Yemen (Yem′-an).

Strategic Geography. The Red Sea is a strategic waterway. Along with the Suez Canal and Gulf of Suez to its north, and

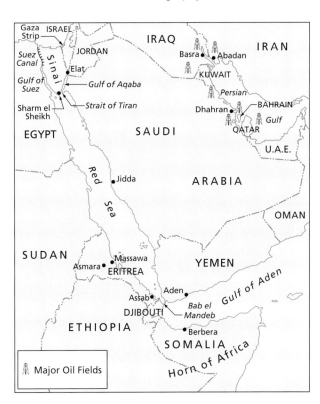

The Suez Canal, the Red Sea, the Gulf of Aden, and the Horn of Africa. The southern entrance to the Red Sea is controlled by the Strait of Bab el Mandeb. The oil fields of the Persian Gulf are at the upper right.

the Gulf of Aden to the south, the Red Sea is the main waterway between Europe and Asia. The northern access is the Suez Canal. The choke point in the south is the Strait of Bab el Mandeb. (The Arabic word *bab* means "gate" or "strait.") Less than twenty miles wide, the strait separates Yemen on the Arabian Peninsula from Ethiopia and the Republic of Djibouti in Africa.

The Persian Gulf and Gulf of Oman

The Persian Gulf area is the leading oil-producing area in the world. The gulf is bounded by Iran on the north, Kuwait and Iraq at the northwest end, Saudi Arabia on the west, and the Arab sheikdoms of Bahrain (Ba-rän′) island, Qatar (Kät′-ar), the United Arab Emirates (UAE), and Oman on the south and southeast. All of these countries are major oil producers. The gulf itself has been divided for oil drilling by these nations, since much of the oil is obtained by offshore rigs. The Persian Gulf has been the scene of major conflicts between Iran, Iraq, and the United States and Western European nations for the last thirty years.

Minerals. Though oil was known to be present in the region in ancient days, the drilling of oil wells there is a comparatively recent development. The first wells in Iran were not drilled until

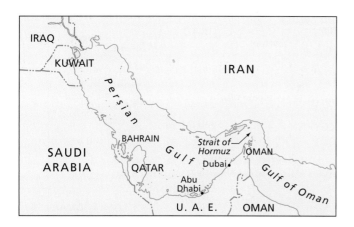

The Persian Gulf and Gulf of Oman. The Strait of Hormuz is a key choke point for all ships entering or leaving the Persian Gulf. It has been the scene of much confrontation between Iran and the navies of the United States and the European Union in recent years.

1935, and those in Kuwait did not start up until 1946. World War II caused a major increase in drilling in both Iran and Saudi Arabia. In the past twenty years, the wells and offshore rigs there have become very important. Today, about a third of the total oil production of the world comes from the Persian Gulf. The United States, Western Europe, and Japan have come to depend on Arab oil in large part. The United States imports about 40 percent of its annual oil needs from the area, Western Europe about 70 percent, and Japan more than 90 percent.

Ports and Naval Bases. The major oil-exporting ports are Ras Tannura (Ta-nur'-a), Saudi Arabia; Abadan and Kharg (Karg) Island, Iran; Sitra, Bahrain; Das Island, UAE; and Mina Abdulla, Mina Shauiba, and Mina Al-Ahmadi, Kuwait. There is a U.S. Navy base at Bahrain, home to the **U.S. Fifth Fleet.** Bahrain is the primary support base in the region for Navy and Marine activities in support of Operation Enduring Freedom in Afghanistan, and it served the same role for Operation Iraqi Freedom.

Fishing. The entire Persian Gulf is shallow. Half of it is less than 120 feet deep, all but a few spots less than two hundred feet. Because it is so shallow, sunlight can reach the bottom in most places, causing lots of plankton to thrive there. Plankton are tiny animals and plants that provide food for small fish. Since there is much plankton, a large variety of fish live in the gulf. Sardines, anchovies, mackerel, and barracuda are the main kinds caught by local fishermen. In the waters controlled by Qatar and the UAE are valuable pearl fisheries.

Strategic Geography. While oil is the big strategic resource, the political and stra-

A satellite picture of the Persian Gulf (top), Strait of Hormuz, and Gulf of Oman (bottom). *NASA*

tegic geography of the gulf is also of great importance. Acquiring a warm-water port on the Persian Gulf has been a major goal of Russia and the former Soviet Union for the past hundred years. A major political goal of Western nations over the same period, especially during the Cold War years, has been to prevent this from occurring.

The Persian Gulf area has been the scene of almost continual conflict since the 1980s, starting with an eight-year war between Iran and Iraq that did not end until 1988. In 1990 Iraq's leader Saddam Hussein staged a brutal invasion of Kuwait, from which he was driven out a year later by a multinational coalition headed by the United States in Operation Desert Storm. Between 2003 and 2011 the United States and allied countries engaged Hussein and his forces during Operation Iraqi Freedom in Iraq, eventually deposing him and sponsoring the formation a new democratic form of government for the country. Unfortunately, this did not end extremist violence against the government and the citizenry, and suicide bombings and other attacks have continued to wreak havoc in the country to the present day.

Indian Ocean

The Indian Ocean is the third-largest in the world. It has an area of about 26 million square miles and an average depth of 12,600 feet. Maximum depth is 24,442 feet in the Java Trench, southwest of the Indonesian islands of Sumatra and Java, on the eastern edge of the ocean.

The main feature of the Indian Ocean floor is a great mid-ocean ridge system, shaped like an upside-down Y. The Southwest Indian Ridge goes around southern Africa and joins the Mid-Atlantic Ridge. The Mid-Indian Ridge continues south of Australia to join with the Mid-Pacific Rise. Many volcanoes lie along the submarine ridges of the Indian Ocean. Many of the islands in the ocean were formed by active and inactive volcanoes.

Two of the world's greatest river systems, the Indus River of Pakistan and Ganges-Brahmaputra (Găn-jēz' Brä-ma-pōō'-tra) of India, have built huge submarine "fans" into the Arabian Sea and Bay of Bengal. These fans are made up of sediments carried from the Himalaya (Him-a-lā'-a) Mountains in those two countries.

In the spring of 2014 the southeastern Indian Ocean about a thousand miles west of Australia was the scene of an extensive months-long search effort for the remains of Malaysian Airlines Flight 370, which mysteriously disappeared while on a flight from Kuala Lumpur to Beijing with 239 passengers and crew in March 2014. It was thought

The island of Diego Garcia in the Indian Ocean. *J. David Rogers*

to have ended up on the ocean bottom there under about 15,000 feet of water after having been diverted about half-way through its flight by person or persons unknown.

Minerals. Tin ore is mined off the shores of Thailand, Malaysia, and Sumatra in the Strait of Malacca. Deposits of sands rich in rare heavy minerals, such as monazite, zircon, and magnetite, are mined off Sri Lanka (Srē-Län'-ka), the Indian state of Kerala (Kĕr'-a-la), the east coast of South Africa, and near Perth in western Australia. A major oil field also lies off western Australia. Rich beds of manganese chunks, as well as nickel, copper, titanium, and lead, have been found on the Indian Ocean floor.

Fishing. The fishing industry in the Indian Ocean produces about ten million tons annually, about 7 percent of the world total, and is mainly carried on at a subsistence level by bordering countries. Tuna and shrimp are the main commercial catches, off the coast of India. Russian, Japanese, Korean, and Taiwanese vessels fish the ocean for these species. Most of the shrimp are canned and sold on the U.S. market. Lobsters are caught off South Africa and western Australia for the U.S. market too. The Indian Ocean catch will continue to grow in value as fishing and canning techniques improve and the demand for fish protein increases.

Ports and Naval Bases. The United States has built a communications station and naval support facility on Diego Garcia, in the mid–Indian Ocean, to support naval communications, space tracking, and deployed Indian Ocean air and surface forces of the U.S. Navy, Marines, and Air Force. Ships of the Military Sealift Command regularly call there, and several are permanently predeployed there, loaded with stocks of combat equipment, supplies, and munitions for use in any future hostilities in the region.

Strategic Geography. We have already discussed two of the main sea routes in the Indian Ocean. They are the oil routes from the Persian Gulf through the Red Sea to Suez, along the east coast of Africa, and around the Cape of Good Hope. The other major sea-lane is past Singapore at the tip of the Malay Peninsula, through the Strait of Malacca, and across the Indian Ocean to Suez. The Strait of Malacca is a main route between Asia and Europe, and it is the route Japanese oil tankers follow from the Persian Gulf to Japan. This strait is one of the world's key strategic choke points for navigation.

In the spring of 1998, much apprehension over nuclear-weapons proliferation in the region arose when India and Pakistan each exploded nuclear test devices. There followed a period of escalating tension between the two nations that might have led to a regional nuclear war but for American intervention, in conjunction with the United Nations. The issue of nuclear nonproliferation continues to be a major concern in the area.

In the late 1990s, the issue of support of terrorist activities in this region became of great concern, particularly in regard to Afghanistan. Bordered by Pakistan to the south and east, Iran to the west, and in the north and northeast by Russia and China, this poverty-stricken and rugged country became the adopted home of one of the foremost terrorist organizations of modern times—al-Qaeda, led by Osama bin Laden. In the fall of 2001 the country became the scene of Operation Enduring Freedom, in which U.S. and allied military forces joined with Afghan rebels to rid the country of bin Laden's terrorist organization and the repressive Taliban government that supported him. Support forces from the United States and other countries have provided security and stability to the country since. Most U.S. forces are scheduled for withdrawal at the end of 2014.

Principal navies of nations around the Indian Ocean are those of South Africa, India, and Australia. Pakistan has a small but efficient navy. The French also have a naval force in the ocean, based at Réunion, to protect their Indian Ocean interests.

Pacific Ocean

The Pacific Ocean is by far the largest of the world's oceans. It covers an area of about 59 million square miles, about 35 percent of the Earth's surface. Its average depth is 12,900 feet. Like the Atlantic Ocean, the part of the Pacific Ocean north of the equator is called the North Pacific, and the part to the south is the South Pacific. The deepest spot in the Pacific Ocean is the Marianas Trench, which, at 36,161 feet at its maximum depth, is also the deepest place on Earth.

The western half of the Pacific sea floor is complex, with thousands of volcanic peaks, trenches, ridges, and submarine plateaus. Many of the volcanoes are no longer active and are in various stages of erosion from sea and weather action. The

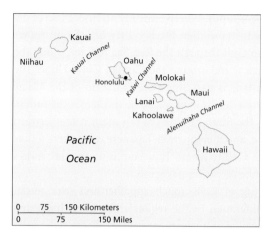

The Hawaiian Islands.

tops of these volcanic peaks are the beautiful Pacific islands one dreams about. There are many coral reefs, teeming with colorful marine life. The most famous and largest reef is the Great Barrier Reef, which runs more than 1,250 miles along the coast of northeastern Australia.

The Hawaiian Islands and the Society Islands, which include Tahiti and Bora Bora, are beautiful places. They are the classic South Sea islands of waving palms and white beaches. Many other South Sea islands, however, especially in the Southwest Pacific, are deadly jungles with disease, stifling heat, incessant rains, and few natural resources.

Minerals. Not much mining is done in the Pacific, but many large mineral deposits have been located in coastal areas and on the ocean floor. Some tin is mined off the Indonesian island of Sumatra; iron ore has been mined for years off Japan; and mineral sands (titanium, zircon, and monazite) are mined off the coast of Queensland, Australia. There are small working oil fields between Australia and Tasmania and off New Zealand's North Island. Other oil drilling is taking place off the coast of southern California and in the Cook Inlet of Alaska. Phosphates are mined along the coasts of Chile, Peru, and Baja California in Mexico.

There are vast fields of manganese chunks in much of the Pacific. An especially heavy belt extends from Baja California to Hawaii and from there to the islands of Palau and northward to Japan. It is said that in these belts, comprising a total area of nearly 1.35 million square miles, the ocean bottom is literally covered with manganese! A number of companies are engaged in mining this vast undersea resource.

Fishing. The annual catch of fish and shellfish from the Pacific greatly exceeds that taken in any other ocean. More than 85 million tons of seafood are taken annually, some 70 percent of the world total. Most fisheries are located within 150 miles of the coasts. The exception to this is tuna fishing, which is carried on throughout the high seas. There are large fisheries for cod, pollock, flounder, rockfish, sea bass, and red snapper all over the Asiatic continental shelf, in the eastern Bering, Yellow, and South China Seas and the seas of Okhotsk (Ō-kŏtsk′) and Japan. Fisheries for sardines and anchovies lie off Peru, California, northern Japan, and Korea. Pollock and salmon are fished in the Gulf of Alaska and off the coasts of the states of Washington and Oregon.

There are very important fisheries for shrimp, crabs, lobsters, and squid in the waters across the northern Pacific. Giant shrimp, called prawns, are caught in the Yellow and South China Seas, off northern Australia, and in the Gulf of Alaska. The largest of all crabs, the Alaskan king crab, is taken in the Gulf of Alaska along the Aleutian (A-lōō′-shan) Island chain and in the Sea of Okhotsk. These huge crabs sometimes grow to more than three feet from claw to tail. Huge lobsters are caught around most of the islands of the Pacific.

Ports and Naval Bases. The major West Coast ports on the U.S. mainland are San Diego, Los Angeles, Long Beach, and Oakland in California; Portland, Oregon; Tacoma and Seattle, Washington; and Anchorage, Alaska. Honolulu, Hawaii, is the major U.S. port in the mid-Pacific. Major foreign ports in the Pacific region include Calleo, the port of Lima, Peru; Santiago, Valparaiso, Chile; Wellington and Auckland, New Zealand; Sydney, Brisbane, and Melbourne, Australia; Jakarta, Indonesia; Singapore (Sĭng′-ga-pôr), on the Malay Peninsula; Bangkok, Thailand; Hong Kong, Canton and Shanghai, China; Manila, in the Philippines; Yokohama (Yō-ka-hä′-ma), Kobe, and Osaka, Japan; Taipei (Ti-pā′), Taiwan; Haiphong (Hi-fŏng′), Vietnam; and Vladivostok (Vlăd-a-vŏs′-tŏk), Russia.

The major U.S. naval base on the West Coast is at San Diego, California, the headquarters of the **U.S. Third Fleet**. Smaller operating bases are located at Seattle. Large naval air stations are located at Point Mogu and North Island, near San Diego, and at Whidbey Island, Washington. There is a large Navy shipyard at Bremerton, Washington. Civilian shipyards with major naval ship contracts are in Seattle, San Francisco, Los Angeles, and San Diego. There is a large Marine base at Camp Pendleton and a Marine air station at Miramar, both near San Diego.

U.S. naval bases in the Pacific are located at Pearl Harbor, Hawaii, Guam, and Yokosuka (Yō-ko-sōō′-ka) Japan. Yokosuka is the home port of the **U.S. Seventh Fleet.** A large naval air facility at Atsugi, near Tokyo, is the primary base for support of U.S. naval aviation in the western Pacific. Although most ships in the Seventh Fleet deploy from home ports on the U.S. West Coast, a carrier battle group has maintained its home port in Yokosuka, Japan, for over forty years.

The Russian Pacific Fleet has its headquarters at Vladivostok, with an important base at Petropavlosk (Pe-tra-pav′-lofsk) on the Kamchatka Peninsula and a major submarine base at Vilyuchinsk (Vil-u-chin′-sk).

The Chinese navy is rapidly growing in strength and capability. It has bases in a number of Chinese ports, including Amoy, Shanghai (Shăng-hi′), Tsingtao (Ching-dou′), and Dairen (Dī-ren′). The Indonesians have a naval base at Surabaja (Sur-a-bi′-a); the Taiwanese at Kaohsiung (Gou′-shyoong′); the South Koreans at Pusan; and the Thais at Sattahip (Sä′-ta-hēp). The Japanese Maritime Self-Defense Force (JMSDF) consists of some 115 ships and submarines and almost two hundred maritime patrol aircraft and helicopters, capable of a broad range of operations in the waters around its home islands. The ships are based at several ports, including Yokosuka, Kure, and Sasebo, and the aircraft operate from several inland airfields.

Strategic Geography. The most impressive thing about the geography of the Pacific is its size. Some examples: the distance from the Panama Canal to Yokohama, Japan, is 7,680 miles, and to Singapore, 10,529 miles; from San Francisco to Manila, Philippines, 6,299 miles, to Melbourne, Australia, 6,970, to Hong Kong, 6,044, to Singapore, 7,350, and to Honolulu, Hawaii, 2,091 miles. From Yokohama to Singapore through the Taiwan (Ti′-wän′) Strait is 2,880 miles. Distance, then, is certainly an important factor to consider when discussing Pacific strategy.

The U.S. Navy has two main tasks in event of a war in the Pacific: (1) protect the long supply lines to our forces and (2) keep the sea-lanes open to our allies, especially Japan, South Korea, the Philippines, Thailand, Australia, and New Zealand. In recent years the Navy has also played a key role in ABM defense of the U.S. West Coast against the potential threat posed by the strategic ballistic missile development program of North Korea.

Japan is a key part of U.S. foreign policy in Asia and the Far East, as evidenced by the fact that the Navy's Seventh Fleet is homeported at Yokosuka. Japan's industries and hardworking people make it the most prosperous country in the area. At the same time, the Japanese constitution prohibits Japan from having armed forces with an offensive capability. Ever since World War II, the United States has been obligated by treaty to defend Japan from foreign attack.

Treaties also commit U.S. forces to help our other Pacific allies in the event of aggression. We have strong mutual-defense ties with Australia and New Zealand. The United States keeps a U.S. Army force permanently deployed in South Korea and participates regularly in military exercises with the armed forces of that country. U.S. forces were supposed to have been withdrawn in the early 1980s, but this withdrawal was never carried out, because of the increasingly belligerent behavior of North Korea over the last several decades.

After the Vietnam War, U.S. relations with China steadily improved. Establishment of full diplomatic relations, including exchange of ambassadors, occurred in 1979. A reversal occurred in mid-1989, however, when Chinese army tanks and troops brutally attacked students demonstrating for demo-cratic reforms in Tiananmen (Tie-nan′-men) Square in Beijing (Be-jing′). The incident marked the beginning of renewed concern over the issue of human rights in China, which has persisted to the present day. Nevertheless China is today one of the largest international trading partners with the United States in Asia and the Far East.

The United States has formal economic and defense ties to several Pacific island groups that were formerly part of the Trust Territory of the Pacific Islands administered by the United States on behalf of the United Nations. These include the Marshall Islands, Caroline Islands, and the Mariana Islands. These were all taken from the Japanese during World War II.

Southern Ocean

The Southern Ocean around Antarctica is **circumpolar**—that is, it surrounds the south polar continent of Antarctica. Its boundary is arbitrarily set at 60 degrees south latitude. In area it totals about seven million square miles. Its average depth is about 13,100 feet. A good portion of it freezes over each winter, and 1.5 million square miles are ice covered year round. The continental shelf of Antarctica is very narrow; ocean depths of 13,000 to 16,500 feet lie beyond the steep continental slope. The northern edge of this basin is the midocean ridge system that separates the Antarctic region from the Atlantic, Indian, and Pacific Ocean basins. It includes several seas surrounding Antarctica, including the Amundsen Sea, Ross Sea, and Weddell Sea.

Minerals. Modern drilling and infrared photography have found many minerals in Antarctica and its surrounding seas, but these deposits are currently too difficult and expensive to mine.

Fishing. Whaling was a thriving business in the Antarctic region for a hundred years until the early 1930s. Then modern floating factory ships and fast whalers with harpoon guns nearly wiped out the whale population. Only about one-tenth of the original whale population still survives, and a number of species are nearly extinct. Iceland and Japan still engage in some whaling, under some degree of control by the International Whaling Commission.

There is some harvesting of krill, small shrimp-like animals that abound in some Antarctic waters during certain seasons of the year. This activity is of only limited commercial value.

Ports and Naval Bases. Some thirty nations presently have either permanent or summer seasonal research stations in Antarctica. The United States has three research stations there, run by the National Science Foundation; the U.S. Navy helps to maintain and supply the stations. The largest, at McMurdo Sound off the Ross Sea, has been manned since the International Geophysical Year explorations in the 1960s. Other smaller ones are located at the South Pole and on Palmer Peninsula. Altogether about 1,200 researchers spend the Antarctic spring and

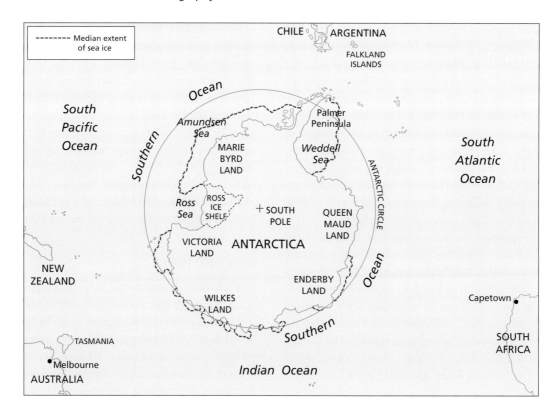

The continent of Antarctica. The continent is completely surrounded by the waters of the Southern Ocean, which includes the Amundsen, Ross, and Weddell Seas, and extends about six degrees above the Antarctic Circle to the South Atlantic, South Pacific, and Indian Oceans. The dashed red lines show the mean (average) extent of sea ice covering the region in a typical recent year.

summer at the stations each year beginning in October. A few of these winter over each year to maintain the facilities and conduct longer-term research projects.

Strategic Geography. No military operations in Antarctica are permitted under international treaty. Antarctica is out of the world's main air and sea-lanes. There is little interest in it at the present time, either for resources or for strategic reasons. Basic research is being conducted in various aspects of the physical sciences, marine life, and the weather. Studies indicate that south polar weather and currents have a great effect on many areas of both the Southern and Northern Hemispheres.

Critical Thinking

1. Research the state of fishing in the world's oceans, including where most of it takes place and what current issues exist as to regulation and conduct of commercial fishing in them.

2. Activist conservation organizations, such as Greenpeace, are often in the news for their activities in regard to safeguarding the remaining numbers of whales and other species of marine life that inhabit the world's oceans. Research the major concerns and goals of these organizations and the methods they use to advance them. Comment on whether or not they are justified in some of the more extreme actions they sometimes take in furtherance of their causes.

3. Research the locations and sponsors of the major research stations and bases in the Antarctic. Are they strategically important? Would you like to spend time at one of them? Justify your reasoning.

Study Guide Questions

1. Why is the Suez Canal important to both Western Europe and the Middle Eastern nations?

2. A. What is the narrow strategic sea located at the southern approaches to the Suez Canal?
   B. What is the key strait at the southern end of this sea?

3. Why is the Persian Gulf important to the United States and its allies?

4. What is the key strait at the southern entrance to the Persian Gulf?

5. A. Where is the headquarters of the U.S. Africa Command?
   B. Where is the home port of the U.S. Fifth Fleet?

6. A. List the three main sea routes in the Indian Ocean.
   B. Which one is the main route between Asia and Europe?

7. Which country in the Indian Ocean region received worldwide attention in 2001 because of the 11 September terrorist attack on the United States?

8. Where has the United States built an important base in the Indian Ocean area?

9. A. Which ocean is the largest in the world?
   B. Where is the deepest spot in this ocean, and what is the depth there?

10. A. What formations are found on much of the western half of the Pacific sea floor?
    B. What often forms around the rims of volcanic islands in the Pacific?

11. A. Where is the major naval base on the West Coast of the United States?
    B. Where is there a large Navy shipyard on the West Coast?

12. Where are the major U.S. naval bases in the middle and western Pacific?

13. Where does the Russian Pacific fleet have its headquarters?

14. What are the two main tasks of the U.S. Navy in the event of war in the Pacific?

15. Which country is considered the key to U.S. foreign policy in the Pacific? Why?

16. A. Where is the home port for the U.S. Third Fleet?
    B. Where is the Seventh Fleet home port?

17. What is meant by the term "circumpolar ocean" when referring to the Southern Ocean basin?

18. A. What valuable Antarctic resource has now been nearly wiped out?
    B. Which two countries still engage in this industry?

19. Where does the United States have research stations in Antarctica?

New Vocabulary

plankton	prawns
manganese	circumpolar
titanium	research station

UNIT 2

Oceanography

The Navy defines oceanography as the "application of the sciences to the phenomena of the oceans, including the study of their forms and their physical, chemical, and biological features." Simply stated, oceanography is the scientific study of what happens on, in, and under the world's oceans.

Greater attention is now being given to the oceans by nearly all nations, including the United States. Some reasons for this are:

- **Social**. The coastal regions of our nation, which include estuaries, mouths of inland rivers, and the Great Lakes, are major population and job centers. More than 40 percent of the U.S. population lives and works near the nation's seacoasts. The coasts extend some 5,400 miles along the Gulf of Mexico and the Atlantic and Pacific Oceans, another 2,800 miles along the shores of the Great Lakes, and over two thousand miles along the beaches of Hawaii, Guam, Puerto Rico, and the Virgin Islands.
- **Economic**. The oceans are rich with natural resources, food, and fuel. They are the "last frontier" for many vital materials on Earth.
- **Political**. The oceans link the continents. The world ocean covers nearly 71 percent of Earth's surface. It is a field for much competition between industrialized nations. It provides the sea lines of communication over which commerce between the United States and many foreign nations takes place.
- **Strategic.** The oceans are vital to U.S. defense. The fleet ballistic-missile submarines that operate in them and their intercontinental missiles give the nation its most important deterrent against aggression by nuclear-armed nations around the world.

In this unit, some of the many features of oceanography are discussed. Oceanography spans the past, the present, and the future of our world. It is especially important to a maritime nation such as the United States.

3

Earth's Oceanographic History

Our study of oceanography will begin with a discussion of the origin of Earth and its seas. Where did it all begin—how and why? A basic idea of how our planet Earth began is essential in our study of the life-giving seas. More about the scientific theory of the formation of the universe and the solar system is given in the astronomy unit (unit 4) of this text.

Formation of the Oceans

Modern science has given us a good idea of how Earth began. This study is a part of astronomy called **cosmology,** the science concerned with the nature of the universe and its origin. Scientists who study cosmology are called "cosmologists."

Cosmologists believe that what is now our solar system (the Sun, the planets, and their moons) began about 4.5 billion years ago as a large cloud of gas and dust. Gradually, gravity and centripetal forces caused this cloud to spin and take the shape of a huge disk, with the infant Sun in its center. From time to time, eddies, swirls, and collisions occurred in this disk, causing a number of smaller clusters of materials to separate and whirl in orbits around the large cluster that was forming the Sun. One of these swirling masses became the planet Earth.

After millions of years of increasing pressure and temperature, metallic crystals of iron and nickel melted and sank toward the core, or center, of the Earth. Because of the intense heat created within the Earth by compression, molten rock (magma) called **lava** often broke through the surface, either in large cracks in the Earth's crust or in active volcanoes that expelled gases and solid materials. The hydrogen molecules, other gases, and water vapor that escaped from the Earth gradually rose. The Sun's rays acted on the released gases and soon distributed them around the new planet to form an **atmosphere.** Meanwhile, the Earth continued to contract into a more solid mass, developing what is now the planet's crust.

The intense heat created by the compression of the Earth continued to cause thousands of volcanoes to bring lava and water vapor to the surface. Radiation from the Sun also continued to form Earth's atmosphere, by breaking up water molecules into separate atoms of hydrogen and oxygen. Because the hydrogen was lighter, much of it escaped into space, while the heavier oxygen atoms were retained in the atmosphere by gravity. Gradually, poisonous ammonia and methane gases in the atmosphere were dissipated by the Sun as both it and Earth cooled. Slowly, the atmosphere cooled enough to cause the water vapor in the air to condense and return to the surface in the form of rain. Falling on Earth's hot surface, some water hissed into steam, joined with new water vapor brought to the surface by volcanoes, and rose to be condensed and fall again and again as rain and, later, as snow.

This continuous **precipitation** (rain and snow) probably went on for thousands, maybe millions, of years. Finally, about four billion years ago, Earth had cooled to about its present size and temperature. Lighter granite (granitic rocks) had risen to higher elevations on the surface, and the heavier basalt (basaltic rocks) had sunk, creating high and low areas. Eventually most of the low spots in the crust filled with rainwater. These gigantic water pools eventually formed the world ocean—not in the same geographic shape we see the oceans today but, nevertheless, covering about 70 percent of Earth's surface.

The cycle of evaporation and condensation continues today, though now only a small percentage of the vapor ascending into the atmosphere comes from volcanoes and other cracks in the Earth. Today most water vapor comes from the ocean surface and trapped groundwater, which is heated and recycled by the Sun. Over millions of years, the oceans have overrun some coastal edges of the early continents as the result of wind and water erosion, earthquakes, and landslides in those areas. At the same time, the buildup of polar icecaps has kept an almost constant amount of water in the seas. Ours is a continually changing geologic world. However, these changes happen too slowly to be seen in the lifetimes of humans, except in instances of violent natural change, such as volcanic eruptions or massive earthquakes.

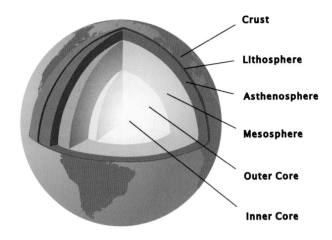

Scientists divide the planet Earth into the crust, mantle, outer core, and inner core. The outer rigid crust is called the lithosphere. The lower layer of the lithosphere, the asthenosphere, and the mesosphere constitute the Earth's mantle. *Base drawing by Matt Halldin*

The Earth's Structure

Earth is made up of several "shells," somewhat like a golf ball. Earth's surface is the **crust,** the only part we can easily see. Consisting of the continents and ocean basins, it is called the **lithosphere.** With an average depth of about twenty miles under continents, Earth's crust may be as much as forty miles deep beneath mountains. Under the oceans, however, it is only three to ten miles thick. Below the lithosphere is the **mantle,** about 1,800 miles of dense rock. The uppermost layer of the mantle is the lower part of the lithosphere. Just below this, several hundred miles thick, is the **asthenosphere.** It is composed of molten rock called **magma.** The lithosphere "rides," or "floats," on this molten part of the mantle. The lower part of the mantle is called the **mesosphere.** In the center of the Earth below the mantle is the **core,** which consists of two parts: a solid inner core of nickel and iron, with a diameter of about 860 miles, and a molten outer core of these metals, about 1,300 miles deep.

The lithosphere, or Earth's crust, is divided into some seven major **geological,** or **tectonic, plates** and a number of smaller ones. The major plates are the North and South American, African, Eurasian, Indo-Australian, Antarctic, and Pacific plates. Most of Earth's volcanic eruptions and earthquakes occur on the boundaries, or **margins,** of these plates.

The Continental Drift Theory

It is not known how many times these plates may have separated, come together, and separated again over the 4.5-billion-year geologic history of our planet. This movement of landmasses is known as the **continental drift theory.** This theory was first seriously proposed about 1912. Many studies and modern oceanographic and geologic instruments have, in general, tended to confirm it. In the late 1960s the theory was modified to take into account all major geological structures of the Earth. The new theory is known as **plate tectonics.**

Let us trace the probable geologic history of our Earth on the basis of continental-drift theory. After millions of years of

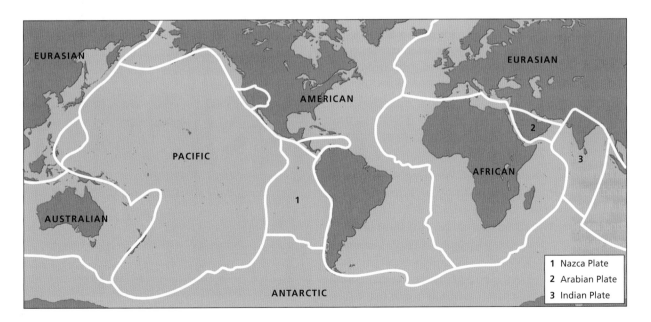

The lithosphere, or outer rigid crust of the Earth, is divided into a number of plates, as shown in the diagram. According to the continental-drift theory, these plates have slowly drifted to their present positions over billions of years. They are still moving today at the rate of several inches a year.

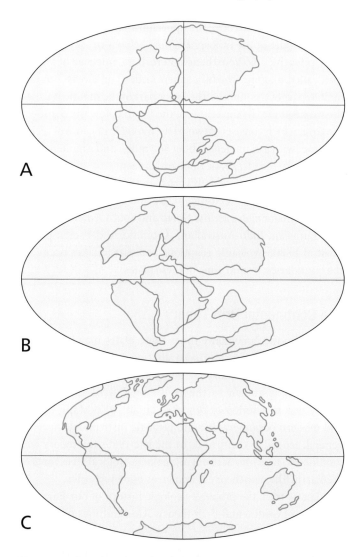

The progression of continental drift. (A) The original supercontinent Pangea, 200 million years ago. (B) The world 135 million years ago. Pangea has split into Laurasia, or the north, and Gondwanaland, to the south. (C) Our world today. India has collided with Eurasia, and Australia has split from Antarctica; North and South America have joined, in Central America.

Alps in France and Switzerland, and the Apennines of Italy. On the other side of the globe, the Pacific plates pushed up the Andes in South America, the Sierras along the West Coast of North America, and the islands of Japan.

The continents gradually took the places on the globe that are familiar to us today. The major ocean basins and numerous seas—once a single ocean mass, with one giant continent—now provide the vital sea lines of communication and commerce between the widely separated continents. The globe as we know it today is the result of a geologic process that has taken billions of years and continues even now.

The Earth's Crust Today

Where these tectonic plates come together, Earth and its inhabitants experience the awesome energy of earthquakes and volcanoes. **Seismographs,** modern instruments that measure the intensity of earthquakes, have helped to locate the boundaries of the plates, called **fault lines.** Also along these boundaries, mountains rise and fall, and volcanic islands push up from the sea. The energy released in the explosion of a nuclear bomb is small compared to these huge geologic forces.

Earthquakes. The great earthquake belts that lie along the plate margins are extremely important to sailors and people who live on seacoasts and in harbors. Volcanoes have created new islands and island chains—the Hawaiian Islands, some of the Aleutian and Japanese islands, and islands in the Caribbean and Mediterranean Seas, among others. In the United States, the entire West Coast is in an earthquake "belt." The best-known feature of this belt is the San Andreas Fault, which runs through the center of California and close to San Francisco. In fact, some

A terrifying photo of the 2004 tsunami coming ashore at Khao Lak, Thailand. Moments after this picture was taken, the area shown was submerged under thirty feet of rushing water. *www.wikipedia.com, D. Rydevik*

pressures and strains, some 65 million years ago Africa and South America had drifted far apart. The Atlantic and Indian Oceans had formed, and North America and Europe were about to split, leaving Greenland to stand between them in the Northern Hemisphere. India moved rapidly (relatively) across the Indian Ocean on its 5,500-mile, 180-million-year trip. It would collide with southern Asia and push up the world's highest mountain range, the Himalayas. Australia began to break away from Antarctica and move northward, while the latter continent moved toward the South Pole. The African plate crashed into the Eurasian plate south of Europe and pushed up the Pyrenees mountain range between Spain and France, the

Part of a huge debris field making its way across the Pacific from the 2011 earthquake and tsunami in Japan. *CHINFO, Dylan McCord*

geologists predict that all of Baja California and much of the present state of California may someday break away from the North American continent and drift toward Alaska, arriving there in about 50 million years!

But not all such catastrophes will happen only in the distant future. In fact, many earthquakes occur daily. Tokyo, Japan, and San Francisco, California, for example, often experience two to three tremors each day. Fortunately, few are ever felt by people, though sensitive seismographs record several hundred of them each year. In 1906 San Francisco was almost totally destroyed by a large quake on the San Andreas Fault. Within the past ten years, devastating quakes have killed tens of thousands of people in Italy, Iran, Turkey, Greece, Guatemala, Nicaragua, Mexico, Pakistan, the Philippines, Russia, and China. A huge earthquake in Haiti in January 2010 killed an estimated 220,000 people and injured and displaced over a million more. The Navy played a major role in the relief efforts, which are still ongoing today. The largest disaster of all time from a single earthquake occurred in 1976 in Tangshan, China, when almost 700,000 people were reported to have been killed.

Tsunami. When a large earthquake, volcanic explosion, or impact of a large asteroid or comet happens near, on, or under the sea, ocean waves radiate from it in ever-widening circles. There may be little movement detectable on the open sea, but as these waves reach shallow waters along coastlines, the waves slow down and pile up in huge crests, sometimes more than a hundred feet high. These huge waves are called **tsunami** (soo-nä-me), a Japanese word that means "surging walls of water." These fantastic walls of water can race across the deep oceans at jet-plane speeds of 450 miles per hour (mph) but then slow to 25–30 mph in coastal waters. Tsunamis are often incorrectly called **tidal waves**; actually, they have no relationship to the tides at all.

The Hawaiian Islands, Alaskan coast, and western Pacific areas are periodically lashed by tsunamis, which have caused great loss of life. The worst tsunami in history occurred in December 2004, when an earthquake under the Indian Ocean generated a huge wave that devastated seacoast areas throughout the region. By some estimates 370,000 people lost their lives in Indonesia, Sri Lanka, Thailand, southern India, and other countries. The devastation prompted a worldwide humanitarian response, including a large relief effort by the Navy. Then in March 2011 a powerful earthquake off the coast of Japan triggered a forty-foot high tsunami that swept ashore on the island of Honshu, demolishing several coastal towns and severely damaging four nuclear-power-plant reactors. The resulting radiation leaks took months to stop, and decontamination efforts are still ongoing. The huge debris field carried out to sea by the receding wave is still washing ashore all along the western shores of the Unites States and Canada.

Other significant historical tsunamis in the western Pacific include a 120-foot high wave caused by an explosion of the volcanic island Krakatoa in 1883 that crashed into the islands of Java and Sumatra and killed 36,000 people, an 1896 tsunami that killed 27,000 people in Japan, and one in 1976 that caused over five thousand deaths in the Philippines.

Critical Thinking

1. Research where the major earthquake belts are and the present state of efforts to predict future earthquakes along them.

Study Guide Questions

1. What is oceanography?

2. Why does our government maintain an active program of oceanographic research?

3. What is the scientific theory explaining the origin of the world ocean?

4. How much of Earth's surface is covered by water?

5. Describe the "construction," or makeup, of Earth, listing and describing the major layers from the surface inward.

6. What are the names of the major plates of the lithosphere?

7. A. Explain the theory of continental drift.
   B. When did the most recent sequence of geologic events leading to the present continental locations begin?

8. Where is the most famous earthquake belt in the United States?

9. A. What is a tsunami?
   B. What events could cause a tsunami?

New Vocabulary

atmosphere	magma
oceanography	mesophere
cosmology	core
eddy, eddies	tectonic plate
lava	margins (of plates)
precipitation	continental drift theory
basalt	plate tectonics
crust	seismograph
lithosphere	fault lines
mantle (of Earth)	earthquake
asthenosphere	

Undersea Landscapes

For many centuries people believed that the sea floor was simply a deep, smooth basin with a bottom covered with oozy mud. In fact, until the twentieth century most knowledge of the ocean floor came from the ancient method of heaving a lead-weighted line overboard in shallow water and looking at the mud, weeds, and sediments that clung to the weight when retrieved. People thought that this ooze covered the bottom and "swallowed up" everything—even sunken ships and lost civilizations. It was not until echo sounders and hydrophones were invented by a U.S. Navy scientist to search for submarines during World War I that oceanographers really began to understand that the ocean bottom has just as varied a geography as the land surface. From that time onward, an intense effort to chart the sea floor has taken place.

Relief of the Earth

The **relief** of the Earth refers to the different elevations and form of its surface, called its **topography.** A relief map, for instance, shows the different heights of a part of the Earth's surface by use of shading, colors, or numbered contour lines (lines along which the elevation is constant).

There are two main levels in the relief: the continents, or continental terraces, including their submerged zones, called the **continental shelves,** and the deep ocean floor. The deep ocean floor is also called the "deep sea," the "deep ocean basin," or the "abyss." The deep-sea floor is described in terms of the individual features constituting it, such as abyssal plains, oceanic ridges, sea floor fractures, deep-sea trenches, islands, and seamounts. It has an average depth of about 12,000 feet (about two to two and a half miles), but there are regions over seven miles deep. Though 71 percent of Earth's crust is covered by water, just two-thirds of that is truly deep oceanic basin.

Echo sounders (sometimes called **fathometers**) provide a rapid means of finding the depth of water over which a vessel is traveling. They measure the time it takes sound pulses to travel from the vessel on the surface to the ocean floor and return as echoes. Echoes that bounce back quickly indicate a shallow bottom or perhaps the top of an undersea mountain. Echoes

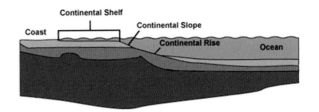

The offshore topography as it generally appears off the continental coasts. There is wide variation in width and smoothness throughout the world. Submarine canyons often cut through the continental shelf and slope.

that take longer indicate deeper water, such as a deep midocean trench. On average, sound travels 4,800 feet per second in water. If an echo takes two seconds to return, then the sound has traveled two times 4,800 feet, or 9,600 feet. Since it is a round trip, half that distance would be the depth of the water—in this case, 4,800 feet. Ocean water depths are customarily given either in units called **fathoms** (one fathom equals six feet) or in meters.

The Ocean Floor

Echo soundings have determined that the ocean floor is divided into three distinct areas: the continental shelf; the deep ocean basin, or abyss; and, lying between them, the continental slope.

The continental shelf borders on continental land areas. Actually, the edges of the continents are under water. The sea, it can be said, spills over the brims of the ocean basins, covering the continental shelves with relatively shallow water. Geologists and oceanographers consider the continental shelf to be an underwater extension of the adjacent land mass, over which water depth gradually increases to between a hundred and two hundred meters (about 328–656 feet). At that point the sea floor transitions to the continental slope and then to the continental rise. In the continental shelf area the exclusive rights of exploration and use of resources belong to the adjacent (littoral) nation, according to international law, extending out at least to 200 nautical miles from shore.

213

The average width of the continental shelves is about forty-two miles. Off parts of North Carolina the shelf extends out to about seventy-five miles. In the Barents Sea off the Arctic coast of Russia it extends eight hundred miles, and off the coast of California it is less than a mile in width. Off parts of Peru and Japan, the plunge begins almost immediately.

The shelves are not always smooth, gradual slopes. They vary from smooth plains to irregular, rough terrain. Many sediments, such as rocks, sand, mud, silt, clay, and gravel, cover the shelves. The most common material is coarse sand, consisting mainly of particles carried away from the continental landmass and deposited by rivers, currents, ice, and wind during the ice age.

Biologically, the continental shelves are sunlit areas that support most of the sea vegetation and saltwater fishes and animals on Earth. Even today, our knowledge about the ocean is mostly limited to the continental-shelf regions. It is here that most fishing is done. Exploration for, and production of, oil and other minerals is done almost entirely on the continental shelves. It is here that nations are most liable to confront each other as their growing populations increase their demands for fuels, minerals, and food.

Beyond the continental shelf, no matter how far from the land, the bottom drops off suddenly. This is where the continental crust of granitic rocks ends and the bottom drops off to the sediments on the ocean floor, which has a base of basaltic rock. The sharp descent is called the **continental slope.** Here is where the deep sea truly begins. Oceanographers and geologists have found that the continental slopes generally drop from a hundred to five hundred feet per mile but that with increasing depth they tend to flatten out and merge into the deep ocean floor.

Humans find this area a bleak and uncomfortable world. There is no light or plant life. The pressure, cold, and silence increase as one descends. The bottom sediments are mainly mud and clay, with small amounts of sand and gravel. There may be rocks in areas with active volcanoes. In some areas the steepness of the slope is dramatic, as along the western coast of South America, where there is an eight-mile descent from the top of the Andes Mountains to the bottom of the Peru-Chile Trench in a horizontal distance of less than a hundred miles.

The continental slopes have some of the most rugged features on Earth. They are scarred with spectacular features like submarine canyons, steep cliffs, and winding valleys. Some places have terraces and plateaus, while others have sheer drop-offs of several thousand feet.

Submarine canyons in the continental slope are similar to canyons found in the southwestern United States. They are often carved out of the shelf and slope by past glaciation, tidal currents, other underwater currents, or landslides. Rapidly moving underwater currents carrying debris and sediments are called **turbidity currents.** They scour the canyon walls much as river or wind erosion does on continental surfaces.

Some submarine canyons are much larger than the Grand Canyon of Arizona. The Hudson Canyon in the western North Atlantic, for example, extends from waters with a depth of three hundred feet at the canyon head, ninety miles southeast of New York Harbor, to a depth of seven thousand feet some 150 miles offshore. The fifty-mile-long canyon is four thousand feet deep in places and has a number of big tributaries entering it. It cuts through the continental slope and joins a low spot in the continental shelf that marks the entrance of the Hudson River channel off New York Harbor. The Hudson Canyon is continuously scoured by currents containing large amounts of silt coming out of the Hudson River. The silt is eventually deposited on an enormous plain of mud called a **submarine fan.** Similar fans extend hundreds of miles out to sea from the mouths of other great rivers of the world, notably the Mississippi, Indus, and Ganges.

The ocean floor lies at the foot of the continental slope and is the true bottom of the ocean. The deep ocean floor extends seaward from the continental slope and takes up one-third of the Atlantic and Indian Oceans and three-quarters of the Pacific Ocean. They are the last large areas to be fully explored, truly the "last frontier" on Earth.

Oceanographers have determined that most of the Pacific deep ocean basin consists of hills forming a rough topography, while plains are widespread in the Atlantic. All these plains are connected by canyons or other channels to sources of sediments on land. These sediments are transported by turbidity currents down the slope to be deposited on the plains.

Ocean Ridges. Every deep ocean floor has impressive mountain ranges called "ridges." The great **Mid-Atlantic Ridge** soars more than six thousand feet above the nearby sea floor in some places, and it rises above the surface to form islands, such as the Azores and Iceland. It extends from north of Iceland to below the tip of South Africa. It continues around Africa and joins the **Mid-Indian Ocean Ridge** coming down from the Arabian Peninsula. The Mid-Indian Ridge continues eastward south of Australia and New Zealand, joining the **East Pacific Rise.**

The East Pacific Rise is the main underwater feature in the southern and southeastern Pacific Ocean. Located about two thousand miles from the west coast of South America, it runs northward to the peninsula of Baja California. The whole 40,000-mile-long mountain chain is sometimes given a single name, the **Mid-Ocean Ridge,** although it is somewhat off center in the Pacific. Many underwater earthquakes occur in a rift running down the ridge's centerline. Large portions of the major plate margins of Earth's surface lie along the centerline of the Mid-Ocean Ridge.

Ocean Islands, Seamounts, and Guyots. All true oceanic islands are volcanic in origin. They differ from island fragments that have broken away from continental masses, such as New Zealand, New Guinea, and Greenland. Almost all of the small islands of the Pacific are oceanic islands—the tops of former

Basin			Mid-Atlantic Ridge											Basin	
Abyssal plain	Abyssal hills	Lower step	Middle step	Upper step	High fractured plateau	Rift mountains	Rift valley	Rift mountains	High fractured plateau	Upper step	Middle step	Lower step		Abyssal hills	Abyssal plain
2,400	2,450	2,450	2,300	2,150	2,000	1,750	800–1,400	1,850	1,000–1,600	1,750	2,100	2,300	2,400		2,600–2,650

Depth (fathoms)

A profile of the Mid-Atlantic ridge.

---

volcanic mountains. When erosion has worn away much of a volcanic peak in the ocean, a strand of coral islands is left around the old volcanic rim. This formation is known as an **atoll** (a'-tôl). The central lagoon of the atoll is what remains of the old volcanic crater.

In some cases, these coral islands continue to subside, finally disappearing beneath the sea surface and leaving what is known as a **seamount.** Many strings of seamounts dot the floor of the central Pacific, the ancient remains of former islands. They are found in all oceans but are most common in the Pacific Ocean.

Scattered underwater mountains with peaks that never reached the surface retain the name seamounts, but those with flattened tops are called **guyots** (ge'-ots). They have been found in the Pacific but not in the Atlantic or Indian Oceans. The stacking of lava from repeated volcanic eruptions is believed to have created these guyots. Their smooth, flat tops indicate that they were probably leveled off by wave action. It is believed that the great weight of the guyots caused them to sink into the sea floor at the same time as the level of the ocean was rising.

The Hawaiian Islands are a volcanic island chain. Spectacular lava eruptions are regular occurrences from a number

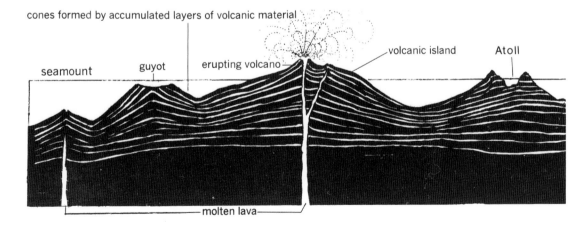

The development of oceanic islands from submarine volcanoes. At the center is a volcanic island with an active volcano. At the far left is a seamount, an underwater volcanic peak that did not reach the surface. At the far right is an atoll, created when seawater invaded an eroding volcanic island to form a lagoon in the former crater, surrounded by coral-covered island fragments of the original rim. Between the volcanic island and seamount is a guyot, once an island or seamount that had its top eroded away by sea action.

The Loihi volcano off the shore of Hawaii adding material to the Big Island. *USGS*

of famous volcanoes in the islands. Kilauea (ke-lou-a'-a) and Mauna Loa (mou'-na lo'-a) on the big island of Hawaii are two of the world's most active volcanoes. Mauna Loa lifts its head 13,677 feet above the blue waters of the Pacific. But this is less than half of its real height, for from its base on the sea floor to its lava-covered summit, Mauna Loa measures more than 31,000 feet. Other island chains of this type include the Caroline, Gilbert, Samoan, and Society Islands.

Critical Thinking

1. It has often been said that more is known about the topography of the surface of the Moon than about the characteristics of the sea floors. Investigate the kinds of equipment now being developed to better map and investigate the nature of the deep ocean floors and their composition.

Study Guide Questions

1. How did Navy hydrophones open a whole new area of study for oceanographers?

2. What are the two main levels in the relief of the Earth?

3. What are other names for the deep ocean floor?

4. A. How does an echo sounder determine the depth of water?
   B. If it takes five and a half seconds for an echo to return to an echo sounder, how deep is the water in that spot?

5. What are the three distinct divisions or areas of the ocean floor?

6. Under international law, to whom do the rights to explore and exploit the continental shelves belong?

7. What is the continental slope?

8. Why are the continental shelves the most valuable part of the ocean floor today?

9. What is a submarine fan, and how does it develop?

10. What are the major segments of the Pacific Mid-Ocean Ridge?

11. Describe the geologic sequence of events in the "wearing down" process of an oceanic island.

12. What is the difference between a seamount and a guyot?

New Vocabulary

ooze	glaciation
topography	turbidity current
relief map	submarine fan
contour line	ocean ridge
terrace	atoll
continental shelf	lagoon
abyss	seamount
echo sounder	guyot
sediment	volcanic eruption
continental slope	

5

Seawater ~ ITS MAKEUP AND MOVEMENTS

Why is the ocean salty? What elements are in water and in the "salts" of the sea? How do waves, currents, and tides move, and why? People have asked these questions for centuries. Matthew Fontaine Maury of the U.S. Navy, who is regarded as the founder of modern oceanography, greatly increased our knowledge of the oceans through his studies of navigational charting and of currents, winds, and storms from 1842 to 1861.

Since then, much has been learned about the oceans, but with each new bit of information, more questions arise. The seas are not only beautiful and interesting but also absolutely essential to the very existence of humankind. In addition to the untold wealth beneath their surface and within their beds, the seas make possible life itself on our planet.

What Is Water?

Water is one of the most abundant, widely distributed, and essential substances on the surface of the Earth. It is an essential requirement for the cells of humans, other animals, plant life, and even crystals of many minerals. Water has many forms. Ice is water in solid form, clouds (and steam) are water in vapor form, and water in liquid form can be found in any lake, river, or ocean.

Snow is probably the purest natural source of water. Rain is next in purity, although both snowflakes and raindrops are formed with a tiny nucleus (center) of salt or dust. Pure water is a compound of two parts hydrogen and one part oxygen. In chemical terms, this is expressed as H_2O. Only when water is between the temperatures of 32 to 212 degrees Fahrenheit (0 to 100 degrees Celsius) at standard atmospheric pressure is it a liquid.

Physical Behavior of Water

In large part, the special characteristics of water make life on Earth possible. For instance, most liquids slowly and continuously contract when cooled, then solidify at some point, and continue to contract in their solid form. Water, however, slowly contracts until cooled to about 4 degrees C (39.2 degrees F), but then, unlike most other liquids, rapidly *expands* as it freezes, increasing in volume about 9 percent as it solidifies and becomes ice. Moreover, this expansion occurs with great force. A plastic milk carton filled with water and placed in a freezer, for example, will expand greatly and may split. A glass bottle will shatter as the ice expands. Once completely frozen, ice follows the normal behavior of most solids and very gradually contracts if its temperature is lowered still further.

If this unique expansion did not take place, ice would sink in water, causing water to freeze from the bottom up. But as we all know, however, ice cubes float. More importantly, ice floats on the surface of the ocean, a lake, or a pond as it forms, serving as an insulating barrier and holding the heat in the water below. If this were not so, much of Earth's oceans would probably be mostly ice most of the time, and life as we know it might have evolved very differently.

Another quality of water is its ability to store heat. Only ammonia has a greater heat-storage capacity than water. Land, on the other hand, has a much lower capacity to store heat. Thus, for any given change in the temperature of the air above it, its temperature rises or falls much faster than water. If the globe were all land, like Mars, it would be scorching hot every day and freezing cold every night. Not many life forms could survive under these conditions. The vast world ocean, however, acts as an enormous heat-controlling thermostat. When it gets hot outside it absorbs more heat, and when it gets cold it gives up more heat, than does any land nearby. Those who live near the seacoasts, or the Great Lakes, are well aware of this characteristic of water. In summer weather air temperatures are cooler near the coast than farther inland, where the Sun quickly heats the ground. In winter, because the water gives up more heat, the exact opposite happens: it is warmer near the coast and colder farther inland. Also, because of the great currents in the sea, the ocean can absorb heat in one area and then transfer it to other areas where some of that heat is released, which land obviously cannot do.

Except under extreme pressure, such as at great ocean depths (or under laboratory conditions), water is not compressible. That is, a given amount of water cannot be made smaller in cubic volume. On the other hand, this liquid can be stirred or mixed easily, in which case the molecules will readily associate with each other, retaining its liquid form. This means that water can "turn over," allowing the heat from the surface to move into deeper depths, colder water to move to the surface, and water to evaporate from the surface, aided by wind and wave action. These processes of heat absorption, convection, and evaporation are vital to the pattern of world climate and to the transfer of heat from equatorial to polar regions.

Water affects sound and light in important ways, too. The speed of sound in water, for example, is very much greater than in air and increases with temperature, pressure, and **salinity** (salt content). Of these factors, temperature is by far the most important in affecting the velocity of sound. The **optical properties** (ability to transmit light) of seawater are of fundamental importance to life in the oceans.

There are many other fascinating things about water. Besides being essential to all animal and plant life, it is also widely used in science and industry as a solvent, as a blending agent, and even as a standard for certain physical measurements and properties, such as **density** (mass per unit volume). The reference points of most thermometers, for example, are the freezing and boiling points of water. Water is also often used as a coolant, a dilutant, a cleansing medium, and in the generation of electricity.

Salts of the Sea

Chemically, seawater is a very pure substance. It is more than 96 percent water—that is, hydrogen and oxygen. About eighty elements, found in solution or suspension, make up the remaining 4 percent. The two main elements in this remaining portion are sodium and chlorine, which combine as common table salt. The most significant of the other elements present in seawater—in concentrations greater than one part per million, or one milligram per liter—are sulfate, magnesium, calcium, and potassium. The remaining additional elements are present in extremely small amounts.

The total salt in seawater is traditionally expressed in parts per thousand (ppt). Scientists use another more precise measure (called *practical salinity units*, or PSU) based on the ratio of the electrical conductivity of a sample of seawater to the conductivity of a standard solution of potassium chloride (KCl) with a salinity equivalent to standard seawater at exactly 35 ppt. The two measures are roughly equivalent.

Ocean salinity varies between 32 and 37 parts per thousand (3 to 4 percent by volume); open-ocean waters are usually about 35. (That is, if a seawater droplet were divided into a thousand tiny parts, there would be 965 parts of water and 35 parts of salt.) Enclosed basins and seas have higher salt concentrations. For example, the Mediterranean Sea has about 38.5, and some areas in the Red Sea, particularly during the summer months, have salinities as high as 41, the highest salinity values in the world ocean. Landlocked lakes that serve as basins for water running off surrounding land, like the Great Salt Lake of Utah or the Dead Sea of Israel, have salinities of 250 and 350, the highest salt content of any bodies of water on Earth. By contrast, freshwater lakes and streams might have a salinity of only a few tenths or less, and rivers and bays open to the sea at only one end—like the Chesapeake Bay, for example—might have salinities varying from a couple tenths at the enclosed end to the mid-20s or higher at the end that opens to the sea.

How did the ocean water get salty? The early world ocean probably was much less salty than today's ocean, since most of the water came from rains caused by the condensation of steam from escaping water vapors of the developing Earth. But for millions of years, rain and melted snow have been running over the land, dissolving various minerals and carrying them down to the sea.

In fact, the salts of the ocean are the results of over two billion years of wearing away of the rocks of Earth's crust. Those materials that are soluble (can be dissolved) remain in the ocean water. Insoluble materials fall (**precipitate**) to the bottom and form sediments and clays that may eventually turn into sedimentary rocks. Though the process continues, much of the material that runs into the ocean now is from sedimentary rocks that have gone through the cycle before. For this reason, the concentration of salts in the sea is fairly stable, having changed very little for millions of years.

Water that has evaporated from the surface of the ocean finally returns to it carrying a microscopic pollutant or mineral. This round trip of evaporation, condensation, and return travel to the sea by way of precipitation is called the **hydrologic cycle** (water cycle—see diagram next page). Plants on land also add to the amount of water vapor entering the air by the process called **transpiration.** This is a special term used to identify the evaporation process through plants and trees.

There are nearly 329 million cubic miles of seawater on our globe. The dissolved minerals carried to the ocean in the hydrologic cycle represent fantastic amounts of every known element. In only one cubic mile of seawater, it is estimated that there are nearly 165 million tons of dissolved minerals, including even small amounts of silver and gold.

Water Temperature

Upper ocean water temperature varies from about 28 degrees F (–2.2 degrees C) in the polar regions to a high of about 95 degrees F (35 degrees C) during summer in the Persian Gulf. The salinity of seawater lowers its freezing point. We know that fresh water freezes at 32 degrees F (0 degrees C); seawater has

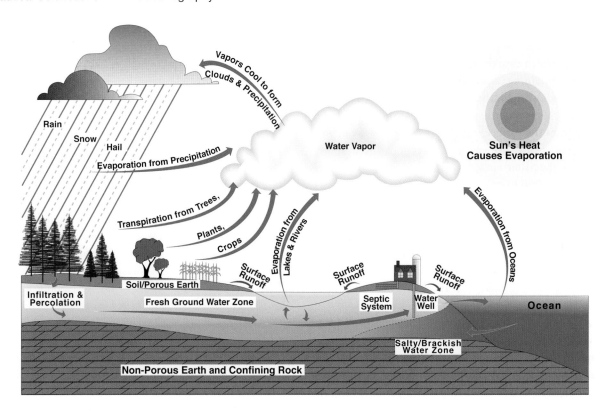

The hydrologic cycle. Water is evaporated from lakes, rivers, and the oceans and transpired from plants and trees into the atmosphere, where it cools, condenses, and falls back to the surface as precipitation. During its journey over the Earth's surface, the water dissolves minerals and carries them and silt, either suspended or in solution, in runoff back to the ocean. *Ohio Department of Natural Resources*

a freezing point of about 28 degrees F (–2.2 degrees C). On the deep ocean bottom, however, the cold, dense water stays at a uniform temperature of about 4 degrees C (39.2 degrees F) all the time in all latitudes.

An instrument called a **bathythermograph** (BT), can be lowered into the water from ships to check water temperatures at various depths (*bathy* means "depth," *thermo* stands for "temperature," and *graph* is "record"). Most Navy USW (undersea warfare) ships have BTs to take readings for continuous monitoring of ocean temperatures for undersea warfare. USW aircraft use what is called an XBT, an expendable bathythermograph, which they drop into the water to get the same data.

Ocean water samples can be taken in **Nansen bottles,** named for a Norwegian oceanographer, Fridtjof Nansen. The Nansen bottle is a metal cylinder with automatic-closing valves on each end. These valves are linked by levers so they work together. The bottles are attached upside down on a long wire. During lowering, water flows through the bottle, until it reaches the desired depth. At sampling depth, a weight called a "messenger" is sent down the wire, releasing the first bottle, which overturns, its valves closing to secure the sample. Another messenger weight, formerly resting on that bottle, then slides down to repeat a similar action on the next bottle below.

As the Nansen bottles capture the water at each desired depth, the mercury column in a thermometer fastened to the outside is automatically fixed. This records the exact temperature of the water when the bottle turned over. In this way, temperatures at any depth in the ocean can be measured. When brought to the surface, the water sample can also be tested for salinity, other chemical content, minute marine life, and so on.

A Nansen bottle being deployed. *NOAA*

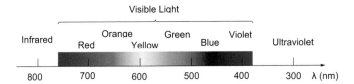

Sunlight consists of light in the infrared, visible, and ultraviolet wavelengths ranging from about three hundred to eight hundred nanometers. The visible light spectrum ranges from about four hundred to seven hundred nanometers.

Sunlight and Water

We know that the main source of energy for life on Earth is the Sun. Its **radiant energy** reaches us after traveling about eight minutes and some 93 million miles through the void of space. This radiant energy consists of both **light waves** (sunlight) and high-energy **X-rays.** **Sunlight** consists of a range or **spectrum** of different wavelengths of light in the infrared, visible, and ultraviolet frequency bands. The infrared and ultraviolet waves are invisible to the unaided human eye. The different colors of the visible light, called the **visible spectrum,** can be seen by using a **prism** (wedge-shaped piece of glass or plastic), or they can be seen in a rainbow.

Some of the visible light striking the surface of the ocean is immediately reflected, but most goes down into the water. As it descends, it changes in quality and quantity. The water acts as a filter, gradually scattering various wavelengths of light, starting at the red end of the visible spectrum, and absorbing its intensity. Therefore, the deeper one goes into the water, the greater the amount of blue light, and the darker it gets. The color of the watery world below about ninety feet (thirty meters) is a dark zone of blues, violets, and black, and nothing else. The depth to which light penetrates varies according to the position of the Sun and the *turbidity* (amount of suspended materials) in the water.

In shallow places, the ocean's water appears light green or brown, while in deeper areas it seems to be blue, gray, or dark green. The colors may change depending on whether the day is cloudy or sunny. Actually, the water itself has no color. What we see as its color is caused by material suspended in it plus the reflection of the sky or scattering of light in the water. Some bodies of water have been given their names because they are colored at times by plant or animal life or sometimes by colored silt flowing into them. The Mid-Eastern Red Sea, for instance, is so named because of the red phytoplankton in the water. The Yellow Sea is so named because of the yellow clay silt carried into it by the rivers of northern China.

The oceans can be divided into three layers, or zones, on the basis of light. The topmost is the **lighted zone,** which ranges in depth from a maximum of about 330 feet (a hundred meters)

in the open, clear sea to about three feet (one meter) in muddy estuaries. Next is the **twilight zone,** which is very dark violet, with only the slightest light penetration. No effective plant production takes place here; this layer ranges from about 260 to 655 feet (eighty to two hundred meters). Below the twilight zone is the area of total and perpetual darkness called the **dark zone**. This is a very thick layer in which no plants grow and animal life consists of carnivores and detritus (particles of plant or animal matter) feeders. This zone has no light at all, except that which is created by an object or animal itself.

Waves

Waves in a liquid are caused by any energy source that disturbs the water surface. The energy transmitted by ocean waves can be very great. Blocks of stone weighing more than 1,300 tons have been moved by waves.

Any disturbance, even a raindrop in a puddle, will create ripples of tiny waves. The tsunami waves caused by an exploding undersea volcano or an earthquake can travel all the way across the ocean. Wind, however, is the most common cause of ordinary sea waves. Sailors often call wind-driven waves "sea," or the state of the sea. A **swell** is a long, smooth wave coming from a distant storm center. Swells may indicate an approaching storm, and they are common in advance of hurricanes.

As the wind begins to blow over a smooth ocean surface, a certain amount of wind energy is imparted by friction and pressure to the underlying sea surface, causing waves to be formed. Wave height depends on three main factors: wind speed, duration of the wind, and the length of the **fetch** (the distance the wind blows over the water). The longer the fetch and the stronger the wind, the higher and longer the wave will be. At about thirteen knots of wind, whitecaps will begin to form. Sea waves twelve to fifteen feet high are not uncommon during a strong sea. Waves twenty-five to thirty feet high or more form during severe storms or hurricanes.

Waves in excess of fifty feet in height are very unusual, although a few are occasionally reported. Years ago the Navy tanker USS *Ramapo* reported a 114-foot wave. What may have been seen and measured by eye in that incident, however, could have been the spray associated with a large, unstable wave. Another huge wave, one that capsized a fictional fishing vessel, was immortalized in the summer 2000 movie *The Perfect Storm* (Warner Bros. Pictures). One of the major difficulties in estimating wave height is the lack of reference points. There is also another factor—the perception of the observer. For example, a small frigate operating with an aircraft carrier will frequently report larger waves than those reported by observers on the carrier.

The storm area of the sea over which wind blows to create waves may extend over more than two thousand square miles on the open ocean. The larger the wave, the more easily the wind can add more energy to its crest. There is a limit to a wave's growth, however. At the edge of the fetch—that is, where the wind effect on the waves ceases—the waves gradually change into smooth swells.

Waves are normally described using certain terms. The top of a wave is called the **crest,** while the lowest part, usually between two waves, is called the **trough.** The **height of a wave** is the vertical distance between the crest and the trough, while the **length of the wave** (the wavelength) is the horizontal distance between two successive crests. The length of time it takes for a complete wave (successive crests or troughs) to pass a given point is called the **period** of the wave. Normally wind waves have short periods, ranging from two to five seconds. Swells far in advance of a major storm may have a period of from twelve to fifteen seconds. The period of tsunami waves ranges from ten minutes to as much as an hour.

Breakers and Surf

Waves that fall over when they encounter the bottom in shallow water are called **breakers.** A line of breakers along a shore is called the **surf,** or surf line. The behavior of the breakers and the surf is highly dependent upon the upward slope, or **gradient,** of the bottom. Generally speaking, the steeper the gradient as the wave approaches a shore, the larger and more violent the oncoming breakers will be.

Knowledge of sea waves, swell, and surf conditions is crucial to naval and Marine amphibious operations. Surf conditions must be predicted accurately in order to determine when troops and vehicles can be safely landed. A four-foot surf is normally considered to be the "critical" height for safe amphibious

The state of the expected surf is always an important consideration in the planning of an amphibious assault. Beaching a landing craft, such as this LCM, is difficult when the surf is heavy. *CHINFO*

landings using traditional landing craft on average beaches. Above that height, boats may **broach**—that is, turn broadside to the beach after grounding. Broaching can cause damage to propellers and cause sand to be ingested into engine cooling-water intakes.

Beach and Coastline Erosion

Coastal landforms owe their shapes to the action of waves, tides, and currents on coastal rocks and sediments. Such wearing down and changing of the coastal outline and makeup is called **erosion.** Repeated ocean action against exposed rocky headlands, and especially sandy shores, constantly remodels beaches and **topography** (land features) near the shore. In addition to the pounding of water itself against the shore, small fragments of rocks and sand carried by the waves also scour away beaches and wear down the shoreline. Seaward of breakers, fine grains of sand and pebbles constantly move back and forth like sandpaper on a tabletop, in a continual grinding action. Often this erosion effect is concentrated more in one area of the shore than in another.

In some cases waves lift up huge rocks bodily or break off rocky outcroppings and throw them ashore. At other times the steady grinding of erosive sands wears away sediments and soil, creating cliffs that may eventually crumble. Occasionally, whole sand beaches are washed out to sea or moved and deposited elsewhere. People who have had the misfortune of having a beach cottage undermined or washed away on the eastern seaboard or on the Gulf of Mexico during gales and hurricanes know what the full impact of this phenomenon can be.

Waves and currents in the seawater cause most major shoreline changes. It is estimated that shorelines of the United States are being worn away at the rate of about one foot each year. Cape Cod, in Massachusetts, may be eroded away completely in about five thousand years if the present rate of erosion by waves continues, for example. Whole communities of homes along the steep seaside cliffs common in many parts of California have had to be abandoned because of water erosion.

On the other hand, waves and currents can cause sediments to accumulate in other places. The great Mississippi River delta continues to grow into the Gulf of Mexico from sediments carried down the river from interior North America. This endless struggle between construction and destruction of the surface of the Earth is one reason that geology and oceanography are so interesting.

An island or a landmass jutting out into the sea often changes the direction of forward motion of incoming ocean waves that encounter them. The waves tend to align themselves with the bottom contours, thus conforming to the general slope of the coastline. When one part of the surf line develops drag and changes direction or bends because of shallower water, this

An example of a breakwater (left) and a groin (right). Notice how sand has piled up along one side of the groin. *Earth Science in Maine*

effect is called **refraction.** Such information is very important when an amphibious assault is being planned. Engineers must also know the ways in which water waves are refracted so they can take advantage of natural phenomena when designing structures to protect shorelines and harbors. They must know where the natural energy is concentrated and where it is weaker, so they can build for greatest effect and economy.

The most common structure built to protect harbors is the **breakwater.** A breakwater is a line of big rocks, sometimes strengthened by steel-reinforced concrete, usually but not always built roughly parallel to, and some distance from, the shoreline. It may be a single structure protecting a harbor entrance or a series of segments that actually create and protect a harbor or an anchorage. In the latter case, there will normally be two or more harbor entrances and exits for shipping. A breakwater is designed to protect ships in a harbor at anchor or alongside piers from external waves, swells, or surf.

Another common structure similar to a breakwater (and sometimes called by the same name along inhabited seacoasts) is the **groin.** Usually built in a series of two or more, groins are barriers of stone or wooden pilings built at right angles to a shoreline to prevent erosion by **longshore currents** parallel to the shoreline. Longshore currents are part of the water movement associated with many beaches. Such currents carry scouring sediments from the beach out to deeper water. In the process, they may destroy the beach and make real estate along that area nearly worthless. They also sometimes create bars that become navigational hazards. Groins serve as dams to stop the movement of sediments by these currents. They may protect a given beach, but such interference with natural processes may also result in more erosion on beaches farther down the shoreline. For this reason careful surveys must be made before such structures are built.

Rip Currents. Rip currents are strong, seaward-moving currents that occur along some shores. They return excess water that has been pushed ashore by a number of different mechanisms, very often creating situations in which a longshore current moving in one direction parallel to a beach hits another longshore current moving in the opposite direction. The result is a strong movement of water outward to the breaker line and even beyond.

Rip currents are often incorrectly called "undertow" (the seaward and downward thrust of a wave after it breaks onto the beach). But these currents do not actually pull swimmers or waders down. They may cause a wader to tumble or pull a swimmer or floater out from shore to deep water. Some rip currents are fast, moving at speeds of up to 8 feet per second.

Rip currents can be very dangerous for those who cannot swim or swimmers who try to fight them. Even a good swimmer may tire quickly trying to swim back toward shore against such a current. If caught in a rip, you must not fight the current. Rip currents are rarely more than a hundred feet wide, so the best procedure is to swim parallel to the shore or breakers until you are past the current. In other words, you should try to swim across the current, without resisting the rip, using just enough strength to avoid being pulled out to deep water beyond the breaker line. By swimming across the current, you should be able to quickly get out of the main pull of the rip and swim back to shore. You must not panic or struggle and overexert yourself.

Ocean Currents and Gyres

The study of ocean currents can be complex. As with everything else in oceanography, new discoveries about the movements of ocean water are being made all the time. The effect that ocean currents have on people, the food cycle, and the weather of the world is profound. We can only introduce this subject here and hope that some students will want to explore this fascinating area of oceanography more on their own.

The movements of the atmosphere (winds) and oceans (currents) are linked to each other. A significant factor in these movements is the rotation of the planet on its axis. Earth's rota-

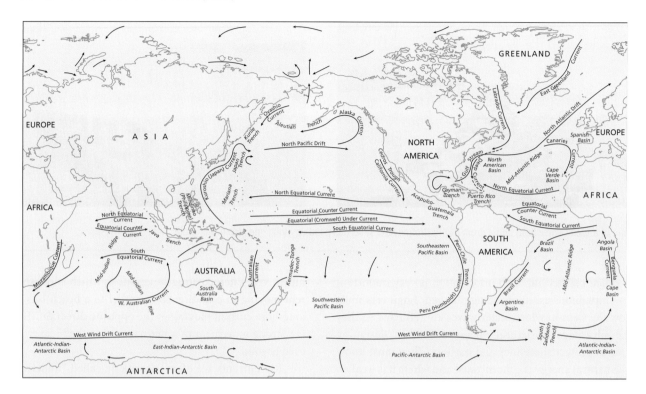

The major ocean currents and gyres.

tion, or spin, creates an invisible force called the **Coriolis effect,** or Coriolis force. This force deflects winds and currents to the right (clockwise) in the Northern Hemisphere and to the left (counterclockwise) in the Southern Hemisphere.

Two other important factors affect global movements of wind and water. These are (1) wind acting on the water surface, and (2) the boundary effects of the continents. Because of the continents, no major ocean current runs all the way around the world.

The heating of water in the equatorial region causes surface water there to rise and then to spread out and flow "downhill" over the surface toward the poles. For example, the water level of the Sargasso Sea in the mid-Atlantic east of Florida is actually about three feet higher than the water level farther north in the North Atlantic basin. As it drifts toward the poles, this water cools and sinks, pushing the water below it toward the equatorial regions. This kind of vertical circular flow, caused by heat differences within the water, is called **convection.** A more important factor affecting global water movements, though, is surface wind. Combined with the landmass placement, surface wind produces a different flow system. The resulting surface-water movements—ocean currents—are a combination of these two flows.

The prevailing winds in the Northern Hemisphere blow from the northeast in the latitude belt from 0 to 30 degrees. These are the **trade winds,** which drive the ocean surface waters to the west. The prevailing winds in the belt from 30 to 60 degrees north blow from the southwest. These are the **prevailing westerlies,** which drive the waters back toward the east. From 60 degrees north to the North Pole, the **polar northeasterlies** blow mainly from the northeast, again causing surface current movement toward the west (see the global winds diagram in chapter 9 of this section).

The combined effect of these winds is to create broad circular currents in the ocean basins in both the Northern and Southern Hemispheres. The movements in the Southern Hemisphere are opposite from those in the Northern Hemisphere, because of the Coriolis effect. These circular systems of currents are called **gyres.** (Keep in mind that winds are named by the direction *from which* they blow, while currents are described in terms of the direction *toward which* they flow.)

While these major currents are well defined, they continuously mingle with other currents, especially in the subpolar (i.e., within the Arctic or Antarctic Circles) regions. Also, there is a constant exchange of Atlantic Ocean water with the Mediterranean Sea through the Strait of Gibraltar. This is mainly due to the difference in salinity between these two bodies of water, which causes lighter Atlantic water to flow into the Mediterranean basin near the surface, while the heavier, saltier water flows out beneath it.

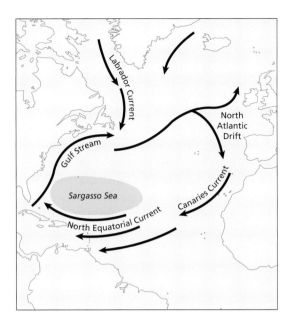

The North Atlantic, showing the gyre formed by the prevailing ocean currents surrounding it with the Sargasso Sea within.

The Gulf Stream. The **Gulf Stream** is the most important current affecting the United States and its entire Atlantic seaboard. The Gulf Stream system flows in a clockwise motion in the North Atlantic. In the center of this moving water mass is the legendary **Sargasso Sea.** This is a vast area of floating plants, thought to be true natives of these waters, which float near the surface by means of air bladders. This is not a thick mass of seaweed that traps ships, as is so often pictured in mystery stories of the sea. On the average about three miles deep, this oval area is about two thousand miles east and west by one thousand miles north and south. The blue waters of the Sargasso Sea form one of the oceanic deserts, and the plant species that inhabit this region are adapted to this environment.

The **North Equatorial Current** carries warmer waters northwestward along the West Indies on the eastern rim of the Caribbean Sea. Part of the current breaks off and enters the Gulf of Mexico. The bulk of it rushes northward to form the Gulf Stream that moves along the Florida, Georgia, and Carolina coasts at the rate of three or four knots and then begins to spread out and turn eastward in the **North Atlantic Drift.** The stream becomes wider and breaks off into *meanders* (different streams) in the northern latitudes. As it goes along the Grand Banks of Newfoundland, it parallels the southward-moving, cold **Labrador Current.** The Labrador Current brings icebergs that have calved (broken away) from the western Greenland glaciers and drifted into the North Atlantic shipping lanes. Here they meet the Gulf Stream's warm water and eventually melt.

In wintertime the warming effect of the Gulf Stream and North Atlantic Drift tends to make the climates in Iceland, Great Britain, and Western Europe much warmer than in other regions in the same latitudes. In the late summer and early fall, the North Equatorial Current region, south of the Sargasso Sea, is the spawning ground for **hurricanes,** which are severe storms with winds greater than 75 mph. These storms, driven by winds higher in the atmosphere, often follow the Gulf Stream into the Caribbean and the Gulf of Mexico or up the East Coast of the United States.

The Kuroshio Current. The **Kuroshio** (koo-ro'-sheo), or **Japan Current,** originates from the greater part of the North Equatorial Current in the Pacific. Like the Gulf Stream, which flows northwestward on the Atlantic side of the state of Florida, the Kuroshio Current flows northwestward from Japan's Ryukyu Islands.

Typhoons are the Pacific equivalent of hurricanes. Spawned in the region of the North Equatorial Current, just north of the equator, they often roar along the track of the Kuroshio, particularly during the late summer months, when high-level hemispheric winds flow in a similar pattern. During the cooler months the normal typhoon track is through the Philippines, into the South China Sea, and eventually into Vietnam. As the warm Kuroshio Current spreads out north of Japan, it passes south of and close to the cold **Oyashio** (o-ya'-sheo) **Current** coming out of the Bering Sea. The Kuroshio Current travels eastward across the North Pacific and splits into two branches. One of these branches is the **Alaskan Current,** which travels counterclockwise around the Gulf of Alaska and westward south of the Aleutian Islands. The other branch becomes the **California Current,** which travels southward along the west coast of the United States.

Tides

Earth's nearest neighbor in space, the Moon, is the main cause of a cyclic rise and fall of the surface of the oceans, along with lesser effects caused by the Sun. This vertical rise and fall of the water level is called **tide.** Anyone who has lived by or visited an ocean shore has seen the ebb and flow of the tide twice daily. The ancient Greeks first recognized the relationship between the tides and the Moon's monthly movement around Earth. It was not until Sir Isaac Newton (1642–1727) worked out his theory of gravity in 1687, however, that this relationship could be explained.

Newton determined that everything in the universe exerts a gravitational force or pull on everything else. The mass (amount of material) of the body and its distance from another object or body determines the gravitational force that each object or body exerts on the other. The pull of gravity is very small for small or greatly distant objects, but in the cases of the Moon and the Sun, the force is enormous, pulling the Earth toward their own centers of gravity, and vice versa. It is this gravitational force that holds the Earth and the other planets in their orbits around the Sun, and keeps the Moon and Earth "tied" together as companions in space.

The pull of the Moon's gravity causes the oceans on the Moon's side of Earth to bulge out toward it. The gravitational pull, however, is not the same everywhere. The points of Earth closer to the Moon are pulled more strongly, and those farther away are pulled less. This effect, in addition to an outward centrifugal force on the far side of Earth caused by the rotation of the Earth-Moon system about its common center of gravity, causes the water on the far side of Earth to bulge outward as well, though not as much as on the near side.

The Sun also helps cause the tides, but its effect is only about two-fifths as strong as that of the Moon. Though it is, of course, much more massive than the Moon, it is 390 times farther away, so the Sun's effect on tides is much smaller.

The variations in position of the Sun and Moon as the Earth rotates beneath them produce the daily cyclic patterns of the tides. On average, successive high and low tides are about six and a half hours apart. At times of the new and full moons, the tides are highest and lowest, respectively, because the forces of the Moon and Sun are either working together or are directly opposed. The result is called the **spring tide.** (The term actually has nothing to do with the spring season.) Halfway between the new and full moons, when we see the half moon during the first and third quarters, the tidal forces of the Moon and Sun are roughly at right angles to one another. At this time the dif-

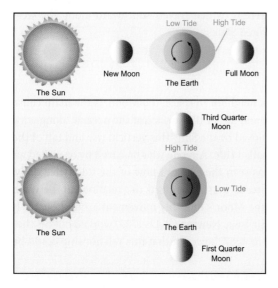

Spring and neap tides. When the Sun, Earth, and Moon are in line with each other (top), their combined gravitational pull results in the largest tidal ranges, known as *spring tides.* When the Sun and Moon are at right angles in relation to Earth (bottom), their combined gravitational pulls tend to reduce tidal ranges to a minimum, resulting in *neap tides.*
www.prancer.physics.louisville.edu

ference between high and low tides is much less than normal. These are called **neap tides.**

The **ebb** of a tide (ebb tide) is the fall of the tide that causes water to flow *away from* the shore. The **flood** of the tide (flood tide) is the rise of the tide that causes water to flow *toward* the shore. These *horizontal* movements of water are called **tidal currents.** The ebb and flood of tides and tidal currents vary widely around the world. They are affected not only by basic gravitational forces but also by the location of the continents and midocean ridges, the shape of the shoreline, the frictional drag between the water mass and the seabed, and the Coriolis force created by Earth's spin. Each tidal system is restricted to its own ocean basin by the continents.

Time and Tides

High tides occur twice a day in most parts of the world because, as mentioned earlier, when it is high tide on the side of Earth nearest the Moon, there is a lower high tide on the opposite side of the Earth. Knowing that Earth turns on its axis once in twenty-four hours, we might presume that these high tides would be exactly twelve hours apart, with low tides midway between them. However, the Moon and Earth are not in fixed positions relative to each other. The Moon revolves around Earth once in about twenty-seven days, in the same direction as the Earth rotates. Because of this motion, it takes twenty-four hours and fifty minutes for a given location on Earth to again be directly opposite the Moon. Therefore, there are twelve hours and twenty-five minutes between high tides.

Because these facts are known precisely, tide tables for each harbor on Earth can be accurately predicted for many years in advance. The National Ocean Service (NOS), a division of the National Oceanic and Atmospheric Administration (NOAA), publishes *Tide Tables* and *Tidal Current Tables* to assist mariners sailing in most parts of the world. Times of high and low tides figured from these tide tables are normally published daily in the **plan of the day** (a daily schedule of events and notes) aboard ships and at naval bases. This information is important in port because responsible officers and the deck department of a ship can use it as a guide to make sure the mooring lines have the right amount of slack. The ship's navigator must also be aware of the range of tides and tidal currents in harbors and channels because variations in water depths and current strengths at some ports are extreme. If tidal currents are strong, boat officers and coxswains must take them into account when planning boat runs and schedules. Tidal information is also routinely printed in most newspapers in communities near large bodies of water, and it is a part of local weather broadcasts by television and radio stations.

Tide and Tidal Current Extremes. The ranges of tides at most locations in the lower and middle latitudes of the world are normally limited to a few feet or less. In some areas of the world, though, tidal effects are extreme. This is especially so in the high northern latitudes. The highest tides in the world are experienced in the Bay of Fundy, between Nova Scotia and New Brunswick, where the spring range of tide often exceeds fifty feet. Another very high tide occurs at the island of Mont-Saint-Michel, France, on the English Channel. This island is surrounded by ten miles of sands at low tide, but when the forty-one-foot tide rises the water moves toward the shore at a rate of 210 feet per minute and completely surrounds the island. Very high tides are also experienced in Alaska, northern Europe, and the northeastern coast of Asia. The harbor at Inchon, Korea, for instance, must enclose its piers with **graving basins.** This is a system of locks that hold in the forty-foot tidal waters during low tide, thereby keeping ships alongside the piers afloat. Were it not for the graving basins, the ships would hit bottom and be severely damaged.

In areas where extreme high tides are common, an associated **tidal bore** (surge current) is often a twice-daily event where the tidal current sweeps up a river whose mouth opens directly on the sea. The world's highest tidal bores sweep up the Amazon River in Brazil and the Hangchow (Tsientang) River in China. During these bores the water level rises from fifteen to twenty-five feet and currents speed up the rivers at 10–16 knots. The Amazon tidal bore affects the river more than three hundred miles inland. Many rivers in Scotland, England, Norway, and Alaska also have tidal bores.

Dangerous tidal currents occur in places where there are big inlets with narrow entrances. This occurs with some fjords (long narrow inlets from the sea) in Greenland, Norway, Alaska, and Chile. Currents rushing past at eight or ten knots make it much too dangerous for boats and ships to attempt passages during much of the day. Tidal currents surge at speeds up to ten knots through channels in the Great Barrier Reef northeast of Australia. The meeting of tidal currents and winds of the Atlantic Ocean and the North Sea in the Pentland Firth, between northern Scotland and the Orkney Islands, creates a bore sometimes ten feet high. Many sailors have lost their lives in the Pentland Firth bore (called the Swelkie by local Scots) since the days of the Vikings. The firth is said to be haunted by the ghosts of the drowned, who howl and call out with the strong northwest winds to sailors passing by on dark winter nights.

Tidal Energy. **Tidal energy** is one of the oldest forms of energy used by humans. A tidal mill built in the Deben Estuary (a wide part of a river where it joins the sea) in Great Britain was mentioned in records as early as 1170 and is still in opera-

The La Rance tidal power plant, located on the estuary of the La Rance River in the province of Brittany, on France's Atlantic coast. Twenty-four two-way turbines are spun by water flowing past as the tides rise and fall, producing a maximum of 240 megawatts per day. *EDF Médiathèque*

tion. Creative engineering has resulted in a large number of schemes that make the tides a reliable source of **green energy** (renewable energy produced without use of fossil fuels).

Tidal electrical power generation requires large capital investments, but once built, tidal power installations may last much longer (with small maintenance costs) than thermal or nuclear power stations. The idea is simple: dam in a basin, let it fill with the incoming tide, and then at low tide release the water through **sluice gates** (regulated-flow channels or gates) so that it can spin turbines and generate electricity. It is more reliable than other green energy solutions such as wind turbines and solar power. The main requirement is a large enough range of tide.

Favorable tidal conditions for such power plants exist at many locations in France and in Brazil, Argentina, Australia, India, Korea, Canada, China, Russia, as well as some other countries. The French built the world's first large-scale successful tidal plant, the La Rance Tidal Power Station, in 1966 near St. Malo, at the mouth of the Rance River estuary. A dam containing turbines spans the estuary. As the twenty-six-foot tides rise and fall, they spin special two-way turbines that drive banks of generators. The station has a generating capacity of 240 megawatts. The world's largest such plant at present is the Shiwa Lake Tidal Power Station in Gyeonggi Province in South Korea. It uses ten 25.4 megawatt submerged turbines that generate power during the rise of each eighteen-foot tide. Several other larger plants are currently in the planning stages in other parts of the country.

The Dutch have for centuries reclaimed land from the sea with dikes and pumps. Their biggest project was the enclosure of the Zuyder Zee, a shallow bay off the North Sea, during most of the last century. Another more recent project was the Delta Works, a series of dams and dikes across the estuaries of the Rhine, Meuse, and Scheldt Rivers, completed in 1997 after nearly fifty years of work. One part of this system generates electricity by tidal flow. At the same time, the project creates freshwater lakes for recreation, reduces and protects the amount of shoreline directly exposed to the storm waves of the North Sea, reclaims land from the sea, and creates a coastal highway system that connects many previously isolated islands in the southern part of The Netherlands.

The first such attempt at tidal power generation in the United States is scheduled for 2015, with the installation of a system of thirty submerged tidal current turbines in the East River in New York City. They will have a total power-generation capacity of approximately a megawatt, enough to power 9,500 homes.

Critical Thinking

1. Identify the major ocean current patterns that exist off the U.S. East and West Coasts and describe the effects that these currents have on the water and air temperatures along the coasts.

2. Research the current state of efforts to generate electrical power from the ocean tides. Do you think this is a valid method of helping to deal with the energy crisis worldwide?

Study Guide Questions

1. Who is the founder of modern U.S. Navy oceanography?

2. What is unique about the cooling and freezing of water?

3. How does the ability of water to store heat make life possible on Earth?

4. A. What are the four main elements in seawater?
   B. What is the percentage of salt in open ocean water?

5. What are the two measures of salinity in common use?

6. A. What are the saltiest bodies of water in the world ocean?
   B. In landlocked lakes?

7. How did the ocean water get salty?

8. Describe the hydrologic cycle.

9. A. What is the freezing point of seawater?
   B. What is the constant temperature of water in the deep sea?

10. What determines the color of water (as seen by the human eye)?

11. What is the most common cause of ocean waves?

12. Upon what three things does wind-generated wave height depend?

13. What are the parts of a wave?

14. A. Why are surf and swell so important to amphibious operations?
    B. What is meant by "critical" height of surf?

15. A. What water actions reshape coastal landforms?
    B. What is such action called?

16. What is the main type of structure built to protect harbors from the sea called?

17. A. What is a longshore current?
    B. What type of structure is built to prevent erosion from these currents?

18. A. What is a rip current, and how may it affect swimmers?
    B. How should a swimmer move to get out of a rip current?

19. A. What force, caused by Earth's rotation, affects the major currents of the world ocean?
    B. In what direction does this force deflect major currents north and south of the equator?

20. What very important current affecting the United States originates on the southern border of the Sargasso Sea?

21. A. Which current brings icebergs into the North Atlantic shipping lanes?
    B. How does the Gulf Stream affect icebergs?

22. A. What important current in the North Pacific has many similarities with the Gulf Stream in the North Atlantic?
    B. What severe storms originate in the same general area as does this current?

23. A. What is the main cause of the ocean tides?
    B. How does the Sun affect the tides?

24. When are tides highest and lowest, and what are these tides called?

25. A. How do naval personnel find out about the tidal situation in their port of call?
    B. Which people aboard ship are particularly concerned about the tides? Why?

26. Where do the world's highest tides occur?

27. A. What is a tidal bore?
    B. Where do the highest tidal bores occur?

28. What is the general theory of operation of a tidal power plant?

New Vocabulary

current
salinity
optical properties
density
precipitate
radiant energy
light waves
X-rays
Nansen bottles
hydrologic cycle
transpiration
bathythermograph
ultraviolet
infrared
visible spectrum
prism
turbidity
swell
fetch (of a wave)
crest (of a wave)
trough (of a wave)
period (of a wave)
breakers
surf
gradient
topography
refraction

broach (in a boat)
erosion
breakwater
groin
longshore current
rip current
undertow
convection (in water)
hurricanes
typhoons
trade winds
gyre
tide
spring tide
neap tide
ebb tide
flood tide
plan of the day
tidal current
graving basin
tidal bore
fjord
tidal energy
sluice gate
turbine
estuary

6

Life in the Seas

So far in this unit we have talked about some physical, geological, and chemical aspects of oceanography. There is a fourth major scientific area: biology. **Marine biology** deals with the living, or organic, content of the sea—its plants and animals.

There are many separate areas of study within modern marine biology, and we cannot explore them all in this text. One important field is biological oceanography, or **marine ecology.** This field is concerned with marine organisms and their environment. It is directly related to (1) human use of the sea for food and employment, and (2) the effect of marine life on naval operations. This latter includes how marine organisms affect ships, installations, and equipment; the ability of people to live and work on and under the sea; the effectiveness of sonar equipment; and many other important things.

Plankton, the Start of the Life Cycle

Plankton, both plant and animal, are billions of tiny floating organisms that wander with the ocean currents or drift in the uppermost layers of the sea. Plankton provides the "ocean pasture" for the smallest animals and fish. Materials in suspension in the sea, including decayed plant and animal life, provide the nutrients plankton need.

Phytoplankton are microscopic marine plants that start the sea **food chain,** the ecological system in which almost every form of life becomes the food for another, usually higher, form of life. Next are the **zooplankton,** tiny animals and larvae of larger sea life. Finally there is a whole range of larger fish and sea animals, which extends from fishes and crabs to the giant blue whale, the world's largest mammal.

To show how small plankton are—and to see if enough could be gathered for a meal—explorer Thor Heyerdahl dragged a plankton net behind his balsawood raft

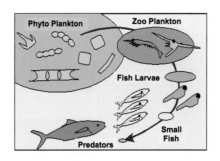

The food chain in the ocean. Beginning with the phytoplankton, which live on the nutrients and decayed matter that upwell from the sea bottom, the system moves around through progressively larger marine animals. To complete the cycle, dead animals drop to the bottom, providing the matter upon which phytoplankton live.

Courtesy of Action Outdoors

Kon-Tiki for many hours across the southern Pacific in 1947. He managed to gather a small amount of edible plankton, which he made into a sort of fish paste. He found it to be very salty. Studies have now proved that this material is almost pure protein. In fact, the sea is believed to contain a large percentage of the world's total protein supply.

Upwelling, El Niño, and La Niña

Upwelling is the movement of deeper layers of water toward the surface. This happens when prevailing winds along a shore cause movement of upper water layers away from the coast. The Coriolis force is also a factor in this process. The resultant vertical circulation from great depths brings decayed materials high in nitrogen and phosphates to the surface. Upwelling occurs near the steepest gradient of the continental slope.

The most remarkable upwelling occurs along the Peruvian and Chilean coasts, between the shoreline and the northward-flowing Humboldt Current. The nutrients and minerals nourish plankton, which in turn attract great numbers of fishes, large and small, to the area. Fishermen catch up to 100,000 tons of anchovies and sardines and the larger fish that feed on them each year. Great flocks of seabirds feed on these fish, and the islands on which the birds nest are covered with tons of their droppings, called **guano.** Over 330,000 tons of guano are "mined" annually for high-grade fertilizer.

Every now and then, for reasons not yet fully understood but probably related to reduced trade winds, the Humboldt Current meanders from its normal course or actually disappears, allowing warmer currents to come along the coast and make the surface layers of water warmer than usual. This stops upwelling, and fish, without their life-supporting nutrients, begin to die. Additionally, millions of sea birds may die in such famines. The hydrogen sulfide from the decaying bodies of both fish and birds is so thick that ships' hulls are turned black. This occurrence is locally called the **Callao Painter,** named after the nearby port of Callao, Peru. The phenomenon that causes upwelling to stop is called **El Niño** ("little boy" in Spanish). The El Niño effect results in unusually warm surface waters in the Equatorial Pacific. For marine life, it is one of the most destructive oceanographic conditions in the world. It can also cause dramatic climatic changes in Central and North America and elsewhere.

A related effect called **La Niña** ("little girl" in Spanish) usually follows when the El Niño subsides. The La Niña effect results in unusually cold surface waters in the Equatorial Pacific. Resulting global climate changes tend to be the opposite of those associated with El Niño. In the continental United States, during El Niño years temperatures in the winter are warmer than normal in the north central states and cooler than normal in the southeast and the southwest. During a La Niña year, winter temperatures are warmer than normal in the southeast and cooler than normal in the northwest.

The Red Tide and Black Sea

In the Red Sea, atmospheric and sea conditions similar to El Niño occasionally occur. There, when the upwelling of cool water stops, the surface layers become heated and bring about a population explosion ("bloom") of tiny red-colored phytoplankton called *dinoflagellata.* They become so numerous that the water takes on a reddish color, giving it the name **Red Tide** (and giving the Red Sea its name). The Red Tide clogs the gills of fish, causing them to suffocate and die. Millions of dead fish are washed ashore, and the resulting stench carries for miles. A similar event occurs, more rarely, along the east coast of Florida.

The Black Sea is essentially a very large saltwater lake. Its only opening is through the Turkish straits (Bosporus and Dardanelles) to the Aegean Sea. The straits are very shallow, so there is little exchange of water between the two seas and no chance for upwelling or the introduction of dissolved oxygen in the Black Sea. As a result, the Black Sea is stagnant. The residue of marine life in the surface layers sinks to the bottom and remains there to decay. The decay of animal and vegetable matter uses up whatever oxygen is available and creates hydrogen sulfide gas. Over thousands of years, this gas and lack of oxygen have completely destroyed bottom life in the Black Sea. The hydrogen sulfide layer begins about two hundred feet below the surface and continues to the bottom. There is no life in this "black zone," which has given its name to the sea.

For navies, the Black Sea poses a special problem. Hydrogen sulfide gas, when mixed with water, has a corrosive effect on metals. Recall how the Callao Painter turns the sides of ships black. The hull fittings of a submarine operating for long periods of time in the hydrogen sulfide zone would run a serious risk of being ruined, thereby endangering the boat and her crew.

The Life Cycle in the Sea

A **biological life cycle** is the chain of natural events in which plants and animals take in foods and chemicals, release wastes during their lifetimes, reproduce, and then die and decompose. In the sea, as on land, sunlight supports the biological life cycle. It does so through the process of **photosynthesis,** the manufacture of food in a green plant. In the sea, floating chlorophyll-bearing (green-colored) phytoplankton are the basic food producers of the sea. They provide the proteins, starches, and sugars necessary to support the sea's smallest life. Phytoplankton are the food for the zooplankton, tiny animals of many shapes, either free-floating or self-propelled. The zooplankton—which also include the eggs and larvae of some larger fishes—are the food for small flesh-eaters (**carnivores**) of the ocean. In turn, the small carnivores are eaten by larger ones. Death and decay complete the cycle. The organic material of both plants and animals decays as the result of bacterial action, releasing again the nutrient raw materials—carbon, phosphorus, and nitrogen—needed to start the process of photosynthesis over again. Since the organic material sinks, most of the decay occurs in deep water. Upwelling currents eventually return the nutrients to the lighted zone in the upper fifteen to twenty fathoms of water, where this life cycle can begin again.

Though phytoplankton can live only in the lighted zone, usually in the upper ninety feet, zooplankton and larger animal life have been found in all parts of the ocean, including the bottom of the deepest part of the 35,800-foot-deep Mariana Trench. Animals that live in these great depths are generally small, ferocious carnivores. They have very soft, scaleless bodies in a wide variety of shapes. They are often snakelike, with narrow fins and very pliant bones, and most are either transparent or black in color, because of the dark environment. Many have developed long, needle-sharp teeth and huge mouths. Others are blind, because they have no need for eyes in the pitch-black world of the abyss. Still others have large bulging eyes, and many have luminescent spots and appendages that glow in the dark. This natural luminescence (light) is believed to attract prey, their mates, or both. Much has yet to be learned about these strange deep-sea animals.

At the shoreline, creatures of the sea live under very difficult conditions. They are subject to the extremes of drying, flooding, baking, and freezing if they are exposed when the tide rises and falls. Waves and currents may also wash them up on the beach to die. And, of course, there are many predators that can get them when they are exposed. Many sea animals that live on the edge of the sea are small, flat, or streamlined, and many have suction-type devices that hold them tightly to rocks. Starfish have hundreds of such suction cups on their five arms. Barnacles attach to underwater surfaces and excrete a chemical that acts as a cement to keep them in place the rest of their lives.

Other marine life is found in tidal pools and hollows of rocks and coral, where it is sheltered from predators and yet has life-sustaining water around it even when the tide is out. In this category are some corals, sponges, sea anemones, sea cucumbers, and sea urchins. Others live on the beaches and burrow into the sand for protection when the tide is out. Able to remain in the air from one high tide to the next, this type includes some crabs, clams, sandworms, and sand dollars, among many others.

A fish with two sea lamprey attached. *USGS*

Life in the Shallow Sea

Most sea animals live in the relatively shallow water seaward of the low-tide level above the continental shelf. Over much of the continental shelf, marine plant life (phytoplankton) is able to float or in some instances attach itself to the bottom and remain within range of sunlight. The plants vary in size from microscopic single cells, such as **algae** and **diatoms,** to huge seaweed plants called **kelp,** which may be 150 feet long. Algae are the most common of all plants. They are a number of different colors; some float, and others attach themselves to rocks. There are also some grasslike plants. In general, however, the sea does not have the wide variety of plants found on land or the advanced members of the plant family, like trees or flowering shrubs. Much of the sea and the sea floor, in fact, is barren.

Where plants exist, however, there is normally an abundance of animal life. The smallest animals of the zooplankton group are the one-celled **protozoans. Jellyfishes** are the largest form of zooplankton. These are beautiful, transparent creatures composed of many white, blue-green, and blue cells, but they often have on their tentacles thousands of stingers that can cause extreme pain, convulsions, and in extreme cases, even death. Others in the group of tiny animals that live off phytoplankton are the **larvae** (young forms) of oysters, snails, and sea worms. More developed animals are the crabs, shrimps, lobsters, clams, oysters, squid, mussels, octopi, and scallops. These animals eat the smaller species of zooplankton and graze upon phytoplankton. Starfish and sea urchins dine on shellfish, such as oysters and clams.

Marine Animals

There are two major divisions of marine animals: those that do not have jaws, and those that do.

There are only two types of jawless fish, the *hagfish* and the *lampreys.* Their mouths are circular and are used to attach to their prey. The hagfish feeds on dead or dying animals, but lampreys attach themselves to living fish, using their rasping tongues to make open sores from which they feed on blood and tissue. The *sea lampreys* in the Great Lakes have caused great damage to the lake trout and whiting fisheries, although in the oceans they are insignificant. The lampreys entered the Great Lakes via the St. Lawrence Seaway, illustrating how human endeavors can in some instances upset an ecological system.

There are four groups of marine animals that have jaws: fish, reptiles, birds, and mammals. **Fish** range throughout the seas, but most live in the shallow, warmer seas. Within this group are five subgroups: (1) *bottom-dwelling fishes* of both shallow and deep seas, which have large heads and whip tails; (2) *large carnivorous fishes* with tough, leathery skins and sharp cutting teeth, such as sharks and rays (this group includes the largest fish—the whale shark, basking shark, and manta ray); (3) *sturgeons,* which have bony plates on the skin and are commercially valuable for their eggs, called **caviar;** (4) *commercial fishes,* the largest group, such as cod, herring, turbot, salmon, tuna, mackerel, flounder, bass, and many others; and (5) *lungfish,* three of which are freshwater types, and one called the **coelacanth.** This oddity, once thought to have died out some 50 million years ago, was found in the Indian Ocean in 1938. An occasional specimen has been caught from time to time since.

The **reptile group** has only a small number of species that live in the sea today—a far cry from the **Age of Reptiles,** when they were the dominant form of life in the world ocean. Reptiles are cold-blooded. That means they cannot regulate their temperatures as mammals do, so they usually inhabit warm tropical seas. There are four groups of living **marine reptiles:** turtles, marine iguanas, sea snakes, and a few ocean crocodiles.

Sea turtles grow to a huge size. The rare leatherback sometimes exceeds six feet in length and weighs over half a ton. Turtles swim with flippers. They come ashore to lay their eggs in holes dug in the sand. There, they are at the mercy of many different kinds of predators. Few of the young make it back to the sea before being eaten by seabirds.

Marine iguanas live only in the Galápagos Islands of Ecuador, off the west coast of South America. They are the only marine lizards. They live in large herds on the rocks near shore and feed on seaweed.

Sea snakes, some related to cobras and kraits, are poisonous. They have paddle-like flat tails, so they can swim. They inhabit sheltered coastal waters, especially near river mouths, and some live in brackish water upstream. There are nearly fifty species of these poisonous snakes living in the tropical Pacific and Indian Oceans. They range from East African waters throughout southern and Southeast Asia, Oceania, Austra-

An American alligator. Alligators have a broad snout with strong jaws and teeth that enable them to eat almost any type and size of prey. Crocodiles have a narrower snout with exposed teeth, better suited for prey like fish and small mammals. *Dev C*

lia, and in the warm Japan Current all the way north to Japan and Korea. A few species live along the Pacific coast of Central and South America. Although sea snakes are poisonous, they do not disturb swimmers and are said not to bite unless forcibly restrained. They feed on fish, mostly at night. This makes them dangerous to fishermen, who may net them when they are attracted by schools of fish and the lights of fishing boats. A number of deaths are caused by sea snakes each year.

Twenty-three species of *crocodiles* inhabit much of the waters of the tropical zones around the world. These include the **American alligator,** found in marshes, swamps, rivers, lakes, tidal areas, and sometimes the ocean in the southeastern United States; the **American crocodile,** found in southern Florida, Central America, South America, and various Caribbean islands; and twenty-one other species found in Asia, Africa, Australia, and other Pacific and Indian Ocean regions. They are very hardy, tough animals that have survived, basically unchanged, from prehistoric times. They range in size from a few feet to as long as twenty feet or more. The smaller ones feed on insects, snakes, turtles, slow-moving fish, small mammals,

and birds. Large adults may eat larger mammals and, on occasion, may attack unwary people.

The **seabird group** includes a number of different species. The *waders,* such as the blue heron, live and feed along the shallows, in estuaries of rivers affected by tides, in ponds, and in mangrove swamps. *Birds of the open sea,* such as the albatross and petrel, live most of the time in the open ocean, coming ashore mainly to breed. They feed mostly on fish, which they catch by pouncing on them from the air above. There are many varieties of flightless birds called *penguins,* all of them in the Southern Hemisphere. The emperor penguin lays its eggs on sea ice in Antarctica. It is the only bird that never comes ashore. As penguins cannot fly, they catch fish by diving and swimming.

The **mammal group** has a limited number of marine species, but they are some of the world's most interesting animals. Marine mammals evolved from land-dwelling ancestors over time by developing adaptations to life in the water. They include the *polar bear* and *sea otter,* which are similar in most characteristics to land animals but are adapted to the sea. The polar bear has extra-long legs, which makes it a powerful swimmer,

Emperor penguins, common throughout Antarctica. *Lin Padgham*

A polar bear at the Buffalo Zoo in New York. *Dave Pape*

and a thick white coat, which insulates it against the icy waters and winds of the Arctic. There are currently between about 20,000 and 25,000 polar bears alive in the wild today, living in Canada, Greenland, northern Russia, islands off the Norwegian coast, and on the northwest Alaskan coast.

The sea otter has webbed feet and is well adapted to life in the sea. It inhabits Pacific coastal regions from Mexico to Alaska, where it feeds in the giant kelp beds on abalone and sea urchins. The sea otter spends most of its life at sea, sleeping, eating, and even giving birth to its young among the kelp. It was almost exterminated for its valuable pelt by the early 1900s, but strict hunting regulations since have allowed it to make a good natural recovery. There are also *river otters,* which inhabit most of the eastern United States and the Gulf region.

Other marine mammals, however, have changed a great deal from the forms they once had on land. There are three groups: the sea cows, the seals, and the whales. The *sea cows* include the manatees of Florida and the jungle rivers of South America. The sea cow eats lily pads. It is cigar shaped with front flippers and a flat tail but no hind flippers.

There are three groups of *seals:* the earless, or true, seals; the eared seals, or sea lions; and the walrus. They are all fish eaters and have streamlined bodies and limbs modified to be flippers. They are fast, expert swimmers and can easily catch their prey in the water. They have a layer of thick blubber beneath the skin to protect them from the cold. The fur seals of Alaska have luxuriant pelts much prized for coats. After many years of overhunting, they are now carefully protected and "harvested" in a managed way for their pelts, a valuable natural resource. The California sea lion is the most common type of seal that performs in zoos and marine shows. The walrus has long ivory tusks and is found only in Arctic waters.

Whales, dolphins, and *porpoises* are all air-breathing marine mammals that bear their young alive, nurse them, and maintain a constant body temperature. They spend their lives entirely in water and breathe through openings called *blowholes.* Movement is aided by horizontal, flattened *tail flukes.* There are two subgroups of whales: the baleen, or whalebone, whale and the toothed whale. Toothed whales have only one

An arctic Harp seal. *Canadian Department of Fisheries and Oceans*

A blue whale display at the American Museum of Natural History. This species is the largest mammal on Earth, often exceeding ninety feet in length. It is also one of the noisiest, making underwater squeals audible for hundreds of miles. *www.wikimedia.com, Shank27*

blowhole, in contrast to the baleen, which have two.

Instead of teeth, the *baleen whales* have a fine mesh sieve with up to eight hundred or more plates of baleen, or whalebone, that hang like a curtain from the upper jaw. When feeding, the whale opens its jaws and takes in seawater. When the jaw closes, the baleen allows the water to flow out but keeps any collected marine life in. The main foods of the baleen whale are plankton and *krill* (a shrimplike animal that grows up to two to three inches long and is found in large numbers in Antarctic waters). Baleen whales range in size from the *minke* (just over thirty feet) to the *blue whale,* which often grows to ninety or a hundred feet in length and weighs a hundred tons.

The giant blue whale, the largest mammal that has ever lived on the Earth, weighs two to three tons at birth, doubles its weight in its first week of life, and seven months later weighs about twenty-four tons! The largest blue whale on record was 108 feet long. From a world population of about 40,000 in 1930, there are now only a few thousand left in the world oceans. Some conservationists fear that it is close to extinction, because its death rate may soon exceed its reproductive rate.

Unlike baleen whales, *toothed whales* have teeth after birth. These teeth number from just a few in some species to as many as 250, although some may be concealed beneath the gum. The narwhal has a single long, tusklike tooth in the upper jaw. This group includes dolphins and porpoises, as well as killer (or orca) and sperm whales. The sizes in this class range from the porpoise, which is about five feet long, to the sperm whale, which can be up to seventy feet long. They eat fish primarily, but the sperm whale also likes *giant squid* found at great depths. Records of sperm whales being entangled with submarine cables at depths down to 3,700 feet indicate that some of the squid on which they feed are browsing on the bottom.

Conservation Laws

In order to help conserve the remaining species of marine mammals, Congress passed the **Marine Mammal Protection Act** in 1972, prohibiting U.S. citizens from hunting any of these animals in U.S. waters or on the high seas, or from importing

Killer, or orca, whales grow to a maximum of thirty-two feet. They get their name from their ferocious attacks on prey like seals and smaller whales, but they seldom if ever attack humans in the wild. Because they are trainable and very agile, they are a mainstay of many marine shows. *NOAA, Robert Pittman*

them or any products made from them into the United States. In 1995 certain of the species had increased in numbers sufficiently that the act was amended to allow Alaskan natives to hunt for subsistence and commercial fishermen to kill members of those species that were inadvertently captured or injured incidental to their operations.

In 1973 Congress passed the **Endangered Species Act,** which places similar prohibitions on hunting *any* species of animal classified as endangered and placed on the *Endangered Species List* maintained under the law. It also prohibits damaging the *habitat* (living environment) of such species. Currently there are over two thousand species listed as endangered; only about thirty have been delisted since the law's inception because their numbers had recovered sufficiently so as no longer to be considered in danger of extinction.

Life in the Open Sea

Beyond the shallow waters of the continental shelf there is much less sea life, because there is little plant or animal food. The animals that do live in the open sea come to the surface to feed on the limited zooplankton and smaller fish, but in general, food is scarce there.

On the edges of the open sea, however, live many of the great game fishes of the world, such as marlin, sailfish, tuna,

and sharks. Especially good fishing grounds for these fish are on the fringes of the Gulf Stream along the eastern seaboard of the United States and on the Mexican coasts in both the Atlantic and Pacific. Tuna species are found throughout the world ocean as they follow the plankton communities and migrate to central ocean spawning grounds.

There are places on continental or island shelves where the ocean floor rises much closer to the surface in high underwater plateaus. These areas have an abundance of marine vegetation for fish to feed on. These plateaus are called **banks.** They are the best fishing grounds in the world: the Grand Banks off Newfoundland, Georges Bank off Massachusetts, the Dogger Bank in the North Sea, and in the Pacific near Japan and Alaska.

The Fishing Industry

According to a recent world fisheries report, some 1.3 million decked and 2.8 million undecked (open) vessels of all sizes and 30 million people are engaged in some phase of the marine fishing industry worldwide. Roughly 80 percent of all decked and open unpowered fishing craft are operated in Asia; most of the remainder are in the Americas and Europe. The annual worldwide consumption of fish and fish products from all sources is some 140 million tons. Of this, some 15 percent comes from **aquaculture** (fish farming). The remaining 85 percent comes from fishing in the world's oceans and inland waters. Of this, about 70 percent comes from the Pacific, 20 percent from the Atlantic, and the rest from the other world oceans and inland waters.

The amount of seafood eaten annually in different parts of the world is related to eating habits that people have developed over centuries and local standards of living. For example, in a recent year in the United States (2010), each person ate an average of only about sixteen pounds (7.3 kg) of fish and other seafood. In Japan in the same year, the average person consumed over sixty pounds (27.3 kg).

The history of the fishing industry is part of the evolution of world commerce and the never-ending search for food. Since the beginning of the twentieth century, many improvements in fishing vessels, nets, and preservation methods have occurred. Progress in fishing methods since 1930 alone has been greater than that in the previous three thousand years. Three main types of commercial vessels have been developed: the purse seiner, a vessel that uses the latest electronic equipment to locate and entrap schools of fish; oceanic long-liners, which can fish for tuna throughout the tropical oceans; and ocean trawlers.

The large *purse seiners* were designed by Americans to pursue tuna on the high seas. They are based in California but cruise the world. Their large nets can catch a whole school of tuna at one "set" of their nets. Many of the larger ships can carry 1,500 tons of frozen fish in their holds.

The *long-liners* originated in Japan and South Korea. These vessels lay out from one to three floating long-lines, each more than twenty miles long and bearing baited hooks every few feet. These vessels seek mainly to catch marlin, sailfish, and tuna.

The *trawler fleets* of the world have greatly increased, especially under Eastern European and Asian flags, and they fish the continental shelves throughout the world. Trawlers gener-

A shrimping boat with nets set. *USCG*

ally stay at sea for several months and bring in a catch of up to 250 tons of fish that have been automatically cleaned and stored in ice. The Japanese and Russians have developed huge fish-factory ships that process and can the catch at sea. They serve as "mother ships" to a fleet of trawlers. They deliver their products directly to foreign markets at prices that cannot be matched by fishermen with less sophisticated equipment.

Aquaculture

The oceans are a good source of food now, but their potential is even greater. The seas alone could provide enough protein for the entire world population of more than seven billion people (2013). At the present time, however, only about 1 percent of the protein in the human diet comes from the sea. A change in people's eating habits, careful conservation and harvesting practices, and cultivation of selected kinds of marine plant and animal life could increase food production from the sea. We must be very careful, however, not to deplete the breeding stock of fish or to overfish given areas. If we do, the disastrous extinction that has occurred with some land animals may be repeated.

The term "aquaculture" refers to the cultivation or raising of marine plants and animals for food. Fish are the most cultivated marine organism, followed by mollusks (oysters, clams, scallops, and mussels) of all kinds and crustaceans (shrimp and crawfish).

Oyster Farming. Oyster farming in Western Europe and in Asia has been carried on for over two thousand years and remains one of the most important commercial enterprises in both regions today. Today most of the world's oysters come from such oyster beds.

An adult oyster can produce as many as 100 million eggs at one laying! But only a few oysters per million eggs survive in their natural environment. Each egg develops into a zooplankton larva and floats about for two to three weeks before settling down on a rock or other surface. People have traditionally cultivated oysters by providing old oyster shells for the larvae to settle on; these old shells are called the *clutch*. Predators, such as starfish, are cleared out, and the area is fenced off. In a few years the oysters are ready to be harvested.

This method has been improved upon, however, because it is too slow. Previously, only the food that fell to the bottom could be eaten by the growing oysters. Now most oyster beds have been replaced by suspension cultures in which the clutch is hung from ropes attached to floating frame rafts suspended in tanks or to stakes driven into the bottom in open waters. This way the oysters have access to plankton floating by in all depths. Using this method, it is possible to harvest 6,400 tons of oyster meat per square kilometer of open water in about two years, and even more in tanks. World oyster production is about 4.8 million tons annually (including oysters taken from the open seas), with China being by far the largest producer, accounting for some 42 million tons, or 84 percent of the world's annual total. The Japanese produce about 260,000 tons annually, followed by French oyster farms that produce some 230,000 tons of oysters annually for the European market. The United States produces an annual total of about 43,000 tons.

Mussel Farming. Even more productive is aquafarming of the common mussel. One mussel aquafarm at Vigo, Spain, nets an unbelievable 27,000 tons of mussel meat annually from each square kilometer of floating farms! World mussel production is about two million tons annually (including mussels taken from the open sea). Again, China is the largest producer, with some 1.4 million tons annually (70 percent of the world total), followed by Spain with about 240,000 tons, Japan with about 115,000 tons, and the United States with about 100,000 tons annually.

Fish Farming. Fish farming has had a high record of success for centuries in Southeast Asia, the Philippines, Indonesia, and China. The raising of milkfish in shallow fish ponds filled with brackish water has reaped some two hundred tons per square kilometer using commercial fertilizers—more than five hundred tons using human sewage as the nutrient fertilizer. In the open ocean, seven tons per square kilometer is the natural production rate. The United Nations has figured that in Southeast Asia alone there are at least 5,500 square kilometers of shallow sea that could be turned over to milkfish production. Such production could supply most of the annual protein requirements of Asia.

Over a thousand years ago the Chinese developed a complex ecological fish farming system that they still use today. They place six different kinds of carp into a single deep pond, knowing that each species occupies a different habitat (water depth) and consumes different food. The grass carp consumes the surface vegetation. There are two midwater dwellers; one eats zooplankton, the other phytoplankton. Finally, there are three bottom feeders, which eat mollusks, worms, and the feces of the grass carp. This is an extremely efficient ecological system that even serves to eliminate "pollution." The system is ancient, but it is naturally organic—and it works.

Woods Hole Oceanographic Institute in Massachusetts has worked out a similar system involving sewage, algae, oysters, seaweed, abalone, sand worms, and flounder. The main crop is oysters, with abalone and flounder as secondary crops. It is a natural sewage-treatment plant. The sewage is used to grow plankton algae, which in turn provide food for oysters. The waste from the oysters is consumed by seaweeds, which is then fed to abalone. The remainder falls to the bottom of the tank and is eaten by sand worms, which are then circulated to a neighboring tank to serve as food for flounder. The cleansed water is then returned to the sea. The system is designed to produce a million pounds of seafood meat annually from a one-acre production facility of fish and shellfish holding tanks and a fifty-acre algae farm using sewage from a community of 11,000 people.

In Southeast Asia, in addition to the milkfish farming described above, fish farmers also harvest mullet, shrimp, and crabs in ponds constructed by clearing mangrove swamps and diking them with mud. These farms are extremely productive. The small fry are first fed in a nursery pond, while algae, bacteria, worms, and other plankton are raised naturally in production ponds with the addition of fertilizer. When the fry get to fingerling size, they are transferred to the production ponds. There they literally gorge themselves, growing to mature size in just a few months. The average annual yield of such ponds is about five hundred pounds per acre.

U.S. Fish Farming. Freshwater commercial fish farming in the United States has become an increasingly widespread and successful endeavor in recent years. The varieties most commonly raised are catfish, trout, salmon, tilapia, and hybrid striped bass. In addition to these fish, several crustacean species are also increasingly being farmed, primarily crawfish and shrimp. Catfish are raised predominantly in the south and southwest. Trout are raised throughout the country, except in the southern states. Maine and Washington state are the main producers of salmon. Tilapia are produced everywhere in the United States, and they are so adaptable that they have to be raised in tanks so as to avoid possible crowding out of native fish if they escaped from open ponds. Most of the striped bass are raised in the eastern seaboard states south of the mid-Atlantic, though some are raised in California and Texas. Louisiana is the primary producer of crawfish, though the other Gulf states also farm them, as well as shrimp. Most freshwater fish marketed in the fish counters of supermarkets or consumed as fish sandwiches in fast-food outlets are products of these fish farms, as are most crustaceans. Aquaculture is currently the fastest-growing sector of agricultural production in the United States.

Bioluminescence

Luminescence means "light created or emitted at low temperatures, not as a result of burning heat." In nature, there are at least four sources of such light: (1) *mineral phosphorus* (phosphorescence); (2) *radioactive minerals* that respond to or reflect certain wavelengths of light; (3) *cool gases* that can be activated by electricity (fluorescent light); and (4) *bioluminescence*—that is, light created by insects (fireflies), certain fishes of the abyss, and microscopic marine dinoflagellata, a single-celled phytoplankton. It is this fourth source of natural light that we shall talk about here.

The bioluminescence of the sea at night is one of the common and yet curious sights of the sea. It is a bluish-green, often sparkling, glow seen in waters disturbed by bow waves, wakes, and cresting waves. In some areas of the world this luminescence is very bright. When these organisms are stimulated by waves, their rhythmic reaction produces a swirling movement of light, like a pinwheel. In calm conditions, the orbital movement of the seawater creates horizontal streaks where the dinoflagellata tend to concentrate. Oceanographers are constantly expanding their study of such natural bioluminescence in the sea.

For the Navy, this bioluminosity of seawater is more than just an interesting natural occurrence. Observed from the air or from the bridge of a large ship, the luminous wake of a ship or periscope traveling at even moderate speed can be detected for some distance. It can clearly reveal the vessel's position and, roughly, its course and speed. During World War II amphibious landings and other naval movements were on several occasions given away by bioluminescence in the warm waters of the Pacific. Naval oceanographers generally know where heavy bioluminescence regularly occurs and can forecast periods of this phenomenon in areas where naval operations are planned.

Fouling and Deterioration

Of the many important problems with which marine biology is concerned, none has greater economic significance to the Navy and commercial maritime interests than the control of **marine fouling** and deterioration. The effects of marine growth on ships' hulls and their saltwater intakes, valves, and piping are costly. Important also is the damage by marine organisms to the wood, plastics, metal, and concrete of shore installations. For the U.S. Navy alone, the protection and maintenance of ships, waterfront structures, and offshore equipment against biological deterioration and fouling costs many millions of dollars annually. More importantly, such uncontrolled fouling and deterioration can reduce the combat readiness of naval ships and shore facilities.

Constant scientific research has developed chemical agents that have successfully protected hull surfaces for as long as twenty-four months. The problem is far from solved, however. New naval equipment constantly requires the development of better **antifouling agents.**

Biological fouling impairs sonar gear by weakening sound transmissions. In some areas of the world such fouling can make sonar gear unfit for use in just a few months. The problem is complicated by the need to develop an antifouling agent that will not itself degrade the acoustic qualities of the equipment.

Large stationary structures built on the continental shelf for both military and commercial projects have additional fouling problems. Offshore oil-drilling platforms, lighthouses, radar stations, and oceanographic research stations are generally intended to be permanent structures. Fouling and deterioration by bacteria, fungi, and marine animals are serious threats to such platforms.

Submarine cables transmitting telephone and electric power, as well as underwater pipelines, have been attacked by shrimplike animals called **gribbles.** They have gnawed through wooden pilings, rubber, and plastic insulation. The famous *teredo,* or "shipworm," can destroy wooden pilings, burrow into rocks and cement, weaken stone seawalls, and destroy insulation on cables. Teredos have even drilled through solid lead sheathing of submarine power cables laid as deep as 7,200 feet!

Dangerous Marine Life

People generally think of danger at sea as attack by fearsome animals. Actually, animal life in the sea is usually more helpful than harmful. Nevertheless, there are two categories of marine species that can be very dangerous to humans: those that are **carnivorous** and those that are **poisonous,** or **venomous.**

Carnivorous Animals. **Sharks** are the leading carnivores of most marine ecosystems. Of the three hundred species identified, the larger species are the top predators in their environments. Although infrequent, shark attack remains a significant threat for bathers along the world's seacoasts and for people who work in the marine environment.

The danger of being attacked by a shark is exaggerated in the minds of many people. The degree of hazard depends both on the location and on the numbers and condition of the people in the water. Sharks are unpredictable and curious; they will investigate any object in the water. They are likely to attack the dead or the wounded. They have an exceptional ability to detect a disabled or wounded animal at long range. Blood in the water attracts and excites them, through their sense of smell.

The largest of all fish in the ocean is the tropical *whale shark,* which may reach more than forty-five feet in length and weigh several tons. The basking shark and well-known *great white shark,* both found in temperate and tropical waters worldwide, may reach lengths in excess of thirty feet and twenty feet, respectively. The tiger shark averages about ten feet in length but may reach as much as twenty feet.

Sharks are found in all oceans from 45 degrees north to 45 degrees south latitude. The danger of shark attack appears to be greatest in tropical and subtropical areas between latitudes of 30 degrees north and 30 degrees south. In 2013 there were a total of seventy-two documented unprovoked shark attacks worldwide, with ten of these fatal. The United States had forty-seven attacks, with twenty-three in Florida, thirteen in Hawaii, six in South Carolina, and one each in North Carolina, Alabama, Texas, California, and Oregon. Although shark attacks can result in serious injury, they are seldom fatal except when the victim is small.

The sharks considered most dangerous to people are the great white shark, considered the most dangerous of all; the *tiger shark,* probably the most common of tropical sharks; the

A great white shark. *Terry Goss w/modifications by César*

sand shark, native to East Indian waters; and the *hammerhead shark,* found throughout the oceans in both tropical and temperate zones.

When sharks are present, people should not dangle arms or legs in the water. Injured swimmers should be removed from the water quickly. Any flow of blood should be stopped as quickly as possible. Dark clothing and equipment are safest for swimmers. All movements should be slow and purposeful, to avoid attracting sharks; if sharks appear, swimmers should remain perfectly still. Some sharks have departed when struck on the snout, but this should be done only as a last resort, because it could aggravate the shark instead.

Barracuda are extremely dangerous. They may reach six to eight feet long. They have knifelike canine teeth and, being swift swimmers, strike rapidly and ferociously. They are feared more than sharks in some areas of the West Indies. Found off the Florida coasts and in the Indian and Pacific Oceans, they are attracted by almost any bright or colored object in the water and attack quickly. Because of the poor visibility, they can be especially dangerous in murky coastal waters, where they will attack at the slightest movement.

Killer whales are found throughout the oceans, from the Arctic to the Antarctic. They are nearly fearless. They reach a length of from fifteen to thirty feet. In packs, they often attack much larger whales. They are very swift swimmers, seeking out seals, walruses, and penguins as prey. Despite their name, attacks against people are rare and are thought to be the result of confusion with their natural prey. The only defense against the killer whale is a hasty retreat from the water.

Moray eels have narrow, powerful jaws with knifelike teeth. They may reach a length of ten feet. They can inflict severe cuts or may hold a bulldog-like grip until either they are killed or their victim is dead. They dwell mostly in crevices and holes under rocks and coral in tropical and subtropical seas. Morays seldom attack unless provoked, so it is very wise not to poke

around in places where they may be lurking. They are common along the California coast.

The **giant devil ray,** or **manta ray,** may reach a spread of twenty feet and a weight of 3,500 pounds. They have a wide range in the topical seas. They are very curious and may investigate air bubbles of divers, possibly getting entangled in air hoses. They have a very coarse skin, which will produce severe abrasion on contact. Otherwise, they usually do not injure humans.

Stinging Animals. Poisonous marine invertebrates that inflict injury by stinging are divided into four main groups:

- Corals, sea anemones, hydroids, and jellyfish
- Mollusks, including octopi and certain shellfish
- Bloodworms and bristleworms
- Sea urchins.

Corals and **sea anemones** have stinging cells that are used to capture food or to repel enemies. These cells inject a paralyzing drug into the victims, causing illnesses among skin divers, sponge fishermen, and other marine workers. This group includes the elk horn coral of the West Indies and rosy sea anemones of the Atlantic. Coral cuts and stings are very painful and slow to heal, and they often become ulcerated. The wounds should be promptly cleaned and any particles removed.

The **hydroids** include poisonous invertebrates like the **Portuguese man-of-war,** often wrongly called a jellyfish. The Portuguese man-of-war floats on the surface of all tropical oceans and the Mediterranean Sea. Its tentacles trail many feet into the water and can give painful stings. The fire coral, a false coral that is sometimes called stinging coral, is found among true corals in the warm waters of the tropical Pacific, Caribbean Sea, and Indian Ocean. Most **jellyfish** look like big, white, wispy mushrooms. They swim by water-jet propulsion at many depths in the oceans. The sea wasp of the tropical seas, especially those of the Australian, Philippine, and Indian Ocean areas, are extremely dangerous. Often they are seen in huge numbers in the South China Sea. The sea wasp jellyfish in particular is very venomous. It can cause death in three to eight minutes. Symptoms are almost immediate shock, muscular cramps, loss of sensation, nausea, constriction of the throat, paralysis, convulsions, and, finally, death.

Swimmers who brush against the Portuguese man-of-war and jellyfish may be stung by their threadlike tentacles. Sting symptoms vary from a mild prickly sensation to a throbbing pain that can render the victim unconscious. Pain may remain in the area of the sting or radiate to the armpit or abdomen. There may be redness and swelling, blistering, or small skin hemorrhaging. There are no specific antidotes, but washing with diluted ammonia or alcohol and swabbing with mineral oil or baking soda may help.

There are two members of the **mollusk** group with a venomous sting or bite: (1) those with spirally twisted single shells,

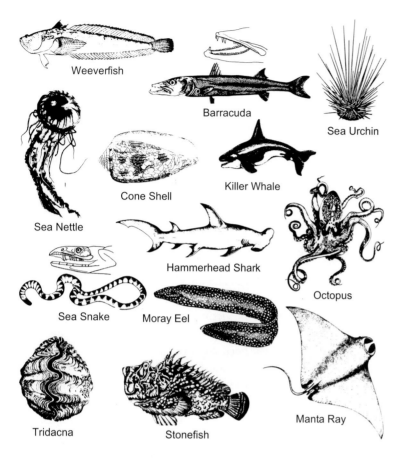

Weeverfish

Barracuda

Sea Urchin

Cone Shell

Killer Whale

Sea Nettle

Hammerhead Shark

Octopus

Sea Snake   Moray Eel

Tridacna   Stonefish

Manta Ray

Some of the more dangerous sea animals.

rot-like beaks and well-developed venom apparatus. They can move rapidly underwater by water-jet propulsion. Fortunately, these perilous-looking animals are timid. Octopi hide in holes in the coral and among rocks of the continental shelves. They are curious but very cautious. The fear of being grabbed by eight choking arms is unfounded. The danger of the octopus is its bite, and a small one can cause as much venom damage as a large one. Bites usually occur when captured specimens are being handled. Bleeding from a bite is profuse, because clotting is retarded by the venom. A burning sensation, nausea, and swelling are likely. With appropriate treatment and rest, the victim usually recovers in a short time.

The **bloodworm** and **bristleworm** have tufted, silky bristles in a row along each side. These bristles can penetrate the skin in the same manner as cactus spines. Their strong jaws can also inflict a painful bite. The bristles and bite of a bloodworm result in a pale area that becomes hot, swollen, and numb or itchy. Bristleworm irritation may last several days. Bristles are best removed with a forceps or by placing adhesive tape over the bristles and pulling them out. Scraping will break them off and may cause infection. The wound should be rubbed with alcohol to soothe discomfort.

Sea urchins are found in large numbers in coastal waters. They have a round body covered with needle-sharp spines, many of them poisonous. They are a danger to swimmers, waders, and divers. The spines, poisonous or not, can inflict deep puncture wounds. Those with poison are long, slender, sharp, and hollow, enabling them to penetrate deeply into the flesh. They are extremely brittle and are likely to break off. The tip of the spine has tiny pincers and a sense bristle that releases the venom. This apparatus will continue to inject poison into the victim for several hours after breaking away from the sea urchin.

Penetration of the skin produces an immediate burning sensation. Redness, swelling, and generalized aching are likely to follow, and deaths from muscular paralysis have been reported.

Vertebrate marine animals that have venomous bites and stings include a number of fishes and sea snakes. Sea snakes were discussed earlier in this chapter. The fishes fall into a number of species: the stingrays, catfish, weeverfish, and scorpionfish.

Stingrays are much-feared flat fish found in warm coastal waters. They may grow to weigh several hundred pounds. They are a serious menace to waders. They lie on the bottom, largely concealed by sand and mud. Stepping on one will cause the ray to drive a venomous barbed tail into the wader's foot or leg with great force. The spines may be driven completely through a

such as snails; and (2) those with no shell, such as the octopus and squid. Those with cone-shaped shells are potentially dangerous. They have a head with one or two pairs of tentacles and a flattened, fleshy foot. Cone shells are favorites of shell collectors. There are some four hundred species, and most have a fully developed venom apparatus. They are found in tropical waters of the Pacific and Indian Oceans and in the Red Sea. They are common on the beaches of the Pacific islands.

The venom apparatus of the cone shell lies near the shell opening. The round teeth at the end of a tubelike appendage are thrust into the victim, and the venom is forced under pressure into the wound. The sting usually produces numbness and tingling, which quickly spread, becoming especially noticeable about the lips and mouth. Paralysis and coma may follow, and finally death as the result of heart failure. Cone shell wounds must be quickly cleaned and suction applied to remove poison. Antibiotics may be desirable. The patient should be kept warm. Stimulants may be required, and hospitalization is recommended.

The octopus has eight arms or tentacles, the squid and cuttlefish ten, around a muscular central body mass. They have par-

foot or well into the leg bone of the victim. The stingray wound causes immediate shooting pain. The wound area will swell and become gray, later red. Severe stings by large specimens can be deadly.

There are about a thousand species of **catfish** in the world. Some of the salt-water catfish are venomous. Their venom glands are located in the sheath of the dorsal and pectoral spines. Some species have curved barbs on the ends of the spines, to make venom absorption more certain. Some freshwater catfishes are delicious to eat, but salt-water catfishes are not often eaten. They usually inhabit rivers, open reef areas, estuaries, and large sandy bays. They are common all along the eastern seaboard, the Gulf of Mexico, India, the Philippines, and Indonesia.

A wound from a catfish spine results in instant stinging and throbbing. The pain may radiate or remain local, numbing an arm or leg. Asian catfish can inflict violently painful wounds that may fester for forty-eight hours and then result in gangrene and death. There are no known antidotes for catfish and other poisonous-fish stings.

Weeverfish are very venomous animals of the temperate zone. They are aggressive, small (less than eighteen inches long) marine fishes. They inhabit sandy or muddy bays. They bury themselves in the mud, with only their heads exposed. With little provocation, they will dart out with poisonous fins erect and strike with unerring accuracy, driving their spines into the victim. The victim suffers instant stabbing pain after being struck. Within thirty minutes, the pain becomes so severe that the victim may scream and thrash about wildly, then lose consciousness and die. The venom attacks both the nervous and blood systems. Immediate first aid and treatment by a doctor may save the patient's life. Recovery takes several months, depending on the condition of the patient and the amount of venom received. There is no antivenom.

The great weever is found along western Africa, in the Mediterranean Sea, and around the British Isles and Norway. The lesser weever inhabits the North Sea, southward along the European coast, and the Mediterranean.

The **scorpionfish** family comprises the most poisonous of all fishes. There are three main groups: zebrafish, scorpionfish, and stonefish. The sting of any of these fish will produce serious results. The deadliness of some of the stonefishes may be ranked with that of the cobra.

The *zebrafish,* also called lionfish, is a beautiful shallow-water fish of tropical and temperate seas. It lives around coral reefs, spreading its fanlike, lacy fins like peacocks. They are usually found in pairs. Beneath the beauty are hidden as many as eighteen long, straight, needle-sharp fin spines. Each spine is equipped with lethal venom. These fish are a menace to anyone exploring tropical coral areas.

The *scorpionfish* inhabits shallow water bays and reefs in the Pacific Ocean. These fishes conceal themselves in crevices among debris, under rocks, or in seaweed. They have nearly perfect protective coloration that makes them almost invisible. When alerted or removed from the water, they erect poisonous spines like zebrafish do.

Stonefish of the Pacific Ocean are found in tide pools and shoal areas. They are hard to see, because they usually lie motionless and partly buried in the mud or sand. They are not afraid of any intrusion in their area, making them a danger to anyone with bare feet. The fish is a mud-brown color and warty like a toad. It has thirteen dorsal, three bottom, and two pelvic spines, all short and heavy, with enlarged venom glands.

Symptoms produced by the scorpionfish family may vary in severity, but the pain is immediate, sharp, and radiates quickly. Pain may cause a victim to thrash about in a wild manner, scream, or lose consciousness. The immediate wound area may be pale, surrounded by a zone of redness, swelling, and heat. Paralysis of an entire arm or leg may result. Death is the usual result of an encounter. A sting should be treated like a snake bite. In some cases the victim may recover after months of treatment, but with impaired general health.

People swimming where scorpionfish live must be alert to the danger and absolutely avoid touching them. Since the species are generally fearless, one should not aggravate them, as they will attack. A direct encounter with any of the scorpionfish is an invitation to disaster.

Underwater Research

In order to see firsthand what goes on in the sea, oceanographers for many years have sought ways to observe the depths. The lack of air, tremendous underwater pressure, utter darkness, and cold have all combined to prevent researchers from descending into the deep ocean and remaining for an extended time. Only in recent years have people succeeded in exploring the sea in meaningful ways. New individual diving gear and methods and advanced undersea research vehicles continue to be developed and successfully operated. They are opening up a whole new scientific frontier.

The traditional deep-diving rubber-canvas suit with metal helmet and lead-filled shoes has given way to two modern types of suits called the *dry suit* and the *hot water suit.* The former is used for cold water dives to moderate depths, and is made of either fabric or neoprene rubber. It has integral boots and is sealed to a diving helmet with a self-contained air supply. Hot water suits are used in deep cold water diving where the air supply is received via an umbilical hose from the surface, along with a continuous supply of heated water to maintain the diver's body heat. Such suits allow professional divers to dive and work at depths ranging to 1,000 feet or more. For even deeper dives a suit called an *atmospheric diving suit,* or ADS, is worn. It consists of an exoskeleton-like suit of armor, supplied with air from

A scuba diver. *NOAA*

The Navy's oceanographic research FLIP (floating instrument platform) ship. It is towed out to a research site, then "flipped" into a vertical position, as shown here, by flooding the stern. The crew's quarters in the bow remain above water, and all equipment and furnishings inside are on swivels so they remain horizontal regardless of the ship's inclination. *CHINFO*

The deep submergence vehicle Alvin (DSV-2) is a research submersible owned by the Navy and operated by the Woods Hole Oceanographic Institution. It is capable of carrying a three-person crew to depths of 21,000 feet. *CHINFO*

the surface at normal atmospheric pressure, which allows divers to reach and work at depths of up to 2,000 feet.

For shallower dives in moderate water temperatures the **self-contained underwater breathing apparatus (SCUBA)** is used. A qualified scuba diver can carry his or her own compressed air tanks and swim freely, if careful, down to two hundred feet or more. A scuba diver normally uses flippers and a mask, and wears a Spandex or Lycra wetsuit for cool water or deeper dives for extended underwater periods. Scuba divers using special breathing gas mixtures can dive to 500 feet or more for short periods.

For much deeper human exploration, the oceanographer Auguste Piccard developed the **bathyscaphe** in 1948. The name comes from two Greek words, *bathy* meaning "deep" and *scaph* meaning "boat." The bathyscaphe is a free-moving underwater research vessel that is somewhat like a submarine. When under the sea, scientists in bathyscaphes can look through strengthened glass ports at an underwater world illuminated by pow-

erful waterproof lights. They can take photos, collect samples with mechanical arms, and stay at great depths for long periods of time.

Another very interesting vessel is the **FLIP (floating instrument platform) ship.** This research platform can flip from a horizontal position to a vertical one. The bow, carrying a marine laboratory, remains fifty feet in the air when the craft assumes a vertical position, while the stern, containing various measuring and sounding instruments, is plunged three hundred feet below the surface. All of the furniture and equipment in the laboratory section is mounted on gimbals, so it stays upright and level during the flip operation. When on station it can support a crew of as many as sixteen.

Another Navy project has been the development of a **deep submergence rescue vessel (DSRV)** to be used in case of submarine accidents.

The Navy has also conducted extensive underwater-living experiments. These have included **underwater habitats**—living and research quarters—where underwater scientists called **aquanauts** have learned to live for long periods at great depths.

In recent years increasing use has been made of remote-controlled, self-propelled exploration vehicles fitted with TV cameras, lights, and a variety of other sensors and grappling devices. Many are capable of operation at great depths, have produced amazing video shots, and have recovered artifacts of sunken ships, such as the famous passenger ship *Titanic* and the German battleship *Bismarck*.

The Threat of Pollution

Human beings are consumers of vast quantities of raw materials and fuels. A tremendous amount of waste material results from this use—individual, societal, industrial, and accidental.

A large part of this waste finds its way into the sea. Fortunately, only a small percentage of this consists of pollutants. **Pollutants** are substances that damage marine processes or cause loss of an ocean resource or restrict its use. Some pollutants interfere with the life processes of marine organisms and reduce biological productivity of the oceans. Others, including oil and litter, are dangerous to people, interfere with recreational activities, or detract from the beauty of the seascape.

It is impossible to completely stop pollution of the oceans. It may be possible to stop pollution of some inland lakes and rivers and to significantly reduce it in others. But the mere fact that people use raw materials makes it impossible to eliminate waste materials. The real issue is what level of pollutants society is willing to accept. This depends directly on the amount of money, research, and effort people are willing to put into reduction and control of individual and industrial waste.

Seven main groups of pollutants presently affect the marine environment and cause international concern: (1) petroleum; (2) heavy metals; (3) radioactive materials; (4) chemical and synthetic fuels, solvents, and pesticides; (5) litter; (6) organic pollutants; and (7) biological pollutants.

Petroleum. Each year, it is estimated that more than 700 million gallons of **petroleum** (oil products) finds its way into the world's oceans. About half of this is oily waste from land. About 20 percent comes from routine ship maintenance, such as fuel-tank cleaning and pumping of bilges (void spaces) and ballast (water taken on to improve stability). Some 13 percent is in the form of *hydrocarbon particles* (oil components containing hydrogen and carbon) blown out to sea from air pollution over land, and the remainder is leakage from oil drilling and production operations and natural seepage from the ocean bottoms.

Unfortunately, scenes like this contaminated Louisiana shore after the BP *Deepwater Horizon* oil spill in 2010 have been all too common on beaches throughout the world in recent years. *Louisiana GOHSEP*

Additionally, there have been terrible spills from undersea oil rigs in the North Sea, the Gulf of Mexico, the California coast, and elsewhere.

The worst oil spill in history was the BP *Deepwater Horizon* oil spill, which occurred in the Gulf of Mexico about forty miles off the Louisiana coast from 20 April to 15 July 2010, when the broken wellhead was finally capped. It happened following an explosion and fire on the drilling platform, 5,100 feet above the well. The resulting oil slick covered nearly 70,000 square miles in the Gulf and contaminated hundreds of miles of Gulf Shore beaches from Texas to Florida. An estimated 4.9 million barrels (210 million gallons) of crude oil were released. The ensuing cleanup efforts have cost billions of dollars to date, and the effects are still in evidence years later.

An oil slick on the high seas can kill plankton in the surface zone, but in general it will dissipate over a period of time. Often it gathers in tarlike balls that eventually sink to the bottom. While such "oil litter" can do no good, it probably does not do much permanent harm either. However, when such an oil slick reaches shore or collects in harbors, coves, or bays, the results are disastrous for seabirds, mollusks, and other shallow-water life. Also, a major oil spill will devastate the economy of a beach resort area and any fishing industry that may be based there.

The Navy's major pollution problem in harbors, ports, channels, and U.S. waters is the discharge of oils and oily wastes. The Navy has an active program to eliminate all such pollution and works closely with the Environmental Protection Agency and the Coast Guard in this effort.

Heavy Metals. The sea's main **heavy metal pollutants** are mercury and, to a lesser extent, barium. These metals are dis-

Fire crews fight fires on the BP *Deepwater Horizon* oil-drilling platform in the Gulf of Mexico in April 2010. The riser pipe 5,100 feet below the rig was severed and the installed blow-out preventer failed, causing leakage of about 60,000 barrels of crude oil a day into the gulf for nearly three months. *USCG*

charged in the effluent from chemical plants, cement works, and other manufacturing processes, a flow that doubles their natural accumulation in the sea. As a result, increased traces of *mercury* have been found in shellfish and other fish species throughout the world, including the Arctic Ocean and the Great Lakes. Sea life, especially shellfish, absorbs the mercury. Fish, oysters, and clams retain mercury, and it continues to build up, never being cast off. In certain coastal areas near where the pollution enters the water, dangerous concentrations occur in the fish. This can cause **mercury poisoning** in humans if they eat the contaminated fish. Periodically in recent years there have been several prohibitions issued by various governments around the world against eating certain kinds of fish and other seafood because of unsafe levels of mercury found in them.

Radioactive Materials. Since World War II, many countries have begun to develop nuclear power plants and fuel-processing facilities to help solve their energy shortages. In theory such plants and facilities can be made safe from leaks, so they will not contaminate nearby land and water environments. The fact is that the cost for so doing is very high, and accidents have occurred. Increasing amounts of **radioactive pollutants** have found their way into the water. One of the worst such cases in recent years was the meltdown of three nuclear-power-plant reactors at Fukushima, on the northeastern coast of the large island of Honshu, Japan, in March 2011, following a large offshore earthquake and tsunami. Much radiation was released onto the land and into adjacent waters of the Pacific Ocean. It took months to accomplish the preliminary cleanup, and at this writing many former residents are still prohibited from returning to their homes there. Some seawater containing elevated levels of radioactive cesium has been detected amongst the debris fields resulting from the catastrophe, making their way across the Pacific toward the United States and Canada.

Much concern has arisen over **radioactive waste products** and reactor parts dumped into the seas over the years. In some cases old sunken sealed drums of radioactive wastes have corroded and leaked, causing contamination of local fish populations. Most countries with nuclear capabilities have agreed to dispose of future wastes in land dumps, as the result of international accords dealing with this issue.

Chemical and Synthetic Compounds. Chlorine, fluorine, bromine, and iodine are proving very dangerous to marine life. These compounds fall into two main groups: (1) **pesticides** and **herbicides,** such as DDT and other chemical weed and insect killers; and (2) the **biphenols,** such as aerosol propellants, solvents, refrigerants, and cleaning agents.

DDT is known to cause reproductive problems in some marine birds. The brown pelican, for instance, is an endangered species in some areas now. When the pelicans eat fish that have absorbed DDT from field and river runoff into coastal bays, their eggs have flimsy shells that break in the nest. Likewise,

the American bald eagle was on the Endangered Species List for some three decades until 2007, by which time the reduction of use of DDT beginning in the early 1970s made possible a comeback.

Most of the adult fish in the Great Lakes have absorbed pesticide and herbicide runoff from farmlands along the rivers that drain into the lakes. Pesticides often kill the eggs and small fry and so have greatly reduced the natural reproduction of game fish in streams, rivers, and ponds, especially in the upper Midwest and in the Great Lakes states. As a result, these states now have to restock their waters annually from fish hatcheries in order to sustain fish populations.

Pesticides running off from farmlands can eventually find their way into drinking water. In some recent studies more than sixty agricultural pesticides were found in the drinking water of people in fourteen states in the mid-Atlantic and southeastern regions. Especially high concentrations were found in parts of Maryland and Virginia that border on the Chesapeake Bay. Prolonged exposure to such contamination can cause cancer in humans.

Litter. **Marine litter** is solid waste of society and ships at sea. It is trucked, barged, and then dumped into rivers and into the oceans at a rate of more than six million tons each year. The ocean floor and coastal areas are littered with this debris. Much of it consists of **packing materials**—plastic, aluminum, wood, and glass—all of which may take centuries or longer to be broken down by the salts of the sea. Much of this litter is not **biodegradable.** In other words, it will never naturally decay and break down. Beaches all over the world are cluttered with this trash, some of which floats to the farthest corners of Earth. It is unsightly, and a hazard to swimmers and small craft navigation. It clogs harbors, and it may destroy the natural habitat of shorebirds and animals. It also congregates in the centers of the great ocean gyres, resulting in growing islands of floating plastic waste materials in the center of the North Atlantic and North Pacific Oceans.

In 1987 an international agreement was put into effect that limits dumping of many types of waste products at sea, including a total ban on the disposal of plastic in the Gulf of Mexico. Although this act helped reduce beach debris worldwide, marine mammals, reptiles, birds, and other sea life continue to sustain injuries by ingesting or becoming tangled in this kind of debris.

One of the worst instances of seaborne debris in history occurred as a result of the major earthquake and associated tsunami that hit Honshu in 2011 (described above). The resulting huge debris field has made its way slowly across the Pacific, impacting the Hawaiian Islands beginning in 2012 and later many beaches on the west coasts of Canada and the United States. Much of it still remains at sea and will undoubtedly continue to wash ashore for many years to come.

On the sea bottom, however, some of this trash actually helps create habitats for plant and animal life. Obsolete ships, car bodies and tires, and cement blocks, among other things, have been used to make **artificial reefs** that are eventually covered by marine growth. The vegetation brings fish, and a flourishing cycle of sea life is created where previously there may have been none. This beneficial result of litter, however, is unique and differs greatly from its usual effect on the environment.

Organic Pollutants. Organic pollutants such as raw sewage and fertilizer are especially troublesome in enclosed water areas. They contain high levels of nutrients that promote rapid plankton and algae growth, in both fresh and salt water. This uses up the available oxygen, upsetting the natural ecosystem. In the United States federal laws prohibiting dumping of sewage and sewage sludge into the oceans were passed in 1972 and 1988. They did much to eliminate the practice after the 1990s, but the problem persists in other areas of the world. Many coastal areas, especially along the shores of the Mediterranean, have been contaminated by unprocessed sewage flow. Coastal wetlands have become "dead" areas, choked with algae and filled with disease-bearing bacteria. When such areas are destroyed, either by raw sewage or by draining, filling, or reclamation projects, devastating blows are struck to the natural reproductive capacity of marine wildlife. Runoff of fertilizers applied to farmlands near waterways emptying into the sea cause many of the same problems as those associated with sewage contamination.

To help prevent pollution of inland waterways and harbors, Navy ships are equipped with one or both of two types of sewage systems: (1) **marine sanitation devices (MSDs),** which enable sewage to be treated before it is discharged from the ship; and (2) **collection, holding, and transfer systems (CHTs),** which collect and hold sewage until it can be transferred ashore in port or pumped overboard in unrestricted waters beyond the territorial limits (at least twelve miles from shore). Many commercial ships and most U.S. pleasure craft are fitted with similar equipment.

Biological Pollutants. Besides the foregoing types of waste pollution, in recent years various kinds of **biological pollutants** have also caused concern. These include both animal and plant organisms that find their way into bilge and ballast water of ships visiting foreign ports, which is then discharged into coastal and inland waters of the United States. Once released into our waterways, these organisms can grow and spread without bound, owing to the absence of any effective control mechanisms that may be present in their native environments.

Two such instances of great concern in the 1990s were the introduction of the **Zebra mollusk** into the Great Lakes and various rivers, such as the upper Mississippi and Susquehanna, by ships arriving from Europe, and a type of sprawling marine weed, called **hydrilla,** that chokes out native vegetation in coastal waters of states from Connecticut to Texas. More recently, an aggressive fish native to Africa and Asia called the **northern snakehead,** which can survive for up to four days out of water on land, was discovered in waters of Hawaii and six other of the lower forty-eight states in the early 2000s. Although it has value as a food fish, if it establishes itself in North America it would have no natural predators and would eventually eliminate many species of food and game fish in U.S. inland waters.

What Is the Answer?

One thing is very clear. If ocean pollution continues at its present pace, the sea, instead of becoming the aquaculture garden of the future, could become a **biological desert.** This would have grave consequences for a world that is going to become increasingly dependent on the sea for food and mineral resources. Instead of becoming a living and recreation area for millions, it could become a polluted, stagnant pool. Wastes that are disposed of in the sea must be treated before dumping so they will not pollute. We must learn to recycle wastes. We must pass effective and practical laws and then enforce them. Life on earth is dependent on the sea and will increasingly continue to be so.

There is still much reason to hope. People are gradually learning about the importance of our relationship with the sea and the ecological balance that exists between the sea, the land, and all plant and animal life. All nations together must develop an international policy that will protect the common heritage of humanity.

Critical Thinking

1. Research the areas in the world in which the major fisheries are located and the status of the yearly catch of fish in these areas. What can be done to increase the yields of food fish in these areas over the next twenty years?

2. What are some techniques and strategies that can be used to reduce the amount of pollution now found in the major ocean basins of the world?

3. Much concern has arisen in recent years over an apparent increase in the rate and severity of shark attacks of swimmers in the coastal areas of the United States, particularly along the Florida seacoast. Do you think the rate of such attacks has in fact increased over the last several years, and if so, what do you think are the primary causes of this phenomenon?

Study Guide Questions

1. What is marine biology?

2. In what areas does marine biology have a direct impact upon naval matters?

3. What are the two basic families of plankton in the seas?

4. A. What is upwelling?
   B. What is the effect of El Niño?

5. What oceanographic phenomenon has given the Red Sea its name?

6. Why has the Black Sea been so named?

7. Describe the steps in the marine food cycle.

8. What are some of the unique characteristics of marine animals that live in the deep sea (abyss)?

9. What are some special characteristics of sea animals living at the edge of the sea?

10. A. What are the smallest animals of the zooplankton group?
    B. The largest?

11. A. What two important conservation laws were enacted by the United States in the 1970s?
    B. What are the major provisions of each?

12. What are the four groups of marine animals with jaws?

13. A. What are the four groups of living marine reptiles?
    B. Where are the most dangerous of these animals found?

14. What part of the world is the penguin's native habitat?

15. A. What are the three groups of seals?
    B. Which are protected by hunting laws?

16. A. What are the two main groups of whales?
    B. What is the main difference between the two groups?

17. A. Why is the Sargasso Sea so named?
    B. Why is this area almost a "desert" in the sea?

18. What are three things that can help increase food production from the sea?

19. To date, what types of ocean fish or shellfish have proved to be most successful in aquafarming?

20. A. What is bioluminescence?
    B. What causes it?
    C. How can this phenomenon affect naval operations?

21. What is the most serious effect of marine fouling and deterioration for the Navy?

22. What are the two categories of marine species that can be dangerous to people?

23. What are the four groups of stinging marine animals that can injure humans?

24. What are the four species of poisonous fish that are particularly dangerous to people?

25. A. What does SCUBA stand for?
    B. Before divers use scuba gear, what qualifications should they have?

26. What is the purpose of a bathyscaphe?

27. What are the seven main groups of sea pollutants?

28. A. What are the main causes of petroleum pollution in the sea?
    B. Where is the most damage caused by an oil spill?

29. What is the particular danger of heavy metal pollution?

30. How does pollution by synthetic compounds affect natural reproduction of seabirds and animals?

31. How do radioactive pollutants affect marine life and humans?

32. How does domestic sewage and fertilizer runoff upset the natural ecosystem in enclosed water areas?

33. What are three instances of biological pollution that have found their way into U.S. waters in recent years?

New Vocabulary

marine biology
ecology
plankton
phytoplankton
food chain
nutrients
zooplankton
upwelling
guano
hydrogen sulfide
life cycle
photosynthesis
chlorophyll
predator
algae
diatoms
kelp
protozoan
banks (water bodies)
aquaculture
oyster
mussel
crustacean
luminescence
antifouling agents
poisonous
venomous
jellyfish
larva, larvae
lamprey
brackish water
flukes

baleen whale
endangered species
habitat
purse seiner
aquaculture
oyster bed clutch
bioluminescence
marine fouling
gribbles
teredo worm
carnivorous
ecosystem
hydroid
mollusks
sea urchin
vertebrate
stingray
dorsal
aquanaut
pollution
biological desert
ballast water
radioactive
pesticide
biphenols
litter
biodegradeable
scopionfish
SCUBA
bathyscaphe
FLIP ship
DSRV

UNIT 3

Meteorology

The men and women who "go down to the sea in ships" fight a continuous battle with the elements. At sea the safety of a ship and her crew can depend on action taken to avoid the full fury of a storm. Extra measures are taken well in advance of approaching bad weather to minimize damage to the ship, her gear, and her cargo.

We have all heard the statement "Everybody talks about the weather, but nobody does anything about it." In the past this statement may have been true, but not today. **Meteorology**—the science of weather—is helping to make our lives safer and easier. Storm forecasts and weather warnings are much more accurate than they have ever been before. A network of weather stations provides information for safe commercial and military flights.

Today **weather satellites** in orbit above Earth provide worldwide meteorological information used in weather prediction and scientific research. Agricultural weather services help farmers plan for planting, harvesting, and marketing. Meteorology enables aircraft to take advantage of air currents, and this improves fuel conservation and flight time. There have even been successful experiments in inducing rain. Also, **meteorologists** (scientists who study weather) are exploring ways to break up dangerous tropical cyclones and tornadoes before they can reach populated areas. Yes, something is being done about the weather!

7

Our Atmosphere

It is not possible to understand much about weather without having a fundamental knowledge of the atmosphere around us. We live at the bottom of a vast ocean of air that completely covers the Earth. This atmosphere has major layers up to about a thousand miles above Earth's surface, though it is believed that traces of gaseous elements, such as helium, are present as far out as 18,000 miles.

Our atmosphere is a mixture of different gases. Near the surface of the Earth, the air is made up of approximately 78 percent nitrogen, 21 percent oxygen, and 1 percent argon and other gases, such as carbon dioxide, hydrogen, and neon. Within the atmosphere is scattered about 1 percent water vapor, called **humidity**. The amount of water vapor is greater in equatorial regions and less in the polar regions.

It is interesting to compare the water ocean with the air "ocean." Water, for instance, is nearly incompressible. A cubic foot of surface water weighs about the same as a cubic foot taken from the bottom of the Marianas Trench. But this is not the case with a cubic foot of air taken from different altitudes. The higher one goes, the lighter the air becomes and consequently the more easily compressed it is.

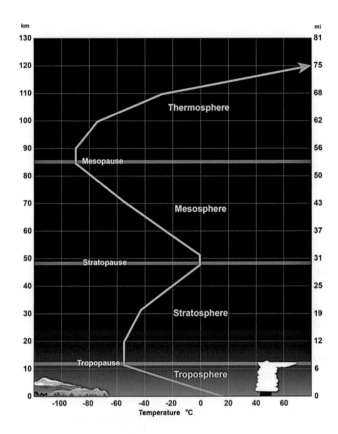

A chart showing the principal layers of the Earth's atmosphere, their boundary layers, and the temperature variation with altitude. The ionosphere extends from above the stratosphere to the thermosphere. *NOAA*

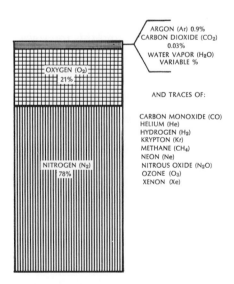

Composition of the Earth's atmosphere. By volume it is composed of about 21 percent oxygen and 78 percent nitrogen, with the remaining 1 percent made up of carbon dioxide, hydrogen, helium, and traces of the rare gases, such as neon, argon, krypton, and xenon.

The atmosphere thins so rapidly that over half of the total atmosphere by weight is in the first three and a half miles. It is within this "air envelope" that almost all of Earth's weather occurs. By the time a balloon has ascended to twenty miles, it has left 99 percent of the atmospheric weight and gases below. Beyond forty-five miles, only helium and hydrogen are present, in very tiny amounts. Within the air envelope, then, lies the tempestuous air ocean, constantly churning and mixing the gases we breathe. Here are all the winds, clouds, rains, and storms that make the weather.

The atmosphere consists of five principal layers. From the Earth's surface outward into space, they are the troposphere, stratosphere, mesosphere, thermosphere, and exosphere. There are also transition zones of vital importance between some of these layers. The tropopause lies between the troposphere and the stratosphere; the chemosphere, or ozone layer, lies mainly between the stratosphere and mesosphere. The ionosphere is the whole area encompassing the mesosphere and the thermosphere. Overlapping the exosphere is the magnetosphere, formed by the interaction of the solar wind with the Earth's magnetic field. In the following sections we will talk about each of these important layers and transition zones.

Troposphere

The **troposphere** is the ocean of air immediately above the Earth's surface. It extends to a height of about eleven miles above the equator, about seven and a half miles in the temperate zones, and only about five miles above the poles. Currents, storms, and waves occur in this air ocean, much as in the seas. Air in the troposphere is constantly turning over. In fact, *tropos* is a Greek word meaning "changing," or "turning." In the troposphere, the temperature and composition of gases change rapidly.

Nearly all clouds are in the troposphere, so it is here that weather occurs. Air heated by the Earth rises, in a process called *convection,* and is replaced by cooler air descending from higher altitudes. As the hot air rises, the pressure decreases, and the air expands, becoming less dense. When it rises, if it cools sufficiently, the moisture in it will condense into clouds and then perhaps into rain or snow. The whole process is determined by the simplest of the laws of gases—expansion is a cooling process, while compression generates heat.

The average temperature of the air at sea level is about 56 degrees F. At the top of the troposphere the temperature is about –60 degrees F. The air cools about five and a half degrees for each thousand feet it travels upward; the reverse occurs in descent.

Air circulation in the troposphere is of great importance to us, because the circulation of air masses determines our weather. As a result, accurate weather prediction is dependent upon a thorough understanding of air movement in the troposphere. Intense study of the atmosphere in recent years has proved that the swift movement of cold-air masses about the vast Antarctic continent is a major factor in determining the world's weather. This is one of the main reasons why many nations, including the United States, have had a continuing interest in Antarctic research.

Tropopause

The **tropopause** is the transitional zone between the troposphere and the near void of the stratosphere. It starts just above the troposphere, at altitudes of from five to eleven miles, and it is divided into three overlapping areas: tropical, extratropical, and Arctic tropopauses. The area between 20,000 and 40,000 feet is of importance to air navigation. This is where the **jet stream** is located, a current of air that moves swiftly from west to east around the Earth. The jet stream is most prominent above the extratropical and Arctic tropopause overlaps.

The jet stream was discovered in World War II, when B-29 bombers flying about four miles high found great assistance from westerly winds of up to 300 mph. Planes were able to get into this stream and greatly increase ground speed, thus shortening flight time and conserving fuel. Staying out of these currents on the return trip also saved time and fuel.

The jet streams have now been charted seasonally, as well as geographically. It has been found that these winds are strongest over Japan and the New England states. Three major jet streams move over the North American continent in winter. One of them nearly blankets the United States. Information on the jet streams is especially significant to commercial airlines, which use the information in plotting their flight plans.

There is a direct relationship between the jet streams and lower atmospheric air masses. Meteorologists have found that the jet streams move with the cool air masses near the Earth's surface. Thus in winter the streams are over the temperate zones, where American and Eurasian pilots can take advantage of them. However, in summer the jet streams move much farther north, out of most of the main commercial air lanes.

Stratosphere

The **stratosphere** lies just above the tropopause and extends to an altitude of about thirty miles. There is almost no weather here, because the air is too thin to create clouds. The temperature in the stratosphere drops much more slowly than in the lower layer. In fact, the temperature averages a fairly constant –40 to –50 degrees F and actually begins to get warmer in the upper limits. By the time a pilot has reached the stratosphere, about three-fourths of the weight of the atmosphere is below the aircraft. Modern commercial aircraft seek to fly in the stratosphere when not using the jet streams, because there is so much less air resistance. This makes much better fuel mileage possible. Pilots also favor this flight level because there is no turbulence and they can fly at top speeds.

A very important transition zone within the stratosphere is the **ozone layer** (sometimes called the *chemosphere*), extending upward into the ionosphere from about twelve to nineteen miles above Earth. *Ozone* is a form of oxygen molecule composed of three atoms of oxygen, rather than the two in a more typical oxygen molecule. Although not present in very high concentrations, the ozone molecules in the ozone layer nonetheless absorb some 98 percent of the biologically damaging medium-

and high-frequency ultraviolet (UV) light in sunlight. Lower-frequency, longer-wavelength ultraviolet light, however, can penetrate the ozone layer and reach the Earth's surface. Though UV light is less potentially damaging, prolonged exposure to it can nevertheless cause eye damage, sunburn, and skin cancers, which is why protection by sunglasses and sunscreen lotion is recommended whenever a person is to be exposed to sunlight for any length of time.

There has been much concern in recent years that the ozone layer is being slowly depleted by *fluorocarbon gas* reacting with the ozone. Fluorocarbons have been widely used as propellants in aerosol cans, for such products as hair spray and spray paint, and also as refrigerants in air conditioning systems in cars, homes, and businesses. As a result of this danger, many spray-can and air-conditioning manufacturers in the United States and elsewhere have switched to other substances, but these alternatives tend to be more expensive. Fluorocarbons are also released by the burning of styrofoam.

Ionosphere

Above the stratosphere lies an area of electrically charged particles called *ions.* This **ionosphere** begins perhaps as low as thirty or forty miles up and extends to about five hundred miles. Turbulences on the Sun, such as sunspots and solar flares, change the ionosphere, and cause magnetic and electrical disturbances within it. It is in the ionosphere that the auroras called the northern and southern lights create their colorful displays over the polar regions.

It is possible to send ordinary radio waves around the world by bouncing them off ionospheric layers. In other words, the ionosphere will reflect radio waves of certain frequencies. By determining the best frequencies and times of day to transmit them,

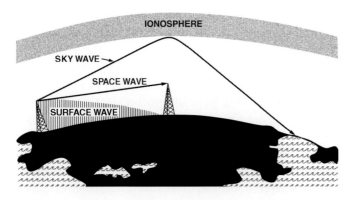

This diagram shows how different types of radio waves interact with the ionosphere. Shorter wavelengths can be reflected off the ionosphere as *sky waves* for considerable distances. Longer wavelengths called space waves pass through it. Radio waves of both kinds that follow the Earth's curvature are called ground or surface waves. *U.S. Army*

communications can be greatly enhanced. This phenomenon is one with which every Navy and ham radio operator is familiar.

The *mesosphere,* the lowest level of the ionosphere, extends from about thirty to fifty miles above the Earth. This layer is one of extreme temperature changes. At the lowest part of the layer the temperature may be as high as 32 degrees F. But it will drop to below –135 degrees F at the mesosphere's upper limits. It will then start to rise again as one moves higher into the thermosphere.

The *thermosphere* is the highest level of the ionosphere; it begins about fifty miles above Earth's surface. The air in the thermosphere is extremely thin, and its molecules are **ionized,** or electrified, by loss of their electrons due to bombardment by X-rays and high-frequency UV light (a combination called "XUV radiation") in solar radiation and **cosmic rays** from outer space. It is in the thermosphere that the principal radio-reflecting layers of the ionosphere are located. Temperatures in this layer increase with altitude, because of the XUV radiation that is absorbed there; temperatures in the upper thermosphere can approach 3,000 degrees F or higher. The air is so thin though that an ordinary thermometer would not register a temperature much above freezing, since there are very few air particles to conduct the heat energy into it.

The **International Space Station** orbits in the middle of the thermosphere, 200–240 miles high. The National Aeronautics and Space Administration (NASA) uses seventy-six miles as the nominal *reentry altitude* for spacecraft returning from space, as this is the level at which atmospheric drag and heating becomes noticeable.

Exosphere and Magnetosphere

The topmost layer or outer fringe of the atmosphere is called the **exosphere.** It begins about four hundred to six hundred miles above the Earth's surface and continues out to about 18,000 miles. **Space** begins in the exosphere. Only light hydrogen and helium atoms exist in the region—in atomic form, because of the intense solar and cosmic radiation. Because of the large amount of unfiltered infrared and ultraviolet light and X-ray radiation present in incoming solar radiation at these altitudes, ambient temperatures may rise as high as 4,500 degrees F in daylight and may drop to near absolute zero (–460 degrees F) at night in the Earth's shadow. Again, as in the thermosphere, the air is so thin that a standard thermometer would not register much of the heating effect in the exosphere.

Surrounding and overlapping the exosphere is the **magnetosphere.** The magnetosphere is formed by the Sun's effect on the Earth's magnetic field.

Earth acts as a huge magnet, surrounded by a magnetic field. But this magnetic field does not dissipate uniformly into space. It is distorted by the **solar wind,** a stream of charged

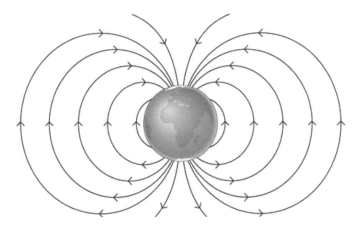

An idealized drawing of the Earth's magnetic field. As the distance from Earth increases, the shape of the magnetic field is actually compressed and distorted by the solar wind. *www.compassadjustment.com*

The Earth's magnetosphere, formed by the interaction of the solar wind with the Earth's magnetic field. The compressed portion in the front facing the Sun is called the *bow shock,* and the drawn-out portion behind is sometimes called the *magnetotail. NASA*

particles emanating from the Sun that rush by at speeds up to 900,000 miles per hour. On the side of Earth nearest the Sun the pressure of the oncoming solar wind compresses the magnetic field down to about 40,000 miles from Earth, a phenomenon called the *bow shock*. On the far side, the solar wind causes the magnetic field to be distended into a huge comet-like tail between three and four million miles long, called the *magnetotail*. The boundary between the magnetic field and the solar wind is called is called the *magnetopause,* and the region within it containing the magnetic field constitutes the magnetosphere. The magnetosphere changes its shape daily as the strength of the solar wind varies. This causes changes closer to Earth that affect radio transmission and the weather.

The magnetosphere is very beneficial to Earth, as it deflects harmful energetic emissions from the Sun and **cosmic rays** (high-energy particles) from distant stars. It also prevents the solar wind from interacting with the ozone layer and the rest of the atmosphere. If not for the magnetosphere, scientists say, the pressure of the solar wind over an extended time would literally blow our atmosphere away, just as it might have on Mars billions of years ago when that planet is thought to have lost its magnetic field.

Inside the magnetosphere are huge numbers of charged particles that have been trapped by Earth's magnetic field. These particles circle Earth in three doughnut-shaped rings, one artificial and two natural. Earth is in the doughnut hole, and there are no trapped particles above or below the north and south poles. These rings are the narrow *Starfish ring,* caused by unforeseen effects of a U.S. hydrogen bomb test explosion at a height of 250 miles in 1962, and the inner and outer *Van Allen radiation belts.*

The **Van Allen radiation belts** were discovered in 1958 by America's first space satellite, *Explorer1,* and mapped out by several of the other early satellites. They encircle Earth in two main doughnut-shaped rings. One is centered about 1,800 miles above Earth and extends to a maximum of about eight thousand miles, while the other is centered between about 9,300 to 12,400 miles up and extends out to about 25,000 miles. The inner belt contains primarily high-energy protons, and the outer belt contains high-energy electrons. In 2013, exploratory space probes orbited by NASA also found evidence of a transitory third belt of charged particles between the other two. There are conical radiation-free zones above both poles, and for a while it was thought that any manned space missions would have to be launched through them to avoid injurious radiation within the belts. Later it was determined that astronauts could safely pass through the belts if their spacecraft were properly shielded and they did not linger in them too long. Manned orbital space missions and the International Space Station are intentionally placed in orbit well beneath the lower limits of the Van Allen belts; satellites operating within them must be shielded against the radiation encountered there.

Atmospheric Pressure

The layer of atmosphere that surrounds us exerts a pressure of nearly fifteen pounds per square inch [14.696 psi, or about 1×10^5 Pascals (SI pressure unit, N/m^2)] at sea level. The weight of the atmosphere varies from place to place, depending on the amount of water vapor present, the temperature, and the height above Earth's surface. Variations in atmospheric pressure are measured by a **barometer.**

The Navy uses two types of barometers: *aneroid* and *mercurial.* Usually the aneroid type is found on board ship. The aneroid, or dry, barometer contains a small metallic cell that contracts when atmospheric pressure increases and expands

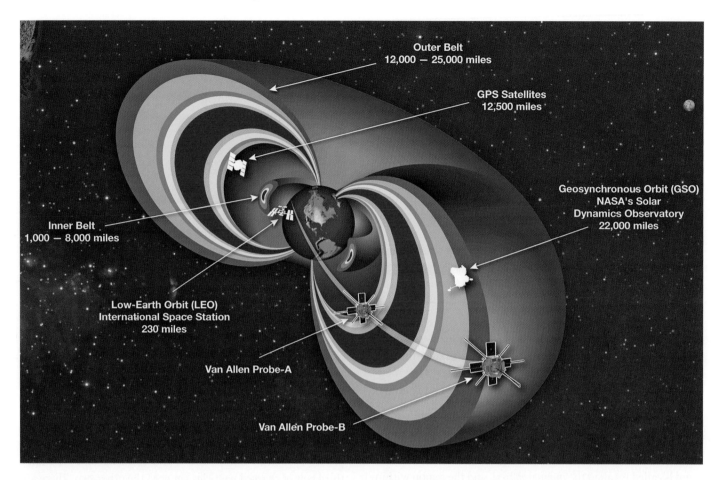

The Van Allen radiation belts, formed by charged particles trapped by the Earth's magnetic field. They encircle the Earth like two gigantic concentric doughnuts, with radiation-free cones over the poles. Two U.S. space probes launched in 2012 to more fully investigate the belts are depicted, and for reference the orbital positions of the International Space Station, GPS satellites, and geosynchronous satellites are also shown. *NASA*

when pressure decreases. The cell is connected to a needle that points to a graduated scale around the face of the barometer. As the cell expands or contracts, the needle indicates the atmospheric pressure on that scale. The mercurial type consists of a calibrated glass tube filled with mercury. It is used at shore activities to check aneroid barometers for accuracy.

Barometers may be graduated in either inches of mercury or millibars. Both inches and millibars are measurements of the height of the mercury column supported at a given time. One "atmosphere" equals 14.696 psi, the pressure at sea level; a bar equals about 0.98 atmosphere, and a millibar equals 1/1,000 of a bar. The average atmospheric pressure at the Earth's surface is 29.92 inches, or 1,013.2 millibars. You will often hear the barometric pressure readings given in inches of mercury on TV weather forecasts. Millibars, however, are normally used on weather charts.

Atmospheric pressure is one of the main factors influencing weather and therefore one of the main indicators used to predict it. Areas of high pressure form when air slowly descends

and warms, inhibiting the formation of clouds with the potential for precipitation. Thus, rising air pressure is generally, but not always, associated with good weather.

The air that descends in high-pressure areas has to get back to higher altitudes in some way, and it does this by rising in areas where the air pressure is low. As the air rises it cools, causing any water vapor in it to condense into clouds and eventually precipitation that begins to fall as rain, ice, or snow. Thus, falling air pressure is generally a sign of the approach of bad weather.

In weather forecasting, areas of rising pressure are called **highs,** and areas of falling pressure are called **lows.** There are no particular pressure readings that divide the two. The relative differences between the two are what is important.

What Makes the Weather?

Weather is the condition of the atmosphere. Changes in weather are caused by changes in the air's temperature, pressure, and water-vapor content; wind causes weather phenomena to move.

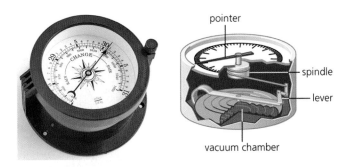

An aneroid barometer (left) has a vacuum chamber (right) that expands and contracts as the atmospheric pressure increases and decreases. A lever connected to the chamber causes a pointer to move across a calibrated scale on the dial. *Precision Graphics*

It can be said, therefore, that weather is the condition of the atmosphere expressed in terms of its heat, pressure, wind, and moisture. All weather changes are ultimately caused by temperature changes in different parts of the atmosphere.

There are some fundamental natural laws that determine these changes. Warm air is lighter in weight and can hold more water vapor than cold air. Cold air is heavier and has a tendency to flow toward the rising warm air, replacing it on the Earth's surface. As this air moves, wind is created, thus beginning the complex forces that cause the changing weather.

Our main source of energy, the Sun, bombards Earth with 126 trillion horsepower each second. This energy is transmitted as **electromagnetic waves** traveling at 186,300 miles (3 × 10^8 meters) per second. It consists of both sunlight and high-energy X-rays. When this radiant energy hits our atmosphere, the atmosphere acts as a giant filter, absorbing a significant portion of the more energetic and dangerous light waves in the sunlight and almost all of the X-rays.

When sunlight hits the top of our atmosphere, about 50 percent of its energy content is in the infrared wavelengths, 40 percent is in the visible spectrum, and 10 percent is in the ultraviolet. About half of this energy is absorbed or reflected on the way down, including most of the dangerous ultraviolet radiation. The remaining half is absorbed by the land and water, then eventually transferred back into the atmosphere as heat, or directly out to space. The absorbed atmospheric heat is also eventually radiated out to space, thus keeping the Earth's "solar energy budget" balanced (see diagram next page).

Because of the balance between the incoming radiant energy and the energy ultimately

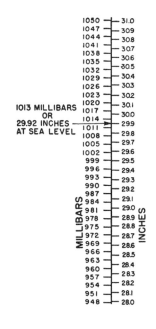

Inches of mercury and the corresponding millibar scale used for measuring barometric air pressure.

reradiated back out into space, the Earth's temperature remains fairly constant, despite the continual inflow of solar radiation. The atmosphere thus acts almost like an automatic thermostat, controlling the Earth's heat. It screens out the dangerous solar radiation and reflects some of the rest, and it acts as an insulator to keep most of the heat from escaping at night. Without the atmosphere the Earth would be like the Moon, with boiling surface temperatures during the day and subfreezing temperatures during the night.

The rates at which the lower atmosphere absorbs heat from the Earth and radiates it out to space have a major effect on the average atmospheric temperature. The concentration of carbon dioxide (CO_2) is thought to play a major role in this, with increases in the concentration resulting in more heat retention for longer periods of time—the so-called **greenhouse effect**. In studies of geological data obtained from polar ice corings, it has been determined that on average over the last several hundred thousand years, the CO_2 level in the atmosphere has consistently been between about two hundred and three hundred parts per million (ppm). Measurements over the last fifty years, however, have shown a dramatic increase in these concentrations, from about 313 ppm in 1960 to about 389 ppm in 2010, and a record high of 400 ppm in May 2013. This increase is thought to have occurred mainly because of deforestation in many areas of the world, coupled with steadily increasing release of CO_2 into the atmosphere by industrialized nations worldwide.

Many scientists and environmentalists assert that this increase in CO_2 levels (the so-called **carbon footprint** of humankind) has resulted in a greenhouse effect that has caused the average temperature to rise to historically high levels everywhere on Earth—a phenomenon referred to by many as **global warming**. Others refute these findings, claiming that the alleged temperature increases, if in fact not just a product of faulty measurements, may be due to normal climatic variations. Whatever the cause, if long-term increases in global temperatures are in fact occurring, this could have many adverse consequences, including sustained heat waves, extensive droughts, increased frequency and intensity of major storms, and additional melting of polar glaciers and sea ice, resulting in a significant rise in the sea level of the oceans worldwide. All of these effects would have dramatic consequences on human habitation throughout the globe. The ultimate example of a greenhouse effect may be the planet Venus, where a thick atmosphere of mainly CO_2 produces an average temperature of almost 900 degrees F (480 degrees C) everywhere on its surface day and night.

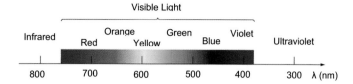

The spectrum of sunlight as it hits our atmosphere. The visible spectrum (400–700 nanometers) contains about 40 percent of the energy content, with 50 percent in the infrared (above seven hundred nanometers) and 10 percent in the ultraviolet (below four hundred nanometers), neither of which we can see. Most of the ultraviolet is absorbed by the atmosphere. The remaining ultraviolet B waves, 315-280 nm, cause tanning effects on human skin, and the infrared causes most of the surface heating effects.

Measuring Temperature

A **thermometer** is an instrument for measuring temperature. There are three different kinds of thermometers in wide use today. They are the alcohol-filled thermometer, the thermocouple-based thermometer, and the infrared thermometer. The **alcohol thermometer** is the most common of all thermometers both in the Navy and in the civilian world. It is a long, narrow glass tube filled with alcohol, usually with red dye added for better visibility. The liquid rises and falls within the bore as the rise and fall of the temperature causes the alcohol to expand and contract. A temperature scale is marked on the tube or mounted alongside it. At one time liquid mercury was also widely used in this type of thermometer, but its use has been discontinued for some years because of potential mercury-poisoning hazards.

The **thermocouple thermometer** is based on the principle that when two dissimilar metals are in contact, a voltage will be produced between them when they are heated. The voltage is proportional to the amount of heat, so that a corresponding temperature scale can be applied. Many of these types of thermometers are in the form of a slender probe that can be inserted into an object or liquid to determine its temperature. The temperature can be presented on a mechanical scale, digitally on a small LCD display, or on a computer or control device, such as a thermostat.

The **infrared thermometer** is based on the measurement of thermal infrared light energy emitted by a body. The amount and frequency of radiation emitted is proportional to its temperature, which allows the application of a corresponding temperature scale. The advantage of this type thermometer is that it can take an object's temperature at a distance by focusing on its surface; the disadvantage is that the *emissivity,* or ability of the object to emit radiation, must be known in order to

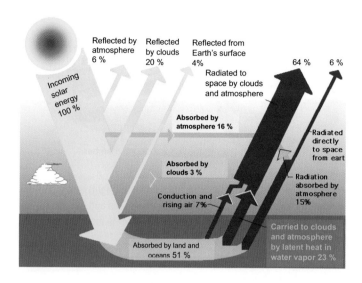

The Earth's solar energy budget. About half of the incoming energy from the Sun is either absorbed on the way down by the atmosphere or reflected by it back out to space. The remainder is absorbed by the land and oceans, then reradiated out into space either directly or via atmospheric heating.

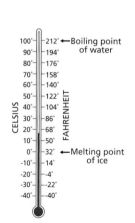

The Celsius and corresponding Fahrenheit temperature scales.

properly calibrate the temperature readout. Ambient heat in the environment can also greatly affect the accuracy of the readout.

The Navy and most civilians in America usually use thermometers with a **Fahrenheit (F) temperature scale.** On that scale, the freezing point of water is 32 degrees and the boiling point is 212 degrees. However, temperatures in meteorology and other sciences, as well as most other countries of the world, are usually expressed according to the **Celsius (C) temperature scale,** in which the freezing point of water is 0 degrees and its boiling point is 100 degrees.

The Celsius scale is in the metric (SI) system, which one day is supposed to be the principal measurement system used in the United States, as it already is most everywhere else. It is likely, however, that for a good many more years conversion of temperatures from one scale to the other will be a common necessity.

There are five degrees of Celsius temperature for every nine degrees Fahrenheit. Since 32 degrees F is equivalent to 0 degrees C, to change a Fahrenheit reading to Celsius you subtract 32 degrees and then multiply the remainder by 5/9. Expressed as a formula this becomes:

$$C = 5/9(F - 32).$$

Let's say you want to change 59 degrees F to Celsius. Subtracting 32 degrees from 59 degrees leaves 27 degrees. Multiply 27 degrees by 5/9 and you get 15 degrees C. To change a Celsius reading to Fahrenheit, the process is reversed. Simply multiply the Celsius temperature by 9/5 and add 32 degrees:

$$F = 9/5 \; C + 32.$$

Using the figures from the previous example, to change 15 degrees C back to Fahrenheit, first multiply it by 9/5, which gives you 27 degrees, then add 32 degrees. You are now back to the original 59 degrees F.

Measuring Relative Humidity and Dew Point

The atmosphere always contains water in the form of vapor. Nearly 71 percent of Earth's surface is covered by water. Heat causes the **evaporation** of millions of tons of water from these surfaces daily. In a process called *transpiration,* additional huge amounts of water enter the air from the green leaves of plants. This water accumulates in the atmosphere in the form of an invisible gas called **water vapor.** As this warm, moist vapor rises, it contracts and cools, at the rate of about 1 degree C (about 2 degrees F) for every hundred meters (about 328 feet) of altitude, eventually condensing into a liquid. The liquid droplets form clouds or fog, and eventually *precipitation* (usually rain or snow) will occur when the droplets become too heavy to remain airborne. This water cycle of evaporation, condensation, and precipitation, is called the *hydrologic cycle.* (See the hydrologic cycle illustration on page 220 of the Oceanography unit.)

The amount of water vapor the atmosphere can contain varies with the atmosphere's temperature and pressure. The **relative humidity** is the ratio of the amount of water vapor the air *actually* contains to the maximum amount that air at that temperature and pressure *could* contain, expressed as a percentage. When the air contains all the water it can at a given temperature and pressure, humidity is said to be 100 percent, called its **saturation,** or **condensation, point.** At this point, the water vapor will begin to condense into water droplets. If the air contains three-quarters of the vapor it could, the relative humidity is 75 percent; half, and the relative humidity is 50 percent; and so on. Since warm air at a given pressure can contain more water than cold air, the relative humidity goes up when air with a given amount of water vapor cools and it drops when that air is heated. Relative humidity in the atmosphere increases with increases in air pressure and decreases with decreases in

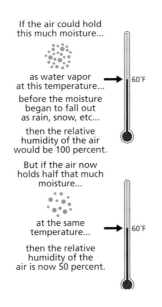

If the air could hold this much moisture...

as water vapor at this temperature...

60°F

before the moisture began to fall out as rain, snow, etc...

then the relative humidity of the air would be 100 percent.

But if the air now holds half that much moisture...

at the same temperature...

60°F

then the relative humidity of the air is now 50 percent.

An illustration of the concept of relative humidity.

pressure, though not as rapidly as changes caused by changes in temperature.

There are several ways in which the air can be cooled. It can rise and expand by convection; it can come into contact with a cooler surface, usually by being blown; it can emit infrared (heat) radiation; or it can be forced upward by being blown over high land masses or mountains. Whatever the cause, when the air cools to its saturation point, the water vapor in it will begin to condense into liquid water.

The **dew point** is the temperature to which air must be cooled—at constant pressure and constant water-vapor content—to reach its saturation (condensation) point (100 percent relative humidity). When the air is cooled to its dew-point temperature near Earth's surface, small water droplets called **dew** begin to condense on objects that are as cool or colder. At higher altitudes, reaching the dew point simply means that the air has been cooled sufficiently to cause a **cloud** to begin to form. If conditions are right and the condensation continues, these cloud droplets grow thicker and will eventually fall as rain or snow.

Relative humidity and dew point are traditionally measured by using a **psychrometer.** A psychrometer is simply two ordinary alcohol thermometers mounted together on a single strip of material. The bulb of one is covered by a water-soaked wick, from which the moisture is allowed to evaporate. The moisture will evaporate until the amount of water remaining in the wick equals the amount of water vapor in the surrounding atmosphere. Since evaporation is a cooling process, the reading on the wet bulb will be lower than on the dry bulb—unless the humidity is 100 percent, at which time both readings are the same. The difference between the wet-bulb and dry-bulb readings is applied to tables developed for that purpose. From the table, the relative humidity and dew point can be read easily. Aboard ship, **sling psychrometers** are often used to speed up the process of getting accurate wet- and dry-bulb readings. A handle and chain are attached to a psychrometer and the apparatus is whirled around in order to rapidly bring the wet bulb into contact with a greater volume of air. The whirling is continued, using a steady, slow swing, until no further change can be detected in the wet-bulb reading. Then the table is referred to by the usual procedure.

More modern electronic instruments called **hygrometers** use a precisely determined dew-point temperature or changes in electrical capacitance or resistance to measure and present readouts of relative humidity.

Critical Thinking

1. Over the last decade there has arisen much debate over the effect of modern industrial gases on the protective upper layers of Earth's atmosphere. What are thought to be the major changes taking place, and what potential or actual effects are these having on Earth's population?

2. Most present-day dermatologists urge the application of sun-block lotion whenever prolonged exposure to sunlight is expected. Research why this concern has arisen and what the eventual effects might be of prolonged unprotected exposure to sunlight during the teenage years.

3. Research the current debate on global warming, including its theorized causes, probable effects, and measures, if any, that might be taken to mitigate or eliminate them.

4. Research the typical weather instruments used aboard U.S. naval vessels and what readings are commonly recorded at sea and by whom.

Study Guide Questions

1. What are the two main elements in our atmosphere and the approximate percentages of each?

2. What changes occur to the air as one ascends into the atmosphere?

3. Where does most of Earth's weather occur?

4. What are the five principal layers of Earth's atmosphere?

5. A. In what layer of the atmosphere are most clouds found?
   B. What are the laws of gases that apply to the development of clouds?

6. Why have the United States and other countries studied Antarctic air masses in recent years?

7. A. What is the tropopause?
   B. Why is it so important to commercial aviation?

8. What is the relevance of the jet stream to modern military and commercial aviation?

9. Why do modern commercial aircraft prefer to fly mostly in the stratosphere?

10. What visual phenomenon occurs in the ionosphere over the polar regions?

11. What is the importance of the ionosphere to communications?

12. A. What is the magnetosphere?
    B. What causes it?

13. A. What is the average air pressure at sea level?
    B. What instrument measures air pressure?

14. What are two types of barometers used by the Navy?

15. How is air pressure related to weather forecasting?

16. What is the "greenhouse effect?"

17. A. What are the two most widely used temperature scales?
    B. What are the freezing and boiling points of each?

18. What is the water or hydrologic cycle?

19. What is the dew point?

20. What instruments measure relative humidity and dew point?

Temperature Conversion Problems

1. Do the following conversions:

   A. 122 degrees F = _____ degrees C

   B. 86 degrees F = _____ degrees C

   C. –4 degrees F = _____ degrees C

   D. 104 degrees F = _____ degrees C

2. Do the following conversions:

   A. 60 degrees C = _____ degrees F

   B. 20 degrees C = _____ degrees F

   C. –10 degrees C = _____ degrees F

   D. 35 degrees C = _____ degrees F

New Vocabulary

meteorology	ionization
exosphere	magnetosphere
atmosphere	magnetopause
humidity	cosmic rays
troposphere	barometer
air mass	millibar
tropopause	highs
jet stream	lows
convection (air)	greenhouse effect
air mass	global warming
stratosphere	dew point
ozone layer	precipitation
chemosphere	relative humidity
ionosphere	psychrometer
mesosphere	hygrometer
thermosphere	carbon footprint

8

Clouds and Fog

Water is always present in the air, in greater or smaller amounts. It can be present in three states: solid, liquid, and vapor. In the last chapter we discussed water vapor in the air, called humidity. Relative humidity was defined as the percentage of the amount of vapor the air contains at a given temperature and pressure relative to the maximum amount it could contain. We also discussed how when cooled to its condensation, or dew, point, the water vapor can condense into liquid water droplets. In this chapter we will discuss how water vapor is formed into clouds and what kind of weather the various kinds of clouds may foretell. This information is vital to meteorologists, but it can also be both helpful and interesting to the average person.

Definition of a Cloud

As discussed in the previous chapter, our atmosphere accumulates large amounts of water vapor from the effects of evaporation and transpiration. Once in the atmosphere, it can be moved from place to place or from one altitude to another by **natural convection** (air movement caused by heating or cooling) and wind. Tiny particles of dust, sand, pollen from plants, factory smoke, and salt particles from oceans are also always present in the air. When water vapor mixes with them and cools sufficiently to condense into tiny droplets around them, these fragments of matter are called **hygroscopic,** or **condensation, nuclei,** terms referring to "particles that readily absorb moisture." A **cloud** is a mass of hygroscopic nuclei that have soaked up moisture from the water vapor in the air. **Fog** is formed in the same way; it is a cloud very close to the ground.

As these hygroscopic droplets ride air currents, one of three things can happen, depending upon the temperature and wind. They may reevaporate back into the atmosphere; they may rise and freeze into ice crystals, sometimes in sufficient amounts to form ice crystalline clouds; or they may collide or **coalesce** with other droplets and form larger drops that become heavy enough to fall as rain, snow, or sleet.

Changes in atmospheric conditions account for the many different shapes of clouds and for their presence at various altitudes. Cloud formations give a clue concerning the forces at work in the atmosphere. Navy and civilian meteorologists must keep accurate records of clouds and must account for cloud cover in their periodic weather reports. Such information is important in forecasting.

Cloud Classifications

There are three basic cloud types: **cirrus** (wispy), **cumulus** (heaped-up), and **stratus** (layered). In addition to the three basic types, there are other types having names that are combinations of these, with the word *nimbus* (meaning "rain") or the prefix *alto-* (meaning "high") identifying clouds in the middle altitudes. Another prefix, *fracto-*, is often used to describe fragmented or windblown clouds.

Clouds are often classified in accordance with the altitudes at which they most frequently occur. The altitude classes are **low, middle,** or **high.** Sometimes a fourth class, **towering,** is used to identify an exceptionally high cloud with its base in the low-altitude area. Altitudes associated with each of these classes are (1) low, surface to seven thousand feet; (2) middle, seven thousand to 20,000 feet; and (3) high, above 20,000 feet.

Middle clouds seldom attain heights greater than 13,000 feet in the polar regions, though they may reach 23,000–45,000 feet in the temperate and tropical zones.

Clouds are usually named according to their appearance. Appearance, though, is largely dependent upon the altitude in which they are found. Grouped by appearance and altitude, there are ten general cloud types.

Low Clouds. Low clouds are of five main types:

1. *Stratus clouds,* the lowest cloud type, are often like a gray layer with a uniform base. They may cause drizzle but never rain. Fog becomes stratus when it lifts.

2. *Nimbostratus* are dark, shapeless, rain-laden clouds, often blanketing the sky. They are true rain clouds and "look wet," because they often have streaks of rain extending to the ground beneath them. They are often seen in the summer at the base of thunderheads. In the winter they bring steady, heavy snow.

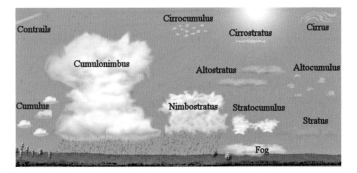

An illustration of the different cloud types. *USDOE*

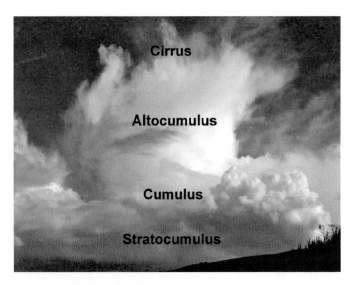

Photo of common cloud types.

3. *Stratocumulus* are irregular, rounded masses of clouds spread out in puffy or rolling layers. These large clouds are usually gray with darker spots or shading. They do not produce rain, but they sometimes fuse at the base and change into nimbostratus. They usually precede bad weather.

4. *Cumulus* clouds are dense, puffy clouds with a beautiful, cauliflower-like appearance. On summer days they look like giant cotton balls in the sky. They rise by day in warm air and usually disappear at night. Fleecy cumulus clouds usually mean fair weather ahead—unless the puffs begin to pile up and the dark edge of a nimbus rain cloud starts to form at the base.

5. *Thunderheads* start at almost any altitude and sometimes extend to heights of as much as 75,000 feet. *Cumulonimbus* is the name given to these clouds. They are very dense clouds of the towering variety. The base of the cloud is the dark nimbus rain cloud. Severe thunderstorms and destructive tornadoes may come from these clouds, which normally are seen only in the summer.

Middle Clouds. Middle clouds are basically stratus or cumulus but with bases beginning about ten thousand feet. They are denoted by the prefix *alto-*:

1. *Altocumulus* are gray or whitish layers of puffy, fleecy clouds. These roll-like clouds are made of water droplets, sometimes laid out in parallel bands. The Sun will sometimes produce a pale blue or yellow corona through altocumulus clouds. The presence of these clouds means that rain will probably occur within twenty-four hours.

2. *Altostratus* clouds are dense sheets of gray or blue, sometimes looking like ridges of frosted glass or flattened vapor trails. The Sun or Moon will glow dimly through altostratus but without a halo, or corona. Light rain will probably occur within twenty-four hours.

High Clouds. High clouds are composed almost entirely of tiny ice crystals. There are three basic types:

1. *Cirrus* clouds are thin, wispy clouds composed mainly of ice crystals. They are often called "mare's tails." In scattered patches, they normally indicate clear, cold weather. But if they are in parallel lines across the high sky, they usually signal a violent change in the weather within thirty-six hours. Spring ice storms, hurricanes, typhoons, or other severe storm conditions will generally appear soon—even if the day when you see the parallel cirrus is beautiful and sunny.

2. *Cirrostratus* clouds may nearly cover the sky with a filmy cloud. They often have a curly appearance at their edges. Because they are made of ice crystals, these clouds form large halos around the Sun and Moon. They indicate that clear and cold weather can be forecast.

3. *Cirrocumulus* clouds are thin, patchy clouds that often form in wavelike patterns. These clouds do not leave shadows on the Earth. Precipitation will usually follow them within twenty-four hours.

Clouds at Sea

Clouds have been leading lost seamen, navigators, and explorers to land since the days of the earliest hardy sea voyagers. Fleecy white clouds on the horizon that are seemingly stationary usually indicate that an island is close by. Clouds form above sunny islands for the same reason that they do above any land—rising air currents containing moisture from vegetation meets cooler air aloft, and condenses into clouds. In the tropics, these clouds often reflect the colors of sandy beaches or coral reefs below. Overhanging clouds may also warn seamen of rocks, reefs, or shoals surrounding islands.

Precipitation

Precipitation (rain, snow, sleet, and hail) cannot occur without clouds. The fact that there are clouds, however, does not necessarily mean that the moisture in them will fall as a form of precipitation. Temperature and the presence of hygroscopic nuclei or ice crystals will determine whether or not there will be precipitation and what form it will take.

Raindrops are formed when moist air is cooled to the point where the moisture condenses into heavy drops. Normally, droplets move about in the cloud somewhat like dust blowing. Cloud moisture droplets are very tiny—only about 0.01 mm (0.0004 in) in diameter—and are too light to fall to Earth. Only if the droplet grows to a diameter of about 0.1 mm (0.004 in) or larger will it begin to fall from the cloud. Cloud droplets grow to a size large enough to fall as rain or snow by combining with one another—a process called **coalescence.** Raindrops range in size from about 0.1 mm to 9 mm (0.004 to 0.35 in) in diameter, above which they tend to break apart. Contrary to popular depiction they are not teardrop in shape, but rather are oval-shaped with a flat surface on the bottom.

Coalescence occurs in two known ways. First, bigger droplets move about slowly in the clouds, eventually bumping into other droplets and combining with them. This is usually the case when rain falls from a nimbostratus or other low cloud. Second, the more important kind of coalescence occurs when, in higher-altitude clouds (such as the middle layer of cumulonimbus), ice crystals and water droplets form near each other. The droplets evaporate, and the resulting vapor collides with the ice crystals and condenses into snow or ice pellets that fall toward Earth, perhaps melting into rain if they pass through warmer air at lower altitudes.

Rainmaking

Rainmaking has been a concern of humans since the most ancient times. Rain dances, sacrifices, drums, cannons, and smoke have all been used to try to make rain, especially when the land was parched with drought. None of these methods worked, of course. But modern rainmaking techniques, based upon the known facts of coalescence, appear in some cases to have successfully induced rainfall.

In modern rainmaking techniques, aircraft or rockets drop dry-ice crystals or silver-iodide crystals into potential rain clouds. This process is called **seeding** the cloud with artificial nuclei. It has been found that one pound of frozen carbon-dioxide (dry-ice) crystals spread by airplane can sometimes start a shower from a large cumulus cloud. Silver iodide can also, using special generators, be sent up from the ground in the form of a gas—a less expensive method. Both methods attempt to cause water droplets to form around the foreign substance and then fall as rain.

Seeding, however, is not successful unless conditions are nearly right for natural rainfall. Even then it often does not work. Seeding may make rain come a bit earlier or cause more rain to fall than might have occurred naturally. It might also cause rain to fall from a cloud that, under natural conditions, would never have produced raindrops. It is difficult to evaluate its effectiveness, however, because it can never be known how much rain might have fallen naturally from any given cloud formation. But seeding definitely cannot cause rain to fall from fair skies or from fair-weather cumulus clouds. Nor is it possible to cause rain to fall over a large area.

Sleet, Hail, Snow, and Frost

Sleet occurs in wintertime when rain or snow falls through a layer of warmer air and then a layer of freezing air as it falls, forming ice pellets that then hit the ground. If the falling precipitation does not completely freeze, it may become a super-cooled liquid or mush that freezes on contact when it hits the cold ground, trees, or telephone wires. Such precipitation, called **freezing rain** or an **ice storm,** can cause power lines to collapse and tree branches to break and fall on power and telephone lines, roofs, and roads. At sea it can cause problems with stability of small craft because of the added weight of such icing topside, and it can cause decks and ladders to become slippery and mooring and rigging lines to be too ice encrusted and stiff to handle.

Hail usually occurs in the summertime. It begins as frozen raindrops in high levels of cumulonimbus thunderheads. The ice pellets may grow if updrafts of air push them upward one or more times after they have been coated with water from lower cloud layers. They will eventually fall, too heavy to be lifted by an updraft. They may grow even more during their descent by picking up moisture that then freezes. Most hailstones are smaller than marbles, but people and animals have been killed or severely injured by hailstones as large as baseballs. Hail can destroy a growing crop in minutes.

People often confuse sleet and hail, as both fall to the ground as ice pellets. Remember that sleet is formed in winter as it falls and freezes from the outside in, whereas hail is formed during summer in clouds and freezes from the inside out.

In winter, when the upper air is very cold, water vapor in clouds will condense into supercooled water droplets, a few molecules of which quickly transform into ice. Then the rest of the droplet freezes around the ice nuclei. The frozen droplets rapidly grow into frozen flakes of random shapes as they acquire more of the available water droplets and vapor. When the flakes grow to sufficient size they begin falling to the ground as **snow.** On the way down the snowflakes may become larger, combining in clumps to form aggregate flakes several centimeters or larger in size.

Advection fog around the San Francisco Golden Gate Bridge that spans the three-mile-long channel between San Francisco Bay and the Pacific Ocean.

Dew and frost do not fall from the skies as do rain, sleet, and snow. As explained in the previous chapter, dew is water vapor that condenses on objects that have cooled below the condensation point of the air around them. **Frost** is similar to dew, but it forms at temperatures below freezing. The water vapor changes directly into ice crystals on contact with the object, without first changing into dew.

Fog

As previously mentioned, what we call fog is really a low-lying cloud that is near or touching the surface of the Earth. It is formed when cool air moves in and mixes with warm air having a high relative humidity, or when warm area passes over a cool area on land or sea. When the air temperature falls below the dew point, fog is formed. As in a cloud, each water droplet in fog has a particle of dust or smoke as its central nucleus.

Fog is hazardous on land, sea, and in the air, because it limits visibility. Although larger aircraft and ships have radar to assist them in foggy conditions, the eyes of alert pilots and ships' lookouts are still necessary for safe navigation. Indeed, the Nautical Rules of the Road explicitly require that ships station lookouts. Many an airplane flight has been delayed, before either landing or taking off, because of poor visibility due to fog. Fog frequently causes vehicle crashes on roads and highways, sometimes involving whole strings of cars and trucks.

Advection fog is the name given to air-mass fog produced by air in motion or to fog formed in one place and transported by wind to another. These fogs occur when the wind moves warm, moist air from a warm ocean surface to a colder land surface, or vice versa. These fogs normally dissipate each day, since the winds producing the fog will change direction when the Sun rises.

Steam fog is a type of advection fog formed by air saturation. It occurs when cold air moves over warm water. When this happens, water evaporating from the warm surface easily saturates the cold air, thus producing the steam fog. This type of fog occurs often in the far north, where it is called "sea smoke." It can be seen in the late fall or winter when a river or pond "steams" as frigid air cools the water until it begins to form a coating of ice.

Radiation fog is caused by the heat that the Earth radiates. It forms only at night, over a land surface. This is a common type of fog, and it may cover a large area, but it usually lifts before noon, after being "burned" away by the Sun's rays. After sunset the Earth receives no more heat from the Sun, but the ground continues to radiate heat. The surface begins to cool, and layers of air close to the surface are cooled by conduction. If the air is sufficiently moist, it will chill to its dew point and form fog. Fog patches may suddenly develop in low areas, drastically reducing visibility.

Critical Thinking

1. In addition to the observation of distinctive cloud types, what other clues did early oceangoing mariners use to indicate the presence of land beneath the horizon, before it could be seen?

2. Why are the fog lights sometimes installed on automobiles always fairly low to the ground and often yellow in color?

Study Guide Questions

1. Of what is a cloud made?

2. What causes water vapor to accumulate in the atmosphere?

3. What are the three basic types of clouds?

4. What are the ranges of altitude for low, middle, and high clouds?

5. What type of weather is associated with these types of clouds?
   A. stratus   D. cumulus
   B. nimbostratus   E. cirrus
   C. cumulonimbus F. altocumulus

6. How were early navigators often able to find previously uncharted islands?

7. What is precipitation?

8. A. How do raindrops form?
   B. What is coalescence, and how does it happen?

9. What two techniques are used in modern rainmaking attempts?

10. A. What is sleet?
    B. What causes it to occur?

11. What is hail, and how are hailstones formed?

12. What is fog, and how is it formed?

New Vocabulary

natural convection	silver-iodide crystals
hygroscopic nuclei	cloud "seeding"
fog	ice storm
coalesce	sleet
nimbus	hail
stratus	hailstone
nimbostratus	dew
cumulus	frost
thunderhead	advection fog
cumulonimbus	"sea smoke"
cirrus	

9

Wind and Weather

Air in motion is called **wind.** Winds blow to achieve a balance in atmospheric pressure. The unequal distribution of atmospheric pressure is caused by the unequal heating of Earth's surface. Winds blow from high-pressure areas to low-pressure areas. The strength of these winds depends on the distance of the high from the low and the difference in pressure (the **gradient**) between the two areas. Since various places on Earth's surface receive more heat than others, temperatures and strengths of winds differ from one area to another.

There is a continual flow of wind over the face of the Earth as the result of this uneven heating. From about two and a half to three miles above the surface to the tropopause, winds are westerly in direction at all degrees of latitude, from the equator to the poles. At the surface, a band of easterly winds called the **trade winds** extends from the equator to 30 degrees, both north and south. Between 30 degrees and 60 degrees, in both the Northern and Southern Hemispheres, there are the **prevailing westerlies.** Finally, between 60 degrees and both poles there are winds called the **polar easterlies.**

Why are there so many different wind directions, and why are there differences in wind circulations in the Northern and Southern Hemispheres? The answers to these questions come from our knowledge of the motions of Earth itself.

Wind and the Earth's Rotation

Two motions of Earth affect the weather. The revolution of Earth around the Sun accounts for the seasonal changes on Earth. We will talk briefly about this a bit later. The other motion is the rotation of Earth on its axis. This rotation causes night and day, with the consequent heating and cooling effects on the atmosphere. It also produces the major wind belts of Earth.

If Earth did not rotate, the warmer air over the equator would rise and move north and south toward the poles, high above Earth's surface. The air would cool and sink as it moved toward the poles. Later, it would move back toward the equator at a steady speed and direction. However, the Coriolis effect (discussed in unit 2) causes the direction of the wind to curve

to the right in the Northern Hemisphere and to the left in the Southern Hemisphere. This curving or deflection effect continues until a balance with other forces is reached.

At this point, we must again bring in the factor of atmospheric pressures in order to explain why there are different belts of prevailing primary winds on Earth. We know that air rises at the equator and begins moving northward at high altitudes. This rising air creates an area of lower air pressure, called a *low*. It eventually sinks and accumulates near the surface, forming a high-pressure area, called a *high*. This sinking and accumulating takes place in the area of 30 degrees north and south latitudes. These areas are called the **Horse Latitudes,** which will be discussed below.

Prevailing Winds

Air must always flow outward from the center of a high-pressure area; this is called **divergence.** Conversely, air flows in toward the center of a low-pressure area; this effect is **convergence.** It follows that when both high- and low-pressure areas are present, air flows from the high- to the low-pressure area, thus creating wind.

The Doldrums. The equatorial belt of light and variable converging winds is called the **doldrums.** The belt varies in position and tends to move north and south of the geographic equator with the Sun. In the doldrums the temperatures are high, and excessive precipitation occurs. Days go by without a

An illustration of vertical convergence and divergence. Unequal heating of the Earth's surface results in unequal distribution of pressure. Warm air rises or converges above lows, and colder air falls or diverges around highs.

The general circulation pattern of winds over the rotating Earth.

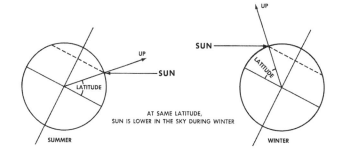

Earth's inclination causes the Sun's position in relation to an observer in northern latitudes to be higher in summer and lower in winter, vice versa in southern latitudes.

breath of wind; thus, in the days of sail, ships avoided this area if possible. Severe tropical storms begin here.

Trade Winds. At the surface and on the poleward sides of the doldrums there are bands of easterly winds called the **trade winds.** The *northeast trades* were a popular route for sailing vessels, and aircraft traveling west in the Northern Hemisphere are favored with a tailwind and clear skies if they fly near 30 degrees north latitude. The winds come from the southeast in the Southern Hemisphere and thus are called the *southeast trades* there.

Subtropical High-Pressure Belt. These are the Horse Latitudes. Because of sinking air from aloft and diverging winds at the surface, these areas generally have fair weather. The diverging winds cause the trade winds found on the equatorial side of this high-pressure belt. The Horse Latitudes tend to be cloudless and calm, with weak, undependable winds. The term "Horse Latitudes" comes from the fact that in the days of sail, ships carrying horses from Europe often were becalmed here. When this happened and horses died for lack of food and water, they were thrown overboard to prevent the spread of disease among the crew and other horses.

Prevailing Westerlies. These winds are found on the poleward side of the subtropical highs and are created by the diverging winds of these highs. They blow from the southwest in the Northern Hemisphere and from the northwest in the Southern Hemisphere. The **prevailing westerlies** provide most of the air flow over the United States.

Polar Front Zone. The belt of low pressure known as the **polar front zone** lies in the area of 60 degrees north and south latitudes. In the north it is called the *Arctic Semipermanent Low,* and in the south it is called the *Antarctic Permanent Low.* These two areas are noted for their bad weather, because the westerlies and the polar easterlies converge in them.

Polar Easterlies. This is a zone of poorly developed surface winds created by outflow from the high pressure at the

poles. These winds have a northeasterly direction in the Northern Hemisphere and a southeasterly direction in the Southern Hemisphere.

Wind and the Earth's Revolution

We have discussed in some detail the effects of the rotational movement of Earth on weather, particularly its effect on winds. Another important movement is the revolution of our planet around the Sun. This movement, combined with Earth's inclination, causes the **seasons.**

Earth is inclined at an angle of 23.5 degrees from the perpendicular to the plane of its orbit of revolution, called the **plane of the ecliptic.** This simply means that Earth tips at this angle all the time, like a top that is beginning to slow down. Because of this fact, the part of Earth receiving the most direct rays from the Sun will vary over a year from 23.5 degrees north (**Tropic of Cancer**) to 23.5 degrees south (**Tropic of Capricorn**), as Earth proceeds in its orbit around the Sun.

Our seasonal weather variations are the result of the angle at which the Sun's rays strike Earth as it revolves around the Sun, not the variations in nearness of the Earth to the Sun as the Earth orbits around it. In summer, because of Earth's inclination, the Sun's rays in the Northern Hemisphere are more direct, even though at this time Earth is farther away from the Sun. Thus, the rays are more concentrated and deliver more energy per unit area, making the weather warm. In winter in the Northern Hemisphere, Earth is actually closer to the Sun, but sunlight hits this hemisphere at a greater angle. Thus, the same amount of sunlight is spread over a larger area, delivering less energy per unit area, so it gets cooler. The reverse of this process happens in the Southern Hemisphere.

Secondary Wind Circulation

We have discussed the primary circulation of winds on Earth. It is the unequal heating of the planet between the equator and

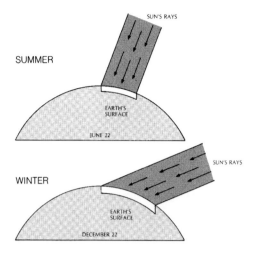

The seasonal temperature variations in middle and high latitudes are a result of the changing angles at which the Sun's rays strike the Earth's surface. Note the difference in the surface areas struck by the same amount of sunshine in summer and winter. Because the energy per unit area is greater in summer (top), it gets hotter than in winter, when the energy per unit area is lower (bottom).

the poles that causes north–south winds. The rotation of Earth turns these winds east or west, depending upon the hemisphere in which they occur. But winds are also affected by the topography of the land and the currents of the seas.

We know that nearly three-fourths of Earth's surface is water. But not many people realize that three-fourths of the world's land surface is in the Northern Hemisphere. Because of its physical properties, land heats up and cools down faster than does water. For this reason, water areas are cooler than land areas during the summer and warmer during the winter. Moreover, the daily average variation of temperature over open water is seldom more than two or three degrees, but three hundred miles inland it is rarely less than fifteen degrees.

The difference between the land and sea temperatures causes the pressure belts of the primary wind circulation to be broken up into enclosed high- and low-pressure areas, called **centers of action**. We see, therefore, that the geography of the continents and seas can also influence the wind and weather.

Highs

In the Northern Hemisphere, air flows in a clockwise manner around high-pressure centers of action. Air subsides (sinks) in the center and diverges (blows outward) from the center of the high-pressure areas. Few clouds are formed. Generally fair weather prevails, either warm or cold, depending upon the season.

Local high-pressure areas develop whenever air cools, compresses, and subsides. The Horse Latitudes and the polar highs are good examples of this. But high-pressure areas can

develop anywhere. When a high develops, the clockwise spiral of air develops and air begins flowing to surrounding lower-pressure areas.

There are large, permanent high-pressure areas near both poles. They produce very cold air, depending on the seasons. A high-pressure area exists over Greenland all the time as well, because of the vast ice cap there. Subtropical highs can usually be found southwest of California and near the Azores in the Atlantic. The high associated with the North Polar zone repeatedly creates icy polar fronts, sometimes called *polar vortexes*, which every winter sweep over most of North America east of the Rockies. This area is called the **North American High**. A similar high-pressure area exists in Siberia, where the temperate zone's coldest temperatures have been recorded.

Lows

The only more or less permanent low-pressure area on Earth is the **Doldrum Belt,** near the equator. The **Aleutian Low** off Alaska is a low-pressure cell associated with the Polar Front and influenced by the Japanese Current. It is intense during the winter but ill defined in summer. Another low-pressure area, lying near Iceland, is called the Icelandic Low. The Gulf Stream influences this low.

Traveling low-pressure cells are frequently found in the area of the Polar Front. These are formed by the interaction of the polar air to the north and the maritime tropical air to the south. These lows are called **migratory lows.** Migratory storms may also move into lower latitudes from the Polar Front. Such storms often occur in the south-central United States and on the U.S. East Coast near Cape Hatteras.

Local lows often form directly below large thunderhead clouds. **Heat lows** form over deserts and other intensely hot areas; a low-pressure area lasts most of the summer over the Arizona and California deserts. Lows sometimes form on the leeward side of mountain ranges and cause rushing winds to "pour" down from the nearby mountains. These lows are common just east of the Rocky Mountains in Colorado.

Mountain Winds

We have just mentioned the lows that sometimes form on the lee side of mountain ranges. These winds are so persistent and predictable in some areas that they have their own names. Topography is a major factor in the formation of such winds, but temperature differences and the rotation of Earth also contribute.

As warm air rises on one side of the mountains, it cools and loses its moisture as rain or snow. The dry, cooler air then rushes down the opposite side, heating the air and pushing it into the low. Famous mountain winds are the **Chinooks of the Rockies,** the **Santa Anas** of southern California, and the **foehns** (fa-ns) of the Swiss and French Alps. These winds sometimes reach gale force and, in the western United States, often become dust storms.

Valley Winds

Probably the most famous valley wind system is the **Mistral** of southern France. This is a cold, dry wind that rushes down the Rhône Valley toward the low-pressure system that often develops over the Mediterranean Sea. Sometimes reaching whole-gale and storm force, over 60 mph, this wind is one the U.S. Sixth Fleet must be on the alert for when involved in western Mediterranean operations.

Monsoons

Monsoons are seasonal winds characteristic of South and Southeast Asia, though they occur elsewhere also, with less intensity and regularity. The monsoon is a very persistent wind that blows on predictable seasonal paths and with definite seasonal characteristics.

Summer (Southwest) Monsoon. As continental Asia begins to warm in the spring, the water area over the Indian Ocean remains relatively cool. The warming effect gradually creates a continental low over the central Asian plateaus and desert. This low draws cooler air from the south. As the moisture-laden Indian Ocean air pushes northeastward over the land, it begins to cool and condense. The rains begin to fall in southern India in mid-May and continue to build up in intensity as the continent warms. The wet air rushes into the southern slopes of the Himalaya Mountains and dumps astounding amounts of rain on the southern Asian countries. It is common for the southeast Burmese coast to have two hundred inches of rainfall during the period between mid-May and late September. At the foothills of the Himalayas, five hundred inches of rain in the same period have been recorded almost every year. The greatest rainfall ever recorded occurred at Cherrapunji, India, during the monsoon: 1,041.78 inches. Squalls and typhoons occur over the Bay of Bengal during this time.

Winter (Northeast) Monsoon. As the cold season of the Northern Hemisphere approaches, the continental high over Siberia regenerates and begins to dominate the air circulation over South and Southeast Asia. The wind now reverses itself and blows from the northeast. The rains of the summer season cease. A warm, low-pressure area now exists over the Indian Ocean. The cooler, dry air from central Asia now blows southwestward across the continent over the Himalayas and into the southern countries. The northeast wind persists from late September until April, when the humidity begins to rise for the next summer monsoon.

During the winter monsoon there is little rain, and by the time January and February arrive the soil is parched and cracked, leaves have curled and died, and dust lies thick over much of the countryside. Dust in Upper Burma around Mandalay is often four to six inches thick along roads and in villages.

Winds and the Beaufort Wind Scale

Meteorologists must always be aware of wind velocity and wind direction. In meteorology wind speeds are always given in **knots**, according to international agreement. The instrument used to measure wind speed is called an **anemometer**, with metal cups attached to arms. The arms are attached to a central spindle, and as the wind blows against the cups, the speed of rotation is calibrated into wind speed. A vane atop the anemometer aligns itself with the direction of the wind. A dial on the instrument readout indicates the apparent wind velocity and direction.

The **Beaufort Wind Scale**, with **Correlative Sea Disturbance Scale**, can also be used to estimate wind speed. This scale is based on careful observation of sea conditions. Adm. Sir Francis Beaufort of the British Royal Navy developed the scale in 1805 to estimate wind speeds from effects on sails. His table numbers the winds from 1 to 12, in order of increasing severity. It compares them to the Sea Disturbance Scale, which describes sea state and mean height of waves on a scale of 1 to 9. Descriptive terms identify the winds and their counterpart waves. The Beaufort Wind Scale enables the shipboard weatherman or sailor to estimate wind speeds merely by looking at the sea state and then comparing the two scales. These scales are also often used to indicate the general wind speeds and sea states existing at given locations of interest.

By convention, wind direction is specified according to the compass direction or compass point of origin from which the wind blows.

An aerographer's mate using an anemometer to measure wind speed on a Navy ship. *CHINFO, Louis Ramirez*

Beaufort no.	Speed in knots	Descriptive terms	Sea criterion	Approximate equivalent sea disturbance scale in open sea		
				Sea state no.	Description	Mean height of waves (in feet)
0	Less than 1	Calm	Sea like a mirror.	0	Calm (glassy)	—
1	1–3	Light air	Ripples with the appearance of scales are formed, but without foam crests.	1	Calm (rippled)	½
2	4–6	Light breeze	Small wavelets, still short but more pronounced. Crests have a glassy appearance and do not break.	1	—	1
3	7–10	Gentle breeze	Large wavelets. Crests begin to break. Foam has glassy appearance. Perhaps scattered whitecaps.	2	Smooth (wavelets)	2½
4	11–16	Moderate breeze	Small waves, becoming longer. Fairly frequent whitecaps.	3	Slight	5
5	17–21	Fresh breeze	Moderate waves, taking a more pronounced long form. Many whitecaps are formed (chance of some spray).	4	Moderate	9
6	22–27	Strong breeze	Large waves begin to form. The white foam crests are more extensive everywhere (probably some spray).	5	Rough	14
7	28–33	Moderate gale	Sea heaps up and white foam from breaking waves begins to be blown in streaks along the direction of the wind. (Spray becomes heavy).	6	Very rough	19
8	34–40	Fresh gale	Moderately high waves of greater length. Edges of crests break into spray. The foam is blown in well-marked streaks along the direction of the wind.	7	High	25
9	41–47	Strong gale	High waves. Dense streaks of foam along the direction of the wind. Sea begins to roll. Spray may affect visibility.	7	—	31
10	48–55	Whole gale	Very high waves with long, overhanging crests. The resulting foam in great patches is blown in dense white streaks along the direction of the wind. On the whole the surface of the sea takes on a white appearance. The rolling of the sea becomes heavy and shocklike. Visibility is affected.	8	Very high	37
11	56–63	Storm	Exceptionally high waves (Small- and medium-sized ships might for a long time be lost to view behind the waves.) The sea is completely covered with long white patches of foam lying along the direction of the wind. Everywhere the edges of the wave crests are blown into froth. Visibility affected.	9	Phenomenal	45 or more
12	Above 64	Hurricane and typhoon	The air is filled with foam and spray. Sea completely white with driving spray. Visibility very seriously affected.	9	—	—

The Beaufort Wind Scale and Correlative Sea Disturbance Scale.

Critical Thinking

1. Research the factors that forecasters use to predict the frequency of hurricanes occurring in the Atlantic and Pacific basins prior to the start of each hurricane season.

2. Investigate the names and locations of the most important weather satellites currently in use for weather forecasting.

3. List the major preparations a homeowner should make when a hurricane is forecasted to strike.

4. How can the power of wind be harnessed to provide a partial solution to the energy crisis?

Study Guide Questions

1. A. What is a simple definition of wind?
   B. Upon what does the strength of wind depend?

2. What are the three primary wind belts in the Northern Hemisphere?

3. A. What two motions of Earth affect the weather?
   B. Which of these motions causes the major wind belts?

4. How does the Coriolis effect cause winds to deflect in the Northern and Southern Hemispheres?

5. A. How does atmospheric pressure affect the primary wind belts?
   B. What are the principal high-pressure belts on Earth's surface?

6. What determines the directional name of a wind?

7. Describe each of the world's prevailing wind and pressure belts.

8. A. What movement of Earth causes the seasons?
   B. What is meant by Earth's "inclination"?

9. What names are given to the 23.5 degrees north and 23.5 degrees south latitude circles?

10. What are the principal causes of secondary wind circulation?

11. What is the effect of the geography of the continents and seas on the primary wind belts in the Northern Hemisphere?

12. How does air "act" in a high-pressure area?

13. Over what countries in the Northern Hemisphere do "permanent" high-pressure areas exist?

14. A. Where do the principal low-pressure areas exist on Earth?
    B. Where do seasonal lows usually develop in the United States?

15. A. What are the most famous mountain winds, and where do they blow?
    B. What type of weather do these winds bring?

16. What valley wind is of particular concern to the Sixth Fleet?

17. A. What are monsoon winds, and where are they most common?
    B. Describe the generation of the southwest and northeast monsoons.

18. What instrument is used to measure wind velocity?

19. A. What is the Beaufort Wind Scale?
    B. How is the Correlative Sea Disturbance Scale used with the Beaufort Wind Scale?

New Vocabulary

gradient
divergence
covergence
trade winds
prevailing westerlies
doldrums

plane of the ecliptic
migratory lows
foehn winds
monsoon
anemometer

10

Fronts and Storms

Mariners have much to fear when they are threatened by severe storms. Gale-force winds can strain rigging, spring seams, bend plates, smash equipment, and tear loose topside equipment, even on aircraft carriers or bulk petroleum tankers. Winds of a hundred knots and waves of sixty feet or more are not uncommon during major storms at sea. The prudent mariner will maneuver to stay clear of storms whenever possible.

An experienced mariner should be able to determine when severe weather disturbances are coming by observing the sky and sea and carefully assessing readings of the meteorological instruments on board. Also, today's radio communications provide regular weather summaries and storm warnings. The mariner at sea will carefully plot such weather information and compare it with the vessel's position and course.

Development of Fronts

An air mass is a large body of air with roughly the same temperature and humidity. An air mass takes on the characteristics of the surface over which it forms. Thus, cold-air masses originate in the cold polar regions, and warm-air masses originate in the tropics. Polar and tropical air masses can develop over either continental or maritime surfaces. These two surfaces give their names to the different kinds of air masses. Since land and sea reflect the Sun's radiation differently, the two kinds of air masses have different characteristics.

It takes more heat per unit of volume to change water temperature than soil temperature, and in seawater, that heat is absorbed to depths in excess of eighty feet. However, on land only a few top inches of the soil will absorb thermal radiation. This means that, as we have seen, oceans are slower to warm up and slower to cool down than are land or continental surfaces. Maritime air, therefore, will tend to bring moderate temperatures, neither too hot nor too cold, as it moves over land areas. In the winter, the United States is swept by continental air masses from the cold Arctic. In the summer, it is swept by warm, moist maritime air masses from the Gulf of Mexico, the Caribbean Sea, and the Pacific Ocean off the Mexican coast.

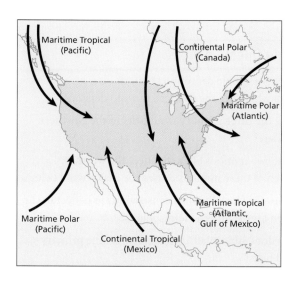

The primary air masses that affect the weather of the United States.

Where warm- and cold-air masses come together, the boundary between them is called a **front**. Air masses rarely fuse unless they are very similar in temperature and moisture content. Fronts are sometimes called **waves**, as in the term "cold wave" or "tropical wave." Along the frontal boundaries a battle for supremacy is fought. There will usually be cloudiness and precipitation in a frontal area. Fronts usually bring unsettled weather. There will often be thunderstorms, especially in summertime. A **cold front** is formed by a cold air mass moving into a warm air mass, pushing the warm air upward. A **warm front** is formed by an approaching warm air mass rising over a cold air mass. When neither mass advances on the other, a **stationary front** is said to exist.

When a cold front moves faster than a warm front moving in the same direction and overtakes it, the warm air mass behind the warm front is forced upward. By the time the advancing cold front meets, or *converges* with, the cooler air mass ahead of the warm front, the warm air has been pushed aloft over both. The convergent front that remains near the surface between the two cold air masses is called an **occluded front**.

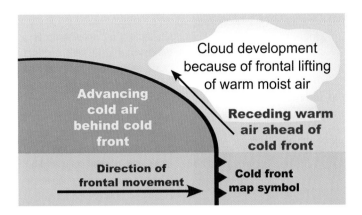 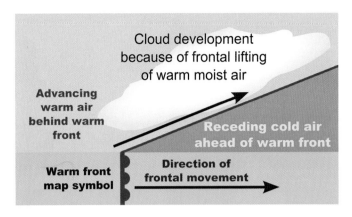

A cold front ahead of an advancing cold air mass (left) causes receding warm, moist air to rise and water vapor to condense, forming clouds and possible precipitation. Warm, moist air behind an advancing warm front (right) rises over a receding cold air mass, causing water vapor to condense and form clouds and possible precipitation. *NASA*

There are two types of occluded front. In what is called a *cold-front occlusion,* the cold air behind the approaching cold front is *colder* than the cool air beyond the warm front air mass, causing the cold front to push both the warm air and the cool

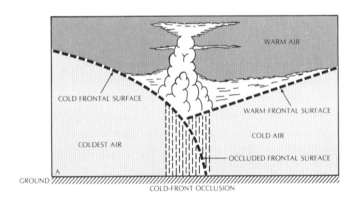

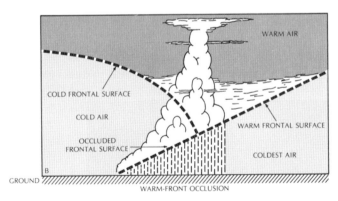

Two types of occluded fronts. In the upper drawing of a cold-front occlusion, the cold air behind the cold front is colder than the cold air ahead of the warm front, pushing the warm air aloft. In the warm-front occlusion on the bottom, the cold air ahead of the warm front is colder that the cold air behind the cold front, forcing the cold front aloft as well. *From Kotsch,* Weather for the Mariner, *133*

air beyond aloft. In the other type, called a *warm-front occlusion,* the situation is reversed. The air behind the advancing cold front is *warmer* than the cool air beyond the rising warm air mass, causing the advancing cold front to ride up over the colder air when the fronts converge. In both cases the occluded front is the convergent front between the two cold air masses. See the accompanying diagrams. A cold front or warm front may extend for hundreds of miles. But the area in which frontal weather disturbances occur is usually a band only fifteen to fifty miles wide behind a cold front. Frontal weather may extend up to three hundred miles behind a warm front.

Thunderstorms

Thunderstorms occur within clouds with vertical development, such as cumulus and cumulonimbus. These storms are characterized by loud thunder, flashes of lightning, very heavy precipitation, strong gusts of wind, and occasional hail or tornadoes. Because the thunderstorm is local in nature and relatively short in duration, it is difficult to forecast.

A thunderstorm develops in three rapid stages. The first stage, called the *cumulus stage,* is an updraft of warm, moist air into the atmosphere. The water vapor cools and condenses into clouds, and the clouds grow taller and taller as the updrafts continue. The second stage, called the *mature stage* of thunderstorm development, is characterized by both updrafts and downdrafts within the storm-producing cloud. The cooler the upper part of this cloud becomes as it towers into the atmosphere, the faster raindrops and sometimes hail will begin to form and fall. The stronger the updrafts, the larger these raindrops and hailstones become. There is frictional drag between the raindrops and the surrounding air, so that air is pulled down with the raindrops as they fall, forming downdrafts. The mature cell usually extends above 25,000 feet. The downdrafts do not extend that high,

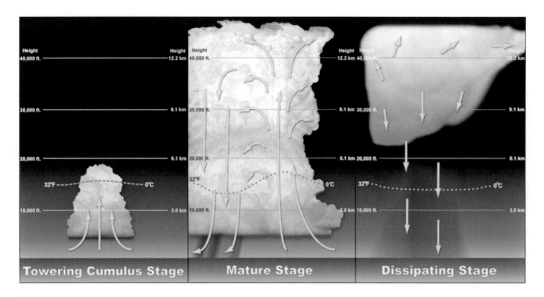

Life cycle of a thunderstorm. In the cumulus stage (left), updrafts cause warm moist air to rise and condense into thick cumulus clouds. In the mature stage (center), both updrafts and downdrafts occur as heavy raindrops, and possibly hail, form and fall. In the dissipating or anvil stage (right), the updrafts cease and the entire cloud becomes downdraft, with lighter rain falling until the storm dissipates. The pink dashed line represents the 0-degree-C temperature level within the clouds. *NOAA*

however, because there is insufficient moisture at the higher altitudes. The final stage is called the *dissipating,* or *anvil, stage.* As more and more air is brought down by raindrop friction, these downdrafts take the place of updrafts and spread out. The entire lower portion of the cloud becomes downdraft, and the high winds in the upper altitudes flatten the top of the cloud into an anvil shape. Lighter rain now falls on the ground; the storm will dissipate in a short time.

Weather Phenomena Associated with Thunderstorms

Precipitation is found in every thunderstorm. Rain will form in regions below freezing level. Hail will form if the updrafts carry melted or partially melted raindrops into the higher, colder altitudes. Snow and ice crystals also may be in any thunderstorm, winter or summer, though in summer they will melt into rain when nearing the Earth. In winter such storms are called "thunder-snowstorms."

A thunderstorm is most turbulent in the area of heaviest precipitation. Icing will often occur just above the freezing level, making thunderstorms very hazardous for aircraft.

The leading gust of wind, sometimes called a **microburst,** is one of a thunderstorm's dangers. This gust occurs just prior to the passage of the storm. The strong winds at the surface are the result of the horizontal spreading-out of the storm's downdraft currents as they approach the surface of the Earth. The speed of the first gust usually is the highest recorded during any thunderstorm and can blow in any direction—even in opposition to the surface wind that is "pushing" the storm. Such conditions can result in "wind shear," which is very dangerous to aircraft in the process of taking off or landing.

Surging air currents in the thunderhead cloud create static electricity, the source of lightning. This process is not com-

pletely understood, but it is generally believed that lightning is caused by the break-up of large water droplets into positively and negatively charged particles. Positively charged particles accumulate near the top of the cloud, and negatively charged particles accumulate in the lower reaches. Equal but opposite charges are also induced on the ground beneath the storm as it passes.

The buildup of electric charge may reach millions of volts. An electrical discharge—lightning—occurs when a pair of these unlike charges reach sufficient strength to overcome the electrical resistance between them. The resulting lightning may flash within the cloud, jump to other clouds, jump from the clouds to the ground, or even jump from the ground up to the cloud. The lightning, then, is nature's way of neutralizing the charges between the two electrical regions of opposite charge.

Lightning occurs in two steps. First, one or more **leaders** (columns) of electrified (ionized) air run between the two oppositely charged regions. This establishes the "circuit" for the main second stroke, which leaps along the leaders to complete the circuit. This second stroke is the one you see and that causes the

Lightning is often produced during thunderstorms. It may go from cloud to cloud or between clouds and the surface. *NOAA*

thunder you hear. The lightning generates brilliant white light and terrific heat, resulting in a rapid heating, compression, and expansion of the air through which it passes. This in turn creates a shock wave that generates the audible thunder in the same manner as an aircraft breaking the sound barrier. Distant lightning may be seen but be too far away for the thunder to be heard.

When a lightning bolt travels between a cloud and the ground, it seeks the shortest path between the two. Thus, high points such as trees, telephone poles, TV antennas, ship and boat masts, and the like are the places most likely to be struck by lightning. Lightning also follows the easiest route to ground after striking, so it will follow electrical wires, plumbing pipes, sailboat rigging, and even saturated drafts of air in its attempt to reach the ground. It is very unwise, therefore, to be near isolated trees or in or on open areas like athletic fields or bodies of water during a thunderstorm; never be out in an open boat. People caught in such situations who have survived lightning strikes often report feeling their body hair standing on end just before the strike, probably due to the large static charge buildup, or possibly even the leaders, immediately prior to the main bolt. In such incidences immediate evasive action could decrease the chances of serious or fatal injury.

Lightning discharges generate a wide range of electromagnetic radiations, including radio-frequency pulses. The U.S. National Weather Service (NWS) and several commercial contractors have installed a network of detectors nationwide that can sense these pulses and triangulate the locations of the lightning bolts that generate them. This allows the discharges to be monitored, logged, and recorded as part of the weather data continuously accumulated by the NWS throughout the country, for dissemination to a wide variety of end users, including local TV weather broadcasts.

The tornado is the most intense and violent of localized storms. The winds in its funnel may rotate at speeds approaching three hundred miles per hour, destroying everything in its path. *NOAA*

A NOAA ship encountering a waterspout in the Gulf of Mexico. *NOAA*

A fundamental rule for airplane pilots is never to fly under or through a thunderstorm. It is safest to fly around the storm. If it must be flown through, it should be penetrated at an altitude of about one-third its height.

Tornadoes

The most intense and violent of localized storms is the **tornado.** It is usually associated with violent thunderstorm activity and heavy rain. Tornadoes are cyclonic wind whirlpools. A tornado forms as a funnel cloud on the forward edge of a fully developed cumulonimbus thunderstorm cloud. Rising air causes a swirling at the base of the parent cloud. As the swirl increases in size and speed, the funnel drops out of the cloud, like an elephant's trunk dangling toward the surface. When it touches ground the funnel is called a tornado; if it forms over water, it is called a **waterspout.**

Winds in the **vortex**—the whirlwind causing the funnel—can exceed 300 mph, with 100–200 mph updrafts in the center. The extreme low pressure in the vortex of a tornado can cause enclosed structures like houses to explode outward as the tornado passes over them, suddenly releasing the pressure of air trapped inside. Roofs may be blown off buildings, cars and trucks may be lifted up and tossed around, and trains may be derailed. The vortex can suck up all manner of dirt and debris, including building materials, animals, and even people. Within the tornado feathers and straws may be propelled by the swirling wind to such speeds that they have the force of power-driven nails. Fortunately, only about one thunderstorm out of a thousand develops a tornado. Tornadoes are normally of fairly small diameter, usually three to four hundred feet, but larger ones are not uncommon. The widest one ever recorded was a 2.6-mile-wide storm that carved out a path of destruction over sixteen miles long near Oklahoma City, Oklahoma, on 31 May 2013. They may continue on an erratic path for anywhere from a mile or less to more than a hundred miles.. But the speed of the storm moving over the Earth's surface is comparatively slow, usually 25–40 mph. The duration over any given spot may be only seconds—but in that short time the devastation can be almost total.

Tornadoes are most common in the temperate zone (the midlatitudes between 23.5 degrees and 66.5 degrees north and south), probably because of the greater atmospheric-temperature contrasts there. The Midwestern United States is the most tornado-ravaged area of the world. Usually these storms hit in the late spring or early summer. But they can occur at almost any time.

Strengths of tornadoes are rated on the **Enhanced Fujita (EF) Scale,** developed by a Japanese-American researcher at the University of Chicago in the 1970s. Tornado ratings on the scale progress from EF1 to EF5, depending on their wind speed and the severity of the damage they cause.

Tropical Cyclones

A **cyclone** is an atmospheric disturbance characterized by a rapid circular air flow around a low-pressure center. These winds are counterclockwise in the Northern Hemisphere and clockwise in the Southern Hemisphere. Although a tornado can be considered a form of cyclone, the term is usually applied to larger storms called **tropical cyclones.** Tropical cyclones are subdivided into three categories: (1) *tropical depressions*—maximum wind less than 34 knots, (2) *tropical storms*—maximum wind 34–63 knots, and (3) *hurricanes* or *typhoons*—maximum wind 64 knots and up.

Large tropical cyclones occur in many places throughout the world and are called by various names. They form over all tropical oceans except the South Atlantic, but they do not form over continents. They are common in the West Indies, often ranging up the East Coast of the United States or into the Gulf of Mexico, where they are called **hurricanes.** Tropical cyclones occurring east of the International Date Line in the Pacific are also called hurricanes. In the western Pacific they are called **typhoons.** Off the west coast of Australia they are called **willy-willies,** and in the Philippines they are called **bagyo,** after a storm that wrecked the city of Baguio in 1911.

Hurricanes, typhoons, and tropical storms with sustained winds in excess of 39 mph are given women's and men's names, alternating up the alphabet in the order in which the storms appear each season. If all the names in the alphabet are used up within a season, successive storms are assigned Greek-letter names. Before 1978, all these storms were given only women's names.

Although the velocities associated with these tropical cyclones are less than those of a tornado, they cover hundreds of times the area and last much longer. Sometimes they will include imbedded tornadoes, especially on their leading edges. The tropical cyclone is the most destructive of all weather phenomena and the one that is of greatest concern to the oceangoing sailor.

Strengths of hurricanes and other tropical cyclones are rated on the **Saffir-Simpson Hurricane Scale,** developed in the 1970s by an engineer and a former director of the National Hurricane Center. Ratings on the scale progress from Category 1 to Category 5, depending on the intensities of the sustained winds, from 74 to 157 mph or greater (64 to ≥137 knots). All five categories are contained within force 12 on the Beaufort Wind Scale.

Characteristics of Hurricanes and Typhoons

Most hurricanes and typhoons form from tropical low-pressure waves near the equator where the trade winds meet called the **Inter-Tropical Convergence Zone (ITCZ).** Tropical cyclones, however, never originate right on the equator, because they require the twisting Coriolis forces of the Earth's rotation to start them spinning, which are not present there. The majority form in a band between about 10 to 30 degrees latitude north and south of the equator. Water temperatures of at least 80 degrees F (26.5 degrees C) are required in order to make the overlaying atmosphere energetic and unstable enough to sustain the necessary convection and thunderstorm formation associated with a tropical low pressure system.

The rotating low causes the warm moist surface air to lift, which in turn pulls more warm moist air toward its center. The lifting causes the moisture to condense. As this moisture condenses, it heats the rotating air more, causing it to rise even more swiftly. As more moist tropical sea air sweeps in to replace this rising air, more condensation takes place, and the cycle intensifies. That is why hurricanes are so violent—because of the tremendous energy released by the continuous condensation and an inexhaustible source of moisture. All the while, the Coriolis effect keeps the air turning more and more rapidly, until it is a giant wheel of swirling winds.

At their strongest, tropical cyclones may vary in diameter from 60 to 1,200 miles (100 to 2000 km) or more. They have moderate winds at their outer edges, increasing toward the center, called the **eye** of the storm; velocities higher than 175 knots (200 mph) have been recorded in the **eye wall**, a band of maximum wind intensity surrounding the eye. The eye of a typical hurricane or typhoon varies between twenty and forty miles (30 to 65 km) in diameter. This area is relatively calm, with light winds and clear or moderately overcast skies and a little drizzle. The heaviest damage caused by these tropical cyclones occurs when the eye wall passes over land.

If the tropical cyclone encounters water temperatures less than 80 degrees F, or if interactions with land or other weather

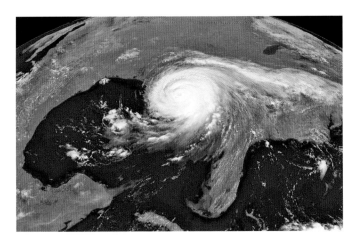

Weather satellite image of Hurricane Katrina approaching New Orleans in 2005. *NOAA*

systems cause vertical wind shear to occur, the storm may lose intensity and degenerate into an **extratropical low** (a low-pressure weather system outside the tropics) and degenerate completely as it moves into higher latitudes.

If the hurricane or typhoon strikes land before this occurs, however, great damage can result. The strong winds and torrential rains can damage or destroy buildings, vehicles, and bridges and turn loose debris into deadly flying projectiles. But the worst effect can be a dramatic rise in the seawater level, called the **storm surge,** near storms making landfall. Storm surges are caused by the effect of hurricane-force winds piling up water along the coastal areas they strike, plus the effect of the low pressure within the storm as it passes over (about 0.4 in, or 1 cm, for each millibar drop in atmospheric pressure). Storm surges of six to eight feet are common in many cases, but may exceed twenty feet or more. The highest surge on record in the United States occurred in Louisiana in August 2005, during Hurricane Katrina, which produced a storm surge of twenty-five feet in several parishes. The storm surge is not a problem at sea, but the large waves (higher than forty to fifty feet in some cases), high winds, and heavy rains generated by these storms can disrupt offshore oil and gas drilling and shipping, cause heavy damage to drilling platforms, and wreck ships.

Once formed, tropical cyclones are **steered** primarily by the trade winds, but they are also affected by other high- and low-pressure systems they may encounter, which makes their individual tracks difficult to predict. In general in the tropical North Atlantic these cyclones move westward from their point of origin, often the west coast of Africa, and upon reaching the West Indies either curve to the northeast off the Atlantic coast of the United States or proceed further westward to either curve up either into Florida or the Gulf of Mexico, or cross Central America. Storms that form in the eastern Pacific mostly pro-

ceed into the central Pacific and dissipate. Those that form in the northwest Pacific generally originate between the Marshall Islands and the Philippines, move toward the east coast of China, and then curve northeastward toward the Philippines, Taiwan, and Japan. Few ever originate in the central Pacific, northern Indian Ocean, or the Mediterranean. In the Southern Hemisphere they generally start out westward and then curve southeastward. Few if any hurricanes ever form in the South Atlantic. Storms that form in the southern Indian Ocean can affect some of the various island nations in the region and various countries along the East African coast. Those that form in the southern and southwest Pacific affect mainly Australia and Indonesia.

Worldwide, the peak of the tropical cyclone season is late summer, when the differences between sea-surface temperatures and the atmosphere above are greatest. In the North Atlantic region, the hurricane season extends from June to November, peaking from late August through September. The northeast Pacific region has a similar season. In the northwest Pacific typhoons occur year-round, with a minimum in February and March and a peak in September. It is the most active ocean basin in the world for tropical-cyclone development. In the Southern Hemisphere the tropical cyclone season extends year-round, with peaks from mid-February to early March, and from April to December in the southern Indian Ocean. There has been only one recorded instance of a hurricane in the South Atlantic (it hit Brazil in 2004), but these storms are fairly common in the other southern ocean basins throughout the world.

Some scientists and media commentators believe that there has been a steady increase in the number and severity of tropical cyclones over the last thirty years or so due to increases in sea water temperature caused by global warming. However, this has been disputed by others who claim that these phenomena may be cyclic over many years and result from natural causes. They cite several storms that occurred in the 1800s that were among the most severe ever recorded and assert that perceived increases in severity of modern storms may in fact be more a result of increased accuracy of modern instrumentation, plus the modern-day trend to build habitations closer to the ocean shores, where they are more susceptible to damage. Whatever the causes, it is indisputable that these huge storms have brought more death and destruction upon humanity than any other natural phenomena.

In the United States the most damaging hurricane in history was Hurricane Katrina, mentioned above, which caused a record $100 billion in damages in Louisiana and Mississippi and killed more than 1,800 people. A hurricane that struck Galveston, Texas, in September 1900 was the deadliest natural disaster in American history, killing somewhere between 6,000 to 12,000 people. The strongest tropical cyclone ever to hit land was Typhoon Haiyan, which struck Samar Island in the

Philippines in November 2013. It hit with sustained winds of 195 mph, with gusts of up to 235, with a twenty-foot storm surge that leveled the city of Tacloban, on neighboring Leyte. It killed at least four thousand people.

Navigation in Tropical Cyclones

As was previously stated above, hurricanes and other tropical cyclones rotate counter-clockwise in the northern hemisphere and clockwise in the southern hemisphere. Because of this, their right-front quarter, or **quadrant,** in the Northern Hemisphere and left-front quadrant in the Southern Hemisphere are called the **dangerous quadrants.** The semicircles on that side are called the **dangerous semicircles,** because here the rotating winds around the eye combine with the forward motion of the storms to produce the highest wind velocities. At landfall, most of the wind damage and greatest storm surge will occur on this side of the storm. Also, vessels caught in the dangerous quadrants tend to be blown in toward the axis of the storm, where the exposure will be the worst. In addition, the heaviest rainfall in the storm is usually concentrated in the quadrant behind the dangerous quadrant.

By contrast, the left semicircle of the storm in the northern hemisphere and the right semicircle in the southern hemisphere are called the **navigable semicircles,** because on this side of the storm the rotating winds are partially canceled by its speed of advance. Less wind damage and storm surge ashore usually results from this side of the storm. Obviously, the best course

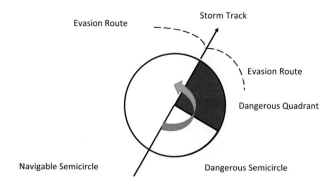

A drawing showing the dangerous quadrant and semicircle, as well as evasion routes around a tropical cyclone whirling counterclockwise in the northern hemisphere. In the southern hemisphere the sides and rotation are reversed.

of action for mariners at sea is to heed warnings of these storms far enough in advance to avoid them altogether, but if caught in them, the best procedure is to maneuver so as to evade the dangerous quadrant or minimize time in it.

Storm Warning Signals

Flags and pennants hoisted at National Weather Service installations and other shore stations indicate the presence or forecast presence of unfavorable winds. These signals are flown over most major marinas in the United States, recreational beaches, and Coast Guard stations:

Type of Warning	Daytime Signals	Night Signals	Equivalent Wind Speeds	
			Knots	MPH
Small Craft			Up to 33	Up to 38
Gale			34–47	39–54
Storm			48–63	55–73
Hurricane			64 or Greater	74 or Greater

Storm warning signals.

- *Small craft warning.* One red pennant displayed by day, or a red light over a white light at night, indicate that winds of up to 38 mph (33 knots) and sea conditions dangerous to small craft are forecast in the area.
- *Gale warning.* Two red pennants displayed by day, or a white light above a red light at night, indicate that winds ranging from 39 to 54 miles an hour (34–47 knots) are forecast.
- *Storm warning.* A single square red flag with a black center displayed during daytime, or two red lights at night, indicate that winds of 55 mph (48 knots) and above are forecast.
- *Hurricane warning.* Two square red flags with black centers displayed by day, or a white light between two red lights at night, indicate that winds 74 mph (64 knots) and above are forecast for the area.

Hurricane Warning System

The U.S. Hurricane Warning System was set up in 1938 as a cooperative effort of the National Weather Service, the Navy, and the Army Air Corps. Previous to that, hurricanes had struck with almost no prior warning. Since then reconnaissance airplanes equipped with radar and weather instruments have been sent out to scout suspected storms whenever they threaten the United States.

In more recent years, weather satellites supplemented by reconnaissance aircraft have been used to collect data on these storms. Bulletins are issued every few hours, giving the latest information on a storm, its intensity, and its present location and probable path, thus furnishing timely warning to all who may be in danger. Vessels at sea and aircraft can change course to avoid the storm; people have time to secure their property to reduce damage and evacuate from areas expected to bear the brunt of the storm. As the storm approaches land, it can be observed by land-based Doppler weather-radar systems. This radar plays a crucial role around landfall, as it can continuously show a storm's location and intensity as it comes ashore.

Two agencies of the National Weather Service track and disseminate information and warnings regarding hurricanes and typhoons that might threaten the United States or its island protectorates. The National Hurricane Center, in Miami, Florida, issues bulletins, watches, and warnings on tropical cyclones from the Prime Meridian (passing through Greenwich, England) west to the 140th meridian in the eastern Pacific; the Central Pacific Hurricane Center based in Honolulu, Hawaii, does the same for the central Pacific between the 140th meridian and the International Date Line (180 degrees west longitude). Agencies of the World Meteorological Organization (WMO) provide the same type of information for other areas worldwide.

Critical Thinking

1. There has been much speculation in the scientific community in recent years about the link between alleged global warming and the increased frequency and intensity of severe weather worldwide. Research the alleged global warming trend and its causes, and the arguments given in support of its link with the increasing incidence of severe weather worldwide.

Study Guide Questions

1. A. How do weather fronts develop?
   B. What usually happens when a cold front meets a warm-air mass?

2. What kind of weather does a front usually bring?

3. What are the three types of frontal systems?

4. Where is the Intertropical Convergence Zone (ITCZ), and why is it of particular importance?

5. What are squalls, and what are their characteristics?

6. Why is the Polar Frontal Zone important to those who live in the temperate zones?

7. What are the first signs of an approaching cold front?

8. What are the signs of an approaching warm front?

9. What is an occluded front?

10. What are the three stages of a thunderstorm, and what happens in each stage?

11. What weather phenomena occur within a thunderstorm?

12. Why should aircraft avoid flying through a thunderstorm?

13. What is lightning, and what causes it to happen?

14. A. What is meant by the statement "Lightning follows the easiest route"?
    B. What causes thunder?

15. A. Where do most tornadoes occur?
    B. What name is given to a tornado over water?
    C. On what scale is the strength of tornadoes rated?

16. A. What are the three categories of tropical cyclone?
    B. What is the established minimum wind velocity for a tropical cyclone?
    C. On what scale is the strength of hurricanes and other tropical cyclones rated?

17. How are the names given to tropical cyclones around the world chosen?

18. How does a hurricane develop, and why is it so violent?

19. What are the most usual tracks or paths of a North Atlantic hurricane?

20. What is the "eye" of the hurricane, and what is unusual about this part of the storm?

21. What aspect of a hurricane usually causes the most damage and casualties?

22. When is "hurricane season"?

23. Explain the "dangerous" and "navigable" semicircles and quadrants of a hurricane.

24. What are the four categories of storm warning signals for unfavorable winds in the vicinity of harbors and beaches in the United States?

25. What means are used to locate and track hurricanes?

26. What are the two National Weather Service agencies that provide information and warnings about hurricanes?

New Vocabulary

cold front	hurricane
warm front	typhoon
stationary front	willy-willies
occluded front	baygo
microburst	eye
leaders (of lightning)	eye wall
tornado	extratropical low
waterspout	storm surge
vortex	dangerous quadrant
tropical cyclone	navigable semicircle
tropical depression	

11

Weather Forecasting

Weather forecasting has developed into a full-time activity of agencies within the U.S. government, the armed services, and many commercial meteorological enterprises. This chapter will discuss some of the procedures used by the National Weather Service and the Naval Meteorological and Oceanography Command to forecast the weather.

National Weather

The principal weather agency in the United States is the **National Weather Service (NWS)**. It is part of the **National Oceanic and Atmospheric Administration (NOAA)**, which is within the Department of Commerce. NOAA is the principal agency within the U.S. government that is focused on the oceans and the atmosphere. In coordination with other federal, state, and local agencies, it collects and disseminates information on the oceans and the atmosphere worldwide and regulates fisheries and marine sanctuaries and protects threatened and endangered marine species. The National Weather Service reports the weather of the United States and its territories and provides weather, hydrologic (water-effect), and climate forecasts and warnings to the general public. It issues warnings about such destructive weather conditions as hurricanes, tornadoes, and floods. It provides special weather services in support of aviation, marine activities, agriculture, forestry, urban air-quality control, and other activities that are sensitive to the weather.

The National Weather Service is composed of a headquarters at Camp Springs, Maryland, near Washington, D.C.; six national centers; six regional support centers, which support field activities throughout the continental United States, Puerto Rico, Alaska, Hawaii, and other islands in the Pacific Ocean; and twelve national specialized centers, which support specialized needs like the Central Pacific Hurricane Warning Center, the Pacific Tsunami Warning Center, and

An automated NWS weather buoy. *NOAA*

the Spaceflight Meteorology Group. The NWS receives weather data from about 11,000 substations, many of which are maintained by volunteers.

Chief among the national centers organization is the National Centers for Environmental Prediction (NCEP), a group of nine specialized centers, each focusing on one aspect of the overall national warning and forecasting process. They are the Aviation Weather Center, in Kansas City, Missouri; the Climate Prediction Center, in Camp Springs; the Space Environment Center, in Boulder, Colorado; the Storm Prediction Center, in Norman, Oklahoma; the National Hurricane Center, in Miami, Florida; the Ocean Prediction Center, in College Park, Maryland; and three others.

The National Weather Service employs thousands of people twenty-four hours a day, seven days a week. It operates some four hundred weather facilities throughout the fifty states, and it also has facilities in overseas locations and on ships worldwide. Each day it receives and processes some 12,000 synoptic (general) and 25,000 hourly reports from a network of automated buoy, ship, and surface observation stations; 1,500 atmospheric soundings; 2,500 reports from aircraft; and all available cloud, temperature, and other data from weather satellites. The NWS operates a nationwide network of Doppler weather radars that can provide continuous information on precipitation and other weather throughout the United States.

The service provides weather information to newspapers, radio and television stations, and other media for the general public. It makes studies of climate and conducts basic and applied research for the purposes of improving future forecasts and services and advancing the science of meteorology.

A major part of the National Weather Service's everyday activity is geared to the service of aviation, through its Aviation Weather Center. It makes available up-to-the-minute flight condition forecasts to all parts of the aviation community.

The Naval Meteorology and Oceanography Command

Because the National Weather Service must serve so many interests in so many ways, it cannot gear its activities to the special needs of the armed services worldwide. Each of the services must maintain its own weather agency. For the Navy, this is the mission of the Naval Meteorology and Oceanography Command (NMOC), headquartered at Stennis Space Center, Mississippi. The command comprises approximately three thousand officer, enlisted, and civilian personnel stationed around the world. It provides global forecast services to meet Navy and other Department of Defense needs throughout the world. It includes elements of the operating forces, shore establishment, and Navy Department, and it cooperates fully with all national, regional, and international weather agencies. It is also an active participant in the WMO.

There are five major component commands within NMOC. The U.S. Naval Observatory (USNO) provides a wide range of astronomical data and products, serves as the official timekeeper for the U.S. Department of Defense (the Navy atomic clock) and supplies time standards for the entire United States. The Joint Typhoon Warning Center (JTWC) is the Department of Defense agency responsible for issuing tropical cyclone warnings for the Pacific and Indian Oceans. The Naval Oceanography Operations Command (NOOC) advises Navy operations on the impact of ocean and atmospheric conditions in every theater and for every operation. NOOC products include those from the Naval Maritime Forecast Center–Norfolk and the Naval Oceanography ASW Center–Yokosuka. The Fleet Numerical Meteorology and Oceanography Center (FNMOC) provides high-quality and timely worldwide meteorology and oceanography support to U.S. and coalition forces from its operations center in Monterey, California. The Naval Oceanographic Office (NAVO) maximizes sea power by applying relevant oceanographic knowledge in support of U.S. national security organizations and forces worldwide.

Also under NOMC are two fleet weather centers (FWCs), one in Norfolk, Virginia, and the other in San Diego, California. FWC Norfolk is responsible for all Navy weather forecasting for fleet operations and training in the Second, Fourth, and Sixth Fleet areas of responsibility in the Atlantic Ocean, Caribbean Sea, Central and South America, and Mediterranean Sea regions. It issues maritime and aviation forecasts; weather warnings to Navy activities located in the Midwestern, mid-Atlantic, and southeastern United States and Europe; it performs ships and aircraft routing; and it organizes, trains, and deploys oceanography teams in support of strike force carriers and large-deck amphibious ships. FWC San Diego does the same for the Third, Fifth, and Seventh Fleet areas of responsibility, providing weather and oceanographic support to Navy activities

The Fleet Aviation Forecast Center pictured here is part of the Fleet Weather Center, Norfolk, located on the naval air station there. *CHINFO*

An automated weather station. This equipment can be mounted on ships and shore stations, and it provides continuous remote readings on temperature, pressure, humidity, and wind speed and direction. *NOAA*

A Navy quartermaster plots the course of his ship. The quartermasters do the tasks of aerographers on smaller ships that do not have meteorological staffs. *CHINFO, Adam Thomas*

throughout the western United States, the Pacific and Indian Oceans, and the Arabian Gulf.

Navy weather units are maintained within all major aviation units, major combatant and auxiliary vessels, fleet flagships, and most naval shore activities. Trained enlisted aerographer's mates and meteorological officers are assigned to these weather units. In addition, many larger ships are equipped with **automated shipboard weather stations** that automatically transmit meteorological data directly to the FNMOC at Monterey. On smaller ships that do not carry aerographers and meteorologists, weather observations and reporting are carried out by the ship's navigator, assisted by trained quartermasters.

Forecast Services and Weather Maps

The National Weather Service publishes many kinds of weather forecasts. Among these are twenty-four-hour detailed forecasts;

three-, seven-, and fourteen-day forecasts; thirty-day general outlooks; twelve-hour aviation forecasts; and special bulletins, weather maps, and storm and frost warnings.

Newspaper, TV, and radio weather reports rely on many of these services. For air safety, complete weather reports are furnished to general and commercial aviation pilots by the Federal Aviation Agency, in cooperation with the National Weather Service. Pilots also get frequent updates of weather information while flying. It is common for commercial airline passengers to hear their captain, just a few minutes after the plane takes off, reporting the weather conditions expected at the destination of the flight, with updates often given en route.

The two kinds of weather reporting are local and long-range forecasting. Local weather reports contain detailed short-range forecasts for thirty-six-hour to seventy-two-hour prediction periods, with less detailed forecasts up to a month or so in advance. The accuracy of these predictions is dependent

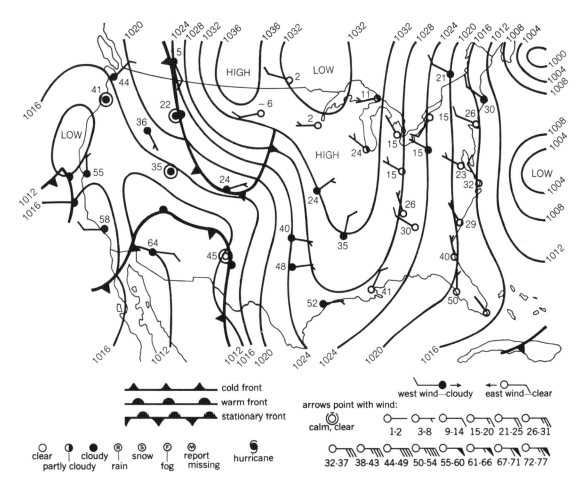

A simplified weather map similar to those issued by the National Weather Service. The symbols shown on the map are identified in the legend beneath it. The curved lines are called *isobars* (lines connecting points of equal pressure) and are labeled in millibars. Closely spaced isobars indicate areas of higher wind intensity. Warm and cold fronts are indicated by heavier lines marked with their associated symbols (see the legend). High- and low-pressure centers are identified, and the small circle symbols indicate the atmospheric conditions. Small arrows attached to them indicate wind direction, with speeds indicated by the number and style of vanes on the ends. Nearby numbers are Fahrenheit temperatures.

upon the timeliness of readings taken at many reporting stations—on land and ships, balloons, and weather satellites. The long-range study is more concerned with an overall view of the climate and with predictions for a year or more in the future. Publications called **almanacs** provide long-range weather predictions for the year ahead; these are based on average weather reported for years past.

Comprehensive weather maps for general public use are generated by the National Centers for Environmental Prediction (NCEP) of the National Weather Service and are available on the NCEP website (www.ncep.noaa.gov). Maps are generated for six-hour intervals for the entire Northern Hemisphere from Western Europe to the Far East (135 degrees east longitude), for the North Atlantic and North Pacific basins, and many subdivisions of the continental United States, for three, seven, and fourteen days in the future. More specialized weather maps intended for a wide variety of other purposes, including general and commercial aviation, are generated by many other agencies within the NWS.

In the Navy, elements of the Naval Meteorological and Oceanography Command prepare these types of forecasts, each for a specific purpose and containing specific information applicable to the types of units and areas of operations in which they are located. Storm warnings are issued by the FWC responsible for the area in which the storm is located. Storms reported are thunderstorms, tornadoes, local wind storms, and major storms. Special warnings are issued for tropical cyclones.

Weather Satellites

Weather satellites are the newest forecasting tool available to the meteorologist. Weather satellites began with the TIROS (TV and Infrared Observation Satellite) in 1960. Since then, many greatly more capable satellites have been developed and placed in orbit. The newest satellites are equipped with high-resolution cameras that transmit pictures of the cloud formations and water-vapor images on the Earth's surface, either by day or by night, in both the visible-light and infrared spectrums. Onboard sensors record surface temperatures and fronts, storms, snow, sea ice, and cloud heights. They can also collect other types of environmental information, such as city lights, forest fires, snow cover, ice mapping, boundaries of ocean currents, effects of pollution, and more. Other **environmental satellites** can detect changes in vegetation, sea states, ocean colors, and ice fields.

There are two types of these satellites: polar orbiting and geosynchronous (geostationary). Weather satellites in **polar orbits** (orbits that pass over the Earth's poles or nearly so) circle the Earth every ninety-six to a hundred minutes at an average

A NOAA weather satellite. *NOAA*

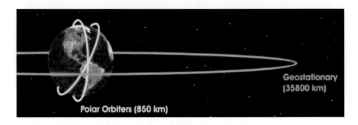

Polar, Sun-synchronous, and geostationary orbits. *NOAA*

height of about 530 miles (850 km), orbiting the entire planet fourteen times a day. They are sometimes called **Sun-synchronous satellites,** because their orbits are actually slightly inclined (98 degrees, versus 90 degrees) to allow them to pass over any given latitude at the same Sun-illumination angle each time. **Geosynchronous satellites** hover 22,300 miles (35,800 km) above the Earth, and, because at this altitude they orbit at the same rate as the Earth rotates, they remain at a fixed location over the equator. NOAA currently has about a half-dozen polar-orbiting weather satellites in orbit at any given time, plus two geosynchronous weather satellites, although at times some of these may become inoperable and require replacement. The geosynchronous satellites are positioned at 75 and 135 west longitudes and provide pole-to-pole coverage between 20 west to 165 east longitudes. Their spectacular pictures of whole weather systems and frontal weather patterns are now a regular part of weather forecasting. There are currently at all times at least two Defense Meteorological Satellite Program (DMSP) satellites maintained by the Department of Defense in polar orbits as well. Other nations such as Russia, China, Japan, and India, as well as the European Union, also have orbiting weather satellites in both orbits.

Critical Thinking

1. Research the qualifications needed to become a meteorologist working for the government or as a television weather forecaster.

Study Guide Questions

1. What is the principal agency in the U.S. government focused on the oceans and the atmosphere?
2. What is the principal weather agency in the U.S. government?
3. What are the main activities of the National Weather Service?
4. A. What is main weather agency of the U.S. Navy?
   B. What are its responsibilities?
5. What are the main component commands within the Naval Meteorology and Oceanography Command?
6. What are the two fleet weather centers responsible for?
7. What kinds of information is presented on weather maps?
8. What is the principal difference between long-range and local forecasting?
9. What are the two types of weather satellites?
10. What weather information is transmitted back to Earth by weather satellites?

New Vocabulary

aerographers	geostationary
meteorologists	Sun-synchronous orbit
polar orbit	geosynchronous

Astronomy

Astronomy is the study of the universe—in particular, the study of the stars and other heavenly bodies, including their composition, motion, position, and size. You might ask, "Why delve into the mysteries of the universe? What does an astronomer produce or achieve?" The product of astronomy is a greater knowledge and understanding of the universe. True, much of this knowledge has not been used directly. However, the study of astronomy led to the discovery of the fundamental laws governing all modern technology. Astronomy is directly responsible for the scientific age, which has fundamentally altered our lives.

The universe is the most awesome concept in the human imagination. The size of the universe is beyond our comprehension. Earth-based and space-based telescopes have found a million galaxies in the region within the Big Dipper alone, and they have observed light coming from distant galaxies and other objects more than thirteen billion light years away.

Origin of the Universe and the Milky Way

There are many theories about the origin of the universe. Ever since ancient times, when humankind first began to study the world and contemplate the heavens, people have wondered how Earth and the universe came to be. Although we certainly know more than the ancients about the origin of things, many questions remain unanswered. Astronomers and other scientists who speculate on the nature of the universe and try to answer these questions are called **cosmologists,** and their science is called **cosmology.**

The modern scientific theory of the origin of the universe is called the **Big Bang,** or expanding-universe, theory. It was first proposed in 1927 by the Belgian astronomer Georges Lemaître. His theory has since been supported by many other scientists and an ever-growing body of scientific data. Lemaître postulated that all matter in the universe was originally concentrated in an incredibly small and dense point-mass. Packed inside was all the material of today's universe, at a temperature greater than 100 trillion degrees C.

According to this theory, our universe began about 13.8 billion years ago when a huge explosion sent dust and gas hurtling outward in all directions. Soon the first galaxies began to form, as parts of this expanding gas and dust began to coalesce. Astronomers believe that this expansion will never cease. Indeed, studies of the movements of other galaxies indicate that all are speeding away from us and from each other at fantastic rates. In May 1992, scientists analyzing data on microwave radiation gathered by an orbiting *Cosmic Background Explorer* (*COBE*) satellite announced that they had been able to verify the existence of slight temperature variations in space that theory predicted would have resulted from the Big Bang. This discovery, along with other subsequent observations, has given further support to the theory—so much so that several prominent cosmologists called it the greatest scientific discovery of the last century.

Our galaxy, the Milky Way, was so named because if observed with the naked eye it appears as a dimly lit band across the night sky. Its formation probably began shortly after the Big Bang. The fact that it is composed of stars was proven in 1610, when Galileo observed them using his telescope. Current estimates are that there are as many as 400 billion stars in our galaxy, many of them perhaps having at least one planet in orbit around them. The oldest known star in the Milky Way has been estimated to be about 13.2 billion years old, almost the age of the universe. The nearest star to our Sun is Proxima Centauri, one of three stars in the Alpha Centaur system, about 4.24 light years from Earth.

Origin of the Solar System

Cosmologists believe that what is now our solar system (the Sun, the planets, their moons, and all the other objects in it) began about 4.6 billion years ago as a large cloud of gas and dust from the Big Bang and subsequent stellar **supernovae** (star explosions) within our galaxy. These materials consisted of the "cosmic mix" of elements observed throughout the universe—74 percent hydrogen by mass, 24 percent helium, and 2 percent heavier elements, such as oxygen, carbon, iron, and others. Small eddies developed within the cloud as it turned in space like a giant whirlpool. A large eddy at the center contracted more rapidly than the rest of the cloud and formed the **proto-Sun.**

In the cold depths of the cloud surrounding the proto-Sun, certain gases combined to form compounds such as water and ammonia. Gradually, forces in the spinning cloud flattened it into the shape of an enormous disk. At a great distance this disk would have looked somewhat like a gigantic revolving phonograph record, with the proto-Sun at the center.

Within this whirling disk, eddies and swirls began to appear at various distances from the central mass. Some were torn apart in collisions, while others were broken up by the growing gravitational pull of the proto-Sun. As this battle continued in the wheeling system, some swirls gained material and others lost it. Finally, a number of these swirls became swirling disks large enough to hold together under the strength of their own gravitational fields. Each was a **proto-planet,** moving through space around the Sun and sweeping up material left over from the original cloud.

As the proto-Sun's mass was pulled together, collisions, compression, and radioactivity heated the mass until temperatures at the center reached millions of degrees C. In a process called **thermonuclear fusion,** hydrogen atoms began to **fuse** (combine under great pressure and temperature) to form helium, causing the proto-Sun to begin to shine—at first a dull red, in time the golden yellow that we see today. Because it was about a hundred times larger in diameter than the largest of the proto-planets, the Sun became a **star** instead of a planet. Its gravitational pull was strong enough to trap light hydrogen atoms in its interior, where they fuel the thermonuclear fusion process.

Meanwhile, proto-Earth and the other proto-planets continued to accumulate ice particles and solid fragments, eventually coalescing into balls. Gradually these proto-planet balls grew by the accumulation of additional gas, dust, and smaller bodies from the region of space near them. (Even today, planets continue to sweep up dust and meteorites.) Smaller rocky, solid, planetary balls formed in the inner part of the whirling disk nearer the proto-Sun. Larger gaseous balls formed farther away, with a band of leftover material revolving between them and in the outer regions of the disk.

The proto-Sun begins to glow in the middle of the rotating disk of gas and dust from which it was formed, with the proto-planets gathering material in orbit around it. *NASA*

In time, radioactive elements and the compressive action within the third ball from the Sun, which would become planet Earth, began to give off heat. After millions of years the temperature became high enough to melt the materials at the planet's center. The iron, nickel, and other heavy metals spread throughout the planet then began to sink, forming a molten core. Later, molten rock outside the core (magma) broke through fissures to the surface. This allowed molecules of hydrogen, water vapor, and other gases to escape, creating an atmosphere above the surface. The oceans were formed when the water vapor released into the atmosphere began to condense and precipitate. The lighter gases, especially hydrogen, did not stay in the atmosphere long. They left behind a high concentration of the heavier, rarer elements of the universe—elements essential for the formation of rocks, plants, and, eventually, our own bodies. Our planet Earth was born.

Similar processes took place on the other three rocky inner planets. Because of their close proximity to the Sun, on the innermost two planets the water mostly boiled off into space, but on the other two it stayed behind. Eventually, for reasons not yet understood, the fourth planet, Mars, lost most if its water, leaving Earth as the only planet in the solar system with large amounts of liquid water and ice on its surface and water vapor in its atmosphere. The large gaseous outer four planets were too cold to harbor liquid water, but some was incorporated into them as vapor, and some formed as ice on some of their moons.

The band of leftover material between Mars and Jupiter, the first of the gas giants, became known as the **asteroid belt.** At some early point in time this material may have coalesced into a planet which later either exploded or collided with another body, but most astronomers believe it just remained a collection of hundreds of thousands of remnant fragments of assorted sizes, as well as larger bodies. The other leftover material in the outer reaches of the disk beyond the last of the gas giants aggregated into many small objects called **dwarf planets** and **comets,** in bands called the **Kuiper Belt** and the **Oort Cloud,** stretching out halfway to the nearest star.

There are other theories of the creation of the universe, the solar system, and our Earth, of course. The foregoing scientific theory is the one accepted by most modern-day cosmologists and other scientists. Perhaps with more numerous and better ground- and space-based telescopes, exploratory bases on the Moon and beyond, and further explorations into outer space, one day we will be able to shed more light on this fascinating topic.

12

Astronomical Observations

Until the twentieth century, observations of the heavens were made visually from Earth's surface, either with the naked eye or, after the Middle Ages, with an optical instrument called the **telescope.** This was a device developed by Dutch eyeglass makers and subsequently improved upon and introduced to early astronomers by the Italian astronomer Galileo Galilei in the early 1600s. But Earth-based observations of celestial bodies with optical telescopes, however large and refined they might be, are hindered by Earth's atmosphere. Sometimes the atmosphere makes observations impossible, as on a cloudy night. Even at the best of times it causes distortion of the incoming light from the body, making it impossible to observe very detailed surface features of even the nearest bodies, like the Moon or the planet Mars.

Fortunately, modern technology has provided methods of observation of the heavens that are far better for many purposes than the Earth-based optical telescope. These include radiotelescopes; aircraft-, balloon- and spacecraft-borne telescopes; and, since the 1960s, manned spacecraft. Each of these will be discussed below.

The Telescope

Because of its wide availability and relatively low cost, the traditional telescope will always have a place in astronomy. There are many different sizes and types of optical telescopes. They range from portable models designed for the amateur, a few inches in diameter and a couple of feet in length, to giant reflecting telescopes with computer-driven aiming machinery, mounted in buildings called **observatories.** These instruments are used primarily by professional astronomers, who make most of their observations by means of time-exposure photography rather than visual sightings. Larger telescopes have **tracking mechanisms** that compensate for the Earth's rotation and revolution by continuous small adjustments of the position of the telescope, keeping it precisely pointed at whatever body it is observing.

If we were to take a trip to an observatory during its working hours, it would be at night. We probably would have to drive up a high hill or even a mountain to get there. The large research observatories are mostly located in high, remote places, away from the lights, smoke, and smog of cities. At high altitudes the air is thinner and clearer, eliminating as much atmospheric distortion as possible. Ideally, the observatory is built where the weather affords a maximum number of clear nights with "steady atmosphere."

The distinguishing feature of an observatory is its large revolving dome. Through a slit-like opening in this dome, the telescope peers into the night sky. Except for the hum of motors and the click of switches, all is quiet as the astronomers direct the telescope toward the desired spot in the heavens. The whole dome can be made to turn, to point the telescope at celestial bodies anywhere in the sky. The environment in the dome must be exactly as it is outside. It must be dark, so that the time-exposure photography used for observations will not be obscured or distorted in any way. The temperature in the dome must be the same as outdoors, with no extra heat, since any such warm air would affect the telescope's lenses and mirrors, blurring the photography. Thus in winter the astronomer must wear heavy clothing as protection from the cold.

Two domes housing telescopes at the Keck Observatory atop a mountain at Mauna Kea, Hawaii. *T. Wynne/JPL*

The **telescope** is the largest and most important object in the observatory. The magnifying power of an optical telescope, which determines how far into the heavens it can peer, is determined by the thickness and curvature of its lens or the radius of curvature of its mirror, while the diameter of its lens or mirror determines how bright and sharp the image will be. The larger the lens or mirror, the greater will be the amount of light that can be gathered from any given celestial body observed and the brighter the image will appear. Because of the physics of a telescope, however, the greater the magnification power of a given telescope, the smaller its field of view and the amount of light it can gather. Each time the magnification is doubled, the image gets four times dimmer. Thus, for each size of telescope there is a maximum amount of magnification that can be achieved without significantly degrading the quality of the image. In astronomy, therefore, successful observation of the dimmer, more distant planets, stars, and galaxies requires **time exposures** (observations made by leaving a camera or electronic detector shutter open for an extended time) by powerful telescopes with very large lenses or mirrors.

Most of the observations made by professional astronomers with large telescopes in observatories use special cameras operated by computers rather than visual observations by eye. At one time, astronomical photographs were taken using traditional cameras that projected the images onto photographic film, then later onto sensitive photographic glass plates. Now special electronic digital cameras called **CCD (charge-coupled device) cameras** are used. They are highly refined and specialized versions of the digital and cell-phone cameras we all use but are capable of much higher resolutions, in the hundreds of megapixels.

Astronomers use single-frame CCD cameras for time exposures and CCD video cameras for real-time (instantaneous) viewing. Images are downloaded into computers and processed with imaging software, much as you might do with digital camera photos and image-manipulating software on your computer at home. Time exposures are the normal method of observation, because the camera must store up the feeble light received from distant stars, nebula (gas clouds), and other celestial objects, perhaps for hours. Such time exposures reveal the movement of the planets, asteroids, meteors, and comets in our solar system against a background of distant and relatively stationary stars and galaxies.

Modern-day astronomers are much more than mere "stargazers." When working at night with the telescopic equipment in an observatory, an astronomer must also be an electronics technician, photographer, and computer operator. During the day, the astronomer must be a mathematician, physicist, chemist, mechanic, research analyst, and office manager. Research and laboratory work goes on every working day, and in observatory shops new and upgraded astronomical instruments are continually being adapted for use in observing the universe.

Types of Telescopes

There are two principal types of astronomical telescopes, refracting and reflecting. Each will be described below.

The **refracting telescope** is the traditional type that is commonly used for rifle gunfights, binoculars, and the like. It uses two lenses. There is a single convex (outwardly curved) lens, called the *objective lens,* at the far end of the telescope. This lens forms a reduced, inverted *image* of a distant object being viewed. The *eyepiece lens,* also convex, at the near end, magnifies this image and reinverts it, making the object appear right side up, closer, and enlarged.

The largest refracting telescope in the world is located at the Yerkes Observatory at Williams Bay on Lake Geneva, Wisconsin. Operated by the University of Chicago, this refractor has an objective lens with a diameter of forty inches (102 centimeters).

Because a refracting lens can be supported only around its edge, the size and weight of a large lens itself produces unavoidable distortions in its shape, which in turn affect the image. The forty-inch Yerkes refractor thus represents the practical upper

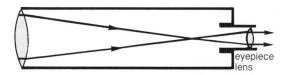

Light-ray diagram for a refracting telescope.

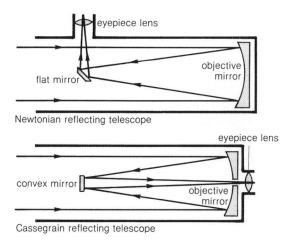

Light-ray diagrams for reflecting telescopes. These may be either Newtonian (top) or Cassegrain (bottom). A Newtonian reflector has a small, flat secondary mirror that focuses the image to the side, while the classic Cassegrain has a convex secondary mirror that focuses the image back through a hole in the primary mirror to the bottom of the telescope. Variants focus the image to the side or to a viewing station at the top of the telescope.

size limit for this kind of telescope. To get around this limitation, the **reflecting telescope** has come into wide use. Sir Isaac Newton is credited with inventing the first one in 1672. This type telescope uses an *objective mirror* in place of the objective lens. This slightly concave (inwardly curving) mirror forms an image that in most cases is reflected by a secondary mirror to where the eyepiece magnifier is mounted.

There are two main types of reflecting telescope. In the *Newtonian reflector,* a flat secondary mirror reflects the light and brings it to a focus at an eyepiece at the side of the telescope. In the classic *Cassegrain reflector,* a curved secondary mirror causes the light to focus behind the objective mirror. Thus the objective mirror must have a hole in the center to allow light to

pass through. The eyepiece is then placed at the bottom of the telescope. Variations of this design reflect the light off the secondary mirror to the side so that a hole in the objective mirror is not required, or to a viewing station at the focal point of the primary mirror near the top of the telescope. Cassegrain reflectors and the other variations are much more expensive than Newtonian reflectors and are utilized for telescopes having very large mirrors.

The largest one-piece primary reflector mirrors in the world today are installed in a telescope in an observatory at Mount Graham near Safford, Arizona. Called the *Large Binocular Telescope,* it actually consists of two twin 8.4-meter (27.5-foot) reflectors mounted side by side that can achieve the same image

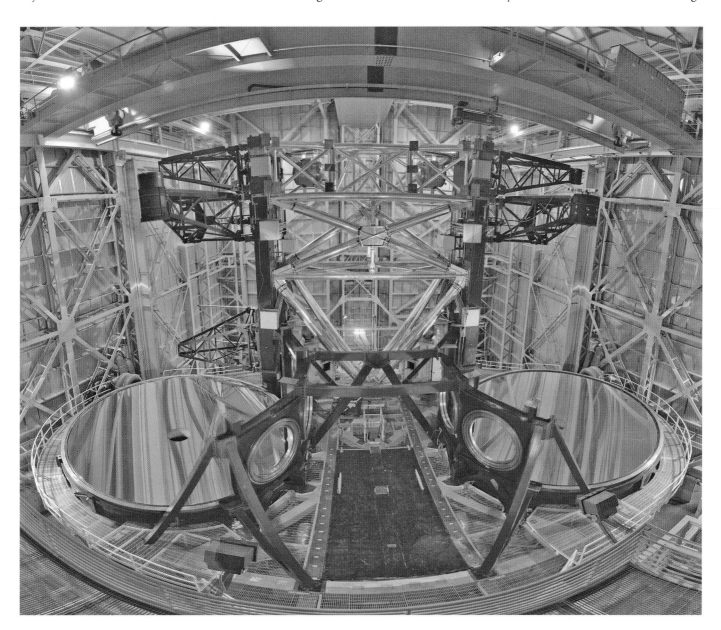

The Large Binocular Telescope at Mount Graham, Arizona. Each of the two mirrors is over eight meters in diameter, and the entire structure is almost thirty meters high. *Large Binocular Telescope Observatory*

sharpness as a 22.8-meter (75-foot) mirror. Each of the cast-glass mirrors weighs over sixteen tons and is almost a meter thick. Another variation of the same idea is the *Very Large Telescope (VLT)* at the European Southern Observatory (ESO), in northern Chile. This observatory can combine the images of an array of four separate 8.2-meter (27-foot) reflecting telescopes in groups of two or three, in a technique called **optical interferometry** (combining images of two or more telescopes) that achieves the same maximum resolution as a 16-meter (52.5-foot) mirror.

To lower the high cost and difficulty of casting one-piece mirrors as large as these, several other more recently constructed large reflecting telescopes have mirrors that consist of a number of smaller mirrored hexagons called *segments*. Each of these is controlled by a computer to a precision within a millionth of an inch. The computer software can make additional continuous tiny adjustments to the overall shape of the mirror to compensate for atmospheric refraction. One such telescope is the *Southern African Large Telescope (SALT)*, located at Sutherland, South Africa. It has an 11-meter (36-foot) mirror made up of ninety-one hexagonal segments. Other such telescopes are located at the Keck Observatory, at Mauna Kea, Hawaii (two telescopes with 10.2-meter [33.5-foot] segmented mirrors), and at La Palma in the Canary Islands in the Atlantic (a 10.4-meter [34-foot] segmented mirror called the *Grand Telescope of the Canaries*).

Because of their huge size and great precision, these large telescopes have much more light-gathering capability and resolution than smaller space-based telescopes like the *Hubble*, described below. Thus, they have enabled Earth-bound astronomers to make observations of such things as planets orbiting distant stars and galaxies at the edges of the universe that would otherwise have been impossible until only a few years ago, when the next generation of more capable space telescopes began to be orbited.

The Radiotelescope

In the early 1900s, astronomers discovered that in addition to radiation in the infrared, visible light, and ultraviolet spectrums, many celestial bodies also emit radiation in the radio-frequency portion of the electromagnetic spectrum. This discovery gave rise to the development of **radiotelescopes**. In a radiotelescope, a dish-like antenna is used to gather the radio waves from space—much as an objective mirror gathers light waves in a reflecting telescope. Like telescopes, they have tracking mechanisms to keep them pointed at their targets as the Earth rotates and revolves, as well as computerized receivers to analyze the signals received.

Radiotelescopes must be very sensitive in order to detect faint radio waves from space. Also, because the wavelengths of

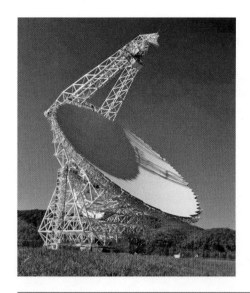

The Robert Byrd radiotelescope at Green Bank, West Virginia, is the world's largest single steerable radiotelescope.
National Radio Astronomy Observatory

many of the radio waves studied are many thousands of times longer than light waves, radiotelescopes must be very large. Like the large telescope observatories, large radiotelescope facilities are mostly located in fairly remote and dry places at higher altitudes to minimize interference from terrestrial radio transmissions and the atmosphere. The world's largest single steerable radiotelescope is the *Robert Byrd* radiotelescope at Green Bank, West Virginia. Its dish is oval shaped, 100 by 110 meters (328 by 361 feet). Other very large ones are at Eifel Mountain, near Bonn, Germany (100 meters [328 feet] in diameter), and Jodrell Bank in Cheshire, England (76 meters [250 feet]). The world's largest stationary radiotelescope, with a diameter of 305 meters (1,000 feet), is near Arecibo, Puerto Rico.

Because some celestial objects are too far away or too cold to radiate detectable light energy, the radio "star map" or radio source map of the sky does not correspond with a visible light map. Radio astronomers have found in deep space many huge regions of gases and remnants of celestial supernovae explosions that had previously been invisible. Sunspots also give off radio waves, as does the corona of the Sun. Radiotelescopes have discovered **quasars.** In an optical telescope these objects look no larger than a single star but are actually regions surrounding massive **black holes** (gravity fields from which nothing can escape) in the centers of distant galaxies that emit hundreds of times more energy than our own Milky Way. They have also discovered **pulsars,** which are bodies that appear to radiate energy at regular, very precise intervals. Once thought to be artificial beacons, they are now known to be rapidly rotating compressed stars in the last stages of stellar life.

Radioastronomers have found that hydrogen and helium account for more than 98 percent of all observable matter in the universe. Of this, some 91 percent is in the form of hydrogen molecules, and 7 percent helium molecules. All the rest of the

The world's largest nonsteerable radiotelescope, with a diameter of a thousand feet, near Arecibo, Puerto Rico. *NOAA*

the basis of all living things, have been found all through space by means of the radiotelescope. More recently, **sugar molecules** were found in gas and dust clouds near a young star some four hundred light years from us. Both these discoveries indicate that the basic substances necessary for life as we know it may be much more plentiful in deep space than previously thought. No optical device could have made these discoveries.

In the 1950s it was found that, like optical telescopes, an array of multiple radiotelescopes can work together to form a giant radiotelescope. The largest such array is located on the Chajnantor Plateau, in Chile's Atacama Desert. Called the *Atacama Large Millimeter Array* (ALMA), it consists of fifty twelve-meter (forty-foot) and sixteen smaller dishes that together are said to be more powerful than all the other existing radiotelescopes in the world combined. The signals from each individual dish are fed into a supercomputer that combines them into a single radio image. Another, even more powerful, array of sixty-four larger dishes is currently under construction in the Northern Cape of South Africa. When completed in 2024 it is designed to be ten times more powerful than the ALMA array. Such arrays can produce amazing images of the distant universe, far more detailed than any optical telescopes can yield, including previously invisible gas clouds and galaxies formed only a few hundred thousand years after the Big Bang.

elements and their molecules add up to only 2 percent of the total. No matter where astronomers have searched in space, the observable universe appears to be made up of the same elements in the same ratios.

Radiotelescope observations have also discovered some more complex and intriguing molecules in space. **Precursor** ("building-block") **molecules** of certain amino acids and DNA,

In recent years radio astronomers have determined that it is possible to combine signals acquired by radiotelescopes widely

A radiotelescope image (left) of the colliding Antennae galaxies, 45 million light years from us, taken by the ALMA array in Chile, and a corresponding visual-light image (right) taken by the European Southern Observatory. The two images illustrate the difference between the two types of images. Note especially the differences in appearance of the galactic centers to the lower left and upper right.

separated throughout the world to form composite radio images of extremely high resolution. This technique became possible only with the development of modern atomic clocks capable of synchronizing the various signals with the required precision, and supercomputers capable of performing the required computations Combining signals from such geographically separated radiotelescopes can yield the same resolution as would be obtained from a radiotelescope as large as the entire globe! More will certainly be done with this in years to come.

Special Uses of the Radiotelescope

While radiotelescopes normally are used only in a passive mode, to detect and receive electromagnetic radio waves, it is possible to modify these devices for other purposes. The radiotelescope can direct powerful microwave-frequency beams at nearby celestial objects and then receive the echoes back when they rebound toward Earth. Radiotelescopes equipped with such transmitters are often called **radar telescopes.** They can furnish very precise data about the distance of celestial bodies within our solar system and about their surface topography. They have been used with success to determine such information for the Moon, all the planets out to Saturn, and for asteroids and comets that pass within range near the Earth.

Radiotelescopes can also be used to control and receive data from spacecraft exploring our solar system. In the controlling mode, they send very strong signals radiated at high power levels (300,000 to 400,000 watts) to reach the distant spacecraft, then listen for the faint replies and data transmissions, which are often only a few fractions of a millionth of a watt strong.

Airborne Observatories

The atmospheric shield that protects Earth from radiation also absorbs and distorts the light and radio waves that get through to our telescopes on Earth. In order to gain more accurate knowledge of the universe, therefore, we have to go beyond our atmosphere. For this purpose, astronomers have used aircraft and balloons fitted with telescopes and other devices to make observations well above most of the atmosphere. Aircraft observations are limited to altitudes of about ten miles, but balloon observations can be made from as high as thirty miles, beyond about 99 percent of the atmosphere.

Aircraft observations made in the 1970s and '80s using a highly modified Lockheed Starlifter jet transport aircraft produced the first sightings of the rings of Uranus in 1977, the discovery of an atmosphere on Pluto in 1988, and infrared investigations of the composition of the planet Mercury in 1995. This aircraft was followed by a modified Boeing 747 jet cargo plane equipped with a larger infrared telescope. Only a few significant balloon-borne telescopic missions have been attempted,

NASA's *SOPHIA* (Stratospheric Observatory for Infrared Astronomy) 747 airborne observatory.

mainly to gather data on high-energy X-rays. Astrophysicists and astronomers in recent years have found the space-based platforms discussed in the following section far more useful.

Satellites and Exploratory Spacecraft

The beginning of the **space age** was 4 October 1957, when the first artificial satellite, *Sputnik 1,* was successfully launched by the Soviet Union. *Sputnik I* was followed four months later by the first U.S. satellite, *Explorer 1.* Since then there has been a steady procession of artificial satellites and other exploratory spacecraft sent into space on scientific astronomical and astrophysical missions.

The astronomical data and new knowledge gained by these spacecraft during the last half-century has greatly exceeded the total knowledge acquired by all previous, earthbound observations since the dawn of history.

A summary of some of the more significant of these efforts to date follows. Although most of this discussion focuses on American space-exploration efforts, led by the National Aeronautics and Space Administration (NASA), other nations and consortiums, including especially the European Space Agency (ESA) in recent years, have also achieved important successes in these endeavors. More detailed information on the exploration of the solar system and the universe beyond is presented in the remaining chapters of this unit and can be found on the NASA website, www.nasa.gov.

The *Explorer 1* satellite mentioned above was followed by some fifty additional Explorer reconnaissance spacecraft, which collectively provided a wealth of information about Earth and its region of the solar system, including the following:

- The nature and effect of the solar wind
- The nature, extent, and behavior of Earth's magnetosphere (Earth's magnetic field)
- A detailed survey of the space between Earth and the Moon
- The nature and density of Earth's upper atmosphere.

Between 1962 and 1975 a total of eight Orbiting Solar Observatories (OSO) were launched into orbit around Earth to study the Sun. Their instruments returned data on solar flares, the Sun's corona (outer atmosphere), and solar activity in the gamma ray, X-ray, and ultraviolet bands of the electromagnetic spectrum.

Concurrent with the OSO investigations of the Sun, from 1962 to 1973 a series of seven Mariner spacecraft conducted investigations of Mars, Venus, and Mercury. Follow-on programs subsequently developed directly from them included the *Magellan* probe to Venus, the Voyager probes, the Viking and later Mars orbiters, and the *Galileo* and *Cassini* probes sent to Jupiter and Saturn.

Skylab, America's first space station, contained a group of eight solar observation instruments and cameras. During the time it was manned, between May 1973 and February 1974, it made more than 150,000 observations of the Sun. These produced many spectacular photos of solar flares and sunspots. The *Skylab* and OSO data "rewrote the book" on solar physics,

The *Skylab* was the first U.S. space station. It was a solar observatory and was manned between May 1973 and February 1974.

our understanding of how and why the Sun functions, and the effects the Sun has on terrestrial weather and communications. *Skylab* reentered the atmosphere and disintegrated in 1979.

While these spacecraft were investigating the nature of near-Earth space, a series of eleven Pioneer space probes began a reconnaissance of the remainder of the solar system. The last of these, *Pioneer 10* and *Pioneer 11,* launched in 1972 and 1973, were the first spacecraft to fly by and photograph Jupiter, and, in the case of *Pioneer 11,* Saturn; they then proceeded outbound to exit the solar system.

Two more capable follow-on Voyager spacecraft were launched in August and September of 1977 and spent more than eleven years exploring Jupiter, Saturn, Uranus, and Neptune before heading off toward interstellar space in 1989. For many years the two Pioneer spacecraft were the most distant human artifacts from Earth, until they were overtaken in 1998 by the later but faster *Voyager 1,* with *Voyager 2* launched a few weeks earlier not far behind. The two Pioneer spacecraft have long since fallen silent, but the two Voyagers are still transmitting useful data from beyond the edges of the solar system. On 12 September 2013 *Voyager 1* was formally proclaimed to be the first spacecraft launched by humanity to exit our solar system. If all goes well, in some 42,000 years *Voyager 1* will pass near the star Polaris, and *Voyager 2* will reach the star Sirius in about 298,000 years.

The two Pioneer spacecraft each carried a golden plaque inscribed with graphics to indicate its origins. The two Voyagers carried gold-plated phonograph records with inscriptions similar to the Pioneers' plaques, plus audio tracks and images that included greetings in fifty-nine languages, contemporary songs, and other sounds and pictures of Earth and its inhabitants.

In 1990 NASA began its **Great Observatories Program,** launching into orbit the first of an eventual four orbiting **space telescopes,** each designed to observe a different band of radiation within the electromagnetic spectrum—visible, gamma rays, X-rays, and infrared. The first and probably best known

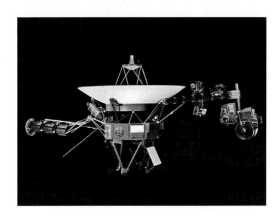

The twin *Voyager 1* and *Voyager 2* space probes.

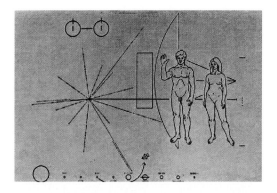

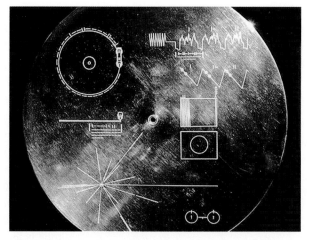

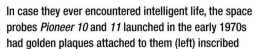

In case they ever encountered intelligent life, the space probes *Pioneer 10* and *11* launched in the early 1970s had golden plaques attached to them (left) inscribed with graphics to indicate their origins. The later probes *Voyager 1* and *2* carried golden phonograph records (right) with similar graphics and also audio tracks and images with many sounds, languages, songs, and pictures of Earth and its people.

of these, the *Hubble Space Telescope,* was placed in orbit around Earth by a space shuttle mission in April 1990. Its telescope system proved flawed and had to be repaired during a subsequent shuttle mission in 1993. A second upgrade mission performed in May 2009 installed new batteries, replaced all gyroscopes, and installed a wide-angle camera and a Cosmic Origins Spectrograph designed for high-resolution spectroscopy of ultraviolet light. The *Hubble* is still in full operation today. It has provided many astounding images that have added much to astronomers' knowledge of the solar system and the universe and its origins.

The *Chandra X-Ray Observatory* was launched into low Earth orbit in 1999 by the shuttle *Columbia,* and the *Spitzer Space Telescope,* which makes observations in the infrared spectrum, was launched into a solar orbit in 2003. Both of these are

still transmitting useful data. The fourth satellite in the series, the *Compton Gamma Ray Observatory,* was launched in 1991 but was deorbited in 2000 after the failure of one of its attitude-control gyroscopes.

In 2009 NASA launched the *Kepler Space Telescope,* equipped with a powerful set of instruments specially designed for discovering planets orbiting other stars, called **exoplanets.** It was placed in an Earth-trailing solar orbit, giving it more stability than if it were in an orbit around Earth. Its optics enabled simultaneous observations of some 145,000 Sun-like stars during its planned three-and-a-half-year mission. *Kepler*'s field of view is about ten times larger than the *Hubble*'s telescope, giving it much greater capability to discover exoplanets than either the *Hubble* or any existing Earth-bound telescope. Its instru-

The *Hubble Space Telescope.*

Artist's rendering of the *Kepler Space Telescope.*

ments detect any periodic dimming caused by planets crossing in front of their host stars (called *transiting* in astronomy), a primary technique used by astronomers to find exoplanets beyond our solar system. By the time it was disabled in May 2013 by an alignment-system failure, *Kepler* had discovered a total of 2,740 potential planets orbiting some 2,000 stars. Early in 2014, scientists announced that they had found an additional 715 new exoplanets from analysis of data gathered before *Kepler* became disabled. Even more may be yet to come.

Along with these unmanned exploratory efforts, in the 1960s the United States made a determined effort to put an astronaut on the Moon by the end of that decade. The effort began with several Ranger and Surveyor spacecraft that conducted orbital mapping of the lunar surface in the early 1960s. It ended with the successful landing of *Apollo 11* on the Moon's surface in 1969. Five additional manned lunar landings and explorations were conducted, the last being *Apollo 17* in late 1972. Many additional unmanned spacecraft from the United States and several other nations have also orbited the Moon and explored its surface and have returned a wealth of additional new information about it.

In 1998 the first components of a new International Space Station (ISS) were launched into a low Earth orbit at altitudes ranging from 330 to 435 kilometers (205 to 270 miles). Two years later, in November 2000, the first crew, of one American and two Russians, arrived at the station; it has been continuously manned since by astronauts and cosmonauts from fifteen nations. A six-member crew of both men and women with six-month stays has been the norm in recent years.

Additional modular components to complete the primary structure were eventually contributed by sixteen nations. New components are still being added, bringing its total mass currently in orbit to just under 420 metric tons (about 925,000

A Soyuz launch from the Baikonur Cosmodrome in Kazakhstan, transporting three astronauts up to the ISS.

The International Space Station, pictured from above.

pounds). For over a decade American space shuttles flew most of the support missions to the ISS, delivering components and supplies and transporting crew members. With the retirement of the U.S. shuttle fleet in 2011, the Russians took over primary responsibility for crew transportation using Soyuz space capsules. Unmanned American, Russian, ESA, and commercial spacecraft now ferry up most of the supplies and new equipment, and bring back any cargo in need of being returned. The ISS is currently funded through at least 2020. In early 2014 the U.S. agreed to a four-year extension of the station's nominal lifetime to 2024. Many proposals to extend its use even further are being continuously submitted.

The Future

The coming years should continue to be exciting ones in the field of astronomy and space exploration. Congress has approved a possible NASA manned mission to one of the asteroids by 2025, followed by a possible manned mission to Mars in the 2030s.

Artist's rendering of the *James Webb Space Telescope*, planned for launch in 2018.

Meanwhile, several more unmanned exploratory missions to Mars are anticipated over the next decade. A NASA mission called *New Horizons*, launched in January 2006, is currently en route to fly by the dwarf planet Pluto and its moons in 2015. It will continue on into the Kuiper Belt beyond and perhaps conduct additional flybys of one or more objects there. A follow-on mission to *Galileo*'s exploration of Jupiter and its moons, called *Juno*, was launched in August 2011 and will arrive at the planet in July 2016. It will be placed in a polar orbit around Jupiter to investigate its gravity field, magnetic field, and magnetosphere.

Several new space telescopes are planned, including the *Space Infrared Interferometric Telescope* (SPIRIT), to consist of two moveable telescopes mounted on a 120-foot beam, scheduled for launch sometime after 2020. A follow-on space telescope to the *Hubble*, the *James Webb Space Telescope*, is scheduled to be launched in 2018. It will have a much larger (6.5-meter, 21-foot) mirror and will search for the first galaxies formed after the Big Bang. Both of these new space telescopes will orbit a million miles above Earth.

The search for extraterrestrial life in the solar system and beyond will be an ongoing quest for the foreseeable future. Undoubtedly there will be many further missions to investigate the possibility of past or present life on Mars, perhaps in the ice-covered oceans of Jupiter's moon Europa, and other places within the solar system. If it could be proven that the formation of Earth-like planets around other stars is a fairly common occurrence everywhere in the universe, statistics would indicate that the probability of at least some form of life existing elsewhere is great. Such a discovery would rank among the greatest scientific achievements of all time, with great consequences for humankind.

Undoubtedly the future holds many more exciting surprises in the field of astronomy!

Critical Thinking

1. Why is the possibility of extraterrestrial life so fascinating to most people and especially to astronomers? What would be some of the possible consequences if life in any form were discovered elsewhere in the universe?

2. Various views of possible alien intelligent life are given in classic science-fiction movies such as *The War of the Worlds* (1953 and 2005), *ET* (1982), the *Alien* film series (1979-97), and many others. How would you conceptualize the nature of extraterrestrial intelligent life (if any), and why?

3. Do you think the current level of effort by the United States on exploration of the solar system and the universe beyond is too little, about right, or too much? Justify your answer.

4. Investigate what academic qualifications are necessary for a career in astronomy and what opportunities exist for employment as an astronomer.

Study Guide Questions

1. What is an observatory, and what is it used for?

2. Where are observatories usually located, and why?

3. Why are most astronomical observations made in modern-day observatories recorded by hi-tech cameras versus traditional photographic plates?

4. What are some of the things an astronomer must be able to do, besides making celestial observations?

5. Name and describe the two main types of telescopes.

6. What does a radiotelescope do?

7. Why is a map of the radio sky different from a visual map?

8. What are quasars?

9. What are pulsars?

10. What has been done with radiotelescopes in recent years to greatly extend their resolution capabilities?

11. What are the other modern-day applications of radio-telescopes, besides analysis of incoming electromagnetic radiations of celestial bodies?

12. What is the main advantage of making astronomical observations from a high-flying aircraft or balloon?

13. When and with what event did the space age begin?

14. What kinds of studies did the Explorer series of spacecraft undertake?

15. What was the main work of *Skylab* in 1973–74?

16. A. What were the missions of the *Pioneer 10* and *11* and *Voyager 1* and *2* space probes?
    B. Where are they now?

17. A. How many Apollo Moon exploration missions were there?
    B. During what period of time did they occur?

18. What was the Great Observatories Program undertaken by NASA in the 1990s?

19. A. What space telescope has discovered many exoplanets since being placed in orbit in 2009?
    B. What method does it use to try to discover these planets?

20. A. What manned space station is currently in orbit around the Earth?
    B. How is it sustained?

21. What manned space exploration missions are in the planning stages by NASA for the 2020s and beyond?

New Vocabulary

supernovae	quasar
thermonuclear fusion	black hole
observatory	pulsar
tracking mechanism	space age
CCD camera	spacecraft
time exposure	space probe
refracting telescope	space telescope
reflecting telescope	exoplanets
optical interferometry	astronaut
radiotelescope	cosmonaut

13

The Moon

Our Moon is the fifth-largest planetary moon in the solar system. At one time most scientists thought that the Moon and Earth had probably formed at the same time and in about the same way (i.e., by accretion), or alternatively, that the Moon had been captured by gravity as it passed by the primordial Earth. However, later measurements showed that their densities were very dissimilar, with the Moon being only about 60 percent as dense as the Earth, which would tend to rule out the former theory. Moreover, analysis of lunar sample material brought back by the Apollo missions showed surprising similarities in the composition of the Earth and the Moon. They have nearly identical amounts of various isotopes of such elements as oxygen, tungsten, and titanium, and these amounts are very different from those in all other bodies in the solar system. This would tend to rule out the capture theory.

Consequently, the favored theory now is that shortly after the Earth cooled, some 4.5 billion years ago, it was struck a glancing blow by a large body about the size of Mars. The impact spewed material from Earth's crust and mantle. Eventually it, along with remnants from the impacting body, came together to form the Moon. To settle the question, more on-site research needs to be done, perhaps using a base camp that might one day be established on the lunar surface.

The Moon's diameter is 2,160 miles, 27 percent that of Earth. The Moon has an elliptical orbit around the Earth, varying from about 226,000 miles at the closest to 252,000 miles at the farthest, with an average distance of about 239,000 miles. It is inclined about five degrees to the plane of Earth's orbit around the Sun (the plane of the ecliptic). Scientists think the Moon was formed only about 14,000 miles above the Earth's surface and then gradually moved farther away to where it is now. It is still moving away, at an average of about three centimeters per year. Its gravitational attraction is only about a sixth that of Earth (0.165 g), so a hundred-pound person on Earth would weigh only about sixteen and a half pounds there and would be able to jump six times higher than he or she could on Earth! The Apollo astronauts enjoyed these effects while walk-

ing on the Moon during their visits there in the late 1960s and early 1970s.

The Moon circles Earth every twenty-seven and a third days. It also completes one rotation about its axis in the same time period, which results in the Moon always having the same near side facing Earth, with the other far side always facing away. In other words, the Moon rotates once on its axis and revolves once around Earth in the same length of time. The effect of this was that until the dawn of the space age in the late 1950s, only the near side was ever visible to Earthbound observers.

The Moon has no atmosphere or liquid water. Thus, there is no gradual daily temperature change from hot to cold, as on Earth. On the Moon, an astronaut partially in the sunlight and partially in the shade would be subjected to extreme heat and cold at the same time. The Moon's surface temperature in

A photo of the Moon's back side, taken from the *Apollo 10* command module from an altitude of sixty miles.

sunlight may get as high as 270 degrees F. In the shadows or darkness of the lunar night, it may go down to as low as –240 degrees F.

Because there is no atmosphere on the Moon, there is no sound either. Since there are no obscuring atmospheric effects, a person on the Moon can see twice as many stars in the sky as from Earth's surface. Also, there is no atmospheric or water erosion on the Moon, which means that its surface features have remained basically unchanged for billions of years, except for the effects of volcanism and bombardment by solar and cosmic radiation and impacts by asteroids, comets, and micro-meteorites.

Moon Geology

The entire surface of the Moon is pockmarked with **craters.** The larger circular craters on the near side, easily seen through binoculars, have been visible for centuries. Many of these have been named for prominent early scientists and Greek philoso-phers, such as Tycho, Copernicus, and Ptolemaeus. Craters on the far side have been named for more modern-day mostly Rus-sian space pioneers, such as Gagarin and Korolev (early Russian cosmonauts). There are also dark, relatively smooth plains and mountain ranges on the Moon's surface, many of them named after mountain ranges on Earth. Galileo mistook the dark plains for bodies of water and called them *maria,* Latin for "sea." The brighter areas were called *terrae,* after the Latin word for "land." Nowadays these areas are referred to as *highlands,* because they are generally higher and brighter than the maria.

The maria are younger than the rest of the Moon. Radioac-tivity measurements of rocks from the Sea of Tranquility gath-ered during the Apollo missions show that they were formed about 3.6 billion years ago, about a billion years after the Moon's formation. The maria cover about 30 percent of the surface on the near side but only about 2 percent on the far side. The term "maria" is still in use, even though now they are known to be filled with solidified lava and dust, not water. They look darker than the lighter highlands because the lunar plains have a lower **reflectance.** (An object that reflected all light would have a reflectance of 100 percent, while one that absorbed all light would have 0 percent.) The dark maria have a reflectance of only about 11 percent, much lower than the highlands. The high-lands are thought to have been formed about 4.4 billion years ago, probably from upwellings of magma beneath the surface.

Besides the maria and highlands, the other major geologi-cal feature on the surface of the Moon is **impact cratering,** the result of crashes of asteroids and comets onto the lunar surface. There are estimated to be over 300,000 such craters of at least one kilometer (0.6 mile) diameter or more on the near side of the Moon alone, with many more on the far side. The most con-spicuous impact crater on the near side is Tycho, in the Moon's

A close-up image of the Moon's fifty-three-mile wide Tycho crater from the *Lunar Reconnaissance Orbiter.* The arrow points to melt features within the crater.

southern hemisphere. It is fifty-three miles wide and three miles deep and has a 1.4-mile-high central peak. It is easily seen when the Moon is full. Tycho has a large system of **rays** (material ejected from impact craters) that radiate as far as 1,500 miles out from the edges of the crater.

Determination of the ages of various impact-melted rocks brought back by the Apollo missions indicates that there was a significant period of extraordinarily heavy bombardment of the Moon between 4.1 and 3.8 billion years ago, known by astrono-mers as the **Late Heavy Bombardment** period. More about this will be discussed later in this unit.

Many smaller craters are almost certainly the result of early volcanic activity, as gases and dusts escaped from the Moon's interior. Some of these can be compared to volcanic craters on Earth, formed when the surface collapsed into an underlying cavity from which lava had flowed.

Other Surface Features

Erosion on the Moon takes place very slowly, because there is no rain or wind. However, the Apollo astronauts learned that the spray of **breccia**—impact material from crashing meteor-ites and other bodies—causes extensive erosion. The constant stream of atomic particles coming from the Sun and the rest of the cosmos also causes a very slow wearing-away of the Moon's surface.

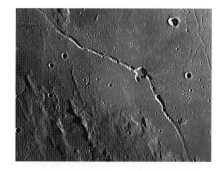

Rilles are cracks in the lunar surface similar to shallow, meandering river beds on the Earth.
Christian Viladrich

Among the lunar rocks that have been returned to Earth are several that scientists have labeled **igneous.** This means that the rock was once molten magma but later became solidified. This is another indication that the Moon, like Earth, has (or once had) a hot interior and volcanoes.

The surface walked on by the Apollo astronauts was coated by a thick dust layer called the **regolith,** which covers the entire surface of the Moon to a depth ranging from a few meters in the maria to ten to twenty meters in the highlands. It is made up mostly of breccia. Various lunar landers and the Apollo astronauts found that the regolith in most places is rather loose on top and compacted underneath.

Moon Mountains and Rilles

The Moon's mountain ranges lie in great arcs bordering the circular maria. Some of their peaks are as tall as the highest Earth mountains. They are concentrated in the Moon's southern hemisphere. With peaks sometimes rising more than 20,000 feet above the plains, lunar mountains are very rugged, since they are not eroded by wind, water, or ice.

The Moon's surface is covered with many cracks, called **rilles.** They are similar to shallow, flat-bottomed river beds on Earth. There seems to be no connection between rilles and other surface features; they sometimes extend hundreds of miles, uninterrupted by mountains, valleys, or craters.

Phases of the Moon

The Moon's motion in its orbit causes its **phases** (progressive changes in the visible portion of the Moon). Since the Moon shines only by reflected sunlight, the relative positions of the Moon, Earth, and Sun determine how much of the Moon we can see at any given time. At new moon, the Moon is between Earth and the Sun, with the dark side facing Earth. A day or so later the Moon is seen as a thin curved shape called a *crescent.* As the lighted part grows in size, the Moon is said to *wax* to full moon. At full moon, the entire illuminated side faces toward Earth, since it is now on the opposite side of Earth from the Sun.

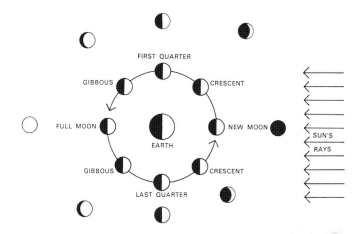

The phases of the Moon. The inner circle shows the Moon's position relative to the Sun and Earth at various points in its orbit. The outer circle shows how the Moon looks from Earth at these times.

The full moon rises in the east as the Sun sets in the west; thus, we can see it all night. Sometimes it is so bright it can be seen well into the morning hours after sunrise. When the Moon is halfway between the new moon and the full moon, one-half of the Moon is illuminated and it is in its first quarter—that is, the Moon is a quarter of a circle (ninety degrees) away from the Sun with respect to the Earth. After full moon, the illuminated part gets smaller, and the Moon is said to *wane.* It goes through its last quarter and back to new moon again. When more than half of the Moon is visible, between the first and last quarters, it is called *gibbous.*

Sometimes the new moon is faintly visible by day, because its otherwise dark night side is illuminated by reflected Earth-light, a phenomenon called **planetshine.** Because of the elliptical orbit of the Moon about the Earth, the apparent size of the full moon is greater at some times than at others, depending on whether the Moon is closer or farther away at the time. Although normally there is only one full moon in each calendar month, every two to three years there will be two in a given month, with the second appearance called a **"blue moon."** The rarity of these events gives rise to the colloquial phrase "once in a blue moon."

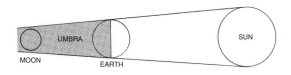

Diagram of a lunar eclipse. Such an eclipse occurs when the Moon passes into the shadow of the Earth, called its *umbra*.

A sequence of photos showing the Moon as it progresses through a lunar eclipse. *CHINFO, Joshua Valcarel*

Because Earth and the Moon are both solid bodies illuminated by the Sun, they both cast cone-shaped shadows in space. Occasionally during its orbits around the Earth, the full moon passes through the conical shadow of Earth, obscuring part or all of its disk. This event is known as a **lunar eclipse.** Such an eclipse can be either partial or total, depending on how much of the Moon enters Earth's shadow. When the Earth passes through the shadow cast by the Moon, part or all of the Sun's disk can be obscured, depending on the position of the observer; the phenomenon is called a **solar eclipse.** This will be discussed more in the next chapter.

If the Moon orbited the Earth in the same plane as the Earth orbits the Sun, these eclipses would occur every month. But because the Moon's orbit is inclined five degrees with respect to the Earth's orbit, they occur on an irregular basis, often several months or more apart. A complete schedule for them can be obtained on the NASA website, www.nasa.gov.

Lunar Exploration Efforts

As was mentioned in the last chapter, American spacecraft exploration of the Moon began in the 1960s with the Ranger and Surveyor series of orbital photography satellites. *Ranger 7* returned many images in 1964, as did two more Ranger orbiters in succeeding years. From 1966 to 1968, NASA sent to the Moon seven Surveyor landers, five of which landed successfully. Their primary objective was to demonstrate the feasibility of soft landings on the Moon's surface, but they also carried instruments to evaluate the suitability of their landing sites for the forthcoming Apollo manned landings.

The Apollo manned lunar landing program ran from 1961 to 1972. For the first several years it was concurrently supported by the two-man Gemini capsule program, conducted from 1962–66. The Apollo program succeeded in its goal of achieving a manned landing on the Moon by the end of the 1960s when *Apollo 11* landed in the Sea of Tranquility in July 1969. Five of the next six Apollo missions also successfully landed on the Moon over the next three years. The exception was *Apollo 13,* which suffered an oxygen-tank explosion in transit to the Moon; the crew made a safe return to earth, using the lunar landing module as a makeshift "lifeboat." The exploits of the *Apollo 13* crew during this crisis were dramatically documented in a classic 1995 movie of the same name. The final manned landing on the Moon was *Apollo 17,* in late 1972.

Astronaut Buzz Aldrin, a member of the *Apollo 11* crew, on the Moon's surface. He and his fellow astronaut Neil Armstrong were the first humans ever to set foot on the Moon in July 1969. Aldrin is standing next to a solar-powered passive seismograph fitted with a radio transmitter; it was left there to transmit readings of lunar moonquakes back to Earth following the mission. The lunar landing module *Eagle* is in the background.

Apollo 16 astronaut Charles Duke gathering rock samples at the Descartes highlands landing site in April 1972. The mission's lunar roving vehicle sits parked in the background.

The Apollo missions brought back some 2,200 samples (altogether 382 kg, 842 pounds) of Moon rocks and soil for later analysis. Analyzed by the Lunar Receiving Laboratory of NASA in Houston, many of the rock samples were found to be rich in iron, titanium, and magnesium but completely lacking in the hydrated minerals common in Earth rocks. Their ages ranged from about 3.2 billion years old for the basaltic samples from the lunar maria to about 4.5 billion years for those derived from the highlands. Analysts found about sixty elements in the soil samples, which were determined to be rich in glass breccias and tiny glass tektites (beads) formed by meteorite impacts on the lunar surface.

Most of the sample material is now in a repository at the Lunar Sample Laboratory facility in Houston, along with sample material from concurrent Soviet *Luna* missions described below. Sample Moon rocks are also on display at the National Museum of Natural History in Washington, D.C., and several other museums throughout the world. Commemorative plaques containing sample fragments were presented to all fifty states and 150 foreign countries by President Richard Nixon in 1973.

During the same time as the American lunar exploration program was taking place, the Soviet Union instituted an ambitious lunar exploration program of its own, intended to achieve the same manned landing results before the Americans did. Though it ultimately failed to put a man on the Moon, it had some notable successes. From 1959 to 1976 the Soviets launched a total of some thirty-four Luna and Zond space probes that conducted flybys, impact probes, and orbital surveys of the Moon. *Luna 1* missed its planned impact of the Moon in January 1959 but became the first man-made object to orbit the Sun; later that year *Luna 2* became the first man-made object to reach the Moon, impacting its surface in September. *Luna 9* in January 1966 achieved a soft landing on the lunar surface, becoming the first spacecraft ever to land on another solar-system body.

Subsequent Luna spacecraft deployed two Lunokhod rovers to the Moon's surface in 1970 and 1973, and three other Luna landers successfully returned small soil samples (0.32 kg, about 11 ounces altogether) from the lunar surface to Earth. However, the Apollo landings ended the space race to the Moon, and the Soviets abandoned further Moon exploration efforts after the mid-1970s, thereafter preferring to concentrate instead on unmanned explorations of Venus and Mars. The fact that many of the surface features on the far side of the Moon are named after prominent figures in the Soviets' Moon exploration program is a testimony to their efforts during these years.

The United States too abandoned further spacecraft exploration of the Moon following the Apollo program, in favor of planetary exploration for the next two decades. In late 1996, however, renewed interest in the Moon as a possible base for a manned expedition to Mars resulted in an exciting discovery of possible water ice on the Moon. Radar signals transmitted by an orbiting Defense Department satellite called *Clementine* indicated the presence of the ice in a large, shady crater near the Moon's south pole, where the temperature is about –387 degrees F (–197 degrees C). The ice was thought to have been deposited there by a comet impact in the distant past. If it does in fact exist, the ice could be used by future Moon-based explorers as a source of both potable water and fuel. The *Clementine* satellite was the first U.S. Moon exploration effort since the last Apollo mission in 1972.

As a follow-up to *Clementine,* a *Lunar Prospector* satellite was placed in orbit around the Moon in January 1998. It was equipped with a neutron spectrometer that could detect the presence of hydrogen or of nine other elements, including iron, titanium, and aluminum. It did in fact detect large amounts of hydrogen at the Moon's poles, thus supporting the possibility of water ice there. After completing its mission in July 1999, it was intentionally crashed into one of the craters near the lunar south pole to try to kick up enough water vapor from suspected ice deposits in the crater to prove the presence of water. However, scientists observing the crash site from more than twenty observatories around Earth and the *Hubble Space Telescope* detected no signs of the impact.

In the new millennium the European Space Agency and several other nations displayed renewed interest in Moon exploration, including Japan, China, India, and Russia. The first three of these placed several reconnaissance satellites in orbit around the Moon in the 2000s, and the latter two have plans to do so in the next decade.

In 2009 the United States launched a *Lunar Reconnaissance Orbiter* spacecraft into low polar orbit around the Moon, the first such American mission since the *Lunar Prospector* in 1998. It has a five-year mission to identify safe landing sites for possible future manned and unmanned rover missions; to make a 3-D map of the entire lunar surface with a high-resolution camera; to look once again for water ice in the polar regions; and to serve as a communications relay for any possible future expeditions to the surface. Two small GRAIL (Gravity Recovery and Interior Laboratory) orbiters were placed in orbit around the Moon by NASA at year's end 2011 to investigate its gravity field and interior structure; upon completion of their mission a year later they were impacted on the surface. In September 2013 NASA launched an orbiter called the *Lunar Atmosphere and Dust Environment Explorer* (LADEE) on a seven-month

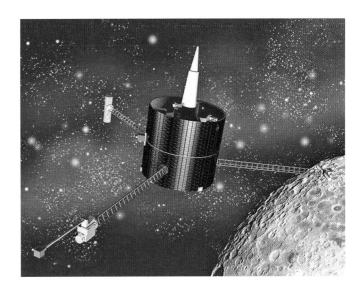

The *Lunar Prospector* orbiter.

mission to study the tenuous lunar atmosphere and dust of the lunar surface. That mission also ended with an intentional plunge into the surface.

Although the current emphasis of most international space programs seems to be on further exploration of Mars and the outer reaches of the solar system and beyond, the Moon will undoubtedly continue to be of interest to future generations of astronomers, astrophysicists, and the general public for many years to come.

Why Explore the Moon?

There are many practical reasons to explore our Moon. It is conceivable that people someday will be able to mine its mineral wealth. The Moon could also serve as a base from which expeditions to Mars or an asteroid could be launched, as it is easier to escape the Moon's gravity than Earth's. Because it has no atmosphere, it would also be an ideal place to set up astronomical observatories and radiotelescopes for observations of other bodies within the solar system and beyond. Communications relays or transportation control stations could serve in a wide variety of constructive ways. Military applications are sure to be developed also, though several international treaties mandate the free use of the Moon and other bodies in the solar system and beyond for the benefit all humankind.

Critical Thinking

1. What is currently the major motivation to travel to and explore the Moon?

2. Research the prevailing scientific theories of the formation of the Moon. Explain each and state which one you think is the most likely. Give the rationale for your choice.

3. Examine the reasons for the resurgence of interest in exploring the Moon in recent years by many nations, including the United States. Speculate on the future uses to which this research could be applied.

Study Guide Questions

1. What is currently the most widely accepted theory of how and when the Moon was formed?

2. Why do we on Earth always view the same side of the Moon?

3. Why is there no gradual daily temperature change on the Moon?

4. What causes erosion on the Moon's surface?

5. What is breccia?

6. What are the maria, and how did they get that name?

7. What is "moonlight"?

8. What probably caused most Moon craters?

9. What significant discovery about the Moon was made in 1996?

10. What are rays and rilles on the Moon?

11. A. What are the phases of the Moon?
    B. What does "gibbous" mean?
    C. What is a "blue moon"?

12. What causes a lunar eclipse to occur?

13. What other nation besides the United States played a major role in Moon exploration efforts from the 1950s through the early 1970s? What was the motivation?

14. What are some practical reasons for exploring the Moon?

New Vocabulary

maria	igneous
craters	rilles
reflectance	phases (of Moon)
impact crating	wax, wane
rays (on Moon)	gibbous
Late Heavy Bombardment	planetshine
breccia	eclipse
regolith	

The Sun

Scientists theorize that our Sun, along with the planets of our solar system, formed about 4.6 billion years ago from the gravitational collapse of a region within a large molecular cloud of light elements left over from the Big Bang, along with heavier elements produced by fusion within generations of earlier large stars within our galaxy that had exploded in supernovae. Most of the matter gathered in the center, while the rest flattened into a revolving disk that would eventually become the solar system. The central mass became increasingly hot and dense, eventually initiating **thermonuclear fusion** (combining two atoms by heat to make a third) in its core and starting to shine.

Earth has been warmed by the light of the Sun for all of its existence. All life is sustained by the solar energy that is converted into chemical energy by plants. Moreover, the power obtained from all fossil fuels, water, and winds can be traced back to the Sun. The Sun, therefore, is the source of most of the world's energy. (The remainder consists of nuclear energy, lunar tidal energy, and the heat produced by pressure and radioactive materials in the interior of the Earth.) Once considered to be an "average" star, it is now thought by astronomers to be bigger and brighter than about 85 percent of the other stars in our Milky Way galaxy, which are predominantly **red dwarfs** (small stars in the final stages of existence).

The Sun contains 99.86 percent of all the matter in our solar system. The Sun's mass is about 330,000 times that of Earth. About three-quarters of its mass is hydrogen, with the rest mostly helium and relatively small amounts of heavier elements, such as oxygen, carbon, and iron. The Sun's gravitational attraction is about twenty-eight times that of Earth (27.9 g); consequently, if it

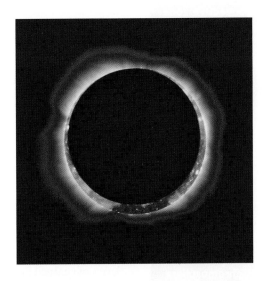

Photo of an annular solar eclipse taken by an orbiting Japanese solar study satellite. The Sun's corona is clearly visible.

were possible to withstand the extreme heat, a hundred-pound keg of nails would weigh about 2,800 pounds on the Sun!

The Sun orbits the center of our galaxy, the Milky Way, at about 25,000 light years from the galactic center, completing one clockwise orbit as viewed from above the galactic north pole in 225–250 million years. The average distance from the Sun to the Earth (that is, Earth's average orbital radius) has been calculated to be 92,870,000—nearly 93 million—miles. It takes eight minutes and nineteen seconds for the Sun's light to reach us over that distance. This average distance is known as an **astronomical unit (AU),** a huge unit of measure often used in describing distances in the solar system. The Sun has a diameter of about 865,000 miles—about 109 times that of Earth. Because it is not a solid body, the Sun rotates at different rates at different latitudes and probably internally. At its surface on its equator it rotates once about its axis about every twenty-four and a half days, somewhat more slowly at the poles.

It is not possible for us safely to look directly at the Sun without first protecting our eyes. Any attempt to do look at the Sun will cause temporary blindness, even permanent damage, unless some sort of filter or special fogged lens is used. *Never look directly at the Sun through a telescope or binoculars.* Doing this would burn the retina of your eye, causing permanently impaired vision or even blindness.

Since the Moon, in its elliptical orbit around Earth, is often the same apparent size as the Sun, when the Moon passes directly between them the Sun's disk can be completely hidden if viewed from within the shadow zone, an event known as a **total eclipse of the Sun.** There is usually only a narrow band across the Earth's surface

307

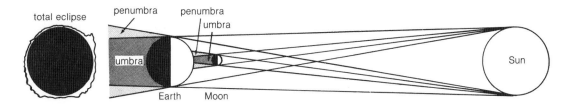

Diagram of a solar eclipse. The darker part of the shadows cast by the Moon and Earth are called the *umbra*, and the lighter part the *penumbra*. Depending on the Moon's distance from the Earth, the eclipse may be *total*, as shown here, or *annular*, when the Moon is farther away, blocking out the Sun's disk but allowing its corona to be visible around it. *U.S. Naval Institute Photo Archive*

where this is observable. At other such times, when the Moon is closer in its orbit to Earth, the Moon will not completely block the Sun's disk but will leave a narrow ring of its corona visible around it, a phenomenon called an **annular eclipse.** This gives astronomers and astrophysicists an opportunity to observe and study this layer of the Sun's atmosphere.

Composition of the Sun

Spectrographic analysis shows that the Sun consists of gases at very high temperatures. Its composition by mass is 74.9 percent hydrogen, 23.8 percent helium, and 1.3 percent other heavier elements, a makeup almost identical to the cosmological mix of these elements throughout the universe. Each second, about 600 million tons of this hydrogen are converted into about 596 million tons of helium by nuclear fusion at the Sun's core, the

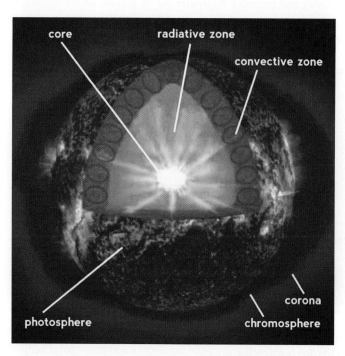

Artist's rendering of the principal layers and zones of the Sun.

other four million tons being converted into energy. Even with this fantastic rate of fuel consumption, the Sun is so massive that astronomers estimate it will take another five billion years or more to exhaust its supply of hydrogen. Temperatures in the core are thought to exceed 16 million degrees C, at which temperatures the fusion reaction is self-sustaining.

The energy generated in the core of the Sun travels outward through two regions called the "radiative" and "convective" zones until it reaches the surface of the Sun, called the **photosphere.** The photosphere is thought to be from a few tens to a few hundreds of kilometers thick; it has a temperature of about 6,000 degrees C. Above the photosphere is the Sun's atmosphere, consisting of five zones: the temperature minimum, the chromosphere, the transition layer, the corona, and the heliosphere. Within the atmosphere temperatures steadily increase until they reach several million degrees in the corona, where the Sun's energy escapes into space as sunlight, other types of electromagnetic radiation, and as energetic particles.

The **corona** is the outer layer of the Sun's atmosphere, much larger in volume than the Sun itself, extending many millions of miles out into space, where it transitions into the **solar wind** (a stream of energetic charged particles, mostly protons and electrons). Average temperatures within the corona vary from about 1 to 2 million degrees C, with some regions as hot as 8–20 million degrees C. No complete theories yet exist to account for why the temperatures increase in the solar atmosphere with increasing distance from the surface or why they are so extreme in the corona.

Beyond the corona lies the **heliosphere,** filled with the energetic particles of the solar wind and extending outward from about twenty solar radii to the edges of the solar system, to a boundary called the **heliopause,** which marks the beginning of deep space. In August 2012 the *Voyager 1* spacecraft passed through this region, as did *Voyager 2* later. Both recorded high levels of charged particles as they approached the boundary.

The interaction of the solar wind with the Earth's magnetic field in the heliosphere creates the Earth's *magnetosphere,* described in chapter 7 in the meteorology unit. The solar wind also causes long-term erosion on the surface of the Moon, and its pressure on the tails of comets causes them always to extend in a direction away from the Sun as the comets pass through the solar system. Spacecraft have to be shielded from the particles in the solar wind to avoid damage to their sensitive electronics, and personnel aboard the International Space Station have to take precautionary measures whenever unusual activity on the Sun causes the intensity of the solar wind to increase to dangerous levels.

Sunspots and Solar Flares

Sunspots are well-defined areas in the photosphere of the Sun that appear darker than their surroundings because they have lower temperatures. Sunspots are regions of intense magnetic activity where convection of heat from the interior is inhibited by strong magnetic fields. The magnetic field above the sunspots causes intense heating in the corona, which generates huge looping fountains of hot gas called **prominences** and **solar flares,** as well as other ejections of mass. The largest sunspots can be tens of thousands of kilometers wide.

There seems to be a cycle of sunspot activity, with greater numbers (maxima) occurring about every eleven years, and

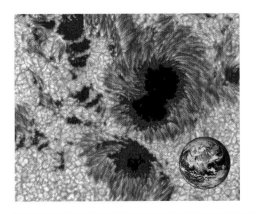

Picture of typical sunspots on the surface of the Sun, with an image of Earth superimposed for size comparison.
Windows to the Universe

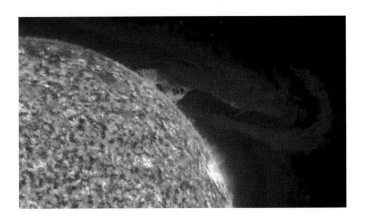

A solar flare. Such flares are of short duration, but they release huge amounts of energy, the largest many times the size of Earth.

lower numbers (minima) in between. Some scientists think there are also longer cycles of sunspot activity, of 40,000 and 100,000 years, that coincide with ice ages experienced on Earth around these times. Since an increase in sunspot and solar flare activity results in an increase in the intensity of the solar wind, these increases in solar activity are directly related to electrical and electronic disturbances on Earth and unusually intense **auroras** (luminous effects in the night sky) at high northern and southern latitudes. The increases in the solar wind intensity also affect the height and ionization of the ionosphere, causing fading and static in shortwave radio transmissions, and can cause problems with communication and Global Positioning System (GPS) satellites. As mentioned above, these increases can also represent a serious health hazard to those aboard the *ISS*.

The Polar Auroras

The interaction of the solar wind with the Earth's magnetic field in the upper atmosphere creates the beautiful and spectacular **aurora borealis (northern lights)** visible in the higher northern latitudes. Similar polar lights, the **aurora australis (southern lights),** appear in the southern hemisphere. As the charged particles within the solar wind pass by the high altitude thermosphere (described in chapter 7, unit 3), some of them are funneled and accelerated down along the Earth's magnetic-field lines. When they collide with nitrogen and oxygen atoms and molecules in the thermosphere, the energy released by these collisions ionizes some nitrogen atoms and causes other nitrogen atoms and oxygen atoms to be *excited* to a higher energy level. When these atoms regain an electron or return to a normal energy level, they release photons of light in the process, tinted green or brownish-red in the case of oxygen, blue or red

The *aurora borealis*, sometimes called the *northern lights*, as seen from a location in Alaska.

in the case of nitrogen. This light creates the auroras we see. As we saw above, increases in the solar wind intensity caused by sunspots and solar flares can cause large increases in the intensities of these auroras.

Solar Exploration

The first satellites designed to observe the Sun were *Pioneers 5 through 9,* launched by NASA between 1959 and 1968. These probes orbited the Sun at about the same distance as Earth and made the first detailed measurements of the solar wind and the solar magnetic field. As previously mentioned, between 1962 and 1975 a total of eight Orbiting Solar Observatories were launched into orbit around Earth to study the Sun. Their instruments returned data on solar flares, the Sun's corona, and solar activity in the gamma-ray, X-ray, and ultraviolet bands of the electromagnetic spectrum.

In addition to the manned *Skylab* solar observatory mentioned earlier, several additional spacecraft were orbited by the United States and other nations throughout the 1980s and 1990s to observe and gather data about the Sun. One of the more important of these is the *Solar and Heliospheric Observatory* (SOHO), a joint project of the European Space Agency and NASA launched in December 1995. Its mission was originally intended to last only two years, but it was later extended through at least 2014. Situated in a so-called *heliospheric* solar orbit at a point between the Earth and the Sun where the gravitational pull from each is equal, SOHO maintains a constant position relative to both, providing a consistent vantage point from which to observe the Sun's atmosphere and measure the

The *Ulysses* space probe. A joint effort of the European Space Agency and NASA, it observed the Sun for the first time from a polar solar orbit, from 1994 to 2009.

solar wind. Besides its solar observations, SOHO discovered a large number of small comets that burn up as they pass the Sun. A follow-on mission, the *Solar Dynamics Observatory* (SDO), was launched in February 2010 into a geosynchronous Earth orbit. It is studying the Sun's magnetic field with an instrument, called the Atmospheric Imaging Assembly (AIA), that allows continuous full-disk observations of the solar chromosphere and corona in seven extreme-ultraviolet wavelengths.

All the foregoing spacecraft that orbited the Sun were placed into equatorial orbits and so could observe only its equatorial regions in detail. The *Ulysses* probe, another joint venture of the European Space Agency and NASA, was launched by the shuttle *Discovery* in 1990 to study the Sun's polar regions from a polar orbit around the Sun. In order to reach the speeds needed to achieve this orbit, it had to get a "slingshot "gravity boost from the planet Jupiter, which it encountered in February 1992. Once *Ulysses* was in its intended orbit, in mid-1994, it began observing the solar wind and magnetic field strength at high solar latitudes with its various sensors, a mission that continued until it was deactivated in 2009, when its power supply ran out.

A *Solar Terrestrial Relations Observatory* (STEREO) mission was launched in October 2006. Two identical spacecraft were launched into the same orbit as Earth around the Sun, one positioned ahead of Earth and the other behind. This placement enables stereoscopic imaging of the Sun and various solar phenomena, such as comets and coronal-mass ejections, by combining images taken at the same time by the two spacecraft. In June 2013 an *Interface Region Imaging Spectrograph* (IRIS) space telescope was launched into a Sun-synchronous polar Earth orbit to further investigate the nature of the interface between the chromosphere and transition region in the Sun's atmosphere, and why the Sun's atmosphere increases in temperature with increasing distance from the photosphere.

Several additional missions to observe the Sun from close orbits are being planned by the United States, Japan, and possibly the ESA over the next decade.

Final Stages of Life

Scientists have deduced from observations of the life cycles of other stars in our galaxy that the Sun is about halfway through its life as an average **main sequence star** (a typical star in our galaxy—see chapter 17). In about five or six billion more years, as we have seen, it will finally have expended most of its supply of hydrogen, whereupon it will expand to some two hundred times its present size over the next half-billion years or so to become a **red giant** (a greatly expanded main-sequence star in the final stages of life). In the process it will engulf the inner two planets but probably will stop just short of the Earth. However, long before that it will have gradually increased in size, luminosity, and temperature, so much so that in about a billion years from now Earth will become hotter than the planet Venus is at present, extinguishing all life. The habitable zone around the Sun will move out to Mars and beyond.

The Sun does not have enough mass to end its life in a *supernova* (huge explosion), as most larger stars do. Instead it will spend another billion years as a red giant, burning helium in its core and losing about a third of its mass, after which it will have only about 120 million years of active life left. It then will go through several expansion and contraction phases, ejecting more mass in the form of a *planetary nebula* (an orbiting cloud of gas and dust), until it is only half as massive as it is today and its core is exposed. It will then undergo a final contraction, cool, and become a dense Earth-sized **white dwarf** (star in the final stage of its existence). The planetary nebula will disperse in a few thousand more years, and the remnant white dwarf will cool for billions of years before fading to black.

Critical Thinking

1. Why is an understanding of the nature and characteristics of the Sun so important to astronomers and meteorologists?

2. Why are many satellites placed in Earth or lunar orbit destroyed after their useful service by crashing them into the terrestrial atmosphere or lunar surface?

Study Guide Questions

1. What is the source of most of Earth's energy?

2. How far is Earth from the Sun?

3. What is an astronomical unit (AU)?

4. Why is it so dangerous to look at the Sun through any kind of lens?

5. What is the composition of the Sun? What are its major layers?

6. How is the Sun its own fuel?

7. What is the Sun's corona?

8. What is the solar wind?

9. What is the importance of sunspots to Earth?

10. What causes the auroras in the high latitudes of the northern and southern hemispheres?

11. What was unique about the *Ulysses* probe launched in 1990?

12. According to scientists what will be the ultimate fate of the Sun and Earth?

New Vocabulary

astronomical unit	sunspots
photosphere	prominences
total eclipse	solar flares
annular eclipse	aurora
corona	aurora borealis
solar wind	aurora australis
heliosphere	red giant
heliopause	white dwarf

15

The Planets

Until the start of the new millennium, the general understanding throughout the scientific community and the general public was that there were nine planets in our solar system, the last and farthest from the Sun being Pluto, discovered in 1930. However, beginning in the late 1990s with the development of more powerful Earth- and space-based telescopes, increasing numbers of bodies were discovered beyond Pluto, in the **Kuiper Belt** (region of the solar system beyond Pluto extending from 30 to 55 AU from the Sun), at least the size of Pluto. Were these to be considered planets as well? For several years this question was debated among the world's leading astronomers and the **International Astronomical Union** (IAU), the internationally recognized authority for assigning designations to celestial bodies.

In 2006 the IAU formally released the following three-part definition of a planet: (1) a planet is a body that orbits the Sun, is (2) massive enough for its own gravity to make it round, and has (3) "cleared its neighborhood" of smaller objects around its orbit. Under this definition the newly discovered bodies of comparable size beyond Pluto were *not* planets, and neither was

Pluto itself, since they did not satisfy the third criterion. They were therefore reclassified into a new category called **dwarf planets**, defined as any body that met the first two criteria but not the third and were not satellites of a larger body.

Traditional and Dwarf Planets

Under the new definition there are now considered to be eight **traditional**, or "classical," **planets** in our solar system, plus Pluto and four other dwarf planets in its outer regions. In order outward from the Sun, the traditional planets are Mercury, Venus, Earth, Mars, Jupiter, Saturn, Uranus, and Neptune. Venus and Mars have some similarities to Earth, but all the other traditional and dwarf planets are very different. Mercury scorches under the intense rays of the Sun. Jupiter and the other three traditional planets beyond it are strange, cold worlds, composed of poisonous gases and chemical compounds uncommon on Earth. The dwarf planets are small, cold, rocky bodies with tenuous if any atmospheres and so far away and dimly lit that they can only be observed by very powerful telescopes. Mer-

The traditional planets and several dwarf planets of the solar system drawn to scale relative to the Sun. The distances separating them are not to scale.

cury, Venus, Earth, and Mars are customarily referred to by astronomers as the **inner planets,** and Jupiter, Saturn, Uranus, and Neptune are referred to as the **outer planets.**

The planets are wanderers in the sky; the word "planet" was derived from *asteres planetai* ("wandering stars"), which ancient Greek astronomers used to describe them. They are called that because they are constantly moving, as they revolve around the Sun in their orbits, against the background of the relatively stationary stars in a mostly easterly direction across the night sky as we observe them from one night to the next. Since they are moving, it is difficult to keep track of them without some sort of chart. A chart that serves as a timetable for the movement and location of the planets is called an **almanac,** or **ephemeris.**

The traditional and dwarf planets all orbit the Sun in the same counterclockwise direction in which the Sun rotates, as viewed from above the Sun's northern pole. Earth's orbit about the Sun, called the **plane of the ecliptic,** is the usual reference to which the orbital planes of all the other bodies in the solar system are compared. It is so named because the Moon must cross this plane in order to cause a solar or lunar eclipse. All the other traditional planets orbit generally in this same plane, but most of the orbits of the dwarf planets are highly inclined with respect to it. You might compare the orbital plane of the traditional planets to an old phonograph record—the Sun is at the center, and each planet's orbit falls into its own groove, each farther outward from the center. Actually, the planets' and dwarf planets' orbits around the Sun, as well as the orbits of all other bodies in orbit around it, are **ellipses** (an egg shape), a slight variation from a circle. The Sun is located at one focus point of these ellipses. The gravitational pull of the Sun keeps all the bodies in the solar system, including the planets and dwarf planets, in their orbits. The time it takes an orbiting body to go around the Sun is called its **orbital period.**

As the bodies in the solar system travel in their elliptical paths, they sweep out equal pie-shaped areas in their orbital planes in equal times. Thus, when they are closer to the Sun, they are traveling faster in their orbits. When they are farther away, they are traveling slower.

Most of the traditional planets rotate about their axes in the same counterclockwise direction as the Sun; the exceptions are Venus and Uranus, which both rotate in the opposite, or retrograde, direction. This backward rotation was probably caused by glancing impacts with other large bodies at some time in the distant past. The dwarf planets rotate as well, with the dwarf Haumea having the fastest known rotational period of any large body in the solar system (3.9 hours).

Although the planets are much smaller than stars, they are also much closer to us, so much so that a telescope can magnify them. Their light also seems to be steadier than the stars, which often seem to twinkle. Five of the traditional planets can be seen without a telescope (except when their orbits take them near the Sun): Mercury, Venus, Mars, Jupiter, and Saturn. Uranus is just at the limit of visibility. Neptune can be seen only with a powerful telescope; that is true also of Pluto and the other dwarf planets.

The traditional planets Venus, Mars, Jupiter, and Saturn are sometimes called the **Big Four,** because they are the most prominent visually. Since its orbit is so close to the Sun, Mercury is hardly ever observable. Likewise, Venus is also always near the Sun as we look at it; however, when it is not crossing the Sun's disk it is readily observable in the western sky just after sunset or in the eastern sky before sunrise. It is thus called the **evening star** or **morning star,** and it is the brightest object in the night sky, after the Moon. Mars, Jupiter, and Saturn have orbits that lie outside the orbit of Earth. Thus when they are observable they can be seen all night. Like our Moon, the planets and dwarf planets shine only by reflected sunlight.

All the traditional planets except Mercury and Venus have satellite moons. Earth has one, Mars has two, and the outer planets all have many, with additional ones continually being discovered in recent years. Several of the dwarf planets have moons as well. A number of the outer planets' moons were first discovered and photographed by the Pioneer and Voyager spacecraft in the 1980s, by the *Galileo* mission to Jupiter in the 1990s, and more recently by the *Cassini* mission to Saturn. Many of these moons, as well as those orbiting the dwarf planets, were also discovered, observed, and photographed by the *Hubble Space Telescope,* as well as by several of the newer large terrestrial telescopes. The pictures of the planets and their moons that appear with their descriptions on the following pages were all taken by these and by some of the other later space probes.

The next sections will briefly describe the other seven traditional planets in our solar system, the dwarf planets, and the many discoveries about them made by spacecraft and telescopes of the United States and other nations. Further information about and spectacular photography from many of the U.S. spacecraft missions can be obtained from the NASA website, www.nasa.gov.

Mercury

Mercury is the closest planet to the Sun, with a mean orbital radius of about 35 million miles, roughly a third of Earth's. It is the smallest of the traditional planets in the solar system, with a radius of 2,440 kilometers (1,516 miles), about 0.4 times Earth's 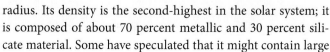 radius. Its density is the second-highest in the solar system; it is composed of about 70 percent metallic and 30 percent silicate material. Some have speculated that it might contain large

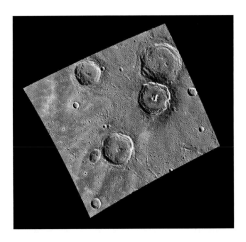

A close-up image of Mercury's cratered surface taken by the *MESSENGER* spacecraft.

deposits of gold. Its gravitational attraction is about 0.4 of Earth's (0.38 g). Its temperature is about 400 degrees C at its equator on the lighted side, –200 degrees C on the dark side, and –93 degrees C at the poles. There is an indication that there might be water ice in shaded impact craters at the poles. Mercury has almost no atmosphere, so there is no erosion on its heavily cratered, Moon-like surface. It rotates only three times about its axis for every two revolutions about the Sun.

Mercury has the shortest period of revolution about the Sun—eighty-eight days, faster than that of any other planet—which may have led to its being named after a Roman deity who was a fast-flying messenger to the other gods. Because it is so close to the Sun, the planet is difficult to observe either by eye or by ground- or space-based telescopes. Its speed in orbit and the intense pull of the Sun's gravity at its location make it difficult for space probes to get into orbit around it. It has thus far been investigated by only two spacecraft.

TV cameras mounted on the *Mariner 10* probe observed Mercury from an elliptical orbit around the Sun during three flybys in 1974 and 1975. A *MESSENGER* (MErcury Surface, Space ENvironment, GEochemistry, and Ranging) spacecraft was launched by NASA in 2004 with more sophisticated instruments to photograph and study the planet more extensively. Following braking fly-bys of Earth and Venus and several of Mercury, the probe settled into a close orbit around the planet in 2011 for a multiyear mission, still ongoing, to investigate Mercury's geology, magnetic field, and tenuous atmosphere, and to confirm the suspected presence of water ice at the poles The probe has returned some 200,000 HD photographic images of the planet to date.

The European Space Agency is planning a joint mission to the planet with Japan in 2015. Two probes are to be conveyed there on a single "bus" spacecraft to further map the planet and study its magnetosphere.

Venus

Venus is the second planet from the Sun, with an average orbital radius of about 67 million miles, some two-thirds that of Earth. It was once believed that Venus was almost a twin sister of Earth and perhaps inhabited, because the two planets are so nearly alike in size, mass, density, composition, and gravity (0.9 g). But actually there the similarities end. Earth rotates once on its axis every day, but Venus rotates only once in 243 Earth days, and in the opposite direction from Earth and most other planets. A Venusian year is 255 Earth days long, and since its axis has only a three-degree inclination with respect to its orbital plane, it has no seasons. Its reverse rotation, in conjunction with its orbital velocity around the Sun results in a solar day on Venus (the length of a day experienced on Venus) of 117 Earth days from one sunrise to the next.

The atmosphere of Venus, composed mainly of carbon dioxide, is the densest of any planet in the solar system. Creating a surface pressure more than ninety times that of Earth, it would bear down on an inhabitant with the weight of the ocean at a depth of 3,300 feet! Moreover, it also traps entering sunlight and prevents the escape of heat energy, resulting in an average temperature greater than 460 degrees C (860 degrees F) everywhere on the planet—hot enough to melt lead and zinc. A forty-mile-thick layer of clouds surrounds the atmosphere. It reflects over 90 percent of the sunlight that strikes it and prevents direct visual observation of the surface. Only an estimated 2 percent of the Sun's light reaches the surface through these clouds and the thick atmosphere beneath them. However, because of the **super-refractivity** (extreme bending of light rays) of the dense atmosphere, no one on Venus would be able to tell the difference between day and night in any case. There would be a dim yellow glow everywhere all the time.

Although it may have had oceans of water billions of years in the past, there is now no water and no free oxygen on Venus. The absence of water and oxygen and the great heat in the Venusian atmosphere are caused by what many scientists call a **runaway greenhouse effect,** an ultimate case of global warming

A picture of the Venusian surface taken by the Soviet *Venera 14* lander in 1982. *NASA*

The *Magellan* orbiter being launched by the space shuttle *Atlantis* in 1989.

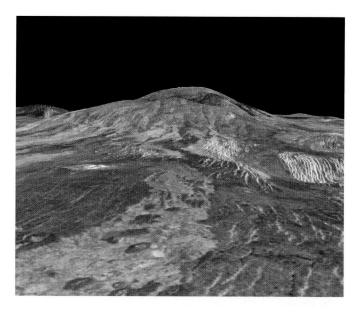

Computer-generated image of a volcanic peak on the surface of Venus based on data obtained by the spacecraft *Magellan*.

caused by buildup of carbon dioxide. The dense atmosphere keeps the intense heat evenly distributed around the planet, with little variation between day and night or from pole to pole.

Since 1962 more than twenty spacecraft have explored Venus. Most of the earlier exploratory missions to the planet were Soviet Venera probes launched from the late 1960s to the early 1980s. Several of these successfully penetrated the Venusian atmosphere and reported its density and pressures before landing on the surface. Once there they recorded surface temperatures of 470 degrees C and returned murky pictures of a barren, lunar-like landscape during the few hours before they melted. Two additional Soviet Vega spacecraft dropped probes and balloons into the Venusian atmosphere in the mid-1980s, and these returned significant information about atmospheric conditions. These observations, plus others by American spacecraft, have shown that the planet is indeed a very unlikely place for life of any kind.

While the foregoing missions to Venus were important, all the data they accumulated were eclipsed by the NASA's *Magellan* orbiter. Launched in 1989, it reached Venus in 1991 and began an extended radar survey of the planet's surface in strips ten to seventeen miles wide. This effort enabled scientists to view details the size of a football field. *Magellan* showed that much of the surface appears to have been shaped by volcanic activity. There are enormous lava flows, unexpected pancake-like structures, and about a thousand large, well-preserved impact craters up to 120 miles in diameter. Large areas of the surface, how-

ever, are relatively smooth, and there are very few small craters, indicating that the surface probably underwent global melting about 400–800 million years ago. The absence of small craters indicates that the planet has had a thick atmosphere for at least that long.

Magellan's radar maps showed no signs, such as shorelines or ocean basins, of past major water bodies. Unlike on Earth, there is no evidence of **plate tectonics** (movements of crustal mass), which may indicate Venus lacks an asthenosphere between its crust and mantle. It has no detectable magnetic field, which indicates its core is probably mostly liquid—or alternatively, solid, though this is unlikely. The distribution of volcanoes is also interesting. Thousands of them appear to be randomly distributed, rather than being located in clusters, such as in the "Ring of Fire" around Earth's Pacific rim.

With its power supplies nearly depleted, *Magellan* ended its mission with a dramatic plunge into the Venusian atmosphere in October 1994, the first time an operating planetary spacecraft was intentionally destroyed. The purpose of the maneuver was to gather data on Venus's atmosphere before *Magellan* ceased to function.

During its second flyby of Venus in 2007, NASA's *MESSENGER* mission to Mercury recorded a variety of scientific data about the Venusian atmosphere. A European Space Agency orbiter called *Venus Express* was placed into polar orbit around the planet in 2006, with an ongoing mission to observe the Venusian atmosphere until at least the end of 2014. Another ESA mission scheduled for launching in 2016 and destined for Mercury will also conduct two flybys of Venus en route, and a Russian *Venera-D* orbiter scheduled for launch the same year will carry a lander capable of soft-landing on the surface and surviving for some time.

So Venus, named for the Roman goddess of beauty, is in fact, hidden behind its clouds, a grim and lifeless inferno. But to us on Earth, Venus is often the brightest object in the sky, besides the Moon and Sun, because of the high reflectivity of its cloud layer. Venus shines most brightly when it is between us and the Sun, even though the sunlight falls on the side away from us, for the planet is closest to us at that time.

Mars

Of all the planets in our solar system, Mars, the fourth from the Sun and the next beyond Earth, has always aroused the greatest interest. Named after the Roman god of war, it is often called the "red planet," because the iron oxide prevalent on its surface gives it a dim red hue as it is observed in the sky. It is not as easily recognized and observed as Venus or Jupiter, because it is not as bright. But Mars's red color and its relatively rapid movement from west to east among the stars make it stand out.

Picture showing the Martian atmosphere and some of the impact craters on the surface, taken by one of the Mars orbiters.

Mars has an average orbital radius of roughly 140 million miles, about one and a half times that of Earth (1.5 AU). Its orbital period is 687 Earth days, and its solar day of twenty-four hours, thirty-nine minutes is only slightly longer than Earth's. Its axis is inclined 25.2 degrees with respect to the plane of its orbit, very comparable with Earth's 23.5-degree tilt, so it exhibits the same kinds of seasons. It is a terrestrial planet, with a thin atmosphere, a little more than half of Earth's size and about a tenth of Earth's mass. Its gravitational attraction is only about 40 percent of Earth's (0.4 g). That means a person weighing 150 pounds on Earth would weigh only about sixty pounds on Mars.

As on Venus, the atmosphere of Mars is composed mainly of carbon dioxide, but the density and atmospheric pressure are only a tiny fraction of what they are on Venus, about equal to Earth's atmosphere twenty miles up. A space suit would be a necessity for any human visitor.

Temperatures on Mars range from near 0 degrees C in summer in the early afternoon to –100 degrees C or cooler just before sunrise. The surfaces of the darker areas may be twenty degrees warmer, due to absorption of the Sun's rays. But because of the thinness of the atmosphere, the air a few feet above the ground may be as much as forty degrees cooler than the surface itself. The daily temperature range of about 100 degrees would be extremely uncomfortable, if not fatal, to Earth's higher organisms. The polar regions seem to have fairly constant temperatures of about –140 degrees C.

Fierce seasonal Martian winds whip up huge dust storms of the iron oxide that covers about three-fourths of the surface. The windstorms may rage for months at speeds of up to three hundred miles per hour, covering much of the planet with swirling reddish-orange dust clouds. The dust of Mars is extremely fine, something like fine talcum powder. It is sometimes carried thirty-five miles above the planet's surface.

The Martian surface, like our Moon, has many impact craters, and also volcanoes, mountain ridges, valleys, and polar caps similar to those on Earth. A primary distinguishing surface feature is the Grand Canyon–like Valles Marineris, which

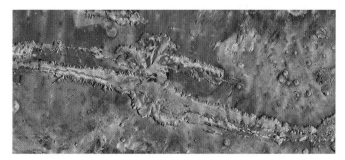

A close-up of the 2,500-mile-long Valles Marineris on the surface of Mars.

Scale photos of the Martian moons Deimos (left) and Phobos (right) obtained by the *Mars Reconnaissance Orbiter.*

runs laterally across the equatorial region on one side. However, it is more than 2,500 miles (4,000 km) long and up to four miles (7 km) deep, in contrast to the 275-mile length and one-mile depth of the Grand Canyon. It probably formed as a rift in the crust some three billion years ago. Many of the larger impact craters date from the Late Heavy Bombardment period, which as previously mentioned lasted from about 4.1 to 3.8 billion years ago, similar to the bombardment that occurred on the Moon (and presumably the Earth and the other inner planets) during the same period. The polar caps grow and shrink with the seasons and are thought to be composed of frozen carbon dioxide and frozen water vapor.

Huge inactive volcanoes are present on the Martian surface. One, named *Olympus Mons* ("Mount Olympus"), is the size of the state of Nebraska. It rises fifteen miles above the surrounding terrain and has a main crater forty miles in diameter. Another, named *South Spot,* has the largest volcanic crater on Mars, seventy-five miles across.

An enduring mystery about Mars is what happened to its liquid water. Analysis of its surface geology by orbiters and rovers over the last several decades has yielded much evidence that there was certainly a lot of it at some time in the distant past, but none has been found anywhere on the surface to date.

Mars has two small moons, Phobos and Deimos, which orbit close to the planet. Their origin is uncertain, although many astronomers theorize they may have been captured by Mars' gravity in the fairly recent past. Photographs of them taken by several Mars orbiters show them to be irregularly shaped and similar in appearance to asteroids. Phobos is only about 27 kilometers (16.7 miles) long, and Deimos is only about sixteen kilometers (ten miles). Both appear barely larger than stars from the Martian surface.

Many astronomers and other prominent scientists in the past thought Mars capable of supporting some kind of life. In

1877 the Italian astronomer Giovanni Schiaparelli caused a sensation when he announced that he had observed a series of long intersecting lines on the Martian surface. He called them *canali,* Italian for "channels," or "canals." Many people believed that the *canali* must have been made by intelligent beings, because they were so straight. Or, they thought, perhaps they had been created by free-flowing water, indicating that Mars could be capable of supporting life. Speculation on the *canali* continued for the next several decades, until more powerful telescopes cast doubt on their existence.

Intelligent life on Mars was also a favorite theme of early science fiction novels, radio programs, and later, movies. In 1938 an American actor and producer, Orson Welles, broadcast over a national radio network a dramatic adaptation of H. G. Wells' 1898 classic novel *The War of the Worlds,* in which a supposed invasion of Earth from Mars seemed to be actually taking place. The realistic radio news-bulletin format he used, uninterrupted by any commercials, caused a panic among many listeners.

Speculation about life on Mars continued for many years. Ultimately, observations and extensive photography by a succession of Soviet and American space probes and orbiters in the 1960s and 1970s definitively proved the *canali* to be illusions and other speculations of life on Mars to be invalid. They sent back numerous, though not well defined, pictures of the Martian surface, measurements of atmospheric pressure and temperatures, and indications that Mars has no magnetic field or radiation belts. They found no sign of living things or of an environment that could support them. The landscape appeared

A replica of the Viking landers with Carl Sagan (1934–96), a prominent American astronomer, cosmologist, and TV science personality who did much to popularize astronomy and the search for extraterrestrial life in the 1960s–90s.

An intriguing view of the alleged "face on Mars" photo taken by one of the Viking orbiters in 1976. Subsequent pictures of the same area taken by later Mars orbiters left little doubt that this was only a transitory wind-erosion effect.

barren, and there were no canals or evidence of liquid water present on the surface. Analysis of the photography did, however, reveal dry river beds and massive canyons that most likely could only have been carved by ancient water erosion.

In 1975 NASA launched two Viking missions to Mars, each consisting of an orbiter to photograph the surface in more detail and a lander to search for signs of microbial life. The two landers made successful soft landings on the surface the following year, the first spacecraft ever to do so. Carrying cameras, sensors, and radio-controlled arms and biological test equipment, both landers sent back pictures of the surface around them and data on the Martian atmosphere. They used their robotic arms to scoop up samples of the Martian soil and deposit them into sealed containers in the craft for analysis. The results were transmitted back to Earth.

In this most detailed search for life on Mars to date, the results were generally considered inconclusive; the first of three tests performed by each lander yielded positive results for the presence of microbes, but the others were all negative. However, reexamination of the test data in recent years indicates that because of some factors not considered relevant at the time, the negative results could well have been misinterpreted, and

the Viking landers may indeed have found proof of microbial life. NASA plans to send a follow-up mission to Mars, equipped with much more sophisticated biological test apparatus, sometime during the next decade to try to find out for sure whether or not such life exists there.

Interestingly, one of the many pictures sent back from the Viking orbiters contained an eerie image of what seemed to some to be a human face carved into a hill. It appeared periodically in many tabloid newspapers for years afterward. Later higher-resolution photos of the same area taken by subsequent orbiters, however, proved the supposed "face" to have been a short-term erosion feature.

In 1996 NASA scientists reported that they had discovered fossilized evidence of ancient Martian bacteria in an Antarctic meteorite determined to have originated on Mars some three billion years ago. Their findings were based on chemical, mineral, and structural evidence found in the interior of the meteorite. The discovery was immediately hailed as one of the most important in the last century by many scientists interested in the possibility of extraterrestrial life. Later, however, other scientists disputed these claims, stating that the alleged "bacteria" were in fact products of natural chemical reactions.

Suffice it to say that these events sparked much renewed interest in the possibility of past or present life on Mars. In response, many innovative new missions were sent to explore Mars further, and many others are planned for the future. One of the first and most successful of these was *Mars Pathfinder*, which made a cushioned landing on the Martian surface on the Fourth of July 1997. Carried aboard was a small 22-pound solar-powered, wheeled rover called *Sojourner*. For nearly three months the little rover roamed the landing area; it and the *Pathfinder* lander returned many images of the surrounding surface features, spectral analyses of nearby rocks, and scientific data regarding the atmosphere. Mission scientists determined that

Three generations of Mars rovers. Two spacecraft engineers stand with test models of the small Mars rover *Sojourner*, the midsized *Spirit* and *Opportunity*, and the large rover *Curiosity*.

many of the rocks at its landing site had very likely been deposited there by a large flood of water in the distant past.

Even more successful than *Pathfinder* were two larger and more capable rovers sent by NASA to Mars in the midsummer of 2003. One of these, called *Spirit,* landed in January 2004 in a rocky outcrop called Gusev Crater; the other, *Opportunity,* landed three weeks later on the opposite side of Mars in a sandy area called the Meridiani Plains. Their mission was to investigate a wide range of rocks and soils that might hold clues to past water activity on the planet. Although they were originally planned to rove the surface for only three months, *Spirit* carried on until March 2010, and *Opportunity* is still operational today.

Ultimately, *Spirit* found much additional evidence of igneous rocks extensively altered by ancient exposure to water. *Opportunity* is still investigating layered bedrock at its location, which has already yielded much geological evidence of an ancient body of shallow water. *Spirit* logged some 4.8 miles of travel on the Martian surface, and *Opportunity* has traveled some twenty-four miles at this writing. *Spirit* sent back, and *Opportunity* continues to send, voluminous data and thousands of detailed panoramic photographs, many showing the rovers' tracks through the Martian terrain.

The latest and most sophisticated rover to investigate Mars is NASA's *Curiosity,* a car-sized vehicle exploring a large feature called Gale Crater. It made a successful wheeled landing on the surface in August 2012 after an innovative descent from orbit lowered by cables from a braking rocket. Collectively called the *Mars Science Laboratory,* it represents the most advanced suite of instruments for scientific study ever sent to the Martian surface. The rover and its advanced payload of scientific instruments are designed to determine the presence of "building block" elements necessary for life, such as carbon and oxygen; investigate the composition of the surface and atmosphere; and investigate the nature and spectrum of all radiation reaching its surface from all sources. *Curiosity* is also fitted with high-resolution cameras, which have already returned some 37,000 images of the geological features around it. In contrast to earlier rovers, which obtained their power from solar panels, *Curiosity* has a self-contained radioisotope power system that generates electricity from heat produced by radioactive decay of plutonium. Its power supply should be capable of sustaining it for ten years or more.

To date the rover has sent back over a hundred gigabits of data, analyzed several ground-up rock samples, and driven over a mile across the surface. Some of the more interesting science results returned by the Mars Science Laboratory thus far include verification of the Martian origin of several meteorites previously found on Earth and of the presence of an unusually high proportion of water (approximately 2 percent) in Martian soil samples analyzed.

Additional missions to Mars planned for the next decade include an orbiter mission by India; several missions by Russia, including a sample-return mission; and several more missions by the United States, including at least one aforementioned biological laboratory specifically designed to try to find a definitive answer as to the existence of microbial life. A U.S. mission may send astronauts to Mars sometime after 2030. Ultimately all these explorations may one day resolve the many questions about water on Mars and the possibility of former or current life there.

The best time for viewing Mars is when it is nearest to Earth, in August and September. In those months it sometimes comes as close as thirty million miles. In February and March, it is over sixty million miles away and much less easily viewed. It is best seen when in direct opposition—in other words, when Earth is directly between the Sun and Mars.

A panoramic view of the Martian surface from Mars rover *Curiosity.*

Jupiter

Jupiter is the fifth planet from the Sun. Largest of all the planets, it has a diameter of 85,500 miles, more than ten times that of Earth, and a volume over 1,300 times as great. It has two and a half times the mass of all the other planets combined. It orbits at an average of about 484 million miles from the Sun (5 AU), with an orbital period of 11.9 Earth years, and never comes closer to Earth than 367 million miles. Because like the Sun it is not a solid body, it rotates at different rates at different latitudes, faster near the equator than at the poles. This, along with the fact that it has the highest rotation rate of any of the traditional planets in the solar system (nine hours, fifty minutes at the equator), creates an easily observable 2,700-mile bulge at the equator. Despite its great distance from Earth, Jupiter usually outshines everything in the night sky except the Moon and Venus.

Named after the king of the Roman gods, Jupiter remained an almost complete mystery until NASA's *Pioneer 10* passed within 82,000 miles of its cloud tops in December 1973. *Pioneer 11* passed within 27,000 miles a year later to find out more. The two U.S. Voyager spacecraft, with more advanced instruments, flew by Jupiter and several of its moons in March and July 1979. Many superb color pictures of the planet and its four major "Galilean" moons (Io, Europa, Callisto, and Ganymede, discussed below) were transmitted back to Earth by all four spacecraft. Several spectacular new discoveries were made, including a set of tenuous rings surrounding the planet, extensive radiation belts, sulfur and sulfur-dioxide volcanism on Io, and water ice on Callisto and Ganymede.

Jupiter can easily retain all kinds of gases in its atmosphere, especially hydrogen and helium. The force of Jupiter's gravity, over two and a half times Earth's (2.5–2.8 g), is such that a 150-pound person would weigh 375 pounds at the equator and 425 pounds at either pole. It is thought that when Jupiter was first formed it was much hotter and about twice the size it is now. It missed becoming a star by only a narrow margin.

The atmosphere of Jupiter is 75 percent hydrogen and 24 percent helium by mass, with small but important amounts of methane, ammonia, and water. The atmosphere is covered by a thirty-mile-thick deck of clouds of ammonia containing wide, roughly parallel horizontal circulation bands (called *zones*) of white, yellow, orange, brown, and gray. The bands vary in thickness from year to year. Their colors are thought to be caused by upwelling compounds that change color when exposed to ultraviolet light. The innermost layer of clouds is probably composed of water vapor suspended in the hydrogen-helium atmosphere. Violent flashes of lightning, a thousand times more powerful than any on Earth, have been observed between this layer and the atmosphere beneath.

We do not yet know for sure what lies beneath the cloud layers. But according to current theory, there is no solid surface as there is on the terrestrial planets. Instead, the hydrogen that makes up most of the atmosphere is believed to be gradually squeezed into a dense, hot fluid under increasing pressure about a thousand kilometers (621 miles) beneath the clouds, with helium droplets precipitating through it. Some 9,500 miles down, under a pressure of three to five million Earth atmospheres and at a temperature of 10,000 degrees C, the hydrogen probably becomes a metal, in a form unknown on Earth.

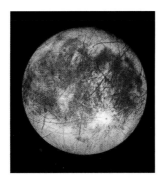

Jupiter's moon Europa is the smallest of the Galilean moons. It is covered by a thick layer of ice, under which is a sixty-mile-deep water ocean that some scientists think may be capable of harboring life.

Since the planet is composed entirely of gas, the depth of its atmosphere is arbitrary; it is usually considered to be the depth at which the pressure is equal to ten times the surface pressure on Earth, which occurs about five thousand kilometers (3,100 miles) beneath the clouds. It is not yet known whether or not the planet has any core. Temperatures range from about –160 degrees C at the cloud tops to 35,000 degrees C or more at the planet's center.

Although Jupiter's atmosphere is kept constantly churning by its interior heat, one feature of the planet remains almost unchanged. That is the **Great Red Spot** in the southern hemisphere. This feature is some 17,000 miles long by 8,500 miles wide. It drifts slowly around the planet, staying generally in the same latitude. Its color sometimes fades to a gray and then returns to its red-orange state. For many years scientists were not sure about the cause of this phenomenon, but observations by the Voyager spacecraft, *Galileo,* and others have convinced most scientists that it is a giant and very-long-lived storm.

Jupiter has a strong magnetic field that traps and accelerates charged particles, creating intense radiation belts similar to Earth's Van Allen belts but thousands of times stronger. They were first reported by *Voyager 1,* and later investigated more thoroughly by the *Galileo* mission in the 1990s and by *Cassini* as it passed by on its way to Saturn in 2000. They extend well beyond the orbit of the innermost of Jupiter's four "Galilean" moons, Io, and present a serious hazard to any spacecraft that come near the planet.

A total of sixty-seven moons have been discovered thus far in orbit around Jupiter. They are loosely divided into four

A close-up photo of Jupiter showing its Great Red Spot.

groups, according to their mass and distance from the planet. The first group contains the four closest moons, of which two are of moderate size and the others are small. They mainly contribute material to and maintain Jupiter's faint ring system.

The second group, the four "Galilean" moons—those discovered by the astronomer in the 1600s—is the most significant, and its members are almost as intriguing as their host planet. All are spherical, larger than the dwarf planets, and together they contain well over 99 percent of the total mass of all sixty-seven moons combined. Several volcanic plumes of sulfur and sulfur dioxide were observed on Io, the fifth moon from the planet, during the *Voyager 1* flyby in 1979, and more were photographed by *Galileo* during its mission from 1995 to 2003. The moon is considered the most geologically active body in the solar system. The ice-covered Europa, sixth from the planet, is the smallest of the four. It is thought to have under its ice a hundred-kilometer-deep (sixty-two-mile) ocean of liquid water, which could possibly harbor life of some kind. Scientists have requested that NASA send a submarine probe there to find out. Ganymede, the seventh farthest and the largest moon, composed of silicate rock and water ice, exceeds Mercury in size. Callisto, the eighth, is larger than Earth's Moon and has long been considered a good candidate for a human exploration base, since it is farthest of the four from Jupiter's intense radiation belts.

The remaining moons, called the **irregular satellites,** are all small, irregularly shaped, and much farther away from the planet. Most of their orbits are much more inclined and more highly elliptical than those of the inner eight. All of them are thought to have been captured by Jupiter's strong gravity field. The inner group of seven all orbit the planet in the same direction as Jupiter rotates (**prograde**), while the forty-five constituting the outer group all rotate in the opposite direction (**retrograde**).

In October 1989 the spacecraft *Galileo* was launched from the space shuttle *Atlantis* with a dual mission to launch a probe it carried into the Jovian atmosphere and then to orbit the planet for at least two years in order to conduct an extensive survey of the planet and its four Galilean moons. *Galileo* entered orbit around Jupiter in December 1995, on the same day as its probe, released months earlier, slammed into the Jovian atmosphere at a speed of about 106,000 miles per hour (47 km/s). The probe carried instruments to measure temperature and pressure along the descent path, locate major cloud decks, and analyze the chemistry of atmospheric gases. The probe also attempted to detect and study Jovian lightning, both by looking for optical flashes and by listening for the radio static they generate. It traveled to between 130 and 160 kilometers below Jupiter's cloud tops before the extreme atmospheric pressure there rendered it inoperable.

Although *Galileo*'s mission was originally planned to last only two years, it ended up exploring Jupiter and its moons for a total of eight years until it was sent on a final plunge into the Jovian atmosphere in September 2003, to avoid any chance of its crashing into and contaminating Europa after it ran out of fuel. Many new discoveries about Jupiter and its moons were made by *Galileo* and its probe, including the finding that (as mentioned above) liquid water probably exists beneath Europa's icy surface. The structure and composition of the rings found earlier by *Voyager 1* were more thoroughly investigated; it was determined that they had been formed and are maintained by dust created by impacts of micrometeorites on the four small inner moons orbiting the planet.

The most recent probe to visit Jupiter was the Pluto-bound spacecraft *New Horizons*, which flew by the planet in February 2007. It took many pictures of Jupiter as it passed by, including several of a newly forming red spot on its surface. In 2011 the probe *Juno* was launched by NASA on a five-year journey to the planet. Upon arrival in 2016 it will be placed in polar orbit above Jupiter, where its array of instruments will attempt to learn more about the planet's origin and structure and will look for evidence of a solid core.

Both Jupiter and Saturn are considered by many scientists to be miniature models of our solar system, displaying many of the fundamental physical processes connected with its formation and early evolution. Undoubtedly, many more amazing discoveries about Jupiter and its moons await us in years to come.

An artist's rendering of the spacecraft *Galileo* in orbit around Jupiter. The blue spots represent its communications with the probe it released into the Jovian atmosphere shortly before its arrival.

Saturn

Named for the Roman god of time, the beautiful ringed planet Saturn is the solar system's second-largest planet. Saturn's rings are made up of billions of tiny solid particles. They extend in bands outward from seven thousand to 171,000 miles above the planet's surface. They are on the plane of the planet's equator, inclined to the orbit at an angle of 26.8 degrees. The rings revolve about the planet, with the inner bands moving faster than the outer ones.

Saturn has a diameter of 71,400 miles, about nine times that of Earth. It has a mean orbital radius of about 870 million miles (9.5 AU) and an orbital period of about twenty-nine and a half years. Like Jupiter, it rotates at different rates dependent on latitude; at the equator it completes each rotation in ten hours, fourteen minutes, but it takes slightly longer at middle and higher latitudes. Also as with Jupiter, this rapid rotational rate gives it a considerable bulge at the equator, about 3,700 miles. It has radiation belts similar to those surrounding Earth and Jupiter but much weaker in intensity, because of absorption by its rings.

Saturn's interior is probably composed of a core of iron, nickel, and rock, surrounded by a deep layer of metallic hydrogen, an intermediate layer of liquid hydrogen and liquid helium, and an outer gaseous layer comprising about 97 percent hydrogen and 3 percent helium. Saturn, like Jupiter, has a layer of

A beautiful photographic portrait, taken by *Cassini*, of a portion of Saturn's rings.

clouds composed of ammonia crystals, and it exhibits the same kinds of horizontal bands, though they are much fainter than those on the larger planet. These bands, which have winds of up to a thousand miles per hour racing through them, were unknown until the flybys of the Voyager spacecraft during the 1980s. Temperatures in the clouds vary from about –170 to –110 degrees C. It is probable that there is no solid surface for thousands of miles under the cloud layers. Core temperatures probably reach about 11,700 degrees C. Because of its low density

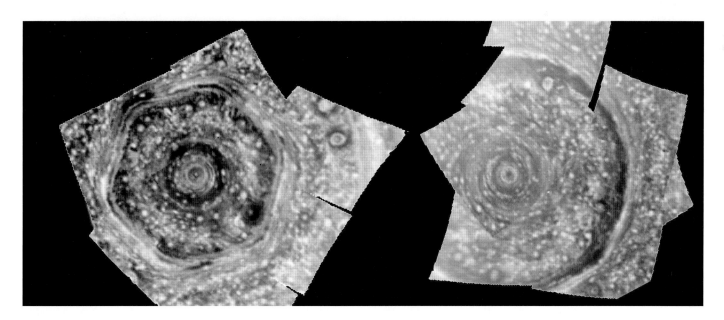

Infrared images by *Cassini* of the amazing hexagonal cloud pattern around Saturn's northern pole (left) and the hurricane-like vortex surrounding its southern pole (right).

Saturn's moons Titan (left) and Enceladus (right), photographed by *Cassini.* Titan is of interest to scientists because its atmosphere is believed to be similar to that of the early Earth, with similar weather phenomena, except that it goes through a methane cycle rather than the water cycle of our terrestrial atmosphere. Enceladus has around its southern pole an ice-covered ocean that could harbor life.

Artist's rendition of the *Cassini* orbiter just after release of the *Huygens* probe toward Titan. Some twenty-two feet long and fourteen feet wide, *Cassini* is one of the larger orbiters ever built. For scale in the picture, the *Huygens* probe heat shield is about nine feet in diameter.

(about 12 percent of Earth's), Saturn's surface gravity is almost the same as Earth's at 1.06 g.

The northern pole has an amazing permanent hexagonal cloud pattern surrounding a circular vortex (whirlpool), which rotates slowly with the rotation of the planet. It was first reported by *Voyager 1* in 1979 and confirmed by the later *Cassini,* as described below. The southern pole has a larger vortex that resembles a huge hurricane, also reported by *Cassini.* Periodic storms, called "Great White Spots," form about every thirty years in the middle latitudes, sometimes growing to extend completely around the planet.

Over 150 moons have been discovered thus far in orbit around Saturn. Many of these are small moonlets either imbedded in Saturn's rings or in very irregular orbits. More like these may be discovered in the future. Of the remainder, only seven are large enough to be of significance, and of these only two, Titan and Enceladus, have drawn much scientific interest. Titan is the largest of Saturn's moons, with about 90 percent of all the mass in orbit around the planet. It is the only known moon in the solar system with an atmosphere. Although it is about one and a half times the size of our Moon, its gravitational attraction is somewhat smaller, at 0.138 g, because it is much less dense.

Titan has surface features very similar to Earth, with dunes, mountains, volcanoes, rivers, and lakes, and it has an atmospheric surface pressure only about one and a half times as great. There similarities largely end, however, as Titan's atmosphere is about 98 percent nitrogen, with about 2 percent methane, at a surface temperature of –180 degrees C. Scientists believe its atmosphere is similar to that of the primordial Earth. Whereas Earth has a hydrologic cycle of liquid water, Titan has an analogous **methane cycle.** Its volcanoes eject ice-water lava, and its rivers and lakes are filled with liquid ethane

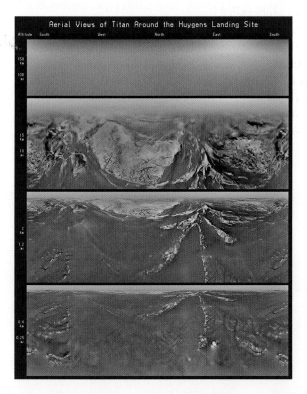

A series of four pictures taken by the *Huygens* probe during its descent through the atmosphere of Titan to its surface.

and methane, which rain in droplets through the atmosphere. Coupled with very low amounts of sunlight—only 1 percent of the amount received on Earth—all this results in a thick yellow haze that makes Titan's surface unobservable from above. Only because of the penetration of the moon's atmosphere by the *Cassini* probe *Huygens,* described below, is anything known about the surface features.

Enceladus, a smaller moon that orbits inside of Titan, is of interest mainly because it may have liquid water beneath its south pole, making it a candidate for extraterrestrial life in some form. It has a relatively smooth, ice-covered surface, with unusual amounts of **water volcanism** in the south polar region. It is very cold, with a surface temperature of –200 degrees C.

The *Pioneer 11* space probe, which flew by Jupiter in late 1973, was redirected to make a flyby of Saturn in September 1979. The two more-capable Voyager spacecraft flew by Saturn and several of its moons in late 1980 and August 1981. A tremendous amount of previously unobtainable knowledge about the planet, its rings, and its moons was gained by all three probes, including dozens of spectacular, high-resolution color pictures.

In 1997 the exploratory spacecraft *Cassini* was launched to proceed to Jupiter for a four-year investigation of the planet and its moons. A joint venture of NASA, the European Space Agency (ESA), and the Italian Space Agency (ISA), *Cassini* is the largest and most sophisticated spacecraft ever built to explore a planet. It carried a probe called *Huygens,* designed by ESA to study the atmosphere and surface of Titan.

In July 2004 *Cassini-Huygens* arrived at Saturn. In December, during its third orbit around the planet, *Cassini* released *Huygens* on a twenty-day journey to Titan, which was reached in January 2005. The probe successfully completed a two-and-a-half-hour descent to the surface. Once there it remained operational for another seventy minutes, sending back data about the moon's atmosphere and amazing pictures of its surface.

The *Cassini* orbiter completed its original mission in 2008 and began several additional new ones that will extend its observation of Saturn to at least 2017. Many new discoveries about the planet and its numerous satellites are sure to result.

Uranus

Uranus, named for the Greek god of the heavens, was discovered by Sir William Herschel in 1781. It is located almost 1.8 billion miles from the Sun (19 AU) and has an orbital period of eighty-four years. Its axis of rotation is unique among the planets, in that it is nearly parallel to the plane of the solar system. It spins once about its axis every seventeen hours and fourteen minutes, though some features in its atmosphere move faster. Its extreme tilt results in each pole's getting forty-two years of continuous sunlight followed by forty-two years of unrelenting darkness.

Uranus has a mass roughly fifteen times Earth's, making it the least massive of the four outer planets. Its diameter of 29,800 miles is about four times that of Earth, but its gravitational attraction is only about 90 percent as strong (0.886 g), because of its lower density. Its atmosphere is 83 percent hydrogen, 15 percent helium, and about 2 percent methane, which gives the planet its greenish color. The interior of Uranus is thought to be composed of a mantle of various kinds of ice, including water, ammonia, and methane, and a small core of iron and nickel. There is no well-defined surface between its mantle and the atmosphere. The planet has a tenuous corona that extends outward for almost 30,000 miles. For reasons not clearly understood, the temperatures of the outer atmosphere and corona range upward of 500 degrees C, then fall off rapidly to around –225 degrees C closer to the surface, making Uranus the coldest planet in the solar system. The planet has a system of wispy rings discovered in 1977 and verified by *Voyager 2* in 1986.

There are twenty-seven known small moons, the largest of which is Titania, with a diameter of only 980 miles. The moons are conglomerates of evenly mixed ice and rock.

Voyager 2 flew by Uranus on 24 January 1986, verifying the presence of the rings and discovering two new ones. It photographed the five larger moons and discovered ten of the smaller ones. Another significant discovery was that the planet's magnetic axis is inclined about 65 degrees with respect to its spin axis, which was thought to make it unique among the planets of our solar system until the probe found a similar situation at Neptune during its flyby in 1989.

Voyager 2 is the only spacecraft to have visited the planet thus far; other missions may be planned in the future. There is some discussion about the possibility of sending *Cassini* to Uranus after its missions at Jupiter are completed, but it would take the spacecraft twenty years to get there.

Neptune

When it was discovered in the early nineteenth century that Uranus sometimes exhibited irregularities (**perturbations**) in its motion in orbit, astronomers inferred that there had to be some object whose gravity pulled the planet out of its path. Astronomers calculated the probable position of such an object—and thus found the planet Neptune in 1846. Uranus and Neptune are often called the "twin planets," even though Neptune is more than a billion miles farther from the Sun, approximately thirty times the Earth–Sun distance (30 AU). They are similar, though, in size (roughly 30,000 miles in diameter) and composition. Neptune has an orbital period of 165 years. Like Jupiter and Saturn, it rotates at a variable rate depending on the latitude, with a period of about eighteen hours at the equator and only twelve hours at the poles.

Neptune's moon Triton. It is the coldest object yet measured in the solar system, and it exhibits water-ice volcanism.

Neptune is the densest of the gaseous planets. It has a composition much like that of Uranus: an atmosphere composed of 80 percent hydrogen, 19 percent helium, and 1 percent methane; an interior consisting of a mantel of water, ammonia, and methane ices; and a small, iron-nickel core. Its gravitational attraction is 1.14 g, roughly one and a third times greater than that of Uranus and 14 percent greater than Earth's. The methane in the atmosphere of Neptune gives it a bluish color, although its atmospheric concentrations of methane are approximately the same as on Uranus; it is not known why it differs so much in color. Like Uranus it has a faint system of rings and a magnetic field strongly tilted, at about 47 degrees with respect to its axis of rotation. Why these phenomena exist on both planets remains a matter of scientific speculation.

Neptune has fourteen known moons. By far the largest of these, with about 99.5 percent of the total lunar mass in orbit, is Triton, discovered just seventeen days after the planet. Unlike all the other larger planetary moons in the solar system, Triton is irregular, with a retrograde orbit (opposite to the direction of planetary rotation) inclined about twenty-three degrees to Neptune's equator, indicating that it is probably a captured body. Its composition and size are similar to those of Pluto, suggesting that it probably came from the Kuiper Belt. It is the coldest object yet measured in the solar system, at a temperature of –235 degrees C. Its surface is covered by frozen nitrogen, water ice, and frozen carbon dioxide and is geologically active, with water-ice volcanism. Its interior is probably 30–45 percent water ice, the remainder rocky material. It has a tenuous atmosphere of nitrogen, probably evaporated from the surface, with a layer of clouds of condensed nitrogen about a mile above the surface.

Like our Moon, it rotates in sync with its revolution around the planet, so the same side always faces Neptune.

Much of what we know about Neptune and its satellites was discovered by *Voyager 2* when it passed about three thousand miles above the planet's north pole in August 1989. The spacecraft reported most of the information about the planet and its moon Triton given above and discovered the rings and six of the small moons. It also reported a "Great Dark Spot" traveling across Neptune's surface, but the spot had disappeared by the time the *Hubble Space Telescope* observed the planet years later. There are no further missions to the planet currently planned.

Dwarf Planets

As defined by the 2006 declaration of the IAU, as we have seen, a dwarf planet is a celestial body that is in orbit around the Sun and is massive enough for its shape to be formed into a sphere by gravitation but, unlike a planet, has not cleared its orbital region of other objects. The IAU currently recognizes five such bodies: Pluto, Haumea, Makemake, Eris, and Ceres. The first four of these are in the Kuiper Belt; Ceres is in the asteroid belt between Mars and Jupiter. For reasons discussed in the following section, it is thought that there may be many more dwarf planets farther out in the Kuiper Belt and even beyond.

The first of the dwarf planets in the Kuiper Belt to be discovered was Pluto. The perturbations in the regular orbit of Uranus were not completely accounted for by the discovery of Neptune. Hence, astronomers looked for further explanation in the form of another planet. Finally, in 1930, an American astronomer, Clyde Tombaugh, discovered Pluto after examining a series of

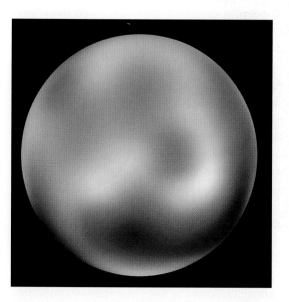

Picture of the dwarf planet Pluto taken by the *Hubble Space Telescope*. It is scheduled to be visited by the spacecraft *New Horizons* in 2015.

telescopic photographs. Its name was selected because Pluto was the Roman god of darkness and the underworld. Because it orbits at an average distance of 3.67 billion miles from the Sun (39 AU), hardly any of the Sun's light reaches it. Mass and density calculations indicate Pluto is composed of rock and methane ice. It is about two-thirds the size of our Moon and has about one-sixth of its mass. It is the largest of the known dwarf planets.

The orbit of this faraway, mysterious body is an oddity in the solar system. Its orbit is inclined to the plane of the rest of the planets and is also highly elliptical, so that for twenty years of each of its 248-year journeys around the Sun, Pluto is actually inside the orbit of Neptune. This occurred most recently between 1979 and 1999.

Pluto and its mate Charon, discovered in 1978, orbit around a center of mass that is outside either of them, about 1,240 miles from Pluto. Because of this, there has been an ongoing controversy, as yet unresolved, among astronomers over whether Charon should be considered a satellite of Pluto, as it was for many years following its discovery, or another dwarf planet, orbiting Pluto as a binary planetary system. Charon is about half the size of Pluto. They orbit each other at a distance of only about 10,600 miles. Their orbital period is 6.4 days, exactly matching their rotation rates, so that each shows the same face to the other all the time. In recent years four additional very small moons orbiting Pluto at distances well beyond Charon have been discovered by astronomers.

The *New Horizons* spacecraft, scheduled to fly by Pluto in 2015.

Because of its unique orbital characteristics, scientists have speculated that Pluto may have been a comet or asteroid, or even a former satellite of Neptune thrown deeper into space by a close encounter with Neptune's large moon Triton. Speculation is that Charon was either formed by a collision of another body with Pluto (in much the same way that our Moon was formed) or that in the early days of the solar system it collided with and was subsequently captured by Pluto.

Ceres, discovered in the asteroid belt between Mars and Jupiter in 1801, was for fifty years considered to be a planet but then was reclassified as an asteroid, and finally as a dwarf planet by the IAU in 2006. Haumea, Makemake, and Eris were all discovered in the Kuiper Belt beyond Pluto within the past several years by astronomers using the *Hubble Space Telescope*. Because they are so distant, not much detail on Pluto, Charon, or the three dwarf planets beyond is observable using earthbound telescopes or the space telescopes currently in orbit.

In early 2014 scientists using data from a now defunct space telescope called the *Herschel*, orbited by the European Space Agency in the early part of the decade, discovered water vapor rising from Ceres' midsection. The source of the water plumes is still unclear. Scientists think there may be a layer of ice just below the surface that gets heated by the sun, or the plumes could be spewed by ice volcanoes. A space probe called *DAWN* launched by NASA in 2007 is due to arrive at Ceres in 2015. The spacecraft carries instruments that can verify the presence of water and that will map the dwarf planet in detail.

In January 2006, as noted above, NASA launched the spacecraft *New Horizons,* which will fly by and photograph Pluto and Charon and the four smaller moons in 2015. It will then probably continue on into the Kuiper Belt to try to photograph at least one of the other known dwarf planets and perhaps discover additional ones.

The Nice Theory of Early Planetary Migration

For many years it was thought that the planets and other bodies that comprise the solar system had been formed and thereafter remained pretty much where they are now, but in the last decade a growing body of evidence seems to indicate otherwise. A growing number of astrophysicists now theorize that in the beginning the planets Saturn, Uranus, and Neptune were much closer to Jupiter, with much leftover material, now called asteroids and comets, orbiting throughout the inner solar system as well as in a dense ring surrounding it, where the Kuiper Belt is now. Uranus and Neptune might even have been in the reverse of their current order from the Sun.

According to the theory, beginning about 600 million years after the formation of the solar system, gravitational forces caused by the accretion of much of the leftover material by the planets caused Saturn, and especially Uranus and Neptune, to

328 ~ Nautical Sciences: Unit 4 ~ Astronomy

move outward. This migration caused a great scattering of the remaining material and smaller bodies within the solar system into the places they now occupy. The solar system was literally turned inside out. Some material from the inner solar system was flung outward to the Kuiper Belt and beyond. Other material from the Kuiper and asteroid belts was propelled inward. It bombarded Mars, the Earth and its Moon, and the other inner planets for at least the next 300 million years, during what is now known as the Late Heavy Bombardment period. This turmoil lasted until about 3.8 billion years ago, when it finally subsided and left the solar system in the form we see now.

The foregoing theory, called the **Nice Theory,** named for Nice, France, where it was formulated in the mid-2000s, is not yet fully accepted by astronomers and astrophysicists. It does, however, explain many of the more recent discoveries about the solar system made by spacecraft and earthbound observatories. In any event, observations of planetary systems around other stars during the last decade indicate that such turmoil may be the norm, rather than the relative tranquility that our solar system has experienced during the last several billion years. This may in turn have a great impact on the probability of life on these exoplanets. It would be difficult for life to arise on planets continually subjected to life-extinguishing impacts of the kind that regularly occurred on Earth and the other inner planets during and after the Late Heavy Bombardment period.

This theory also gives rise to speculation that there may be many as yet undiscovered dwarf planets in the Kuiper Belt and the Oort Cloud region, perhaps even additional cold and dark Earth- and Mars-sized planets.

Critical Thinking

1. List some of the more important of the astronomical and other physical factors and scientific conditions that combine to make life as we know it on Earth possible. Could these same conditions possibly exist at other locations in our solar system or around nearby stars?

2. Why do you think that there has long been such fascination among astronomers, other scientists, and the general public concerning the possibility of life on the planet Mars?

3. Research the characteristics required for a body orbiting a planet in space, such as the Pluto-Charon system, to be classified as a satellite moon, another planet, or dwarf planet. List some examples of ambiguities that might cause a body to be classified in more than one way, depending on one's point of view.

4. Ever since the International Astronomical Union downgraded Pluto from planetary status in 2006 there has been a great deal of controversy about that decision and attempts to reinstate it. List the pros and cons of the argument and how you feel it ought to be resolved. Justify your conclusion.

Study Guide Questions

1. What are the three criteria necessary for a celestial body to be classified as a planet?

2. Name the eight traditional, or "classical," planets in order from the Sun.

3. What are the timetables used to keep track of the movement and location of the planets?

4. What is an orbital period?

5. What are the only two U.S. spacecraft to have visited Mercury thus far?

6. What have space probes revealed about Venus?

7. When do we usually see Venus best, and what do we call it at these times?

8. What planet is called the "red planet"?

9. A. What were the *canali*?
   B. What happened to the *canali* theory?

10. What American robotic vehicles have explored Mars?

11. Which planet is the largest of our solar system?

12. What feature near Jupiter would be a major concern for any astronauts traveling to that planet in the future?

13. What spacecraft has performed the most comprehensive investigation of Jupiter?

14. What is the Great Red Spot of Jupiter?

15. What were the significant discoveries made about Jupiter by the *Galileo* spacecraft and probe in the 1990s?

16. Why were the explorations of Saturn by *Pioneer 11* and the two Voyager spacecraft of such importance?

17. How was the planet Neptune discovered?

18. What is unusual about the magnetic fields of Uranus and Neptune?

19. What discoveries led to the reclassification of Pluto as a dwarf planet?

20. A. What are dwarf planets?
    B. How many have been discovered thus far?

21. What is the "Nice Theory" about the early solar system?

22. A. What was the Late Heavy Bombardment period of Earth and the other bodies in the inner solar system?
    B. What do scientists speculate was its cause?

New Vocabulary

Oort Cloud
Kuiper Belt
International Astronomical Union (IAU)
planet
dwarf planets
almanac (celestial)
ephemeris
plane of the ecliptic
ellipse
orbital period
super-refractivity
runaway greenhouse effect
orbital radius
rotational axis
orbital inclination
prograde motion
retrograde motion
perturbation
binary system (of two celestial bodies)
water
water-ice volcanism

16

Asteroids, Comets, and Meteorites

Asteroids are small bodies referred to by astronomers as **minor planets** that revolve around the Sun in the same direction as the planets. It is thought that there are millions of asteroids within the solar system, with many located between the orbits of Mars and Jupiter in a region called the **asteroid belt.** An equal number, called *Trojans,* share the same orbits as Neptune, Jupiter, and Mars, with the Jupiter Trojans being most numerous. Others, called *near-Earth asteroids,* are in orbits between Mars and Earth. According to the International Astronomical Union (IAU), over 630,000 of these minor planets have been discovered to date. Of these, some 16,000 are large enough to be named, and over ten thousand are in near-Earth orbits.

For centuries astronomers had wondered why the large gap between Mars and Jupiter was without a planet. In 1801, after several hundred years of searching, the first and largest asteroid, Ceres, was discovered there. Orbiting at a mean distance of 257 million miles from the Sun, Ceres, 480 miles in diameter, is so large that it is now classified as a dwarf planet. It is estimated to contain about a third of the entire mass of the asteroid belt. Besides Ceres, we now know there are hundreds of thousands of these minor planets in the asteroid belt that can be seen using terrestrial and space telescopes, and probably a million or more smaller ones.

Most astronomers think the asteroids represent material left over when the solar system was formed about 4.6 billion years ago. Others believe that they are the remnants of a large planet that once orbited in the asteroid belt but then exploded for some unknown reason, and some believe that they are leftovers from collisions of smaller dwarf planets in the distant past. Because of their extreme age and pristine, unchanged condition, they are of great interest to astronomers, and several have been investigated by various spacecraft in recent years. One of the long-term goals of NASA is to land a human exploration team on one, possibly as soon as the mid-2020s.

The asteroid Gaspra photographed by the spacecraft *Galileo* while on its way to Jupiter in 1991.

None of the asteroids has any kind of atmosphere. They appear to be little more than irregular chunks of rock, carbon, and common metallic substances, though it has been speculated that some might contain other, more valuable minerals, even gold or diamonds.

On its way to Jupiter in the early 1990s, the spacecraft *Galileo* twice passed through the asteroid belt while getting gravity assists from Earth. During these transits it passed close by the asteroids Gaspra in 1991 and Ida in 1993, photographing them and in the process discovering a small satellite, named Dactyl, orbiting the latter. In June 1997 a *Near Earth Asteroid Rendezvous* (NEAR) spacecraft came within 750 miles of the carbon-rich asteroid Mathilde while on its way to a year-long encounter with the asteroid Eros, which it reached in February 2000. In February 2001, NEAR landed on Eros' surface, after having transmitted some 200,000 detailed pictures of the asteroid back to Earth. The pictures reveal a surface strewn with boulders, craters, and mysterious bright spots. Eros is considered a geologic relic from the formation of the solar system.

Comets

Comets appear as bright plumes of light in the night sky, sometimes visible without the aid of a telescope. They number perhaps in the millions. They are the travelers of the solar system, wandering through it in huge elliptical orbits, out of the Plane of the Ecliptic. Most originate far beyond the Kuiper Belt in the **Oort Cloud,** a region of space beginning at 50,000 AU from the Sun and extending halfway to the nearest star. Most astronomers think that they, like asteroids, are material left over from the formation of the solar system 4.6 billion years ago. Astronomers, therefore, have great interest in exploring them as opportunities arise, in order to find out about the composition and formation of the early solar system.

There are two categories of comets, based on the amount of time they take to complete an orbit around the Sun. "Long-period" comets take over two hundred years per orbit, and "short-period" comets with smaller orbits take less than two hundred.

Most comets are thought to have little mass. They are believed to be composed of a nucleus of water ice, frozen gases, and dust-like particles of such elements as carbon and sodium, altogether rather like a dirty snowball. When a comet approaches the interior of the solar system, radiation from the Sun begins to heat it, causing particles of material and vapor to be released. These form a halo around the nucleus called a **coma**. The nucleus and coma together form the *head* of the comet.

As the comet comes closer, pressure from the solar wind causes the vapor and dust particles in the coma to fan out from the head in a direction opposite the Sun, forming a *tail*. Certain gases in the coma, stimulated by the sunlight, begin to glow, much like a fluorescent bulb. When sunlight is reflected from the dust particles in the tail, the effects combine to make the comet visible from Earth. Luminous tails more than 100 million miles long have been observed. As the comet swings around the Sun, its tail appears to continually change direction, since it always points away from the Sun as a result of the solar wind. As the comet moves away from the Sun, its tail is pushed in front of the head. Eventually the tail either disintegrates or is collected again by the nucleus. The comet then returns to the darkness of outer space.

Every trip around the Sun causes comets to lose some of their mass. Eventually they may break up completely, leaving debris all along the path that was once their orbit. Sometimes Earth crosses a part of a former comet path. The tiny particles then collide with our atmosphere, producing a **meteor shower.**

Until comparatively recent times a comet was usually named for the first person or persons to report its discovery, and then later they were given alphanumeric designations. In 1994 the IAU approved the current system. Comets are now designated by the year of their discovery, followed by a letter and number indicating the half-month of their discovery and the order in which they were discovered. One of several prefixes are added to indicate the type or nature of the comet, and the sequence of its discovery. For example, **Halley's Comet,** the earliest and best known of all short-period comets, first observed and recorded as such by the British astronomer Edmund Halley on 15 September 1682, carries the designation 1P/1682 Q1. This indicates that it was the first periodic comet discovered (1P) and the first comet discovered in the second half of September (Q1)

Halley's Comet during its transit of the inner solar system in 1986.

A reconstruction of the head of Halley's Comet, based on close observations by two Soviet and a European Space Agency spacecraft that flew by it during its last transit of the solar system in 1986.

in 1682. If there had been a second periodic comet discovered later that same month, its designation would have been 2P/1682 Q2; and so on. In addition, some especially significant discoveries are still given the names of their discoverers or of the instruments or programs that helped to find them, and these are also attached to their designations. A similar system is also used to designate asteroids.

There are currently over 3,700 cataloged comet discoveries in IAU records, going back to Halley's Comet in 1682. Most of these are long-period comets that have been seen only once. Some three hundred have been seen more than once, with almost all of these having short periods of ten years or less.

After computing its orbit, Halley found that his comet had the same orbit as comets seen in 1531 and 1607. Halley suspected that all three were the same comet, which he calculated had a predictable orbital cycle of about seventy-five years. This prediction proved to be correct when the comet reappeared in 1758. Sightings of Halley's Comet have continued into more recent history. It was sighted in 1834 and again in 1910. It reentered the inner solar system in 1986 and was photographed from close up during flybys by two Soviet Vega spacecraft and a European Space Agency probe called *Giotto*. They reported its composition to be mainly dirty water ice. Its nucleus appeared to be potato shaped, rather than spherical as had been expected.

NASA has thus far successfully launched two space-probe missions to study comets. The first, called *Stardust*, was launched in 1999 and collected from the comet Wild 2 dust that was returned to Earth in a capsule in 2006. Surprisingly, analysis of the dust found many compounds and particles that could only have been formed by heat, much nearer to the Sun. This gives support to the Nice Theory of migration of Neptune and Uranus in the early days of the solar system, according to which material like that discovered in the Wild 2 dust would have been flung outward from near the Sun to where it could be acquired by the comet.

In late 2004 NASA launched a spacecraft called *Deep Impact* to travel some 260 million miles (430 million km) from Earth to the comet Tempel-1 and send an 820-pound copper probe crashing into it, in order to investigate what lies within its interior. The probe struck the comet in July 2005 with a kinetic energy equivalent to 4.5 tons of TNT. On impact there was a large double flash, followed by a plume of debris that soon

Artist's rendition of the *Deep Impact* probe striking the comet Tempel-1 in July 2005.

extended several thousand miles into space. A crater was formed in the comet's surface about the size of a small sports stadium. The impact was observed by instruments in the spacecraft and by several space telescopes, as well as by astronomers on Earth. By analyzing the results of the impact, scientists learned that the comet is tightly packed, rather than a loose conglomerate of material as some had speculated, and that it contains less water than expected.

Following its mission to Wild 2, *Stardust* returned to the comet Tempel-1 in 2011 to more fully assess the *Deep Impact* crash site. It was found that the impactor had not in fact penetrated to the comet's core as had been suspected, instead leaving only a 150-meter crater that had mostly filled in with debris following the mission.

More missions to comets are planned for the future as opportunities arise.

Meteoroids, Meteors, and Meteorites

A **meteoroid** is a chunk of rock or metal orbiting in space, similar to an asteroid but much smaller, by current convention not exceeding a meter in size. Meteoroids by the countless tens of thousands orbit the Sun. Some are dust particles that may eventually drift down through Earth's atmosphere. Others weigh anywhere from a few ounces to several tons or more. Most meteoroids are invisible, because of their small size—until, by chance, one is drawn into the Earth's atmosphere by gravity. Then, as the meteoroid plunges through the atmosphere at great speed, it heats up from friction with the air. This causes it to burn and sparkle brilliantly as it streaks across the sky toward Earth, producing the brief trail of light high in the atmosphere called a "shooting star." This is actually the fiery death of a golf-ball-sized meteoroid, now referred to as a **meteor** once the fiery track becomes visible.

Most meteors burn up long before reaching the Earth's surface. Occasionally, however, a meteor is large enough to hit the ground. Such meteors, called **fireballs,** often streak brightly low across the sky and sometimes explode like a bomb just before they hit, creating shock waves that damage anything on the ground beneath. One such air burst occurred in the skies over Chelyabinsk, Russia, in February 2013. Recorded on camcorders by the local townspeople, it shattered many windows and injured some 1,200 people. Several large pieces were later found at the bottom of a nearby lake.

Such remnants of meteors that strike the ground are called **meteorites.** They are usually irregularly shaped, pock-marked chunks about the size of a soccer ball or smaller, though there have been some much bigger. One of the largest meteorites ever found in the Western Hemisphere was discovered in Greenland by Robert Peary in 1894. It weighed thirty-four tons and was put on display at the American Museum of Natural History in New York City, where it remains today. There are two main kinds of meteorites: stony meteorites called *aerolites* and iron and nickel ones called *siderites*. Aerolites are much like stones on Earth, composed of oxygen, silicon, magnesium, and some iron. The siderites, however, are about 90 percent iron, 8 percent nickel, and a mixture of other minerals. Of the meteorites that have been found, some 94 percent are aerolites and about 5 percent are siderites, with the remainder a mix of both.

A third kind of meteorite, called a *tektite,* has been found in widely scattered parts of the globe. These small meteorites usually weigh between an ounce and a pound. They are composed of a glassy compound having high silicon content, along with oxides of aluminum, magnesium, iron, calcium, sodium, and potassium. Some are nearly transparent, while others come in various shades of green, amber, and brown. Tektites do not resemble any rock or glass substance on Earth. They may have come from the interior of a destroyed planet where materials

A still from one of the camcorder recordings of the meteor fireball that exploded over Chelyabinsk, Russia, in February 2013. *www.RussiaTrek.org*

A nickel-iron meteorite found near Diablo Canyon in Arizona in 1897. It has been dated as about 4.5 billion years old, close to the estimated age of the solar system. *Smithsonian Institution, Laurie Minor-Penland*

A contemporary photo showing part of the effects from an air burst of a small asteroid or comet near Tunguska, Siberia, in 1908. *Leonid Kulik Expedition*

were subjected to extremely high temperatures, or from impacts on the Moon. Considerable research is being devoted to tektites, for they may shed light on the origin of the solar system.

Impacts with Earth

Every day it is estimated that between ten to forty tons of interplanetary material finds its way into Earth's atmosphere. Most of this is in the form of small particles called *micrometeorites* less than 2 millimeters in size, and dust left over from ancient asteroid and meteoroid collisions. Traveling at high speed, most of this material is incinerated after a few seconds. Rarely, larger meteors survive to hit the surface as meteorites or explode as fireballs above it. However, on an average of about once every ten thousand years an asteroid or comet larger than a hundred meters strikes the Earth and causes local disasters or tidal waves. Such an event is thought to have occurred in the wilderness near Tunguska, Siberia, in 1908, when a probable air-burst of a small asteroid or comet leveled trees within a radius of fifteen to twenty miles and broke windows hundreds of miles away.

In recent years there has been great concern about the effect that an even larger asteroid or comet would have if it were to strike Earth. Scientists think that such impacts have already occurred many times in Earth's early history, most notably during the Late Heavy Bombardment period from 4.1 to 3.8 billion years ago. They probably deposited large amounts of water on the surface, and they may have conveyed to Earth the chemical building blocks of life that we now know permeate much of space. Many scientists also believe that another such impact off the Yucatán Peninsula in Central America about sixty-five million years ago raised a planetary dust cloud that persisted for years and caused the extinction of the dinosaurs. In recent years NASA has sponsored an ongoing effort called the **Near Earth Object Program** with the goal of identifying and tracking 90 percent of all near-Earth objects of sizes greater than 140 meters. If any of these are determined to be possible strike threats, it is hoped that sufficient warning could be given to minimize damage or perhaps even deflect or destroy the object before it hits.

Critical Thinking

1. Why are astrophysicists interested in sending more missions such as 2005's *Deep Impact* to investigate the composition of comets and asteroids?

2. In the event that it is ever determined that a large comet or asteroid may strike Earth, what are some measures that might be attempted to either avoid the impact or reduce the damage such an impact might cause? Why would there be such a large release of energy involved in an impact such as this?

Study Guide Questions

1. How is it thought that the asteroids originated?

2. Where are the asteroids located in the solar system?

3. Of what are comets composed?

4. What causes a comet to be visible?

5. Of what are the tails of comets composed?

6. What happens when a comet breaks up, leaving debris that eventually enters Earth's atmosphere?

7. A. What is the name of the most famous comet?
   B. How often can it be seen from Earth?

8. What remarkable mission was conducted in 2005 to study the composition of comets?

9. What causes a meteor to become a "fireball"?

10. What happens to most meteors?

11. What are the main kinds of meteorites?

12. A. What are tektites?
    B. Where did they probably originate?

13. What would be some of the possible effects of a large asteroid or comet striking the Earth?

New Vocabulary

asteroids	meteor
minor planets	meteorite
comet	fireball
coma	aerolites
meteor shower	siderites
nucleus (of comet)	tektites
meteoroid	

17

The Stars

The stars are distant suns in space. The closest one, of course, is our Sun, one of an estimated 400 billion stars in our Milky Way galaxy. But the universe contains billions of galaxies, each of which contains billions of stars, so there is an unimaginable number of stars in the universe.

The next closest star is Proxima Centauri, about 26.4 trillion miles distant. Most of the rest are far beyond it. When discussing stars, therefore, it soon becomes apparent that we are talking of distances that are mind-boggling. Miles or kilometers are useless in describing such distances. Thus, the **light-year** has been adopted as a common unit of astronomical distances in deep space. Sometimes even this is inadequate, leading to the use of a distance unit called a **parsec,** defined as 3.26 light years.

A *light-year* is the distance that light travels in a year. This distance is, for practical purposes, nearly six trillion miles. Remember that a light-year is a unit of distance, not of time, even though the word "year" is used. It is a bit like describing the distance to some location as a "twenty-minute drive" or a "fifteen-minute walk." When astronomers say a star is "ten light-years away," they mean that it takes light ten years to travel from the star to their observatory. On this scale, our nearest neighboring star, Proxima Centauri, is about 4.24 light years away.

Even when using light-years or parsecs to measure cosmic distances, the numbers can become huge. Modern telescopes can see out to distances in excess of thirteen billion light-years. This means, in effect, that astronomers are looking "back in time." They see distant stars and galaxies as they were millions or billions of years ago, since it has taken their light that long to reach us on Earth. The light that is leaving distant stars tonight will not arrive here for countless centuries. Since radio waves and light waves travel at the same speed, any "communication" directed at us from these distant stars would not get here for at least that long. Thus, even if many of these stars had orbiting planets that supported intelligent life, any interaction with it on our part would be problematic, especially considering that we have only had radio communications for a little over a century.

Constellations

When the ancients observed the stars in the sky, the patterns in which many of the brighter stars are arranged reminded them of various common terrestrial shapes. Over time many of these patterns, now called **constellations,** were given names of objects, animals, and even people that they seemed to resemble. The oldest of these date from Babylonian astronomy in the Bronze Age and were later adopted by the Greeks and Romans. Various constellations were also identified by many other cultures, including the Chinese, the Aztecs and Incas of Central America, and pre-Columbian Native Americans of North America. Many of their names survive today, such as *Ursa Major* (the Big Bear), *Orion* (the Hunter), and *Ares* (the Ram). There are some eighty-eight constellations presently recognized by the International Astronomical Union. They have not changed much since ancient times, because the stars that form them are so far distant that their positions in the sky have not shifted much over the last few thousands of years.

Stars Classified

As we look at them in the sky, some stars appear brighter than others, and some can barely be seen with the naked eye. The relative brightness of a celestial body is called its **magnitude.** The Greek astronomer Ptolemy divided the visible stars into six groups according to their magnitude and the order in which they appeared at night. The first group of stars to become visible at twilight are called the *first-magnitude stars*. They are considered to be a hundred times brighter than the faintest stars visible to the naked eye in full night, the *sixth-magnitude stars*. Hence, there is a magnitude ratio of the fifth root of 100, or 2.51, between each magnitude group. The magnitude of a celestial body with an intensity between two groups is denoted by a decimal fraction, as for example, a 2.6-magnitude star. The two brightest stars in the sky, Sirius and Canopus, are actually more than a hundred times brighter than a sixth-magnitude star. Consequently, they are assigned *negative* magnitudes, –1.6 and

It was natural for the ancients to visualize the shapes of common things around them when they viewed the stars, as with this depiction of the constellation Orion, the hunter. Note the three stars of Orion's belt, easily visible on most nights, and the other bright stars that outline his form. His prey in this drawing is sometimes portrayed as a bow instead.

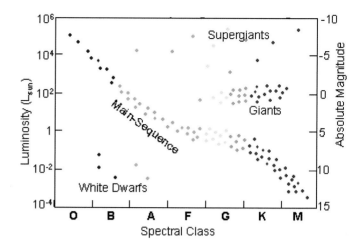

A spectrum-luminosity, or Hertzsprung-Russell, diagram. Our Sun is about in the center, with an assigned luminosity of 1 and absolute magnitude of 5. The colors on the diagram correspond to the type classifications along the bottom. *University of Arizona Astronomy Department*

–0.9, respectively. The Moon varies in magnitude from –12.6 to –3.3, and the Sun has a magnitude of about –26.7. Astronomers call the brightness of a star as it appears to an observer on Earth its **apparent magnitude.**

The nature of a star can best be determined from its *spectrum* (light and other electromagnetic wavelengths emitted), plus some other pertinent information. Different stars have different spectra, as the wavelengths and intensities of light and other radiations they emit vary with their size, composition, and temperature. Astronomers classify stars into several groups according to their size, color, *luminosity* and *absolute magnitude.* The term **luminosity** refers to the brightness of a star as compared to the brightness of the Sun, and the **absolute magnitude** is the brightness that a star would have at a standard distance from Earth of ten parsecs—32.6 light-years. Since they are both measures of a star's brightness, there is a unique value of luminosity that corresponds with every value of absolute magnitude.

Stars are customarily plotted on a graph of luminosity and corresponding absolute magnitude (vertical scale) versus their spectral color and temperature (horizontal scale), producing a kind of chart called a **spectrum-luminosity diagram,** or **Hertzsprung-Russell (H-R) diagram,** after its inventors. On the diagram our Sun, because it is the reference for this measure, is assigned a luminosity of 1, which corresponds to a value of 5 on the absolute-magnitude scale. The horizontal spectral scale is divided into lettered groups called *types* by color and temperature, with the hottest type O blue stars on the left, and

proceeding through types B (blue-white), A (white), F (yellow-white), G (yellow), K (orange), to M (red), the coolest stars, on the far right. When a number of stars are plotted on the diagram, they bunch into groups—*supergiants, giants, main-sequence stars,* and *white dwarfs.* When astronomers discuss a star, they describe it in terms of its position on the diagram, as, for example a "yellow main-sequence type G star (e.g., our Sun)," or a "type M red dwarf," and so on.

Our Sun is about in the middle of the yellow portion of the main sequence. As stated above, it has an absolute magnitude of +5. The giant stars are given an absolute magnitude of 0, thus making them a hundred times brighter than the Sun. Even brighter are the supergiants, which are as much as a million times as bright. Their absolute magnitudes are therefore negative (–5 to –10), corresponding to luminosities ten thousand (10^4) to a million (10^6) times that of our Sun. Of the more familiar stars, Rigel, Polaris (the North Star), and Antares are supergiants; Arcturus and Capella are giants. Vega, Altair, and the Sun are medium-sized main-sequence stars on the spectrum-luminosity diagram. The main sequence comprises 98 percent of all stars visible to astronomers. Hydrogen fusion is their main energy source. The bright blue stars on the upper left of the diagram are so hot that they burn up their hydrogen fuel in only a few million years, while the white and red dwarf stars to the lower left and lower right are far more numerous but often so dim that they cannot be observed in the visible light spectrum.

The most interesting group, however, is the one called white dwarfs. Most once were main-sequence stars like our Sun but are in their final stages of life after having expended all of their hydrogen fuel collapsing to about the size of Earth, and dropping off the main sequence. They lost much of their mass in the process but still have densities much greater than any substance on Earth. A cubic inch of material from one of these stars could weigh as much as a ton. White dwarfs will continue to radiate energy obtained by fusion of helium and other higher-weight elements at a low level for several billions of years before they eventually fade to black. Most do not shine brightly enough to be seen in the visible-light spectrum.

Another kind of dwarf stars are the red dwarfs, to the lower right on the main sequence. Astronomers estimate that about 75 percent of all the stars in our Milky Way galaxy are red dwarf stars. They were considerably smaller than our Sun when formed and burn with thousands of times less intensity. They emit light mostly in the infrared part of the spectrum and therefore, like white dwarfs, are not visible to observers using optical telescopes. Because of their low rate of hydrogen consumption, they are extremely long-lived, by some estimates having expected life cycles tens of billions of years longer than that of our Sun. No one knows for sure, because on the time scale of the age of our universe, they are still in their infancies. Our nearest neighbor, Proxima Centauri, is this kind of star. There are also even smaller, cooler, less radiant, and far less numerous stars called *brown dwarfs* lower and to the right of the red dwarfs on the spectrum-luminosity diagrams. They are not considered main sequence stars and are not shown on most diagrams.

The stars in our galaxy are also classified according to their *location*. All the stars in our galaxy are placed into one of two distinct groups, called **Population I** and **Population II**. Population I stars are found in regions where there is a great deal of dust and gas. These are young stars that are still forming, growing, and adding mass. The stars in the neighborhood of our Sun all belong to Population I. Population II stars are older stars, located in regions essentially free of dust and gas. They have used up the available supply of raw material from space and are, relatively speaking, near the ends of their lives as luminous stars.

Life Cycle of Stars

A star begins as a huge, cold, dark cloud of gas and dust called a **nebula,** as did our Sun. Such nebulae are observable throughout the universe. Precisely where or how these nebulae form is not known. Some astronomers believe they came from the ashes of stars long gone; others say they originated from the Big Bang; and still others say they are a mixture of the two. But we do know that stars are being born today out of the gas and dust nebulae of the Milky Way, our galaxy of stars. The *Hubble Space Telescope* and ground-based optical and radiotelescopes have provided many spectacular images of this process taking place.

Because of advances in astronomy and astrophysics, the major stages in the life of a star have been fairly well established.

The main factor determining what kind of star will be born is how much gas and cosmic dust become locked together by gravity in that particular area. Most stars in our Milky Way and other galaxies begin life as main-sequence stars that shine by the fusion of hydrogen into helium. If there is a lot of material available there, the star will probably form as a brilliant blue giant, with a life cycle of a few billion years. If it is like most of the visible stars, it will be a bright yellow star like our Sun, with a much longer life cycle than a blue giant, averaging about ten billion years. With even less dust and gas, it will be a red dwarf that will shine dimly for many tens of billions or perhaps trillions of years.

It perhaps seems somewhat odd that the brighter stars have shorter lives, but it is easily explained. The more fuel there is to burn, the greater the heat and the fuel-consumption rate; so, comparatively speaking, the brighter bigger star is burning itself out faster. The rate of fuel consumption is set at the beginning and does not vary. Once the hydrogen-to-helium fusion cycle begins, it will continue until the hydrogen is exhausted.

In the introduction to this unit, we described the probable birth of the Sun. We need not go through the entire sequence of the birth of a star again, but by way of review, we know that heat and pressure eventually build up toward the center of the proto-star as it grows by acquiring mass from the surrounding gas and dust. As the temperature and pressure increase still further, the ball begins to glow. Eventually the proto-star shines, sending its energy out into space in the form of visible light and other electromagnetic radiation.

Most astronomers believe there is a "normal" evolution of stars thereafter. As the helium content builds up in the center, stars like the Sun begin to fuse hydrogen along an expanding spherical shell surrounding the core. This causes the star to gradually grow in size, increasing in luminosity and temperature until it finally becomes a red giant. During this process stars with at least half the mass of our Sun can begin to fuse helium at their cores, producing heavier elements. More massive stars can fuse these heavier elements along a series of expanding shells as well. As a red giant, the star consumes fuel at a tremendous rate, until its nuclear fuel is used up.

Once a star like the Sun has exhausted its nuclear fuel, its core slowly collapses until the star becomes a dense white dwarf. During this process it throws off its outer layers as a *planetary nebula* (a nebula that surrounds the starlike planets) that dissipates in a few tens of thousands of years. The white dwarf can survive for many billions of years thereafter, gradually cooling and turning black. Giant stars, with five to eight times the mass of the Sun or more, once they exhaust their fuel can explode as *supernovae,* their cores collapsing to form extremely dense **neutron stars.** Supergiant stars, with masses greater than ten

A black hole is theorized to be the remnants of supernovas of massive stars. They are so massive that not even light can escape them.

times the mass of the Sun, collapse even further following such explosions to become **black holes,** superdense bodies with gravitational attraction so strong that it prevents even light from escaping, insofar as is currently theorized. Although the universe is not old enough to allow them to know for sure, astrophysicists theorize that red dwarfs will slowly burn brighter and hotter until they expend their hydrogen fuel and become white dwarfs.

Most of the brightest stars we can see in a clear evening are the giants or supergiants, edging closer to their last bursts of glory. A few are bright new stars, and others are ordinary main-sequence stars like our Sun in the middle stages of life and close enough to appear very bright.

Exoplanets

Beginning in the early 1990s, larger more powerful Earth-based telescopes began to have sufficient magnification and resolution to allow astronomers to discover planets orbiting other stars, called *extrasolar planets,* or *exoplanets.* Two primary techniques have been used to find them. The first involves searching for stars that appear to "wobble" as they move through space, periodically surging forward then slowing down before surging forward once again. Such motion is indicative of a planet revolving around the star: the planet's gravity alternately accelerates the star forward when it circles ahead of the star, then slows the star down as it circles behind. A second primary technique involves searching for stars that exhibit minor periodic dimming, possibly caused by planets passing across, or *transiting,* their disks. A number of other more highly refined techniques have also been developed, but these remain the most successful methods that astronomers and astrophysicists use to find these planets using modern ground-based and space telescopes. Once found, some

of these exoplanets have been directly observed by the largest ground-based telescopes.

Thus far over 3,500 exoplanets orbiting distant stars have been discovered, with even more possible candidates yet to be identified by further analysis of data from the *Kepler* space telescope described in chapter 12. Many of these are thought to have potential Earth-like characteristics. Based on the *Kepler* data, astronomers now believe that almost all of the estimated 400 billion stars in our galaxy may have at least one planet in orbit around them, at least seventeen billion of them Earth-sized, and over half in orbits within the **habitable zones** (regions neither too hot nor too cold to support life) around their stars! Many of these, however, orbit around small red dwarf stars, which for several reasons too technical to discuss here are not considered conducive to life.

As interesting as the discovery of exoplanets orbiting around distant stars is, an even more recent revelation suggests that there may be many exoplanets that roam freely through interstellar space, away from any central stars. These are referred to as **rogue,** or **interstellar planets.** In theory many of these may have originally formed in accretion disks surrounding distant stars but were later ejected into space. Other, Jupiter-sized ones may have formed in isolation from interstellar gas and dust but never became large enough to become stars. Over the last few years astronomers using several of the newer large ground-based telescopes claim to have identified some four hundred of these nomad planets, the closest one being about a hundred light years from Earth. Some estimate that there may be more than twice as many of these rogue planets as there are stars in our Milky Way galaxy! These are indeed exciting times for astronomy.

Artist's conception of a rogue planet, wandering alone through space.

Novae and Supernovae

Sometimes an apparent new star appears in the sky for the first time in recorded astronomical history. Since ancient times these events have been called **novae** (plural of *nova*, the Latin word for "new"). Even more rarely this "new" star is a **supernova,** which blazes forth with a luminosity as much as a million times that of an ordinary star, sometimes outshining an entire galaxy of stars. Records of these events appear in accounts as far back as 134 BC, when the ancient Greek astronomer Hipparchus observed one in the constellation Scorpius. Chinese records tell of a brilliant star appearing in the daytime sky in AD 1054. Tycho Brahe, a German astronomer, found one in the constellation Cassiopeia in 1572 and observed it until it disappeared in 1574. Others have been observed throughout history, including one in 1987.

Since these phenomena appear suddenly and usually disappear relatively quickly—after only a few days or weeks for supernovae, and three to six months for other novae—they are now more correctly called "temporary stars." But we now know these phenomena really are not new stars at all. *Novae* are thought to be caused by the accretion of hydrogen by white dwarf stars from companion red-giant stars orbiting around them. After a period of time the hydrogen is heated and then explodes, resulting in the burst of light that we call a nova. Astrophysicists theorize that such white dwarf stars may be capable of multiple novae over time. *Supernovae* are thought to originate from the implosions of either large white dwarfs or remnant neutron stars formed after the collapse of giant stars, or from the sudden collapse of supergiant stars in the last stage of life. Astronomers estimate there are about forty novae in the Milky Way galaxy each year, with about ten visible from Earth. On average there are only about three supernovae observed each century within the Milky Way.

Cepheid Stars and Pulsars

One way astronomers can determine a star or distant galaxy's brightness and distance from us is by using stars called **cepheid** (se´-fid) **variables** as a reference. The brightness of these stars changes by about one magnitude over regular cycles lasting from less than thirty to over sixty days. There are also changes in their radiation spectra as their brightness varies, indicating that these cycles are caused by temperature changes as the stars expand and contract. When the cepheid cools and contracts, it becomes dimmer. At some point the contraction causes its internal pressure and temperature to increase, causing it to expand and grow brighter. Once the star has expanded, the balance is again upset—so the star contracts again, under its gravitational attraction. Another name for the cepheid variable, because of this alternating phenomenon, is *pulsating star*.

The discovery that there is a constant relationship between the cyclic period of cepheid variables and their magnitudes enables astronomers to use them both as references for brightness and as means of measuring distances in space. By noting how many days it takes a cepheid to grow bright and dim, they can quickly deduce its absolute magnitude at any time. Thus, if there is a cepheid anywhere near a distant celestial body of interest, its brilliance can be compared to that of the cepheid to determine its absolute magnitude, and from that its luminosity. Moreover, there is a distance relationship between the absolute magnitude of a star and its apparent magnitude as seen from Earth. Starlight decreases in intensity proportionally to the square of the distance. Using this relationship, once astronomers know the absolute magnitude of a star, they can easily compute the approximate distance to it. Since most observable galaxies have many of them, cepheid variables provide a valuable method for calculating astronomical distances to the galaxies and their stars when other methods are not possible.

Pulsars are relatively young, very dense neutron stars spinning at incredible rates, most likely the remnants of supernova explosions. They emit intense rotating beams of electromag-

Spiral galaxy NGC 5584, 72 million light years away in the constellation Virgo. It contains many cepheid variables, identified by small circles. Blue circles indicate those with periods less than 330 days; green, those with periods between thirty and sixty days; and red, those with periods greater than sixty days. There is a supernova visible just below and to the right of the galaxy's center. The blue glow of young stars illuminates the spiral arms. Most of the small reddish dots scattered through the galaxy that look like bright stars are actually other more distant galaxies.

netic energy, similar to a rotating lighthouse beam. The emissions occur in radio frequencies and at visible-light, X-ray, and gamma-ray wavelengths, at periods ranging from less than a second to some 8.5 seconds, corresponding to their amazing rotation rates. Some 1,800 have been discovered to date.

When first observed in 1967, they were thought to be beacons or signals originated by intelligent alien life, but soon they were determined to be natural phenomena. Over time their periods slow as they lose energy, and after some 10–100 million years they stop radiating altogether. This means that of all the pulsars in the 13.6 billion years of the universe's existence, 99 percent no longer pulsate.

Pulsars rotate with such regularity that the timing of their beams rivals atomic clocks in precision. This enables them to be uniquely identified and located by their periods. For this reason they can be used as navigational beacons in space. Diagrams of our Sun's position relative to fourteen pulsars were included on the golden plaques and records on the Pioneer and Voyager spacecraft, so that any extraterrestrials who one day might discover them will know where in the galaxy we are located (see illustration on page 296).

Binaries and Star Clusters

Stars have a tendency to cluster together, due to gravitational attraction. Pairs of stars that orbit each other are called **binaries,** or double stars. Such binaries often orbit around each other at fantastic speeds and exchange material with each other. As mentioned above, if one of them is a white dwarf and the other is a star in the red-giant stage, nova explosions may occur as a result of this exchange.

Larger groups of stars are referred to as **star clusters.** Clusters are classified by both their appearance and their population. A *moving cluster* contains a few stars that travel in parallel lines. *Open clusters* are loosely grouped stars, often found in areas where there are glowing masses of dust and gas. Most open clusters are found in the Milky Way, so they often are called *galactic clusters. Globular clusters* contain many thousands of stars—too many to count, even with the best photography. Some globular clusters contain background galaxies as well. They may have as many as several hundred thousand stars and galaxies. *Star clouds* are clusters in which the stars are so thick that they look like glowing clouds.

Nebulae

As previously mentioned, nebulae are clouds of gas and dust visible in the heavens. They are among the most beautiful of

Infrared view of the Horsehead nebula, the *Hubble Space Telescope*'s twenty-third-anniversary image. The nebula is about 1,600 light years distant, in the constellation Orion.

A globular star cluster within a galaxy some 28,000 light years distant from us.

all astronomical phenomena. Some nebulae are easily visible through an optical telescope; thus, they can be studied using a spectrograph. Many others are far easier to observe in the infrared, ultraviolet, or radio-frequency portions of the electromagnetic spectrum using a radiotelescope.

There are three kinds of nebulae observable in the visible light spectrum. The *bright nebula* glows and is easily visible because there is a bright star nearby that illuminates it. A *dark nebula* is composed of the same gas and dust as the bright nebula but is visible only because it is silhouetted against the stars behind it; there is no illuminating star in the region of a dark nebula. The third kind is the *planetary nebula,* resulting from a nova or supernova explosion. These nebulae show considerable surface detail, though they are much less dense than planets. They may have dim dwarf stars in the middle, remnants of the explosion that formed them.

Galaxies

On a clear night you can often see what appears to be a wispy cloud extending across the northern sky. Actually, it is a vast

Spiral galaxy NGC 1300, similar in size and shape to our Milky Way galaxy, except that it does not have a central massive black hole. It is about 70 million light years away, in the constellation Eridanus, and has a span of over 100,000 light years.

The beautiful Sombrero galaxy, an elliptical galaxy seen on edge, about 28 million light years distant in the constellation Virgo. It has a supermassive black hole in its center.

band of stars called the Milky Way—our own galaxy. A **galaxy** is a huge collection of stars, star clusters, dust, and gas, all held together by gravitation.

The Milky Way is shaped like a giant spiral or pinwheel, with more stars in the center than at the edges. It is estimated to be about 100,000 light years across, with the central hub about 10,000 light years in diameter, and the spiral arms about 1,000 light years thick. The Milky Way contains over 400 billion stars revolving about a massive black hole in the constellation Sagittarius.

Our Sun is located in a spiral arm about two-thirds of the distance from the center of the Milky Way to its outer rim, about 25,000 light years from the center. The Sun and the rest of our solar system, as well as the other stars in the galaxy, revolve around its center at a speed of about 135 miles per second. Even going this fast, it takes about 240 million years for us to complete one circuit. The whole galaxy itself is also moving through space at an approximate speed of about 370 miles per second.

The galaxy looks much like a spiral nebula. In fact, earlier astronomers thought the Milky Way was a nebula. But modern telescopes clearly show that the galaxy is composed of billions of stars too far away to be distinguished as separate points of light. The Milky Way is best seen on a clear summer night, running across the sky from north to south.

As crowded as the stars in the Milky Way appear, we see only a fraction of the actual number, because of the huge amount of gas and dust nebula fogging the space between the stars. Most of the stars in the center of the galactic swirl are thus blocked from our view.

Up until the 1920s astronomers thought that all the stars in the heavens were within the Milky Way galaxy, but after that groundbreaking astronomers like Edwin Hubble showed that the Milky Way is just one of many galaxies, each containing billions of stars. Although some galaxies are currently colliding or appear to have collided at some time in the distant past, most are separated from neighboring galaxies by oceans of space. All but one of the more distant galaxies appear to be accelerating away from us, and most from each other, at rates proportional to their distances. The exception is the spiral Andromeda galaxy, some 2.5 million light years distant, that is proceeding toward our Milky Way galaxy at speeds that will cause it to collide with the Milky Way in about 3.75 billion years, forming a large ellipsoidal galaxy (see below) thereafter. Because of the vast distances between stars, our solar system will probably emerge unscathed, though as previously mentioned, all life on Earth will have long before ceased due to the expansion of our Sun over the next few billion years. Most of the observable galaxies have cepheid variables scattered throughout them, as well as occasional novae and some supernovae. As explained previously, the cepheids enable astronomers to calculate roughly how far distant these galaxies are from us.

Galaxies may be classified, according to their shapes, into three different groups (1) *ellipsoidal galaxies,* which have rather clearly defined, symmetrical shapes, ranging from spheres to circles; (2) *spiral galaxies,* like our Milky Way, which have a distinct nucleus with one or more spiral arms; and (3) *irregular galaxies,* which have no well-defined shape.

Supermassive Black Holes and Dark Matter and Energy

Observations by the *Hubble* and *Spitzer* space telescopes and newer, more powerful ground-based telescopes have led astronomers to conclude that there are supermassive black holes in the centers of most galaxies, including our own. The masses of these black holes are proportional to the masses of the galaxies containing them. The one in the center of our galaxy may have a mass equal to nearly two million times our Sun. How these formed is not known, since they greatly exceed the masses of black holes formed by supernova explosions of even the largest supergiant stars.

In addition, observations that all the stars in our galaxy revolve around its center at the same speed, rather than at increasing speeds farther from the center, as well as other discrepancies in the observed motion of other matter in the universe at odds with currently accepted theory, have led astrophysicists and cosmologists to believe that there must be some as yet undiscovered material present throughout space. This material, which they call **dark matter,** cannot be seen with telescopes; it neither emits, reflects, nor absorbs light or any other electromagnetic radiation. Its existence and properties are inferred from its gravitational effects on the visible matter and structure of the universe. It is theorized to be composed of an as yet undiscovered kind of subatomic particle and is estimated to constitute some 23 percent of the total matter in the universe. The search for this particle is one of the major ongoing efforts in modern subatomic particle physics.

There is also a theoretical **dark energy,** which accounts for some remaining observational anomalies, especially the continuous acceleration of distant galaxies already speeding away from us at very high rates. Insofar as is presently understood, "normal" matter and energy and conventional theories of gravity and relativity cannot account for this motion. Taken together, dark matter and dark energy are theorized to account for some 96 percent of all matter and energy in the universe, with the observable universe as we know it constituting only the remaining 4 percent!

Obviously, much about the true nature of our universe remains to be discovered in the coming years.

Critical Thinking

1. Research the various methods that astronomers and astrophysicists use to determine whether there are bodies such as planets in orbit around distant stars.

2. Research how cosmologists have determined the probable age of the universe.

3. The prominent astrophysicist Stephen Hawking has spent a lifetime investigating the origin and nature of black holes. Research his work and summarize his more important findings regarding these celestial phenomena.

4. Research the latest theories of dark matter and dark energy and how these affect scientific views of the nature of the universe.

Study Guide Questions

1. What are the stars?

2. After the Sun, what star is closest to Earth?

3. A. What is the most commonly used unit of astronomical distance in deep space?
   B. In miles, what distance does it represent?

4. Why is communication with distant galaxies implausible at the present time?

5. What is the difference between the apparent and absolute magnitude of stars?

6. A. How are stars classified by their characteristics?
   B. What are the principal star colors?

7. A. What is the spectrum-luminosity diagram?
   B. What is a "main sequence" star?

8. What are the main groups of stars depicted on a spectrum-luminosity diagram?

9. What is a white dwarf star?

10. How are stars classified by their position within our galaxy?

11. What is the principal factor determining what kind of star will be "born"?

12. Why do brighter stars have shorter lives?

13. What is believed to be the sequence in the life cycle of a typical star such as our Sun?

14. What are the two main methods by which exoplanets orbiting around other stars are discovered?

15. What are "rogue" planets?

16. What are novae and supernovae?

17. What are cepheid stars?

18. What are pulsars?

19. What are binaries?

20. A. What is a nebula?
    B. What are the three kinds of nebulae?

21. A. What is a galaxy?
    B. To which galaxy does our solar system belong?
    C. What is the shape of our galaxy?

22. A. How are galaxies classified?
    B. What are the three classifications?

23. What mysterious object has been discovered at the center of the Milky Way and many other galaxies?

24. What are dark matter and dark energy?

New Vocabulary

light-year	neutron star
parsec	nova, -ae
constellation	supernova, -ae
H-R diagram	cepheid variable
main sequence star	pulsar
apparent magnitude	binaries
luminosity	ellipsoidal galaxy
absolute magnitude	spiral galaxy
main-sequence star	irregular galaxy
supergiant	dark matter
white dwarf	dark energy
population I and II stars	black hole
nebula, -ae	exoplanet
blue giant	rogue planet
red giant	

UNIT 5

Physical Science

Since the dawn of recorded history, humans have sought to investigate and explain the world around us. In seeking to gain this understanding, we have made much progress in almost every field of human endeavor. Broadly speaking, **science** is the search for relationships that can be used to explain and predict how and why people, animals, and things behave as they do. The application of these relationships to devices designed to assist us in satisfying our everyday needs and goals gives rise to **technology.**

There are many branches of science. One branch consists of the **biological sciences,** which deal with the study of living things. Another branch is collectively referred to as the **physical sciences,** concerned with nonliving matter, energy, and the physical properties of the universe. Three of the main topics in the physical sciences are physics, chemistry, and astronomy. **Physics** is the study of how forces, matter, and energy in various forms interact. **Chemistry** is the study of matter and how it changes under various conditions. **Astronomy** is the study of the universe beyond the Earth. Other topical areas included in physical science are **geology,** the study of the Earth's structure; **meteorology,** the study of the atmosphere; and **oceanography,** the study of the oceans.

The physical sciences used in the study of the planet are often referred to as the **Earth sciences.** While they are often studied individually, all the physical sciences are ultimately related, and they are often interdependent on one another. For example, an oceanographer must know about the chemistry of water; a chemist must know about the physics of atomic structure; and astronomers must know how both apply to everything in the universe beyond Earth.

Those who engage in the search for scientific truth are called **scientists.** Although some important scientific discoveries are made by chance, most are the result of prolonged investigation over time, called **research.** Doing research involves generating ideas, creating **hypotheses** (possible explanations), performing experiments to verify or sometimes disprove the hypotheses, and then publishing the results so others in the scientific community can verify the results and carry the progress forward.

Scientists use many methods and techniques in their investigations, but all use some form of a systematic approach called the **scientific method.** It involves some or all of the following steps: (1) making observations, (2) forming questions, (3) forming hypotheses or explanations, (4) conducting experiments to test the hypotheses, (5) collecting data and analyzing the results, and (6) drawing conclusions. As the result of their applications of the scientific theory, scientists form *theories* and *laws* to help make predictions concerning the future. A **theory** is a reasoned explanation of observed events, while a **law** is a statement that describes and predicts the future outcome of these events. Scientific theories and laws are often expressed as mathematical equations and formulas that may be used to predict outcomes of natural events.

In this unit we will take a brief look at several physical science topics of key importance to today's Navy that have not already been covered in other parts of the nautical sciences section of this text.

18

Motion, Force, and Aerodynamics

The riddle of how and why things move has fascinated humankind since ancient times. About 2,300 years ago, Greek philosophers studied motion. It seemed to them that all matter should be at rest (motionless) in its normal state. Things that they observed to be in motion always seemed to tend to slow down and eventually stop. To their way of thinking, in order to keep moving an object had to have some unbalanced force—that is, not balanced by an opposing force—acting on it. In the absence of such a force, a moving object would slow down and eventually stop.

The famous Greek philosopher Aristotle (384–322 BC) concluded from this assumption that the speed of an object depends entirely on the force being applied to it and the resistance it meets. Aristotle's conclusion, however, was later proven to be inaccurate.

In the sixteenth century AD, the Italian scientist Galileo Galilei (1564–1642) determined that in the absence of friction an object in horizontal motion could continue to move at the same speed with no additional force. Later in the same century this statement was accepted by Sir Isaac Newton (1624–1727), and with some elaboration it became the basis of the first of his three now-famous laws of motion.

Newton's Laws of Motion

Newton based his laws of motion largely on observation and experimentation, using Galileo's work as a starting point. Like all theoretical laws, Newton's laws were originally based upon what Newton saw around him. Then, with some brilliant insight, he expanded his results to include new phenomena and possibilities.

Newton's first law of motion states that a body at rest tends to remain at rest and that a body in motion tends to remain in motion, in a straight line, unless an outside force acts on the body. Newton defined this resistance to change as **inertia**. This law is sometimes therefore called the *law of inertia*.

Sir Isaac Newton from a 1689 portrait.

Newton's second law of motion states that the acceleration of a body is directly proportional to the force acting on it and inversely proportional to the mass of the body, and is in the same direction as the applied force. Mathematically, this is often expressed by the formula

$$F = ma.$$

There may, of course, be more than one force acting on a body at the same time. The F in the formula, then, refers to the **net** or **resultant** force applied to a body after all forces acting on it are combined.

Newton's third law of motion states that whenever one body exerts a force upon a second body, the second exerts an equal but opposite force back upon the first. Stated another way, for every action there is an equal but opposite reaction.

As an example of Newton's laws, suppose you want to take a trip in your car. When you first get in you are **at rest** (motionless), because no unbalanced forces are acting on you. When you press on the accelerator, the car's engine exerts a force on the car and everything attached to it. The car therefore accelerates forward, taking you along with it. Within the car, your seat pushes forward on you, and you in turn push back on the seat with an equal but opposite force as long as the car is accelerating. Eventually you reach cruising speed—say, thirty miles per hour—and ease up the pressure on the accelerator. Though the engine is still producing some forward force, at this cruising speed the forward force of the engine is exactly matched by opposing forces, such as air friction, thus producing a state of no net, or unbalanced, forces acting on either you or the car. Therefore you stay at a steady speed of thirty miles per hour.

When you want to slow down, you apply the brakes and disengage the engine (either automatically or manually), thus generating a net force on the car in a direction opposite to its motion. It begins to slow down. Meanwhile, you tend to keep moving forward inside, restrained only by your seat belt and friction with the seat. While the seat belt restrains you, you and the seat belt each exert an equal but opposite force on each other. Eventually you and the car stop, at which point, once again, no net forces are acting on either you or the car.

Taken together, Newton's three laws describe the relationships among force, mass, acceleration, and velocity for all bodies in motion at speeds that are relatively low as compared to the **speed of light,** 3×10^8 meters per second, or 186,000 miles per second. Such motion is often called **Newtonian motion.** Almost all motion on Earth falls into this category. We can therefore easily use Newton's laws to make all manner of predictions about things undergoing Newtonian motion. However, bodies in space can travel much faster. At extremely high speeds, time, mass, and length become distorted, and different rules, devised by Albert Einstein (1879–1955), apply. These rules are collectively called **Einstein's Theory of Relativity,** which he formulated early in the last century.

Forces

Let us take another look at Newton's second law of motion. How do we define acceleration? **Acceleration** is change in velocity per unit of time, normally one second. **Velocity** is the rate of motion (speed) in a given direction. In the example above, the speed was expressed in terms of miles per hour (mph), and the implied direction was the way the car was headed. Other widely used speed units are feet per second (ft/s^2) and, in the metric system, meters per second (m/s^2) or kilometers per hour (km/hr). In the marine environment, speeds are customarily expressed in **knots,** which are *nautical miles* (1.15 statute miles, about 6,070 feet) per hour. Velocity and speed are often used interchangeably, but to be technically correct a velocity must always include some directional reference. The units of acceleration are derived from velocity units divided by time units, usually seconds; the most common are written ft/s^2 and m/s^2. **Force** can be defined as power or energy exerted against a body in a given direction. Its units are **pounds** in the English system and **newtons** (N) in the metric system. **Mass** is the quantity of material contained in an object. In the metric system the unit of mass is the **kilogram.** In the English system the pound is often erroneously used to indicate mass, although it is really a force unit.

One kind of force that must be dealt with for all moving earthbound objects is **friction.** Friction is caused by contact between the moving object and other substances around it. The amount of the friction is dependent on the nature of the materials in contact, the force between them, and sometimes their velocity relative to each other. Solids moving against each other generate **contact friction.** Bodies moving through fluids, such as water or air (considered a fluid in these cases), generate **fluid friction,** which increases with the speed of travel through the fluid. This type of friction is often called **drag.** Friction always

acts in a direction opposite to the direction of motion. The energy generated by friction is usually dissipated in the form of heat.

Gravitational Attraction and g-Forces

In the science of motion, acceleration is often measured in terms of the **standard acceleration of gravity,** abbreviated by the letter *g*. A freely falling frictionless body is attracted to the Earth by a force equal to its weight, with the result that it accelerates at a constant rate of approximately thirty-two feet (9.8 meters) per second each second (written as 32 ft/sec^2 [9.8 m/sec^2]). Its acceleration while in this condition, called **free fall,** is thus said to be 1 g. The values given for it above are standard values at the Earth's surface.

The value of *g* may change, of course, if you ascend some distance above the Earth's surface or go into space or to some other celestial body, like the Moon, where the acceleration due to gravity is different. You may have noticed in the astronomy unit of this text that the gravitational attraction of the Moon, planets, and other bodies can be expressed in terms of multiples of *g*, such as 0.165 g in the case of the Moon or 0.4 g in the case of Mars.

Weights of objects may be calculated as a special case of Newton's second law, F = ma, by substituting *g* for *a*:

$$W = mg.$$

If you know the mass of the body and the value of *g* at the location at which you wish to calculate its weight, you can easily do so using this formula. For example, the weight of a person with a mass of 100 Kg on Earth's surface would be given by

$$W = 100 \text{ Kg} \times 9.8 \text{ m/s}^2 = 980 \text{ newtons (1 Kg} \bullet \text{m/s}^2 = 1 \text{ newton), or } 220.5 \text{ pounds (1 newton} = 0.225 \text{ pound).}$$

If the person were to go to the Moon, where the acceleration due to gravity is 0.165 g, then their weight would be given by

$$W = 100 \text{ Kg} \times 0.165 \text{ (9.8 m/s}^2) = 161.7 \text{ newtons, or } 36.4 \text{ pounds.}$$

In space, where there is no gravity, a person would have no weight, since there mg = 0. It is important to note the distinction between weight and mass—the weight can change, depending on location, while mass does not.

Bodies making rapid turns will experience other accelerations, and therefore forces, due to **centripetal force** (which can be many times that of gravity), often expressed as multiples of *g*. As an example, if a jet fighter making a tight turn experiences a sideways force of 5 g's, there is a centripetal force on it equal to five times its weight. A missile or aircraft is designed to withstand only a certain number of g's, and if that is exceeded,

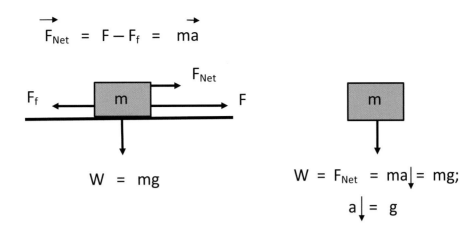

$$\vec{F}_{Net} \;=\; F - F_f \;=\; \vec{ma}$$

$$W = mg$$

$$W = F_{Net} = ma{\downarrow} = mg;$$
$$a{\downarrow} = g$$

Illustration of Newton's second law. On the left, a body of mass *m* and weight *W* is being pulled by force *F* across a surface generating friction force F_f. Its acceleration, *a*, results from the net force F_{Net} acting on it, equal to the difference between *F* and F_f. Nothing happens vertically, because its downward weight is balanced by the upward force of the surface on it. On the right, the body is in free fall. Since its weight is now the only force acting on it, its downward acceleration is equal to the acceleration due to gravity, *g*.

damage to its structure, its payload, or its instruments may occur. In the case of manned aircraft, the pilot may black out (become unconscious).

Energy, Work, and Power

There are many forms of energy. Some of these are kinetic and gravitational energy, chemical and thermal (heat) energy, electrical energy, and nuclear energy; there are many others. Under the proper conditions, energy can be transformed or converted from one form to another or, in the case of nuclear energy, from energy into matter and vice versa. No matter the kind of energy, however, it follows the **law of conservation of energy**, which states that within a closed (isolated) system, energy may neither be created nor destroyed, only changed from one form to another.

Kinetic energy is energy of motion. The faster an object moves, the more kinetic energy it is said to have. **Gravitational energy** is energy of position within a gravitational field; the higher an object is, or the more distant from a center of gravitational attraction, the more **gravitational potential energy** it has. Many other kinds of energy have potential energy associated with them as well. The sum of an object's kinetic and gravitational potential energy is called its **mechanical energy.** **Chemical energy** is energy within a substance that can be released as heat by a chemical reaction such as burning, or sometimes absorbed when combining with other compounds or elements. **Electrical energy** is energy that is made available by the flow of electrical charge through a conductor. It can be converted into other forms of energy by passage through devices like heating elements or motors. **Nuclear energy** is the energy that binds particles within the nucleus of an atom. It can be

released as heat by radioactive decay, nuclear fission, or nuclear fusion. Once released, the heat can be converted into the other forms of energy described above.

In the metric system (International System, known by its French abbreviation, SI), the unit used for all types of energy is called a *joule*. In the English system, the units vary according to the type of energy: mechanical energy is measured in *foot-pounds,* heat in *calories,* electrical energy in *kilowatt hours,* and nuclear energy in *electron-volts.*

When a force acts through a distance, **work** is said to have been done. The formula is:

$$W = F \times d.$$

In the English system the units of work are **foot-pounds,** and in the SI system **newton-meters.** One newton-meter is called a **joule.**

Doing work on a body increases its level of energy. In mechanical systems, for example, it may gain height or velocity, or both. Under the proper conditions, some of a body's energy can be transformed back into work, thus lowering its energy, as when falling water drives a turbine. There is, therefore, an equivalence between work and energy, indicated by the fact that they both have the same unit in the metric system, the joule.

The rate at which work is done or energy is gained or expended is **power.** The formula is:

$$P = W/t \text{ or } E/t,$$

where *P* is power, *W* is work, *E* is energy, and *t* is the time in seconds. In the English system the unit of power is the **horsepower,** and in the metric system it is the **watt.** There are 746 watts in one horsepower. For example, if ten newtons of force acted over a distance of ten meters for five seconds, the power generated would be (10 × 10)/5, or 20 watts (0.013 horsepower). A larger unit of power called the **kilowatt** (KW), equivalent to a thousand watts or 1.34 horsepower, is commonly used, especially in connection with electrical power consumption. If the United States ever fully adopts the metric International System of units, all products such as automobile engines that produce or use power will be rated in kilowatts instead of horsepower. Most American-built marine engines used on boats already use kilowatts as their standard measure of power.

The Physics of Flight

The path of a body in flight is determined by Newton's laws of motion, according to the forces acting upon it. Some of these forces are natural, and others are man-made. Various combinations of these forces produce different effects on the flight path. **Aerodynamics** is the science that deals with the motion of bodies moving through air and other gases. Missiles and aircraft use aerodynamic forces to maintain their flight path. The surface of a body in flight is called its *airfoil*. The aerodynamic forces acting on a moving airfoil are *thrust, drag, gravity* (weight), and *lift*. Other factors that can affect a body in flight are the *angle of attack* between the airfoil and the *airstream* (air flowing past it) and, in the case of a body flying in a curved path, *centripetal force.*

Each of the forces described above is a **vector quantity**, meaning something that has both magnitude (length or size) and direction. All forces acting on a body can be resolved into a single *net force* by mathematically combining their vectors to form the *resultant force* vector. The net or resultant force determines the motion of the body, in accordance with Newton's laws.

Daniel Bernoulli (1700–82) postulated that since the total energy in any closed system remains constant, if one element in

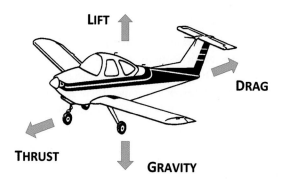

The aerodynamic forces acting on a moving airfoil, such as an airplane, are thrust, drag, gravity, and lift. The combination of these forces produces a resultant force that will determine where the plane goes.
Courtesy of www.allstar.fiu.edu

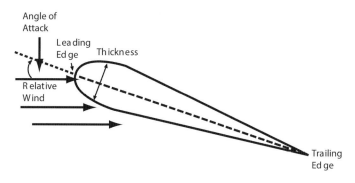

An illustration of an *angle of attack* between the inclination of an airfoil and the oncoming airstream.

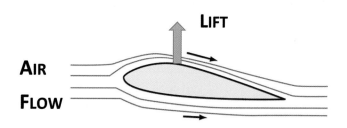

Illustration of the Bernoulli principle. Air that passes over the top of a convex wing must travel farther and therefore faster than the air beneath it. This results in a lower pressure on top of the wing than the bottom, creating an upward force called lift.

any system of streamlined fluid flow is decreased another must increase to counterbalance it. This is called **Bernoulli's principle.** The airstream flowing past the fuselage and over the wing of an aircraft or guided missile forms a system to which this principle can be applied.

When air passes over the convex wing of an aircraft, it must travel a greater distance than the air passing under it. Since the two parts of the airstream reach the trailing edge of the wing at the same time, the air that flows *over* the wing must move faster than the air that flows *under* it. According to Bernoulli's principle, this results in a lower pressure on the top than on the bottom surface of the wing. This pressure difference tends to force the wing upward, thereby giving it lift. For takeoffs and landings, larger aircraft have *wing flaps* that can be extended from the trailing edge and sometimes projections called *slats* from the leading edge, which increase the lift even more. Since most missiles and high-performance jet aircraft use flat wings rather than the curved wings of slower aircraft, in order to reduce drag, they must get the necessary lift entirely from the angle of attack between the oncoming airstream and the wing.

Here is an example of the physics of flight. Consider an airplane taking off from a runway. Before it starts rolling, its speed is zero, and there is no drag. When its brakes are released, the force of thrust developed by its engines at full power is unbal-

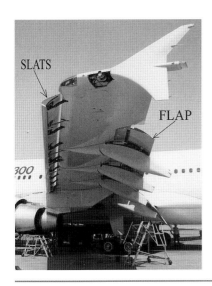

Wing flaps and slats on a typical large commercial airliner. *Arpingstone*

A vapor cone created by the shock wave of a Navy FA-18 going supersonic. *CHINFO*

anced, and as a result the plane begins to accelerate rapidly down the runway, in accordance with Newton's second law. As its speed increases, the lift force produced by its wings grows rapidly, by Bernoulli's theorem.

As its takeoff run progresses, the plane's forward acceleration decreases as the opposing drag force steadily increases. When the nose rises off the runway, the angle of attack increases, adding still more upward force. Soon the total lift force overcomes the downward weight produced by gravity, and the plane lifts off. Shortly after takeoff the plane's forward acceleration falls off to zero as increasing drag matches thrust. The plane continues climbing at a steady speed, by Newton's first law, until it decreases drag by raising the landing gear and retracting any wing flaps and slats. Now the plane can accelerate once again as it climbs to cruising altitude and attains cruising speed, when all forces acting on it are once more in balance.

Should the propulsive force be decreased for any reason, such as to slow down for landing, the force of drag will exceed the thrust. The plane will then slow until the forces are again in balance.

Mach Numbers and Sonic Booms

Speeds of missiles and high-performance aircraft are often expressed in terms of **Mach numbers** rather than in miles per hour or knots. The Mach number is the ratio of the body's speed to the speed of sound in that particular part of the atmosphere. For example, if an aircraft is flying at a speed equal to one-half the local speed of sound, it is said to be flying at Mach 0.5. If it moves at twice the local speed of sound, its speed is Mach 2.

The speed expressed by the Mach number is not a fixed quantity, because the speed of sound in air varies directly with

the square root of air temperature. Because of air temperature changes in the atmosphere with increasing altitude, the speed of sound decreases from 770 mph (344 meters per second) at sea level, on an average day when the air is 68 degrees F (20 degrees C), to 661 mph at the top of the troposphere. The speed of sound remains constant between 55,000 feet and 105,000 feet then rises to 838 mph, reverses, and falls to 693 mph at the top of the stratosphere.

When an object travels through air it creates a series of pressure waves in front of and behind it, similar to the bow wave and wake of a boat traveling through water. As the object increases speed, the waves are forced together and compressed. If the object reaches the speed of sound or greater (called **supersonic speeds**), the waves merge to form a conical shock wave and an associated explosion-like noise called a **sonic boom.** These spread out together from the object at the speed of sound. The strength of the shock wave and the sonic boom produced by it increases with the size and speed of the object and decreases with altitude and distance. Thus a high-flying jet aircraft traveling at supersonic speeds may not be heard on the ground beneath it, but if the plane were close to the ground, the shock wave could cause damage such as broken windows and spilled liquids, and the loud sonic boom would be deafening.

The shock wave and sonic-boom effects can be greatly reduced by **streamlining** a body that travels at supersonic speeds. For supersonic aircraft this includes such measures as decreasing the thickness of fuselage and wings, sweeping the wings back, decreasing the wingspan, and extending the length of the nose. All these features are readily apparent in the designs of modern supersonic jet aircraft and missiles.

Critical Thinking

1. In the first part of this chapter the motion of a car was used to illustrate how Newton's laws of motion operate. Do the same thing for a guided missile being fired from the ground at an airborne target.

2. Discuss some of the ways that drag can be reduced for a body moving through air.

Study Guide Questions

1. A. According to ancient Greek philosophers, what keeps an object in motion?
   B. According to Isaac Newton, what keeps an object in motion?

2. State Newton's three laws of motion.

3. A. How fast is light speed?
   B. What theory describes the motion of bodies with speeds near light speed?

4. A. What are the units of force in the English system of units?
   B. In the metric system?

5. A. Is the weight or the mass of an object subject to change with its location?
   B. How is the weight of an object determined?

6. What kind of force must be reckoned with for all earth-bound objects in motion?

7. What are the four aerodynamic forces on bodies in flight?

8. According to Bernoulli's theorem, how is lift developed by a curved wing?

9. What is meant by g forces?

10. How are Mach numbers derived?

11. A. What is a sonic boom?
    B. What causes it?

12. What are some measures that can be taken to decrease the shock wave and sonic boom produced by aircraft flying at supersonic speeds?

New Vocabulary

research	potential energy
hypothesis	mechanical energy
scientific method	chemical energy
theory	electrical energy
net force	nuclear energy
Newtonian motion	energy
friction	metric system
drag	joule
free fall	work
acceleration	horsepower
velocity	watt
knots	aerodynamics
mass	thrust
drag	lift
g-force	angle of attack
free fall	vector quantity
centripetal force	shock wave
kinetic energy	sonic boom

19

Buoyancy

oats, ships, and submarines are of course closely related to our Navy and the people who serve in it. You may have had experience with a rowboat, canoe, or raft. You know instinctively that such craft float, especially if they are made of wood or light plastic, even if they happen to fill with water. But why does a *metal* ship float? How can a submarine hover submerged at a desired depth? To answer questions such as these it is necessary to know something about what is called the **buoyant force.**

Over two thousand years ago the Greek scientist Archimedes (287–212 BC) found that an object immersed in a fluid is pushed up with a force that equals the weight of the fluid it displaces. This force has come to be called the *buoyant force,* and the principle that describes it is named **Archimedes' Law** in honor of its discoverer. For purposes of Archimedes' Law, it does not matter what the object is made of or whether the "fluid" is a liquid or a gas. The law applies equally to both.

Why Objects Float

Suppose that a stone with a volume of half a cubic meter weighs 9,800 newtons in air. If submerged in water, by Archimedes' law it would feel an upward force equal to the volume of water displaced—4,900 newtons in this case, since the weight of a cubic meter of water is 9,800 newtons. The *apparent weight* of the stone in the water—its weight in air minus the buoyant force—would now be 4,900 newtons (9,800 – 4,900 = 4,900), and it would sink.

Now let us suppose that instead of a stone we had a hollow iron boat also weighing 9,800 newtons. We place the boat in the water and it begins to sink. As it does so, it begins to displace some of the water, so again by Archimedes' Law it begins to feel an upward force equal to the weight of the water being displaced. After it has sunk into the water to the point at which a cubic meter of water has been displaced, it feels an upward force exactly equal to its weight, 9,800 newtons. At this point the upward buoyant force exactly equals the downward weight, so there is no longer any net downward force on the boat (9,800 – 9,800 = 0). By Newton's first law, described in the first chapter

of this unit, objects with no net force on them tend to remain at rest. Thus, our boat would now float, assuming there was still some part of it above water, called the *freeboard.* The line around the boat where the surface of the water meets it when it floats is called the *waterline,* and the depth of the keel is called its *draft.*

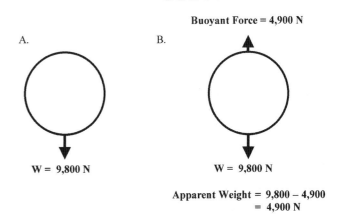

An object with a volume of half a cubic meter that weighs 9,800 N in air (A) has an apparent weight of 4,900 N in water (B) because of the upward buoyant force on it equal to the weight of the water displaced.

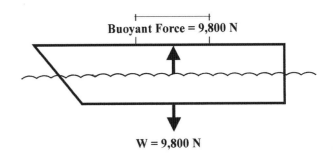

A hollow boat weighing 9,800 N will sink into the water until it displaces an equal weight of water, whereupon it floats at that depth, called its "draft."

Now suppose a hole were drilled in the hull of our boat below the waterline, allowing the water to flow in. As it fills, the combined weight of the boat plus the water inside would be always be greater than the weight of the water being displaced, no matter how far down it sinks. Thus in this situation the boat would eventually fill completely and sink to the bottom, just as in the example of the stone above. So it really does not matter what material is used to construct the boat. It could be made of wood, fiberglass, steel, or even concrete. A hollow boat will always float as long as there is still some part of its hull above water keeping water out when it has sunk to a depth at which its weight is matched by the upward buoyant force provided by the water being displaced.

Density is a scientific term used to describe how much of a material is present per unit of its volume. By convention it is usually specified using the SI system, in kilograms per cubic meter or sometimes grams per cubic centimeter. Anything with a density less than that of water, such as wood, will always float, since when it sinks into water it will always achieve equality between the upward buoyant force and the downward weight before it is totally submerged. On the other hand, solids having a greater density than water will always have a greater downward weight than upward buoyant force, so they will always submerge completely and sink.

Gases as well as liquids exert upward buoyant forces. Instead of a boat, suppose we experiment with a small rubber balloon. If we blow up the balloon with air at the same or lower temperature than the air surrounding it, by Archimedes' Law an upward force will begin to act on it equal to the weight of the outside air being displaced. But the weight of the balloon's skin plus the air inside it will be greater, thus causing the balloon to fall to the floor, just as the boat filled with water sank to the bottom.

But now suppose we blew hot air, or a light gas such as helium, into the balloon. Heated air and light gases like helium are less dense than regular air, so they weigh less per unit volume. If we inflated our balloon to the same size as before, the same upward force as before would be felt by it. But the downward weight force would be less. The balloon, therefore, would rise into the air, since there is an unbalanced upward net force on it. In the case of a large balloon launched into the atmosphere, as the balloon goes up the air gets thinner, so even though the balloon expands somewhat as it rises, eventually at some altitude the upward buoyant force decreases to the point that it equals the downward weight; the balloon floats at this altitude.

The Submarine

When cruising on the surface of a body of water, a submarine acts just like the boat described above. It will sink only partially into the water, to a depth at which its weight is balanced by the upward buoyant force of the water it displaces. For most submarines this happens when the hull is about two-thirds submerged.

Now suppose that the submarine wants to submerge completely. To do this, it needs more weight to compensate for the upward buoyant force exerted on it by the weight of the water displaced by its totally submerged hull. To provide the weight, submarines are fitted with fillable water tanks inside them called *ballast tanks*. When water is pumped into these tanks, their weight and the structural weight of the submarine now combine to weigh more than the upward buoyant force, so the submarine dives. To level off at some desired depth, the submarine adjusts the amount of water in the ballast tanks until the downward weight and upward buoyant force are roughly in

Aerographer's mates on an aircraft carrier release a weather balloon. Once released the balloon will rise and expand until its weight matches that of the volume of air it displaces. *CHINFO*

A submerged submarine will remain at a given depth as long as the weight of its hull plus ballast water inside equals the weight of the water it displaces. *CHINFO*

balance. The propulsion system of the submarine and its diving planes can now keep the submarine at the desired depth, like an airplane flying at some level in the atmosphere. If the weight and buoyant force were exactly matched, the submarine would be able to hover at the desired depth without any forward propulsion, much like the balloon hovering in air.

To surface from a submerged depth, the submarine forces water out of the ballast tanks with compressed air until the upward buoyant force is once again greater than the downward weight. At this point the submarine will surface, aided by its propulsion system. Thus, a submarine in water acts much like a balloon in air, even though the densities of the media in which they operate are much different.

Ship Stability

One of the considerations in ship design is that the ship should be stable in a wide variety of sea conditions and if damaged. The stability of a ship is basically dependent on the location of its *center of gravity* and its *center of buoyancy* at various angles of inclination, or *roll*. The **center of gravity** is defined as the center of mass of the ship, around which the ship seems to move. The center of gravity does not change position as the ship moves. The **center of buoyancy** is the geometric center of the portion of the ship's hull that is underwater. It tends to move in an arc as the ship rolls. For good stability a ship's center of gravity should be as low as possible in the hull, so that there is a large amount of horizontal distance between the downward force through the center of gravity and upward force through the center of buoyancy. This will generate *torque* (force of rotation) called a **righting arm** that will tend to right the ship whenever it rolls. If the center of gravity rises, either because of damage or intentional

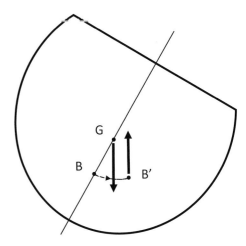

When a ship rolls, the center of buoyancy *B* moves in an arc to the new position *B'*, creating a torque called a *righting moment* between the upward force of buoyancy and the downward force acting through the center of gravity *G*. The lower the center of gravity, the greater the horizontal distance between the two forces, thus increasing both the righting moment and the ship's stability.

addition of weight higher in the ship, this righting torque will tend to decrease, and the ship's stability may be impaired to the point that it might capsize if it rolls too far.

Because of the foregoing, if a lightly loaded ship is operating in heavy weather, it will sometimes take on additional water in tanks near the keel (bottom) or fill empty fuel tanks with water in order to lower its center of gravity as low as possible. In this condition it will be less likely to experience dangerous rolls in stormy seas. The additional water is called **ballast.**

Critical Thinking

1. Why is it important for anyone connected with water-craft to know something about the laws of buoyancy and stability?

Study Guide Questions

1. Who is credited with discovering the law of buoyant force?

2. State the principles of Archimedes' Law.

3. What is the apparent weight of an object in water, and how is it computed?

4. How can a boat constructed from a material more dense than water float?

5. What is density, and how is it computed?

6. Why does a hot-air balloon tend to rise in the air, while one filled with cold air does not?

7. With what equipment is a submarine fitted to allow it to submerge?

8. Upon what basic factors does a ship's stability depend?

9. What might happen if excessive weight is added high in a ship?

10. What will a ship sometimes do to lower its center of gravity in stormy seas?

Problems

1. A steel cube with a volume of one cubic meter and a density of 7,800 kg/m^3 is submerged in water (density 1,000 kg/m3). If each kilogram weighs 9.8 newtons,
   A. What is the weight of the cube in air?
   B. What is the upward force on the cube when it is completely submerged?
   C. What is the apparent weight of the cube in water?

2. A wooden cube of density 600 kg/m^3 is floating in water.
   A. How much water in m^3 will it have to displace in order to float?
   B. What percentage of its volume will be above water when it floats?
   C. How deep into the water will it sink?

New Vocabulary

buoyant force
apparent weight
freeboard
waterline
ballast tanks

center of gravity
center of buoyancy
righting arm
ballast

20

Basic Electricity

The study of electricity began with the ancient Greeks. They discovered that by rubbing a mineral called amber with a cloth, they could create a mysterious force of attraction between the cloth and the amber. They also observed that after they rubbed two different ambers with two different cloths, the two cloths would repel one another—as strongly as they were attracted to amber. These forces were called "electric" (from the Greek word for amber), and the cloths and ambers were said to be electrically charged.

Although the Greeks discovered electric force, they could not explain it. In fact, it was not until the atomic theory of matter was developed that the true cause of electricity was found. When scientists discovered that atoms are composed of negatively charged particles (electrons) that orbit around positively charged particles (protons), they could explain electrical charge. Normally there is a balance between the negative charge of electrons and the positive charge of protons. Therefore, under most conditions an atom will have no charge. But if the number of electrons is increased, the atom will become negatively charged. On the other hand, if electrons are taken away, the atom will have a positive charge. Charged atoms are called **ions**.

One of the fundamental laws of electricity is that like charges repel each other and unlike charges attract each other. In the atom, the electrons are held in their orbits by the attractive force between them and the protons in the nucleus. In the Greeks' experiments with amber, the cloth picked up electrons from the amber, thus becoming negatively charged. This left the amber with a positive charge—and unlike charges attract one another.

Conductors and Insulators

An electric charge can move through a material if it has a large number of *free electrons*—that is, electrons that can easily move from atom to atom in the material. Substances that permit the free motion of a large number of electrons because of their atomic structure are called **conductors**. Any metal is a good conductor, but gold, silver, copper, and aluminum, in that order, are the best conductors. Wire made from copper or alu-minum is generally used to conduct electricity from one place to another, as those materials are less expensive than the other good conductors. Electrical energy is conveyed at the speed of light through conductors by the free electrons. As the electrical energy passes, each electron moves a very short distance to the neighboring atom, where it replaces one or more electrons by forcing them out of their orbits. The replaced electrons repeat the process in other nearby atoms.

Most nonmetallic substances have very few free electrons and are therefore poor conductors. These substances, such as rubber, glass, plastic, or dry wood, are called **insulators.** Wire conductors are covered by this insulating material to prevent the electricity from being diverted from the conductors.

Voltage

The force that causes electricity to move through a conductor is called **voltage,** or **electromotive force,** symbolized by E or, sometimes, by *EMF*. There are six basic ways to generate voltage:

1. *Friction.* Voltage can be produced by rubbing two materials together. *Static electricity* is the most common name for this type. It occurs frequently in dry climates or on days of low humidity.

2. *Pressure.* Voltage can be produced by squeezing crystals, such as natural quartz or, more usually, manufactured crystals. Compressed electrons tend to move through a crystal at predictable frequencies. Crystals are frequently used in communications equipment.

3. *Heat.* Voltage can be produced by heating the place where two unlike metals are joined. The difference in temperature between this junction and another reference junction between the two metals at a known temperature, called the "cold junction," produces a voltage that varies with the temperature difference. This voltage can then be calibrated against a temperature scale. This arrangement is called a *thermocouple.* As a result, thermocouples are often used to measure and regulate temperature, as in a thermostat.

357

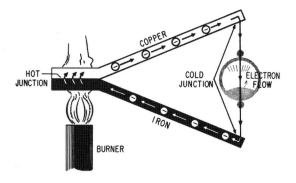

Voltage produced by heat in a thermocouple.

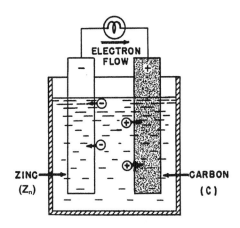

A simple one-cell battery.

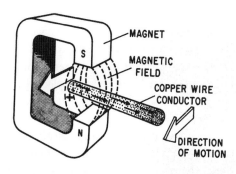

Voltage produced by magnetism. The faster the wire transits the magnetic field, the more voltage is produced. In a generator, many such wires are formed into a coil, which is made to rotate within the magnetic field by some form of engine or turbine.

4. *Light.* Voltage can be produced when light strikes a *photosensitive* (light-sensitive) substance. The light dislodges electrons from their orbits around the surface atoms. Voltage produced in this manner is called *photoelectric*. A *photoelectric cell* is a device that operates on this principle. Although among the more expensive ways to generate voltage and electricity, this method is coming into wide use in modern times because it is one of the few methods that can produce large amounts of electricity without using natural resources or generating carbon-based waste products. Besides large-scale electrical power production using solar panels, applications include auxiliary outdoor lighting, battery replenishment for isolated lights (such as highway signs and navigational lights on waterways), and as integral components of such electronic devices as automatic door openers and burglar alarms.

5. *Chemical action.* Voltage can be produced by chemical reactions, as in a battery cell. The simple voltaic battery consists of a carbon strip (positive) and a zinc strip (negative) suspended in a container with a solution of water and sulfuric acid. This solution is called the *electrolyte*. The chemical action that results from this combination causes electrons to flow between the zinc and carbon electrodes. Batteries are used as sources of electrical energy in a wide variety of applications, such as vehicles, aircraft, ships and boats, and portable equipment of all kinds.

6. *Magnetism.* Voltage can be produced when a conductor moves through a magnetic field, or a magnet moves through an electric field, in such a manner as to cut the field's lines of force. This is the method used by the most common source of electric power, the **electric generator.** Essentially, in a generator a coil of copper-wire conductors is moved through the magnetic field created by a U- or C-shaped electromagnet.

As mentioned above, most voltage and electricity used for applications requiring more that a few watts of electrical energy is produced by electric generators. Today most of these are powered either directly or indirectly by fossil fuels, such as gasoline, diesel oil, natural gas, and coal. However, over the past several decades these fuels have become increasingly expensive, mostly because supplies of the natural resources from which they are derived have gotten progressively smaller, and also because of increased production and distribution costs. Also, there has been a heightened awareness of the detrimental effects on the environment of continued heavy use of these fuels. Consequently, there has been a trend toward increasing the use of "green energy" for electrical power generation. This includes solar panels, geothermal energy, wind, and tidal energy. Nuclear energy has also been extensively used as a source of heat for electrical power generation over the last half-century.

An instrument designed to measure voltage in an electrical circuit is called a **voltmeter.** Voltages are measured in units called **volts.** A difference in voltage from one place to another in an electrical circuit is called a *potential difference,* measured in volts.

Current

The flow of electricity through a conductor is called **electric current.** Electric current is classified into two general types, depending on how it is generated: *direct current* and *alternating current.* Direct current flows continuously in the same direction, while an alternating current periodically reverses direction. An **ampere** (or amp) is the unit used to measure the rate at which current flows. The symbol for current flow is *I.* An instrument designed to measure current in an electrical circuit is called an **ammeter.**

Every material offers some resistance, or opposition, to the flow of electric current. Good conductors offer very little resistance, while insulators or poor conductors offer high resistance. The size and composition of wires in an electric circuit are designed to keep electrical resistance as low as possible. A

A number of different means can be used to provide the motive force that rotates the coils of a generator through a magnetic field in order to produce electricity. Here, a group of NJROTC cadets visit a *wind farm*, a group of wind turbines used to generate electricity. Ambient wind spins the blades, which in turn spin the shafts of the generators located at the top of the towers. *CHINFO, Mike Miller*

wire's resistance depends on its length, diameter, composition, and temperature.

Manufactured circuit elements that provide a specific amount of resistance are called **resistors.** Resistance is measured in **ohms,** symbolized by Ω, the Greek letter *omega,* or sometimes just the letter *R.* One ohm is the resistance of a circuit element (or circuit) that permits a steady current of one ampere to flow when a potential difference of one volt is applied to that circuit. An instrument designed to measure resistance in an electrical circuit is called an **ohmmeter.**

When electrical experiments were first conducted in the 1800s, the electron was as yet undiscovered, so it was assumed that current was a flow of positive charges from the positive to the negative terminals of a source in a circuit. This idea became so widespread that still today for many applications electrical current is said to proceed from positive to negative terminals of a battery or generator. We now know that the reverse is true. An electrical current is conveyed through a conductor primarily by negatively charged electrons that can move within it. Thus, in the scientific community the more accurate concept of an electron current flowing from negative to positive is more prevalent; it is also probably easier to understand, so that is the concept used herein for our discussion of electricity.

Batteries

A battery consists of a number of cells assembled in a common container and connected to function as a source of electrical power. A *cell* is the fundamental unit of a battery. A simple cell consists of two electrodes placed in a container holding the electrolyte.

The *electrodes* are the conductors by which the current leaves or returns to the electrolyte. In a simple cell they are carbon and zinc strips, placed in the electrolyte. In the dry cell there is a carbon rod in the center and a zinc container in which the cell is assembled. The electrolyte may be a salt, an acid, or an alkaline solution. In the automobile storage battery the electrolyte is in liquid form. In the dry cell battery, the electrolyte is a paste.

A *primary cell* is one in which the chemical action eats away one of the electrodes, usually the negative. Eventually the electrode must be replaced or the cell discarded. In the case of the common dry cell, as in a flashlight battery, it is usually cheaper to buy a new cell.

A *secondary cell* is one in which the electrodes and the electrolyte are altered by the chemical action that generates current. These cells may be restored to their original condition *(recharged)* by forcing an electric current through them in the direction opposite to that of discharge. The automobile storage battery and the batteries within portable devices such as cell phones are common examples of rechargeable batteries composed of secondary cells.

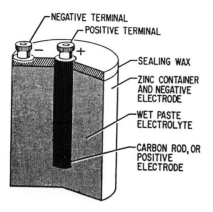

Cross section of a dry cell battery.

The Electrical Circuit

Whenever a potential difference (voltage) exists across a conductor, a pathway for electrons and thus current flow is created. An **electric circuit** is a conducting pathway consisting of the conductor and the path through the voltage source. For example, a lamp connected by wires to a dry cell's terminals forms a simple electric circuit. The electron current flows from the negative (–) terminal of the battery through the lamp to the positive (+) battery terminal and continues by going through the battery from the (+) terminal to the (–) terminal. As long as this pathway is unbroken and the voltage is maintained, current will flow. Such an electrical circuit is called a *closed circuit*. An *open circuit* is one in which the flow of electricity is interrupted, as by a switch.

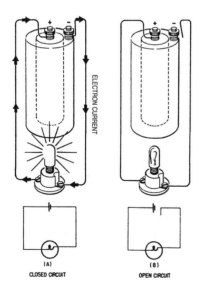

Simple closed (A) and open (B) electric circuits and their associated schematic diagrams.

A **schematic** is a diagram in which symbols, instead of pictures, are used for a circuit's components. These symbols are used in an effort to make the diagrams easier to draw and easier to understand. Schematic symbols aid the technician who designs or repairs electrical or electronic equipment.

Some of the more common symbols in an electrical schematic appear in the drawing below. A long bar over or alongside a short one is the symbol for a battery or battery cell. A sawtooth is the symbol for resistance, and a line connecting them symbolizes a wire. There are many other standard symbols for other possible components as well.

Ohm's Law

In the early 1800s, George Simon Ohm proved that a definite relationship exists among current, voltage, and resistance. This relationship, called **Ohm's Law,** is stated as follows: the current in a circuit is directly proportional to the applied voltage and inversely proportional to the circuit resistance. Ohm's Law may be expressed as the equation:

$$I = E/R,$$

where I = current in amperes, E = voltage in volts, and R = resistance in ohms. If any two of the quantities in the equation are known, the third may be easily found.

Example: a circuit contains a resistance of 1.5 ohms and a source voltage of 1.5 volts. How much current flows in the circuit?

Solution: I = E/R = 1.5 V/1.5 Ω = 1 ampere.

In many circuit applications, the current is known and either the voltage or the resistance will be the unknown quantity. To solve a problem in which current and resistance are known, the basic formula for Ohm's Law must be transformed to solve for E. Multiplying both sides of the equation by R, the formula for finding voltage is:

$$E = IR.$$

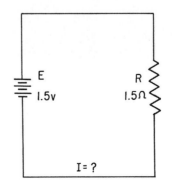

Determining current in a simple circuit. *E* is the designation for a voltage source like a battery, symbolized by long and short lines; *R* is the designation for resistance, symbolized by a sawtooth line, with its associated value in ohms labeled with the Greek letter *omega* (Ω); *I* is the designation for current.

Similarly, to transform the basic formula when resistance is unknown, multiply both sides of the basic equation by R and then divide both sides of the equation by I. The resulting formula for resistance is:

$$R = E/I.$$

Power

Electrical power, like mechanical power discussed earlier, refers to the rate at which work is being done. Work is done whenever a force acts through a distance, causing motion. Therefore, since voltage makes current flow in a closed circuit, work is being done below. The rate at which this work is done is called the *electric power rate,* and its measure is the *watt*—the basic SI unit of power. Power is equal to the current through the circuit, multiplied by the voltage across the circuit, or in equation form,

$$P = IE.$$

As an example, if a current of two amps flows through a circuit in which the potential difference is two volts, the power being expended is four watts.

When voltage in a circuit is doubled and resistance remains unchanged, the power is doubled twice. This occurs because the doubling of voltage causes a doubling of current which therefore doubles both of the factors that determine power. In other words, the rate of change of power, in a circuit of fixed resis-

tance, is the square of the change in voltage. Thus the basic power formula P = IE may also be expressed as

$$P = E^2/R, \text{ or } P = I^2R.$$

These equations can easily be derived by simple substitution from the ones above. All these relationships are shown in the electrical equation circle illustration.

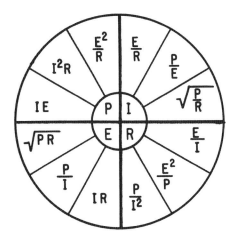

A graphic summarizing the basic formulas for Ohm's Law and for power *(P)*. In each quadrant are three formulas, each of which can be used to find the unknown factor whose symbol appears in the adjacent quadrant of the central circle.

Critical Thinking

1. List some basic safety precautions one should observe when working with any type of electrical equipment or circuitry.

2. Analogies are often drawn between the way in which water flows downhill and through pipes and the way electricity is generated and travels through wires and resistances. Describe some of these analogies and how they can be used to help understand how electricity works.

3. List the various energy transformations that take place in a conventional electrical power distribution network from the time that a fossil fuel is burned to provide energy in the generating plant until the electrical power is consumed in a person's home.

Study Guide Questions

1. What are the positive and negative charged particles in an atom?

2. What force keeps the electrons of an atom revolving in regular orbits?

3. How is electricity conveyed?

4. A. What substances are the best conductors of electricity?
   B. Why?

5. What is an insulator?

6. What is the fundamental law concerning electrical charges?

7. What unit is used to measure electromotive force?

8. What are the six common methods of producing voltage?

9. What is a thermocouple?

10. For what applications is the photoelectric cell used?

11. What is the most common source of chemically created electricity?

12. What is the unit of measure for current?

13. What is the unit of measure for resistance?

14. What factors determine the amount of resistance in a wire conductor?

15. What is an electrical circuit?

16. How does electricity flow in a circuit?

17. What is a schematic diagram?

18. A. Describe Ohm's law.
    B. What does it enable us to find?

19. What is the unit of measure for power?

20. What are the three formulas for electrical power?

Simple Circuit Problems

1. A simple circuit consists of one sixty-watt bulb and a standard 120-volt source of electricity.
   A. What is the current I in amperes?
   B. What is the resistance R in ohms?

2. A simple circuit powered by a 115-volt battery has two hundred ohms of resistance in it. What is the current I in amperes?

3. A simple battery-powered circuit has 0.75 ampere running through one 150-ohm resistor. Using this information, find the voltage of the battery.

Power Problems

1. What power in watts is being dissipated in a resistance of a hundred ohms if two amperes of current are flowing through it?

2. What is the resistance of a hundred-watt light bulb connected to a 120-volt power supply?

New Vocabulary

electricity	current
conductor	ampere
insulator	ammeter
voltage	resistance
electromotive force	ohm
thermocouple	ohmeter
photoelectric	battery
voltmeter	schematic

21

Electronics

There are a great many devices used in modern life in general and in the Navy that are based on electricity, electronics, and the electromagnetic wave. Some of these include computers, cell phones, audio equipment of all kinds, radio, television, radar, and sonar. The previous chapter of this unit covered the subject of basic electricity. In this chapter we will discuss the nature of the electromagnetic wave, upon which all of the electronic devices mentioned above are based, and some of the more common modern-day applications, including radio and radar. Computers and sonar will be discussed in the following chapters.

In general there are two kinds of waves, by type: mechanical and electromagnetic. **Mechanical waves** require some sort of material in which to travel or propagate (spread). Many of these waves can be felt and seen. Examples of this type of wave would be water waves through water, sound waves through air, or vibrations along a taut string. The other type is **electromagnetic waves,** so called because these have both electrical and magnetic components. Waves of this type are nonmaterial and cannot be directly felt or seen. They travel best through a complete vacuum, in which there is no material present. If there is material present it may impede them. Examples of this kind of wave would be radio, TV, radar, light, and infrared (heat) waves. The material or space through which waves travel is called the **medium.**

Regardless of the type of wave, all need some sort of energy source to originate. Waves can be thought of as nature's means

of dissipating energy from this source. They will continue to propagate until the energy level in the surrounding medium is the same as the energy at the source location.

Waves can also be classified by their form. There are two kinds. *Longitudinal waves* cause the medium through which they travel to be displaced back and forth along the path of the wave, like a spring bouncing back and forth. Longitudinal waves are thus mechanical waves that require a material medium to propagate. Sound is a wave of this kind. *Transverse waves* cause the medium to be displaced perpendicularly to the direction of travel of the wave, in a pattern often called a *sine wave*. They can be both mechanical and electromagnetic. Examples of this kind of wave are water waves, and waves produced in a stringed musical instrument when a string is plucked. All electromagnetic waves are also waves of this kind.

The figure on the next page depicts a sample mechanical or electromagnetic transverse, or sine, wave, and the terms used to describe it:

- A *cycle* is one complete sequence of values of the strength of the wave as it passes through a point in space.
- The *wavelength,* abbreviated in electronics by the Greek letter λ *(lambda),* is the length of a cycle expressed in

P waves are longitudinal waves

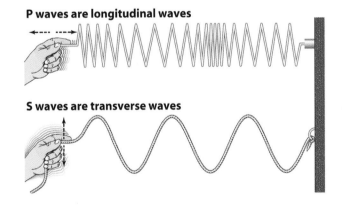

S waves are transverse waves

Illustration of a longitudinal mechanical pressure (P) wave like a sound wave and a transverse sine (S) wave like a radio wave. *www.spot.pcc.edu*

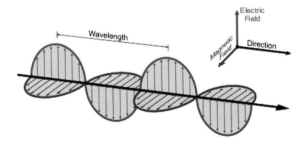

Schematic diagram of an electromagnetic wave. *NOAA*

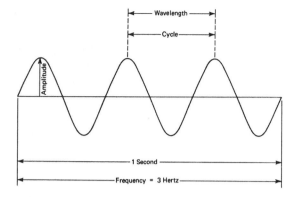

Characteristics of an electromagnetic wave with a frequency of three hertz.

distance units, usually either meters (m) or centimeters (cm, 10^{-1} m). Extremely short waves can be measured in terms of nanometers (nm, 10^{-9} m) or sometimes *angstroms* (A), a distance unit of 0.1 nanometer (10^{-10} m).

- The *amplitude* is the wave strength at particular points along the wave. It is a measure of the energy contained in the wave. Large-amplitude waves convey more energy than do those having small amplitude.
- The *frequency,* abbreviated as *f,* is the number of cycles repeated during one second of time. Since the time frame shown in the figure is one second, for example, it could be said that the frequency of the wave shown is three cycles per second.
- The *period,* abbreviated by the Greek letter τ *(tau),* is the time required to complete one cycle of the wave. In the figure, the period would be a third of a second. Period and frequency are related by the formula

$$\tau = 1/f.$$

Electromagnetic Waves

All electronic devices use electromagnetic waves as the basis of their operation. Very briefly, in an electronic device an electromagnetic wave is produced by a rapidly expanding and collapsing magnetic field, which is in turn produced by alternately energizing and deenergizing an electronic circuit especially designed to generate such waves. Such a generating circuit is often referred to as an *oscillator.* For many applications such as radio, an amplifier of some type is used to boost the power of the oscillator output, and an antenna is used to form the outgoing wave.

In the vacuum of space or in Earth's atmosphere an electromagnetic wave is theorized to travel at a velocity approaching the **speed of light,** or 3×10^8 meters per second (186,000

miles per second). Frequency and wavelength of an electromagnetic wave are related by the formula

$$\lambda = 3 \times 10^8/f,$$

where λ is the wavelength in meters and f the frequency in cycles per second. Thus, every specific electromagnetic frequency is radiated at a specific wavelength, so any given electromagnetic wave can be described either by its frequency or by its wavelength, or sometimes both. There is an inverse relationship between the two, so that as frequency increases, the wavelength gets shorter, and vice versa.

In most of the physical sciences the term **hertz**, abbreviated Hz, has come to be used in place of cycles per second, in honor of the German pioneer in electromagnetic radiation, Heinrich Hertz (1857–94). One hertz is defined as one cycle per second. Higher frequencies are expressed in terms of numbers of thousands *(kilo, k),* millions *(mega, M),* or billions *(giga, G)* of hertz. For example, ten thousand cycles per second is expressed as 10

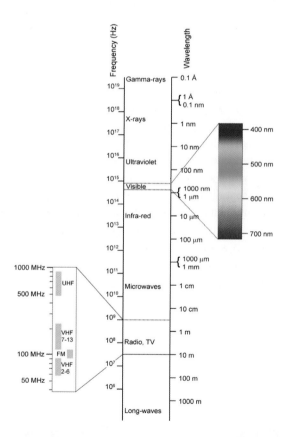

The electromagnetic spectrum. Each frequency has a corresponding wavelength. The spectrum ranges from long waves at the lower end, through radio, TV, and microwaves, then infrared, visible, and ultraviolet light, to various kinds of rays at the upper end. The expanded segments show the more commonly used radio and TV channel bands and their designations, as well as the wavelengths of the various visible light colors. *Victor Blacus*

kilohertz, abbreviated 10 kHz; 2.5 million cycles per second would be 2.5 megahertz, or 2.5 MHz.

The behavior of an electromagnetic wave is dependent upon its frequency and corresponding wavelength. For descriptive purposes, electromagnetic waves can be arranged in order of frequency and wavelength on an "electromagnetic spectrum" diagram. Electromagnetic waves are classified as *long waves* at the lower end of the spectrum; *radio waves* from about 3kHz to 300 GHz; *microwaves* from about 300 MHz to about 300 GHz; and infrared, visible, and ultraviolet *light* and various kinds of *rays* at the upper end of the spectrum. The prefix *micro* in microwaves does not designate a wavelength in the micrometer range; rather it refers to electromagnetic waves that are shorter than radio waves typically used in radio broadcasting. The boundaries on both ends of the microwave range are fairly arbitrary.

Though electromagnetic wave frequencies within the range of 20 to 20,000 Hz are sometimes called the "audible" frequencies, it must be remembered that to be heard such waves must be transformed into mechanical sound waves through devices called **speakers.**

Propagation Effects

The medium through which electromagnetic waves travel affects their path. Weather, atmospheric conditions, or obstructions can cause variation from the straight path the waves might otherwise take in a vacuum. These variations are called refraction, reflection, diffraction, and trapping.

Refraction (bending) occurs when there is a change in the density of the medium in which the wave is traveling. Take, for example, a radio wave transiting the atmosphere. Because the atmosphere gradually decreases in density with altitude, the wave is refracted, or bent downward. This increases the distance the radio wave will have to travel to get out of the atmosphere, and tends to make it bend down over the horizon and follow the

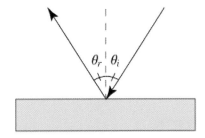

Reflection of a radio wave follows the law of reflection, which states that the angle of incidence (θ_i) is equal to the angle of reflection (θ_r).

Earth's curvature. Low-frequency waves are bent more readily than high-frequency waves, so long, low-frequency radio waves are used for long-range radars and long-distance radio communication.

Reflection of an electromagnetic wave can occur whenever it encounters a surface or other medium that it cannot easily penetrate. Like all waves, it follows the **law of reflection,** which states that the *angle of incidence* at which they hit such surfaces is equal to the *angle of reflection* off of them. In addition, radio waves transmitted from Earth's surface are reflected from the *ionosphere,* which is generally from 30 to 250 miles above Earth. The distance between the transmitter and the point where the reflected radio wave returns to the ground is called the *skip distance.*

Diffraction causes spreading of electromagnetic waves behind obstructions. It results from the generation of secondary waves by the primary wave at the edges of the obstruction.

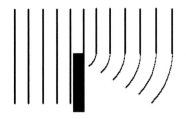

Diffraction causes spreading of electromagnetic waves behind obstructions, by means of the generation of secondary waves by the primary wave at the edge of the obstruction.

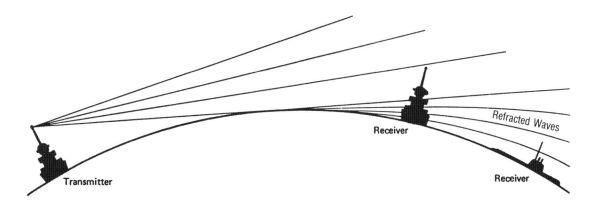

Refraction is the bending of radio waves over the horizon, extending their range to receivers beneath Earth's curvature.

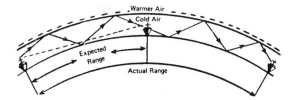

Trapping. The duct acts as a wave guide.

Trapping, sometimes called *ducting*, occurs when a temperature inversion in the atmosphere traps cold air close to Earth's surface. Under those circumstances radio signals may be reflected from the warmer air above back to Earth a number of times. This will increase the range of the transmitted signal. This trapped cold air is called a *duct*. This effect can also occur with light waves under certain circumstances.

Radio

As mentioned above, radio frequency waves are electromagnetic waves transmitted in the range from about 3 kHz to 300 GHz. On Earth most of these waves are intentionally generated by electronic devices such as radio and TV transmitters, though some are unintentional by-products of other electric and electronic gear. There are also a number of natural radio-frequency transmitters—for example, interstellar gas and celestial bodies such as planets and stars.

Although called the "radio-frequency band," there are many kinds of electronic devices whose signals are transmitted at frequencies within it that are not radios in the traditional sense. Examples include television, radar, and cellular telephones. Most of the following discussion about radio waves generally applies to all these devices as well, but there are significant differences in the way certain of them make use of the radio spectrum, particularly those that incorporate new technology developed in recent years.

Traditional radio transmissions use a series of electromagnetic waves transmitted at constant frequency and amplitude, called **continuous waves.** Because an unmodified continuous wave cannot convey much information, the wave is normally modified, or **modulated,** in some way. When this is done, the basic continuous wave is referred to as a **carrier wave.**

There are three main methods by which a carrier wave may be modulated to convey information. These are *amplitude, frequency,* and *pulse modulation.* In **amplitude modulation,** abbreviated AM, the amplitude of the carrier wave is modified in accordance with the amplitude of a modulating wave, such as voice or music. In the radio receiver the signal is *demodulated* by removing the modulating wave, which is then amplified and related to the listener by means of a speaker. This type

of modulation is widely used in the commercial radio broadcast band, with carrier wave frequencies in the range from 550—1,700 kHz. In **frequency modulation,** abbreviated FM, the frequency of the carrier wave instead of the amplitude is altered in accordance with the frequency of the modulating wave. This type of modulation is used for FM commercial radio broadcasts and the sound portion of television broadcasts, with FM radio carrier wave frequencies in the range from 88—108 MHz. As in AM radio, the FM or TV receiver demodulates and amplifies the sound modulation and conveys it to a listener via speakers. **Pulse modulation** is different from either amplitude or frequency modulation in that there is usually no impressed modulating wave. In this type of modification, the continuous wave is broken up into very short bursts, or "pulses," separated by relatively long periods of silence during which no wave is transmitted. This is the type of transmission used by most types of radars.

In radio technology, sinusoidal carrier waves and AM/FM modulations are collectively referred to as *analog waves.*

The rapid expansion of electronic digital technology over the last decade gave rise to the need to integrate digital signals into carrier-wave modulation, particularly in applications like cell phones and WiFi. Also, the technique of **multiplexing** was developed, wherein multiple analog signals and digital data streams are incorporated into a single carrier wave. For analog signals this is usually done by transmitting them on additional frequencies slightly above and below the carrier-wave frequency, and for digital data streams, embedding such signals into the modulation of the carrier wave. The multiplexed signal can then be *demultiplexed* by suitably designed receivers.

In the case of AM and FM radio, digital multiplexing gave rise to so-called *HD radio,* wherein digital audio and sometimes accompanying digital data signals are embedded into the radio signal along with the traditional analog modulation. An HD radio receiver will then play or display the digital parts of the transmission, reverting to the basic analog carrier-wave modulation whenever the digital signals cannot be received for some reason. Music transmitted digitally in this manner is said to

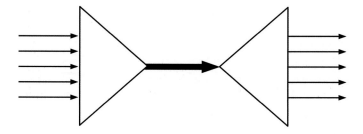

In multiplexing, multiple signals or digital data streams can be incorporated into a single carrier wave, then demultiplexed at the receiving end.
The Anome

rival CDs in quality. The "HD" in HD radio has nothing to do with HD television; it is the name applied to this technology in the United States by the company that originated it. In foreign countries different techniques are used to convey the digital portion of the signal, so different names are used for the systems, and different receivers are required.

Radio Applications

There are countless applications of radio wave technology in today's world. Radio-frequency waves are used for commercial ground-based and satellite radio and TV broadcasts, radar, wireless Internet connectivity, and voice and data transmission by all manner of consumer electronic devices, including two-way radios, cellular telephones, and computers. Other examples of common consumer products that use radio waves include microwave ovens, GPS devices, garage-door openers, and a host of portable electronic devices, like tablets and media players.

Household microwave ovens use a standardized radio frequency of 2.4 GHz, well within the lower microwave frequencies, to heat food. Water and fat molecules are particularly sensitive to electromagnetic radiation of this wavelength, readily absorbing energy from it in the form of heat. This is why foods relatively high in water and fat content heat relatively quickly in these devices, whereas other nonmetallic substances do not. Metals and other electrically conductive materials—especially wire, pointed objects, and crumpled foil—act as antenna within the oven. They quickly absorb the microwave energy and will spark, arc, and burn anything in contact, thus representing safety hazards.

Military applications of radio include radar; ground and satellite-based communication systems; weapons control systems; drone (UAV) and manned aircraft communications; control, navigation, and landing systems; guided-missile and cruise-missile guidance and control systems; and many constantly emerging new technologies.

Cellular Telephones

One of the most widely used applications of radio technology in the modern world is the cellular telephone, or **cell phone.** There are an estimated six billion cell-phone users throughout the world today, and cell-phone networks are in operation in almost every country. Various cell phone models allow for both voice and data transmission, including GPS displays, Internet links, text messages, photographic images and videos, and a wide variety of applications tailored to individual user needs.

In order to communicate with the cellular networks, each cell phone contains a miniaturized low-power *transceiver* (transmitter and receiver), an antenna, and control circuitry. Two radio frequencies are required for communications between cell phones and the base stations (transmitting towers) within the cellular network. One, called the *uplink channel,* transmits the electromagnetic radio signal from the cell phone to the nearest cell tower; the other, called the *downlink channel,* transmits signals from the towers to the cell phone. Older cell phones use analog signal modulation, but newer ones use digital modulation, greatly increasing data transmission rates and enabling the use of many additional functions besides voice transmission. The radio-frequency bands currently designated for use by cellular systems in North America range from about 700 to 2,700 MHz. Somewhat different frequency bands are used in South America, Europe, and Asia, so cell phones designed for use in the United States and Canada may not work in other countries. Worldwide travelers need specially designed multiband phones capable of "roaming" internationally.

Cell phones are so named because they operate within "cells" of communication established around each *base station,* which normally consists of a transmission tower and related equipment. In urban areas each base-station tower may have a range of up to a half-mile, while stations in rural and open areas may have ranges of from five to twenty-five miles, depending on the surface topography. Ranges are limited to these relatively short distances so that cell phone transmissions can be done at very low power levels, in order to avoid interference with adjacent cells and to extend the time that cell phones may be used before recharging their batteries. New developments in cell-

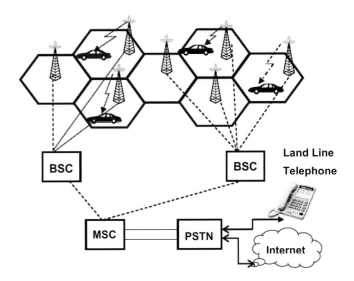

Illustration of a cell-phone network. Clusters of towers called "base stations" are connected to base station control centers (BSCs), which communicate via either microwave radio or land-line links with mobile switching centers (MSCs). These interface with the public switched telephone network (PSTN), the infrastructure that in turn connects with other MSCs, the land-line telephone system, and the Internet.
From Rao, Mobile Cellular Communications, *Fig. 1.12*

phone system technology, called 4G LTE (described below), are extending these ranges further.

Clusters of base stations are connected to *base station control centers* (BSCs), which manage the transfer of cell-phone signals from one tower to another as the user moves around within the system. The BSCs are in turn connected via either microwave radio or land-line links with *mobile switching centers* (MSCs). These interface with the public telephone network infrastructure, which in turn connects with other MSCs, the land-line telephone system, and the Internet. The MSCs maintain encrypted data bases containing the last known locations of all active cell phones within their systems, as well as user-authentication and billing information.

Radar

Radar (short for radio detection and ranging) was developed originally as a means for detecting and determining the ranges to targets in warfare. But it has since been adapted to a wide range of other applications, from speed detection to storm tracking. Radar is based on the principles that electromagnetic waves can be formed into a beam, and that some of the waves so transmitted will be reflected back if the beam encounters an object in its path.

Radar uses electromagnetic wave frequencies from 50 MHz to 40 GHz, most of them in the microwave band. The microwave band is subdivided into a number of narrower bands identified by letter designations that contain the frequencies used for different types of radars and other high-frequency radio transmissions. In general, the lower the frequency, the more the wave will bend in conformance to the curve of the Earth, and the longer will be the range of the radar.

Navy radars are grouped into three general categories: search, fire control, and special. **Search radars** are of two categories: air search and surface search. Most naval aircraft and warships are equipped with the former, and surface ships have the latter as well. Both are used for early warning, and surface-search radars are used for general navigation as well. Search radars detect targets at maximum range, at the sacrifice of some detail. They use wave frequencies from about 50 MHz to about 8 GHz. **Fire-control radars** are important parts of gun and missile fire-control systems. They are used after a target has been located by search radar to guide gunfire and other weapons to it. Because more precision is required, they use waves of relatively high frequencies, about 8–12 GHz, which form tight beams that radiate outward in almost straight lines. Precision marine navigation and mapping radars also use this frequency band. **Special radars** are used for specific purposes, which include ground-controlled approach (GCA) at airfields, carrier-controlled approach radar, and height finding. They use frequencies of about 27 GHz and higher.

A parabolic radar-dish antenna. The antenna both forms the outgoing radar beam and collects any returning echoes. Radar antennas can also take other shapes and forms, depending on the type of radar and wavelengths it uses. *CHINFO, Troy Clarke*

Radar operates very much like a sound-wave echo reflection. If you shout in the direction of a cliff, you will hear an echo of your shout return from the direction of the cliff. What actually takes place is that the sound waves generated by the shout travel through air until they strike the cliff. There they are reflected, and some return to the originating spot, where you hear them as an echo. There is a time interval between the instant you shout and when you hear the echo. The farther you are away from the cliff, the longer the interval before the echo returns. The distance to the cliff is proportional to the length of the time interval. If a directional device is built to transmit and receive this echo, it can be used to determine the direction and distance to the cliff, since we know the speed of sound.

Radar equipment works on the same principle. Pulse-modulated radio waves of extremely high frequency are beamed out, and the radar set is programmed to receive their echoes. This out-and-back cycle is repeated up to four thousand times per second. If the outgoing wave is sent into empty space, no energy is reflected back to the receiver. But if the wave strikes an object—such as an airplane, a ship, a building, or a hill—some of the energy comes back, at the speed of light, as a reflected wave.

In the case of search radar, the echoes received by the radar receiver appear as marks of light on a cathode ray tube (CRT), a device similar to a TV screen. It is commonly called a **scope,** or **PPI** (plan position indicator). The scope is marked with a scale of yards or meters, miles or kilometers (a thousand meters), and degrees. It provides a bird's eye view of the area covered by the radar, showing the transmitter in the center of the screen. Each time a target is detected it appears as an intensified spot on the scope. Thus an observer watching the PPI can tell the range and bearing to the target. Other radars can tell the altitude of incoming aircraft and missiles.

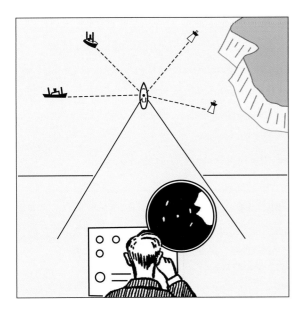

A PPI (plan position indicator) radarscope presentation. On this scope targets appear as light-colored dots called "pips." Here the inset shows the PPI scope presentation of the physical targets.

Radar in the Navy

Radar has many uses in the Navy. Surface-search and navigational radars are used extensively to assist Navy ships in navigating through constricted waters and during times of poor visibility and stormy weather, as well as tracking other shipping in the area. Air-search and height-finding radars are used to track both friendly and potentially threatening aircraft, and fire-control radars of various kinds are used to guide shipboard weapons to their targets.

The information gathered by most shipboard search radars is presented and analyzed in a space called the Combat Information Center (CIC), or in surface warships the Combat Direc-tion Center (CDC). Quite often on today's ships during General Quarters the commanding officer (CO) assumes a battle station in the CIC or CDC and leaves the executive officer as the senior officer on the bridge. As the head evaluator of the information coming into the center, the CO must quickly decide which targets to engage and with what means—aircraft, guided missiles, or radar-directed gunfire. The CO must also decide how to maneuver in order to escape or engage enemy ships, submarines, and aircraft.

Electronic Warfare

Electronic warfare (EW) refers to any action involving the use of the electromagnetic spectrum or directed electromagnetic energy to control the spectrum, attack an enemy, or impede enemy attempts to impede or prevent our own use of the spectrum. Electronic warfare can be conducted from air, sea, land, or space by manned and unmanned systems, and it can target humans, communications, computer networks, radar, or other electronic assets. Electronic warfare includes three major subdivisions: electronic attack (EA), electronic protection (EP), and electronic warfare support (ES). Electronic warfare systems include (1) collection of information on the enemy without his knowledge and without divulging one's own presence; (2) hindering or rendering the enemy's electronic spectrum useless by jamming circuits with electronic countermeasures (ECM), now referred to as *electronic attack* (EA) measures; and (3) electronic counter-countermeasures (ECCM), now called *electronic protection* (EP), which ensure the continued use of our electronic spectrum in spite of any enemy attempts to direct EA against it. *Electronic warfare support* (ES) is the subdivision of electronic warfare involving actions to search for, intercept, identify, and locate sources of intentional and unintentional radiated electromagnetic energy, for the purposes of threat recognition, targeting, planning, and conduct of future operations.

Critical Thinking

1. Why is a basic understanding of electronics important for almost everyone in today's society?

Study Guide Questions

1. A. What are the two types of waves?
   B. What are the two forms these waves can take?

2. A. What is the standard unit of measurement of frequency?
   B. What does this measurement represent?

3. What is the audible frequency range?

4. What four variations from the straight wave path are caused by atmospheric or weather elements?

5. Define the following wave terms:
   A. Cycle
   B. Wavelength
   C. Amplitude
   D. Period.

6. What range of frequencies in the electromagnetic spectrum comprise radio waves?

7. What basic methods are used to modulate a radio wave?

8. What is multiplexing?

9. What are some of the military applications of radio?

10. Why are cell phones so named?

11. What is the fundamental principle of radar?

12. What are the three general categories of U.S. Navy radars?

13. What does a fire-control radar do?

14. What are the functions of EA, EP, and ES?

New Vocabulary

electromagnetic wave	frequency modulation
medium (waves)	pulse modulation
wavelength (radio wave)	multiplexing
amplitude	microwave oven
frequency	cell phone
hertz	radar
microwave	search radar
diffraction	fire-control radar
trapping	electronic warfare
continuous wave	jamming
modulation	electronic attack
carrier wave	electronic protection
amplitude modulation	electronic warfare support

22

Computers and the Internet

A *computer* is a device that can carry out a finite set of arithmetical or logical operations. The **electronic digital computer,** the most common type of modern computer, consists of at least one processing element, called a *central processing unit* (CPU), and some form of memory. It may have additional internal components, such as *modems* for communication or secondary memory for data storage. *Peripheral devices* (external components attached to the computer wirelessly or with cables) enable information to be input or output, stored, retrieved, transmitted, displayed, or printed.

The first electronic digital computers were developed in the United Kingdom and the United States in the early 1940s. They were made of vacuum tubes, were about the size of a small room, and consumed vastly more power than modern computers. Since the advent of the digital computer, constant advances in solid state electronics technology have made possible corresponding advances in architecture, size, and operation, to the point where modern computers bear little resemblance to the early prototypes.

Modern Digital Computers

Modern digital computers are based on **integrated circuits** (a set of electronic components connected by ultrathin conductors printed on small silicon wafers called *chips*). Several chips may be combined with other electronic components on a printed circuit board, groups of which make up the various components of the computer. These chips are millions of times faster and more capable than the vacuum-tube components of the early computers built in the 1940s.

Digital computers can be programmed using a variety of machine and computer languages to perform limitless tasks. It is difficult to think of many aspects of life in the modern-day world that are not affected in some way or another by computers. Common uses range from information processing, computation, social networking, and communication using small desktop **personal computers** (PCs) and portable **laptop** computers to large applications, such as corporate and government accounting, transaction processing, and high-capacity data processing, using large, immobile computers called **main frames.** In industry, computers are widely used to control all manner of manufacturing processes, and electrical grids rely on them to control and regulate the production and transmission of electrical power. They are integral parts of almost all motor vehicles,

The ENIAC computer, built in 1946 at the University of Pennsylvania. It was one of the world's first prototype electronic computers.
U.S. Army photo

RADM Grace Hopper (1906–92) played a leading role in the development of the electronic computer. She helped to design and build early prototypes in the 1950s and later the first compiler and the first widely used computer programming languages, COBOL and FORTRAN, in the 1960s. After her retirement in 1986 she continued to work in the computer industry as a consultant until her death in 1992. *The Naval History and Heritage Command*

airplanes, and ships. Computers are also used as components in consumer electronic devices, such as smartphones, tablets, digital music players, and GPS units. Computers can communicate with one another and be linked together via specially designed computer data networks and the Internet (described below).

Individuals operate computers by means of user-friendly **operating system programs,** such as Microsoft Windows and Apple Mac OS, that control applications and continuously monitor all critical computer systems and functions. Programming that controls computers and their processes and enables them to perform tasks is collectively called **software,** and all physical components of computers and devices attached to them that carry out the programming are collectively referred to as **hardware.**

A typical laptop computer, with screen and integral keyboard. *Hewlett-Packard*

Computer Architecture

Electronic digital computers are designed to perform computations and store data on the basis of the **binary number system,** wherein all numbers are represented as powers of two, using only the digits 0 and 1. In computers this corresponds to processing and storage elements that have either no charge (0) or some charge (1), or in some cases, two different standard charges. Computers perform these discrete binary computations millions, even billions of times per second using groups of eight such binary numbers, called **bytes** (B). Each byte is therefore able to represent 2^8 or 256 different numbers. To represent larger numbers, several consecutive bytes may be used. Fractions are represented by fractional powers of two (represented digitally) and negative numbers by an auxiliary data bit. All keyboard functions, such as spacing, and data, such as letters, special characters and multimedia objects (images, video

A typical personal computer (PC), with separate monitor, keyboard, and mouse. There are also newer types called "all-in-ones" that combine the monitor and computer in a single module. *Hewlett-Packard*

and sound recordings), and color hues are linked, or *coded,* to unique combinations of these numbers. A single function or character might take a single byte to encode, while other data may take multiple bytes. Standards for this coding include *ASCII* (American Standard Code for Information Exchange) for keyboard functions and characters, *JPEG* (Joint Photographic Experts Group) for images, and *MPEG* (Moving Picture Experts Group) for video.

Digital computers are rated according to their computational speed and memory capacity. **Computer speed** is expressed as the number of computational cycles that the computer's CPU can perform per second, expressed in Hertz (Hz). Early computers operated in the kilohertz (KHz) range (thousands of cycles per second), but over time computational speeds increased into the millions (MHz) and later billions (GHz) of cycles per second.

Computer memory capacity is expressed in multiples of the number of bytes that can be stored. Early computer memories were limited to a few thousand bytes (kilobytes, KB), but over time memory capacities increased exponentially into the millions (megabytes, MB), billions (gigabytes, GB), and trillions (terabytes, TB) of bytes. In the computer technology world, these memory capacities are expressed in powers of two, in keeping with the binary system, so that a kilobyte of memory capacity is actually defined as 2^{10} (1,024) bytes, a megabyte as 2^{20} (1,048,576) bytes, and so on. For all other computer applications, however, these large numbers are expressed in the traditional way, as powers of ten.

The *internal,* or *main, memory* of a digital computer is accessed directly by the CPU and is located close to it so as to minimize data-transmission time. Memories are made up of a large number of microscopic semiconductor cells called *random access memory* (RAM). Computers also have *secondary memories,* in which much larger quantities of data may be stored, usually in the form of devices called **hard drives.** For many years hard drives contained rapidly rotating discs coated with magnetic material so their data would not be lost when the computer was powered down. More recent hard-drive technology is based on solid-state memory that does not use rotating discs. Solid-state memory allows for faster access, creates less heat, and is more durable than traditional spinning hard drives. Main-memory access times are measured in nanoseconds (billionths of a second), whereas secondary memory speeds were traditionally measured in milliseconds (thousandths of a second). That is why it sometimes takes a relatively long time to start up, or *boot,* some older computers, as their start-up programming is stored in secondary storage. Modern secondary memory speeds are much faster.

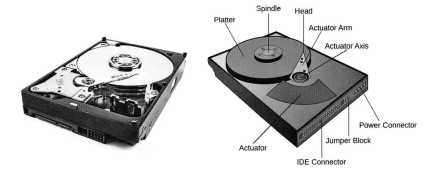

Left: A typical mechanical hard drive. *William Warby*
Right: A schematic identifying the parts of a mechanical hard drive. *Surachit*

As previously mentioned, computers interface with the external world by means of input/output devices called **peripherals.** These include such hardware as the keyboard and computer mouse, monitors, printers, microphones and speakers, cameras, and auxiliary storage media, such as CD and DVD drives. Almost all peripherals can now be connected to the computer either by cables or wirelessly. They interface with the computer through software called **device drivers** that act as translators between the peripheral devices and the applications or operating-systems programming that use them.

In addition to electronic digital computers, there is another type of computer, called an **analog computer**, which can be electronic or electrical (using electrical current), hydraulic (using water or oil), or mechanical (using a system of gears and levers or slide-rule or circular scales). Analog computers are called that because they can simulate mathematical calculations or the physical behavior of mechanical systems by *analogous* current or fluid flow through a properly designed array of components, or gear rotations, or scale manipulations. Analog computers were once widely used as thermostats, for process control, military aircraft bombsights, and large-caliber naval gunfire control and torpedo solutions on surface warships and submarines. Math calculations done by students, engineers, and scientists were done using linear or circular *slide rules.* The superior capabilities of modern digital computers, controllers, and electronic calculators in all these applications have reduced present-day analog computer use to a few specialized needs.

As in the civilian world, computers are extensively used in the Navy and Marine Corps for a wide variety of applications both ashore and afloat. They are integral parts of almost every major shipboard system and enable instant communications

A GTE EA22 analog computer built in the 1960s. Circuits built of plug-in wires and electronic components on its face could simulate the behavior of many kinds of mechanical systems. *Technikum29*

between sailors at sea, Marines on deployment, and their families at home. They are also used for many applications in naval aircraft, cruise missiles, and guided munitions of all kinds.

The Internet

Although some attempts were made in the 1950s to link computers together after their prototypes were developed a decade earlier, the birth of the modern **Internet** occurred in the 1960s with work funded by the Defense Advanced Research Projects Agency (DARPA). DARPA's efforts led to the development of the first computer network, intended to facilitate communication and research among various federal government agencies and contractors. It was called the *ARPANET.* By the end of 1969 there were four host computers linked together in the fledgling network. It grew to hundreds of linked computers a few years later.

Though originally restricted to Department of Defense users, soon the ARPANET's usefulness convinced many other potential user communities to build additional networks, wherever funding could be obtained for the purpose. Soon the need for a standardized system of network operating procedures to link various networks together became obvious. By the late 1970s the first such network standards had been developed and implemented, under the leadership of DARPA.

From the beginning, computer networks were extensively used for messaging among remote users. Although at first they had no established format, eventually these messages became standardized and were called *electronic mail,* or e-mail**s.** At first such communication over the ARPANET was done between host names assigned by a monitoring Stanford University research group, but this quickly became cumbersome, leading to the establishment of the **Domain Name System** in 1983. This is a standardized system of addresses wherein various types of information, or *domains,* are associated with multi-level *domain names* assigned to the various entities, such as individual computers, servers (described below), or **websites** (network locations where information is stored) that support them. Domain names provide easy human-friendly linkage to corresponding thirty-two-bit numerical *Internet Protocol* (IP) addresses needed by computers to identify and access interconnected computers and other entities and devices on the network worldwide. Examples of top-level domain names most commonly used in the United States are gov, edu, com, mil, org, and net; there are currently about fifteen others as well. In late 2013 it was announced that over the next few years some 1,400 new "strings" (names) of various lengths would be added, some them in Arabic, Cyrillic, and Chinese. For communications between users in different countries, there are also some 250 top-level two-letter *country codes*, such as uk for the United Kingdom and fr for France. Lower-level domain names are progressively added to the left of the top-level domain names and separated by a period, called a "dot." There are an infinite variety of domain names. They are administered by a number of government and private organizations called *domain name registrars,* and they range from e-mail addresses assigned by e-mail mailbox providers to registered domain names based on the titles of entities such as a commercial company or government organization—as, for example, irs.gov (the U.S. government's Internal Revenue Service).

As the number of interlinked computer systems continued to grow in the mid-1980s, facilitated by such standardization as the domain-name system, the term *Internet* came into common usage as an abbreviation of the term "internetworking," which had been used up to that point for such networks. In the late 1980s the term *World Wide Web* (www) was coined by a contractor at the CERN atomic research facility in Switzerland. It subsequently became the prefix for all Internet addresses and has often come to be used as a synonym for the Internet itself, though the web is actually a service that operates over the Internet, like e-mail. The underlying set of standard procedures by which the World Wide Web operates is called the *Hyper Text Transfer Protocol* (http). This protocol defines how transmissions on the Internet are formatted and transmitted and what actions web servers and search programs (described below) should take in response to various user commands. The letters "http" or "https" precede all Internet website addresses accessed by Internet users, with the latter designation used for secure sites.

Servers

A **server** is a system of software run on one or more linked computers to provide a resource to a user on a computer network and/or the Internet. They may serve limited users within a large organization, such as a government department, or general-

A typical main-frame server rack.
Edmondo

public users via the Internet. There are database servers, e-mail servers, web servers, and gaming servers, among many others.

Any computer may function as a server, but those supporting large networks and the Internet are typically main-frame computers with features such as faster CPUs, huge memory capacities, multiple hard drives, and redundant power supplies. Like other network components, each server is given a numerical IP address that allows it to be accessed by any qualified user.

Internet Features

A major milestone for the Internet was the development of the **browser,** a software tool used to locate information on the web. Rudimentary browsers were developed in the 1980s, but the first of the more capable browsers that popularized the World Wide Web was developed in 1993 by a computer-applications group at the University of Illinois. It formed the basis for more sophisticated browsers and modern **search engines** (computer-based software designed to facilitate key-word Internet searches) developed commercially by Netscape, Microsoft Corporation, and others in the years since.

A second major milestone for the Internet in the mid-1990s was the formation of commercial companies, called *Internet service providers* (ISPs), that facilitated consumer access to the Internet. They provided access at first via standard telephone lines, and later by high-speed service via telephone lines or TV cable or broadband wireless transmission, described below. A key service of ISPs is to assign email addresses to their clients and to provide e-mail mailbox hosting services for them, via servers that send, receive, accept, and store their e-mails. ISPs also enable clients to use various commercially available browsers and search engines to research and access whatever information they might desire and to enable such services as *webcasting* (broadcasts delivered via the Internet), Internet-based voice and video telephone service, and *instant messaging* (IM).

A more recent milestone for Internet technology with great promise for the future is the increasing use of so-called **cloud computing,** wherein application programming and data is stored on a number of remote sites accessible via the Internet and referred to as "the cloud," as opposed to on a user's own device. This greatly increases the capabilities of these devices while decreasing their cost and making better more efficient use of available Internet resources.

Connectivity to the Internet may be done in a variety of ways and using a number of different types of devices, ranging from personal and lap-top computers to cell phones and tablcts. Methods of connection include *traditional telephone lines* (**dial-up** and **DSL**), dedicated *hard-wired lines* (e.g., **Ethernet**), television *coaxial cable service,* and *wireless radio* (**WiFi**) transmission. Dial-up telephone allows only *narrowband* transmission, versus *broadband* in the case of DSL (Digital Subscriber Line) and the other three.

The term **broadband** refers to the simultaneous use of a broad range of carrier-wave frequencies with bandwidths of 6 MHz. This allows at least 1.5 megabits (1.5 million bits) of information or higher to be transmitted each second, as opposed to a maximum of 56 kilobits (56 thousand bits) per second for **narrowband** dial-up telephone, which uses a single carrier-wave frequency with a bandwidth of only 3 kHz. Modern-day **fourth-generation (4G)** WiFi (*Wireless Fidelity)* peak download rates are as high as 1 gigabits (1 billion bits) per second. Thus, a modern 4G WiFi system can transmit about 18,000 times more bits per second than traditional voice telephone service, though for data the download rates are typically much slower. A recent technology upgrade to 4G networks called **LTE** (Long Term Evolution) achieves increased data upload and download speeds through use of new digital signal processing (DSP) technology.

The Internet itself has no formal international governing or regulating body. Each of the various computer networks that make it up sets its own policies, with guidance and regulation by the various countries in which they are located. The only restriction is that each network must conform to the established Internet Protocol address and domain-name systems. It is estimated that over a third of the world's current population of seven billion now makes use of the Internet, an amazing increase from the few thousands of mostly scientific and military users at its beginnings in the early 1990s. Satellite-based communication systems facilitate its use worldwide and by American military personnel wherever they may be on land, at sea, and in the air. Its use has even been extended into near-Earth space, with the installation of Internet links aboard the International Space Station in 2010.

Information technology (IT) refers to anything related to computing or networking technology, such as hardware, software, the Internet, or the people who work in these fields. Most government agencies and many private companies have IT departments for managing and supporting the computer and networking facilities within their organizations.

Cyberspace and Security

The sum total of all the world's computers, servers, and networks interconnecting these is called **cyberspace.** Despite all the advances in communication and dissemination of knowledge and scientific advances made possible for legitimate users of cyberspace, there are, unfortunately, those who would try to do damage to it or use it for illegal gain. Individuals who engage in this kind of illegitimate activity are called **hackers.** Sometimes they attempt to break into various kinds of financial networks to steal personal information (called **identity theft**) or divert funds for illicit personal gain, or into corporate, industrial, or government systems to conduct espionage (spying). Others try to infect various systems with "glitch" programs called **viruses** that partially or completely impair the systems or the computers in them. Such attempts by extremists or terrorists in furtherance of their objectives are called **cyber terrorism;** if done by foreign governments or other foreign entities on a large scale, they are called **cyber warfare.**

Countermeasures against this activity, including but not limited to such measures as *data encryption, antivirus programming,* and *firewalling* (isolating sensitive data and programming from outside interactions) is called **cyber security.** There are a number of both government and private organizations that are engaged in this endeavor. They include the U.S. Cyber Command for military applications, and for other user communities the Department of Homeland Security, federal, state, and local law enforcement agencies, and a number of corporate and industrial groups and commercial firms. The U.S. Cyber Command has components within each of the military services.

Critical Thinking

1. Identify and describe the major advances in computer technology that you think will happen by the year 2100.

2. Investigate what academic qualifications are necessary for a career in computer science, and what opportunities exist for employment as an IT professional.

Study Questions

1. A. What are the main components of a modern electronic digital computer?
   B. What number system is the basis for all operations performed within a computer?

2. A. What are computer peripherals?
   B. How are they accessed by the computer's operating system programming?

3. What is an analog computer?

4. What early Defense Department computer system was the forerunner of the modern-day Internet?

5. What is a server?

6. A. What is a browser?
   B. What is a search engine?

7. What is cloud computing?

8. What do the terms "broadband" and "narrowband" mean?

9. What does the term "information technology" (IT) relate to?

10. What is cyberspace?

11. A. What are large-scale attempts by foreign countries to damage U.S. computer networks called?
    B. What are countermeasures against this called?

New Vocabulary

central processing unit (CPU)
modem
peripheral device
integrated circuits
personal computer (PC)
laptop computer
main frame computer
operating system
software (computer)
hardware (computer)
binary numbers
byte
random access memory (RAM)
hard drives
device driver

analog computer
e-mails
website
server (computer)
browser
search engine
Internet service provider (ISP)
webcasting
cloud
computer broadband
information technology (IP)
hacker, -s
identity theft
cyber terrorism

23

Sound and Sonar

Earlier in this unit we described the different forms that wave energy can take. Classified by type, these are mechanical and electromagnetic waves. **Sound** is a mechanical wave. Like all waves, it originates at a source of energy, which in the case of sound causes matter to vibrate. These vibrations are passed along into the material surrounding the source—the medium—in the form of a series of longitudinal (in the direction of travel) pressure waves. Each wave carries with it a certain amount of energy imparted to it by the source as it vibrates. Once started, if the medium through which it travels is of uniform temperature and density, the individual waves spread through the medium in the form of expanding three-dimensional spheres, much like ripples expanding over a two-dimensional water surface from the point of impact of a stone.

Because the available energy in the wave is spread over an ever-increasing area as each sphere expands, with the area of a sphere being $4\pi r^2$, the energy per unit area falls off rapidly as the distance (the radius, r) from the sound source increases. The amount of energy or power in a sound wave at any given location is called the **sound intensity.** It is expressed in terms of watts per square centimeter or per square meter. In order for a human to hear a sound, it must hit the eardrum with an intensity of at least 10^{-12} watts per square meter. Anything less will not deflect the eardrum sufficiently for the sound to be heard.

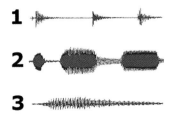

Representation of three longitudinal mechanical-pressure sound waves from a drum (1), a French horn, (2) and a flute (3), plotted as amplitude (vertical scale) vs time (horizontal scale). *Cralize*

A human's ability to hear a sound also depends on the frequency of the sound, or the number of times per second that a sound wave passes by. As was also stated earlier, the audible frequency range for the human ear is 20 to 20,000 Hz. Sounds in the extreme high and low ends of this frequency range require more power per unit area to be heard than do sounds in the mid-range.

The Physics of Sound

Because sound is a mechanical wave that propagates in a material medium, it stands to reason that the more material there is per unit volume in the medium—in other words, the greater its density—the more readily sound will travel through it. Because of the increase in molecular motion within a material as temperature increases, temperature of the medium also affects sound transmission. Sound travels better within a given material if its temperature is higher than when its temperature is lower. The table below gives the speed of sound in meters per second at sea level for different materials at different temperatures:

MATERIAL	SPEED OF SOUND (M/SEC)
Air at 0 degrees C	332
Air at 20 degrees C	344
Air at 100 degrees C	392
Kerosene at 25 degrees C	1,324
Water at 25 degrees C	1,498
Wood (oak)	3,850
Steel	5,200

Sound waves exhibit the same general behavior as other types of waves. They can be reflected by media having a significantly greater density than the mediums they originate in, as, for example, when a sound wave traveling through air hits the wall of a room. The reflected sound is called an **echo.** Sound waves can be bent or refracted as they pass from one medium to another, if the densities are not too dissimilar. They can also be diffracted, spreading after they pass through a narrow opening. They obey the formula

$$V = f\lambda,$$

where V is the velocity of the wave, f is its frequency, and λ is the wavelength. Thus, if we know the speed of sound for a given medium and either the frequency or wavelength, we can easily calculate the unknown quantity. When a sound wave is reflected from an object creating an echo, one can easily compute the distance to the object if the speed of sound in the medium containing it is known, using the simple formula

$$\textbf{Distance = rate} \times \textbf{time.}$$

For instance, if the speed of sound in air is 344 m/sec and it takes four seconds for an echo to return to a source, then the one-way distance is (4 sec ÷ 2) × 344 m/sec = 688 meters. Besides specifying the intensity of a sound in terms of its power per unit area, as described above, there is another widely used measure of sound intensity relative to the quietest sound the ear can hear. This measure, called *relative intensity,* or noise level, is calculated in units called decibels. A sound having 0 decibels is equal in intensity to the lowest that can be heard, 10^{-12} watts per square meter (W/m^2). On the decibel scale a sound of a hundred decibels would be 10^{10} times as intense as a sound of 0 decibels, or 10^{-2} W/m^2. A sound of 120 decibels is the loudest sound that the ear can stand without pain; above that, the eardrum begins to tear. Sound decibel levels that are negative indicate a sound that is too faint to be heard without amplification—for example, distant fish sounds in the ocean.

The Physiology of Sound

Without a human ear to hear a sound wave there would be no sound, only noise. The sound waves are gathered and funneled by the outer ear into an opening through the skull called the *ear canal.* At the inner end of the ear canal is a very thin and very sensitive membrane called the *eardrum.* Its extreme sensitivity is indicated by the fact that, as stated above, it can detect sound intensities of 10^{-12} watts per square meter, equivalent to a pressure of only 2×10^{-5} newtons (the metric unit of force) per square meter—a pressure level that will displace the eardrum only about a billionth of a centimeter! It is obvious that you should be very careful to protect your eardrums from loud or highly focused sound, such as that produced by highly amplified music or earphones.

Beyond the eardrum is the *middle ear.* Here three delicate bones called the "hammer," "anvil," and "stirrup" transmit the sound from the eardrum to the inner ear, where a liquid-filled structure called the *cochlea* is located. Sound vibrations in the liquid are sensed by special cells that translate the mechanical vibrations to electromagnetic nerve impulses. These impulses

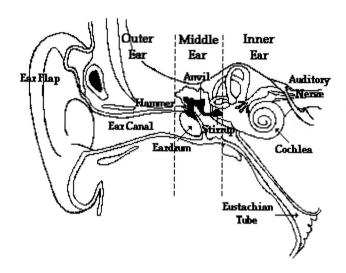

Physiology of the ear. *Encyclopedia of Science*

travel through the auditory nerve to the brain, which interprets them as sound.

Some animals, such as bats and dogs, have ears that are sensitive to sounds above the 20,000 Hz upper frequency limit that humans can hear. Sounds in this region are called ultrasound. Bats use these high intensities to navigate by means of echoes returned from objects around them, and dog owners may use ultrasonic dog whistles to call their pets.

The Doppler Shift

You may have noticed the apparent change in frequency or *pitch* of a train whistle or automobile horn as the train or auto approaches, passes, and departs. Actually, there is no change in the frequency emitted by the source. There is, however, a change in the frequency reaching the ear, because of the relative motion between the source and you. As the train or auto approaches, the effect is of an increase in frequency caused by compression of the distance between waves. When the source is opposite you, you hear the frequency the whistle or horn actually puts out. When the train or auto moves away, the effect is to increase the distance between waves, thus causing a decrease in the frequency reaching your ear. This phenomenon is known as the Doppler effect, named for the Austrian physicist Christian Doppler (1803–53). The change between the highest and lowest frequencies heard and the source frequency is called the Doppler shift.

The Doppler shift can be used to determine the speed and direction of motion of a sound's source, such as a submarine in the ocean. This phenomenon also occurs with electromagnetic waves, such as radio and light. By analyzing the Doppler shift in light from a distant star, for instance, astronomers can determine the speed at which it is moving away from us. Radar

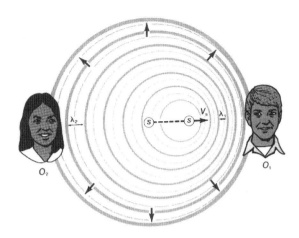

An illustration of the Doppler effect. As the sound source *S* moves to the right, observer O_1 hears a higher frequency than observer O_2 because of the compression of the sound's wavelength λ_1 as the source approaches. The observer O_2 hears a lower frequency because of the stretching of the wavelength λ_2 resulting from the source's motion away. The difference between the frequencies heard by the two observers and the source frequency is called the Doppler effect. *From Leyden et al.,* Introduction to Physical Science

detectors use the Doppler shift to determine the speed of baseballs and automobiles, as well as wind speeds in storms.

Sound in the Sea

Since Navy ships and submarines operate in the sea, the characteristics of sound in seawater are of special interest to Navy people. The speed of sound waves traveling through seawater is affected by three factors: (1) its temperature; (2) its pressure, a function of depth; and (3) its salinity, or salt content.

Temperature is by far the most important of these factors. The speed of sound changes from four to eight feet per second for every degree of temperature change. The temperature of the sea varies from freezing in the polar seas to more than 85 degrees F in the tropics. It may decrease by more than thirty degrees from the surface to a depth of 450 feet. So temperature changes in the sea have a great effect on the speed of sound in the seawater.

Sound also travels faster in water under pressure, since the density increases somewhat as pressure increases. Pressure increases as depth increases, so the deeper a sound wave is, the faster it travels. This pressure effect is smaller than temperature effect, but it cannot be neglected, since it increases about two feet per second for each hundred feet of depth.

Seawater has high mineral content, or salinity. The density of seawater is about sixty-four pounds per cubic foot; that of fresh water is only about 62.4 pounds per cubic foot. This vari-

ation is the result of the salt content in the seawater. The saltier the water, the greater its density, and hence the faster the speed of sound in it. The speed of sound increases about four feet per second for each part-per-thousand increase in salinity—a lesser effect than that of temperature but greater than that of pressure.

Sonar

The principal means of detecting and tracking submarines at sea is called **sonar** (short for sound navigation and ranging). The earliest sonar device, used in World War I, was a simple hydrophone that could be lowered into the water to listen for noises generated by submerged submarines. Three ships equipped with this equipment could, working together, pinpoint the location of U-boats by *triangulation*—plotting the bearings of the hydrophone noise from the three ships and seeing where the bearings crossed.

Today's sonar gear is much more sophisticated. It provides highly accurate ranges and bearings to the submerged submarine. Analysis of Doppler data provides accurate courses and speeds for the submarine. The sonar information is normally presented visually on a CRT screen rather than by sound, as the early devices did. In addition, very sophisticated sonars for use by helicopters and fixed-wing aircraft have been developed.

There are two basic modes of operation of sonar systems employed for the detection of targets. They are referred to as active and passive.

Active sonars transmit underwater sound pulses that strike targets and return in the form of echoes. The returned echoes indicate the range and bearing of the target. Surface undersea warfare (USW) ships often employ the active (pinging) mode when seeking out submarines. Active sonar is also used by submarines and ships to analyze shorelines, bottom characteristics, and ocean depths. Submarines can switch to active modes to locate ships or other submarines, but they rarely do so, because it would give away their locations.

Passive sonars do not transmit sound. They only listen for sounds produced by the target and from them obtain accurate bearing and estimated range information. Target detection is achieved at great ranges through the use of highly sensitive hydrophones. Passive sonar is the normal mode used by submarines, but surface ships can employ passive modes in addition to their active sonar. USW aircraft, helicopters, and shore stations also use passive sonar. A prime example of the latter was a once-secret extensive array of hydrophones placed along the seabed by the Navy in the northern Atlantic and Pacific oceans to track Soviet submarines during the Cold War. It could pick up, identify, and track many of the submarines sometimes at distances of hundreds of miles based on the unique sound characteristics each emitted. Called the SOSUS (Sound Surveillance System), much of it was deactivated after the end of the Cold

Bow-mounted sonar dome on the guided-missile destroyer *Lassen*, in dry dock at Yokosuka, Japan. *Kenneth Abbate*

A Navy helicopter lowering a dipping sonar during an undersea warfare exercise. *CHINFO*

War, but there are still three facilities in operation—at Dam Neck, Virginia; Whidbey Island, Washington; and St. Mawgan, in southwest England. They are now used mostly to track migrating whales and detect illegal driftnet fishing on the high seas.

For many years most shipboard sonar systems were mounted in domes beneath USW ships' bows or mounted on submarines' hulls and were therefore called **hull-mounted systems.** In more recent years a type of passive sonar system called a **towed array** has also been installed in many USW surface ships and submarines. This consists of a semibuoyant tube several thousand feet long that is fitted with numerous hydrophones. The tube is unreeled and towed behind the ship or submarine. Such an array is extremely sensitive and can pick up noise generated by submarines operating many miles away.

Sonar equipment called **dipping sonar** can be used by helicopters to detect submerged submarines. The helicopter can hover and lower a hydrophone or pinging transducer into the sea to a depth of about four hundred feet. The sonar searches a 360-degree area. After searching, the helicopter hauls in the cable and goes quickly to another spot. When a submarine is detected, the helicopter can attack it with homing torpedoes or bring in other USW units to assist.

Radio sonobuoys are small, expendable floating hydrophone units that are dropped in the area of a suspected submarine, usually by aircraft. They are dropped one at a time in a circular pattern around the contact area. By analysis of the radio signals received from each sonobuoy, the location and direction of movement of the submarine can be determined. It can then be attacked by the aircraft itself or by other available USW forces.

Most ships and many pleasure craft have on board a **fathometer** (echo sounder) for determining water depth under the hull. A sound pulse is transmitted toward the bottom, and its echo is received back. The water depth is then displayed on a

LED screen, along with the bottom contour. The fathometer is normally used as a navigational aid, particularly when entering shallow water. It also is used regularly in oceanographic research to determine the contour of the sea bottom. Most Navy ships keep their fathometer on continuously to have an accurate recording of the water depths on their course. The information can be displayed numerically and stored for later analysis. A variety of fathometer called a *fish finder* is used by many fishermen to locate schools of fish beneath their boat; in addition to the water depth, the fish-finder screen displays echoes returned from fish as separate dots drifting across it above the bottom contour line.

A Navy aviation ordnanceman loads sonobuoys into the belly of a Navy P-3 Orion aircraft searching for the lost Malaysia Flight 370 airliner in the Indian Ocean in April 2014. *CHINFO, Keith DeVinney*

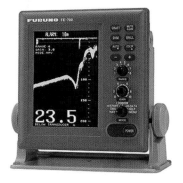

The Furuno Model FE-700 fathometer, typical of the type used by Navy surface ships. *Furuno product catalog*

An LED display of a typical fish finder, a product of Piranha Technologies Inc. *Piranha Technologies*

Critical Thinking

1. Compare and contrast the similarities and differences between a mechanical sound wave and an electromagnetic wave like light or radio.

2. In this chapter the Doppler shift principle was explained relative to the behavior of sound. Research how the same principles can be used with electromagnetic radiations such as radar and light to determine the same kinds of information.

Study Guide Questions

1. A. What kind of a wave is sound?
   B. What form do sound waves have?

2. How does sound spread through a uniform medium?

3. A. What is the minimum intensity in watts/m^2 that a sound must have in order to be heard?
   B. What pressure in newtons/m^2 does this correspond to?

4. What is the audible frequency range?

5. In what units is relative intensity or noise level measured?

6. Why should people be careful to protect their eardrums against loud sounds?

7. A. What is the apparent frequency shift of a passing whistle or horn called?
   B. What causes this shift?

8. What three factors affect the speed of sound in water?

9. What does the Doppler effect enable a sonar technician to do when analyzing returning sonar echoes from a submarine?

10. What are two modes of operation of shipboard sonar systems?

11. Why do submarines rarely use active sonar?

12. How do helicopters use sonar to detect submarines?

New Vocabulary

sound intensity	active sonar
eardrum	passive sonar
ear canal	sonobuoy
inner ear	fathometer
hydrophone	fish finder

Bibliography

Maritime History

Books

American Military History. Washington, D.C.: Center of Military History, U.S. Army, 1989.

Bradford, James C., ed. *Admirals of the New Steel Navy, 1880–1930.* Annapolis, Md.: Naval Institute Press, 1990.

———. *Captains of the Old Steam Navy, 1840–1880.* Annapolis, Md.: Naval Institute Press, 1986.

———. *Command under Sail: Makers of the American Naval Tradition, 1775–1850.* Annapolis, Md.: Naval Institute Press, 1985.

Cutler, Thomas. *Brown Water, Black Berets: Coastal and Riverine Warfare in Vietnam.* Annapolis, Md.: Naval Institute Press, 1988.

Dull, Paul S. *A Battle History of the Imperial Japanese Navy, 1941–1945.* Annapolis, Md.: Naval Institute Press, 2007.

Engle, Eloise, and Arnold S. Lott. *America's Maritime Heritage.* Annapolis, Md.: Naval Institute Press, 1975.

Luraghi, Raimondo. *A History of the Confederate Navy.* Annapolis, Md.: Naval Institute Press, 1996.

Lyon, Jane D. *Clipper Ships and Captains.* New York: American Heritage, 1962.

Miller, Edward S. *War Plan Orange: The U.S. Strategy to Defeat Japan, 1897–1945.* Annapolis, Md.: Naval Institute Press, 2007.

Miller, Nathan. *The U.S. Navy: A History.* 3rd ed. Annapolis, Md.: Naval Institute Press, 1997.

Morison, Samuel Eliot. *The Two-Ocean War.* Boston: Little, Brown, 1963.

Polmar, Norman, Eric Wertheim, Andrew Bahjat, and Bruce W. Watson, Jr. *Chronology of the Cold War at Sea, 1945–1991.* Annapolis, Md.: Naval Institute Press, 1997.

Potter, E. B., ed. *Sea Power.* 2nd ed. Annapolis, Md.: Naval Institute Press, 1981.

Pratt, Fletcher. *The Compact History of the United States Navy.* 3rd ed. New York: Hawthorne Books, 1967.

Rickover, H. G. *How the Battleship* Maine *Was Destroyed.* Annapolis, Md.: Naval Institute Press, 1976.

Ridgway, GEN Matthew B., USA (Ret.). *The Korean War.* Garden City, N.Y.: Doubleday, 1967.

Robinson, Charles M., III. *Shark of the Confederacy: The Story of the CSS* Alabama. Annapolis, Md.: Naval Institute Press, 1994.

Rodgers, VADM William L. *Greek and Roman Naval Warfare.* Annapolis, Md.: Naval Institute Press, 1964.

Rohwer, Jürgen. *War at Sea, 1939–1945.* Annapolis, Md.: Naval Institute Press, 1996.

Rohwer, Jürgen, and Gerhard Hummelchen. *Chronology of the War at Sea, 1939–1945.* Annapolis, Md.: Naval Institute Press, 1992.

Still, William N. J. *The Confederate Navy.* Annapolis, Md.: Naval Institute Press, 1997.

Stillwell, Paul, ed. *Air Raid: Pearl Harbor!* Annapolis, Md.: Naval Institute Press, 1981.

Tarrant, V. E. *Jutland: The German Perspective.* Annapolis, Md.: Naval Institute Press, 1995.

Periodicals

Byram, LTCOL Michael J., USMC. "Fury from the Sea: Marines in Grenada." U.S. Naval Institute *Proceedings* (May 1984).

Gaillard, Lee. "The Great Midway Crapshoot." U.S. Naval Institute *Proceedings* (June 2004).

Griffin, CDR Jim, USN. "Still Relevant After All These Years." The Falklands War. U.S. Naval Institute *Proceedings* (May 2012).

Guérout, Max. "The Wreck of the C.S.S. *Alabama.*" *National Geographic* (December 1994).

Halpern, Paul. "Jutland: A Battle in One Dimension." U.S. Naval Institute *Proceedings* (June 2006).

Nott, John. "The Falklands Campaign." U.S. Naval Institute *Proceedings* (May 1983).

Parker, Commodore Foxhall A. "The *Monitor* and the 'Merrimac.'" U.S. Naval Institute *Proceedings* (March 2012).

Simmons, Dr. Dean, et al. "Air Operations over Bosnia." U.S. Naval Institute *Proceedings* (May 1997).

Tillman, Barrett. "Into the Rising Sun: The Doolittle Raid." U.S. Naval Institute *Proceedings* (April 2007).

Truver, Scott C. "U.S. Navy in Review." Annual. U.S. Naval Institute *Proceedings* (May 2007–10).

Truver, Scott C., and Robert Holzer. "U.S. Navy in Review." Annual. U.S. Naval Institute *Proceedings* (May 2011–13).

Internet

Columbia Electronic Encyclopedia. "Vichy Government." infoplease.com.

Encarta Online Encyclopedia. "Iran-Iraq War." encarta.msn.com.

Federation of American Scientists. "Strategic Arms Reduction Treaty (START I) Chronology." fas.org.

Gordon Leidner. "Causes of the Civil War: A Balanced Answer." members.tripod.com.

Magazine Web. "The Confederate Navy, 1861–1865." magweb.com.

Mariners' Museum. "Monitor Expedition." mariner.org.

Mark F. Jenkins. "Famous Blockade Runners." ameriteck.net.

U.S. Army. "World War II: The War against Japan." army.mil/cmh.

U.S. Navy. [Numerous topics and illustrations]. navy.mil and history.navy.mil.

USS *Pueblo* Veterans Association. "The Attack." uspueblo.org

War and Military Records. "The Siege of Vicksburg." myheritage.com.

Wikipedia, The Free Encyclopedia. [Numerous topics and illustrations]. wikipedia.org.

Leadership

Books

Chalker, Edsel O. *Leadership Education 1.* Air Force Junior ROTC Textbook. Maxwell Air Force Base, Ala.: Air Training Command/Air University, 1979.

Department of Leadership and Law, U.S. Naval Academy. *Fundamentals of Naval Leadership.* Annapolis, Md.: Naval Institute Press, 1984.

Johnson, Brad W., and Gregory P. Harper. *Becoming a Leader the Annapolis Way.* New York: McGraw-Hill, 2005.

Montor, Karel, et al. *Naval Leadership: Voices of Experience.* Annapolis, Md.: Naval Institute Press, 1998.

Wray, RADM Robert O., USN. *Saltwater Leadership.* Annapolis, Md.: Naval Institute Press, 2013.

Periodicals

Fiedler, 2/LT Nicole, USMC. "The Distance between Selfish & Selfless Leadership." U.S. Naval Institute *Proceedings* (August 2008).

Harrison, CDR Holly, LCDR Mike Sharp, SCPO Albert Fernandez, USCG. "It's All about the Bystanders." U.S. Naval Institute *Proceedings* (August 2013).

Harrison, MCPO Michael, USN. "True Mentorship Is Never Scripted." U.S. Naval Institute *Proceedings* (February 2004).

Rogers, LT Daniel, USCG. "Leadership before the Mast." U.S. Naval Institute *Proceedings* (February 2006).

Stewart, MSGT Billy D., Jr., USMC. "If You're the Chief, Be the Chief." U.S. Naval Institute *Proceedings* (February 2004).

Nautical Sciences

Books

Kotsch, RADM William J., USN. *Weather for the Mariner.* 3rd ed. Annapolis, Md.: Naval Institute Press, 1983.

Leyden, Michael B, Gordon P. Johnson, and Bonnie B. Barr. *Introduction to Physical Science.* Menlo Park, Calif.: Addison-Wesley, 1988.

Rao, Gottapu Sasibhushana. *Mobile Cellular Communications.* Noida, India: Pearson Education India, 2012.

Roberson, Patricia Q., and Naomi L. Mitchell, eds. *Aerospace Science: The Science of Flight.* Maxwell Air Force Base, Ala.: Air Force Junior ROTC, 1993.

Sears, Francis W., Mark W. Zemansky, and Hugh D. Young. *College Physics.* 7th ed. New York: Addison-Wesley, 1991.

Periodicals and Booklets

Carmel, Stephen M. "The Cold, Hard Realities of Arctic Shipping." U.S. Naval Institute *Proceedings* (July 2013).

Craig, CDR John A., USN. "Don't Give Up the Ship(s)!" UUVs. U.S. Naval Institute *Proceedings* (July 2013).

Evans, LCDR Brian, USN, and Rick Lanchantin. "Lifting the Fog on Cyber Strategy." U.S. Naval Institute *Proceedings* (October 2013).

Gore, Rick. "Neptune: Voyager's Last Picture Show." *National Geographic,* August 1990.

Morrison, David. "Voyages to Saturn." Washington, D.C.: U.S. Government Printing Office, 1982.

Newcott, William R. "Galileo Mission." *National Geographic* (September 1999).

Spaner, CAPT Jonathon S., USCG, and Hillary LeBail. "The Next Security Frontier." Climate change. U.S. Naval Institute *Proceedings* (October 2013).

Internet

Absolute Astronomy. "Overwhelmingly Large Telescope," "Southern Africa Large Telescope," "Very Large Telescope." absoluteastronomy.com.

Aeronautics Learning Laboratory for Science Technology and Research (ALLSTAR). "Principles of Aeronautics." allstar.fiu.edu.

Australia Telescope Outreach and Education. "Obtaining Astronomical Spectra." outreach.atnf.csiro.au.

Columbia Electronic Encyclopedia. "Evolution of Telescopes." factmonster.com.

Furuno Corp. "FE-700 Navigational Echo Sounder." furuno.com.

How Stuff Works. "How Cell Phones Work." electronics.howstuffworks.com.

National Aeronautics and Space Administration. "Hubble," "The Planets," and numerous other topics and picture galleries on space exploration. nasa.gov.

———. "Images." spacetelescope.org.

National Geographic Education. "Sleet," "Our Solar System." education.nationalgeographic.com.

National Oceanic and Atmospheric Administration. "National Weather Service" and numerous other topics on meteorology and weather. nws.moaa.gov

———. "NOAA's Geostationary and Polar-Orbiting Weather Satellites." noaasis.noaa.gov.

National Radio Astronomy Observatory. "How Radio Telescopes Work," "Robert C. Byrd Green Bank Telescope." nrao.edu

National Weather Service. "Ocean Prediction Center," and many additional meteorological and weather-related topics. opc.ncep.noaa.gov.

SETI Institute. [Various topics regarding extraterrestrial life investigations]. seti.org.

Starizona. "Understanding Magnification." starizona.com.

USA Today. "FAQ: Hurricanes and Global Warming." usatoday.com.

U.S. Navy. [Numerous articles and photos relating to the U.S. Navy]. navy.mil.

U.S. Navy Surface Warfare Officer School. "Stability and Buoyancy Lessons." fas.org/man/dod.

NASA. "The James Webb Space Telescope." jwst.nasa.gov.

———. "IRIS," "The Planets," " Missions," and many other topics related to the U.S. space program. nasa.gov

———. "Near Earth Object Program." neo.jpl.nasa.gov

———. "Results of Analyses of Sample Material Returned by Apollo and Luna Missions." curator.jsc.nasa.gov

Universe Today. "Plane of the Ecliptic." universetoday.com.

Wikipedia, The Free Encyclopedia. [Numerous topics and illustrations]. wikipedia.org.

Index, Maritime History

(Italicized numbers indicate a photo, line art, or map)

Index, Leadership

(Italicized numbers indicate a photo or line art)

Index, Nautical Sciences

(Italicized numbers indicate a photo, line art, or map)

About the Author

CDR Richard Hobbs has been involved with the Navy's NJROTC program for more than thirty years as a writer/editor of many of its instructional textbooks and other materials. A 1966 graduate of the U.S. Naval Academy, Commander Hobbs had thirty-plus years of service as a former Sailor, midshipman, and surface line officer in the regular and reserve Navy. He has also worked in industry as a ceramics engineer and production manager, in publishing as an editor on the staff of the Naval Institute Press, and in education as a navigation instructor at the Naval Academy and as a community college instructor and high school AP and honors physics teacher.

In addition to instructional materials for the NJROTC program, Commander Hobbs has also written the widely acclaimed *Marine Navigation: Piloting, Celestial and Electronic*, a standard text and reference book in the field for the last forty years, and is a contributor of several articles on marine navigation and other related topics to *World Book Encyclopedia*. A certified tennis instructor, he retired after twenty years of teaching physics and coaching tennis at a local high school near Annapolis. An avid sailor, after many years living aboard their motorsailor *R n R*, he and his family reside in Maryland and in Florida.